**Fodor's** 1st Edition

# Andalusia

D0802237

The Guide
for All Budgets

Completely
Updated

Where to Stay, Eat,
and Explore

On and Off
the Beaten Path

When to Go,
What to Pack

Maps, Travel Tips,
and Web Sites

Fodor's Travel Publications • New York, Toronto, London, Sydney, Auckland
**www.fodors.com**

# Fodor's Andalusia

**EDITOR:** Matthew Lombardi

**Editorial Contributors:** Nuha Ansari, Linda Cabasin, Mark Little, Edward Owen, George Semler, AnneLise Sorensen
**Editorial Production:** Kristin Milavec
**Maps:** David Lindroth, Inc.; Mapping Specialists, *cartographers;* Rebecca Baer and Bob Blake, *map editors*
**Design:** Fabrizio La Rocca, *creative director;* Guido Caroti, *art director;* Jolie Novak, *senior picture editor;* Melanie Marin, *photo editor*
**Cover Design:** Pentagram
**Production/Manufacturing:** Angela L. McLean
**Cover Photo** (Tile fountain with pigeons, Seville): Carlos Navajas/The Image Bank/Getty Images

## Copyright

First Edition

ISBN 0–679–00778–4

ISSN 1541–2903

## Important Tip

Although all prices, opening times, and other details are based on information supplied to us at press time, changes occur all the time in the travel world, and Fodor's cannot accept responsibility for facts that become outdated or for inadvertent errors or omissions. So **always confirm information when it matters,** especially if you're making a detour to visit a specific place.

## Special Sales

Fodor's Travel Publications are available at special discounts for bulk purchases for sales promotions or premiums. Special editions, including personalized covers, excerpts of existing guides, and corporate imprints, can be created in large quantities for special needs. For more information, contact your local bookseller or write to Special Markets, Fodor's Travel Publications, 1745 Broadway, New York, NY 10019. Inquiries from Canada should be directed to your local Canadian bookseller or sent to Random House of Canada, Ltd., Marketing Department, 2775 Matheson Boulevard East, Mississauga, Ontario L4W 4P7. Inquiries from the United Kingdom should be sent to Fodor's Travel Publications, 20 Vauxhall Bridge Road, London SW1V 2SA, England.

PRINTED IN THE UNITED STATES OF AMERICA

10 9 8 7 6 5 4 3 2 1

# CONTENTS

# Maps

# ON THE ROAD WITH FODOR'S

A trip takes you out of yourself. Concerns of life at home completely disappear, driven away by more immediate thoughts—about, say, what marvels will beguile the next day, or where you'll have dinner. That's where Fodor's comes in. We make sure that you know all your options, so that you don't miss something that's around the next bend just because you didn't know it was there. Mindful that the best memories of your trip might have nothing to do with what you came to Andalusia to see, we guide you to sights large and small all over the country. You might set out to see one of the region's great Moorish palaces, but back at home you find yourself unable to forget the lively tapas bar or pottery-laden *cerámica* just around the corner. With Fodor's at your side, serendipitous discoveries are never far away.

## About Our Writers

Our success in showing you every corner of Andalusia is a credit to our extraordinary writers. Although there's no substitute for travel advice from a good friend who knows your style, our contributors are the next best thing—the kind of people you would poll for travel advice if you knew them.

Raised in Cornwall, England, journalist **Edward Owen** has worked in London, Toronto, and Sydney, and, since 1980, Madrid. Long a foreign correspondent for London's *Times, Sunday Times,* and *Daily Express,* he now specializes in travel, wine, gastronomy, and restaurant reviews.

Born and educated in Connecticut, writer and journalist **George Semler** has lived in Spain for the last 30-odd years. During that time he has written on Spain, France, Morocco, Cuba, and the Mediterranean region for *Forbes, Sky, Saveur,* the *International Herald Tribune,* and the *Los Angeles Times* and published walking guides to Madrid and Barcelona. When not fly-fishing or hiking the Pyrenees, he continues a passionate romance with Andalusia that began in 1971.

Writer and editor **AnneLise Sorensen** currently splits her time between Barcelona, where she's reconnecting with her Catalan roots, and California. For this book she combed the Costa del Sol, fortified by platters of *fritura malagueña*—Málaga's famed fried fish—at beachside *chiringuitos*; explored the sparkling *pueblos blancos* sprinkled atop Spain's southern mountaintops; chatted up local historians on the geranium-filled balconies of Archidona's red-and-ocher ocatagonal square; and joined in many a raucous regional fiesta along the way. AnneLise writes for various magazines and travel publications and has contributed to numerous Fodor's guides, including those to Spain, San Francisco, Denmark, and Ireland.

You can rest assured that you're in good hands—and that no property mentioned in the book has paid to be included. Each has been selected strictly on its merits, as the best of its type in its price range.

## How to Use This Book

Up front is **Smart Travel Tips A to Z**, arranged alphabetically by topic and loaded with tips, Web sites, and contact information. **Destination: Andalusia** helps get you in the mood for your trip. **Subsequent chapters** are arranged regionally. Each chapter is divided geographically; within each area, towns are covered in logical geographical order, and attractive stretches of road between them are indicated by the designation *En Route*. To help you decide what you'll have time to visit, all chapters begin with our writers' favorite itineraries. (Mix itineraries from several chapters, and you can put together a really exceptional trip.) The A to Z section that ends every chapter lists additional resources. At the end of the book you'll find Background and Essentials, including Portraits—essays about Andalusian culture—followed by several pages of handy vocabulary.

## Icons and Symbols

★      Our special recommendations
✕      Restaurant
🏠      Lodging establishment
✕🏠   Lodging establishment whose restaurant warrants a special trip
☺      Good for kids (rubber duck)
☞      Sends you to another section of the guide for more information
✉      Address

☎    Telephone number

🕐    Opening and closing times

📷    Admission prices (those we give apply to adults; substantially reduced fees are sometimes available for children, students, and senior citizens)

Numbers in white and black circles ③ ❸ that appear on the maps, in the margins, and within the tours correspond to one another.

For hotels, you can assume that all rooms have private baths, phones, TVs, and air-conditioning unless otherwise noted and that all hotels operate on the European Plan (with no meals) if we don't specify another meal plan. We always list a property's facilities but not whether you'll be charged extra to use them, so when pricing accommodations, do ask what's included. For restaurants, it's always a good idea to book ahead; we mention reservations only when they're essential or are not accepted. All restaurants we list are open daily for lunch and dinner unless stated otherwise; dress is mentioned only when men are required to wear a jacket or a jacket and tie. Look for an overview of local dining-out habits in Smart Travel Tips A to Z and in the Pleasures and Pastimes section that follows each chapter introduction.

## Don't Forget to Write

Your experiences—positive and negative—matter to us. If we have missed or misstated something, we want to hear about it. We follow up on all suggestions. Contact the Andalusia editor at editors@fodors.com or c/o Fodor's, 1745 Broadway, New York, NY 10019. And have a fabulous trip!

*Karen Cure*

Karen Cure
*Editorial Director*

# Spain

Ferrol
A Coruña
Vilalba
Ribadeo
Luarca
Gijón
Ribadesella
Santander
Santiago de Compostela
Oviedo
Cangas de Onís
Bilbao
Muros
Lugo
Mieres
PICOS DE EUROPA
CANTABRIAN MTS.
Pontevedra
Ourense
Ponferrada
León
Vigo
Astorga
Burgos
Tui
Benavente
Palencia
Log
Valladolid
Zamora
Tordesillas
Duero
Salamanca
Adanero
Segovia
SIERRA DE GUADARR
Avila
Guadalaj
Ciudad Rodrigo
El Escorial
MADRID
PORTUGAL
SIERRA DE GREDOS
Toledo
Plasencia
Talavera de la Reina
Ta
Aranjuez
Tajo
Alcázar de San Juan
Cáceres
Guadalupe
Trujillo
Guadiana
Ciudad Real
Mérida
Abenójar
Valdepe
Badajoz
Almadén
Jerez de los Caballeros
Zafra
SIERRA MORENA
Fregenal de la Sierra
Bailén
Linares
Ube
Córdoba
Jaén
Baeza
Aroche
Ecija
Baena
Seville
Guadalquivir
Guadix
Carmona
Lucena
Granada
Huelva
SIERRA
Sanlúcar de Barrameda
Antequera
Loja
Gulf of Cadiz
Ronda
Nerja
Jerez de la Frontera
Torremolinos
Málaga
Motril
Cádiz
Estepona
Fuengirola
COSTA DE LA LUZ
Marbella
COSTA DEL SOL
ATLANTIC OCEAN
Algeciras
Gibraltar
TO CANARY ISLANDS
Strait of Gibraltar
Bay of Biscay

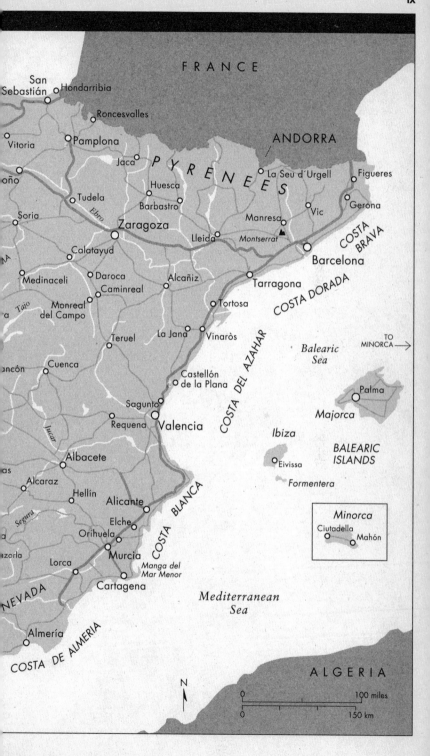

## Andalusia

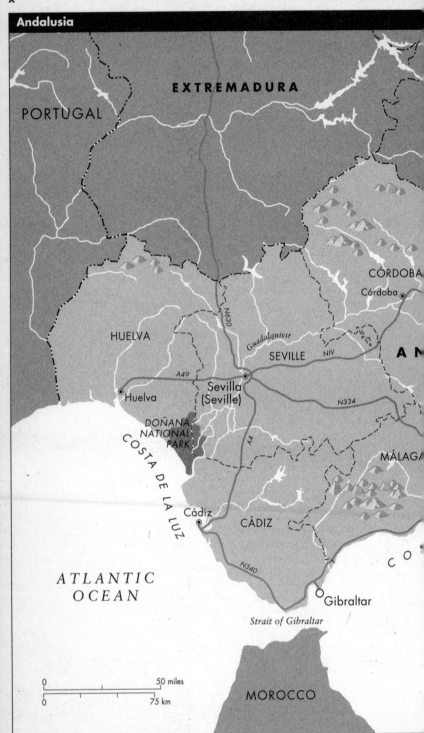

PORTUGAL

EXTREMADURA

CÓRDOBA

Córdoba

HUELVA

*Guadalquivir*

SEVILLE

A N

N630

NIV

Huelva

Sevilla
(Seville)

N334

DOÑANA
NATIONAL
PARK

MÁLAGA

C O S T A   D E   L A   L U Z

A4

Cádiz

CÁDIZ

C O

N340

*ATLANTIC
OCEAN*

Gibraltar

*Strait of Gibraltar*

| 0 | | 50 miles |
| 0 | | 75 km |

MOROCCO

CASTILE-LA MANCHA

JAÉN
*Guadalquivir*

CAZORLA
NATIONAL
PARK

MURCIA

Jaén

*N323*

*NIV*

DALUSIA

*N342*

ALMERÍA

*N340*

Granada

GRANADA

Almería

*N331*

*N340*

Málaga

COSTA DE ALMERÍA

TA   DEL   SOL

*Mediterranean
Sea*

N

KEY
—·—·— Regions
— — — Provinces
⊙ Provincial
capitals

# ESSENTIAL INFORMATION

The following information addresses many of the questions that arise when you're planning your trip and when you're on the road. In addition, the organizations listed here can supplement the information in this guide book. Note that most of the information pertains to all of Andalusia and in some cases all of Spain; for specific details about the various topics covered below *within* the regions covered in this book—Seville, Huelva, and so on—additionally consult the A to Z sections at the end of each regional chapter.

## ADDRESSES

Apartment addresses in Spain include the street name, building number, floor level, and apartment number. For example, "Calle Cervantes 15, 3°, 1ª" indicates that the apartment is on the *tercero* (third) floor, *primera* (first) door. In older buildings, the first floor is often called the *entresuelo;* one floor above it is *principal* and, above this, is the first floor. The top floor of a building is the *ático* (attic). In more modern buildings, there is often no entresuelo or principal.

## AIR TRAVEL

Regular nonstop flights serve Spain from the eastern United States; flying from other North American cities usually involves a stop. Flights from the United Kingdom to Spain are more frequent, cover small cities as well as large ones, and are priced very competitively, particularly if you travel on a low-cost carrier such as EasyJet or Go.

There are no direct flights from the United States to Andalusia; you'll have to connect in Madrid for flights to the south. If you're coming from North America and would like to land in a city other than Madrid or Barcelona, consider flying a British or other European carrier; just know that you may have to stay overnight

in London or another European city on your way home. There are no nonstop flights to Spain from Australia or New Zealand.

There are numerous daily flights from Madrid and Barcelona to Andalusia's main hubs, including Málaga, Seville, and Granada.

### BOOKING

When you book **look for nonstop flights** and **remember that "direct" flights stop at least once.** Try to avoid connecting flights, which require a change of plane. Two airlines may operate a connecting flight jointly, so ask if your airline operates every segment of the trip; you may find that the carrier you prefer flies you only part of the way. To find more booking tips and to check prices and make on-line flight reservations, log on to www.fodors.com.

### CARRIERS

From North America, American, Continental, US Airways, Air Europa, and Spanair fly to Madrid; American, Delta, and Iberia fly to Madrid and Barcelona.

Iberia, British Airways, and numerous other British carriers fly from London to Málaga and Seville. Most major European cities have direct flights to Málaga and Seville on Iberia or their own national airlines.

Within Spain, Iberia is the main domestic airline, but Air Europa and Spanair fly a number of domestic routes at lower prices. Iberia flies eight times daily from Madrid to Seville and Málaga, and four times daily to Granada, Jerez, and Almería. Iberia flies from Barcelona to Málaga, Seville, Jerez, and Granada, and also from Bilbao to Seville. Iberia also has regular flights to the south from other Spanish cities. Spanair flies from Madrid to Málaga five to seven times daily during the week and three times daily on the weekends; and from Barcelona to Málaga two to three times daily. Air Europa flies from Madrid to Málaga one to two times daily, and from Barcelona to Seville once daily.

➤ FROM NORTH AMERICA: **Air Europa** (☎ 888/238–7672). **American** (☎ 800/433–7300). **Continental** (☎ 800/231–0856). **Delta** (☎ 800/221–1212). **Iberia** (☎ 800/772–4642). **Spanair** (☎ 888/545–5757). **US Airways**(☎ 800/622–1015).

➤ FROM THE U.K.: **British Airways** (☎ 0845/773–3377). **EasyJet** (☎ 0870/6000000). **Go** (☎ 0870/6076543). **Iberia** (☎ 0845/601–2854).

➤ WITHIN SPAIN: **Air Europa** (☎ 902/401501). **Iberia** (902/400500). **Spanair** (☎ 902/131415).

## CHECK-IN AND BOARDING

Always **ask your carrier about its check-in policy.** Plan to arrive at the airport about two hours before your scheduled departure time for domestic flights and 2½ to 3 hours before international flights. Assuming that not everyone with a ticket will show up, airlines routinely overbook planes. When everyone does, airlines ask for volunteers to give up their seats. In return, these volunteers usually get a certificate for a free flight and are rebooked on the next flight out. If there are not enough volunteers, the airline must choose who will be denied boarding. The first to get bumped are passengers who checked in late and those flying on discounted tickets, so **get to the gate and check in as early as possible,** especially during peak periods.

Always **bring a government-issued photo I.D. to the airport;** even when it's not required, a passport is best.

## CUTTING COSTS

The least expensive airfares to Spain are priced for round-trip travel and must usually be purchased in advance. Airlines generally allow you to change your return date for a fee; most low-fare tickets, however, are nonrefundable. It's smart to **call a number of airlines and check the Internet;** when you are quoted a good price, **book it on the spot**—the same fare may not be available the next day. Always **check different routings** and look into using alternate airports. Also, price off-peak flights, which may be significantly less expensive than others. Travel agents, especially low-fare specialists (☞ Discounts and Deals), are helpful.

Consolidators are another good source. They buy tickets for scheduled international flights at reduced rates from the airlines, then sell them at prices that beat the best fare available directly from the airlines. Sometimes you can even get your money back if you need to return the ticket. Carefully read the fine print detailing penalties for changes and cancellations, purchase the ticket with a credit card, and **confirm your consolidator reservation with the airline.**

You can **fly as a courier** to Spain, though not within Spain. When you do travel this way, you trade your checked-luggage space for a ticket deeply subsidized by a courier service. There are restrictions on when you can book and how long you can stay. Some courier companies list with membership organizations, such as the Air Courier Association and the International Association of Air Travel Couriers; these require you to become a member before you can book a flight.

Many airlines, singly or in collaboration, offer discount air passes that allow foreigners to travel economically in a particular country or region. These visitor passes usually must be reserved and purchased before you leave home. Information about passes can be difficult to track down on airline Web sites, which tend to be geared to travelers departing from a given carrier's country rather than to those intending to visit that country. Try typing the name of the pass into a search engine, or search for "pass" within the carrier's Web site.

If you buy a round-trip trans-Atlantic ticket on **Iberia,** you might want to purchase a Visit Spain pass, good for four domestic flights during your trip. The pass must be purchased before you arrive in Spain, all flights must be booked in advance, and the cost starts at $165 ($290 if you want to include flights to the Canary Islands).

On certain days of the week, Iberia also offers *minitarifas* (minifares), which can save you 40% on domestic flights. Tickets must be purchased at least two days in advance, and you must stay over Saturday night.

➤ CONSOLIDATORS: **Cheap Tickets** (☎ 800/377–1000 or 888/922–8849, WEB www.cheaptickets.com). **Discount Airline Ticket Service** (☎ 800/576–1600). **Unitravel** (☎ 800/325–2222, WEB www.unitravel.com). **Up & Away Travel** (☎ 212/889–2345, WEB www.upandaway.com). **World Travel Network** (☎ 800/409–6753).

➤ COURIER RESOURCES: **Air Courier Association** (☎ 800/282–1202, WEB www.aircourier.org). **International Association of Air Travel Couriers** (☎ 352/475–1584, WEB www.courier.org). **Now Voyager Travel** (☎ 212/431–1616).

### ENJOYING THE FLIGHT

**State your seat preference** when purchasing your ticket, and then repeat it when you confirm and when you check in. For more legroom, you can request one of the few emergency-aisle seats at check-in, if you are capable of lifting at least 50 pounds—a Federal Aviation Administration requirement of passengers in these seats. Seats behind a bulkhead also offer more legroom, but they don't have underseat storage. Don't sit in the row in front of the emergency aisle or in front of a bulkhead, where seats may not recline.

Ask the airline whether a snack or meal is served on the flight. If you have dietary concerns, **request special meals when booking.** These can be vegetarian, low-cholesterol, or kosher, for example. It's a good idea to pack some healthful snacks and a small (plastic) bottle of water in your carry-on bag. On long flights, try to maintain a normal routine, to help fight jet lag. At night, **get some sleep.** By day, **eat light meals, drink water** (not alcohol), and **move around the cabin** to stretch your legs. For additional jet-lag tips consult *Fodor's FYI: Travel Fit & Healthy* (available at bookstores everywhere).

The Spanish predilection for cigarettes notwithstanding, most airlines serving Spain, including Iberia, do not allow smoking on either international or domestic flights. It's nonetheless wise to ask your carrier about its policy.

### FLYING TIMES

Flying time to Madrid from New York is seven hours; from London, just over two hours. From Madrid to Seville or to Málaga, flying time is one hour; from Barcelona to either city, it's an hour and a half.

### HOW TO COMPLAIN

If your baggage goes astray or your flight goes awry, complain right away. Most carriers require that you **file a claim immediately.** The Aviation Consumer Protection Division of the Department of Transportation publishes *Fly-Rights,* which discusses airlines and consumer issues and is available on-line. At PassengerRights.com, a Web site, you can compose a letter of complaint and distribute it electronically.

➤ AIRLINE COMPLAINTS: **Aviation Consumer Protection Division** (✉ U.S. Department of Transportation, Room 4107, C-75, Washington, DC 20590, ☎ 202/366–2220, WEB www.dot.gov/airconsumer). **Federal Aviation Administration Consumer Hotline** (☎ 800/322–7873).

### RECONFIRMING

Check the status of your flight before you leave for the airport. You can do this on your carrier's Web site, by linking to a flight-status checker (many Web booking services offer these), or by calling your carrier or travel agent. Always confirm international flights at least 72 hours ahead of the scheduled departure time.

### ▶ AIRPORTS

Most flights from the United States and Canada land in, or pass through, Madrid's Barajas (MAD). The other major gateway is Barcelona's El Prat de Llobregat (BCN). From England and elsewhere in Europe, regular flights also land in Málaga (AGP), Alicante (ALC), Palma de Mallorca (PMI), and on Gran Canaria (LPA) and Tenerife (TFN).

Andalusia's main airports are in Málaga, Seville, and Granada, all of which have plenty of public transportation options for reaching the city center.

➤ AIRPORT INFORMATION: **Madrid–Barajas** (☎ 91/305–8343). **Barcelona–El Prat de Llobregat** (☎ 93/298–3838). **Aeropuerto de Almería** (☎ 950/213700). **Aeropuerto de Granada** (☎ 958/245223). **Aeropuerto de Málaga** (☎ 952/048804). **Aeropuerto de Sevilla** (☎ 95/444–9000).

## BIKE TRAVEL

Long distances, an abundance of hilly terrain, and the blistering summers (which can begin as early as April in some parts of Andalusia, such as Seville and Málaga) make touring Andalusia by bike less than ideal for all but the fittest bikers. That said, Andalusia's numerous nature preserves, particularly around Ronda, are perfect for mountain biking, especially in spring and fall, and many have specially marked bike paths.

It's usually better to rent a bike locally than deal with the logistics of bringing your own bike with you. Bikes are not usually allowed on trains, for instance; they must be packed and checked as luggage. At most nature preserves, at least one agency rents mountain bikes and, in many cases, leads guided bike tours. Check with the park's visitor center for details. In addition, rural hotels often make bikes available to guests, sometimes free of charge. Rental costs for a mountain bike range between €12 and €18 per day. Guided bike excursions, which include the bikes and support staff, generally start at about €54 a day.

### BIKES IN FLIGHT

Most airlines accommodate bikes as luggage, provided they are dismantled and boxed; check with individual airlines about packing requirements. Airlines sell bike boxes, which are often free at bike shops, for about $15 (bike bags start at $100). International travelers often can substitute a bike for a piece of checked luggage at no charge; otherwise, the cost is about $100.

## BOAT AND FERRY TRAVEL

Spain's major car-ferry line is Trasmediterránea, which operates in Andalusia out of Málaga and Almería. Direct Trasmediterránea ferries head from Málaga's port to the Spanish city of Melilla on the north African coast. From Almería's port, Trasmediterránea ferries sail to Melilla and Nador in Morocco. The ferry line Ferrimaroc also travels between Almería and Nador. Ferries sail once daily; in the summer, from late June to early September, service usually increases to two to three daily trips.

From outside of the country, regular car ferries connect the United Kingdom with northern Spain. Brittany Ferries sails from Plymouth to Santander; P&O European Ferries sails from Portsmouth to Bilbao. If you want to drive from Spain to Morocco, you can take a car ferry from Málaga, Algeciras, or Tarifa, run by Trasmediterránea; the ferry line Buquebus sails from Algeciras to Ceuta, in Morocco, up to 14 times a day. Both ferry lines also offer a catamaran service that takes half the time of the standard ferry.

➤ FROM THE U.K.: **Brittany Ferries** (☎ 0239/289–2200). **P&O European Ferries** (☎ 0239/230–1000).

➤ IN SPAIN: **Buquebus** (☎ 902/414242). **Ferrimaroc** (☎ 950/274878). **Trasmediterránea** (☎ 902/454645).

## BUS TRAVEL

Buses from Spain's principal cities, including Barcelona, Madrid, and Valencia, travel to at least one, if not more, of Andalusia's main cities. Enatcar, Spain's major national long-haul bus line, travels from Barcelona to Málaga, Granada, Almería, and Seville. Continental Auto travels from Madrid to Granada.

Within Andalusia, an array of private companies provide bus service that ranges from knee-crunchingly basic to luxurious. Bus fares are lower than the corresponding train fares, and the service is more extensive than the train; if you want to reach a town not served by train, you can be sure a bus will go there. There are regular bus services between the main cities of Andalusia, including Almería, Málaga, Granada, Seville, and Córdoba, operated by the Alsina Graells Sur company. Additionally, a slew of private companies operate within each of Andalusia's provinces, connecting the province's capital city to the smaller towns of the province, and also providing services between the small towns. However, note that if you are traveling between smaller towns, you will often have to make bus connections in the capital and/or hub city, which can add quite a few hours to your journey, especially if you have to wait a long time for the connection. Note, too, that tracking down which companies go where can be a trying task. You'll find the main companies of each province listed in the appropriate chapters. However, if you plan on traveling extensively throughout the province by bus, your best bet is to call—or even better, to visit—the capital city's bus station upon arrival to get all the up-to-date schedules and fares. Note that bus service is often extremely limited—if not nonexistent—on Sunday and holidays. Smaller towns don't usually have a central bus depot, so ask the tourist office for buses to your destination and where to wait for the bus.

For a longer haul, you can travel to Spain's main cities—Barcelona and Madrid—by bus from London, Paris, Rome, Frankfurt, Prague, and other major European cities. To Andalusia, there are two or three buses a week from London to Málaga and the Costa del Sol. A word about trip lengths: the 25-hour bus journey from, for example, London to Barcelona, is bearable, but note that it's then another 9 hours to cross Spain to Málaga, making the total journey time a whopping 34 hours. Although bus fares are generally considerably less than flying with a major carrier such as Iberia, they may not be cheaper than traveling on a low-cost carrier such as EasyJet, especially during the low season. Therefore, it might be a good idea to hunt around first for cheap airfares before committing yourself to the day-and-a-half bus journey.

## CLASSES

Most of Spain's larger bus companies have buses with comfortable seats and adequate legroom; on longer journeys (of two to three hours or more), a movie is often shown on board, and earphones are provided. Except for smaller regional buses that travel only short hops, all buses have a bathroom on board. Nonetheless, most long-haul buses usually stop at least once every two to three hours for a snack and bathroom break. That said, the downside to traveling by bus is, of course, that you can't roam the aisles quite as freely as on the train; also, the bus is prey to road and traffic conditions, which can make or break the journey. Fortunately, Spain's highways, particularly along major routes, are well maintained. That may not be the case in Andalusia's more rural areas, where you could be in for a bumpy ride—which is sometimes made worse by older buses equipped with shock absorbers that have long since ceased to absorb. Enatcar, Spain's largest national bus company, offers two luxury classes in addition to its regular line. At the top of the line is the Supra Clase, with roomy leather seats and on-board meals; also, you have the option of *asientos individuales* (individual seats, with no other seat on either side) that line one side of the bus. The next class is the Eurobus, with comfortable seats and plenty of legroom but no asientos individuales or on-board meals. The Supra Clase and Eurobus usually cost, respectively, up to one-third and one-fourth more than the regular line.

## CUTTING COSTS

If you plan on returning to your initial destination, note that you can always save by buying a round-trip ticket instead of one-way. Also, some of Spain's smaller, regional bus lines offer multitrip bus passes, which are worthwhile if you plan on making multiple trips between two fixed destinations within the region. Generally, these tickets offer a savings of 20% per journey; you can buy these tickets only in the bus station (not on the bus). The general rule for children is that if they occupy a seat, they pay.

## FARES AND SCHEDULES

In Spain's larger cities, you can pick up all schedule and fare information at the bus station. Smaller towns may not have a bus station but just a bus stop. Schedules are sometimes listed at the bus stop; otherwise, you should call the bus company directly or check at the tourist office, which can usually supply schedule and fare information.

## PAYING

At the bus station ticket counter, generally all major credit cards (except for American Express) are accepted. If you buy a ticket on the bus, it's cash-only. Traveler's checks are almost never accepted.

## RESERVATIONS

During peak travel times (Easter, August, and Christmas), it's always a good idea to make a reservation at least three to four days in advance.

➤ BUS TOURS: **Marsans** (✉ Gran Vía 59, Madrid,☎ 902/306090). **Pull-mantur** (✉ Plaza de Oriente 8, Madrid, ☎ 91/541–1805).

➤ FROM THE U.K.: **Eurolines/National Express** (☎ 01582/404511 or 0990/143219).

➤ WITHIN ANDALUSIA: **Alsina Graells Sur** (✉ Seville, ☎ 95/441–8811; ✉ Málaga, ☎ 952/318295; ✉ Granada, ☎ 958/185480; ✉ Almería, ☎ 950/235168; ✉ Córdoba, ☎ 957/278100; ✉ Jaén, ☎ 953/255014).

➤ WITHIN SPAIN: **Continental Auto** (✉ Avenida de América 1, Madrid, ☎ 91/7456300 or 902/422242, WEB www.continental-auto.es). **Enatcar** (✉ Estación Sur de Autobuses, Calle Méndez Álvaro, Madrid, ☎ 902/422242).

## BUSINESS HOURS

### BANKS AND OFFICES

Banks are generally open Monday–Friday 8:30 or 9 until 2 or 2:30. Some banks occasionally open on Saturday 8:30 or 9 until 2 or 2:30. From October to May, savings banks are also open Thursday 4:30–8. Currency exchanges at airports and train stations stay open later; you can also cash traveler's checks at El Corte Inglés department stores until 10 PM (some branches close at 9 or 9:30).

Most government offices are open weekdays 9–2.

### GAS STATIONS

Gas stations on major routes and in big cities are open 24 hours. On less-traveled routes, gas stations are usually open 7 AM–11 PM. If a gas station is closed, it's required by law that it post the address and directions to the nearest station that is open.

### MUSEUMS AND SIGHTS

Most museums are open from 9:30 to 2 and 4 to 7 (or 5 to 8) six days a week, usually every day but Monday. Note, however, that many of Andalusia's major tourist sights—in an ongoing effort to accommodate more visitors—do not close in the middle of the day. These include Granada's Alhambra, Seville's Alcázar, Córdoba's Mezquita, and Málaga's Alcazaba. Schedules are subject to change, of course, particularly between the high and low seasons, so **confirm opening hours before you make plans.**

### PHARMACIES

Pharmacies keep normal business hours (9–1:30 and 5–8), but every midsize town (or city neighborhood) has a duty pharmacy that stays open 24 hours. The location of the duty pharmacy is usually posted on the front door of all pharmacies.

### SHOPS

When planning a shopping trip, remember that **many shops in Spain close at midday** for at least three hours. The exceptions are large supermarkets and the department-store chain El Corte Inglés. Stores are generally open from 9 or 10 to 1:30 and from 5 to 8. Most shops are closed on Sunday, and in some cases are also closed Saturday afternoon. That said, larger shops in tourist areas may stay open Sunday in summer and over the Christmas holiday. The Costa del Sol, with its gargantuan summer tourist population, operates on a different schedule entirely, particularly in the resort towns of Torremolinos, Benalmádena-Costa, and Fuengirola. Tourist restaurants are open more or less continuously throughout the day and evening, as are souvenir shops. And you'll never lack for little "mom-and-pop"-style grocery stores open from early morning until 10 or 11 PM, where you can buy groceries and alcohol—albeit at marked-up prices—and often beach accessories such as suntan oil and cheap sunglasses.

## CAMERAS
## AND PHOTOGRAPHY

All major brands of film are readily available in Spain, and at reasonable prices. Try to **buy film in large stores or photography shops**; film sold in smaller outlets may be out of date or stored in poor conditions. To have film developed, **look for shops displaying the Kodak Q-Lab sign**, a guarantee of quality. If you're in a large town or resort, you will find shops that can process film in a few hours.

The *Kodak Guide to Shooting Great Travel Pictures* (available at bookstores everywhere) is loaded with tips.

➤ PHOTO HELP: **Kodak Information Center** (☎ 800/242–2424, WEB www.kodak.com).

### EQUIPMENT PRECAUTIONS

**Don't pack film and equipment in checked luggage,** where it is much more susceptible to damage. X-ray machines used to view checked luggage are becoming much more powerful and therefore are much more likely to ruin your film. Try to **ask for hand inspection of film,** which becomes clouded after repeated exposure to airport X-ray machines, and **keep videotapes and computer disks away from metal detectors.** Always **keep film, tape, and computer disks out of the sun.** Carry an extra supply of batteries, and **be prepared to turn on your camera, camcorder, or laptop** to prove to airport security personnel that the device is real.

### VIDEOS

The standard videotape available in Spain is for the PAL system (used in Britain and much of continental Europe, though not France). Tapes for other systems are hard to come by, so take a good supply with you. In airports, keep videotapes away from metal detectors.

## CAR RENTAL

Avis, Hertz, Budget, and National (partnered in Spain with the agency Atesa) all have branches at major Spanish airports and in large cities. Smaller, regional companies often offer lower rates. All agencies have a wide range of models, but virtually all cars in Spain have a manual transmission. **If you don't want a stick shift, reserve weeks in advance and specify automatic transmission,** then call to reconfirm your automatic car before you leave for Spain. Rates in Madrid begin at the equivalent of $65 a day and $300 a week for an economy car with air-conditioning, manual transmission, and unlimited mileage. Add to this a 16% tax on car rentals.

Although you should always rent the size car that makes you feel safest, a small car, aside from saving you some money, can be a good bet for the tiny roads and parking spaces in many parts of Spain.

➤ MAJOR AGENCIES: **Avis** (☎ 800/331–1084; 800/879–2847 in Canada; 0870/606–0100 in the U.K.; 02/9353–9000 in Australia; 09/526–2847 in New Zealand; WEB www.avis.com). **Budget** (☎ 800/527–0700; 0870/156–5656 in the U.K.; WEB www.budget.com). **Hertz** (☎ 800/654–3001; 800/263–0600 in Canada; 020/8897–2072 in the U.K.; 02/9669–2444 in Australia; 09/256–8690 in New Zealand; WEB www.hertz.com). **National Car Rental** (☎ 800/227–7368; 020/8680–4800 in the U.K.; WEB www.nationalcar.com).

### CUTTING COSTS

For a good deal, **book through a travel agent who will shop around.** Remember to ask about required deposits, cancellation penalties, and drop-off charges if you're planning to pick up the car in one city and leave it in another. If you're traveling during a holiday period, also make sure that a confirmed reservation guarantees you a car. Note that it is almost always cheaper to book your car before leaving your home country, through your local branch of an international rental company.

Do **look into wholesalers,** companies that do not own fleets but rent in bulk from those that do and often offer better rates than traditional car-rental operations. Prices are best during off-peak periods. Rentals booked through wholesalers often must be paid for before you leave home.

➤ LOCAL AGENCIES: Avis (☎ 902/135531). Budget(☎ 901/201212). Europcar (☎ 902/105030). Hertz (☎ 902/402405). National/Atesa (☎ 902/100101).

➤ WHOLESALERS: Auto Europe (☎ 207/842–2000 or 800/223–5555, FAX 207/842–2222, WEB www.autoeurope. com). Destination Europe Resources (DER; ✉ 9501 W. Devon Ave., Rosemont, IL 60018, ☎ 800/782–2424, WEB www.der.com). Europe by Car (☎ 212/581–3040 or 800/223–1516, FAX 212/246–1458, WEB www. europebycar.com).

## INSURANCE

When driving a rented car you are generally responsible for any damage to or loss of the vehicle. Collision policies that car-rental companies sell for European rentals typically do not cover stolen vehicles. Before you rent—and purchase collision or theft coverage—see what coverage you already have under the terms of your personal auto-insurance policy and credit cards.

## SURCHARGES

Before you pick up a car in one city and leave it in another, **ask about drop-off charges or one-way service fees,** which can be substantial. Note, too, that some rental agencies charge extra if you return the car before the time specified in your contract. To avoid a hefty refueling fee, **fill the tank just before you turn in the car,** but be aware that gas stations near the rental outlet may overcharge. It's almost never a deal to buy the tank of gas in the car when you rent it; the understanding is that you'll return it empty, but some fuel usually remains.

## CAR TRAVEL

Your own driver's license is valid in Spain, but you may want to get an International Driver's Permit for extra assurance. Permits are available from the American or Canadian Automobile Association, or, in the United Kingdom, from the Automobile Association or Royal Automobile Club. Note that although anyone over 18 with a valid license can drive in Spain, some rental agencies will not rent cars to drivers under 21.

Driving is the best way to see Andalusia's rural areas and get off the beaten track, particularly if you want to explore the hill villages. The main cities are connected by a network of excellent four-lane *autovías* (freeways) and *autopistas* (toll freeways; "toll" is *peaje*), which are designated with the letter A and have speed limits of up to 120 kph (74 mph). The letter N indicates a *carretera nacional* (basic national route), which may have four or two lanes. Smaller towns and villages are connected by a network of secondary roads maintained by regional, provincial, and local governments.

Andalusia's major routes bear heavy traffic, especially during holiday periods. Drive with care: the roads are shared by a potentially perilous mixture of local drivers, Moroccan immigrants traveling between North Africa and northern Europe, and non-Spanish vacationers, some of whom are accustomed to driving on the left side of the road. Be prepared, too, for heavy truck traffic on national routes, which, in the case of two-lane roads, can have you creeping along for hours.

## EMERGENCY SERVICES

The rental agencies Hertz and Avis have 24-hour breakdown service. If you belong to an auto club (AAA, CAA, or AA), you can get emergency assistance from the Spanish counterpart, RACE.

➤ LOCAL AUTO CLUBS: RACE (✉ José Abascal 10, Madrid,☎ 900/200093).

## GASOLINE

Gas stations are plentiful, and most of those on major routes and in big cities are open 24 hours. On less-traveled routes, gas stations are usually open 7 AM–11 PM. If a gas station is closed, it's required by law that it post the address and directions to the nearest gas station that is open. Most stations are self-service, though prices are the same as those at full-service stations.

You punch in the amount of gas you want (in euros, not in liters), unhook the nozzle, pump the gas, and then pay. At night, however, you must pay before you fill up. Most pumps offer a choice of gas, including leaded, unleaded, and diesel, so **be careful to pick the right variety** for your car. All newer cars in Spain use *gasolina sin plomo* (unleaded gas), which is available in two grades, 95 and 98 octane. *Super,* regular 97-octane leaded gas, is gradually being phased out. Prices vary little among stations and were at press time €.82 a liter for leaded, 97 octane; €.76 a liter for sin plomo, 95 octane; and €.89 a liter for sin plomo, 98 octane. Credit cards are widely accepted.

### ROAD CONDITIONS

Spain's highway system now includes some 6,000 km (3,600 mi) of beautifully maintained superhighways. Still, you'll find some stretches of major national highways that are only two lanes wide, where traffic often backs up behind slow, heavy trucks. Autopista tolls are steep but as a result are often less crowded than the free highways. On the autopistas, you'll find that many of the rest stops are nicely landscaped and have cafeterias with good food.

Most Spanish cities have notoriously long morning and evening rush hours. Traffic jams are especially bad in and around Seville and Málaga. If possible, **avoid the morning rush hour, which can last until noon, and the evening rush hour, which lasts from 7 to 9.**

### ROAD MAPS

Detailed road maps are readily available at bookstores and gas stations.

### RULES OF THE ROAD

Spaniards drive on the right. Horns are banned in cities, but that doesn't keep people from blasting away. Children under 10 may not ride in the front seat, and seat belts are compulsory everywhere. Speed limits are 50 kph (31 mph) in cities, 100 kph (62 mph) on N roads, 120 kph (74 mph) on the autopista and autovía, and, unless otherwise signposted, 90 kph (56 mph) on other roads.

Spanish highway police are particularly vigilant about speeding and illegal passing. Fines start at €90, and police are empowered to demand payment from non-Spanish drivers on the spot. Although local drivers, especially in cities such as Madrid, will park their cars just about anywhere, you should **park only in legal spots.** Parking fines are steep, and your car might well be towed, resulting in fines, hassle, and wasted time.

### CHILDREN IN SPAIN

Children are greatly indulged in Spain. You'll see kids accompanying their parents everywhere, including bars and restaurants, so bringing yours along should not be a problem. Shopkeepers will shower your child with *caramelos* (sweets), and even the coldest waiters tend to be friendlier when you have a youngster with you. And although you won't be shunted into a remote corner when you bring kids into a Spanish restaurant, **expect no high chairs or special children's menus.** Children eat what their parents do, so it's perfectly acceptable to ask for an extra plate and share your food. Be prepared for late bedtimes, especially in summer—it's common to see toddlers playing cheerfully outdoors until midnight. Because children are expected to be with their parents at all times, few hotels provide baby-sitting services, but those that don't can often refer you to an independent baby-sitter (*canguro*).

A favorite destination among visiting Northern European families is the Costa del Sol, with its cheerful range of fun-for-the-whole-family diversions, from amusement and water parks to the miles of sandy beaches (many posted with vigilant lifeguards) where kids can build sand castles and splash about in the warm Mediterranean waters. The Costa, particularly in the family resort of Fuengirola, is also liberally dotted with kid-friendly restaurants, with (an exception to the rule) colorful children's menus and hotels that offer family discounts and deals.

If you are renting a car, don't forget to **arrange for a car seat** when you reserve. For general advice about traveling with children, consult

*Fodor's FYI: Travel with Your Baby* (available in bookstores everywhere).

## FLYING

If your children are two or older, **ask about children's airfares.** As a general rule, infants under two not occupying a seat fly at greatly reduced fares or even for free. When booking, **confirm carry-on allowances** if you're traveling with infants. In general, for babies charged 10% of the adult fare you are allowed one carry-on bag and a collapsible stroller. If the flight is full, the stroller may have to be checked or you may be limited to less.

Experts agree that it's a good idea to use safety seats aloft for children weighing less than 40 pounds. Airlines set their own policies: U.S. carriers usually require that the child be ticketed, even if he or she is young enough to ride free, since the seats must be strapped into regular seats. Do **check your airline's policy about using safety seats during takeoff and landing.** Safety seats are not allowed everywhere in the plane, so get your seat assignments as early as possible.

When reserving, **request children's meals or a freestanding bassinet** (not available at all airlines) if you need them. But note that bulkhead seats, where you must sit to use the bassinet, may lack an overhead bin or storage space on the floor.

## FOOD

Visiting children may turn up their noses at some of Spain's regional specialties. Although kids seldom get their own menus, most restaurants are happy to provide simple dishes, such as plain grilled chicken, steak, or fried potatoes, for the little ones. *Fritura malagueña,* Málaga's famous fried fish, is one dish that most kids do seem to enjoy. If all else fails, familiar fast-food chains such as McDonald's, Burger King, and Pizza Hut are well represented in the major cities and popular resorts.

## LODGING

Most hotels in Spain allow children under a certain age to stay in their parents' room at no extra charge, but others charge for them as extra adults; be sure to **find out the cutoff age for children's discounts.**

## SIGHTS AND ATTRACTIONS

Museum admissions and bus and metro rides are generally free for children up to age five. We indicate places that children might especially enjoy with a rubber duckie (🦆) in the margin. Andalusia's plethora of magical Moorish castles and forts, from the Granada's Alhambra to Seville's Alcázar, will appeal to museum-weary (and -wary) kids.

## SUPPLIES AND EQUIPMENT

Disposable diapers (*pañales*), formula (*leche maternizada*), and bottled baby foods (*papillas*) are readily available at supermarkets and pharmacies.

## COMPUTERS ON THE ROAD

A few of Spain's newer hotels, mainly in the major cities, provide data ports for Internet access in guest rooms. If you need to bring your computer, *see* Electricity.

Virtually every town with more than two traffic lights has at least one cybercafé, most with hourly rates under €3; Andalusia's big cities, particularly Seville, Granada, and Málaga (with its large foreign student presence), have dozens of Internet centers, all competitively priced.

## CONSULATES

➤ AUSTRALIA: **Seville** (✉ Federico Rubio 14, Santa Cruz, ☎ 954/220971 or 954/220240).

➤ CANADA: **Málaga** (✉ Plaza de la Malagueta 3, ☎ 952/223346). **Seville** (✉ Avda. de los Pinos 34, Casa 4, Mairena del Aljarafe, ☎ 954/229413).

➤ UNITED KINGDOM: **Málaga** (✉ Mauricio Moro 2, ☎ 952/352300). **Seville** (✉ Plaza Nueva 8, ☎ 95/422–8874 or 95/422–8875).

➤ UNITED STATES: **Fuengirola** (✉ Centro Comercial Las Rampas, ☎ 952/474891). **Seville** (✉ Paseo de las Delicias 7, Arenal, ☎ 95/423–1885).

## CONSUMER PROTECTION

Whether you're shopping for gifts or purchasing travel services, **pay with a major credit card** whenever possible, so you can cancel payment or get reimbursed if there's a problem (and you can provide documentation). If you're doing business with a particular company for the first time, **contact your local Better Business Bureau and the attorney general's offices** in your state and (for U.S. businesses) the company's home state as well. Have any complaints been filed? Finally, if you're buying a package or tour, always **consider travel insurance** that includes default coverage (☞ Insurance).

➤ BBBs: **Council of Better Business Bureaus** (✉ 4200 Wilson Blvd., Suite 800, Arlington, VA 22203, ☎ 703/ 276–0100, ℻ 703/525–8277, WEB www.bbb.org).

## CRUISE TRAVEL

Málaga is the cruise capital of Andalusia, and in the summer its port is often filled to capacity with cruise ships that dock for a day or two before gliding to their next port of call. Among the many cruise lines that call at Spain are Royal Caribbean, Holland America Line, Renaissance Cruises, the Norwegian Cruise Line, and Princess Cruises.

To learn how to plan, choose, and book a cruise-ship voyage, consult *Fodor's FYI: Plan & Enjoy Your Cruise* (available in bookstores everywhere).

## CUSTOMS AND DUTIES

When shopping abroad, **keep receipts** for all purchases. Upon reentering the country, **be ready to show customs officials what you've bought.** If you feel a duty is incorrect, appeal the assessment. If you object to the way your clearance was handled, note the inspector's badge number. In either case, first ask to see a supervisor. If the problem isn't resolved, write to the appropriate authorities, beginning with the port director at your point of entry.

### IN AUSTRALIA

Australian residents who are 18 or older may bring home A$400 worth of souvenirs and gifts (including jewelry), 250 cigarettes or 250 grams of tobacco, and 1,125 ml of alcohol (including wine, beer, and spirits). Residents under 18 may bring back A$200 worth of goods. Prohibited items include meat products. Seeds, plants, and fruits need to be declared upon arrival.

➤ INFORMATION: **Australian Customs Service** (Regional Director, ✉ Box 8, Sydney, NSW 2001; ☎ 02/9213– 2000 or 1300/363263; 1800/020504 quarantine-inquiry line; ℻ 02/9213– 4043; WEB www.customs.gov.au).

### IN CANADA

Canadian residents who have been out of Canada for at least seven days may bring in C$750 worth of goods duty-free. If you've been away fewer than seven days but more than 48 hours, the duty-free allowance drops to C$200. If your trip lasts 24 to 48 hours, the allowance is C$50. You may not pool allowances with family members. Goods claimed under the C$750 exemption may follow you by mail; those claimed under the lesser exemptions must accompany you. Alcohol and tobacco products may be included in the seven-day and 48-hour exemptions but not in the 24-hour exemption. If you meet the age requirements of the province or territory through which you reenter Canada, you may bring in, duty-free, 1.5 liters of wine *or* 1.14 liters (40 imperial ounces) of liquor *or* 24 12-ounce cans or bottles of beer or ale. If you are 19 or older you may bring in, duty-free, 200 cigarettes and 50 cigars. Check ahead of time with the Canada Customs and Revenue Agency or the Department of Agriculture for policies regarding meat products, seeds, plants, and fruits.

You may send an unlimited number of gifts (only one gift per recipient, however) worth up to C$60 each duty-free to Canada. Label the package UNSOLICITED GIFT—VALUE UNDER $60. Alcohol and tobacco are excluded.

➤ INFORMATION: **Canada Customs and Revenue Agency** (✉ 2265 St. Laurent Blvd. S, Ottawa, Ontario K1G 4K3, ☎ 204/983–3500, 506/ 636–5064, or 800/461–9999, WEB www.ccra-adrc.gc.ca/).

### IN NEW ZEALAND

All homeward-bound residents may bring back NZ$700 worth of souvenirs and gifts; passengers may not pool their allowances, and children can claim only the concession on goods intended for their own use. For those 17 or older, the duty-free allowance also includes 4.5 liters of wine or beer; one 1,125-ml bottle of spirits; and either 200 cigarettes, 250 grams of tobacco, 50 cigars, *or* a combination of the three up to 250 grams. Meat products, seeds, plants, and fruits must be declared upon arrival to the Agricultural Services Department.

➤ INFORMATION: **New Zealand Customs** (Head office: ✉ The Customhouse, 17–21 Whitmore St., Box 2218, Wellington, ☎ 09/300–5399 or 0800/428–786, 🌐 www.customs.govt.nz).

## IN SPAIN

European Union residents who have traveled only within the EU need not pass through customs upon returning to their home country. If you plan to come home with large quantities of alcohol or tobacco, check EU limits beforehand.

From countries that are not part of the European Union, visitors age 15 and over may *enter* Spain duty-free with up to 200 cigarettes or 50 cigars, up to 1 liter of alcohol over 22 proof, and up to 2 liters of wine. Dogs and cats are admitted as long as they have up-to-date vaccination records from their home country.

## IN THE UNITED KINGDOM

If you are a U.K. resident and your journey was wholly within the European Union, you probably won't have to pass through customs when you return to the United Kingdom. If you plan to bring back large quantities of alcohol or tobacco, check EU limits beforehand. In most cases, if you bring back more than 200 cigars, 800 cigarettes, 10 liters of spirits, and/or 90 liters of wine, you have to declare the goods upon return.

➤ INFORMATION: **HM Customs and Excise** (✉ Portcullis House, 21 Cowbridge Rd. E, Cardiff CF11 9SS, ☎ 029/2038–6423 or 0845/010–9000, 🌐 www.hmce.gov.uk).

## IN THE UNITED STATES

U.S. residents who have been out of the country for at least 48 hours may bring home, for personal use, $800 worth of foreign goods duty-free, as long as they haven't used the $800 allowance or any part of it in the past 30 days. This exemption may include 1 liter of alcohol (for travelers 21 and older), 200 cigarettes, and 100 non-Cuban cigars. Family members from the same household who are traveling together may pool their $800 personal exemptions. For fewer than 48 hours, the duty-free allowance drops to $200, which may include 50 cigarettes, 10 non-Cuban cigars, and 150 milliliters of alcohol (or perfume containing alcohol). The $200 allowance cannot be combined with other individuals' exemptions, and if you exceed it, the full value of all the goods will be taxed. Antiques, which the U.S. Customs Service defines as objects more than 100 years old, enter duty-free, as do original works of art done entirely by hand, including paintings, drawings, and sculptures.

You may also send packages home duty-free, with a limit of one parcel per addressee per day (except alcohol or tobacco products or perfume worth more than $5). You can mail up to $200 worth of goods for personal use; label the package PERSONAL USE and attach a list of its contents and their retail value. If the package contains your used personal belongings, mark it PERSONAL GOODS RETURNED to avoid paying duties. You may send up to $100 worth of goods as a gift; mark the package UNSOLICITED GIFT. Mailed items do not affect your duty-free allowance on your return.

➤ INFORMATION: **U.S. Customs Service** (for inquiries, ✉ 1300 Pennsylvania Ave. NW, Washington, DC 20229, 🌐 www.customs.gov, ☎ 202/354–1000; for complaints, ✉ Customer Satisfaction Unit, 1300 Pennsylvania Ave. NW, Room 5.5A, Washington, DC 20229; for registration of equipment, ✉ Office of Passenger Programs, 1300 Pennsylvania Ave. NW, Room 5.4D, Washington, DC 20229, ☎ 202/927–0530).

## DINING

Spaniards love to eat out, and restaurants in Spain have evolved dramatically thanks to a favorable economic climate and burgeoning tourism. A new generation of Spanish chefs—some with international reputations—has transformed classic dishes to suit contemporary tastes, drawing on some of the freshest ingredients in Europe.

The restaurants featured in this book are the cream of the crop in each price range. Restaurants are identified by a crossed knife-and-fork icon ✕; establishments with a ✕📷 symbol are hotels with restaurants that stand out for their cuisine and are open to nonguests.

| CATEGORY | COST* |
|---|---|
| $$$$ | over €18 |
| $$$ | €13–€18 |
| $$ | €8–€13 |
| $ | under €8 |

*per person for a main course at dinner

## MEALS AND SPECIALTIES

Most restaurants in Spain do not serve breakfast (desayuno); for coffee and carbohydrates, head to a bar or cafetería. Outside major hotels, which serve buffet breakfasts, breakfast in Spain is usually limited to coffee and toast or a roll. Lunch (comida or almuerzo) traditionally consists of an appetizer, a main course, and dessert, followed by coffee and perhaps a liqueur. Dinner (cena) is somewhat lighter, with perhaps only one course.

Between meals, the best way to snack is to sample some tapas (appetizers) at a bar, for which Andalusia is rightly famous. It is said that Andalusia has more tapas bars than any other region in Spain, and after a night or two on the streets of Seville, Granada, or Málaga, you'll likely agree that this is true. The origin of the tapa (which means a "cover" or "lid") stems from a time when bartenders would place a morsel of something or other—say, a slice of ham, or a moist wedge of cheese—atop the glass of wine or sherry they served up. These days, tapas are no longer as simple or, most often, gratis (free). A sampling of tapas has become a meal in itself, and normally you can choose from quite a variety, including excellent seafood. As for the tradition of being served a free nibble, this depends entirely on where you roam. In the touristy quarters of

Andalusia's capitals, the only free tapas may be a handful of nuts or olives—if that. However, as you explore the more out-of-the-way towns, you'll come across plenty of small, old-time tapas joints where your vino tinto (red wine) comes generously accompanied with a slice of pungent cheese or perhaps a wedge of tortilla de patatas (potato omelette). Note that a racion is just a larger helping of a tapa.

In addition to an à la carte menu, most restaurants offer a daily fixed-price menu (menú del día), consisting of two courses, coffee, and dessert at an attractive price. If your server does not suggest the menú del día when you're seated (perhaps on the assumption that foreigners will order à la carte), feel free to ask for it—"Hay menú del día, por favor?" Restaurants in many of the larger tourist areas will have the menú del día posted outside. Usually, the fixed-price menu is served at lunchtime, though increasingly—particularly in tourist centers—it is also served in the evening; again, you may have to ask for it.

Spain as a whole does not have a single cuisine but rather various cuisines representing its distinct regional cultures. Andalusia's most famous contribution to the culinary world is its cold soup, gazpacho and the almond-based ajo blanco, gastronomic godsends in the summer heat. Another Andalusian favorite is pescadito frito (fried fish), delicious and served everywhere. The sherry wines from Jerez de la Frontera are of high renown, from the pale, dry fino to the nutty amontillado.

## MEALTIMES

Mealtimes in Spain are later than elsewhere in Europe. Lunch starts around 2 or 2:30, dinner between 8 and 10 (9 and 11 in Madrid). In the Costa del Sol, with its heavy tourist traffic, restaurants often open a bit earlier, whereas restaurants catering to tourists may not close at all in the middle of the day.

Unless otherwise noted, the restaurants listed in this guide are open daily for lunch and dinner.

## PAYING

Credit cards are widely accepted in Spanish restaurants. If you pay by credit card, leave the tip in cash (☞ Tipping).

## RESERVATIONS AND DRESS

Reservations are always a good idea: we mention them only when they're essential or not accepted. For top restaurants, book as far in advance as you can, and confirm when you arrive in Spain. We mention dress only when men are required to wear a jacket or a jacket and tie.

## WINE, BEER, AND SPIRITS

Apart from its famous wines, Spain produces many brands of lager, the most popular of which are San Miguel, Cruzcampo, Aguila, Mahou, and Estrella. Jerez de la Frontera is Europe's largest producer of brandy and is a major source of sherry. Catalonia produces most of the world's *cava* (sparkling wine). Spanish law prohibits the sale of alcohol to people under 16.

## HEALTH CONCERNS

At the end of 2000, the first cases of bovine spongiform encephalopathy (BSE, or "mad cow disease") were detected among Spanish cattle, raising questions about the safety of eating beef in Spain. Cattle is subject to testing, and local health authorities have declared it safe to eat Spanish beef and veal, but dishes containing brains or cuts including the spinal cord should be avoided.

## DISABILITIES AND ACCESSIBILITY

Unfortunately, Spain has done little to make traveling easy for visitors with disabilities. Many of Andalusia's museums and Moorish monuments are not wheelchair-accessible. In the rest of Spain, only the Prado and some newer museums, such as Madrid's Reina Sofía and Thyssen-Bornemisza, have wheelchair-accessible entrances or elevators. Most of the churches, castles, and monasteries on a sightseer's itinerary involve quite a bit of walking, often on uneven terrain.

## RESERVATIONS

When discussing accessibility with an operator or hotel reservations agent, **ask hard questions.** Are there any stairs, inside *or* out? Are there grab bars next to the toilet *and* in the shower/tub? How wide is the doorway to the room? To the bathroom? For the most extensive facilities meeting the latest legal specifications, **opt for newer accommodations.** If you reserve through a toll-free number, consider also calling the hotel's local number to confirm the information from the central reservations office. Get confirmation in writing when you can.

➤ COMPLAINTS: **Aviation Consumer Protection Division** (☞ Air Travel) for airline-related problems. **Departmental Office of Civil Rights** (for general inquiries, ✉ U.S. Department of Transportation, S-30, 400 7th St. SW, Room 10215, Washington, DC 20590, ☎ 202/366–4648, FAX 202/366–3571, WEB www.dot.gov/ost/docr/index.htm). **Disability Rights Section** (✉ NYAV, U.S. Department of Justice, Civil Rights Division, 950 Pennsylvania Ave. NW, Washington, DC 20530; ☎ ADA information line 202/514–0301, 800/514–0301, 202/514–0383 TTY, 800/514–0383 TTY, WEB www.usdoj.gov/crt/ada/adahom1.htm).

## TRAVEL AGENCIES

In the United States, the Americans with Disabilities Act requires that travel firms serve the needs of all travelers. Some agencies specialize in working with people with disabilities.

➤ TRAVELERS WITH MOBILITY PROBLEMS: **Access Adventures** (✉ 206 Chestnut Ridge Rd., Scottsville, NY 14624, ☎ 716/889–9096, dltravel@prodigy.net), run by a former physical-rehabilitation counselor. **Care-Vacations** (✉ No. 5, 5110–50 Ave., Leduc, Alberta T9E 6V4, Canada, ☎ 780/986–6404 or 877/478–7827, FAX 780/986–8332, WEB www.carevacations.com), for group tours and cruise vacations. **Flying Wheels Travel** (✉ 143 W. Bridge St., Box 382, Owatonna, MN 55060, ☎ 507/451–5005, FAX 507/451–1685, WEB www.flyingwheelstravel.com).

➤ TRAVELERS WITH DEVELOPMENTAL DISABILITIES: **Sprout** (✉ 893 Amsterdam Ave., New York, NY 10025, ☎ 212/222–9575 or 888/222–9575, FAX 212/222–9768, WEB www.gosprout. org).

## DISCOUNTS AND DEALS

Be a smart shopper and **compare all your options** before making decisions. A plane ticket bought with a promotional coupon from travel clubs, coupon books, and direct-mail offers or purchased on the Internet may not be cheaper than the least expensive fare from a discount ticket agency. And always keep in mind that what you get is just as important as what you save.

### DISCOUNT RESERVATIONS

To save money, **look into discount reservations services** with Web sites and toll-free numbers, which use their buying power to get a better price on hotels, airline tickets, even car rentals. When booking a room, always **call the hotel's local toll-free number** (if one is available) rather than the central reservations number—you'll often get a better price. Always ask about special packages or corporate rates.

When shopping for the best deal on hotels and car rentals, **look for guaranteed exchange rates**, which protect you against a falling dollar. With your rate locked in, you won't pay more, even if the price goes up in the local currency.

➤ AIRLINE TICKETS: Air-4-Less (☎ 800/247–4537).

➤ HOTEL ROOMS: Hotel Reservations Network (☎ 800/964–6835, WEB www.hoteldiscount.com). International Marketing & Travel Concepts (☎ 800/790–4682, WEB www. imtc-travel.com). Turbotrip.com (☎ 800/473–7829, WEB www. turbotrip.com). Steigenberger Reservation Service (☎ 800/223–5652, WEB www.srs-worldhotels.com). Travel Interlink (☎ 800/888–5898, WEB www.travelinterlink.com).

### PACKAGE DEALS

Don't confuse packages and guided tours. When you buy a package, you travel on your own, just as though you had planned the trip yourself. Fly/drive packages, which combine airfare and car rental, are often a good deal. If you **buy a rail/drive pass,** you may save on train tickets and car rentals. All Eurail and Europass holders get a discount on Eurostar fares through the Channel Tunnel.

## ELECTRICITY

To use electric-powered equipment purchased in the United States or Canada, **bring a converter and adapter.** Spain's electrical current is 220 volts, 50 cycles alternating current (AC); wall outlets take Continental-type plugs, with two round prongs.

If your appliances are dual-voltage, you'll need only an adapter. Don't use 110-volt outlets marked FOR SHAVERS ONLY for high-wattage appliances such as blow-dryers. Most laptops operate equally well on 110 and 220 volts and so require only an adapter.

## EMERGENCIES

The pan-European **emergency phone number (112)** is operative in some parts of Spain but not all. If it doesn't work, dial the emergency numbers below for national police, local police, fire department, or medical services. On the road, there are emergency phones marked SOS at regular intervals on *autovías* (freeways) and *autopistas* (toll highways).

Most of Andalusia's main cities have a Red Cross (*Cruz Roja*) that can also dispatch an ambulance in case of an emergency. Additionally, there are numerous private ambulance services, which are often listed under *ambulancias* (ambulances) in the *Paginas Amarillas* (Yellow Pages). For non-emergencies, there are private medical clinics throughout Andalusia. Every town also has at least one pharmacy that is on-duty for 24 hours; the address of the on-duty pharmacy is generally posted on the front door of all pharmacies. You can also dial Spain's general information number for the location of a doctor's office or pharmacy that's open nearest you.

If your documents are stolen, contact both the local police and your embassy. If you lose a credit card, phone the issuer immediately (☞ Money).

➤ CONTACTS: **General medical information** (☎ 1003). **National police** (☎ 091). **Local police** (☎ 092). **Fire department** (☎ 080). **Medical service** (☎ 061).

## ENGLISH-LANGUAGE MEDIA

In cities and major resorts, you'll have no trouble finding newspapers and magazines in English. U.K. newspapers are available on the day of publication. From the United States, you'll see major news magazines, such as *Time,* along with *USA Today* and the *International Herald Tribune.* The *Tribune* includes a truncated (eight page), English-language version of *El Pais,* one of Spain's largest daily newspapers.

### BOOKS

Major airports sell books in English, including the latest paperback bestsellers. Bookshops across the Costa del Sol also sell English-language books.

### NEWSPAPERS AND MAGAZINES

Befitting its status as the coastal tourist magnet of Spain, the Costa del Sol offers its vast visitor population a host of local English-language newspapers and magazines. Throughout Málaga you'll find the weekly *Sur, Entertainer,* and *Costa del Sol News* and the monthly magazine *Essential.* In Marbella, there's *Absolute Marbella,* a glossy magazine covering the resort town's glitterati along with restaurant and hotel reviews and listings of all the sumptuous villas and estates you might want to rent or buy. In Nerja, look for the monthly *Insight,* with news and cultural tidbits about the Costa Tropical. Distributed throughout the country is the U.K.-published monthly *Spain,* with articles on travel, lifestyle, property, and gastronomy.

### TELEVISION

Spain is served by two state-owned national television channels, two private networks, regional channels in some parts of Spain, and local channels serving individual towns. Many hotels have satellite service, which usually includes at least one news channel in English (CNN, BBC World, or Sky News).

## ETIQUETTE AND BEHAVIOR

The Spanish are very tolerant of foreigners and their strange ways, but you should always behave with courtesy. Be respectful when visiting churches: casual dress is fine if it's not gaudy or unkempt. Spaniards do object to men going bare-chested anywhere other than the beach or poolside and generally do not look kindly on public displays of drunkenness.

When addressing Spaniards with whom you are not well acquainted, use the formal *usted* rather than the familiar *tu* (☞ Language).

### BUSINESS ETIQUETTE

Spanish office hours can be confusing to the uninitiated. Some offices stay open more or less continuously from 9 to 3, with a very short lunch break. Others open in the morning, break up the day with a long lunch break of two–three hours, then reopen at 4 or 5 until 7 or 8. Spaniards enjoy a certain notoriety for their lack of punctuality, but this has changed dramatically in recent years: you are expected to show up for meetings on time. Smart dress is the norm.

Spaniards in international fields tend to conduct business with foreigners in English. If you speak Spanish, address new colleagues with the formal *usted* and the corresponding verb conjugations, then follow the lead in switching to the familiar *tu* once a working relationship has been established.

## GAY AND LESBIAN TRAVEL

Since the end of Franco's dictatorship, the situation for gays and lesbians in Spain has improved dramatically: the paragraph in the Spanish civil code that made homosexuality a crime was repealed in 1978. Along the coastal resorts and in the major cities, particularly Seville, Granada, and Cádiz, attitudes toward gays and lesbians are relatively tolerant and open. This is due, in part, to the heavy influx of foreign visitors from the progressive parts of Europe, such as Holland and the Scandinavian countries. In Andalusia's smaller towns and rural areas, gay travelers may experience unwanted attention, particularly if they engage in public displays of affection. In summer, the Torremolinos and Benidorm beaches of the Costa del Sol are gay and lesbian hot spots.

➤ GAY- AND LESBIAN-FRIENDLY TRAVEL AGENCIES: **Different Roads Travel** (⊠ 8383 Wilshire Blvd., Suite 902, Beverly Hills, CA 90211, ☎ 323/651–5557 or 800/429–8747, ℻ 323/651–3678, lgernert@tzell.com). **Kennedy Travel** (⊠ 314 Jericho Turnpike, Floral Park, NY 11001, ☎ 516/352–4888 or 800/237–7433, ℻ 516/354–8849, WEB www.kennedytravel.com). **Now, Voyager** (⊠ 4406 18th St., San Francisco, CA 94114, ☎ 415/626–1169 or 800/255–6951, ℻ 415/626–8626, WEB www.nowvoyager.com). **Skylink Travel and Tour** (⊠ 1006 Mendocino Ave., Santa Rosa, CA 95401, ☎ 707/546–9888 or 800/225–5759, ℻ 707/546–9891), serving lesbian travelers.

➤ LOCAL RESOURCES: **Gai Inform** (⊠ Fuencarral 37, 28004 Madrid, ☎ 91/523–0070). **Nos Asociación Andaluza de Lesbianas y Gais** (⊠ Calle Lavadero de las Tablas 15, Granada, ☎ 958/200602).**Teléfono Rosa** (⊠ C. Finlandia 45, Barcelona, ☎ 900/601601).

## GUIDEBOOKS

Plan well and you won't be sorry. Guidebooks are excellent tools—and you can take them with you. If you plan on exploring the rest of Spain, you may want to check out *Fodor's Spain,* or the color-photo-illustrated *Fodor's Exploring Spain,* which is thorough on culture and history. They are available at on-line retailers and bookstores everywhere.

## HEALTH

Sunburn and heatstroke are real risks in summertime Spain. On the hottest sunny days, even those who are not normally bothered by strong sun should cover themselves up, carry sunblock lotion, drink plenty of fluids, and limit sun time for the first few days. Andalusia simmers with the highest temperatures in Spain, and Seville, in particular, is legendary for its blistering summer heat waves, which often reach 100°F (38°C) or more. There is a very good reason why Andalusians, indeed, most

Spaniards, take a long lunch break and, traditionally, a siesta between 2 and 5—it's to escape the heat and cool down before emerging once again after the sun has dipped lower in the sky.

If you require medical attention, ask your hotel's front desk for assistance or go to the nearest public Centro de Salud (day hospital); in serious cases, you'll be referred to the regional hospital. Medical care is good in Spain, but nursing is perfunctory, as relatives are expected to stop by and look after inpatients' needs. In some popular destinations, such as the Costa del Sol, there are volunteer English interpreters on hand.

Spain was recently documented as having the highest number of AIDS cases in Europe. Those applying for work permits will be asked for proof of HIV-negative status.

## FOOD AND DRINK

The major health risk in Spain is *diarrea,* or traveler's diarrhea, caused by eating contaminated fruit or vegetables or drinking contaminated water. So **watch what you eat.** Avoid ice, uncooked food, and unpasteurized milk and milk products, and **drink only bottled water** or water that has been boiled for several minutes, even when brushing your teeth. Mild cases may respond to Imodium (known generically as loperamide) or Pepto-Bismol, both of which can be purchased over the counter. In Spain, ask for *un antidiarreico,* which is the general term for antidiarrheal medicine; Fortasec is a well-known brand. You don't need a prescription to buy it. Drink plenty of purified water or tea—chamomile is a good folk remedy. In severe cases, rehydrate yourself with a salt-sugar solution consisting of ½ teaspoon salt (*sal*) and 4 tablespoons sugar (*azúcar*) per quart of water.

### OVER-THE-COUNTER REMEDIES

Over-the-counter remedies are available at any *farmacia* (pharmacy), recognizable by the large green cross outside. Some medications will look familiar, such as *aspirina* (aspirin), whereas others are sold under various brand names. If you regularly take a nonprescription medicine, take a sample box or bottle with you, and the Spanish pharmacist will provide you with its local equivalent.

### HOLIDAYS

Spain's national holidays are January 1, January 6 (Epiphany), Good Friday, Easter, May 1 (May Day), August 15 (Assumption), October 12 (National Day), November 1 (All Saints'), December 6 (Constitution), December 8 (Immaculate Conception), and December 25. In addition, each region, city, and town has its own holidays honoring political events and patron saints.

If a public holiday falls on a Tuesday or Thursday, note that **many businesses also close on the adjacent Monday or Friday** for a long weekend, called a *puente* (bridge). If a major holiday falls on a Sunday, businesses close on Monday.

### INSURANCE

The most useful travel-insurance plan is a comprehensive policy that includes coverage for trip cancellation and interruption, default, trip delay, and medical expenses (with a waiver for preexisting conditions).

Without insurance you will lose all or most of your money if you cancel your trip, regardless of the reason. Default insurance covers you if your tour operator, airline, or cruise line goes out of business. Trip-delay covers expenses that arise because of bad weather or mechanical delays. Study the fine print when comparing policies.

When you're traveling internationally, a key component of travel insurance is coverage for medical bills incurred if you get sick on the road. Such expenses are not generally covered by Medicare or private policies. U.K. residents can buy a travel-insurance policy valid for most vacations taken during the year in which it's purchased (but check preexisting-condition coverage). British and Australian citizens need extra medical coverage when traveling overseas.

Always **buy travel policies directly from the insurance company**; if you buy them from a cruise line, airline, or tour operator that goes out of business you probably will not be covered for the agency or operator's default, a major risk. Before making any purchase, **review your existing health and home-owner's policies** to find what they cover away from home.

➤ INSURANCE INFORMATION: In the U.K.: **Association of British Insurers** (✉ 51 Gresham St., London EC2V 7HQ, ☎ 020/7600–3333, FAX 020/7696–8999, WEB www.abi.org.uk). In Canada: **RBC Travel Insurance** (✉ 6880 Financial Dr., Mississauga, Ontario L5N 7Y5, ☎ 905/791–8700 or 800/668–4342, FAX 905/813–4704, WEB www.rbcinsurance.com). In Australia: **Insurance Council of Australia** (✉ Level 3, 56 Pitt St., Sydney, NSW 2000, ☎ 02/9253–5100, FAX 02/9253–5111, WEB www.ica.com.au). In New Zealand: **Insurance Council of New Zealand** (✉ Level 7, 111–115 Customhouse Quay, Box 474, Wellington, ☎ 04/472–5230, FAX 04/473–3011, WEB www.icnz.org.nz).

➤ TRAVEL INSURERS: In the U.S.: **Access America** (✉ 6600 W. Broad St., Richmond, VA 23230, ☎ 800/284–8300, FAX 804/673–1491 or 800/346–9265, WEB www.accessamerica.com). **Travel Guard International** (✉ 1145 Clark St., Stevens Point, WI 54481, ☎ 715/345–0505 or 800/826–1300, FAX 800/955–8785, WEB www.travelguard.com).

### LANGUAGE

Although Spaniards exported their language to all Central and South America, you may be surprised to find that Spanish is not the principal language in all of Spain. The Basques speak Euskera; in Catalonia, you'll hear Catalan; in Galicia, Gallego; and in Valencia, Valenciano. Although almost everyone in these regions also speaks and understands Spanish, local radio and television stations may broadcast in these languages, and road signs may be printed (or spray-painted over) with the preferred regional language. Spanish is referred to as Castellano, or Castilian.

Fortunately, Spanish is fairly easy to pick up, and your efforts to speak it will be graciously received. **Learn at**

**least the following basic phrases:**
*buenos días* (hello—until 2 PM),
*buenas tardes* (good afternoon—until
8 PM), *buenas noches* (hello—after
dark), *por favor* (please), *gracias*
(thank you), *adiós* (good-bye), *sí*
(yes), *no* (no), *los servicios* (the toi-
lets), *la cuenta* (bill/check), *habla
inglés?* (do you speak English?), and
*no comprendo* (I don't understand).
For more helpful expressions, *see* the
Spanish Vocabulary at the end of this
guide or, better yet, pick up a copy of
Fodor's *Spanish for Travelers*.

You should have no trouble finding
people who speak English in major
cities and coastal resorts, but you
won't necessarily be able to count on
the bus driver or the passerby on the
street. Those who do speak English
may speak the British variety, so don't
be surprised if you're told to queue
(line up) or take the lift (elevator) to
the loo (toilet). Many guided tours
offered at museums and historic sites
are in Spanish; ask about the language that will be spoken before you
sign up.

## LANGUAGES FOR TRAVELERS

A phrase book and language-tape set
can help get you started. *Fodor's
Spanish for Travelers* (available at
bookstores everywhere) is excellent.

## LANGUAGE PROGRAMS

Málaga has the distinction of offering
Spain's first Spanish-language program for foreigners, begun in 1947.
Since then, Málaga has grown into
one of Spain's principal centers to
learn Spanish, with more than 24
accredited schools and a notable
Spanish-language program at the
University of Málaga. Programs may
last anywhere from 2 to 12 weeks, or
more, and often combine classes with
a host of outdoor and social activities,
such as tapa tasting and sightseeing
excursions.

Salamanca is also renowned for its
Spanish-language programs, particularly its distinguished, long-running
program at the University of Salamanca. In the rest of Spain, you'll
find a number of private schools that
offer Spanish-language courses of
various durations for foreigners. Don
Quijote is one network with schools

in several locations around Spain.
The international network Inlingua
has 30 schools in Spain.

The state-run Instituto Cervantes,
devoted to promoting Spanish language and culture, teaches in its
offices worldwide and can advise you
on other courses in Spain.

➤ LANGUAGE PROGRAMS: **Don Quijote**
(⊠ C. Placentinos 2, Salamanca,
37998, ☎ 923/268860). **Escuela
Acacias** (⊠ Avda. Juan Sebastián 117,
Málaga, 29017, ☎ 952/295902, WEB
www.acacias.org). **Inlingua International** (⊠ Belpstrasse 11, Berne, CH-
3007, Switzerland, ☎ 4131/388–
7777). **Instituto Cervantes** (⊠ 122 E.
42nd St., Suite 807, New York, NY
10168, ☎ 212/689–4232).

## LODGING

The Spanish government has spent
decades buying up old castles and
historic buildings and converting
them into outstanding lodgings called
paradors. In contrast, most of Spain's
private hotels are modern high-rises,
though more and more innkeepers are
restoring historic properties. By law,
hotel prices must be posted at the
reception desk and should indicate
whether or not the value-added tax
(IVA; 7%) is included. Breakfast is
normally *not* included. Note that
high-season rates prevail not only in
summer but also during Holy Week
and local fiestas.

The lodgings we list are the cream
of the crop in each price category.
We always list the facilities that
are available, but we don't specify
whether they cost extra; when pricing
accommodations, always ask what's
included and what's not. Properties
are assigned price categories based on
the range from their least-expensive
standard double room at high season
(excluding holidays) to the most
expensive. Properties marked ✕🖭 are
lodging establishments whose restaurants warrant a special trip.

| CATEGORY | COST |
| --- | --- |
| $$$$ | over €140 |
| $$$ | €100–€140 |
| $$ | €60–€100 |
| $ | under €60 |

*All prices are for a standard double
room, excluding tax.*

➤ INTERNATIONAL AGENTS: **El Sol** (✉ Box 320, Wayne, PA 19087, ☎ 610/687–9066, WEB www.elsolvillas.com). **Hideaways International** (✉ 767 Islington St., Portsmouth, NH 03801, ☎ 603/430–4433 or 800/843–4433, FAX 603/430–4444, WEB www.hideaways.com; membership $129). **Hometours International** (✉ Box 11503, Knoxville, TN 37939, ☎ 865/690–8484 or 800/367–4668, WEB http://thor.he.net/~hometour/). **Interhome** (✉ 1990 N.E. 163rd St., Suite 110, North Miami Beach, FL 33162, ☎ 305/940–2299 or 800/882–6864, FAX 305/940–2911, WEB www.interhome.com). **Villas and Apartments Abroad** (✉ 1270 Ave. of the Americas, 15th floor, New York, NY 10020, ☎ 212/897–5045 or 800/433–3020, FAX 212/897–5039, WEB www.ideal-villas.com). **Villas International** (✉ 4340 Redwood Hwy., Suite D309, San Rafael, CA 94903, ☎ 415/499–9490 or 800/221–2260, FAX 415/499–9491, WEB www.villasintl.com).

## CAMPING

Camping in Spain is not a wilderness experience. The country has more than 500 campgrounds, and many have excellent facilities, including hot showers, restaurants, swimming pools, tennis courts, and even nightclubs. Be aware that in summer, especially August, the best campgrounds fill with Spanish families, who move in with their entire households: pets, grandparents, even the kitchen sink and stove. You can pick up an official list of all Spanish campgrounds at tourist offices.

It can be hard to find a site for independent camping outside established campgrounds. For safety reasons, you cannot camp next to roads, on riverbanks, or on the beach, nor can you set up house in urban areas, nature parks (outside designated camping areas), or within 1 km (½ mi) of any established campsite. To camp on a private farm, seek the owner's permission.

## HOME EXCHANGES

If you would like to exchange your home for someone else's, **join a home-exchange organization,** which will send you its updated listings of available exchanges for a year and will include your own listing in at least one of them. It's up to you to make specific arrangements.

➤ EXCHANGE CLUBS: **HomeLink International** (✉ Box 47747, Tampa, FL 33647, ☎ 813/975–9825 or 800/638–3841, FAX 813/910–8144, WEB www.homelink.org; $106 per year). **Intervac U.S.** (✉ 30 Corte San Fernando, Tiburon, CA 94920, ☎ 800/756–4663, FAX 415/435–7440, WEB www.intervacus.com; $90 yearly fee for a listing, on-line access, and a catalog; $50 without catalog).

## HOSTELS

No matter what your age, you can **save on lodging costs by staying at hostels.** In some 4,500 locations in more than 70 countries around the world, Hostelling International (HI), the umbrella group for a number of national youth-hostel associations, offers single-sex, dorm-style beds and, at many hostels, rooms for couples and family accommodations. Membership in any HI national hostel association, open to travelers of all ages, allows you to stay in HI-affiliated hostels at member rates; one-year membership is about $25 for adults (C$35 for a two-year minimum membership in Canada, £13 in the United Kingdom, A$52 in Australia, and NZ$40 in New Zealand); hostels run about $10–$30 per night. Members have priority if the hostel is full; they're also eligible for discounts around the world, even on rail and bus travel in some countries.

➤ ORGANIZATIONS: **Hostelling International—American Youth Hostels** (✉ 733 15th St. NW, Suite 840, Washington, DC 20005, ☎ 202/783–6161, FAX 202/783–6171, WEB www.hiayh.org). **Hostelling International—Canada** (✉ 400–205 Catherine St., Ottawa, Ontario K2P 1C3, ☎ 613/237–7884 or 800/663–5777, FAX 613/237–7868, WEB www.hihostels.ca). **Youth Hostel Association of England and Wales** (✉ Trevelyan House, Dimple Rd., Matlock, Derbyshire DE4 3YH, U.K., ☎ 0870/870–8808, FAX 0169/592–702, WEB www.yha.org.uk). **Youth Hostel Association Australia** (✉ 10 Mallett St., Camperdown, NSW 2050, ☎ 02/9565–1699,

FAX 02/9565–1325, WEB www.yha.com. au). **Youth Hostels Association of New Zealand** (⊠ Level 3, 193 Cashel St., Box 436, Christchurch, ☎ 03/ 379–9970, FAX 03/365–4476, WEB www.yha.org.nz).

## HOTELS

The Spanish government classifies hotels with one to five stars. Although quality is a factor, **the rating is technically only an indication of how many facilities the hotel offers.** For example, a three-star hotel may be just as comfortable as a four-star hotel but lack a swimming pool. Similarly, Fodor's price categories ($–$$$$) indicate room rates only—they aren't a measure of comparative quality. You might find a well-kept $$$ inn more charming than the famous $$$$ property down the street.

All hotel entrances are marked with a blue plaque bearing the letter H and the number of stars. The letter R (standing for *residencia*) after the letter H indicates an establishment with no meal service. The designations *fonda* (F), *pensión* (P), *casa de huéspedes* (CH), and *hostal* (Hs) indicate budget accommodations. In most cases, especially in smaller villages, rooms in such buildings will be basic but clean; in large cities, they can be downright dreary. Note that a *hostal* and *hostel* are not the same thing; although both are budget options, a *hostal* should be perceived as a less-expensive hotel, though not as inexpensive as a dorm room–style hostel.

Spain's major private hotel groups include the Sol Meliá, Tryp, and Hotusa. The NH chain, which is concentrated in major cities, primarily serves business travelers. Dozens of reasonably priced beachside high-rises along the Costa del Sol and Costa Tropical cater to package tours.

There is a growing trend in Spain toward small country hotels. Estancias de España is an association of more than 40 independently owned hotels in restored palaces, monasteries, mills, and post houses, generally in rural Spain; contact them for a free directory.

Although a single room (*habitación sencilla*) is usually available, singles are often on the small side. Solo travelers might prefer to pay a bit extra for single occupancy of a double room (*habitación doble uso individual*). All hotels we review have private bathrooms unless otherwise noted.

➤ MAJOR SPANISH CHAINS: **NH Hoteles** (☎ 902/115116, WEB www. nh-hoteles.es). **Sol Meliá** (☎ 902/ 144444, WEB www.solmelia.com). **Tryp** (☎ 901/116199, WEB www. trypnet.es).

➤ SMALL HOTELS: **AHRA** (Andalusian Association of Rural Hotels; ⊠ C. Cristo Rey 2, 23400 Úbeda, Jaén, ☎ 953/755867). **Estancias de España** (⊠ Menéndez Pidal 31-bajo izq., 28036 Madrid, ☎ 91/345–4141). **Hosterías y Hospederías Reales** (hotels in Castile–La Mancha; ⊠ Frailes 1, 13320 Villanueva de los Infantes, Ciudad Real, ☎ 902/ 202010).

➤ TOLL-FREE NUMBERS: **Best Western** (☎ 800/528–1234, WEB www. bestwestern.com). **Choice** (☎ 800/ 424–6423, WEB www.choicehotels. com). **Hilton** (☎ 800/445–8667, WEB www.hilton.com). **Holiday Inn** (☎ 800/465–4329, WEB www. sixcontinentshotels.com). **Westin Hotels & Resorts** (☎ 800/228–3000, WEB www.starwood.com/westin).

## PARADORS

The Spanish government runs more than 80 paradors—upmarket hotels in historic buildings or near significant sites. Some are in castles on a hill with sweeping views; others are in monasteries or convents filled with artistic treasures; still others are in modern buildings on choice beachfront, alpine, or pastoral property. Andalusia is well endowed with paradors, from Ronda's lovely parador perched above the Tajo gorge to the spectacular mountaintop parador in Jaén—one of the stars of the parador chain—built in the Moorish Castillo de Santa Catalina.

Parador rates are reasonable, considering that most have four- or five-star amenities; and the premises are invariably immaculate and tastefully furnished, often with antiques or reproductions. The paradors offer 35% discounts to senior citizens 60 and over, usually in the months of

May and June, though the months may vary. Those who are 30 and under also qualify for special discounted deals (with the buffet breakfast included in the price), generally from May to December. Each parador has a restaurant serving regional specialties, and you can stop in for a meal or a drink without spending the night. Breakfast, however, is an expensive buffet, so if you just want coffee and a roll, you'll do better to walk down the street to a local café.

Because paradors are extremely popular with foreigners and Spaniards alike, **make reservations well in advance.**

➤ INFORMATION: In Spain: **Paradores de España** (⊠ Central de Reservas, Requena 3, 28013 Madrid, ☎ 91/516–6666, WEB www.parador.es). In the U.S.: **Marketing Ahead** (⊠ 433 5th Ave., New York, NY 10016, ☎ 212/686–9213 or 800/223–1356). In the U.K.: **Keytel International** (⊠ 402 Edgeware Rd., London W2 1ED, ☎ 0207/402–8182).

### RURAL LODGINGS

Throughout Andalusia, a growing number of *casas rurales* (country houses similar to bed-and-breakfasts) offer a pastoral lodging experience either in guest rooms or in self-catering cottages. Comfort and conveniences vary widely; it's best to book this type of accommodation through one of the appropriate regional associations. Ask the local tourist office about casas rurales in your chosen area.

➤ CONTACTS: **AHRA** (Andalusian Association of Rural Hotels; ⊠ C. Cristo Rey 2, 23400 Úbeda, Jaén, ☎ 953/755867). **Red Andaluza de Alojamientos Rurales** (⊠ Apartado 2035, 04080 Almería, ☎ 950/265018, WEB www.raar.es; ⊠ Calle Sierpes 48, Oficina D, 41004 Seville, ☎ 95/421–1266). **Viajes Rural de Almería** (⊠ Centro Comercial Oliveros 27, 04004 Almería, ☎ 950/254–178, WEB www.ruralesalmeria.com).

### MAIL AND SHIPPING

Spain's postal system, the *correos,* does work, but delivery times can vary widely. An airmail letter to the United States may take anywhere from four days to two weeks; delivery to other destinations is equally unpredictable. Sending your letters by priority mail ("*urgente*") ensures speedier arrival.

### OVERNIGHT SERVICES

When time is of the essence, or when you're sending valuable items or documents overseas, you can use a courier (*mensajero*). The major international agencies, such as Federal Express and UPS, have representatives in Spain; the biggest Spanish courier service is Seur. MRW is another local courier that provides express delivery worldwide.

➤ MAJOR SERVICES: **DHL** (☎ 902/122424). **Federal Express** (☎ 900/100871). **MRW** (☎ 900/300400). **Seur** (☎ 902/101010). **UPS** (☎ 900/102410).

### POSTAL RATES

Airmail letters to the United States and Canada cost €.75 up to 20 grams. Letters to the United Kingdom and other EU countries cost €.50 up to 20 grams. Letters within Spain are €.25. Postcards carry the same rates as letters. You can buy stamps at post offices and at licensed tobacco shops.

### RECEIVING MAIL

Because mail delivery in Spain can often be slow and unreliable, it's best to have your mail sent to American Express. Mail can also be held at a Spanish post office; have it addressed TO LISTA DE CARREOS (the equivalent of poste restante) in a town you'll be visiting. Postal addresses should include the name of the province in parentheses, e.g., Marbella (Málaga).

➤ INFORMATION: In the U.S., call **American Express** (☎ 800/528–4800) for a list of offices overseas.

### MONEY MATTERS

Spain is no longer a budget destination, but prices still compare slightly favorably with those elsewhere in Europe. Coffee in a bar generally costs €.75 (standing) or €.90 (seated). Beer in a bar: €.95 standing, €1 seated. Small glass of wine in a bar: around €1. Soft drink: €1–€1.20 a bottle. Ham-and-cheese sandwich: €1.80–€2.70. Two-km (1-mi) taxi ride: €2.40, but the meter keeps ticking in traffic jams. Local bus ride: €.80–€1.20. Movie ticket: €3–€4.80. Foreign newspaper: €1.80.

Prices throughout this guide are given for adults. Substantially reduced fees are almost always available for children, students, and senior citizens. For information on taxes, *see* Taxes.

## ATMS

All decent-size towns in Spain have ATMs. The majority of ATMs are found in banks, but increasingly you can also find ATMs in large shopping centers. All major Spanish banks are members of the Cirrus and Plus networks and therefore the majority of local bank cards work in Spanish ATMs simply by punching in the same PIN (Personal Identification Number) you use at home. Nevertheless, it's a good idea to check with your bank before leaving home to confirm that your PIN will work abroad. The word "PIN" in Spanish is the same, though pronounced *"peen."* Most Spanish ATMs require a PIN with a minimum of four digits. It is important that you know your PIN by its digits (and not just by the corresponding letters) because some ATM keypads in Spain aren't marked with letters, just numbers; also, some keypads are the reverse of the U.S., with "9,8,7" on the first row, "6, 5, 4" on the second row (and so on), instead of starting with "1, 2, 3" on the first row as they commonly do in the U.S. You can also use credit cards in ATMs but before leaving home you must **make sure your credit cards are programmed for ATM use in Spain.** If you don't already have one, you will have to request a PIN before leaving your home country in order to access money from your credit card at a foreign ATM. Make sure to request your PIN at least a two to three weeks before leaving on your trip, because most credit card companies will not issue PIN numbers over the phone, but only by sending it to your home address. Note, too, that if the magnetic strip on your credit card or debit card is somehow demagnitized and doesn't work in an ATM, you can go into most main banks and request a cash advance or cash withdrawal via a manual transaction. It's a good idea to warn your credit card company that you're going abroad—sometimes they see exotic destinations on charges and suspend service for security reasons.

## CREDIT CARDS

Credit cards are generally accepted throughout Andalusia. The most common exception is that some restaurants don't accept American Express. Throughout this guide, the following abbreviations are used: **AE,** American Express; **DC,** Diners Club; **MC,** MasterCard; and **V,** Visa.

➤ REPORTING LOST CARDS: **American Express** (☎ 900/941413). **Diners Club** (☎ 901/101011). **MasterCard** (☎ 900/974445). **Visa** (☎ 900/971231).

## CURRENCY

On January 1, 2002, the European monetary unit, the euro (€), went into circulation in Spain and the other countries that have adopted it (Austria, Belgium, Finland, France, Germany, Greece, Ireland, Italy, Luxembourg, the Netherlands, and Portugal). Euro notes come in denominations of 5, 10, 20, 50, 100, 200, and 500; coins are worth 1 cent of a euro, 2 cents, 5 cents, 10 cents, 20 cents, 50 cents, 1 euro, and 2 euros. At press time, exchange rates were €1.02 to the U.S. dollar, €1.57 to the pound sterling, €.66 to the Canadian dollar, €.56 to the Australian dollar, €.48 to the New Zealand dollar, and €.10 to the South African rand.

## CURRENCY EXCHANGE

For the most favorable rates, **change money through banks.** Although ATM transaction fees may be higher abroad than at home, ATM rates are excellent because they are based on wholesale rates offered only by major banks. You won't do as well at exchange booths in airports or rail and bus stations, in hotels, in restaurants, or in stores. To avoid lines at airport exchange booths, **get a bit of local currency before you leave home.**

➤ EXCHANGE SERVICES: **International Currency Express** (☎ 888/278–6628 orders). **Thomas Cook Currency Services** (☎ 800/287–7362 orders and retail locations, WEB www.us.thomascook.com).

## TRAVELER'S CHECKS

Do you need traveler's checks? It depends on where you're headed. If you're going to rural areas and small towns, go with cash; traveler's checks are best used in cities. Lost or stolen checks can usually be replaced within 24 hours. To ensure a speedy refund, buy your own traveler's checks—don't let someone else pay for them: irregularities like this can cause delays. The person who bought the checks should make the call to request a refund.

## OUTDOORS AND SPORTS

Andalusia's fair weather is ideally suited to outdoor sports virtually year-round, though in summer you should restrict physical activity to early morning and late afternoon. Spain has more golf courses than any other country in Europe and is also kind to hikers, water-sports enthusiasts, and, believe it or not, skiers. The country's sports federations have the best information; local tourist offices (☞ Visitor Information) can also be helpful.

### GOLF

Andalusia, with more than 70 courses, is a golfer's paradise. Spain's—if not Europe's—highest concentration of golf courses are sprinkled across the Costa del Sol, whose nearly year-round balmy weather, combined with vistas of the glittering Mediterranean, make it a memorable spot to play. The celebrated Valderrama, once host of the Ryder Cup, is in Sotogrande, near San Roque. You'll also find plentiful courses along the balmy coasts of Almería and Cádiz. The best season for golf is October through June; greens fees are lower during the hot summer months. Many hotels linked to golf courses offer all-inclusive deals, or offer guests reduced greens fees.

➤ INFORMATION: **Real Federación Española de Golf** (✉ Capitán Haya 9, 28020 Madrid, ☎ 91/555–2682).

### HIKING

Andalusia's vast and varied natural treasures are a boon for hikers. From the looming Sierra Nevada in Granada to the lush natural parks— more than 12 in all—that unfold across the region, the opportunities are endless. With its pine forests, waterfalls, and gorges, the Cazorla Nature Park in the Jaén province is an outdoors wonderland for hikers. It also boasts the *Cañada de las Fuentes,* the source of Andalusia's grand river, the Guadalquivir. Throughout Andalusia, the parks' visitor centers and local outing clubs usually have plenty of information.

➤ INFORMATION: **Agencia de Medio Ambiente (AMA) de Jaén** (✉ Avda. de Andalucía 79, 23001 Jaén, ☎ 953/215000). **Federación Española de Montañismo** (✉ C. Floridablanca 75, 08015 Barcelona, ☎ 93/426–4267).

### SKIING

Not everyone thinks of sunny Spain as a skier's destination, but it's the second-most mountainous country in Europe (after Switzerland) and has an impressive 28 ski centers. The best slopes are in the Pyrenees and also in the Sierra Nevada, near Granada. The Sierra Nevada, with the highest peak in mainland Spain, has one of Europe's best-equipped ski stations, with 21 lifts and about 60 km (40 mi) of marked trails.

➤ INFORMATION: **Federación Española de Deportes de Invierno** (Spanish Winter Sports Federation; ✉ Arroyo Fresno 3A, 28035 Madrid, ☎ 91/376–9930). **Recorded ski report** in Spanish (☎ 91/350–2020). **Sierra Nevada snow conditions** in Spanish (☎ 958/249119).

### WATER SPORTS

Water sports abound in Andalusia. Yacht harbors dot the region's Mediterranean coast, and virtually every coastal city and resort has several clubs and outfits that rent equipment and/or offer courses and tours. The coast near Tarifa, on Spain's southernmost tip, is the windsurfing capital of mainland Europe. Spain's best dive sites are Granada province and the Cabo de Gata (near Almería); regional tourist offices can direct you to the local diving clubs. The Guadalquivir River, churning across Andalusia, presents numerous boating opportunities, from canoeing to paddleboat trips.

➤ INFORMATION: **Federación Española de Vela** (Spanish Sailing Federation; ✉ Luís de Salazar 9, 28002 Madrid, ☎ 91/519–5008).

## PACKING

Pack light. Although baggage carts are free and plentiful in most Spanish airports, they're rare in train and bus stations.

On the whole, Spaniards dress up more than Americans or the British. Summer is hot nearly everywhere; visits in winter, fall, and spring call for warm clothing and, in winter, boots. It makes sense to wear casual, comfortable clothing and shoes for sightseeing, but you'll want to **dress up a bit in large cities, especially for fine restaurants and nightclubs.** American tourists are easily spotted for their sneakers—if you want to blend in, wear leather shoes.

On the beach, anything goes; it's common to see females of all ages wearing only bikini bottoms, and many of the more remote beaches allow nude sunbathing. Regardless of your style, **bring a cover-up** to wear over your bathing suit when you leave the beach.

In your carry-on luggage, **pack an extra pair of eyeglasses or contact lenses and enough of any medication** you take to last a few days longer than the entire trip. You may also ask your doctor to write a spare prescription using the drug's generic name, since brand names may vary from country to country. In luggage to be checked, **never pack prescription drugs or valuables.** And don't forget to carry with you the addresses of offices that handle refunds of lost traveler's checks. Check *Fodor's How to Pack* (available in bookstores everywhere) for more tips.

To avoid customs and security delays, carry medications in their original packaging. Don't pack any sharp objects in your carry-on luggage, including knives of any size or material, scissors, manicure tools, and corkscrews, or anything else that might arouse suspicion.

## CHECKING LUGGAGE

You are allowed one carry-on bag and one personal article, such as a purse or a laptop computer. Make sure that everything you carry aboard will fit under your seat or in the overhead bin. Get to the gate early, so you can board as soon as possible, before the overhead bins fill up.

If you are flying internationally, note that baggage allowances may be determined not by piece but by weight—generally 88 pounds (40 kilograms) in first class, 66 pounds (30 kilograms) in business class, and 44 pounds (20 kilograms) in economy.

Airline liability for baggage is limited to $2,500 per person on flights within the United States. On international flights it amounts to $9.07 per pound or $20 per kilogram for checked baggage (roughly $640 per 70-pound bag) and $400 per passenger for unchecked baggage. You can buy additional coverage at check-in for about $10 per $1,000 of coverage, but it excludes a rather extensive list of items, shown on your airline ticket.

Before departure, **itemize your bags' contents** and their worth, and label the bags with your name, address, and phone number. (If you use your home address, cover it so potential thieves can't see it readily.) Inside each bag, **pack a copy of your itinerary.** At check-in, **make sure that each bag is correctly tagged** with the destination airport's three-letter code. If your bags arrive damaged or fail to arrive at all, file a written report with the airline before leaving the airport.

## PASSPORTS AND VISAS

When traveling internationally, **carry your passport** even if you don't need one (it's always the best form of I.D.) and **make two photocopies of the data page** (one for someone at home and another for you, carried separately from your passport). If you lose your passport, promptly call the nearest embassy or consulate and the local police.

U.S. passport applications for children under age 14 require consent from both parents or legal guardians; both parents must appear together to sign the application. If only one parent appears, he or she must submit a written statement from the other parent authorizing passport issuance for the child. A parent with sole authority must present evidence of it when applying; acceptable documentation includes the child's certified birth certificate listing only the applying parent, a court order specifically permitting this parent's travel with the child, or a death certificate for the nonapplying parent. Application forms and instructions are available on the Web site of the U.S. State Department's Bureau of Consular Affairs (www.travel.state.gov).

### ENTERING SPAIN

Visitors from the United States, Australia, Canada, New Zealand, and the United Kingdom need a valid passport to enter Spain. Australians who wish to stay longer than a month also need a visa, available from the Spanish embassy in Canberra.

### PASSPORT OFFICES

The best time to apply for a passport or to renew one is in fall and winter. Before any trip, check your passport's expiration date, and, if necessary, renew it as soon as possible.

➤ AUSTRALIAN CITIZENS: **Australian State Passport Office** (☎ 131–232, WEB www.passports.gov.au).

➤ CANADIAN CITIZENS: **Passport Office** (to mail in applications: ✉ Department of Foreign Affairs and International Trade, Ottawa, Ontario K1A 0G3; ☎ 800/567–6868 toll free in Canada or 819/994–3500, WEB www.dfait-maeci.gc.ca/passport).

➤ NEW ZEALAND CITIZENS: **New Zealand Passport Office** (☎ 0800/22–5050 or 04/474–8100, WEB www.passports.govt.nz).

➤ U.K. CITIZENS: **London Passport Office** (☎ 0870/521–0410, WEB www.passport.gov.uk).

➤ U.S. CITIZENS: **National Passport Information Center** (☎ 900/225–5674, 35¢ per minute for automated service or $1.05 per minute for operator service, WEB www.travel.state.gov).

### REST ROOMS

Spain has some public rest rooms, including, in larger cities, small coin-operated booths. Your best option,

however, is to use the facilities in a bar or cafeteria, remembering that it's customary to order a drink in such cases. Gas stations have rest rooms; you usually have to request the key to use them.

### SAFETY

Petty crime is a huge problem in Spain's most popular tourist destinations. In Andalusia, you should be particularly careful in the city of Málaga, which has one of the highest unemployment rates in Spain. Many muggings have been reported, though the most frequent offenses are pickpocketing, something that also happens with alarming frequency in Seville, Granada, and, elsewhere in Spain, in Madrid and Barcelona. In airports, laptop computers are choice prey. The best way to protect yourself against purse snatchers and pickpockets is to **wear a concealed money belt or a pouch** on a string around your neck. **Don't wear an exterior money belt or a waist pack,** both of which peg you as a tourist. Store only enough money in your wallet or purse to cover casual spending. Distribute the rest of your cash and any valuables (including credit cards and your passport) between a deep front pocket, an inside jacket or vest pocket, and a hidden money pouch. Do not reach for the money pouch once in public. If you carry a bag or camera, be absolutely sure it has straps; you should sling it across your body bandolier-style, adjusting the height to hip level or higher. Men should carry their wallet in the front pocket; women carrying purses should strap them across the front of their bodies. Leave the rest of your valuables in the safe at your hotel.

On the beach, in cafés and restaurants (particularly in the well-touristed areas), and in Internet centers, always keep your belongings on your lap or tied to your person in some way. Additionally, be cautious of any odd or unnecessary human contact, verbal or physical, whether it's a tap on the shoulder, someone spilling their drink at your table, and so on. Thieves often work in twos, so while one is attracting your attention, the other could be swiping your wallet.

Theft from cars occurs all over the country. We cannot overemphasize the fact that you should **never, ever leave anything valuable in a parked car,** no matter how friendly the area feels, how quickly you'll return, or how invisible the item seems once you lock it in the trunk. Thieves can spot rental cars a mile away, and they work very efficiently.

## WOMEN IN SPAIN

The traditional Spanish custom of the *piropo* (a shouted "compliment" to women walking down the street) is fast disappearing, though women traveling alone may still encounter it on occasion. The piropo is harmless, if annoying, and should simply be ignored.

## SENIOR-CITIZEN TRAVEL

Although there are few early bird specials or movie discounts in Spain, senior citizens generally enjoy discounts at museums. Spanish social life encompasses all ages—it's very common to see senior citizens next to young couples or families in late-night cafés.

To qualify for age-related discounts, **mention your senior-citizen status up front** when booking hotel reservations (not when checking out) and before you're seated in restaurants (not when paying the bill). Be sure to have identification on hand. When renting a car, ask about promotional car-rental discounts, which can be cheaper than senior-citizen rates.

➤ EDUCATIONAL PROGRAMS: **Elderhostel** (✉ 11 Ave. de Lafayette, Boston, MA 02111-1746, ☎ 877/426–8056, FAX 877/426–2166, WEB www. elderhostel.org).

## SHOPPING

Andalusia has plenty to tempt the shopper, from simple souvenirs to high-quality regional crafts. Clothing is highly fashionable, if expensive. Shoes and leather accessories are as chic as you'll find. Many of the best buys are food items; just check customs restrictions in your home country before purchasing edibles. Spanish wines make lovely souvenirs.

Spain's major department store is El Corte Inglés, with branches in all major cities and towns.

## SMART SOUVENIRS

Andalusia—the quintessential steamy, flamenco-and-torero Spain of your imagination—is, not surprisingly, a prime region to pick up archetypal Spanish souvenirs. Andalusian ceramics and pottery, such as those decorated in the typical Sevillana pattern of flowers against a white background, or the Granada style of blue and green on white with a bright pomegranate in the middle—are known throughout Spain. Andalusia's Moorish legacy left an indelible mark on many of the region's crafts, which include copperware, painted azulejo tiles, woven textiles, and marquetry (varnished boxes, tables, and other furniture inlaid with colorful pieces of wood). As for gastronomic gifts, Andalusia is king: Spain's finest cured ham, *jamón ibérico*, comes from the Iberian black pig, and the best known—and most expensive, costing up to €120 for a kilo—is the ham that hails from Jabugo in the province of Huelva. However, you'll find top-notch cured ham (the general name is *jamón serrano*) throughout Andalusia, and most ham shops sell vacuum-sealed packets of sliced, cured ham, which pack easily, weigh little, and make for tasty souvenirs to take home. An exquisite accompaniment to the salty cured ham is the famous dry *fino* sherry of Jeréz de la Fontera—a bottle or two of which may be your most popular gift among the folks back home. A special mention also goes to the superb olive oil of Jaén.

Spain's leather is highly esteemed for its top quality—and reasonable price tag. Shoe lovers, especially, are spoiled in Spain, where there is a wide variety of fashionable shoe stores with high-quality leather shoes at decent prices, particularly in the larger cities. For more traditional footwear, pick up a pair of *alpargatas*, better known internationally by their French name, *espadrilles*. Originally farmers' shoes, these canvas shoes with rope soles are comfortable and cheap (you can pick up a basic pair for as little as €7), and come in a rainbow of colors. Spain's Riojan wines are world renowned—and after one sip of a pungent Riojan red, you'll understand why. You can buy

Riojan wines all over Spain, though the best prices are, of course, in the region of La Rioja itself.

## STUDENTS IN SPAIN

Students can often get discounts on admission to museums and other sights. Remember to bring your valid student IDs with you.

➤ IDs AND SERVICES: **Council Travel** (CIEE; ✉ 205 E. 42nd St., 15th floor, New York, NY 10017, ☎ 212/822–2700 or 888/226–8624, FAX 212/822–2719, WEB www.counciltravel.com). **Travel Cuts** (✉ 187 College St., Toronto, Ontario M5T 1P7, Canada, ☎ 416/979–2406 or 888/838–2887, FAX 416/979–8167, WEB www.travelcuts.com).

## TAXES

### VALUE-ADDED TAX

Value-added tax (VAT), similar to sales tax, is called IVA in Spain (pronounced "*ee*-vah," for *impuesto sobre el valor añadido*). It is levied on both products and services such as hotel rooms and restaurant meals. When in doubt about whether tax is included, ask, "*Está incluido el IVA?*"

The IVA rate for hotels and restaurants is 7%. Menus will generally say at the bottom whether tax is included (*IVA incluido*) or not (*más 7% IVA*).

Whereas food, pharmaceuticals, and household items are taxed at the lowest rate, most consumer goods are taxed at 16%. A number of shops, particularly large stores and boutiques in holiday resorts, participate in Global Refund (formerly Europe Tax-Free Shopping), a VAT refund service that makes getting your money back relatively hassle free. On purchases of more than €90, you're entitled to a refund of the 16% tax. **Ask for the Global Refund form** (called a Shopping Cheque) in participating stores. You show your passport and fill out the form; the vendor then mails you the refund, or—often more convenient—you **present your original receipt to the VAT office at the airport** when you leave Spain. (In both Madrid and Barcelona, the office is near the duty-free shops. Save time for this process, as lines can be long.) Customs signs the original and refunds your money on the spot in

cash (euros) or sends it to the central office to process a credit-card refund. Credit-card refunds take a few weeks.

➤ VAT REFUNDS: **Global Refund** (✉ 99 Main St., Suite 307, Nyack, NY 10960, ☎ 800/566–9828, FAX 845/348–1549, WEB www.globalrefund.com).

## TELEPHONES

Spain's phone system is perfectly efficient. Direct dialing is the norm. The main operator is Telefónica. Note that only cell phones conforming to the European GSM standard will work in Spain.

### COUNTRY CODES

The country code for Spain is 34. When dialing a Spanish number from abroad, drop the initial "0" from the local area code. The country code is 1 for the United States and Canada, 61 for Australia, 64 for New Zealand, and 44 for the United Kingdom.

### DIRECTORY AND OPERATOR ASSISTANCE

For general information in Spain, dial 1003. International operators, who generally speak English, are at 025.

### INTERNATIONAL CALLS

International calls are awkward from coin-operated pay phones because of the enormous number of coins needed; and they can be expensive from hotels, as the hotel often adds a hefty surcharge. The best way to phone home is to use a public phone that accepts phone cards (☞ Phone Cards) or go to the local telephone office, the *locutorio*: every town has one, and major cities have several. The locutorios near the center of town are generally more expensive; farther from the center, the rates are sometimes as much as one-third less. You converse in a quiet, private booth, and you're charged according to the meter. If the call ends up costing around €3 or more, you can usually pay with Visa or MasterCard.

To make an international call yourself, dial 00, then the country code, then the area code and number.

### LOCAL CALLS

All area codes begin with a 9. To call within Spain—even locally—dial the area code first. Numbers preceded by a 900 code are toll free; those starting with a 6 are going to a cellular phone. Note that calls to cell phones are significantly more expensive than calls to regular phones.

### LONG-DISTANCE SERVICES

AT&T, MCI, and Sprint access codes make calling long distance relatively convenient, but you may find the local access number blocked in many hotel rooms. First ask the hotel operator to connect you. If the hotel operator balks, ask for an international operator, or dial the international operator yourself. One way to improve your odds of getting connected to your long-distance carrier is to travel with more than one company's calling card (a hotel may block Sprint, for example, but not MCI). If all else fails, call from a pay phone.

Before you leave home, **verify your long-distance company's access code in Spain.**

➤ ACCESS CODES: **AT&T Direct** (☎ 900/990011). **MCI WorldPhone** (☎ 900/990014). **Sprint International Access** (☎ 900/990013).

➤ GENERAL INFORMATION: **AT&T** (☎ 800/222–0300). **MCI WorldCom** (☎ 800/444–4444). **Sprint** (☎ 800/793–1153).

### PHONE CARDS

To use a newer pay phone you need a special phone card (*tarjeta telefónica*), which you can buy at any tobacco shop or newsstand, in various denominations. Some such phones also accept credit cards, but phone cards are more reliable. You can use the tarjeta telefónica to make long-distance calls, and you can also buy phone cards exclusively for international calls, often at low rates.

### PUBLIC PHONES

You'll find pay phones in individual booths, in special telephone offices (locutorios), and in many bars and restaurants. Most have a digital readout so you can see your money ticking away. If you're paying with coins, you need at least €.15 to call locally, €.45 to call another province. Simply insert the coins and wait for a dial tone. (With older models, you

line coins up in a groove on top of the dial and they drop down as needed.) Note that rates are reduced on the weekends and after 8 PM Monday–Friday.

### TIME

Spain is on Central European Time, one hour ahead of Greenwich Mean Time, six hours ahead of Eastern Standard Time. Like the rest of the European Union, Spain switches to daylight-saving time on the last weekend in March and switches back on the last weekend in October.

### TIPPING

Waiters and other service staff expect to be tipped, and you can be sure that your contribution will be appreciated. On the other hand, if you experience bad or surly service, don't feel obligated to leave a tip.

Restaurant checks almost always include a service charge, which is not the same as a voluntary tip. **Do not tip more than 10% of the bill,** and leave less if you eat tapas or sandwiches at a bar—just enough to round out the bill to the nearest €1. Tip cocktail servers €.30–€.50 a drink, depending on the bar.

Tip taxi drivers about 10% of the total fare, plus a supplement for a long ride or extra help with luggage. Note that rides from airports carry an official surcharge plus a small handling fee for each piece of luggage; these charges do not substitute for a tip.

Tip hotel porters €.50 a bag, and the bearer of room service €.50. A doorman who calls a taxi for you gets €.50. If you stay in a hotel for more than two nights, tip the maid about €.50 per night. The concierge should receive a tip for any help he or she provides.

Tour guides should be tipped about €2, ushers in theaters or at bullfights €.15–€.20, barbers €.50, and women's hairdressers at least €1 for a wash and style. Rest-room attendants are tipped €.15.

### TOURS AND PACKAGES

Because everything is prearranged on a prepackaged tour or independent vacation, you spend less time planning—and often get it all at a good price.

## BOOKING WITH AN AGENT

Travel agents are excellent resources. But it's a good idea to collect brochures from several agencies, as some agents' suggestions may be influenced by relationships with tour and package firms that reward them for volume sales. If you have a special interest, **find an agent with expertise in that area**; the American Society of Travel Agents (ASTA; ☞ Travel Agencies) has a database of specialists worldwide.

Make sure your travel agent knows the accommodations and other services of the place being recommended. Ask about the hotel's location, room size, beds, and whether it has a pool, room service, or programs for children, if you care about these. Has your agent been there in person or sent others whom you can contact?

Do some homework on your own, too: local tourism boards can provide information about lesser-known and small-niche operators, some of which may sell only direct.

## BUYER BEWARE

Each year consumers are stranded or lose their money when tour operators—even large ones with excellent reputations—go out of business. So **check out the operator.** Ask several travel agents about its reputation, and try to **book with a company that has a consumer-protection program.** (Look for information in the company's brochure.) In the United States, members of the National Tour Association and the United States Tour Operators Association are required to set aside funds to cover your payments and travel arrangements in the event that the company defaults. It's also a good idea to choose a company that participates in the American Society of Travel Agents' Tour Operator Program (TOP); ASTA will act as mediator in any disputes between you and your tour operator.

Remember that the more your package or tour includes the better you can predict the ultimate cost of your vacation. Make sure you know exactly what is covered, and **beware of hidden costs.** Are taxes, tips, and transfers included? Entertainment and excursions? These can add up.

➤ TOUR-OPERATOR RECOMMENDATIONS: **American Society of Travel Agents** (☞ Travel Agencies). **National Tour Association** (NTA; ✉ 546 E. Main St., Lexington, KY 40508, ☎ 859/226–4444 or 800/682–8886, WEB www.ntaonline.com). **United States Tour Operators Association** (USTOA; ✉ 275 Madison Ave., Suite 2014, New York, NY 10016, ☎ 212/599–6599 or 800/468–7862, FAX 212/599–6744, WEB www.ustoa.com).

## TRAIN TRAVEL

Andalusia is well linked to the rest of Spain by train, especially with the advent of the wonderful high-speed train, the 290-kph (180-mph) AVE, which travels between Madrid and Seville (with a stop in Córdoba) in less than three hours at prices starting around €60 each way. The fast Talgo service is also efficient. However, the rest of the state-run rail system—known as RENFE—remains below par by European standards. Local train travel can be tediously slow, and most long-distance trips run at night. Although overnight trains have comfortable sleeper cars, first-class fares that include a sleeping compartment are comparable to airfares.

Andalusia's main cities are connected by train, but many of the region's smaller towns and villages are not, which means that you'll have to bus it around Andalusia if you want to veer even slightly off the well-traveled tourist track. Trains chug regularly between Granada, Seville, Málaga, Córdoba, Jaén, Cádiz, and other main cities, though note that you will more often than not have to make a connection in Bobadilla, a small town whose claim to fame is that it sits smack in the center of Andalusia's train network. As you're planning your train journeys (and if you speak Spanish), it's well worth calling the 24-hour RENFE phone number for up-to-date schedules and also to determine the quickest routes, with as few train changes as possible. Changes can slow you down immeasurably, especially if you have to wait a long time for your connection.

If you purchase a same-day round-trip ticket while in Spain, you'll get a 20% discount; if you purchase a different-day round-trip ticket, a 10% discount applies.

International overnight trains run from Madrid to Lisbon and from Barcelona to Paris (both 11½ hours). A daytime train runs from Barcelona to Grenoble and Geneva (10 hours).

You can buy train tickets in advance at the train station, which is what most Spaniards do. Note that the lines can be long, so give yourself plenty of time if you plan on buying same-day tickets. For popular train routes, you will need to reserve tickets more than a few days in advance; call RENFE to inquire. The ticket clerks at the stations rarely speak English, so if you need help or advice in planning a more complex train journey you may be better off going to a travel agency that displays the blue-and-yellow RENFE sign. The price is the same. For shorter, regional train trips, you can often buy your tickets directly from machines in the main train stations. Note that if your itinerary is set in stone and has little room for error, you can buy RENFE tickets through Rail Europe before you leave home.

Commuter trains and most long-distance trains forbid smoking, though some long-distance trains have smoking cars.

## CUTTING COSTS

If you're coming from the United States or Canada and planning extensive train travel, **look into rail passes.** If Spain is your only destination, consider a **Spain Flexipass.** Prices begin at $155 for three days of second-class travel within a two-month period and $200 for first class. Other passes cover more days and longer periods.

Spain is one of 17 European countries in which you can use the **Eurailpass,** which buys you unlimited first-class rail travel in all participating countries for the duration of the pass. If you plan to rack up the miles, get a standard pass. These are available for

10 days ($554), 21 days ($718), one month ($890), two months ($1,260), and three months ($1,558). If your needs are more limited, look into a **Europass,** which costs less than a Eurailpass and buys you a limited number of travel days, in a limited number of countries (France, Germany, Italy, Spain, and Switzerland), during a specified time period.

In addition to the Eurailpass and Europass, Rail Europe sells the Eurail Youthpass (for those under age 26), the Eurail Saverpass (which gives a discount for two or more people traveling together), a Eurail Flexipass (which allows a certain number of travel days within a set period), the Euraildrive Pass, and the Europass Drive (which combines travel by train and rental car). Whichever you choose, remember that you must **buy your pass before you leave** for Europe.

Many travelers assume that rail passes guarantee them seats on the trains they wish to ride: not so. You need to **reserve seats in advance** even if you're using a rail pass. Seat reservations are required on some trains, particularly high-speed trains, and are a good idea on any train that might be crowded. You'll also need a reservation if you want a sleeping berth.

➤ RAIL PASSES: **CIT Tours Corp.** (☎ 800/248–8687, WEB www.cit-tours. com). **DER Tours** (☎ 800/782–2424). **Rail Europe** (☎ 877/456–7245; ☎ 800/361–7245; WEB www. raileurope.com).

➤ TRAIN INFORMATION: RENFE (☎ 902/240202, WEB www.renfe.es).

## FROM THE UNITED KINGDOM

Train services to Spain from the United Kingdom are not as frequent, fast, or affordable as flights, and you have to change trains—and stations—in Paris. Allow 2 hours for the changing process, then 13 hours for the trip from Paris to Madrid. It's worth paying extra for the Talgo express or Puerta del Sol express to avoid changing trains again at the Spanish border. If you're under 26 years old, Eurotrain has excellent deals.

➤ INFORMATION: Eurotrain (✉ 52 Grosvenor Gardens, London SW1W OAG, U.K., ☎ 0207/730–8832).

Transalpino (✉ 71–75 Buckingham Palace Rd., London SW1W ORE, U.K., ☎ 0207/834–9656).

## LUXURY TOURING TRAINS

The luxurious turn-of-the-20th-century *Al Andalus Expreso* makes five-day trips in Andalusia with sightseeing in Córdoba, Granada, and Seville. The cost, which includes most meals, is about $2,600 per person.

➤ RESERVATIONS: **Marketing Ahead** (✉ 433 5th Ave., New York, NY 10016, ☎ 212/686–9213 or 800/ 223–1356). **Club ABC** (✉ 200 Broadacres Dr., Bloomfield, NY 07703, ☎ 973/338–1122, Ext. 2273). **DER Tours** (✉ Box 1606, Des Plaines, IL 60017, ☎ 800/782–2424).

➤ IN SPAIN: **Iberrail** (✉ Capitán Haya 55, 28020 Madrid, ☎ 91/571–6692).

## TRANSPORTATION

## WITHIN SPAIN

After France, Spain is the largest country in Western Europe, so seeing any more than a fraction of the country involves considerable domestic travel. If you want the freedom of straying from your fixed itinerary to follow whims as they come, driving is the best choice. The roads are generally fine, although traffic can be heavy on major routes, trucks can clog minor routes, and parking is a problem in cities (☞ Car Travel).

Spain is well served by domestic flights, though of course these cost more than ground options. Train service between the largest cities is fast, efficient, and punctual, but trains on secondary regional routes can be slow and involve frequent changes of train (☞ Train Travel). In such cases, buses are far more convenient (☞ Bus Travel).

## TRAVEL AGENCIES

A good travel agent puts your needs first. Look for an agency that has been in business at least five years, emphasizes customer service, and has someone on staff who specializes in your destination. In addition, **make sure the agency belongs to a professional trade organization.** The American Society of Travel Agents (ASTA)—the largest and most influential in the field with more than 24,000 members in some 140 countries—maintains and enforces a strict code of ethics and will step in to help mediate any agent-client disputes involving ASTA members if necessary. ASTA (whose motto is "Without a travel agent, you're on your own") also maintains a Web site that includes a directory of agents. (If a travel agency is also acting as your tour operator, *see* Buyer Beware *in* Tours and Packages.)

➤ LOCAL AGENT REFERRALS: **American Society of Travel Agents** (ASTA; ✉ 1101 King St., Suite 200, Alexandria, VA 22314, ☎ 800/965–2782 24-hr hot line, FAX 703/739–3268, WEB www.astanet.com). **Association of British Travel Agents** (✉ 68–71 Newman St., London W1T 3AH, ☎ 020/7637–2444, FAX 020/7637–0713, WEB www.abtanet.com). **Association of Canadian Travel Agents** (✉ 130 Albert St., Suite 1705, Ottawa, Ontario K1P 5G4, ☎ 613/237–3657, FAX 613/237–7052, WEB www.acta.ca). **Australian Federation of Travel Agents** (✉ Level 3, 309 Pitt St., Sydney, NSW 2000, ☎ 02/9264–3299, FAX 02/9264–1085, WEB www.afta.com.au). **Travel Agents' Association of New Zealand** (✉ Level 5, Tourism and Travel House, 79 Boulcott St., Box 1888, Wellington 6001, ☎ 04/499–0104, FAX 04/499–0827, WEB www.taanz.org.nz).

## VISITOR INFORMATION

Before you go, consult the Tourist Office of Spain in your home country or on the World Wide Web.

➤ TOURIST INFORMATION: **Chicago** (✉ Water Tower Pl., 845 N. Michigan Ave., Suite 915-East, Chicago, IL 60611, ☎ 312/642–1992). **Los Angeles** (✉ 8383 Wilshire Blvd., Suite 960, Beverly Hills, CA 90211, ☎ 213/ 658–7188). **Miami** (✉ 1221 Brickell Ave., Suite 1850, Miami, FL 33131, ☎ 305/358–1992). **New York** (✉ 666 5th Ave., 35th floor, New York, NY 10103, ☎ 212/265–8822). **Canada** (✉ 2 Bloor St. W, Suite 3402, Toronto, Ontario M4W 3E2, ☎ 416/ 961–3131). **United Kingdom** (✉ 22– 23 Manchester Sq., London W1M 5AP, U.K., ☎ 0207/486–8077).

➤ U.S. GOVERNMENT ADVISORIES: **U.S. Department of State** (✉ Overseas

Citizens Services Office, Room 4811, 2201 C St. NW, Washington, DC 20520, ☎ 202/647–5225 interactive hot line or 888/407–4747, 𝖶𝖤𝖡 www. travel.state.gov); enclose a business-size SASE.

## WEB SITES

Do check out the World Wide Web when planning your trip. You'll find everything from weather forecasts to virtual tours of famous cities. Be sure to **visit Fodors.com** (www.fodors. com), a complete travel-planning site. You can research prices and book plane tickets, hotel rooms, rental cars, vacation packages, and more. In addition, you can post your pressing questions in the Travel Talk section. Other planning tools include a currency converter and weather reports, and there are loads of links to travel resources.

Andalusia has a host of Web sites covering the region. Both www. andalucia.org and www.andalucia. com are in Spanish and English, and provide listings and write-ups on Andalusia's sights and attractions. For general Spain Web sites, www. okspain.org provides a basic introduction; the Spain-based www. tourspain.es is more sophisticated. For a virtual brochure on Spain's paradors, go to www.parador.es.

## WHEN TO GO

May and October are the optimal times to come to Andalusia, as the weather is generally warm and dry. May gives you more hours of daylight, whereas October offers a chance to enjoy the harvest season, which is especially colorful in the wine regions.

In April you can see some of the region's most spectacular fiestas, particularly Seville's Semana Santa (Holy Week), and by then the weather is warm enough to make sightseeing comfortable. For listings of Fiestas by region, *see* Pleasures and Pastimes at the beginning of each chapter.

Spain is the number-one destination for European travelers, so **if you want to avoid crowds, come before June or after September.** Crowds and prices increase in the summer, especially along the coasts, as the Mediterranean is usually too cold for swimming the rest of the year. Spaniards vacation in August, and their migration to the beach causes huge traffic jams on August 1 and 31. Major cities are relaxed and empty for the duration; small shops and some restaurants shut down for the entire month, but museums remain open.

### CLIMATE

Summers in Andalusia are hot: temperatures frequently hit 100°F (38°C), and air-conditioning is not widespread. Try to **limit summer sightseeing to the morning hours.** That said, warm summer nights are among Spain's quiet pleasures.

To avoid the sweltering heat, visit in spring, when the sun is less fierce and sea breezes cool the coast. Temperatures begin to rise in late spring, particularly in the inland cities. Andalusian winters are fairly mild along the coastline, but wetter and chillier inland. The Sierra Nevada mountains looming near Granada see plenty of snow in the winter and offer some of Spain's best skiing.

➤ FORECASTS: **Weather Channel Connection** (☎ 900/932–8437), 95¢ per minute from a Touch-Tone phone.

The following lists the average daily maximum and minimum temperatures for Seville.

**SEVILLE**

| Jan. | 59F | 15C | May | 81F | 27C | Sept. | 90F | 32C |
|------|-----|-----|------|-----|-----|-------|-----|-----|
|      | 43  | 6   |      | 55  | 13  |       | 64  | 18  |
| Feb. | 63F | 17C | June | 90F | 32C | Oct.  | 79F | 26C |
|      | 45  | 7   |      | 63  | 17  |       | 57  | 14  |
| Mar. | 68F | 20C | July | 97F | 36C | Nov.  | 68F | 20C |
|      | 48  | 9   |      | 68  | 20  |       | 50  | 10  |
| Apr. | 75F | 24C | Aug. | 97F | 36C | Dec.  | 61F | 16C |
|      | 52  | 11  |      | 68  | 20  |       | 45  | 7   |

# 1  DESTINATION: ANDALUSIA

Arabian Nights, Andalusian Days

What's Where

Pleasures and Pastimes

Fodor's Choice

Great Itineraries

# ARABIAN NIGHTS, ANDALUSIAN DAYS

**N**AMED FOR AL-ANDALUS (Arabic for "land of the west"), the 781-year Moorish empire on the Iberian Peninsula, Andalusia is where the authentic history and character of the Iberian Peninsula and Spanish culture are most palpably, visibly, audibly, and aromatically apparent.

Though church- and Franco regime–influenced historians attempted to sell a sanitized, Christians-versus-infidels portrayal of Spanish history, what has most distinctively imprinted and defined Spanish culture, the factor that most enriched and singularly marked the art, architecture, language, thought, and even the cooking and dining customs of most of the Iberian Peninsula, was the almost eight-century reign of the Arabic-speaking peoples who have become known collectively as the Moors. Nowhere is this more dramatically evident than in Andalusia.

Arabic Muslims led an army of Berbers across the Strait of Gibraltar in 711 and went on to develop, under the leadership of survivors of the fugitive Persian Umayyad dynasty from Damascus, a flourishing civilization that extended nearly to the Pyrenees. This dynasty reached its apogee at Córdoba in the 9th century; Seville fell to the Christian "reconquest" in 1248, and Granada held out for another 244 years before surrendering to Ferdinand and Isabella in 1492. In all, the Moorish sojourn on the Iberian Peninsula lasted 300 years longer than the Roman tenure and some 270 longer than the current Christian regime. That Andalusia was the region most influenced by the Moors becomes obvious in the maze of horseshoe arches in Córdoba's mosque, in the Mudéjar splendor of Seville's Alcazar, and in the ultimate expression of Moorish refinement and taste at Granada's Alhambra.

Gypsies, bulls, flamenco, horses—Andalusia is the Spain of story and song, the one Washington Irving romanticized in the 18th century. Andalusia is, moreover, at once the least and most surprising part of Spain: least surprising because it lives up to the hype and stereotype that long confused all of Spain with the Andalusian version, and most surprising because it is, at the same time, so much more.

To begin with, five of the eight Andalusian provinces are maritime, with colorful fishing fleets and a wealth of seafood usually associated with the north. Secondly, there are snowcapped mountains and ski resorts in Andalusia, the kind of high sierra resources long thought most readily available in the Alps, or even the Pyrenees . . . but the Sierra Nevada is within sight of North Africa. Thirdly, there are wildlife-filled wetlands and highland pine and oak forests rich with game and trout streams, not to mention free-range Iberian pigs. And lastly, there are cities such as Seville that somehow manage to combine all of this natural plenty with the creativity and cosmopolitanism of a London or a Lyon.

Another Andalusian surprise is its historical wealth. In modern times, this has been Spain's poorest region, the one whose economy remained closest to feudalism, the one from which workers long needed to emigrate to find jobs in the more industrialized cities of northern Spain and beyond. It is easy to forget the shipping and commercial wealth it generated during Spain's Golden Age, especially in Cádiz and Seville. And before that, the Moors, whose hydraulic engineers made Andalusia an agricultural power, flourished here, making Córdoba the Manhattan of the 9th century, the western city where patients were sent for brain surgery.

Although an exploration of Andalusia must begin with the cities of Seville, Córdoba, and Granada as the fundamental triangle of interest and identity, Huelva's Sierra de Aracena and Doñana wetlands, Jaén's Parque Natural de Cazorla, Cádiz's Pueblos Blancos (White Villages), and Granada's Alpujarras are unforgettable natural settings to balance the urban treasures of the Andalusian capitals. Meanwhile, the smaller cities such as Cádiz—the Western world's oldest metropolis, founded by Phoenicians more than 3,000 years ago—and Jerez, with its sherry cellars and purebred horses, have much to explore as well. And in between the urban and rural attractions is another entire chapter of Andalusian life: the noble towns of the countryside, ranging from Carmona—Alfonso X's Lucero de España (Morning Star of Spain)—to Jaén's Renaissance gems of Úbeda and Baeza, Córdoba's Priego de Córdoba, Málaga's Ronda, and Cádiz's Arcos de la Frontera.

Andalusia is, like Spain, infinitely varied and diverse within its apparent unity. Seville and Granada are like feuding sisters, one vivaciously flirting, the other darkly brooding; Córdoba and Cádiz are estranged cousins, one landlocked, the other virtually under sail; Huelva and Almería are universes apart, the first a verdant Atlantic Arcadia and the second a parched Mediterranean sunbelt; and Jaén is an upland country bumpkin—albeit with its Renaissance palaces—compared with the steamy cosmopolitan seaport of Málaga.

Seville poet Manuel Machado (1874–1947) said it best in his classic "Oda a Andalucía":

*Cádiz, salada claridad,*

*Granada, agua oculta que llora.*

*Romana y mora, Córdoba callada,*

*Málaga, cantaora,*

*Almería, dorada.*

*Plateado Jaén.*

*Huelva, la orilla de las tres caravelas.*

*Y Sevilla!*

(Cádiz, salty dazzling, / Granada, hidden waters weeping. / Roman and Moorish, silent Córdoba, / Málaga, flamenco songstress, / Golden Almería. / Silvery Jaén. / Huelva, shore of Columbus's three caravelles. / And Seville!)

— George Semler

# WHAT'S WHERE

Andalusia is Spain's southernmost autonomous community, bordered by Portugal to the west, the province of Murcia to the east, Extremadura and Castilla–La Mancha to the north, and the Mediterranean Sea and the Atlantic Ocean to the south. The five coastal provinces—Huelva, Cádiz, Málaga, Granada, and Almería—stretch along the southern edge of Andalusia, whereas Seville, Córdoba, and Jaén are landlocked. The two east-west mountain ranges, the Sierra Morena to the north and the Sistema Penibético to the south, are divided by the valley of the Guadalquivir River. The Sistema Penibético boasts the Iberian Peninsula's highest mountain, the 3,478-ft peak of Mulhacén.

A basic fact that you should keep in mind when getting to know the region: every province in Andalusia bears the name of its capital. So Seville is both a city and a province, as are Huelva, Cádiz, and so on.

## Seville

The world's most enduring and indelible impression of things Spanish is rooted in a place about which native poet Manuel Machado could manage no more than a breathless ". . . y Sevilla!" Dazzling Seville brings to life the most romantic visions of Spain: passionate flamenco dancers, dashing bullfighters, flower-choked streets, whitewashed villas perfumed by thousands of orange blossoms; no wonder Bizet's *Carmen* and Rossini's *Barber of Seville* were set here. Hispalis for the Romans, Isbyllia for the Moors, Seville has always been Spain's chief riverine port, astride the Guadalquivir River that launched Columbus to the New World and Magellan around the globe. Perhaps more important for the history of Spain and the development of the European Renaissance, the relative ease of maritime travel and transport in medieval times made Seville much closer to North Africa than to Madrid or, at that time, Toledo. Seville's Campiña, the fertile countryside south of the capital, the Sierra Norte with its cooling highland villages, and the rugged Sierra Sur where romantic bandits once roamed complete Seville province's rich offering of urban and rural attractions.

## Huelva

Famed as live oak-forested grazing grounds for the treasured *cerdo ibérico,* the free-range, semiwild Iberian pig, Huelva's Sierra de Aracena is a surprisingly fresh and leafy mountain getaway at Spain's far southwestern corner bordering Portugal. Along with the ham factories and pig farms around Jabugo, these mountain villages contain extraordinary architectural gems, such as the former mosque at Al-monaster and the *iglesias manuelinas* (Portuguese-influenced churches). Moorish fortresses such as the one in the town of Cortegana, and the famous Gruta de las Maravillas (Cavern of Marvels) at Aracena provide natural scenery and civilization in this highland retreat known for powerful mountain cooking and superb hiking opportunities. Huelva's Costa de la Luz stretches from the border with Portugal at the Guadiana River to the Guadalquivir estuary. The Marismas del Odiel (Odiel Wetlands) west of Huelva are a rich repository of wilderness. The Ruta Colombina (Route of Columbus) east of the city of Huelva traces the explorer's prevoyage steps. Doñana National Park, with a total area of more than 500 square km (200 square mi) and another 250 square km (100 square mi) of protected peripheral lands, was once a game preserve for the Spanish royal family and is one of Spain's greatest natural treasures. Astride the main Eurasian-African migratory flyway, Doñana harbors a diversity of bird species unique in Europe, with some 300 in all. Deer, wild boar, semi-wild horses, and, the star of Doñana, the Iberian lynx, are also found in the higher parts of the park. With three distinct habitats—beaches and moving sand dunes, the forested higher ground, and the marshes that make up more than half of the park's total area—there is something for everyone here. Visitor centers at Matalascañas (El Acebuche), La Rocina, the Palacio de Acebrón, Cerrado García, and, in Sanlúcar de Barrameda, at the Fábrica de Hielo (formerly an ice factory for refrigerating fish) can put visitors in the middle of Doñana by boat, horseback, all-terrain personnel carrier, or foot.

## Cádiz

The city of Cádiz is often compared to Havana for its size and the baroque architecture that became the colonial trademark in the New World; the saying goes (liberally translated) that "Havana is Cádiz with more salsa, and Cádiz Havana with more *salero* (charm)." Dazzling Cádiz is a surprise for longtime Spain hands and Spanish natives as well. The city's carnival is among the most cleverly creative and hilarious of all of Spain's many hundreds of fiestas, with satirical street theater events competing for first prize in a city elaborately costumed for nearly two weeks.

With a surfeit of fresh seafood pouring in from all around this virtual island trapped between the Mediterranean and the Atlantic, tapas and fish stews such as that of the famous *urta* (a rockfish said to be endemic to the waters around Cádiz) are exquisite in this southernmost provincial capital originally colonized by the Phoenicians more than 3,000 years ago. The vineyards around Sanlúcar de Barrameda produce the sherrylike Manzanilla prized throughout Spain, while Jerez de la Frontera is world famous for fine sherries. Beyond Cádiz the beaches of Sancti Petri, La Barrosa, and El Palmar lead past Barbate and Zahara de los Atunes, past the Roman ruins at Baelo Claudia, and down to the windsurfing capital at Tarifa. Beginning at Arcos de la Frontera, the drive through the famous *pueblos blancos* (white villages) in the eastern and upland part of the province reveals the characteristic architecture of houses, castles, and churches. The list of towns reads like an Hispano-Arabic sonnet: Algar, Bornos, Espera, Villamartín, Prado el Rey, Puerto Serrano, Algodonales, Olvera, Torre-Alhaquime, Acalá el Valle, Setenil, El Gastor, Zahara de la Sierra, Grazalema, Benaocaz, Ubrique, Villaluenga, and El Bosque. The highest peak in Cádiz, the 4,950-ft El Torreón, the unique Spanish fir (*pinsapo*) forest in the Sierra de Grazalema, and the arts, crafts, and cuisine of each mountain town are all good reasons to explore these highlands as carefully as time allows.

## Málaga

This cosmopolitan maritime town is in some ways more an international free port than Andalusian, though the stupendous Alcazaba and the tapas taverns in the town's historic center are soundly southern Spanish. The Gibralfaro castle above the Alcazaba is even older, dating from the 8th century, while the cathedral and the Iglesia de el Sagrario are also key Málaga sights. Pablo Picasso was born in Málaga in 1881, when his father was an art professor here; his birthplace and the Picasso Museum offer several interesting early Picasso works, including a strikingly wide-eyed, lantern-jawed self-portrait of the artist. The parador at Gibralfaro, the Málaga bullring, and the *chiringuitos* (shacks) serving fresh fish in the sand at El Palo, 6 km (4 mi) east of the port are among Málaga's most memorable and characteristic spots. Málaga province veers from the tourist beaches of the Costa del Sol to the stunning mountain towns of Ronda and Antequera.

## Córdoba

Córdoba's *Mezquita* (mosque), with a cathedral built in the middle of it, is the perfect metaphor for the history and civilization of the Iberian Peninsula. Córdoba, center of world culture in the 9th and 10th centuries, is a living monument to its past glories. The city has a unique set of Mudéjar churches, flower-bedecked patios, the stunning Julio Romero de Torres collection of paintings, Spain's only perfectly preserved synagogue, and the Torre de Calahorra with its living display of Al-Andalus detailing the city's Islamic and Jewish roots. In addition, there are the thought-provoking monuments to some of the most brilliant scholars in modern intellectual history, from Seneca and Averroës to Lucan and Maimonides. Madinat al Zahra, the ornate summer palace built just west of the city for Caliph-King Abderraman III's beloved Zhara, is the crown jewel in Córdoba's surprising historical splendor. Northern Córdoba's Sierra Morena is a natural arcadia of pine and live oak with wide-open ranges, the Andalusian and Castilian *dehesa,* where wild Iberian pigs roam freely looking for the acorns that make them so delicious. An exploration of this stark countryside will take you through the Valle de los Pedroches, through the town of Hinojosa del Duque with its famous Catedral de la Sierra (Highland Cathedral), and through towns such as Añora, known for its carefully preserved Cruces de Mayo (May Crosses) celebrations. Bélmez has a 13th-century castle on a promontory offering panoramic views of the valley, and Belalcázar, on the northern edge of the province, has a massive 15th-century tower overlooking the town. For mountain cuisine and an intimate look at the Córdoba most visitors don't see, this is a fine one-day excursion. Córdoba's Sierra Subbética, from the olive groves around Baena through the highland crag at Zuheros and on to the elegant town of Priego de Córdoba, follows a route eventually leading to Granada. Filled with baroque monuments, churches, and elaborate fountains nestled around an intricate medieval Jewish quarter with whitewashed facades and flower-bedecked balconies, Priego rises out of the rugged sierra like an architectural and hydraulic oasis.

## Jaén

Andalusia's northwesternmost province of Jaén, divided by the upper Guadalquivir River, is a striking contrast of olive groves, pristine wilderness, and Renaissance towns with elegant palaces and churches. The Parque Natural de Cazorla, Segura y Las Villas contains miles of trout-infested rivers and fauna ranging from deer to mink to several strains of mountain goat. The main towns of Jaén, Úbeda, Baeza, and Cazorla are filled with some of Spain's most impressive 16th-century architecture. Úbeda's parador, the Capilla del Salvador, and the Iglesia de San Pablo are each superb examples of the austere yet ornate Spanish late Gothic style. Baeza is rich in plateresque gems such as the town hall and the Plaza del Pópulo, and punctuated with shady terraces and taverns under the porticoed arches along the Paseo de la Constitución. Cazorla's Moorish castle and the ruins of the Iruela fortress are no less impressive than Andujar's Puente Romano, while the capital city of Jaén, famous for its silver mines in Roman times, has a Renaissance cathedral and Spain's most extensive 11th-century Arab baths.

## Granada

The Granada of Federico García Lorca, of the final Nasrid Sultan Boabdil, of the Catholic Monarchs Ferdinand and Isabella, and of the Spanish and Holy Roman Emperor Charles V, is a brooding, poetic place at once dark and luminous. The Albayzín, once the Moorish quarter over the Darro River, overlooks the Alhambra, at night red and gold in the floodlights around its ramparts. The contrasting Christian and Moorish cultures are never more dramatically counterposed than in this sultry enclave huddled under the snowcapped Sierra Nevada. The elaborately sculpted plateresque Cartuja sacristy, the fortresslike Carlos V palace plunked down in the middle of the Alhambra, and the stunning Capilla Real in the Granada cathedral provide a response to the delicate Moorish aesthetic of the Alhambra, the Palacio de la Madraza, Dar al-Horra palace, and the 11th-century Arab baths. Granada, as Washington Irving discovered in 1829, is a visual feast to savor carefully. As the old saying goes, "Give alms, woman! There is no greater misfortune than to be blind in Granada." Towering over the city, with snowcapped peaks gleaming whitely even in the dog days of summer, this ski resort and natural paradise is situated closer to a cultured metropolis than any other mountain getaway on the planet. A 30-minute drive from the Alhambra places you just under Spain's highest peak, the 11,427-ft Mulhacén. The road up to the Pico de Veleta is Europe's highest, and the 360 degrees of panoramic views are some of Iberia's most memorable, including the Cordillera Bética to the north, the Sierra de Sagra to the northwest, Mulhacén to the east, and the Sierras de Tejeda and Almijara to the west. Across the flat, blue expanse of the Mediterranean, on a clear day, the coast of North Africa is often visible. South and east of Granada, the Alpujarra, foothills of the Sierra Nevada, are studded with whitewashed villages that could have been conjured over from the Moroccan Rif. A hiker's paradise with trails and equestrian excursions up into the peaks of the Sierra Nevada, the Alpujarra were the final refuge for the Moriscos, Moors allowed to remain in Spain, exiled to the mountains, until the final re-expulsion decree in 1609. Artisanal rugs and blankets woven in striking colors, and simple mountain cuisine, based on the famous Trevélez ham and natural mountain products from game to goat and sheep cheeses, are characteristic of this fresh slice of alpine Andalusia perched between the Mediterranean coast and the high sierra.

## Almería

With its colossal 10th-century Alcazaba walled fortress presiding over the city as a reminder of its past glory, Almería reached its zenith during the Córdoban caliphate of the 9th and 10th centuries. As Córdoba's most important seaport, al–Mariyat (maritime lookout), early Almería was a commercial and textile giant. The fortresslike cathedral, the porticoed Plaza Vieja, and the Templo de San Juan, with remnants of the Moorish mosque including the restored 12th-century *mihrab* (prayer niche), are among the city's star attractions, along with the Gypsy and fishermen's quarter, La Chanca, with its colorful cave dwellings. The Parque Nacional Cabo de Gata offers birdwatching and diving options, and the towns of Sorbas, Mojácar, and Níjar are among the province's most picturesque.

# PLEASURES AND PASTIMES

## Architecture

Mudéjar Spain—the Spain built under Christian rule by Moorish architects, engineers, and craftsmen—has been called the most distinctive and characteristic Iberian contribution to western European art and architecture. The Mezquita de Córdoba and the Alhambra at Granada, in a sense the two bookends of Moorish architecture, coming as they did at the outset and the sunset of the Moorish empire on the Iberian Peninsula, are the two best examples of purely Moorish art and architecture. Seville's Alcázar comes third only because it was built in the Moorish style by the Christian King Pedro I. Equally fascinating are the Iglesias Fernandinas, the Mudéjar churches built after Fernando III conquered Córdoba and Seville and set about converting Islamic mosques to Christian churches. The pueblos blancos of the Cádiz sierra and the Alpujarra villages of Granada have a distinctive mountain style with North African overtones, and the ruins of Moorish castles and former mosques in Huelva's Sierra de Aracena are consistently surprising eye candy for the curious traveler. Jaén's Renaissance palaces in the towns of Úbeda and Baeza, the Ronda bullring, and Córdoba's synagogue are further examples of the truly staggering variety of architectural treasures throughout Andalusia.

## Art

Seville's Museo de Bellas Artes is the finest museum in Andalusia and one of the best two or three in Spain, with its superb collection of La Escuela Sevillana (The Seville School) of Murillo, Zurbarán, and Valdés Leal. Córdoba's fine arts museum and, especially, the Julio Romero de Torres collection just across the patio, offer hauntingly sensual works by the Córdoban artist and his father and teacher. Picasso was born in Málaga, which, along with Barcelona and Paris, claims the greatest 20th-century artist as its own. The Picasso Museum holds several notable works by the Cubist master. Granada's Museo de Bellas Artes in the Palacio de Carlos V at the Alhambra has famous work by Fray Juan Sanchez Cotán (whose paintings are also in abundance in Granada's Monasterio de la Cartuja) as well as interesting paintings by José María Rodríguez-Acosta from the late 19th and early 20th century. Granada's Fundación Rodríguez-Acosta is another notable fund of art.

## Dining

Andalusia is the great bastion and master of *las freiduras* (fried foods), a skill inherited (along with much of Andalusian cuisine) from the Moors. The least impressive-looking glass and aluminum corner emporium is likely to be serving *boquerones en adobo* (5-inch anchovies fried in batter) fresh from the Guadalquivir estuary with such a strong taste of cumin that you may wonder which side of the Strait of Gibraltar you've washed up on. *Espinacas con garbanzos* (chickpeas and spinach) in Seville, laced with cumin, is nothing like its counterpart in Catalunya. Seafood tapas along the Atlantic coast from Cádiz to Sanlúcar de Barrameda are so fresh that the use of bread and other accoutrements is superfluous. Inventive chefs such as Seville's Willy Moya (Poncio) and Enrique Becerra (Becerra) are restoring and modernizing ancient Moorish recipes such as *alboronía* (eggplant and zucchini–based vegetable stew). From the Iberian hams of Huelva to their Granada cousins at Trevelez, there is plenty of acorn-fed, free-range bounty on the hoof, and game and the produce from the Campiña make once-hungry Andalusia a place where it's not difficult to be on a permanent feast.

## Equus and Taurus

Horses and bulls are major themes in Andalusia. Jerez de la Frontera's Real Escuela Andaluza de Arte Ecuestre is arguably the world's finest equestrian ballet. Sanlúcar de Barrameda's August horse race on the beach bordering the Guadalquivir is a unique grassroots event. Seville's Maestranza bullring is the sanctum sanctorum of the art of tauromachy, and a chance to see Curro Romero perform in the Feria de Abril is one of bullfighting's most exquisite and riveting moments. Ronda's bullring is the oldest in Spain, and the aesthetic power of a bullfight in this context is undeniable. El Puerto de Santa María has one of Spain's biggest bullrings and puts on some of the season's top events, and all over Andalusia, where tauromachy is considered part of the local culture, bullfights generate an atmosphere and intensity rarely encountered north of the Desfiladero de Despeñaperros.

## Fiestas

Andalusia is often thought of as a permanent fiesta anyway, so it's no surprise that official celebrations in the south of Spain are among the peninsula's most spectacular. Seville's Semana Santa (Easter Week) is the reigning queen of Andalusian festivals, a full week of hauntingly beautiful religious processions highlighted by spontaneous *saetas* (flamenco song, literally "arrows" to and from the heart). Feria de Abril begins 10 days later, a decidedly more secular event featuring horses, bulls, and Andalusian beauties. Cádiz's Carnival, held in late February and early March, is the calendar year's opening bash, with clever satirical street theater mocking local and international figures and phenomena. Córdoba's mid-May Festival de los Patios combines flamenco performances with lavish floral displays in the city's finest courtyards. Jerez de la Frontera's Feria del Caballo (Horse Fair) shows off Andalusia's famous equestrian culture with accompanying sherry tasting and flamenco dancing until dawn. El Rocío, the annual late-May, early-June pilgrimage from all over Andalusia to the Hermitage of the Virgen del Rocío (Our Lady of the Dew) is one of Spain's most picturesque explosions of gypsy, flamenco, and religious fervor. Huelva's Fiestas Colombinas, held in late July and early August, Jaen's June 11 Virgen de la Capilla procession, Andújar's Romería de la Virgen de la Cabeza pilgrimage, and Sanlúcar de Barrameda's Exaltación del Río Guadalquivir, complete with horse races on the beach at the mouth of southern Spain's greatest river, are just a few of Andalusia's thousand and one fiestas.

# FODOR'S CHOICE

No two people agree on what makes a perfect vacation, but it's fun and helpful to know what others think. Here's a compendium drawn from the must-see lists of hundreds of tourists. For detailed information about these memories-in-the-making, refer to the appropriate chapters in this book.

## Dining

**Poncio, Seville.** Willy Moya has put together Andalusia's finest fusion of Moorish and French cooking in this delightful spot in the heart of Triana, the city's traditional Gypsy and sailor quarter across the Guadalquivir. *$$$*

**Casa el Pisto, Córdoba.** Out of reach of the somewhat overvisited Judería, this authentic Córdoban tavern and restaurant next to the San Miguel church serves fine fare and even better ambience at its gleaming mahogany bar. *$$–$$$*

**Mirador de Morayma, Granada.** The most spectacular of the restaurants overlooking the Alhambra, this lovely spot in the Albayzín is as beautiful as the view it offers. *$$–$$$*

**La Giralda, Seville.** A favorite of locals and visitors alike for its stellar interpretations of tapas and small dishes from the Andalusian culinary canon, this little slot just up from the Giralda is superb. *$$*

**Parador de Santa Catalina, Jaén.** Inside a castle on top of a hill, the surroundings alone are worth a lunch or dinner break. *$$*

**Terraza Carmona, Vera, Almería.** Feast on classic Almerían dishes, such as *gurullos con conejo* (pasta with rabbit), at this spacious, long-established restaurant. *$$*

**El Tintero, Málaga.** Join hundreds—literally—of other diners at this massive, cacophonous seafood restaurant overlooking Málaga's Playa de Dedo, where you select your dinner from large silver platters—paraded through the restaurant by nimble waiters—that are piled high with the freshest fish around. *$–$$*

## Lodging

**Alfonso XIII, Seville.** No one doubts that this is Seville's greatest hotel, a neo-Mudéjar colossus with a relaxed and graceful air about it. The lush patio and the coffered ceilings are cool and dark redoubts, with dazzling Seville awhirl outside. *$$$$*

**Casa Morisca, Granada.** A restored Moorish town house in the Albayzín, this classically graceful palace with its *alberca* (fountain) on the ground floor and hand-carved, hand-painted wood ceilings is one of Granada's aesthetic gems. *$$$–$$$$*

**Parador Condestable Dávalos, Úbeda, Jaén.** This 16th-century palace around a central patio with balconies and balustrades leading to the rooms upstairs is one of the best of Spain's paradors, set in the context of Úbeda's oasis of Renaissance architecture. *$$$*

**Parador de Ronda, Málaga.** Bask in the sensational views from this elegant parador balanced at cliff's edge atop Ronda's plunging Tajo gorge. *$$$*

**La Casa Grande, Arcos de la Frontera, Cádiz.** Just down from the Parador, this intimate spot has just a few rooms, but each is memorable for its design and taste. The breakfast terrace vertiginously overlooking the Guadalete River and the flat plains beyond is breathtaking. *$$*

## Quintessential Andalusia

**Alcazaba, Almería.** Once the largest fortress ever built by the Moors in Spain, this impressive castle perched on a hill affords spectacular views of Almería and its bay.

**Alhambra, Granada.** One of Spain's most enduringly popular attractions, this Moorish citadel is an endlessly intricate fantasy of lavishly carved and colored patios, arches, and cupolas.

**Bérchules, La Alpujarra, Granada.** This Alpujarran town in the foothills of the Sierra Nevada is a mountain retreat and jumping-off point for walking excursions in some of Andalusia's most beautiful countryside.

**Carmona, Seville.** Dubbed *Lucero de Europa* (Morning Star of Europe) by King Alfonso X el Sabio, this is one of Seville province's best Renaissance towns, with Mudéjar churches and a Roman necropolis as well. In the Alcazar del Rey Pedro I el Cruel, an excellent parador overlooks the plains to the south.

**Grazalema, Pueblos Blancos, Cádiz.** At this quintessential pueblo blanco in the mountains east of Arcos de la Frontera, Grazalema's Muslim roots are palpable in its whitewashed, flat-roofed houses with window boxes filled with geraniums.

**Mezquita, Córdoba.** Built between the 8th and 10th centuries, the Mezquita (mosque) is a fine example of Spanish Muslim architecture. Some 850 columns create a forest of onyx, jasper, marble, and granite, all topped with red-and-white-striped horseshoe arches and surrounded by mosaics and plasterwork.

**Priego de Córdoba, Córdoba.** In Córdoba province's Sierra de la Subbética, this surprising oasis of baroque architecture and lavish fountains was developed in the 18th century by rich silk merchants. The *Barrio del la Villa,* the Moorish quarter, is honeycombed with picturesque narrow streets.

**Ronda, Málaga.** A favorite haunt of German romantic poet Rainer Maria Rilke and a scenario for a chilling episode in Hemingway's *For Whom the Bell Tolls,* Ronda also boasts one of Spain's oldest and most beautiful bullrings.

## Special Memories
**Bajo de Guía Beach, Sanlúcar de Barrameda, Cádiz.** Whether or not you catch the August horseraces galloping down Sanlúcar de Barrameda's beach at the mouth of the Guadalquivir River, the beach itself, and the taverns that parallel it, are superb, especially at sunset.

**Concurso de Guitarra Flamenca, Córdoba.** For new talent and the most authentic flamenco, this May guitar festival in Córdoba is a guaranteed success performed in the city's finest patios and churches.

**Fiesta Internacional de Musica y Danza, Granada.** With the Alhambra's Patio de los Arrayanes or the Carlos V Palacio as a setting, the world's top classical music and dance ensembles are never more moving than in Granada in June.

**Semana Santa, Seville.** La Madrugá (dawn) of Good Friday, when La Virgen de la Macarena and La Virgen de Triana are both in the streets, is the culminating point of this explosion of color and passion.

## Where Art Comes First
**La Cartuja, Granada.** Thought to be a Christian response to the sumptuous Moorish Alhambra across town, La Cartuja's baroque carvings in the ceiling of the sacristy are some of the best in Spain.

**Museo de Bellas Artes, Seville.** This elegant former convent houses an excellent collection of paintings by "The Seville School" of Murillo, Zurbarán, and Valdés Leal.

**Museo Julio Romero de Torres, Córdoba.** Córdoba's most famous painter lived in the house across from the fine arts museum. His dreamlike and sensual themes of love and death in a flamenco key are superb.

# GREAT ITINERARIES

## Andalusian Uplands
More widely known for beaches and the flat and fertile *vega* (farmland), Andalusia has surprising highlands rich in hiking and trekking options as well as varied and interesting architectural and gastronomic treasures. With six national parks to choose from, the mountain resources of southern Spain should not be overlooked.

**Sierra de Aracena, Huelva** *2 days.* This lush mountain retreat in Spain's southwestern corner is home to, among other wildlife, the free-range Iberian pig. Jabugo is synonymous with this acorn-fattened delicacy. Cortegana, Almonaster la Real, and Aracena have lovely Mudéjar churches.

**Sierra de Grazalema, Cádiz and Málaga** *2 or 3 days.* The Cádiz highlands are famous for the pueblos blancos from Arcos de la Frontera up to Grazalema and into the province of Málaga to Ronda.

**Sierra de Segura, Jaén** *2 days.* The Parque Natural de Cazorla, Segura y Las Villas is rife with flora and fauna from mountain goats to royal eagles. Trout thrive in the clear mountain streams, headwaters of the historic Guadalquivir.

**Sierra Nevada and the Alpujarra, Granada** *3 or 4 days.* Spain's highest peak at Mulhacén, the skiing in the Sierra Nevada, and the hiking trails in the Alpujarra foothills along the Sierra Nevada's southern flanks are some of the Iberian Peninsula's finest mountain resources.

**Sierra Morena, Córdoba** *2 or 3 days.* Northern Andalusia's Sierra Morena is rough up-country that seems closer to Castilla and the Iberian meseta than to Andalusia and the Mediterranean. Belalcázar's castle and Hinojosa del Duque's "Catedral de la Sierra" are highlights.

**Sierra Norte, Seville** *2 days*. Due north of Seville, the mountain villages of Constantina and Cazalla de la Sierra are weekend retreats from the heat and pace of Andalusia's greatest metropolis.

## Roman, Moorish, and Mudéjar Highlights

Colonized by Rome, followed from the 4th through 7th centuries by Visigoths, who were then superseded by the Moors in 711, Andalusia offers opportunities to explore Roman, Moorish, and neo-Moorish or Mudéjar sites of various kinds. In 206 BC, Itálica was the Roman city on the Guadalquivir River before commerce moved closer to the port at Hispalis, now Seville. Nearby Carmona's Roman necropolis contains some 900 tombs dating from the 2nd century BC. The other major Roman site is at Baelo Claudia, near Tarifa in the province of Cádiz. Abderraman III's summer palace at Madinat al-Zahra near Córdoba may have been even more opulent than Granada's Alhambra before Berbers sacked and pillaged it in AD 1010. Córdoba's Mezquita and Granada's Alhambra are the most important manifestations of Moorish architecture on the Iberian Peninsula, and Seville's Alcazar is the main example of neo-Moorish construction. The many Mudéjar churches of Córdoba and Seville, as well as more remote chapels in places such as Huelva's Almonaster la Real and Córdoba's Montoro, each have their own distinct character.

**Seville, Itálica, and Carmona** *2 or 3 days*. The Moorish-style Alacazar, the medieval Barrio de Santa Cruz Jewish quarter, and the city's many Mudéjar churches are Seville's patrimony, but the Roman ruins at Itálica and Carmona's Roman cemetery reverberate with history.

**Córdoba and Madinat al-Zahra** *2 or 3 days*. Córdoba's Mezquita-Catedral (a mosque with a Gothic cathedral in the middle of it), the Judería with its unique synagogue, and the remains of the Umayyad summer palace at Madinat al-Zahra are all two hours from Madrid by the high-speed AVE train.

**Granada and Sierra Nevada** *2 or 3 days*. The Alhambra with the snowcapped Sierra Nevada behind it is one of Spain's great sights, but even more unusual is the chance to combine sizzling Granada's urban and cultural resources with the high sierra skiing and trekking opportunities less than an hour away.

**Cádiz, the Costa de la Luz, and Baelo Claudia** *1 or 2 days*. The city of Cádiz, western Europe's oldest, and the coast between Cádiz and Tarifa offer a variety of urban and natural opportunities. Baelo Claudia is a well-preserved Roman town to explore.

# 2 SEVILLE PROVINCE

Andalusia at its most colorful and characteristic, dazzling Seville is where the most wildly romantic visions of Spain all merge and come to life. A fantasy of passionate flamenco, dashing bullfighters, and flower-choked streets winding past whitewashed villas perfumed by thousands of orange blossoms: it is no wonder that Bizet's *Carmen* and Rossini's *Barber of Seville* were set here or that the world's most indelible impression of things Spanish is rooted in a place about which native poet Manuel Machado could only manage a breathless *"Y Sevilla!"*

By George
Semler

THE CITY OF SEVILLE IS SO LUMINOUS and aesthetically astounding that it's hard not to rub your eyes in disbelief at some of the things you see here. That the cathedral, the world's largest Gothic structure, and the Real Alcázar, one of Spain's finest Moorish (or Moorish-style) palace-fortresses, stand side by side seems almost impossible, and yet, there they are. Add to that a gleaming white, flower-festooned medieval Jewish quarter and dozens of redbrick Mudéjar, Gothic, baroque, and Renaissance churches, Moorish ramparts, civil structures, and noble palaces sprinkled liberally around the city's historic center and you may find yourself wondering whether you can see it all in much less than a lifetime. And then there's the river; the graceful bridges, in both traditional and postmodern design, that span it; and the popular and colorful Barrio de Triana beyond.

Europe's only deepwater riverine seaport, Seville owes much of its opulence to the river the Romans called Betis and the Moors afterward named Oued al-Kebir (Great River)—the modern-day Guadalquivir. Flowing west at its own sluggish pace from the Sierra Morena in Jaén to meet the Atlantic Ocean at Sanlúcar de Barrameda, southern Spain's most important waterway has carved the landscape and shaped the history of western Andalusia's provinces of Seville, Huelva, and Cádiz.

The landscape you see here today is very different from that of three millennia ago. Then the Guadalquivir widened into a broad estuary just south of present-day Seville. Along the banks of this inland sea dotted with islands, the civilization of Tartessus (the Biblical land of Tharsis) thrived, drawing its wealth from the gold- and silver-rich mountains of northern Huelva. This near-legendary realm traded actively with the seafaring Phoenicians from the Middle East, who founded their first Iberian settlement in Cádiz around 1100 BC. But then Tartessus vanished without a trace, apparently swallowed up by the waters, Atlantis style.

No one knows exactly where its capital stood, but its ruins probably lie somewhere buried beneath the marshes that formed as the Guadalquivir silted up. Today these marshes constitute one of the most precious natural treasures of Europe, Doñana National Park, a vital staging post for countless migrating bird species and permanent home to some of the continent's last surviving lynx and imperial eagles.

Two thousand years ago, as the river shifted course, it left the thriving Roman city of Itálica, birthplace of emperors Trajan and Hadrian, high and dry, prompting the rise to prominence of another early town, Hispalis, on the banks of the river 7 miles away. Known to the Moors as Isbiliyya, its name would eventually evolve into Seville. The city's fortunes continued to increase under the Moors, and later after its conquest by the Castillian Christians under King Ferdinand III in the 13th century, when the city acquired its massive cathedral and its exquisite royal palace, the Real Alcázar.

With the European discovery of the Americas, Seville would reach even greater splendor, outshining Madrid in riches and culture, as ships loaded with the booty sailed upriver past the Torre de Oro (Tower of Gold) and into Seville's port. Much of this treasure was siphoned off to pay for the Spanish throne's increasingly expensive foreign entanglements and bankers' debts, but enough was left over to fuel a cultural flowering and a building bonanza that can still be seen today in an endless array of palaces and monuments.

Seville is where all the romantic images of Andalusia—and Spain in general—spring vividly to life, in vibrant fiestas, fiery flamenco, thrilling bullfights and colorful streets perfumed by the blossoms of thousands of orange trees. The attractions and temptations of the Andalusian capital often blind visitors to the western Andalusian countryside, where myriad surprises await the inquisitive traveler. From the aristocratic towns and Roman ruins of Seville's Campiña to the rolling farmlands, sandy coastline, and tree-clad sierras of the inland and upland province of Seville, there is much to see beyond the capital city.

## Pleasures and Pastimes

### Bullfighting

Seville is home to one of Spain's most celebrated bullrings, the Maestranza. Few *toreros* (bullfighters) gain nationwide recognition until they have fought in this "cathedral of bullfighting." The season runs from Easter until late October, but it peaks early on, when Seville's April Fair draws Spain's leading toreros for a string of daily *corridas* (bullfights) of exceptional intensity, purity, and beauty. Though bullfighting, within Spain and abroad, is met with ever-more-critical opposition, the words of taurine phenomenon "El Juli" are worth pondering: "I respect the opinion of those who oppose bullfighting. But they should also respect the fact that this ancient fiesta, an artistic creation descended from prehistoric Mediterranean religious ritual, provides work, inspiration, and entertainment to many people and forms an essential part of the Spanish identity."

### Dining and Grazing

Drawing on the resources surrounding Seville, from the seafood of Andalusia's coast and the Guadalquivir, to the vegetables of the Campiña, to the free-range Iberian pig of the highlands, Seville is a food lover's paradise. Spicier, meatier, and more Moorish than its downriver neighbors at Cádiz and Sanlúcar de Barrameda, Seville freely combines all of the Andalusian countryside's rich produce, from vines to bovines, olives to garbanzos, sheep to nuts.

Seville's cuisine is distinct from those of the rest of Andalusia. Whereas on the coast chefs try to stay out of the way of the pure taste of seafood and the open ocean, in Seville there is a more exciting variety of tastes produced by a wider range of products. Possibly Spain's best blend of Iberia and North Africa, Seville features interesting combinations of superb vegetables, chickpeas, cumin seed, coriander, acorn-fed Iberian ham, and cheeses from southern La Mancha. *Guisos* (stewed combinations) are typically served in small *cazuelitas* (earthenware casseroles) and may be accompanied by anything from La Rioja wines to the local sherrylike *Manzanillas* and Moriles.

Favorite Seville dishes include: gazpacho, *pesca'ito frito* (fried whitefish); *espinacas con garbanzos* (spinach with garbanzos) with cumin seed; *cordero con miel* (lamb with honey); *albondigas de cordero* (lamb meatballs); *jarrete de ternera* (veal hock); guisos of *perdiz, liebre, ternera,* and *cordero* (partridge, hare, veal, and lamb); *puchero* (Andalusian stew); *lentejas con cordero* (lentils with lamb); *espárragos trigueros* (wild asparagus); *cola de toro a la Sevillana* (Seville-style bull's tail); *chocos* (cuttlefish) served in a cazuelita with tiny carrots, olive oil, and thyme; cazuelita of *champiñónes, gambas,* and *jabugo* (mushrooms, shrimp, and Iberian pig) in a dark sauce; and *patatas importancia* (potatoes "of importance," a gratin of baked potato with cheese and jabugo ham).

**Seville Province**

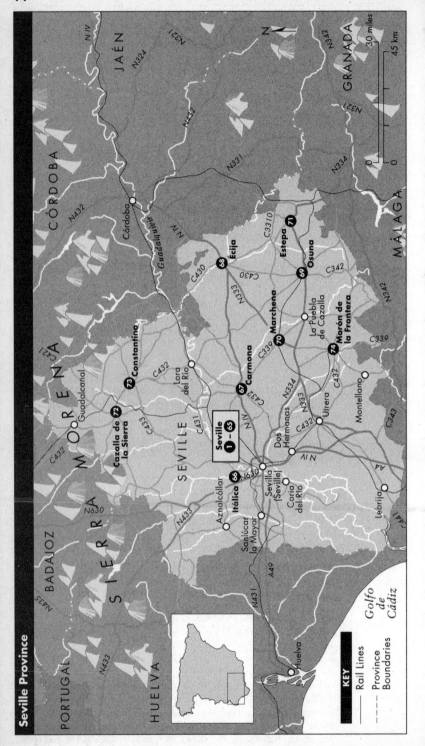

KEY
— Rail Lines
--- Province Boundaries

The local beverages of choice feature the *fino* (a dry and light sherry from Jerez) and Manzanilla (a dry and delicate sherry with a hint of saltiness from Sanlúcar de Barrameda). Cold beer is also popular, especially during the torrid summers, and fine wines from La Rioja or La Ribera de Duero impeccably accompany Seville fare.

| CATEGORY | COST* |
|---|---|
| $$$$ | over €18 |
| $$$ | €13–€18 |
| $$ | €8–€13 |
| $ | under €8 |

*per person for a main course at dinner*

## Fiestas

Seville's dramatic **Semana Santa** (Holy Week) processions are the most famous in Spain. For a solid week, penitents in pointed hoods carry floats back and forth from the cathedral while crowds watch their favorite icons come to life and flamenco singers explode into moving *saetas* (literally "arrows") sung to the representations of the grieving Virgin Mary. A week or two later (depending on the full moon that determines the date of Easter Sunday) the **Feria de Abril,** Seville's annual city fair, is celebrated with another uproarious week of flamenco singing, dancing, and fireworks nightly at the *casetas* (party tents) in the fairground across the river from the city center. The season's World Series of bullfights, comparable only to those of Madrid's Feria de San Isidro, unfolds in La Maestranza bullring, and processions of horses carrying women dressed in flamenco costumes parade through the streets. The Assumption of the Virgin Mary is celebrated with special devotion and fanfare in Seville on August 15, in part because it's the day of the city's patron, **Nuestra Señora de los Reyes** (Our Lady of the Kings). The cathedral opens its doors at 4:30 in the morning for the first mass of the day.

The June 3 **Corpus Christi** celebration is famous for the traditional dance of *los seises,* featuring six young boys dressed in Renaissance costumes of red and silver silk performing a mysterious and elegant mazurka in front of the cathedral's main altar.

**La Velá de Santa Ana,** from July 21 to 26, is the annual fiesta of the seafaring neighborhood of Triana. La Velá (Andalusian for *velada,* or soirée) brings all of Triana's flamenco and Gypsy atmosphere into the street for a week of revelry. Calle Betis is lined with casetas and stands sell everything from shrimp to almonds and Manzanilla. *La Cucaña,* a contest in which young men attempt to climb a greased pole and capture the prize, usually a leg of ham, is a favorite event.

During the second week of November the annual **Feria de la tapa sevillana** (Seville Tapas Fair), in the Palacio de Exposiciones y Congresos, is a chance to sample the city's finest culinary art in miniature.

## Flamenco

Seville, along with Jerez de la Frontera in Cádiz, is widely acknowledged as the headquarters of this quintessentially Andalusian art form, which combines dance, singing, guitar, and percussion. Seville offers a gamut of flamenco opportunities ranging from professional clubs to the grassroots amateur *cante jondo* (literally, "deep song") heard in little taverns and *tablaos* (clubs) all over town. What the commercial clubs lack in spontaneity they partly make up for in skill and polish, though the true emotion, the *duende* (witchcraft) of authentic flamenco song and dance is best found in performances that tend to break out well off the beaten tourist track in the *tascas* (bars) of popular barrios such as Triana and La Macarena, or in the great flamenco factory of Las Tres Mil Viviendas, Seville's outlying, largely Gypsy, community. Ask around—at the tourism office, your hotel, or just about any bar—for the *peñas* (societies), semiprivate clubs that are happy to have an interested visitor or two (though not busloads). If you blend in and don't look like you're about to flash photographs or behave like a tourist, a seemingly improvised flamenco event is likely to materialize, and these are the most memorable.

### Lodging

The city of Seville has accommodations ranging from grand old hotels to recently converted palaces to traditional warm family-run hotels. La Campiña, the farmland and countryside south of the Guadalquivir, offers *agroturismo* accommodations in a wide range of farmhouses, manor houses, and *cortijos,* Andalusian country estates with varying degrees of luxury.

It *is* possible to sleep cheaply in Seville, but your room will be tiny, and you'll have to scour areas far from the city center. Prices fluctuate dramatically with the seasons—much more so than in most other parts of Spain—so it's best to inquire in advance. Always ask about discounts; but even if you don't ask, you will often find that outside the busiest dates the offered room rate is lower than the officially listed price.

For the top lodging spots during Seville's Holy Week or April Fair you *must* book early—four to eight months in advance in Seville, though for the odd pensione, *hostal,* or one-star hotel, you can nearly always do quite nicely (and cheaply) if you show up unannounced. Most hotel prices in Seville rise steeply—by at least half, usually doubling or tripling—during Holy Week and the April *ferias.*

| CATEGORY | COST |
|---|---|
| **$$$$** | over €140 |
| **$$$** | €100–€140 |
| **$$** | €60–€100 |
| **$** | under €60 |

*All prices are for a standard double room, excluding tax.*

## Exploring Seville and Seville Province

Although exploring the city of Seville can (and should) be the main objective here, there is also much to see and admire in the fertile farmland south of the Guadalquivir river known as La Campiña, along La Vega of the Upper Guadalquivir, and in the Sierra Norte and Sierra Sur areas at Seville province's northern and southern extremities.

Itálica, with its elaborate Roman ruins, is nearly walking distance from Seville (though walking isn't advised—there is no picturesque route), and just south of Seville, Alcalá de Guadaira's mills and fortresses are the town's most interesting attractions.

La Vega, or river basin, is a flat and fertile expanse north of the Guadalquivir river with a series of small towns—Villanueva del Río y Minas, Lora del Río, Alcolea del Río, and Peñaflor—each of which has a memorable building, square, or church to offer.

Farther afield, the Ruta de Artealia encompasses the four main towns of the Campiña: Carmona, Marchena, Écija, and Osuna, all within 100 km (60 mi) of Seville and each richly endowed with fortresses, bastions, churches, and noteworthy noble palaces. In the Sierra Norte that, along with the Sierra Morena, separates Andalusia from the plains of Castile, Cazalla de la Sierra is a lively mountain stronghold popular with weekenders and famous for its anise liqueur, whereas Constantina is a quieter and more reflective village with splendid views over the surrounding hills. In the Sierra Sur, Morón de la Frontera is the best base camp for an exploration of the charming mountain villages along the "Ruta del Tempranillo," named for the bandit who once controlled this highland region.

## Great Itineraries

As a general overview, a visitor to Seville should never fail to see the cathedral, the Alcázar, the Barrio de Santa Cruz, Triana, the Museo de Bellas Artes, Calle Sierpes, the Puerta de la Macarena, and the Convento de Santa Paula. Itálica and Carmona are the two out-of-town musts.

### IF YOU HAVE 3 DAYS

With home base in ⛫ **Seville** ①–㊿, on your first day, visit the **cathedral** ① and the Giralda. After lunch at the Bar Giralda on Calle Mateos Gagos, take a walk through the orange blossom–scented lanes of the Barrio de Santa Cruz. In the afternoon explore Arenal and cross the Puente de Triana to get the feel of this traditional sailor and Gypsy quarter on the far side of the river. On the second day, carefully explore the **Real Alcázar** ③ before walking through the shady **Parque de María Luisa** ㉚. Briefly tour the monumental **Plaza de España** ㉝ before heading over past the onetime tobacco factory, now the **University of Seville** ㉟, to the **Torre de Oro** ㊳. Taxi or bus out to the far side of the old part of Seville to the Murallas Arabes (Arab Walls) and visit **La Basílica de la Macarena** ㊸ and the Barrio de la Macarena in the afternoon and early evening. At night, take in some flamenco: the Salve Rociera at midnight at El Tamboril or a professional show at Los Gallos, both in Plaza de Santa Cruz. Devote the next day to Anadalusia's Roman heritage: explore the ancient town of **Carmona** ㊻, with its Roman necropolis, and then the Roman ruins at **Itálica** ㊺ before returning to Seville.

### IF YOU HAVE 5 DAYS

Starting in ⛫ **Seville** ①–㊿, on the first day see the **cathedral** ① and Giralda. After lunch at the Bar Giralda on Mateos Gagos, walk through the narrow lanes of the Barrio de Santa Cruz. The next day, explore the **Real Alcázar** ③ in the morning. In the afternoon take in the **Museo de Bellas Artes** ㊷; then head toward the river and walk the Paseo de Colón, where you can see **Plaza de Toros Real Maestranza** ㊵ (Seville's bullring) and visit the **Torre de Oro** ㊳. On your third day, wander the **Parque de María Luisa** ㉚, stopping at the Plaza de América and monumental **Plaza de España** ㉝. On your way back to the city center, look for the **University of Seville** ㉟, the former tobacco factory of *Carmen* fame. In the afternoon, start at the Murallas Arabes, visit the **La Basílica de la Macarena** ㊸, and explore the Barrio de la Macarena. On Day 4, leave Seville for ⛫ **Carmona** ㊻ for a careful exploration of this ancient gem of a town. Spend your last night in the town of ⛫ **Osuna** ㊽ after exploring **Marchena** ㊾ and **Écija** ㊼. On your last day, explore the country town of **Morón de la Frontera** ㊿ before returning to Seville or heading south to Ronda.

## When to Tour

Seville's Ferias de Abril, Semana Santa (Holy Week) and Feria (the more secular bash that follows a week or 10 days later) may take place anytime between late March and early May and are certainly, although crowded, the most exciting weeks to be in Seville. If you want to experience the pomp and crackle of one of the greatest of all Spanish fiestas, this is the time to come—just reserve a room far in advance (and read, with allowances for important changes that have taken place over the last three decades, the Seville chapter of James Michener's classic *Iberia*). The big fiestas aside, spring and late fall are particularly nice, when the weather is warm but not unpleasantly hot. Winters are mild and uncrowded and the Andalusian sun never feels better.

# SEVILLE

*550 km (340 mi) southwest of Madrid, 220 km (140 mi) northwest of Málaga.*

Seville's whitewashed houses bright with bougainvillea, its ocher-color palaces, churches, and convents, and its baroque facades have long enchanted both Sevillanos and travelers. Lying on the banks of the Guadalquivir, bustling Seville is Spain's fourth-largest city, with a population of almost 800,000, and is the capital of Andalusia. It may at times seem an unchecked free-for-all, with traffic-choked streets and high unemployment that undoubtedly contributes to its notorious petty-crime rate. But Seville's artistic heritage, its aesthetic obsession bordering on narcissism, and its residents' charm and zest for life more than compensate for its big-city disadvantages.

Seville has a long and noble history. It was conquered in 205 BC by the Romans, who called it Hispalis, according to one theory because of the *palos* (sticks or stilts) upon which many of the houses were constructed to elevate them over the Guadalquivir's then-more-ample marshland. The Moors invaded in the early 8th century and held Seville for more than 500 years, leaving behind one of their greatest works of architecture, the Giralda, now a bell tower but constructed as a sister minaret to Marrakesh's landmark Kutoubia. King Ferdinand III lies enshrined in the glorious cathedral, along with his rather less saintly descendant, Pedro the Cruel, builder of the splendid Alcázar.

Seville is justly proud of its literary and artistic heritage. Painters Diego Rodríguez de Silva Velázquez (1599–1660) and Bartolomé Estéban Murillo (1617–82) were sons of Seville, as were the poets Gustavo Adolfo Bécquer (1836–70), Antonio Machado (1875–1939), and Nobel Prize winner Vicente Aleixandre (1898–1984). The tale of the ingenious knight of La Mancha was begun in a Seville jail—Don Quixote's creator, Miguel de Cervantes, twice languished in a debtors' prison here. Tirso de Molina's Don Juan wooed and seduced in Seville's mansions, later scheming as Don Giovanni in the Barrio de Santa Cruz; the Barrio was also the setting for the nuptials of Rossini's barber, Figaro. Nearby, at the old tobacco factory (now the University of Seville), Bizet's sultry Carmen first met Don José.

Seville's color and vivacity are most intense during Semana Santa (Holy Week), when lacerated Christs and bejeweled, weeping Virgins from the city's 24 parishes are paraded through the streets on floats borne by penitents or *Nazarenos,* who often walk barefoot. Some penitents carry crosses or chains, having promised during an illness or crisis of some kind that, if they overcame their troubles, they would publicly offer gratitude and, in the process, atone for their sins.

A week later, and this time in full flamenco costume, Sevillanos throw their April Fair, the greatest party of the year. This celebration began as a horse-trading fair in 1847 and still honors its equine origins: midday horse parades feature men in broad-brimmed hats and Andalusian riding gear astride prancing steeds, with their women in long, ruffled dresses riding sidesaddle behind them. Bullfights, fireworks, and all-night singing and dancing in the fairground's casetas complete the spectacle.

# Exploring Seville

The layout of the historic center of Seville makes exploring easy. The central zone around the cathedral, the Alcázar, Calle Sierpes, and Plaza Nueva is splendid and monumental, but it's not where you'll find Seville's greatest charm. El Arenal, home of the Maestranza bullring, the Teatro de la Maestranza concert hall, and a concentration of picturesque taverns, still buzzes the way it must have when stevedores loaded and unloaded ships from the New World. Just north of the center, the medieval Jewish quarter, Barrio de Santa Cruz, is a lovely, white-washed tangle of alleys. The immense Barrio de la Macarena to the west is rich in sights and authentic Seville atmosphere. The fifth and final neighborhood to explore, on the far side of the river Guadalquivir, is in many ways the best of all: Triana is the traditional habitat for sailors, Gypsies, bullfighters, and flamenco artists, as well as the main workshop for Seville's renowned ceramics artisans.

## Centro

This stroll takes in the major sights of central Seville, the high ground wedged in between the Barrio de Santa Cruz, the Barrio de la Macarena, and Arenal.

### A Good Walk

Start with the **cathedral** ①, in the Plaza Virgen de los Reyes. Climb the Giralda, the minaret of the former Moorish mosque—from the top you have a panoramic view over the city. Walk down Avenida de la Constitución and visit the **Archivo de Indias** ②, which holds the surviving documents related to the discovery of the New World. Behind the archive is the **Real Alcázar** ③, a Moorish-style palace surrounded by high walls.

From the Alcázar and the cathedral, it's a 10-minute walk north to the **ayuntamiento** ④, with its intricate plateresque southern facade. **Plaza Nueva** ⑤ is on the far side of the city hall. Two blocks north through narrow alleys filled with taverns and bars is the baroque **Capilla de San José** ⑥. Farther north the pedestrian **Calle Sierpes** ⑦ is Seville's most famous shopping and strolling street. From there, backtrack down Calle Cuna, which runs parallel to Sierpes, stopping at No. 8 to see the **Palacio de la Condesa de Lebrija** ⑧. Continue down Calle Cuna to the Plaza del Salvador and the **Iglesia del Salvador** ⑨, a former mosque. Walk up Alcaicería to **Plaza de la Alfalfa** ⑩ and along Calle Sales Ferrer toward Plaza Cristo del Burgos—in a small alley off the square is the **Casa Natal de Velázquez** ⑪, where the painter Diego de Velázquez Silva was born in 1599.

TIMING

Allow at least half a day for the central Seville tour, including either the Alcázar *or* the cathedral, but preferably not both at once—these essential Seville sights can be overwhelming when viewed back to back. The Alcázar, especially, is worthy of a good half day on its own.

### Sights to See

❷ **Archivo de Indias** (Archives of the Indies). Opened in 1785 in the former Lonja (Merchants' Exchange), this dignified Renaissance building was designed by Juan de Herrera, architect of El Escorial, in 1572. The archive holds an impressive collection of documents relating to the discovery of the New World—drawings, trade documents, plans of South American towns, even the autographs of Columbus, Magellan, and Cortés. Many of the 38,000 documents have yet to be sorted and properly cataloged, so the selection of items on display changes regularly. ⊠ *Avda. de la Constitución, Centro,* ☎ *95/421–1234.*

**20**

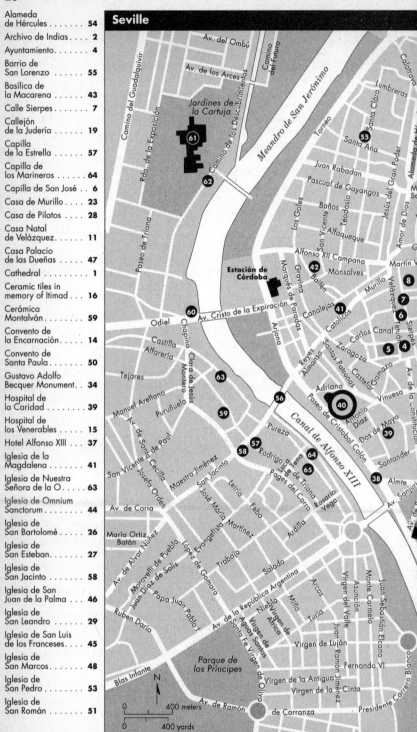

Seville

**KEY**

*i* Tourist Information

✉ *Free.* ☿ *Weekdays 10–1, 8–3 for researchers; temporarily closed to nonresearchers for renovation, scheduled to reopen end of 2003.*

❹ **Ayuntamiento** (City Hall). This Diego de Riaño original, built between 1527 and 1564, stands in the heart of Seville's commercial center, the Plaza Nueva. The side of the building overlooking the plaza dates from the 19th century, but if you walk around to the other side, on the Plaza de San Francisco, you'll see Riaño's intricate plateresque facade. Look for the *arquillo* (little archway) on the west end of the building with the plaque commemorating Cervantes' novel *Rinconete y Cortadillo*, scenes from which are placed here. ✉ *Plaza Nueva 1, Centro,* ☎ *95/ 459–0101,* WEB *www.sevilla.org.* ✉ *Free.* ☿ *Mandatory tours Tues.– Thurs. 5:30 and 6:30; Sat. 11 and 12:30. No tours mid-July–mid-Sept.*

❼ **Calle Sierpes** (Serpentine Street). Reportedly named not for snakes, per se, but for the way this once watery thoroughfare originally twisted, serpentlike, through the marshes and tidal pools that formerly collected here, this is Seville's main shopping and people-watching street. The Café de la Campana, possibly named for the bell (*campana*), belonging to the fire station once located here at the northern end of Calle Sierpes, is the most famous meeting point in Seville, *the* place to see and be seen for the movers and shakers of the Seville bourgeoisie. Café Ochoa, nearby, is nearly as fashionable. All during Holy Week, floats pass in review through La Campana, where the *plana mayor* (the top drawer) of Seville's politicos and well-to-do reserve seats far in advance. From La Campana, the floats proceed through Calle Sierpes past the town hall to the cathedral before starting back to their respective parishes. Look for the spectacularly colorful *azulejos* (tiles) advertising the 1924 Studebaker at the corner of Calles Tetuan and Sierpes. At the corner of Calle Pedro Caravaca is the Real Círculo de Labradores, an exclusive men's club since 1856, which you can catch a glimpse of while being shown out. Near the southern end of Calle Sierpes, at No. 85, a plaque marks the spot where the Cárcel Real (Royal Prison) once stood. The plaque explains that Miguel de Cervantes began writing *Don Quixote* in one of its cells while imprisoned for losing a handsome sum of money he had collected as taxes for the Crown. Ironically, the site is now occupied by a bank.

❻ **Capilla de San José.** This tiny 18th-century baroque chapel is a thimble of peace in this commercial neighborhood. The intricately coffered cedar ceiling comes to life as your eyes adjust to the penumbra, and the ornate gilt carving of the main altar grips the eyes. Listen carefully and you can hear birds chirping in the organ over the choir loft. ✉ *Calle Jovellanos s/n, Centro.* ✉ *Free.* ☿ *Mon.–Sat. 8–12:30 and 6:30–8:30.*

⓫ **Casa Natal de Velázquez.** One of Spain's greatest painters, Diego de Velázquez, was born in this *casa de vecinos* (town house and patio shared by several families) in 1599. The house—whose modest ocher facade belies its size—fell into ruin, but was bought in the 1970s by the well-known fashion designers Victorio y Lucchino, who carefully restored it for use as their studio. The house is not open to the public. ✉ *Padre Luis María Llop 4, Centro.*

★ ❶ **Cathedral.** The best place to start exploring Seville is the Plaza Virgen de los Reyes: from next to the central fountain you can gaze up at the magnificent Giralda, symbol of Seville; and the east facade of the great Gothic cathedral. After Ferdinand III captured Seville from the Moors in 1248, the great mosque begun by Yusuf II in 1171 was reconsecrated to the Virgin Mary and used as a Christian cathedral, much as the mosque at Córdoba was. But in 1401 the people of Seville decided to erect a new and glorious cathedral, one that would equal the status of their great city. They promptly pulled down the old mosque, leaving only its minaret and outer court, and set about their task with unparalleled zeal. The mighty building before you was completed in just over a century—a remarkable feat for the time. The clergy renounced their incomes for the cause, and a member of the chapter is said to have proclaimed, "Let us build a church so large that we shall be held to be insane." This they proceeded to do, for today Seville's cathedral can be described only in superlatives: it is the largest and tallest cathedral in Spain, the largest Gothic building in the world, and the world's third-largest church, after St. Peter's in Rome and St. Paul's in London.

You enter the cathedral grounds via the **Patio de los Naranjos** (Courtyard of Orange Trees), part of the original mosque. The old fountain in the center was used for ritual ablutions before entering the mosque. Near the Puerta del Lagarto (Lizard's Gate), in the corner near the Giralda, see if you can find the wooden alligator—thought to have been a gift from the emir of Egypt in 1260 as he sought the hand of the daughter of Alfonso X el Sabio (the Wise)—and the elephant tusk, found in the ruins of Itálica.

The cathedral's exterior, with its rose windows and magnificent flying buttresses, is a monument to pure Gothic beauty. Aside from the well-lit high altar, the dimly illuminated interior can be disappointing, its five naves and numerous side chapels shrouded in gloom; Gothic purity has been largely submerged in ornate baroque decoration. Still, there is a great deal worth seeing here, even if you have to strain your eyes.

Enter the cathedral itself through the Puerta de la Granada or the Puerta Colorada. Before you, in the central nave, rise the **Capilla Mayor** (Main Chapel) and its intricately carved altarpiece, begun by a Flemish carver in 1482 and finished by both Spanish and Flemish artists by 1564. This magnificent *retablo* (altarpiece) is the largest in Christendom (65 ft by 43 ft), depicting some 44 scenes from the life of Christ. The scenes are populated by more than 200 figures, and the whole work is lavishly adorned with gold leaf. Binoculars would help to study these scenes carefully, many of them luridly illustrated with, for example, babies impaled on spears (in the "slaughter of the innocents" scene) and voluptuous female figures in the representation of hell.

Make your way to the opposite (southern) side of the cathedral, where you can't miss the flamboyant **Tomb of Christopher Columbus.** The great explorer knew both triumph and disgrace, but found no repose after dying, bitterly disillusioned, in Valladolid—the Spanish royal court at the time, 191 km (115 mi) north of Madrid—in 1506. Initially buried in Valladolid, his remains were taken to Hispaniola (now Santo Domingo) by his son, Hernando. When Santo Domingo fell to the French in 1697, the tombs of Columbus and his son were removed to Havana. In 1898, when Spain lost Cuba in the Spanish-American War, the remains were returned to their final resting place in the Seville cathedral. Columbus's coffin is borne aloft by four kings representing the medieval kingdoms of Spain: Castile, León, Aragón, and Navarre. Columbus's son, Hernando Colón (1488–1539), is also interred here; his tombstone, inscribed with the words A CASTILLA Y A LEÓN, MUNDO NUEVO DIO COLÓN (to Castile and León, Columbus gave a new world), lies between the great west door, the Puerta Mayor, and the central choir.

Between the elder Columbus's tomb and the Capilla Real, at the eastern end of the central nave, the cathedral's treasuries display a wealth of gold and silver (much of it from the New World), relics, and other works of art. In the **Sacristía de los Cálices** (Sacristy of the Chalices), look for Martínez Montañés's wood carving *Crucifixion, Merciful*

*Christ,* Valdés Leal's *St. Peter Freed by an Angel,* Zurbarán's *Virgin and Child,* and Goya's *St. Justa and St. Rufina.* The **Sacristía Mayor** (Main Sacristy) holds the keys to the city, which Seville's Moors and Jews presented to their conqueror, Ferdinand III. Finally, in the dome of the **Sala Capitular** (Chapter House), in the cathedral's southeastern corner, is Murillo's *Immaculate Conception,* painted in 1668.

One of the cathedral's highlights, the **Capilla Real** (Royal Chapel), is reserved for prayer and concealed behind a ponderous curtain, but you can duck in if you're quick, quiet, and properly dressed. To do so, after exploring the rest of the cathedral and the Giralda, enter again from a separate door, the Puerta de los Palos, on Plaza Virgen de los Reyes (signposted ENTRADA PARA CULTO—entrance for worship). Along the sides of the chapel are the tombs of the wife of Ferdinand III, Beatrix of Swabia, and his son, Alfonso X el Sabio (died 1284); in a silver urn before the high altar rest the precious relics of Ferdinand III himself, Seville's liberator (canonized in 1671), who was said to have died from excessive fasting. In the (rarely open) vault below lie the tombs of Ferdinand's descendant Pedro the Cruel and Pedro's mistress, María de Padilla. Above the entrance grille, you can see a Jerónino Roldán sculpture of Ferdinand III receiving the keys to Seville, with the chained and defeated Moors at his feet.

Before you duck into the Capilla Real, climb to the top of the **Giralda,** the undisputed symbol of Seville. It dominates the skyline and can be glimpsed from almost every corner of the city. Once the minaret of Seville's great mosque, from which the faithful were summoned to prayer, it was built between 1184 and 1196, just 50 years before the reconquest of Seville. The Christians could not bring themselves to destroy this tower when they tore down the mosque, so they incorporated it into their new cathedral. In 1565–68 they added a lantern and belfry to the old minaret and installed 24 bells, one for each of Seville's 24 parishes and the 24 Christian knights who fought with Ferdinand III in the reconquest. They also added the bronze statue of Faith, which turned as a weather vane—*el giraldillo,* or "something that turns," thus the name Giralda. To give it a rest after 400 years of wear and tear, the original statue was replaced with a copy in 1997.

With its baroque additions, the slender Giralda rises 322 ft. Inside, instead of steps, 35 sloping ramps—wide enough for two horsemen to pass abreast—climb to a viewing platform 230 ft up. It is said that Ferdinand III rode his horse to the top to admire the city he had conquered. If you follow in his horse's footsteps, you'll be rewarded with a glorious view of tile roofs and the Guadalquivir shimmering beneath palm-lined banks. ⊠ *Plaza Virgen de los Reyes, Centro,* ☎ *95/421–4971.* 🎫 *€6 for cathedral, museum, Giralda, and Patio de los Naranjos.* ☉ *Mon.–Sat. 11–5, Sun. 2–6, and for mass.*

**❾ Iglesia del Salvador.** Built between 1671 and 1712, the Church and Colegiata de San Salvador stand on the site of Seville's first great mosque. The deep reddish maroon *sangre de toro* (bull's blood) facade conceals a dizzyingly ornate altar and overlooks one of Seville's most popular gathering points. The patio of the mosque, used for ablutions prior to prayer, is still partly preserved on the east side of the colegiata, accessible from inside the church and from Calle Córdoba to the northeast. Inside, the ornate gilt altarpiece is a stunningly rich example of early baroque exuberance. Look especially for the image of *Jesús de la Pasión,* carved by Juan Martínez Montañés (1568–1649), whose monument centers the square outside. This sculpture is borne through the streets on Holy Thursday in one of Holy Week's most moving processions. The square outside and the steps of the church fill with midday and evening crowds of young people sipping beer or fino from the bars, Bodeguita Los Soportales and La Antigua Bodeguita, across the way. The baroque facade of the **Iglesia de San Juan de Dios** (also known as the Hospital de Nuestra Señora de la Paz), largely concealed by the orange trees across the square from the Iglesia de San Salvador, leads into a lush baroque interior with complex molded plaster sculptures in the cupola. ⊠ *Plaza San Salvador, Centro,* ☎ *95/421–1679.* ⊠ *Free.* ☉ *Mon.–Sat. 9–1 and 6:30–8:30.*

**❽** **Palacio de la Condesa de Lebrija.** Until the early 1990s, this 16th-century palace was the private residence of its aristocratic owner, the late countess of Lebrija. Her heirs have opened the ground floor to the public, including a spectacular courtyard graced by a Roman mosaic purloined from the ruins in Itálica and surrounded by Moorish arches and fine tiles. The side rooms house an eclectic collection of archaeological goodies. ⊠ *Cuna 8, Centro,* ☎ *95/422–7802.* ⊠ *€3.60 ground floor, €6.60 first floor.* ☉ *Weekdays 10:30–1 and 4:30–7 (May–Oct. 5–8), Sat. 10–1.*

**❿** **Plaza de la Alfalfa.** Originally the Roman forum and later Seville's grain and livestock market, Plaza de la Alfalfa, (named for, yes, alfalfa) is an extraordinarily warm and quirky space that comes hilariously alive on Sunday mornings with an animal market like no other in Andalusia or anywhere in Spain. Any kind of animal—from a kitten to a donkey to an iguana—could turn up in this square known to have housed a lion in a pet store and where, on the corner of Plaza de la Alfafa and Calle Luchana, an urban *vaquería* (milk cow stable) operated until the last quarter of the 20th century. ⊠ *Centro.*

**❺** **Plaza Nueva.** Once site of the Inquisition's autos-da-fé and home of the church and convent of San Francisco (torn down in the mid-19th century), this relatively new expanse, centered around the equestrian statue of King (and Saint) Fernando III, stretches out to the west of the neoclassical facade of the ayuntamiento (town hall). A sort of intermediate breathing space between El Arenal, Barrio de Santa Cruz, and La Macarena farther north, Plaza Nueva is a pivotal area that could as well have been christened Plaza Neutral. The Hotel Inglaterra and its dark, wood-paneled Trinity Pub anchor the west end of the square, and Calle de Zaragoza off to the left has a handful of excellent bars and cafés, from the Casablanca at No. 50 to the diminutive Casa Paco at No. 32 to the Taberna del Alabardero farther up at No. 20. A short walk into the edge of Arenal will take you to the excellent Enrique Becerra restaurant at the corner of Gamazo and Zaragoza. In Plaza Nueva proper, look for the intricate paving stone mosaics representing everything from geometrical designs to bulls' heads, fish, and doves, or the coat of arms of "Er Beti," Seville's beloved (though usually second best after the Real Sevilla) soccer club, Real Betis Balompié. Look also for Seville's NO8DO symbol, awarded to the city by Alfonso X el Sabio for remaining loyal to him during the 13th-century rebellion organized by his son Sancho. The cryptogram means, with reference to Seville, *"No me ha dejado"* (It didn't leave me), using as a symbol the figure eight–shaped form of the *madeja* (ball of yarn) between NO and DO for "NO-madeja-DO," in the typical phonetics of Andalusian speech. ⊠ *Plaza Nueva, Centro.*

**★ ❸** **Real Alcázar.** The Plaza Triunfo forms the entrance to the Mudéjar palace built by Pedro I (1350–69) on the site of Seville's former Moorish *alcázar* (fortress). Don't mistake the Alcázar for a genuine Moorish palace, like Granada's Alhambra—it may look like one, and it was indeed designed and built by Moorish workers from Granada, but it was commissioned and paid for by a Christian king more than 100 years after the reconquest of Seville. In its construction, Pedro the Cruel incorporated stones and capitals he pillaged from Valencia, from Córdoba's Medina Azahara, and from Seville itself. The Alcázar is the finest example of Mudéjar architecture in Spain today, though its purity of style has been much diluted by the alterations and additions of successive Spanish rulers. The palace serves as the official Seville residence of the king and queen of Spain.

You enter the Alcázar through the Puerta del León (Lion's Gate) and the high, fortified walls. These are of genuine Moorish origin, but they belie the exquisite delicacy of the interior. You'll first find yourself in a garden courtyard, the **Patio del León.** Off to the left are the oldest parts of the building, the 14th-century **Sala de Justicia** (Hall of Justice) and, next to it, the intimate **Patio del Yeso** (Courtyard of Plaster), part of the original 12th-century Alcázar of the Almohad dynasty. Cross the **Patio de la Montería** (Equestrian Court) to Pedro's Mudéjar palace, arranged around the beautiful **Patio de las Doncellas** (Court of the Damsels), resplendent with delicately carved stucco. Its name probably refers to the annual gift of 100 virgins to the Moorish sultans. Although its Granadan craftsmanship recalls the Alhambra, the upper galleries were added by Carlos V. Opening off this patio, the **Salón de Embajadores** (Hall of the Ambassadors), with its cedar cupola of green, red, and gold, is the most sumptuous hall in the palace. It was here that Carlos V married Isabel of Portugal in 1526, for which occasion he added the wooden balconies.

Other royal rooms include the dining hall of Felipe II (1527–98) and the three baths of Pedro's wily mistress, María de Padilla. María's hold over her royal lover—and apparently over his courtiers, too—was so great that they supposedly lined up to drink her bathwater. The **Patio de las Muñecas** (Court of the Dolls) takes its name from two tiny faces carved on the inside of one of its arches, no doubt as a joke on the part of its Moorish creators. Here Pedro reputedly had his half brother, Don Fadrique, slain in 1358, and here, too, he murdered guest Abu Said of Granada for his jewels. Pedro presented one of these, a huge, uncut ruby, to the Black Prince (Edward, Prince of Wales [1330–76], eldest son of England's Edward III) in 1367. It now sits among other priceless gems in the Crown of England.

You come next to the Renaissance **Palacio de Carlos V,** built by the emperor at the time of his marriage and endowed with a rich collection of Flemish tapestries depicting Carlos's victories at Tunis. Look for the map of Spain: it shows the Iberian Peninsula upside down, as was the custom in Arab mapmaking. There are more goodies—rare clocks, antique furniture, paintings, and more tapestries—on the Alcázar's upper floor, in the **Estancias Reales** (Royal Chambers). These are the apartments used by King Juan Carlos I and his family when in town. The required guided tour leads you through the dining room, other protocol rooms, and the king's office. Tours depart in the morning only, every half hour in summer and every hour in winter.

At the end of your visit, pause in the **gardens,** where you can breathe the fragrance of jasmine and myrtle, wander lovely terraces and ornamental baths, and peer into the well-stocked goldfish pond, covered with water lilies. In the midst of this green oasis is an orange tree said to have been planted in the time of Pedro the Cruel. From the gardens, a passageway leads to the **Patio de las Banderas** (Court of the Flags), which has a classic view of the Giralda. ⊠ *Plaza del Triunfo, Centro,* ☎ *95/450–2324,* W̲E̲B̲ *www.patronato-alcazarsevilla.es.* ⊠ *€5; tour of Royal Chambers €3.* ☉ *Apr.–Sept., Tues.–Sat. 9:30–8, Sun. 9:30–6; Oct.–Mar., Tues.–Sat. 9:30–6, Sun. 9:30–2:30.*

# Barrio de Santa Cruz

Home of Seville's Jewish community in the Middle Ages, Barrio de Santa Cruz is a shady warren of lanes, whitewashed buildings, courtyards, and banks of bougainvillea and flowers of every kind. The area was much favored by the city's nobles in the 17th century, and the houses are beautifully preserved, some still ranking among Seville's most elegant and expensive properties. The atmosphere is unbeatable: wrought-iron lanterns cast shadows on the whitewashed walls, and ocher-framed windows hide behind rectangular grilles. On some streets, bars alternate with antiques stores and souvenir shops, but most of the quarter is residential. The Callejón del Agua, beside the wall of the Alcázar's gardens, has some of the quarter's finest mansions and patios.

## A Good Walk

Begin in **Plaza Virgen de los Reyes** ⑫ at the eastern end of the cathedral. The baroque facade of the **Palacio Arzobispal** ⑬ stands on the north side of the central fountain, and the 16th-century **Convento de la Encarnación** ⑭ is the church on the opposite corner. Walk up Calle Mateos Gagos past La Giralda (the bar, not the tower) possibly Seville's most famous tapas emporium, and turn right into Calle Rodrigo Caro. Pass the Bodega Santa Cruz on your left and turn right into Calle Jamerdana where, just past No. 4, a giant studded wooden door announces the back of the **Hospital de los Venerables** ⑮, just around the corner in the Plaza de los Venerables. From there, Calle Gloria leads past the **ceramic tiles in memory of Itimad** ⑯, the beautiful slave girl the last Moorish king of Seville, Almotamid, fell in love with and made his queen. In **Plaza de Doña Elvira** ⑰ with its fountain and azulejo benches, young Sevillanos gather to play guitars. Walk out to the right to the antiques shops and outdoor café in Plaza de la Alianza, where a simple crucifix hangs on the dazzling white wall shrouded in bougainvillea. From Plaza de la Alianza take Calle Romero Murube to **Plaza del Triunfo** ⑱, highlighted by its Inmaculada Concepción monument. Cut through the Patio de Banderas and the passageway at the far left corner, the **Callejón de la Judería** ⑲, leading through a low, tightly curved medieval Mudéjar archway into Calle Vida. Bearing right into el Callejón del Agua you will pass the plaque marking the Casa de Washington Irving at No. 2. **Plaza Alfaro** ⑳ is at the end of the Callejón del Agua, a lovely little square at the edge of the **Jardines de Murillo** ㉑, complete with a statue of Christopher Columbus. Cutting through the edge of the gardens past the two Moorish watchtowers, walk left into the **Plaza de Santa Cruz** ㉒, with its wrought-iron cross in the center and the elegant Albahaca restaurant. The 17th-century filigree iron cross marks the site of the erstwhile church of Santa Cruz, destroyed by Napoléon's General Soult. The painter Murillo was buried here in 1682, though his current resting place is unknown. The **Casa de Murillo** ㉓ is just up Calle de Santa Teresa. From Plaza de Santa Cruz, cut through Calle Mezquita (Mosque), past the Roman columns exposed on the corner, and into **Plaza de los Refinadores** ㉔ with the monument to Don Juan Tenorio in the center. As you emerge into Calle de Cano y Cueto you will miss the intimate hush of the Barrio de Santa Cruz. Take a left on Calle de Santa María la Blanca and go two blocks to what was once a medieval synagogue, the **Iglesia de Santa María la Blanca** ㉕. Just past this church, one of Seville's most fascinating, is Calle Marqués de Céspedes, with the lovely hotel Casas de la Judería at the end of this dead-end alley. Back out on Calle de Santa María la Blanca, a right onto Calle Cespedes and another right onto Calle de la Virgen de la Alegría brings you to the 18th-century **Iglesia de San Bartolomé** ㉖. From here, Calle Levíes leads to Plaza de las Mercedarias, where a right onto Calle Vidrio leads you past a series of lush patios on the way out to

Calle de San Esteban. To the left are the 14th-century **Iglesia de San Esteban** ㉗ and the 16th-century **Casa de Pilatos** ㉘, one of Seville's three most important Renaissance palaces. Nearby, look for the giant marble eagles over the door at the Casa de las Águilas (eagles) at No. 16 on the street of the same name and the **Iglesia de San Leandro** ㉙ on Calle de las Caballerizas.

TIMING

The Barrio de Santa Cruz, with Seville's largest pedestrian zone, is a maze that's best wandered haphazardly. The route suggested here merely hits the highlights—navigating from one sight to another offers many opportunities for surprises, and getting lost may be the best way to capture the essence of the place. Allow four hours for your walk, including the Casa de Pilatos. Try to time it so that you get a look into Santa María la Blanca, or make a special trip back when it's open.

## Sights to See

㉓ **Casa de Murillo.** This house on Calle Santa Teresa is named for the painter Bartolomé Esteban Murillo (1617–82), who lived here for a time; the street is named for Santa Teresa de Ávila (1515–82), who once stayed here and was so enchanted by Seville she decreed that anyone free from sin in this city was indeed on the path to God. The building now houses the Andalusian Department of Culture, but the courtyard and lower floor can be visited. One of the rooms has instructive panels giving the locations of all of Murillo's works on display in Seville. Another room illustrates the history of the building. ⊠ *C. Santa Teresa 8, Barrio de Santa Cruz.* ☎ *Free.* ☉ *Weekdays 10–2 and 4–7.*

㉘ **Casa de Pilatos.** This Renaissance town house and palace was built in the first half of the 16th century by the dukes of Tarifa, ancestors of the current owner, the duke of Medinaceli. It's known as Pilate's House because the original marquis of Tarifa, Don Fadrique, modeled it after Pontius Pilate's house in Jerusalem after a 1518 pilgrimage to the Holy Land. The superb azulejo decorations and the hybrid of Spanish Mudéjar, Gothic, and Renaissance architecture make this one of Seville's most rewarding visits.

Through the marble entryway is an arcaded, bougainvillea-choked carriage area. On the wall of the four-sided tower overhead is the coat of arms of the Duques de Medinaceli. Moving right into the main patio, you will enter a Mudéjar enclosure with ceramic tile mosaics and midpoint arches of varying sizes under a Gothic second-story balustrade. The Renaissance Genovese fountain in the center of the patio is flanked by classical sculptures representing the goddesses Minerva, Athena, Ceres, and a dancing muse. Moving right through the Salón del Pretorio, also known as the Salón de los Azulejos for its massive display of geometrically designed tiles, you enter the Corredor del Zaquizamí (Arabic for corridor), where a naked Carrara marble Venus reclines beneath a relief of "Trofeos de Venus," representing the swords and shields of the goddess's countless conquests. The chapel is known as the Capilla de la Flagelación (Chapel of the Flagellation) for the column representing the one at the house of Pontius Pilate where Christ was scourged. The upstairs apartments, which you can see on an optional guided tour, contain dozens of frescoes, paintings, and priceless pieces of antique furniture. Look for the little Goya painting of the Ronda bullring entitled *El Arrastre* on the left entering the Salón de Oviedo. The next room, the Salón de Pacheco, is named for the teacher and father-in-law of Velázquez, Francisco Pacheco, whose painting, the *Apotheosis of Hercules,* adorns the ceiling. On the north wall is a Murillo (a copy, the original is in the Hospital de la Caridad) of *Moses in the Desert.* The jagged cuts still visible across the painting are the result of the hasty cutting and rolling of the canvas at the beginning of the Spanish Civil War, when anarchist looting threatened the houses of Seville's aristocracy. ⊠ *Plaza Pilatos 1, Barrio de Santa Cruz,* ☎ *95/422–5298.* ⌨ *€8; €5 lower floor only.* ⊙ *Lower floor: Oct.–June, daily 9–6; July–Sept., daily 9–8. Apartments daily 10–1 and 4–6.*

**⓰ Ceramic tiles in memory of Itimad.** Near the Plaza de los Venerables is the homage to Itimad, *"esclava y reina"* (slave and queen). The message in the tiles translates to read, "Almotamid, last Moorish king of Seville, fell in love with Itimad, a slave. Her beauty, a poem, and the love of the king made her Queen of Seville." As the story goes (some of it documented history, some legend), Almotamid, last Moorish monarch of Seville, an avid poet, was walking along the Guadalquivir with adviser and friend Abenamar, debating the best way to describe in verse the reflections and ripples on the river, when a feminine voice perfectly finished the couplet Almotamid had begun. Itimad, a slave girl who worked in the azulejo factory in Triana, was as beautiful and charming as her poetry; the king sent for her, moved her into the royal palace, fell in love with her, and made her his queen. Almotamid was eventually deposed and imprisoned in North Africa; Itimad followed and survived by working as a seamstress until her death in 1095. Almotamid, who once presided over Seville's most glorious era, died in prison shortly thereafter. ⊠ *Calle de la Gloria at corner of Plaza de los Venerables, Barrio de Santa Cruz.*

**⓮ Convento de la Encarnación.** This convent was constructed in 1591 on a spot once occupied by a mosque and later by the hospital of Santa Marta, founded in 1385 by the archdeacon of Ecija, Fernán Martinez. Look for the plaque on the convent wall citing the mention of the Corral de los Olmos, a gathering place for grifters, hustlers, and the picaresque characters, in the Miguel de Cervantes novel *Rinconete y Cortadillo.* Don't miss a visit to the peaceful Plazuela de Santa Marta next to the convent. ⊠ *Plaza de la Virgen de los Reyes s/n, Barrio de Santa Cruz.* ⌨ *Free.* ⊙ *Weekdays 10–2 and 4–7.*

**⓯ Hospital de los Venerables.** Once a retirement home for priests, this baroque building in the heart of the Barrio de Santa Cruz now houses a private cultural foundation that presents exhibitions and concerts here. A mandatory 20-minute guided tour takes in a splendid azulejo patio with an interesting sunken fountain (designed to cope with the low water pressure in this part of town) and upstairs gallery, but the highlight is the chapel and its frescoes by Juan Valdés Leal. The pews are arranged with their backs to the altar, facing the imposing pipe organ, built in 1991 but based on a 17th-century design and made with pieces cannibalized from original instruments. It's used for concerts. The pews are reversed once a year, for mass on May 30, the feast day of Seville's patron, San Fernando. ⊠ *Plaza de los Venerables 8, Barrio de Santa Cruz,* ☎ *95/456–2696.* ⌨ *€3.61 with guide.* ⊙ *Daily 10–2 and 4–8.*

**㉖ Iglesia de San Bartolomé.** In the heart of the Barrio de Bartolomé, which along with the Barrio de Santa Cruz forms Seville's medieval Jewish quarter, this neoclassical structure was designed by José Echamorros and inaugurated in 1806. The church is laid out in the shape of a Latin cross under a cupola supported by an octagonal cylinder. The ceramic representation of La Virgen de la Alegría on the cupola is a reproduction of the 16th-century sculpture inside by the Flemish sculptor Roque de Balduque. The Calle de Levíes leading away from San Bartolomé is one of the most representative streets in the Jewish quarter, named for an illustrious Jewish family of early economic advisers to the crown. Calle Levíes leads down to the house and birthplace of Miguel de

Mañara, one of Seville's great 16th-century philanthropists and said to be the model for Tirso de Molina's original Don Juan Tenorio, who reformed from his sinful life and dedicated himself to works of charity. For a surprising sight, don't fail to look back at the barber pole–like polychrome dome of San Bartolomé as you enter the Plaza de las Mercedarias. ⊠ *C. Virgen de la Alegría s/n, Barrio de Santa Cruz,* ☏ *95/441–9357.* ☏ *Free.* ☉ *Weekdays 10–2 and 4–7.*

**㉗ Iglesia de San Esteban.** This late-14th-century Mudéjar church is interesting for its high relief plaster moldings in the Capilla del Sacramento (Chapel of the Sacrament) and for the Zurbarán paintings along the side naves of the main altar. In a chapel on the east side of the church is the sculpture of a seated Christ, *Nuestro Padre de la Salud y de Buen Viaje* (Our Father of Good Health and a Safe Journey); it was placed here for medieval travelers leaving the city by the Puerta de Carmona, once the eastern exit through the city walls but now long gone. ⊠ *C. San Esteban s/n, Barrio de Santa Cruz.* ☏ *Free.* ☉ *Weekdays 10–2 and 4–7.*

**㉙ Iglesia de San Leandro.** The convent of San Leandró is famous for its *torno,* the turntable through which the cloistered Clarist order of nuns sold *yemas* (pastries made of sugar and egg yolk) and, more important, received a dozen eggs from the friends and family of brides-to-be in return for a rain-free wedding day. The torno was also, for centuries, a standard way of delivering unwanted or illegitimate infants into the hands of orphanages. The entrance to the convent church is in the Plaza de San Leandró, which has at its center the Pila del Pato (Duck's Font). Juan Martinez Montañes, Seville's most prolific early sculptor of liturgical images, made the church's two St. Johns (the Evangelist and the Baptist, sculpted in 1621 and 1632 respectively), as well as the two altarpieces. ⊠ *C. de los Caballerizos s/n, Barrio de Santa Cruz.* ☏ *Free.* ☉ *Weekdays 10–2 and 4–7.*

**㉕ Iglesia de Santa María la Blanca.** This former 13th-century synagogue is one of Seville's most interesting churches. The left-hand wall, facing the altar, is the only remaining element of the synagogue that was one of three (along with what is now the Iglesia de San Bartolomé and another in the Plaza de Santa Cruz) that served the approximately 5,000 Jews who lived in Seville's *aljama* (Jewish quarter) until a June 6, 1391, pogrom all but ended Seville's Jewry. The doors on Calle Archeros, now the lateral facade of the church, were the original entryway into the synagogue. Note the 10 stars of David on the cupboard behind the confessional on the left side of the church. The 1650 Murillo *Santa Cena* (Holy Supper) on the left-hand wall is the church's best painting, despite being a copy (the original is in the Prado). Murillo also painted the arches overhead, though the originals were stolen by Maréchal Soult during the 1810 French invasion and later replaced with copies. The church's crowning glory is the 17th-century baroque cupola swarming with plaster molds of putti, cherubim, and winged infants of all descriptions, the work of the Borja brothers. ⊠ *C. Santa María la Blanca s/n, Barrio de Santa Cruz,* ☏ *95/441–5260.* ☏ *Free.* ☉ *Weekdays 10–1:30, 4:30–7:30.*

**㉑ Jardines de Murillo.** From the Plaza Santa Cruz you can embark on a stroll through these shady gardens, where you'll find a statue of Christopher Columbus topped with a lion (representing León, one of the realms—along with Castile and Aragon—of the unified Spain that controlled the land "discovered" by Columbus). At the Plaza Alfaro corner of the gardens, don't miss the elaborate wooden balcony with carved eaves overlooking giant ficus trees. This was where Rossini's Figaro serenaded Rosina. ⊠ *Plaza Santa Cruz, Barrio de Santa Cruz.*

**⑬ Palacio Arzobispal.** The spectacular churrigueresque (Spanish baroque) *portada* (entryway) of the Palacio Arzobispal is often literally over-shadowed by the neighboring Giralda. Constructed from the 16th through the 18th century, the palace was used as military headquarters by Maréchal Soult during the Napoleonic occupation of 1810. Beyond the dazzlingly sculpted plateresque entryway, the three flights of the speckled jasper (a colorful quartzlike stone) stairway and the Murillo and Zurbarán paintings are among the palace's finest treasures. ⊠ *Plaza Virgen de los Reyes s/n, Centro.* 🎫 *Free.* ☉ *Weekdays 10–2 and 4–7.*

**⑳ Plaza Alfaro.** This little square at the intersection of Callejón del Agua and Calle Lope de Rueda merits some careful scrutiny. Up Calle Lope de Rueda is the Institut Français de Seville at No. 30, a onetime music school with a graceful doorway and facade. Across the street at No. 21 is the house of the Pickmans, an English family prominent in Seville during the early to mid-20th century. The spectacular doorway is said to have been rescued from the Palacio Arzobispal de Úbeda; the tombstone is Roman, and the column's capital is from the Visigothic tenure in Seville (from the 5th to the 8th century). At No. 7 is another handsome doorway and patio. Back in Plaza Alfaro, an excellent Renaissance facade is nearly concealed by orange trees, and to its right is the intricately carved balcony where Figaro serenaded Rosina in Rossini's 1816 *Barber of Seville.* A walk through the giant ahuehuete trees in the Jardines de Murillo will take you past two more watchtowers, with their coats of arms showing castles and lions, for Castile and León, the realms of Pedro the Cruel. ⊠ *Plaza del Alfaro s/n, Barrio de Santa Cruz.*

**㉔ Plaza de los Refinadores.** This shady square filled with palms and orange trees is separated from the Murillo gardens by an iron grillwork and ringed with stately glass balconies. At its center is a monument to Don Juan Tenorio, the famous Don Juan known for his amorous conquests. Originally brought to literary life by the Spanish Golden Age playwright Fray Gabriel Téllez (better known as Tirso de Molina) in 1630, the figure of Don Juan has been portrayed in countless variations through the years, usually changing to reflect the moral climate of the times. As interpreted by such notables as Molière, Mozart, Goldoni, Byron, and Bernard Shaw, Don Juan has ranged from merciless seducer to helpless victim, fiery lover to coldhearted snake, voluptuous hedonist to pleasureless sufferer. The plaques around his effigy in Plaza de los Refinadores (so-named for the olive oil refineries once located here) can be translated as follows: "Here is Don Juan Tenorio, and no man is his equal. From haughty princess to a humble fisherwoman, there is no female he doesn't desire, nor affair of gold or riches he will not pursue. Seek him ye rivals; surround him players all; may whoever values himself attempt to stop him or be his better at gambling, combat, or love." ⊠ *Plaza de los Refinadores s/n, Barrio de Santa Cruz.*

# El Arenal and Parque María Luisa

This walk combines two very different worlds that abut one another along the banks of the Guadalquivir. Parque María Luisa is part shady midcity forestland and part monumental esplanade. On what was a site of the Inquisition's autos-da-fé, when victims were burned in what was then known as the Prado de San Sebastián, the present complex was constructed for the 1929 Exposición Iberoamericana. Along with the wooded parkland, you'll find here an excellent archeological museum, a museum dedicated to popular art and folklore, and the Plaza de España, with its colorful ceramics representing historic highlights from each Spanish province and region. Between the Parque María Luisa and Arenal is the university area, once site of the famous Real Fábrica de Tabacos (Royal Tobacco Factory).

The heart of El Arenal, named for its sandy riverbank soil and originally a neighborhood of shipbuilders, stevedores, and warehouses, lies between the Puente de San Telmo just upstream from the Torre de Oro and the Puente de Isabel II (Puente de Triana). El Arenal extends as far north as Avenida Alfonso XII to include the Museo de Bellas Artes; other major sights are the Iglesia de la Magdalena, the Maestranza bullring, the Teatro de la Maestranza, the Casa de la Caridad, and the Torre de Oro.

## A Good Walk

Beginning at the southern end of **Parque María Luisa** ㉚ at the Plaza de América, visit the **Museo Arqueológico** ㉛, then stop in at or just walk past the **Museo de Artes y Costumbres Populares** ㉜ on the way to **Plaza de España** ㉝. From Plaza de España's far end, cut into the park, pass the **Gustavo Adolfo Becquer Monument** ㉞, and walk out to the **University of Seville** ㉟, once the Real Fábrica de Tabacos. After visiting the **Palacio San Telmo** ㊱, take a spin around the **Hotel Alfonso XIII** ㊲ on the way through to the Puerta de Jerez and the Palacio de Yanduri. Take Calle Almirante Lobo to the **Torre de Oro** ㊳, and from there cross to the Teatro de la Maestranza and the **Hospital de la Caridad** ㊴ just behind it. Then cut in to the Arco del Postigo, also known as the Postigo del Aceite, the minor entryway through the Arab walls where olive oil was once delivered to the city. From there a short walk out Calle Adriano, named for the Roman emperor Hadrian, leads to **Plaza de Toros Real Maestranza** ㊵, Seville's and Spain's bullfighting sanctum sanctorum. A short walk up Paseo Colón leads past the Bar Isbiliyya to Avenida de los Reyes Católicos, where a right turn leads four blocks into the **Iglesia de la Magdalena** ㊶. Two blocks north is Seville's excellent **Museo de Bellas Artes** ㊷.

TIMING

Depending on how many of the museums you explore and how thoroughly you explore them, this could be a full-day tour with lunch at one of El Arenal's many taverns and restaurants. A straight walk-through would take about two hours.

## Sights to See

㉞ **Gustavo Adolfo Becquer Monument.** The Becquer memorial is one of the highlights of Parque María Luisa and a shady respite from the nearby Plaza España. The Carrara marble sculpture of Cupid surrounded by swooning women under an immense ahuehuete tree is dedicated to Spain's greatest romantic poet, whose famous *Rimas* includes verses ranging from breathless ("Today I saw her; today I saw her and she looked at me; today I believe in God!") to despairing ("Bitter is the pain, but at least to suffer is to live!"). In his passionate poetic descriptions of the cycle of romantic love from hope to joy to despair to bitterness, Becquer (1836–70) was a forerunner of 20th-century romantic poets such as Pablo Neruda. ⊠ *Parque María Luisa.*

㊴ **Hospital de la Caridad.** Behind the Maestranza Theater is this almshouse for the sick and elderly, where two gruesome works by Valdés Leal (1622–90) depicting the Triumph of Death and six paintings by Murillo (1617–82) are displayed. The baroque hospital was founded in 1674 by Miguel de Mañara (1626–79), the man who inspired the character of Don Juan. A nobleman of licentious character, Mañara was returning one night from a riotous orgy when he had a vision of a funeral procession in which the partly decomposed corpse in the coffin was his own. Accepting the apparition as a sign from God, Mañara renounced his worldly goods and joined the Brotherhood of Charity, whose un-savory task was to collect the bodies of executed criminals and bury them. He devoted his fortune to building this hospital and is buried before the high altar in the chapel. The artist Murillo was a personal friend of Mañara's, which accounts for La Caridad's chief attractions. ✉ *C. Temprado 3, El Arenal,* ☎ *95/422–3232.* ☞ *€2.50.* ☉ *Mon.–Sat. 9–1:30 and 3:30–6:30, Sun. 9–1.*

**㊲ Hotel Alfonso XIII.** Seville's most emblematic hotel, this grand, Mudéjar-style building next to the university was constructed—and named—for the king's visit to the 1929 fair. You don't have to stay here to admire the inner courtyard or sip a cool martini in the bar and enjoy the ornate Moorish decor. ✉ *San Fernando 2, El Arenal,* ☎ *95/491–7000,* WEB *www.westin.com.*

**㊶ Iglesia de la Magdalena.** This rambling monolith midway between Plaza Nueva and the Museo de Bellas Artes includes the Mudéjar Capilla de la Quinta Angustia (Chapel of the Fifth Anguish), where Bartolomé Esteban Murillo was baptized in 1618, and a baroque section finished in 1709 by architect Leonardo de Figueroa. The colorful bell tower and the domes and cupolas extending above the church are a visual feast. Inside, look for the painting *Santo Domingo en Soria* by Zurbarán and the frescoes depicting the *Alegoría del triunfo de la fé* (Allegory of the Triumph of Faith) by Lucas Valdés over the altar. Don't miss the mural on the north wall of the nave depicting an auto-da-fé, a reminder of Seville's important role in the Spanish Inquisition as headquarters of Inquisitor General Tomás de Torquemada. ✉ *C. San Pablo 10, El Arenal,* ☎ *95/422–9603.* ☞ *Free.* ☉ *Mon.–Sat. 8–11, 6:30–9; Sun. 8–1.*

**㉛ Museo Arqueológico.** Housed in a fine Renaissance-style building, Seville's Museum of Archaeology holds artifacts from Phoenician, Tartessian, Greek, Carthaginian, Iberian, Roman, and medieval times. Some of the best displays are marble statues and mosaics from the Roman excavations at Itálica and a faithful replica of the fabulous Carambolo treasure found on a hillside outside Seville in 1958: 21 pieces of jewelry, all of 24-karat gold, dating from the 7th and 6th centuries BC. ✉ *Plaza del Mercado s/n,* ☎ *95/432–2401.* ☞ *€1.66.* ☉ *Sept.–mid-June, Tues.–Fri. 10–2 and 4–7, weekends 10–2:30; mid-June–Aug., Tues.–Sun. 10–2:30.*

**㉜ Museo de Artes y Costumbres Populares.** The Mudéjar pavilion opposite the Museum of Archaeology houses this museum of mainly 19th- and 20th-century Spanish folklore. The first floor has re-creations of a forge, a bakery, a wine press, a tanner's shop, and a pottery studio. Upstairs, exhibits include 18th- and 19th-century court dress, regional folk costumes, carriages, and musical instruments. ✉ *Plaza de América 3, Parque de María Luisa,* ☎ *95/423–2576.* ☞ *€1.50; EU citizens free.* ☉ *Wed.–Sun. 9–8.*

★ **㊷ Museo de Bellas Artes.** Along with, perhaps, its counterpart in Bilbao, this museum is widely considered second only to Madrid's Prado in Spanish art. Certainly, no other museum in the world has as many paintings by Bartolomé Esteban Murillo (1617–82), and no Spanish museum contains as comprehensive a collection from the Escuela de Sevilla (Seville School) of painting: from the hard-edged, static work of Francisco de Zurbarán (1598–1664) to the more dynamic, expressive, and increasingly human work of the Murillo school through Juan de Valdés Leal (1622–90). Opened in 1841, the museum occupies the former convent of La Merced Calzada, most of which dates from the 17th century. The building is filled with lovely details, from the quiet patios and ancient azulejos to the carved ceiling beams in the refectory. The excellent collection, presented in chronological order on two floors, shows works from the 14th century to 16th-century Mannerism on the lower floor and from the baroque to the 20th century on the upper floor. Disappointingly, there is only one work by Seville's greatest artist, Velázquez; most of Seville's Velázquezes were purloined by the French during the Peninsular War, and what remained was picked over by the British in the 19th century. The museum's first few rooms have outstanding examples of Seville Gothic art, including sculpture and a church retablo. There are also fine examples of baroque religious sculpture in wood, a quintessentially Andalusian art form. Paintings not to miss include Murillo's *La Servilleta*, a portrait of the Virgin and Child allegedly painted on a *servilleta* (napkin) in 1665; *La Inmaculada* by Valdés Leal, a 1672 painting of great movement and expressiveness; and Zurbarán's *San Hugo en el Refectorio* (1655), an unusually harmonious chromatic work by this master of sharp chiaroscuro contrast. Upstairs, in the rooms dedicated to the 19th and 20th centuries, look for Gonzalo de Bilbao's *Las Cigarreras,* a group portrait of the famous Seville cigar makers that inspired Mérimée and Bizet's Carmen. ⊠ *Plaza del Museo 9, El Arenal,* ☎ *95/422–0790.* ☒ €*1.50; EU citizens free.* ☉ *Tues. 3–8, Wed.–Sat. 9–8, Sun. 9–2.*

**㊱** **Palacio San Telmo.** This splendid baroque palace is largely the work of architect Leonardo de Figueroa. Built between 1682 and 1796, it was at first a naval academy, then the private residence of the Dukes of Montpensier, outshining the royal court in Madrid in brilliance, and included extensive gardens that are now the María Luisa park. It is now the seat of the Presidencia de Junta de Andalucía, the regional government's chief executive. Look for the exotic main portal, vintage 1734, a superb example of the powerful churrigueresque style. The interior can be visited on a guided tour on Monday and Wednesday by contacting the Departamento de Protocolo. ⊠ *Avenida de Roma, El Arenal,* ☎ *955/035558 (Protocolo); 95/421–3412.* ☒ *Free.* ☉ *Guided tours Mon. and Wed. by appointment only.*

**㉚** **Parque María Luisa.** At one of the loveliest parks in Spain, you'll find a statue of El Cid by Rodrigo Díaz de Vivar (1043–99), who fought both for and against the Muslim rulers during the reconquest, and the old Casino building from the 1929 Hispanic-American Exhibition, now the Teatro Lope de Vega. The park itself, formerly the garden of the Palacio de San Telmo, is a blend of formal design and wild vegetation. It was redesigned for the 1929 Exhibition, and the impressive villas on the grounds are the fair's remaining pavilions, many of them now consulates or schools. At the south end of the park, past the Isla de los Patos (Island of Ducks), is the Plaza de América, designed by Aníbal González. This blaze of color, with deep-orange sand, flowers, shrubs, ornamental stairways, and fountains tiled in yellow, blue, and ocher, is surrounded by three impressive buildings in neo-Mudéjar, Gothic, and Renaissance styles built by González for the 1929 fair. Two of them now house Seville's museums of archaeology and folklore. ⊠ *Main entrance: Glorieta San Diego, El Arenal.*

**㉝** **Plaza de España.** This monumental attraction is on the eastern edge of the Parque de María Luisa. Designed by architect Aníbal González, the grandiose half-moon was Spain's centerpiece pavilion at the 1929 Exhibition. The brightly colored azulejo pictures in its arches portray decisive historical moments from the 50 provinces of Spain, and the four bridges over its ornamental lake symbolize the medieval kingdoms of the Iberian Peninsula. ⊠ *El Arenal.*

**㊵** **Plaza de Toros Real Maestranza.** Built between 1760 and 1763, the Plaza de Toros de la Maestranza is named for the naval dockyard that

Arenal used to be. It's generally considered the spiritual heart of Spanish bullfighting, the most beautiful major bullring and the most romantic. Bizet's *Carmen* culminates here, with the passionate heroine slain by her spurned lover. The ancient brick bleachers with Triana ceramic numbering, the red-tiled roof, and the ornate presidential box all contribute to a powerful aesthetic excitement even before the opening bull bursts out of the chute. The adjoining museum has posters, prints, and photos.

The most intense corridas take place during the Feria de Abril, and no Feria de Abril is complete without an appearance by Curro Romero, aka "El Faraón" (The Pharoah), the supreme figure, though far from the most talented, among contemporary matadors. Romero, now in his sixties, is as famous for provoking riots of protest for cowardly (and even illegal) performances as he is for making some of the slowest and most beautiful and moving passes ever constructed. ⊠ *Paseo de Colón 12, El Arenal,* ☎ *95/422–4577.* 🖭 *Plaza and bullfighting museum €4.* ☉ *Daily 9:30–2 and 3–7 (9:30–3 only on bullfight days).*

**㊳ Torre de Oro.** One of Seville's great landmarks, the Tower of Gold, so-named for the golden tiles that once covered its facades, stands on the banks of the Guadalquivir near the Puerta de Jerez. A 12-sided tower built by the Moors in 1220 to complete the city's ramparts, it once served to close off the harbor when a chain was stretched across the river from its base to another tower on the opposite bank. In 1248 Admiral Ramón de Bonifaz succeeded in breaking through this barrier, a major strategic move that allowed Ferdinand III to capture Seville. The tower now houses a small but well-presented naval museum. ⊠ *Paseo de Colón, El Arenal,* ☎ *95/422–2419.* 🖭 *€1; free Tues.* ☉ *Tues.–Fri. 10–2, weekends 11–2.*

**㉟ University of Seville.** At the far end of the Jardines de Murillo, opposite Calle San Fernando, stands what used to be the **Real Fábrica de Tabacos** (Royal Tobacco Factory). Built between 1750 and 1766, the factory employed some 3,000 *cigarreras* (female cigar makers) less than a century later, including, of course, the heroine of Bizet's opera *Carmen,* who rolled her cigars on her thigh. Although it's not formally a tourist site, you are free to wander around the lower floors and courtyards of the building, usually teeming with students. Note the old signs above the doors indicating the various functions each section fulfilled when this was still a tobacco factory. Today's factory is across the river. ⊠ *C. San Fernando, El Arenal,* ☎ *95/455–1000.* 🖭 *Free.* ☉ *Weekdays 9–8:30.*

# Barrio de la Macarena

This immense neighborhood covers the entire northern half of historic Seville and deserves to be walked not once but many times. Most of the best churches, convents, markets, and squares are concentrated around the center of the Barrio de la Macarena in an area delimited by the Arab ramparts to the north, the Alameda de Hercules to the west, the Santa Catalina church to the south, and the Convento de Santa Paula to the east. The area between the Alameda de Hercules and the Guadalquivir is known to locals as the Barrio de San Lorenzo, a Barrio de la Macarena subdivision most conveniently approached as an entity of its own, ideal for an evening of tapas grazing.

## A Good Walk

Beginning on Seville's northeast edge at the church of San Hermenegildo, built into the 12th-century Arab ramparts at the corner of Ronda de Capuchinos and Calle Madre Dolores de Márquez, cut through the Arab walls and walk along Calle Macarena. Continue along the walls (in springtime sprouting yellow wildflowers called *jaramago*) for some 200 yards to a stairway leading down into the now dry moat, and from there follow along the edge of the lawns outside the ramparts another 300 yards down to the giant, freestanding Puerta de la Macarena. Just inside is the **Basílica de la Macarena** ㊸, home of Seville's most revered image, the Virgen de la Macarena. Down Calle San Luis, past the Mudéjar bell tower and striped arches of the Iglesia de San Gil, at Plaza de Pumarejo No. 3 is the handsome Palacio de Pumarejo, built in 1883 for the then-powerful Pumarejo family; a look inside reveals an elegant but crumbling courtyard.

From Plaza Pumarejo walk west on Calle Relator to where Callejón de la Amargura curves off to the left. Give Pasaje de Amores a pass and continue on Amargura into the deliciously fishy smelling Plaza de Calderón de la Barca, the back of the Mercado de Abastos, the vibrant Calle Feria food market. After a browse through the market, take a careful look at the **Iglesia de Omnium Sanctorum** ㊹, then slip through Calle Arrayan to the Iglesia de Santa Marina and the **Iglesia de San Luis de los Franceses** ㊺ just across the street. Walk west on Calle de la Divina Pastora down to Calle Gonzalez Cuadrado, go left to Plaza Montesino and Calle Feria. Two blocks farther is the Convento del Espíritu Santo and the **Iglesia de San Juan de la Palma** ㊻. A left on Calle San Juan de la Palma will take you to Calle Dueñas and the **Casa Palacio de las Dueñas** ㊼, home of the Dutchess of Alba, Spain and Europe's most titled aristocrat. From there, continue on to the corner of Calle Bustos Tavera and turn left over to the **Iglesia de San Marcos** ㊽, one of Seville's best Mudéjar churches. Just behind it is the **Iglesia y Convento de Santa Isabel** ㊾ and the square of the same name. A few steps down Calle de Santa Paula is one of the finest gems of Seville's vast liturgical architecture, the **Convento de Santa Paula** ㊿.

From the Convento de Santa Paula, take a right on Calle Enladrillada and walk a block to the Plaza de San Roman, with its lovely Gothic-Mudéjar **Iglesia de San Román** (51), known as the favorite church of many of Seville's Gypsies. From Plaza de San Roman, a five-minute stroll southwest on Calle del Sol will take you to the **Iglesia de Santa Catalina** (52), one of Seville's most ancient and charming churches, directly across from El Rinconcillo, the city's oldest tavern, a perfect stopping point for this ambitious tour.

Still to see are the nearby **Iglesia de San Pedro** (53), **La Alameda de Hércules** (54), and **El Barrio de San Lorenzo** (55), tucked away at the western edge of the Barrio de la Macarena, a perfect evening grazing ground.

TIMING

You could spend days and days exploring the Barrio de la Macarena. This walk through the heart of the barrio could be completed in two hours of forced march, but it would be better to spend four or five and browse through some of the convents, churches, and markets. The Thursday flea market in the Alameda de Hércules is a side visit worth reserving time for.

## Sights to See

㊸ **Basílica de la Macarena.** This neobaroque basilica built in 1949 by Aurelio Gómez Millán holds Seville's most revered image, La Virgen de la Esperanza Macarena (the Virgin of Hope, Macarena). The name Macarena comes from the Puerta de la Macarena, an entryway through the ramparts named for one Macarius Ena, a Roman centurion whose palace stood here in the 2nd century AD. Sculpted in the late 17th century by Luisa Roldán, La Macarena is considered *la mas guapa* (the most beautiful) of all of Seville's Marian images. A dark splotch on her right cheek, restored years ago and now weathering differently from the rest of her countenance, is a cause for citywide concern and debate. Covered in candles and carnations, her cheeks streaming with glass tears, La Macarena is the focus of the Holy Week's most emotional procession on La Madrugá, the early morning of Good Friday (*madrugada* means "dawn"). One of La Madrugá's most beloved processions is the march of Los Armaos (the armed ones), also known as La Centuria, in which 100 Roman soldiers are sent by La Macarena to ask her son, Jesus del Gran Poder in the Iglesia de San Lorenzo, for permission to be taken from the basilica and carried through the streets.

La Macarena is a favorite patron of Gypsies and non-Gypsies alike, and protector of many matadors; the Sevillian bullfighter Joselito was said to have spent half his fortune buying her four emeralds. When in 1920 he was killed in the ring at the age of 25, the Macarena was dressed in widow's weeds for a month. El Misterio de la Sentencia (The Mystery of the Sentence) is the *misterio* (as floats with the representations Christ are called) that you'll see on display in the basilica along with La Macarena. ⊠ *Puerta de la Macarena, Barrio de La Macarena,* ☎ *95/490–1800.* ⌨ *Basilica free, treasury €2.70.* ☉ *Basilica daily 9–1 and 5–8, treasury daily 9:30–1 and 5–8.*

NEED A BREAK?  
Just to the left of Basílica de la Macarena is the **Bar Macarena** (⊠ Calle San Luis 140), a wonderfully boisterous and unsophisticated little tavern. Down Calle San Luis from the basillica, at the corner of Plaza de Pumarejo, is the **Bodega Camacho,** a little old-time Seville tavern with heaving wooden floors, a counter well out of kilter, and a throng of happy people.

**47 Casa Palacio de las Dueñas.** One of Seville's finest pieces of late-15th- to early 16th-century architecture, this lovely palace is a good example of the transition from the Gothic-Mudéjar to the Renaissance style. The 11 patios, nine fountains, and more than 100 marble columns are indicative of the amplitude and splendor of this residence, now the property of the Duchess of Alba. The main entrance leads into a spacious garden ringed by stables, carriage houses, and a landing leading into the two-tiered, rectangular main patio. The salons and chapel are decorated with lovely ceramics and wrought-iron grills leading to the surrounding gardens and patios. The mural in the upper gallery is notable, as are the ceiling and ceramic work in the chapel, the prehistoric *león ibérico* (Iberian lion), and, on the upper floors, the Italian paintings, the works by Zuloaga, Madrazo, and Sorolla, and the Mariano Benlliure sculpture.

To the left of the main entrance on Calle Dueñas, don't miss the plaque commemorating the birth of Antonio Machado (1875–1939), Spain's greatest 20th-century poet (with due respect to Federico García Lorca, who would probably agree). The plaque reads as follows: "In a room in this palace born on the 26th of July of 1875 the poet Antonio Machado. Here he knew the light, the bright garden, the fountain, and the lemon tree." The mosaic coat of arms over the entryway is that of the Duchess of Alba. The flat azulejos are good examples of Triana ceramic artisanry of the 17th and 18th centuries. You can arrange to visit the interior by contacting the Departamento de Protocolo of the Casa de Alba in Madrid. ⊠ *Calle Dueñas s/n, Barrio de la Macarena,* ☎ *91/422–0956 (Casa de Alba, Madrid).* ☉ *Guided tours by appointment only.*

**50 Convento de Santa Paula.** Both the church and the convent museum here are among Seville's most serene semisecret hideaways. The entrance

# EASTER WEEK IN SEVILLE

**H**OLY WEEK IN SEVILLE is a sparkling eruption of religious emotion laced with Gypsy passion and pagan joy. From Palm Sunday to Good Friday some 65 *cofradías* (brotherhoods) take to the streets bearing more than 120 pasos with vivid representations of Christ on the cross followed by the grieving Virgin Mary.

More than 50,000 pointy-hooded penitents, known as *Nazarenos* (20,000 of them lugging wooden crosses), accompany processions through the streets, while central Seville becomes a vast wine and tapas fest and crowds gather to watch their most beloved icons moving in eerily lifelike rhythms through the city's squares and corners. Throughout Holy Week, and the Feria de Abril a week later, Seville is officially "de fiesta," partying, both men and women slicked up and turned out as if headed for weddings, possibly their own.

The week builds to a crescendo with *La Madrugá* (dawn), from midnight Thursday into the early hours of Good Friday, a date so cherished in Seville that calendars on bar counters and café walls count off the days until its arrival. La Madrugá features Seville's most revered icons: El Cristo del Calvario, El Cristo del Gran Poder, El Cristo del Silencio, El Cristo de los Gitanos, La Virgen de la Esperanza de Triana, and, most important of all, La Virgen de la Esperanza Macarena. The Holy Thursday pasos and the processions of Good Friday's dawn overlap in the early hours of La Madrugá when spectators, penitents, and floats achieve such density that many Semana Santa fans prefer to miss this part, rising early to catch the sunrise as numbers thin.

A typical procession consists of two floats, carried by 40 to 50 *costaleros* (so-called because these burly porters carry the 2,000-lb floats "a cuestas," on their backs) and accompanied by anywhere from 200 to 2,000 Nazarenos and (lately) Nazarenas, often barefoot, in ankle-length black, white, cream-colored, maroon, or purple tunics with pointed conical hoods, or *capirotes*. Nazarenos carry either baseball bat–sized candles or, if they are penitents, wooden crosses. The penitents come first, then the "Misterio" or crucifixion, then the remaining Nazarenos, then the Palio, the canopied platform carrying the Virgin Mary. Behind the Palio comes the brass, woodwind, and percussion orchestra, unless it's a silent (black-clad) procession, in which case there is no music at all other than the spontaneous and hair-raisingly moving saetas—spontaneous flamenco solos sung from balconies or from the streets. These powerful, improvisational outbursts of pain and joy are where religious fervor and Andalusian Gypsy musical tradition meet. The saetas—good, bad, or sensational—are the highlights of every procession.

Nothing about Semana Santa fails to fascinate: the saeta, the costaleros, the capataz who directs the maneuvering of the floats in and out of their churches and through the streets, the artisans who restore and create icons, composers of new music for the processions, the selection and performance of traditional marches and fugues . . . every aspect is analyzed and evaluated by radio and television commentators, print journalists, and doctoral students. The term *muy capillita* (chapel-minded) was coined to describe those Sevillanos—and there are many—who think of little but Semana Santa throughout the year.

*El Llamador*, the official program, has timetables for every procession, along with information about the cofradías, the icons, the music, and the number of Nazarenos. With the program, you can map your way from one procession to another, catching the best moments: a saeta here, the paso at a tight corner there. In the meantime, wine, acorn-fed Iberian ham, manchego cheese, and Seville tapas flow freely.

to the museum is at No. 11 Calle Santa Paula, and the wooden door to the left, usually closed, leads through the orange-grove garden to the church. The convent church was built between 1483 and 1489, and the church doorway, completed in 1503, is Santa Paula's finest treasure, a singular fusion of Mudéjar brickwork, Gothic arches, and ceramic Renaissance medallions by Niculoso Pisano. It's representative of a style called Reyes Católicos (Catholic Monarchs), in allusion, somewhat ironically, to Ferdinand and Isabella. The royal couple's motto is inscribed on the door in early Castilian: *tato mota mota tato, tanto monta, monta tanto, Isabela como Fernando* (roughly translatable as "even-steven"), reflecting (along with the symbol of the yoke in reference to two oxen both pulling at once), Ferdinand and Isabella's equally shared power.

In the one-naved church, don't miss the richly coffered Mudéjar ceiling crafted by Diego López de Arenas in 1623, the gigantic Juan de Roelas fresco of St. Christopher (portrayed, as is the norm, with a pair of enormous legs in reference to Christopher's biblical role of carrying Christ across a raging river). The 1730 baroque altar is by José Fernando de Medinilla; the 16th-century image of Santa Paula is the work of Andrés de Ocampo. The wood sculpture of St. John the Evangelist is by Alonso Cano, Spain's most famous baroque painter, sculptor, and architect, and the wood carving of St. John the Baptist is the work of Juan Martínez Montañes, Seville's leading Renaissance sculptor.

The museum next door is packed with priceless objects and paintings ranging from gold and silver chalices to a canvas of *San Jerónimo Penitente* by Lucas Jordán. By no means least are the views through the lovely ancient windowpanes into the convent cloister, or the Mudéjar coffered ceiling on the upper floor and in the church choir. The convent, home for 40 members of the religious community, is famous for its excellent marmalade, available for purchase in the museum. ⊠ C. *Santa Paula 11, Barrio de la Macarena,* ☎ *95/453–6330.* 🖾 *Museum €2; church free (small donation expected).* ⊙ *Tues.–Sun. 10:30–1; 4:30–6:30 (museum closed afternoons).*

**⑤⑤** **El Barrio de San Lorenzo.** A walk through this neighborhood might begin at the **Convento de San Clemente,** near the Puente de la Barqueta, the modern sailboatlike bridge designed by Santiago Calatrava. The **Convento de Santa Clara** is at Calle Santa Clara No. 40; a look into the courtyard will reveal the **Torre de Don Fadrique,** built by the younger brother of King Alfonso X el Sabio, ostensibly as a defensive tower but in fact as a love nest for his mistress, his stepmother, and King Fernando III's widow, Juana de Pontiheu. (Don Fadrique was eventually beheaded in Toledo for "offending royal decorum.") Don't miss the lower Romanesque and upper Gothic windows on the tower, or the gargoyles peering over the corners. Three blocks south on Calle Santa Clara and through Calle Eslava is the back of the **Iglesia de San Lorenzo. Plaza San Lorenzo** is a shady little square with a choice of churches: Jesus del Grand Poder and San Lorenzo itself. In San Lorenzo, the Holy Week float *La Bofetá* (the slap), one of Seville's favorites, portrays the provocation of Christ. The barrio has an abundant supply of *tascas* (bars) and taverns.

**㊹** **Iglesia de Omnium Sanctorum.** This 14th-century Mudéjar church named for All Saints is the home of the sculpture of the Virgen de Todos los Santos, which, covered by a canopy, is reminiscent of St. Peter's basilica in Rome. There the resemblance ends; the exposed brickwork bell tower and geometrically decorated facade over a Gothic entryway are further examples of Seville's unique blend of European and North African decorative motifs. Take a close look at the blue-and-white ceramic tile–encrusted arches around the minuscule slit windows, and, on the Mudéjar bell tower, at the all-but-vanished representations of Seville's three most revered figures: Alfonso X el Sabio, Fernando III el Santo, and San Isidro. ⊠ *Calle Amargura s/n, Barrio de la Macarena,* ☎ *95/470–0233 or 95/490–6754.* ▨ *Free.* ◷ *Mon.–Sat. 9–1 and 6:30–8:30.*

NEED A BREAK? Don't miss the **Cantina,** the little café and restaurant with outside tables wedged under the back of the Iglesia de Omnium Sanctorum.

**㊻ Iglesia de San Juan de la Palma.** This corner church, a 14th-century Mudéjar structure with a gem of a bell tower constructed in 1788, is on a sweet little plaza of the same name, the culminating point for the Cofradía de la Amargura's Palm Sunday procession, the last one to retire from the streets, usually about four o'clock on Holy Monday morning. *Nuestra Señora de la Amargura* (Our Lady of Bitterness, or Sorrow), an early 18th-century sculpture by Pedro Roldán, is one of Seville's most moving representations of the grieving Mary, and the San Juan Evangelista that accompanies her on the procession float is a 1760 work by Benito de Hita y Castillo. The Easter moon lighting the Plaza de San Juan de la Palma, the emblematic palm tree, the square's main tavern with its lights off, and the inevitable "spontaneous" saeta habitually sung from the balcony across from the church door all make this a prime spot to be for the Palm Sunday finale. ⊠ *Calle Feria s/n, Barrio de la Macarena.* ▨ *Free.* ◷ *Mon.–Sat. 9–1 and 6:30–8:30.*

**㊺ Iglesia de San Luis de los Franceses.** Billed as the high point of Seville's baroque liturgical architecture, this 1699–1731 construction was carefully assembled using elements of Italian baroque custom-built to suit local tastes. Light floods into the cupola, illuminating the frescoes by Lucas Valdés in the upper reaches of the Greek cross–shaped nave. ⊠ *Calle San Luis s/n, Barrio de la Macarena.* ▨ *Free.* ◷ *Mon.–Sat. 9–1 and 6:30–8:30.*

**㊽ Iglesia de San Marcos.** Placed astride the Moorish *hara mayur* (main street), a prolongation of the earlier Roman *Cardus Maximus,* and now Calle San Luis, this classic Mudéjar structure is one of Seville's finest. The bell tower, like the Giralda, was constructed over the minaret of an earlier mosque in the 14th century, and in shape and proportion, as well as the arches and tracery on the upper part of the tower, it's a perfect echo of Seville's most emblematic landmark. One of the original 24 parishes established after the Christian conquest in 1248, San Marcos has been burned and restored twice. During the restoration process after the 1936 burning by anticlerical anarchists at the outbreak of the Spanish Civil War, the graceful Moorish horseshoe arches in the interior were rediscovered. The exquisite Gothic-Mudéjar portal, model for the doorways of the churches of San Juan de la Palma and San Esteban, is composed of eight fluted arches edged with diamond-shaped points. The *sebka* motif in the interlaced arches above is an Almohad tradition. Over the center is a representation of the Eternal Father, and the figures on either side are St. Gabriel on the left and the Virgin Mary on the right. Overhead are a dozen tiny lions, evangelistic symbol of St. Mark. ⊠ *Plaza de San Marcos 10, Barrio de la Macarena,* ☎ *95/ 421–1425.* ▨ *Free.* ◷ *Mon.–Sat. 9–1 and 6:30–8:30.*

NEED A BREAK? The **Taberna León de San Marcos** (⊠ 3 Calle Vergara), to the left of the Iglesia de San Marcos, is a handy place to fill up on cumin seed–laced *espinacas con garbanzos* (spinach with garbanzos) while overlooking the church's bite-sized minaret-turned-bell tower.

**⑤② Iglesia de Santa Catalina.** Built over a former mosque, this 14th-century Mudéjar beauty has a miniaturesque quality, especially when observed through the open windows of the equally irresistible tavern, El Rinconcillo, just across the way. From the Plaza Ponce de León you can best see the bell tower and former minaret. Curiously, on the Calle Alhóndiga side, the Gothic doorway of the former church of Santa Lucía, destroyed in 1930, leads to an antechamber from which a deeply curved horseshoe arch opens into the Santa Catalina church. Inside, the Capilla del Sacramento (Chapel of the Sacrament) on the left is one of Seville's finest baroque gems, the work of Leonardo de Figueroa. On the right, La Capilla de la Exaltación (The Chapel of the Exaltation) is covered with a ceiling painted in 1400; the figures of Christ and Santa Lucía were sculpted by Pedro de Roldán. ⊠ *Calle Alhóndiga s/n, Barrio de la Macarena,* ☎ *95/421–7441.* 🎫 *Free.* ☉ *Mon.–Sat. 6:30–7:30 PM.*

**⑤③ Iglesia de San Pedro.** This originally Gothic-Mudéjar church, established here in the 15th century, is a compendium of architectural styles. Its main treasures include the coffered Mudéjar-style ceiling, the geometrical tracery decorating the vaulted chapel ceiling, the Zurabarán painting of the *La Cara Sagrada* (The Sacred Face) in the Capilla del Sacramento, and the intricate Moorish-influenced wooden tracery on the chapel doorway. The baroque carved stone facade was added in 1624; the bell tower, with its Mudéjar lobed arches, is finished with a baroque belfry. Diego de Velázquez was baptized here on June 8, 1599. Behind the church is the torno of the Convento de Santa Inés, where sweets famous among Sevillanos are sold. Also in Santa Inés is the *cuerpo incorrupto* (miraculously undecomposed body) of the convent's 14th-century founder, Doña María Coronel, who was driven there to escape the unrequited love of King Pedro the Cruel. The convent's baroque organ was made famous by poet Gustavo Adolfo Bequer's story of Maese Perez, the organist who returned from the tomb to complete the greatest Christmas oratory ever played in Seville. ⊠ *Calle de Doña María Coronel 1, Barrio de la Macarena,* ☎ *95/421–6858.*

**⑤① Iglesia de San Román.** This 14th-century Gothic-Mudéjar church (undergoing restoration through 2004) is a lovely ocher-colored hue with deep maroon and brick-red trim. Note the Córdoba mosque-style red-and-white-stripe stone in the slit windows on either side of the main door and the telescoping horseshoe arches over the openings. The church is a favorite of the barrio's Gypsy population; the Cofradía de los Gitanos (Gypsy Brotherhood) is the Holy Week guild that carries the Nazareno de la Salud, a dark-skinned, purple-robed representation of Christ most favored by Gypsies, on La Madrugá, Holy Week's most emotional moment. ⊠ *Plaza de San Román s/n, Barrio de la Macarena.*

NEED A
BREAK?

In **Bar La Uno** (⊠ Plaza de San Román 1), you can see the chalkboard calendar to the right of the bar counting the days until La Madrugá, as well as photographs of Iglesia de San Roman's El Nazareno with his heavy crown of thorns. A compendium of Gypsy lore, with photos and images of everyone from Gypsy bullfighter Rafael de Paula to *cantaora* La Mujer del Lebrijano, Bar La Uno is one of Seville's vanishing grass-roots neighborhood bars.

**④⑨ Iglesia y Convento de Santa Isabel.** Built in 1490 and used as the city's prison for women during the 19th century, the Convent of Santa Isabel stands just behind the Iglesia de San Marcos. The baroque doorway facing the orange tree–choked Plaza de Santa Isabel is decorated with a 1609 bas-relief by Andres de Ocampo depicting the Visitation of Mary to her cousin Santa Isabel. The church facade, built in 1602, has a magnificently weathered and studded door framed by fluted Corinthian columns. ⊠ *Plaza de Santa Isabel s/n, Barrio de La Macarena,* ☎ *95/421–6013.* ⧠ *Free.* ⊙ *Mon.–Sat. 6:30–8:30* PM.

**54  La Alameda de Hércules.** The leafy, dusty length of the Alameda de Hércules, so-named for the legendary founder of Seville, comes to life on Thursday and Sunday when a riotous flea market covers the *alameda* (tree-lined promenade) with goods of every design and description. The two pillars at the north end of the alameda, topped with badly weathered representations of Hercules and Julius Caesar, were moved there in 1574 from the remains of the Roman temple on Calle Mármoles. At the south end are two columns topped with lions holding shields placed there in the mid-18th century. In the little park north of the columns you'll find the **monument to Pastora Pavón "Niña de los Peines"** (Girl of the Combs). The four sides of the monument, inscribed *Bulería, Seguirilla, Soleá,* and *Petenera,* represent the different *palos* (movements) or styles of flamenco song and dance.

The Alameda de Hércules, even on nonmarket days, has an easy, disheveled grace. A traditional Seville meeting point, this Rambla-like strip has been popular with Sevillanos since 1574 when it was reclaimed from the marshes that once festered in this part of town. Caravaning Scandinavians in VW campers tend to set up here and late-night bars on either side of the Alameda continue into early morning. You might see a painter lost in concentration rendering the fuzzy linden trees, or a fledgling writer actually hunched over, pecking at a portable typewriter while parachute seeds gather on his shoulders. The cafés, bars, and taverns around the Alameda de Hercules are invariably colorful and atmospheric, and many are open late.

# Triana

Located on the western bank of the Guadalquivir, Triana is a colorful quarter traditionally inhabited by sailors, Gypsies, and bullfighters. It could be said that Triana is to Seville as Seville is to Spain, or indeed as Spain is to northern Europe, with a rough, devil-may-care sense of freedom and spontaneity almost palpable in the air. The Iglesia de Santa Ana, the Capilla de los Marineros, the ceramics shops, the flamenco bars and clubs, and even the view back across the river of the Seville skyline from Calle Betis all rank among the city's highlights.

## A Good Walk

Enter Triana by the **Puente Isabel II** ⑤⑥, better known as the Puente de Triana. (At the Triana end of the bridge is the María Angeles, an excellent café and restaurant with wonderful views; La Esquina del Puente, down on the corner of Calle Betis is another good choice.) Continue straight across Plaza del Altozano and up Calle San Jacinto to the **Capilla de la Estrella** ⑤⑦, with its enigmatic six-pointed Star of David, and on to the immense **Iglesia de San Jacinto** ⑤⑧ at the intersection with Calle Pagés del Corro. Turn back down Calle San Jacinto and, on your way back toward the bridge, noting the blue-and-white ceramic–tiled Tenencia de Alcaldía (Triana Town Hall) with its thick straw roll-up blinds on the far side of the street at No. 55, turn left onto Calle Alfarería, Seville's main pottery street, with its richly decorated ceramic facades, many of them further adorned with flowers. You will soon begin to hear the sounds of tapping and sawing from the ceramics workshops. Many of the artisans are creating or restoring figures for Holy Week. At No. 8 is a plaque to a famous *capataz* (boss or captain), Manolo Bejarano (and to his father and maestro, Eduardo), commanders of the Holy Week floats so beloved and revered in Seville. Cerámica Santa Isabel at No. 12 is intensely decorated with colorful tile, and **Cerámica Montalván** ⑤⑨ at No. 23 offers a fascinating workshop and showroom visit. Continue to the end of Calle Alfarería to the junction with Calle de Castilla, passing the spectacular Cerámica Antonio Japón facade at No. 43 and the important, semi-clandestine flamenco redoubt El Mantoncillo at No. 103.

From here either continue north past the Puente del Cachorro to see the **Iglesia del Cachorro** ⑥⓪ and, farther north, the **Monasterio de Santa María de las Cuevas** ⑥① and **La Cartuja** ⑥②, or return to Plaza del Altozano on Calle de Castilla. Along Calle de Castilla, take a careful look at the **Iglesia de Nuestra Señora de la O** ⑥③. Take a loop through the Paseo de Nuestra Señora de la O down along the riverbank, covered in spring with wildflowers. The concrete jetties at the edge of the Guadalquivir are platforms used equally by lovers and anglers. Cut back up to Calle de Castilla through the next passageway, called Callejón de la Inquisición (Inquisition Alley) in memory of the Castillo de Triana fortress and prison that once stood here. This was where the Inquisition held its prisoners for interrogation; the walls of the castillo were again used for executions during and after the Spanish Civil War. Don't miss the *corralas* at Nos. 7 and 16 Calle de Castilla, typical traditional Spanish apartment buildings built around inner courtyards, directly descended from medieval North African *fondouks* (inns), complete with flower-festooned balconies and cool air circulating through. Coming to Calle San Jorge, note Cerámica Santa Ana at No. 12, with its ornate ceramic facade. The former *lechería* (dairy) at No. 23 Calle San Jorge also has interesting tilework, and at No. 19 there is yet another corrala to have a look through.

Back out in Plaza del Altozano, check out the sensuous bronze sculpture dedicated to flamenco guitar, song, and dance, then dive down into Calle Pureza across the square, along with Calle Betis one of Triana's two most characteristic streets. Walk down Calle Pureza (past good nighttime haunts such as the Molino Pintado at No. 43, Bar Pureza at No. 45, and La Cañera at No. 49) to the tiny **Capilla de los Marineros** ⑥④, home of the Esperanza de Triana, whom Trianeros fanatically claim to be more beautiful than the rival Virgen de la Esperanza Macarena across the river. From the chapel, continue down Calle de la Pureza to Seville's oldest church, **Iglesia de Santa Ana** ⑥⑤. After a careful look, move back to the river and walk along Calle Betis, which, along with one of the best views across the river, has some of the most colorful bars, clubs, and restaurants in Seville.

TIMING

Two to three hours would be the minimum length for a vigorous march through Triana; add another hour or two for a trip downstream to La Cartuja. Though there are no two-hour museum visits here, the ceramics shops, cafés, and restaurants where the authentic feel of Triana is best experienced can make rushing back across the river seem like a bad idea.

## Sights to See

⑤⑦ **Capilla de la Estrella.** The entryway of the tiny chapel on Calle San Jacinto is somewhat curiously decorated with the six-pointed star of David, symbol of Judaism. Queries to the chaplain bring the explanation that Christ was, after all, a Jew, and thus the star is in no way illogical. Nuestra Señora de la Estrella, one of Palm Sunday's favorite and final pasos, is the most cherished icon here, designed by sculptor Martínez Montañés. La Estrella passing through the Postigo del Aceite and on her way across the Puente de Triana are among Palm Sunday's most stirring moments. ✉ *Calle San Jacinto 62, Triana,* ☎ *95/410–1356.* ⊡ *Free.* ☽ *Mon.–Sat. 9–1 and 6:30–8:30.*

㉜ **Capilla de los Marineros.** This little 18th-century chapel, the home of La Virgen de la Esperanza de Triana, is staggeringly ornate. Its Holy Week float representing the purple-robed Nazarene Christ dragging his cross is impeccably painted in bright gold. The representation of La Esperanza de Triana is of great pride to the neighborhood; it's fiercely contended to be *mas guapa* (more beautiful) than La Macarena, the favorite rendering of the Virgin on the other side of the river. ✉ *Calle Pureza 53, Triana.* 🎟 *Free.* ⏱ *Mon.–Sat. 9–1 and 6:30–8:30.*

㉝ **Cerámica Montalván.** Ceramic azulejos (the name derives from the Arabic *az-zulayjz*, meaning small stone) are a Seville specialty introduced by the Moors. Islamic religious law forbade human and animal iconography, so the Moors became expert at making mosaics in complex geometric patterns. Cerámica Montalván has a showroom as well as workshops in action in Triana's most interesting artisanal street. ✉ *Calle Alfarería 23, Triana,* ☎ *95/433–3254.* 🎟 *Free.* ⏱ *Weekdays 9–2, 5–8; Sat. 9–2.*

㉞ **Iglesia del Cachorro.** In northern Triana close to La Cartuja, this popular chapel is dedicated to La Virgen del Patrocinio and el Cristo de la Expiración. It's popularly known as El Cachorro (the cub, or pup), so-named for the elegant, lovelorn Gypsy who, according to legend, inspired late-17th-century sculptor Francisco Ruiz Gijón's rendering of Christ expiring on the cross. According to the story, Ruiz Gijón chanced upon Triana's most admired and mysterious flamenco cantaor of the moment, nicknamed El Cachorro, breathing his last after being stabbed by a jealous husband. The artist quickly drew El Cachorro's face and later sculpted the expression so perfectly that all of Triana recognized El Cachorro being carried through the streets during the following Holy Week. ✉ *Calle Virgen del Patrocinio s/n, Triana,* ☎ *95/433–3341.* 🎟 *Free.* ⏱ *Mon.–Sat. 9–1 and 6:30–8:30.*

㉟ **Iglesia de Nuestra Señora de la O.** Built near the end of the 17th century, this colorful baroque structure is home for the sculpture of *La Virgen con el Niño* by Duque Cornejo and of a much admired sculpture group by Pedro Roldán that includes Santa Ana and San Joaquín, grandparents of Christ, and of the Virgin. The Nazarene Jesus on the wall opposite San Joaquín and Santa Ana is by Pere Roldán as well. Look for the ceramics decorating the bell tower and the tiles of Christ bearing the cross on the upper facade. ✉ *Calle de Castilla 30, Triana,* ☎ *95/433–7539.* 🎟 *Free.* ⏱ *Mon.–Sat. 9–1 and 6:30–8:30.*

㊱ **Iglesia de San Jacinto.** Built in the 18th century after a design attributed to architect Mateo Figueroa, the Iglesia de San Jacinto is most notable for the jumble of towers, spires, and parapets on its somewhat overpopulated roof. The ceramic-tile representation of La Virgen del Rocío (Our Lady of the Dew) on the Calle San Jacinto facade is a key feature, as are the dogs with bones high up over the door. ✉ *Calle de San Jacinto 47, Triana,* ☎ *95/433–2351.* 🎟 *Free.* ⏱ *Weekdays 7:30 AM–9 PM.*

㊲ **Iglesia de Santa Ana.** Founded in 1276 and constructed shortly thereafter by order of Alfonso X el Sabio, this was the first church built following the reconquest of Seville from the Moors. The main vault is similar to that of the Burgos cathedral in northern Castile, leading historians to suspect that the same architect may have been responsible for both. The Cistercian Gothic style with Mudéjar touches is the result of extensive restoration efforts after the 1755 Lisbon earthquake. The church's main altar is one of the finest in Seville, decorated with a sculptural composition of Santa Ana, the Virgin, and the infant Christ. The baptismal font in the baptistry, *La Pila de los Gitanos* (the

Gypsies' Font) is said to confer *duende*, the gift of flamenco inspiration, to children of the faithful. ⊠ *Calle Pureza 80, Triana,* ☎ *95/427-1382.* ☞ *Free.* ⊙ *Mon.–Sat. 9–11 and 7–9.*

NEED A BREAK?

**Bar Santa Ana** (⊠ corner of Calle Pureza and Calle Santa Ana) is a good spot for a break, filled with *ambiente cofrade* (clubby atmosphere) and windows opening out into the lateral facade of Iglesia de Santa Ana.

**62 La Cartuja.** Named after its 14th-century Carthusian monastery, the island of La Cartuja, across the river from northern Seville, was the site of the decennial Universal Exposition in 1992. Five new bridges were built across the river for the event. The island is home to the Teatro Central, used for music and theater performances; the vast green expanse of the Parque del Alamillo, Seville's largest, and least known, park; and the Estadio Olímpico, a 60,000-seat covered stadium opened in 1999. Part of the island is a technology park. The eastern shore of the island holds the largest theme park in Andalusia, **Isla Mágica**, with 14 different attractions, including the hair-raising Jaguar roller coaster. ⊠ *Av. Américo Vespucio 2,* ☎ *95/448–7000,* WEB *www.islamagica.com.* ☞ *Apr.–May €19, June–Oct. €21.* ⊙ *Apr.–May, weekends 11 AM–midnight; June–Oct., daily 11 AM–midnight.*

**61 Monasterio de Santa María de las Cuevas.** Commonly known as the Monasterio de la Cartuja, this former Carthusian monastery dates from the 14th century. Christopher Columbus, a regular visitor, was buried here for a few years. From 1841 to 1980 the building housed a ceramics factory, where Seville's famous Cartuja china was made. The monastery was fully restored for use as the Royal Pavilion during the 1992 Exposition and is now open to the public; part of the building houses the Centro Andaluz de Arte Contemporáneo, which has permanent and temporary art exhibits. ⊠ *Isla de la Cartuja,* ☎ *95/503–7083,* ☞ *€1.80; free Tues. for EU citizens.* ⊙ *Tues.–Fri. 10–8, Sat. 11–8, Sun. 10–3.*

**56 Puente de Isabel II.** This bridge, commonly known as the Puente de Triana, is an important Seville landmark. It was the first permanent bridge to span the Guadalquivir and is a key symbolic space, as both nexus and barrier between the hurly-burly of Gypsy and working-class Triana and the more elegant, bourgeois Seville. Built of steel in 1845, the bridge culminates on the Triana side with **La Capillita del Carmen,** a tiny ceramic-tiled chapel and miniature tower built by Aníbal González in 1926 and dubbed "El Mechero" for its resemblance to early cigarette lighters. Some of the most memorable Holy Week moments take place on the Puente de Triana: the crossings of La Virgen de la Estrella at sunset on Palm Sunday, La Virgen de la Esperanza de Triana at dawn on Good Friday, and El Cachorro (Cristo de la Expiración) just after midnight at the beginning of Holy Saturday.

## Dining

**$$$$** ✕ **Egaña-Oriza.** One of Seville's most acclaimed restaurants, the Egaña-★ Oriza is beautifully situated on the edge of the Murillo Gardens. The decor is modern, with walls of deep peach. José Mari Egaña, the owner, is Basque, but he is now considered one of the fathers of modern Andalusian cooking. The menu changes with the seasons, but might include favorites such as *lomos de lubina con salsa de erizos de mar* (sea bass fillets with sea-urchin sauce) or *solomillo con foie natural y salsa de ciruelas* (fillet steak with foie gras and plum sauce). The adjoining Bar España is a good place for refined tapas. ⊠ *San Fernando 41, Barrio de Santa Cruz,* ☎ *95/422–7211. AE, DC, MC, V. Closed Sun. and Aug. No lunch Sat.*

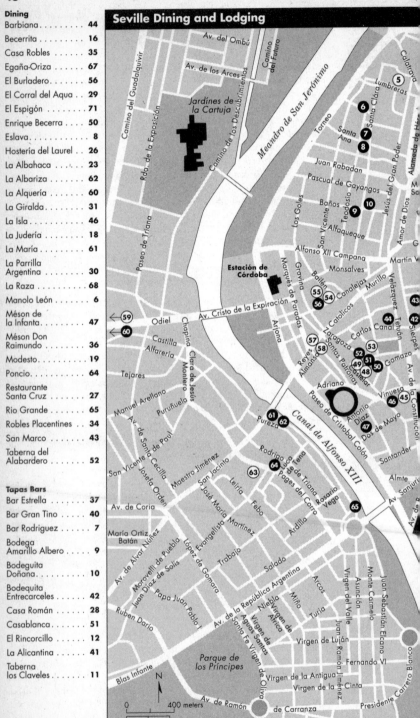

**Seville Dining and Lodging**

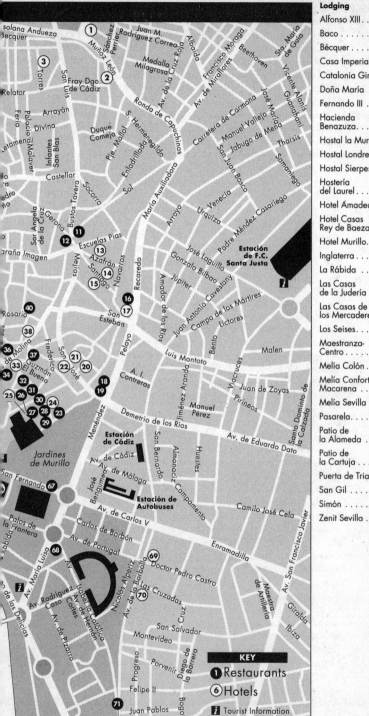

**KEY**

❶ Restaurants

❻ Hotels

🛈 Tourist Information

$$$$  ✕ **La Alquería.** For one of Seville's best dining experiences, make the
★     15 km (10 mi) trip out of the city to this country estate—or better yet,
      spend the night at Hacienda Benazuza, the hotel that adjoins the
      restaurant. At midday, you'll find traditional Spanish and interna-
      tional dishes; in the evening the menu offers creative cuisine heavily
      influenced by the recipes of acclaimed Catalan chef Ferran Adrià. ⊠
      *Virgen de las Nieves, Sanlúcar la Mayor,* ☎ *95/570–3344. AE, DC,
      MC, V.*

$$$$  ✕ **Taberna del Alabardero.** Installed in a 19th-century mansion near
      the Plaza Nueva, this elegant restaurant is also a small hotel, with seven
      guest rooms furnished with antiques. Fronted by a courtyard and a bar,
      the dining area is decorated in Sevillian tiles. The modern Spanish cui-
      sine includes *milhojas de pulpo con patatas y pimientos asados* (octo-
      pus in pastry with potatoes and roast peppers) and the classic Basque
      dish *bacalao con kokotxas al pil-pil* (cod cheeks sizzling in olive oil).
      The *menú de degustación* (tasting menu), though expensive, is a good
      value for its culinary tour of the kitchen's finest achievements. ⊠
      *Zaragoza 20, El Arenal,* ☎ *95/456–0637. AE, DC, MC, V.*

$$$   ✕ **La Albahaca.** One of Seville's prettiest restaurants is ensconced in
      one of its prettiest neighborhoods, the Barrio de Santa Cruz. This typ-
      ical Andalusian house was built by the celebrated architect Juan Ta-
      lavera as a home for his own family; inside, three dining rooms are
      colorfully decorated with ceramic tiles and leafy potted plants. Service
      is friendly and professional. The menu changes seasonally, but there
      will always be some variation on *lubina al horno* (baked sea bass) and
      the restaurant's star dish, *foie de oca salteado* (lightly sautéed goose
      liver perfumed with honey vinegar). ⊠ *Plaza Santa Cruz 12, Barrio
      de Santa Cruz,* ☎ *95/422–0714. AE, DC, MC, V. Closed Sun.*

$$$   ✕ **La Isla.** Fresh fish is hauled daily from the Cádiz and Huelva coasts
      to supply the many bars and restaurants in the Arenal district, between
      the cathedral and the bullring. La Isla is one of the best, and *parril-
      lada de mariscos y pescados,* a fish and seafood grill for two people,
      is one of its best meals. *Zarzuela,* the Catalan seafood stew, is another,
      and simple meat dishes are also served. The two attractive dining
      rooms feature blue-and-white tile designs and cream-colored stucco walls.
      ⊠ *Arfe 25, El Arenal,* ☎ *95/421–5376. AE, DC, MC, V. Closed Aug.*

$$$   ✕ **Becerrita.** Around the corner from the Hotel Giralda, this restau-
      rant is favored by Sevillanos and known to few tourists. It's a small
      establishment—cozy verging on cramped—with diligent service and tasty
      modern treatments of classic Spanish dishes, such as *carrillada de de
      ibérico estofado* (Ibérico pork stew) and *dados de merluza frita* (fried
      hake medallions). Inquire about the fresh dish of the day as well. ⊠
      *Recaredo 9, Barrio de Santa Cruz,* ☎ *95/441–2057. AE, MC, V. No
      dinner Sun.*

$$$   ✕ **Casa Robles.** One block north of the cathedral is one of Seville's clas-
      sic restaurants, established in 1954. The busy bar downstairs does a
      roaring trade in tapas. The dining room is upstairs, where the yellow
      tablecloths match the walls. The food is classically Andalusian: try the
      *ensalada de pimientos asados* (roast-pepper salad with tuna), followed
      by the herb-flavored *cordero asado* (roast lamb). Service is efficient and
      discreet, but the wine list is limited. ⊠ *Alvarez Quintero 58, Barrio
      de Santa Cruz,* ☎ *95/456–3272. AE, DC, MC, V.*

$$$   ✕ **El Corral del Agua.** Abutting the outer walls of the Real Alcázar on
      one of the prettiest streets in the Barrio de Santa Cruz, this restaurant
      is in a restored 18th-century house centered around a delightful patio
      with a central fountain and a profusion of potted plants. The menu
      features Andalusian specialties such as *cola de toro al estilo de Sevilla*
      (Seville-style bull's tail) prepared with modern flair. ⊠ *Callejón del Agua*

6, *Barrio de Santa Cruz,* ☎ *95/422–4841 or 95/422–0714. AE, DC, MC, V. Closed Sun. and Jan.–Feb.*

**$$$**  ✕ **Hostería del Laurel.** This restaurant—also a small hotel—is geared toward tourists, capitalizing on its location in the Barrio de Santa Cruz. In summer you can dine outdoors on the plaza, surrounded by beautiful white and ocher houses. The indoor dining rooms are decorated in traditional Castilian style, with wood paneling, white walls, heavy wooden tables and chairs, and ceilings laden with hanging hams, dried herbs, peppers, and vegetables. The menu offers a wide selection of traditional Spanish fare. ⊠ *Plaza de los Venerables 5, Barrio de Santa Cruz,* ☎ *95/422–0295. AE, DC, MC, V.*

**$$$**  ✕ **La Judería.** This cozy restaurant with traditional decor has long been a mainstay on the Seville dining scene. Fish dishes from northern Spain and meats from Ávila are specialties. Try *cordero lechal* (roast lamb) or *urta a la roteña* (a fish dish from Rota, on the coast of Cádiz). ⊠ *Cano y Cueto 13, Barrio de Santa Cruz,* ☎ *95/441–2052. Reservations essential. AE, DC, MC, V. Closed Aug.*

**$$$**  ✕ **Manolo León.** This elegant town house not far from the Puente de
  ★   la Barqueta in the northwestern corner of the Barrio de la Macarena has an enticing selection of excellent offerings from savory black olives to acorn-fed Iberian ham. The service is abundant, professional, and friendly, and the upstairs terrace offers a breath of river-cooled air in hot weather. Manolo León's other location at Calle Juan Pablos 8 is equally impressive. Try the gazpacho in summer, or the *ajo blanco,* a white gazpacho made primarily of almonds instead of tomato. ⊠ *C. Guadalquivir 12, Barrio de la Macarena,* ☎ *95/437–3735. AE, DC, MC, V.*

**$$$**  ✕ **Poncio.** Around the corner from Calle de Rodrigo de Triana and
  ★   named for the seaman who first sighted the New World, this happy place combines Andalusian tradition with a French flair. Chef Willy Moya trained in Paris and blends local and cosmopolitan cuisine flawlessly. Try the *salmorejo encapotado* (thick, roughly chopped gazpacho topped with diced egg and chunks of acorn-fed ham), or the *besugo con gambitas* (sea bream with shrimp). Don't miss the nearby Iglesia de Santa Ana, Seville's oldest church. ⊠ *C. Victoria 8, Triana,* ☎ *95/434–0010. AE, DC, MC, V.*

**$$–$$$**  ✕ **Barbiana.** Stuck deep in the heart of Seville's business and shopping district near Plaza Nueva, this low-key spot is a surprisingly fine seafood emporium with a tapas bar in the front room. The place is simple and unself-conscious, and the tastes and aromas sneak up on and ambush your senses. Look for the *corvina sanluqueña* (sea bass cooked in spices in the Sanlúcar style) or the *lenguado al azahar* (sole in bitter orange). At midday the place is packed with bankers, merchants, and the *prohombres* (industrial leaders) of Seville, but in the evening things are quieter. ⊠ *C. Albareda 11, Centro,* ☎ *95/421–1239. AE, DC, MC, V.*

**$$–$$$**  ✕ **Eslava.** What's best at the daily market determines the menu at this
  ★   restaurant near the Iglesia de San Lorenzo serving Andalusian specialties. *Chuleta de buey al ajo tostado* (beefsteak with toasted garlic) and *magret de pato a la naranja agria* (duck breast cooked in bitter orange) are two house favorites; the *bonito con patatas* (tuna with potatoes) and *urta a la roteña* (sea bream stewed with shrimp and shellfish) are also excellent when available. ⊠ *C. Eslava 3–5, Barrio de San Lorenzo,* ☎ *95/490–6568. AE, DC, MC, V.*

**$$–$$$**  ✕ **La Albariza.** Overlooking the Guadalquivir at the edge of the Triana district, this restaurant and tapas bar has the feel of a wine cellar (a Manzanilla sherry cellar, to be exact) and Iberian ham museum rolled into one. Aromatic marinated olives and *chacina* (Iberian ham and sausage) are good starters, with seafood close behind. The *tor-*

*tillitas de camarones* (tiny shrimp cooked in a light batter) are de rigueur, as is the calamari. ⊠ *C. Betis 6, Triana,* ☎ *95/433–2016. AE, DC, MC, V.*

**$$–$$$** ✕ **La Parrilla Argentina.** For a change of pace from Andalusian cuisine, try beef from Argentina at this little spot tucked in behind the Alzácar. In addition to steaks and chops cooked over coals, the kitchen can put together creditable combinations ranging from *ternera con alcachofas* (veal with artichokes) to a *salmorejo con perdiz* (an unchopped gazpacho with partridge). ⊠ *C. Rodrigo Caro 7, Barrio de Santa Cruz,* ☎ *95/456–0726. AE, DC, MC, V.*

**$$–$$$** ✕ **Río Grande.** Famous for rice dishes and gazpachos served on a terrace overlooking the Guadalquivir, this spectacular spot, though a tourist standard, is an excellent choice for alfresco dining. In addition to the paellas and *fideuás* (paellas made with noodles), Río Grande has a repertory of local Andalusian specialties ranging from chickpeas and spinach cooked with cumin seed and other herbs to North African–derived sweet and savory combinations such as pork with figs. ⊠ *Calle Betis s/n, Triana,* ☎ *95/427–8371. AE, DC, MC, V.*

**$$** ✕ **El Burladero.** One of Seville's universally top-ranked dining establishments, this rustic yet chic place in the Hotel Colón serves local Andalusian cuisine, from the simplest country dishes such as *rabo de toro* (bull tail) to cosmopolitan fare all the way past filet mignon and foie gras to Russian caviar. ⊠ *C. Canalejas 1, El Arenal,* ☎ *95/450–5599. AE, DC, MC, V.*

**$$** ✕ **El Espigón.** This *marisco* (seafood) specialist not far from the south-
★ ern end of the Parque de Maria Luisa in the Barrio El Povenir is known for some of the best *camarones en adobo* (shrimp in herb sauce) and *besugo con ajos* (sea bream with garlic) in town. The *bacalao a la vinagreta con romero* (cod with rosemary vinaigrette) is another favorite, and the jabugo ham and inland produce are also first-rate. ⊠ *C. Bogotá 1, Parque María Luisa,* ☎ *95/462–6851. AE, DC, MC, V.*

**$$** ✕ **Enrique Becerra.** Clued-in locals come to this cozy corner house in the Arenal district just off Plaza Nueva for home-cooked Andalusian dishes with North African overtones, served in small earthenware cazuelitas. Sample specialties such as *pez espada al amontillado* (swordfish cooked in dark sherry) and *cordero a la miel* (honey-glazed lamb)—or let owner Enrique organize a culinary symphony for you. The lively bar and dining room, with wooden beams overhead and ceramic tiles decorating the walls, are favorite meeting places among Sevillanos. ⊠ *Gamazo 2, El Arenal,* ☎ *95/421–3049. AE, DC, MC, V. Closed Sun.*

**$$** ✕ **La Giralda.** Just up from the Giralda and Plaza Virgen de los Reyes,
★ this superb tapas bar and restaurant built into the remains of Arab baths serves a staggering selection of fine tapas and cazuelitas. Moorish tiles and marble columns add atmosphere to this simple spot, but what sets it apart are the extraordinary taste combinations: *patatas importancia* (roast potato gratin), *cazuelita de chocos* (a casserole with cuttlefish and tiny carrots cooked in oil and thyme), and the *cazuelita Tío Pepe* (a stew of shiitake mushrooms, shrimp, ham, and dogfish) are highlights. ⊠ *C. Mateos Gago 1, Barrio de Santa Cruz,* ☎ *95/422–7435. AE, DC, MC, V.*

**$$** ✕ **La María.** Run by a Basque family, this handy spot at the Triana end of the Puente de Isabel II commands wonderful views over the river from its breezy upstairs terrace. Specialties from the north such as *bacalao al pil-pil* (cod cooked in oil kept at a low temperature) contrast interestingly with the gazpachos and *freiduría de pescado* (fish fried dry in very hot oil) typical of Seville. La María also serves a noteworthy *tortilla española de patatas* (Spanish potato omelette) for the quick bite on your way into or out of Triana. ⊠ *C. Betis 12, Triana,* ☎ *95/433–8461. AE, DC, MC, V.*

**$$** ✕ **La Raza.** The main attraction here is the unbeatable location on the edge of the Parque María Luisa. In fair weather you can dine outside under the shade of enormous rubber trees and palms. Specialties include rice dishes, such as *arroz con langostinos y puntillas* (rice with prawns and baby squid), and the classic paella (for two). There are also inexpensive set menus. ⊠ *Avenida Isabel la Católica 2, El Arenal,* ☎ *95/423–2024. AE, MC, V.*

**$$** ✕ **Mesón de la Infanta.** Between the two Maestranzas (bullring and theater) in the Arenal district, this tapas bar and restaurant gives you a choice of sitting in one of the intimate dining rooms or taking a spot at the bar. Specialties include hellfish, peppers both *piquillo* (sweet, usually stuffed with cod or hake) and *de Padrón* (fiery hot from the Galician town of Padrón), and *cazuelita de gambas al ajillo* (shrimp cooked with garlic, oil, and chili pepper). ⊠ *C. Dos de Mayo 26, El Arenal,* ☎ *95/456–1554. AE, DC, MC, V.*

**$$** ✕ **Mesón Don Raimundo.** Tucked into an alleyway off Calle Argote de Molina (which leads up from the cathedral's Plaza Virgen de los Reyes), Don Raimundo is decorated with an odd collection of blue-and-white tiles, marble columns, stained glass, farm implements, and assorted other bric-a-brac. The house specialties are meat dishes, such as Mozarab-style wild duck (braised in sherry) and *solomillo a la castellana* (Castilian-style steak), but you'll find fish, too. Open with the crunchy *tortillitas de camarones* (batter-fried shrimp pancakes) or stuffed peppers. Portions are generous. Unfortunately, the restaurant is often packed with tour groups. ⊠ *Argote de Molina 26, Barrio de Santa Cruz,* ☎ *95/422–3355. AE, DC, MC, V.*

**$$** ✕ **Modesto.** Sevillanos come to this restaurant on the edge of the Barrio de Santa Cruz for an excellent value. Downstairs is a lively, crowded tapas bar; upstairs is the dining room, whose stucco walls are decorated with blue and white tiles. You can dine outside on the terrace in warm weather. The house specialty is a crisp *fritura Modesto* (a selection of small fish fried in top-quality olive oil); another excellent choice is the *cazuela al Tío Diego* (Uncle Jim's casserole—ham, mushrooms, and shrimp). Though you can dine inexpensively here, ordering pricy *mariscos* (shellfish) takes your bill to another level. ⊠ *Cano y Cueto 5, Barrio de Santa Cruz,* ☎ *95/441–6811. AE, DC, MC, V.*

**$$** ✕ **Restaurante Santa Cruz.** This stately 18th-century town house across from the Hospital de los Venerables in the Plaza de Santa Cruz serves chacina as well as an ample variety of other fish and meat dishes—*Lubina a la parilla* (grilled sea bass) or *rabo de toro* (bull tail stew) are two favorite dishes here. The town house, said to be the birthplace of Don Juan Tenorio, also has a garden, a patio, and a bullfighting museum. ⊠ *Plaza de los Venerables s/n, Barrio de Santa Cruz,* ☎ *95/422–1710. AE, DC, MC, V.*

**$$** ✕ **Robles Placentines.** This alternate Robles location offers the same high-quality Andalusian cooking as the traditional Robles establishment on Calle Alvarez Quintero, but there are fewer tourists here, and somehow you sense that they're trying harder to please local palates. Sample the *potaje de garbanzos* (chickpeas stewed with Iberian ham) for a true taste of the Campiña, Seville's fertile farmland. ⊠ *C. Placentines 2, Barrio de Santa Cruz,* ☎ *95/421–3162. AE, DC, MC, V.*

**$$** ✕ **San Marco.** Set in an old neoclassical house in the shopping district, this Italian restaurant has a leafy patio and is furnished with antiques. The menu is a happy combination of Italian, French, and Andalusian cuisines. Count on good pastas, such as ravioli stuffed with shrimp and pesto sauce. The restaurant now has four satellites, but this one, the original, is the most charming. ⊠ *Cuna 6, Centro,* ☎ *95/421–2440. Reservations essential. AE, DC, MC, V.*

## Cafés and Tapas Bars

Seville may have more bars and cafés than residents, or so it seems, yet they're usually full to the brim. In a culture where there is prestige attached to at least appearing to be a man or woman of leisure, cafés serve as outdoor living rooms, meeting points, neutral turf, and raucous parties to which the whole world is invited. Mixing the Vienna coffeehouse concept ("together but alone") with a natural southern European gift for joyful and boisterous improvisation, Seville's cafés can be intimate, hyperactive, and romantic—designed equally for lovers and for parties out on a rage.

Hangouts range from rustic taverns and tapas emporiums to sunny outdoor cafés to tearooms and chocolaterias. There are also wine-tasting cellars, beer halls, and Irish pubs. Establishments operate at a wide range of hours, though most of the hot spots in and around the Alameda de Hércules are open until 2:30 AM or later.

### CAFÉS

**Café España.** More bar than classic café, this busy spot across from the university and the facade of the former Fábrica de Tabacos is a popular haunt for students and visitors alike. ⊠ *C. San Fernando 41, El Arenal,* ☎ *95/421–2990.*

**Confitería La Campana.** If Seville is the capital of the province, La Campana is the capital of Seville, which is saying a lot in a city that has a town hall, a cathedral, and a dazzling Alcázar as well. Founded by Antonio Hernández Merino in 1885 on the site of a former fire station (the only *campana*, or bell, historians have been able to place here), La Campana has been Seville's social nerve center since the day it opened. The central location, fine artisanal pastry, and a warm and friendly family at the helm are the reasons why. ⊠ *C. Sierpes 1, Centro,* ☎ *95/422–3570.*

**Horno San Buenaventura.** Don't be surprised if the Horno de San Buenaventura seems to follow you around Seville: there are seven in all, all good. Pastry and bread are staples, along with coffee, tea, and beer. The Plaza de la Alfalfa address, ex-Roman forum that it is, is one of the liveliest, a good observation post for the Sunday animal market. ⊠ *Plaza de la Alfalfa 9, Centro,* ☎ *95/422–3542.*

**Javier Ochoa.** About midway through Seville's most popular promenade, this famous café and pastry shop has been packing in happy, excitable coffee drinkers and conversationalists since 1910. ⊠ *C. Sierpes 45, Centro,* ☎ *95/422–8223.*

**Laredo.** A well-known Calle Sierpes hangout, this traditional alternative to the often full-to-the-gills Campana serves, in addition to coffee and pastries, beer and *montaditos* (canapés). ⊠ *C. Sierpes 90, Centro,* ☎ *94/268–2181.*

### TAPAS BARS

The tapa (literally, "lid"), originally a piece of cheese or ham covering a wayfarer's glass of wine, evolved into one of Spain's great contributions to world culinary culture, and it's generally understood to have been invented in Andalusia. Seville has so many excellent tapas emporiums that the list could be endless. These are a few of the best.

**Bar Estrella.** This prizewinning tapas emporium does excellent renditions of everything from *paté de esparragos trigueros* (wild asparagus paté) to *fabas con pringá* (stewed broad beans). ⊠ *C. Estrella 3, Barrio de Santa Cruz,* ☎ *95/422–7535.*

**Bar Gran Tino.** Named for the giant wooden wine cask that once dominated the bar, this busy spot on the funky Plaza Alfalfa is always alive and serves a representative range of Andalusian tapas, from *chocos* (cuttlefish) to chacina. ⊠ *Plaza Alfalfa 2, Centro,* ☏ *95/421–0883.*

**Bar Rodriguez.** At this clean, well-lighted (if slightly over-aluminumized) corner bar in the Barrio de San Lorenzo, the cumin seed–laced *adobo de boquerón* (bread-crumbed herring) is as good as it gets, and the *pijotas fritas* (fried fish) and the *pavía de bacalao* (strips of cod in batter) are fried tight, dry, and rigid—that is, to perfection. ⊠ *Plaza San Antonio de Pádua 6, Barrio de San Lorenzo,* ☏ *95/438–7354. Closed Sun.*

**Bodega Amarillo Albero.** One of a cluster of good bars on the northwestern corner of Plaza de la Gavidia, this handy saloon serves delicious chacinas and a wide selection of cazuelitas. ⊠ *Plaza de la Gavidia 5, Barrio de San Lorenzo,* ☏ *95/421–1346.* ☉ *Daily 10 AM–2 AM.*

**Bodeguita Doñana.** This bric-a-brac-filled place is a feast for the eye as well as for the palate. It's a good next stop after the Amarillo Albero across the street. ⊠ *Plaza de la Gavidia 6, Barrio de San Lorenzo,* ☏ *95/438–6758. Closed Sun.*

**Bodeguita Entrecarceles.** Literally meaning "between jails," this rustic spot just around the corner from Plaza del Salvador is roughly where Miguel de Cervantes, serving time for squandering the king's taxes, started *Don Quijote.* Try the montaditos and cazuelitas, some of the best in Seville. ⊠ *C. Manuel Cortina 3, Centro,* ☏ *95/422–1365. Closed Sun.*

**Casablanca.** This little slot is easy to overlook on busy Calle de Zaragoza, but everything they serve here is carefully selected, well presented, and delicious, from *crianzas* (aged wines) to finos, cheese to chacina. The small dining room in the back serves the same excellent fare. ⊠ *C. Zaragoza 50, El Arenal,* ☏ *95/422–2498. Closed Sun.*

**El Bacalao.** The specialty here is, of course, *bacalao* (salt cod), prepared countless ways. ⊠ *Plaza Ponce de León 15, El Arenal,* ☏ *95/421–6670. Closed Sun.*

**El Rinconcillo.** Founded in 1670, just too late for Miguel de Cervantes to have hoisted a libation here, this lovely spot continues to chalk your tally on the wooden counters and serve a classic selection of dishes such as the fabas con pringá, *caldereta de venao* (venison stew), a superb *salmorejo* (cold vegetable soup), and espinacas con garbanzos. The views of the Iglesia de Santa Catalina out the front window are unbeatable. ⊠ *C. Gerona 40, Barrio de la Macarena,* ☏ *95/422–3183. Closed Wed.*

**La Alicantina.** This is just one of Plaza del Salvador's clutch of hyperactive watering holes, a tapas bar with pastoral scenes of wine- and beer-making on its azulejo walls. ⊠ *Plaza del Salvador 2, Centro,* ☏ *95/422–6122. Closed Sun.*

**Taberna los Claveles.** Just a few steps down Calle del Sol from El Rinconcillo, this traditional Seville tavern marks up your tally in chalk on the wooden counter and serves nicely chilled finos, *cañas* (draft beers), and Manzanillas. To eat, try the hot *bocadillo de jamón ibérico* (Iberian ham sandwich). ⊠ *C. del Sol 15, Barrio de la Macarena,* ☏ *95/422–6527.*

# Lodging

**$$$$** ▦ **Alfonso XIII.** Inaugurated by King Alfonso XIII on April 28, 1929, ★ this grand hotel is a splendid Mudéjar Revival palace, built around a huge central patio. The public rooms are resplendent with marble floors, wood-paneled ceilings, heavy Moorish lamps, stained glass, and ceramic tile in the typical Sevillian colors. Unfortunately, meals are no longer served in the spectacularly sumptuous Salón Real (reserved for banquets) but in a smaller, modern restaurant; there is also a Japanese restaurant. ⊠ *San Fernando 2, El Arenal, 41004,* ☎ *95/491–7000,* FAX *95/491–7099,* WEB *www.westin.com. 127 rooms, 19 suites. 2 restaurants, minibars, cable TV, pool, hair salon, bar, meeting rooms, parking. AE, DC, MC, V.*

$$$$   🏨 **Casa Imperial.** Adjoining the Casa de Pilatos, and at one time connected to it via underground tunnel, this restored 16th-century palace was once the residence of the Marquis of Tarifa's majordomo. Public areas surround four different courtyards. The 24 suites are approached by a stairway adorned with trompe l'oeil tiles. Each suite is different—one has a private courtyard complete with trickling fountain—but all have kitchenettes. The bathroom fixtures are stylishly old-fashioned, and the curvy bathtubs are made of masonry. Some rooms have king-size beds. *Imperial 29, Barrio de Santa Cruz, 41003,* ☎ *95/450–0300,* FAX *95/450–0330,* WEB *www.casaimperial.com. 14 suites, 10 junior suites. AE, DC, MC, V.*

$$$$   🏨 **Catalonia Giralda.** This modern hotel in a cul-de-sac off Recaredo caters largely to the tour-bus crowd, but service is friendly and professional, and rates are reasonable. The rooms, dressed in relaxing, contemporary beige tones, are comfortable, spacious, and light. Some are carpeted; newer ones have bright wood floors. ⊠ *Sierra Nevada 3, Barrio de la Macarena, 41003,* ☎ *95/441–6661,* FAX *95/441–9352. 113 rooms. Restaurant, minibars, cable TV, bar, meeting rooms. AE, DC, MC, V.*

$$$$   ✕ **Hacienda Benazuza.** Live the life of a true Andalusian *señorito,* or
   ★   country squire, at this rambling palace on the edge of the village of Sanlúcar la Mayor, 15 km (10 mi) outside Seville off the road to Huelva. Surrounded by olive and orange trees and centered on a courtyard with towering palm, the building incorporates an 18th-century church. The interior, with clay-tile floors and ocher walls, is tastefully furnished with antiques. The restaurant, La Alquería, is one of the best in the province. A second restaurant, La Alberca, opens for outdoors dining when weather permits. ⊠ *Virgen de las Nieves, 41800 Sanlúcar la Mayor,* ☎ *95/570–3344,* FAX *95/570–3410,* WEB *www.hbenazuza.com. 41 rooms, 3 suites. Restaurant, tennis court, putting green, pool, paddle tennis. AE, DC, MC, V.*

$$$$   🏨 **Los Seises.** This stylish hotel occupies a section of Seville's 16th-cen-
   ★   tury Palacio Episcopal (Bishop's Palace). The combination of modern and Renaissance architecture is striking: segments of the original structure appear intriguingly in hallways and even in the guest rooms. Room 219, for instance, is divided by a 16th-century brick archway, and breakfast is served in the old chapel. Each room is a different shape, and most are split-level. A pit in the center of the subterranean restaurant reveals the building's foundations and some archaeological finds, including a Roman mosaic. The rooftop pool and summer restaurant are in full view of the Giralda. ⊠ *Segovias 6, Barrio de Santa Cruz, 41004,* ☎ *95/422–9495,* FAX *95/422–4334,* WEB *www.seises.es. 40 rooms, 2 suites. Restaurant, minibars, cable TV, pool, bar, parking (fee), some pets allowed. AE, DC, MC, V.*

$$$$   🏨 **Meliá Colón.** The grand old Colón was built for the 1929 Exhibition. A white-marble staircase leads up to the central lobby, which has a magnificent stained-glass dome and crystal candelabra. The reception area, La Fuente restaurant, and Bar Majestic open off this circular space. Downstairs is the El Burladero restaurant, with a bullfight theme, and La Tasca tavern. The old-fashioned rooms are elegantly fur-

nished with silk drapes and bedspreads and wood fittings. ⊠ *Canalejas 1, El Arenal, 41001,* ☎ *95/450–5599,* 𝔽𝔸𝕏 *95/422–0938,* 𝕎𝔼𝔹 *www. solmelia.com. 204 rooms, 14 suites. 2 restaurants, minibars, cable TV, hair salon, 2 bars, meeting room. AE, DC, MC, V.*

$$$$ 🖭 **Meliá Sevilla.** This vast, modern hotel behind the Plaza de España resembles the best American business hotels. Ask for a room at the front, facing the pool and the Plaza de España, which is illuminated on weekends; those in the back have poor views. The best rooms and suites are on the ninth floor. Travelers with disabilities are well accommodated here. ⊠ *Dr. Pedro de Castro 1, Parque María Luisa, 41004,* ☎ *95/442–2611,* 𝔽𝔸𝕏 *95/442–1608,* 𝕎𝔼𝔹 *www.solmelia.com. 364 rooms, 5 suites. Restaurant, coffee shop, pool, hair salon, bar, meeting room, parking (fee). AE, DC, MC, V.*

$$$–$$$$ 🖭 **Doña María.** This is one of Seville's most charmingly old-fashioned
★ hotels, tucked in under the cathedral and the Giralda just off the Plaza Virgen de los Reyes. Some rooms are small and plain; others are luxuriously furnished with antiques. Room 310 has a four-poster double bed, and 305 has two single four-posters; both have spacious bathrooms. There's also a rooftop pool with a good view of the Giralda, just a stone's throw away. ⊠ *Don Remondo 19, Barrio de Santa Cruz, 41004,* ☎ *95/422–4990,* 𝔽𝔸𝕏 *95/421–9546,* 𝕎𝔼𝔹 *www.hdmaria.com. 67 rooms. Dining room, cable TV, pool, bar. AE, DC, MC, V.*

$$$–$$$$ 🖭 **Pasarela.** Behind the Plaza de España, the Pasarela is cozier than its larger neighbor, the Meliá Sevilla. Several ground-floor sitting rooms, some with oil paintings and table lamps, give the place a homey atmosphere. Guest rooms are large and fully carpeted, with predominantly green-and-beige modern decor. ⊠ *Avda. de la Borbolla 11, Parque María Luisa, 41004,* ☎ *95/441–5511,* 𝔽𝔸𝕏 *95/442–0727. 77 rooms, 5 suites. Dining room, minibars, cable TV, gym, sauna, bar, meeting room. AE, DC, MC, V.*

$$$ 🖭 **Bécquer.** The Bécquer is well maintained and well located near the main shopping district. Marble floors, dark wood, and leather furniture dominate the public areas, which include a small sitting room dedicated to the poet Gustavo Adolfo Bécquer. The guest rooms are traditionally Spanish, with peach-color walls, floral prints, matching woven bedspreads, and carved-wood headboards. ⊠ *Reyes Católicos 4, Centro, 41001,* ☎ *95/422–8900,* 𝔽𝔸𝕏 *95/421–4400,* 𝕎𝔼𝔹 *www.hotelbecquer.com. 137 rooms, 2 suites. Dining room, cafeteria, cable TV, bar, meeting rooms, parking (fee), some pets allowed. AE, DC, MC, V.*

$$$ 🖭 **Fernando III.** At the edge of the Barrio de Santa Cruz, near the whitewashed and flower-filled Judería (Jewish quarter), you'll find this shady oasis. The traditional dark furnishings and somber surroundings are surprisingly welcoming here. The bar and cafeteria are cavernlike—but all the cozier for it—and rooms are spare and spacious. The location on the Plaza de Altamira offers a plethora of nearby cafés, restaurants, and art galleries, as well as the churches of San Nicolás and Santa María la Blanca. ⊠ *C. San José 21, Barrio de Santa Cruz, 41004,* ☎ *95/421–7708,* 𝔽𝔸𝕏 *95/422–0246. 154 rooms, 1 suite. Restaurant, pool, bar. AE, DC, MC, V.*

$$$ 🖭 **Hotel Casas Rey de Baeza.** This traditional 18th-century *corrala* or *casa de vecinos* (apartments distributed around a central courtyard), up behind the Casa de Pilatos is one of several lodgings (along with Casas de Judería and Casas de los Mercaderes) set up in and around historic Seville sites. The rooms are bright and airy and look out into the Plaza de Jesús de la Redención or into interior ceramic-tiled patios around central fountains. ⊠ *Plaza Jesús de la Redención 2, Barrio de Santa Cruz, 41003,* ☎ *95/456–1496,* 𝔽𝔸𝕏 *95/456–1441. 41 rooms. Cafeteria, minibars, cable TV, pool, bar, parking (fee). AE, DC, MC, V.*

$$$ ⊞ **Inglaterra.** This classic hotel, next to the British Consulate on the
★    central Plaza Nueva, has long been known for warmly welcoming
     British and American visitors. Room decor is understated in a comfortably
     old-world way. Fifth-floor rooms have large balconies overlooking the
     plaza. The second-floor dining room seems perched in the orange trees
     around the edge of the square outside, and the spacious lobby lounge
     and the hotel's Irish tavern, the Trinity Pub, are always buzzing. The
     Gallery restaurant is an excellent place for fine Andalusian, Mediter-
     ranean, and international cuisine. ⊠ *Plaza Nueva 7, Centro, 41001,*
     ☎ *95/422–4970,* FAX *95/456–1336,* WEB *www.hotelinglaterra.es. 109
     rooms. Restaurant, bar, lobby lounge, pub, some pets allowed. AE, DC,
     MC, V.*

$$$ ⊞ **Las Casas de la Judería.** Tucked into a passageway just off the Plaza
★    Santa María, in the heart of the Barrio de Santa Cruz, this graceful and
     labyrinthine hotel occupies three of the barrio's old palaces, each ar-
     ranged around inner courtyards. Ocher predominates in the suitably
     palatial common areas; the guest rooms are dressed in tasteful pastels
     and decorated with prints of Seville. ⊠ *Callejón de Dos Hermanas 7,
     Barrio de Santa Cruz, 41004,* ☎ *95/441–5150,* FAX *95/442–2170. 79
     rooms, 26 suites. Dining room, minibars, cable TV, bar, lounge, park-
     ing (fee). AE, DC, MC, V.*

$$$ ⊞ **Meliá Confort Macarena.** Aimed primarily at business travelers,
     this attractive modern hotel—with the coolly efficient service typical
     of the Meliá chain—is a good choice if you want to be in the north-
     ern part of the city, close to the Macarena basilica and the Andalusian
     parliament. Rooms sport blue furnishings, wood paneling, and large
     mirrors. Most of those on the lower floors have balconies, but the best
     views are to be had from the west-facing rooms on floors 4 and 5. ⊠
     *San Juan de Ribera 2, Barrio de la Macarena, 41009,* ☎ *95/437–5800,*
     FAX *94/438–1803,* WEB *www.solmelia.com. 326 rooms, 5 suites. Restau-
     rant, minibars, cable TV, pool, bar, Internet, meeting rooms. AE, DC,
     MC, V.*

$$$ ⊞ **San Gil.** Near the Puerta and Basílica de la Macarena, this hand-
     some early 20th-century town house includes a quiet garden and patio.
     The rooms are spacious, decorated in light colors, and furnished with
     traditional pieces that, although not priceless antiques, give a sense of
     the building's relative seniority. Certain corner rooms look out over
     the Macarena procession during Holy Week. ⊠ *C. Parras 28, Barrio
     de la Macarena, 41002,* ☎ *95/490–6811,* FAX *95/490–6939. 61 rooms.
     Dining room, cable TV, pool. AE, DC, MC, V.*

$$$ ⊞ **Zenit Sevilla.** If you want to base yourself in the Triana area this
     comfortable modern hotel is an excellent choice. It's hidden behind the
     main police station, where a spacious courtyard leads to the bright,
     airy reception area. Rooms are carpeted and handsomely dressed in
     blue-on-white fabrics. ⊠ *Pagés de Corro 90, Triana, 41010,* ☎ *95/
     434–7434,* FAX *95/434–2797,* WEB *www.zenithoteles.com. 128 rooms.
     Restaurant, cafeteria, minibars, bar, meeting rooms, parking (fee),
     some pets allowed. AE, DC, MC, V.*

$$–$$$ ⊞ **Las Casas de los Mercaderes.** Occupying a zone once (and to some
     degree still) known as the central commercial district of Seville, this
     hotel is distributed around a central patio in the style of the Moorish
     *fondouk* (inn) that once stood here. The double rooms are of medium
     size, the singles on the small side, and the decor unimposing: modern
     furnishings in a discreet beige or cream tone. Surrounded by the city's
     main attractions, equidistant between the town hall and Plaza del Sal-
     vador, this is a handy and economical option for Seville lodging. ⊠
     *Álvarez Quintero 9, Centro, 41004,* ☎ *95/422–5858,* FAX *95/422–
     9884. 47 rooms. Cafeteria, parking (fee). AE, DC, MC, V.*

**$$–$$$**    ⊞ **Hostería del Laurel.** The greatest drawback at this little spot on one of the Barrio de Santa Cruz's best squares is its popularity with tourists. The rooms are adequate, the restaurant acceptable, the prices reasonable, and the history of the place includes an 1844 visit from no less than José de Zorrilla, the romantic novelist most responsible for launching the legend of Don Juan Tenorio. Remember that the Barrio de Santa Cruz is pedestrianized; there is public parking two blocks away at Avda. Menendez Pelayo and Plaza Refinadores. You'll need to travel light or have rolling suitcases to get baggage to the Plaza de los Venerables. ⊠ *Plaza de los Venerables 5, Barrio de Santa Cruz, 41004,* ☎ *95/422–0295,* 𝖥𝖠𝖷 *95/421–0450. 22 rooms. Restaurant, bar. AE, DC, MC, V.*

**$$–$$$**    ⊞ **Maestranza-Centro.** A modest little hideaway in a 19th-century
★    town house near the bullring and many of Seville's top restaurants, La Maestranza is a low-cost winner. The typical Seville patio with colorful tiles leads up to rooms with high ceilings decorated in bright tones and equipped with modern conveniences, including air-conditioning and television. It's a good "old but new," inexpensive but modern option. ⊠ *Gamazo 12, El Arenal, 41004,* ☎ *95/422–6766,* 𝖥𝖠𝖷 *95/421–4404. 18 rooms. Dining room. AE, DC, MC, V.*

**$$**    ⊞ **Baco.** The inside of this traditional 19th-century Seville town house has been renovated, with fully equipped modern rooms surrounding the various patios. The hotel's well-known restaurant, El Bacalao, is part of the same building though not in the hotel proper. The rooms to ask for are the quieter ones at the back overlooking tile-covered patios. ⊠ *Plaza Ponce de León 15, Barrio de la Macarena, 41003,* ☎ *95/456–5050,* 𝖥𝖠𝖷 *95/456–3654. 25 rooms. Restaurant, bar. AE, DC, MC, V.*

**$$**    ⊞ **Hotel Amadeus.** You'll find here a musical haven in the heart of Seville.
★    With pianos in the soundproofed rooms and a music room off the central patio and lobby, this acoustical oasis is ideal for touring professional musicians and music fans in general. The breakfast terrace on the roof terrace overlooks the Judería and the Giralda. The 18th-century palace has been charmingly restored and equipped with such modern amenities as in-room Internet, satellite TV, and a small glass-walled elevator whipping quietly up and down a corner of the central patio. ⊠ *Calle Farnesio 6, Barrio de Santa Cruz, 41004,* ☎ *95/450–1443,* 𝖥𝖠𝖷 *95/450–0019,* 𝖶𝖤𝖡 *www.hotelamadeussevilla.com. 14 rooms. Dining room, minibars, cable TV, Internet. AE, DC, MC, V.*

**$$**    ⊞ **Patio de la Alameda.** This charming small hotel in what was once a hospital is not especially convenient to the major Seville sights, but it's a good choice for exploring the Barrio de la Macarena, and you'll discover much that's attractive about Seville as you walk across Calle Sierpes to the cathedral or down Calle Feria to the Convento de Santa Paula. Convenient to the Alameda de Hércules, the pristine hotel, filled with plants and fountains, is a surprise after the dusty hubbub outside. Rooms, centered around small courtyards painted an attractive ocher, are modern and have kitchenettes and sitting rooms. ⊠ *Alameda de Hércules 56, Barrio de la Macarena, 41002,* ☎ *95/490–4999,* 𝖥𝖠𝖷 *95/490–0226,* 𝖶𝖤𝖡 *www.patiosdesevilla.com. 22 apartments. Kitchenettes, cable TV, bar, parking (fee). AE, DC, MC, V.*

**$$**    ⊞ **Patio de la Cartuja.** These leafy, sunlit apartments are fully equipped, with sitting rooms and water trickling in the interior patios outside your door. The impeccably bright and cheery setting is a 30-minute walk to the city's main sights through the Barrio de San Lorenzo (or directly across via Calle Sierpes), a stroll that will allow you to get to know Seville as you can no other way. ⊠ *C. Lumbreras 8–10, Barrio de la Macarena, 41002,* ☎ *95/490–0200,* 𝖥𝖠𝖷 *95/490–2056. 57 apartments. Cafeteria, bar, parking (fee). AE, DC, MC, V.*

**$$** ⊞ **Puerta de Triana.** You'll find a good value at this friendly, modern establishment, conveniently located for shopping and sightseeing one block east of the Puente de Triana. The common areas have a bright, modern look, and the rooms are dressed in light blue-green fabrics and light wood furnishings. ⊠ *Reyes Católicos 5, Arenal, 41001,* ☎ *95/421–5404,* ℻ *95/421–5401,* ☉ *www.puertadetriana.com. 65 rooms. Dining room, cable TV, bar. AE, DC, MC, V.*

**$$** ⊞ **La Rábida.** A converted Andalusian house in the Arenal district retains a traditional atmosphere with its large, covered central patio. The location is convenient to both sights and shops, and many rooms overlook a second, leafy patio with oblique views of the Giralda. Decor in the guest rooms is dreary, but the mattresses are firm and the price is right. ⊠ *Castelar 24, El Arenal, 41001,* ☎ *95/422–0960,* ℻ *95/422–4375. 87 rooms. Restaurant, bar. AE, DC, MC, V.*

**$$** ⊞ **Simón.** Located in a rambling turn-of-the-19th-century town house, the Simón is a good choice for inexpensive, basic accommodation near the cathedral. The spacious, fern-filled, azulejo-tiled patio makes the initial impression, and the elegant marble stairway and the high-ceilinged and pillared dining room are cool and stately spaces. The rooms are less grand, but the mansion's old-world style permeates throughout the house. ⊠ *García de Vinuesa 19, El Arenal, 41001,* ☎ *95/422–6660,* ℻ *95/456–2241,* ☉ *www.hotelsimonsevilla.com. 29 rooms. Dining room, some pets allowed. AE, DC, MC, V.*

**$–$$** ⊞ **Hotel Murillo.** This quirky and inexpensive hotel hidden deep in the
★   Barrio de Santa Cruz is known for the little three-wheeled cart that collects guests at the nearest taxi stand. It's named for Seville's most famous painter, and room keys are attached to little palettes. The lobby is filled with antiques, armored warriors, and a British phone box. The guest rooms are unimpressive but adequate, and the silence of the Barrio de Santa Cruz is golden. ⊠ *C. Lope de Rueda 9, Barrio de Santa Cruz, 41004,* ☎ *95/421–6095,* ℻ *95/421–9616,* ☉ *www.hotelmurillo. com. 57 rooms. Bar. AE, DC, MC, V.*

**$** ⊞ **Hostal la Muralla.** This simple spot just inside the medieval Moorish walls on the northern edge of the Barrio de la Macarena. Rooms are small but decorated in bright colors with fresh wood trim. The best overlook the walls and the leafy courtyard behind the Iglesia de San Hermendgildo. Prices double here during Holy Week and the April Fair but remain rock bottom the rest of the year. ⊠ *Fray Diego de Cádiz 39, Barrio de la Macarena, 41003,* ☎ *95/437–1049,* ℻ *95/437–9411. 15 rooms. Dining room. AE, DC, MC, V.*

**$** ⊞ **Hostal Londres.** Located on a quiet street near the Museo de Bellas Artes, this simple but comfortable hostelry is a good value. Rooms are plain but clean, and some have balconies. Between the nearby art treasures, the lively nightlife around the Barrio de San Lorenzo, and the good vibrations emanating from the plaque to Manuel Machado (fellow poet and brother of the more famous Antonio) across from the door of the hotel, this is a find. ⊠ *San Pedro Mártir 1, El Arenal, 41001,* ☎ *95/421–2896,* ℻ *95/450–3830. 23 rooms. Dining room. MC, V.*

**$** ⊞ **Hostal Sierpes.** This pleasant hostelry near the cathedral, with covered courtyard graced with arches, Seville tiles, and easy chairs, is in one of the quieter parts of the Barrio de Santa Cruz. The best rooms are upstairs, around a smaller, glass-roofed patio. ⊠ *Corral del Rey 22, Barrio de Santa Cruz, 41004,* ☎ *95/422–4948,* ℻ *95/421–2107,* ☉ *www.hsierpes.com. 36 rooms. Restaurant, bar, some pets allowed. AE, MC, V.*

# Nightlife and the Arts

Seville has a vibrant nightlife and plenty of cultural activity. To find out what's on, the best source of information is the monthly *El Giraldillo* magazine, which lists classical concerts, jazz, films (for films in English, look for "v. o."), plays, art exhibits, and dance performances in Seville and all major Andalusian cities. It is available free at tourist offices, or for a small fee at newsstands.

## Flamenco Shows

Flamenco presents a conundrum, in Seville and elsewhere. To get the real thing, spontaneous flamenco song and dance, tourists, almost by definition, must not be present at all, and certainly not in great numbers, and especially not paying steep prices. There are spots in Seville where authentic flamenco can be found: approach carefully, try to blend in, or pretend not to be paying much attention. The other part of this Catch-22–like riddle is that street or grassroots flamenco often has more emotion but less technique than commercial flamenco. So at the *tablaos* (flamenco clubs), which are more accommodating to tourists, you might see performances that communicate less passion, but do so with consummate skill and professionalism. Trying to find it both ways is the challenge. Ask around discreetly for likely venues for *juergas* (binges), as spontaneous flamenco outbursts are called. Bars and cafés in Triana occasionally come to life, as do places around the Alameda de Hércules.

Seville has a handful of regular flamenco clubs, patronized more by tourists than by locals. Tickets are sold in most hotels; otherwise, make your own reservations (essential for groups, advisable for everyone in high season) by calling the club in the evening.

**El Arenal** is in the back room of the picturesque Mesón Dos de Mayo tavern and restaurant. Here you get your own table, rather than having to sit in rows. ⊠ *Rodo 7, Arenal*, ☏ *95/421–6492.*

**Bar El Mundo** in the Plaza Alfalfa area holds Tuesday night flamenco functions after 11. These are noncommercial performances by up-and-coming flamenco talent. ⊠ *C. Siete Revueltas 5, Centro*, ☏ *no phone.*

**Casa Anselma** in Triana's Pagés del Corro offers Anselma herself, a popular Seville flamenco personality. This is the real thing. Blend in and don't (for God's sake) show them this book! Flamenco performances are scheduled for Thursday night but can break out at any time. ⊠ *C. Levíes 18, Triana*, ☏ *no phone.*

**El Patio Sevillano** caters mainly to tour groups. The show is a mixture of regional Spanish dances (often performed to taped music) and pure flamenco by some outstanding guitarists, singers, and dancers. ⊠ *Paseo de Colón 11, Arenal*, ☏ *95/421–4120.*

**El Rejoneo** on Calle Betis in Triana is a likely spot for a semispontaneous juerga on a daily basis. ⊠ *C. Betis 31 B, Triana*, ☏ *no phone.*

**La Carbonería** offers exhibitions of paintings, flamenco fusion performances, and spontaneous flamenco and *cante jondo* (flamenco song) in the Barrio de Santa Cruz. ⊠ *C. Levíes 18, Barrio de Santa Cruz*, ☏ *95/456–3749.*

**Lo Nuestro** in Triana has flamenco performances daily. Just across the river on Calle Betis, this is a hot place for the latest in young talent. ⊠ *C. Betis 31 A, Triana*, ☏ *95/434–1911.*

**Los Gallos** is an intimate club in the heart of the Barrio de Santa Cruz. Performances are good and reasonably pure. Dinner at the elegant La Albahaca restaurant next door followed by flamenco at Los Gallos—with a break for *El Salve Rociera* (a liturgical song) sung at midnight at El Tamboril across the Plaza de Santa Cruz—is a comprehensive and complete outing. ⊠ *Plaza Santa Cruz 11, Barrio de Santa Cruz,* ☎ *95/ 421–6981. Jan. 8–31.*

**Quejio** near Plaza Alfalfa is a store specializing in music, books, and flamenco art. Top-quality flamenco performances often accompany book presentations here. ⊠ *C. Huelva 34, Centro,* ☎ *95/456–2491.*

**Sala El Cachorro** in the Triana district is an open-mike–type of flamenco promotion venue well worth seeking out. Check *El Giraldillo* for listings. ⊠ *C. Procurador 19, Triana,* ☎ *no phone.*

**Sevillanas** near the Hotel Colón has live groups and generalized rumba and sevillana dancing from 11 until dawn every night. This is more a place to dance flamenco than to watch performances. ⊠ *C. Canalejas 2, El Arenal,* ☎ *no phone.*

**Taberna Pata Negra** in Plaza de San Leandró near the Casa de Pilatos offers tapas, wine, and flamenco performances on Wednesday after 10. ⊠ *Plaza de San Leandró s/n, Barrio de Santa Cruz,* ☎ *95/421–2191.*

## Music and Theater

Long prominent in the opera world, Seville is particularly proud of its opera house, the **Teatro de la Maestranza** (⊠ Paseo de Colón 22, El Arenal, ☎ 95/422–3344). Be sure to check out what's on here—it's usually the best show in town. Classical music and ballet are performed at the **Teatro Lope de Vega** (⊠ Avda. María Luisa, Parque María Luisa, ☎ 95/459–0853). Flamenco, classical music, and occasional ballet performances are held at **Escuela Superior de Ingenieros** (⊠ Universidad de Sevilla, Pabellón de Uruguay, Parque María Luisa, ☎ 95/ 455–1047). Flamenco and music from the Al-Andalus tradition are the specialty at the **Casa de la Memoria de Al-Andalus** (⊠ C. Ximénez de Enciso 28, Barrio de Santa Cruz, ☎ 95/456–0670). The Fundación El Monte organizes musical events ranging from flamenco to the Academy of St. Martin in the Fields at the Sala Joaquín Turina. Look for listings under **Fundación el Monte—Sala Joaquín Turina** (⊠ C. Laraña 4, ☎ 95/421–3041). The **Teatro Central** (⊠ José de Gálvez s/n [Isla de la Cartuja], Triana, ☎ 95/446–0780, [WEB] www.teatrocentral.com) is a modern theater built for Expo 92 that stages theater, dance, classical concerts, and contemporary music. You can catch classical concerts at the **Conservatorio Superior de Música** (⊠ Baños 48, San Vicente, ☎ 95/ 491–5630). The **cathedral** (⊠ Plaza Virgen de los Reyes, Centro, ☎ 95/421–4971), in its vastness, is acoustically challenging for classical music, but there are occasional concerts held in the *coro* (choir) and in the *trascoro* (behind the choir), the space between the central choir stalls and the main door on Avenida de la Constitución. The church of **San Salvador** (⊠ Plaza San Salvador, Centro, ☎ 95/421–1679) offers occasional choral and classical concerts. The **Teatro Alameda** (⊠ Crédito 13, Barrio de la Macarena, ☎ 95/438–8312) stages a variety of productions in Spanish, including some children's plays.

# Outdoor Activities and Sports

## Boating

The Guadalquivir is prime territory for boating enthusiasts. Paddleboats, canoes, and river cruises are great ways to see Seville and the surrounding countryside from the water. Among the many options are paddleboats and canoes; inquire at the tourist office or on the riverbank near the Torre del Oro. **Cruceros Turísticos Torre del Oro** (⊠ Paseo Alcalde Marqués de Contadero beside Torre del Oro, Arenal, ☎ 95/421–1396) runs river cruises every half hour, April–October, 11 AM–midnight, and November–March 11–7 and at 8 PM and 9 PM, for €12 per person.

## Bullfighting

*Corridas* (bullfights) take place at the **Maestranza Bullring** (⊠ Paseo de Colón 12, ☎ 95/422–4577). The season runs from Easter Sunday until October 12, with most corridas held on Sunday except during special fiestas. The season highlight is the April Fair, when daily fights feature Spain's leading toreros. Other key dates for fights are Corpus Christi, August 15, and the last weekend in September. Tickets for these fights are expensive (€30 to €60), and you should buy them in advance from the official *despacho de entradas* (ticket office: ⊠ Calle Adriano 37, ☎ 95/450–1382) alongside the bullring. Other legitimate *despachos* sell tickets on Calle Sierpes, but they charge a 20% commission.

# Shopping

Seville is the region's main shopping center and ground zero for archetypal Andalusian souvenirs. Most souvenirs are sold in the Barrio de Santa Cruz and on the streets around the cathedral, especially Calle Alemanes.

The main shopping area for Sevillanos themselves is Calle Sierpes, along with its neighboring streets Tetuan, Velázquez, Plaza Magdalena, and Plaza Duque. Fashionable boutiques abound here. Near the Puente del Cachorro bridge, the old Estación de Córdoba train station has been converted to a stylish shopping center, the **Centro Comercial Plaza de Armas** (⊠ enter on Plaza de la Legión, Centro), with swish boutiques, bars, fast-food joints, a microbrewery, and a cinema complex. **El Corte Inglés** (main branch: ⊠ Plaza Duque de la Victoria 8, Centro, ☎ 95/422–0931) is a well-run department store that stays open throughout the day, with several branches in the city.

## Antiques

For antiques, look along Mateos Gago, opposite the Giralda, and in the Barrio de Santa Cruz on Jamerdana and on Rodrigo Caro, between Plazas Alianza and Doña Elvira. **Populart** (⊠ Pasaje de la Villa no. 40, Barrio de Santa Cruz) is an excellent spot for artisanal ceramics and antiques.

## Books

A large assortment of books in English, Spanish, French, and Italian is sold at the American-owned **Librería Vértice** (⊠ San Fernando 33–35, El Arenal, ☎ 95/421–1654), near the gates of the university. The tiny secondhand bookstore **Trueque** (⊠ Pasaje de la Villano no. 2, Barrio de Santa Cruz) specializes in books on Seville.

## Ceramics

A good place to look for Seville's famous azulejo tiles and other ceramics is in the **potters' district** in Triana, centered around Calle Alferería and Calle Antillano Campos. **Cerámica Santa Isabel** (⊠ Alferería 12, Triana, ☎ 95/434–4608) is one of a string of ceramics shops in Triana. In central Seville, **Martian Ceramics** (⊠ Sierpes 74, Centro, ☎ 95/421–3413) has a good range of high-quality plates and dishes, especially the flowers-on-white patterns native to Seville. It's a bit touristy, but fairly priced. In the **Barrio de Santa Cruz,** try along Mateos Gago; Romero Murube, between Plaza Triunfo and Plaza Alianza, on the edge of the barrio; and between Plaza Doña Elvira and Plaza de los Venerables.

### Fans

**Casa Rubio** (⊠ Sierpes 56, Centro, ☎ 95/422–6872) is Seville's premier fan store—no mean distinction. It has everything from traditional to entirely contemporary fans.

### Flamenco Culture and Dress

Beware: flamenco paraphernalia is prohibitively expensive—a *mantón de Manila,* a typical Andalusian silk shawl, can range from €200 to €800, although cheaper versions can be found. One of the best flamenco shops, with a wide range of prices, is **María Rosa** (⊠ Cuna 13, Centro, ☎ 95/422–2143). For privately fitted and custom-made flamenco dresses, try **María del Mar Nuñez Pol** (⊠ Cardenal Ilundain 3, Centro, ☎ 95/423–6028), which is among the best. For music, books, and everything related to flamenco art, **Quejio** (⊠ Huelva 34, Centro, ☎ 95/456–2491) is the place to go.

### Guitars

**Cayuela** (⊠ Zaragoza 4, El Arenal, ☎ 95/422–4557) is run by the second generation of a family of guitar makers from Andújar, near Jaén. They carry unique, handcrafted guitars and high-quality factory-made instruments. **Casa Damas** (⊠ C. Sierpes 61, Centro, ☎ 95/422–3476) sells music and instruments on Seville's main shopping street.

### Pastries

The most famous outlet for artisinal pastries, founded in 1885, is **La Campana,** (⊠ Sierpes 1, Centro, ☎ 95/422–3570). Andalusia's convents are known for their homemade pastries. A wide selection from a number of convents is sold at **El Torno** (⊠ Plaza El Cabildo, Centro, ☎ 95/421–9190), a tiny shop on a quiet square near the cathedral.

### Porcelain

La Cartuja china, originally crafted at La Cartuja Monastery but now made outside Seville, is sold at **La Alacena** (⊠ Alfonso XII 25, Centro, ☎ 95/422–8021). The department store **El Corte Inglés** (main branch ⊠ Plaza Duque de la Victoria 8, Centro, ☎ 95/422–0931) has a good porcelain selection.

### Street Markets

The **Plaza del Duque** has a crafts market on Friday and Saturday. Sunday morning brings the **Alameda de Hercules** crafts market. On Sunday in the **Plaza del Cabildo,** there is a coin and stamp market. The Sunday pet market in **Plaza de la Alfalfa** brings together as interesting variety of humans as beasts.

### Textiles

You'll find all kinds of blankets, shawls, and embroidered tablecloths woven by local artisans at the three shops of **Artesanía Textil** (⊠ García de Vinuesa 33, Arenal, ☎ 95/456–2840; ⊠ Sierpes 70, Centro, ☎ 95/422–0125; ⊠ Plaza de Doña Elvira 4, Barrio de Santa Cruz, ☎ 95/421–4748). **Sevilla Mágica** (⊠ Miguel de Mañara 11, Barrio de Santa Cruz, ☎ 95/456–3838) sells *mantoncillos* (flamenco shawls) and orange blossom perfume and rents bicycles as well.

## Side Trip from Seville

### Itálica

**66** *12 km (7 mi) north of Seville, 1 km (½ mi) beyond Santiponce.*

This ancient city was founded by Scipio Africanus in 206 BC as a home for veteran soldiers. By the 2nd century AD, it had grown into one of Roman Iberia's most important cities and given the Roman world two great emperors, Trajan (52–117) and Hadrian (76–138). Ten thousand people once lived here, in 1,000 dwellings. About 25% of the site has been excavated, and work is still in progress.

The most important monument is the huge, elliptical **amphitheater,** which held 40,000 spectators. You'll also find traces of city streets, cisterns, and the floor plans of several villas, some with mosaic floors, though all the best mosaics and statues have been removed to Seville's Museum of Archaeology.

Itálica was abandoned and plundered as a quarry by the Visigoths, who preferred Seville. It fell into decay around AD 700. Some of its other remains, including a **Roman theater** and **Roman baths,** are visible in the small town that has grown up next door, Santiponce. ☎ 95/599–7376. 🖼 €1.50; EU citizens free. ☉ Oct.–Mar., Tues.–Sat. 9–5:30, Sun. 10–4; Apr.–Sept., Tues.–Sat. 9–8, Sun. 9–3.

# LA CAMPIÑA

The province of Seville is officially broken down into the administrative and touristic subdivisions of Sierra Norte at the northern tip; Sevilla Vía de Plata between the Guadalquivir and the northern Sierra Moreno; Sevilla capital around the city itself; Sevilla Guadalquivir-Doñana between the metropolitan area and the Guadalquivir estuary; La Campiña, the fertile *vega* or alluvial floodplain south of the Guadalquivir; and Sierra Sur, the thin southern slice of mountainous terrain bordering the provinces of Malaga and Granada. General usage, however, tends to refer to nearly all of Seville province, with the exception of the sierra, as La Campiña and, indeed, it is in La Campiña where most of Seville province's treasures are to be found. The four main towns of the Campiña are Carmona, Marchena, Écija, and Osuna, all within radius of 100 km (60 mi) around Seville. Each is endowed with castles, churches, and noble *palacetes* (town houses).

## Carmona

★ ⑰ *32 km (20 mi) east of Seville off N-IV.*

Christened "Lucero de Europa" (Morning Star of Europe) by no less than Alfonso X el Sabio, Carmona is one of the oldest continuously inhabited places in western Europe. After the Phoenicians and Carthaginians had established settlements here and at Cádiz as early as 1100 BC, Carmona later became an important town under both the Romans and the Moors. Its extraordinary Roman necropolis contains about 900 tombs dating from the 1st century AD. Today Carmona is a quiet Andalusian town with a dramatic position on a steep, fortified hill. As you wander its ancient, narrow streets, you'll see a wealth of Mudéjar and Renaissance churches, medieval gateways, and simple whitewashed houses of clear Moorish influence, punctuated here and there by a baroque palace. Artists from around the world are discovering this eddy in the greater flow of time, and Carmona is quietly but steadily becoming a cosmopolitan painters' and writers colony.

Park your car near the Puerta de Sevilla in the imposing **Alcázar de Abajo** (Lower Fortress), a Moorish fortification built on Roman foundations at the edge of the old town. In the tower beside the gate is the tourist office, where you can grab a map.

On the edge of Carmona's "new town," across the road from the Alcázar de Abajo, stands the church of **San Pedro,** begun in 1466. Its extraordinary interior is an unbroken mass of sculptures and gilded surfaces, and its baroque tower, erected in 1704, is an unabashed imitation of Seville's Giralda. The **Plaza de San Fernando,** in the heart of the old town, is bordered by 17th-century houses with Moorish overtones. The Gothic church of **Santa María,** up Calle Martín from Plaza San Fernando, was built between 1424 and 1518 on the site of Carmona's former Great Mosque. Santa María is a contemporary of Seville's cathedral, and it, too, retains its Moorish courtyard, once used for ritual ablutions. The 18th-century **Palacio del Marqués de las Torres** has been restored to house a small museum on the history of Carmona (☎ €2; ☺ Oct.–May, Wed.–Mon. 11–7, Tues. 11–2; June–Sept., Wed.–Mon. 10–2 and 6:30–9:30, Tues. 10–2).

The **Puerta de Córdoba** (Córdoba Gate) on the eastern edge of town is an old gateway built by the Romans around AD 175, then altered by Moorish and Renaissance additions. The Moorish **Alcázar de Arriba** (Upper Fortress) was built on Roman foundations and later converted by King Pedro the Cruel into a fine Mudéjar palace. Pedro's summer residence, it was destroyed in 1504 by an earthquake, but the parador that now stands amid its ruins commands a breathtaking view.

At the western end of Carmona lies the city's most outstanding monument, the **Roman necropolis.** Here, in huge underground chambers, some 900 family tombs were chiseled out of the rock between the 2nd and 4th centuries BC. The walls, decorated with leaf and bird motifs, are punctuated with niches for burial urns. The most spectacular tombs are the **Elephant Vault** and the **Servilia Tomb,** which resembles a complete Roman villa with its colonnaded arches and vaulted side galleries. Its lone occupant, a young woman, was embalmed, unlike the rest of the dead in the necropolis, who were cremated. ☒ *C. Enmedio,* ☎ *95/ 414–0811.* ☒ *Free.* ☺ *Mid-Sept.–mid-June, Tues.–Fri. 9–4:45, weekends 10–1:45; mid-June–mid-Sept., Tues.–Fri. 8:30–1:45, Sat. 10–2.*

## Dining and Lodging

$$$ ✕ **San Fernando.** You enter from a side street, but this second-floor restaurant looks out onto the Plaza de San Fernando. The beige dining room is pleasant in its simplicity, with nothing to distract from the view of daily life below. The kitchen presents modern versions of Spanish dishes with a bit of flair—as in thin, fried potato slivers shaped as a bird's nest. Kid and partridge are perennial favorites, and there's a fine range of desserts. ☒ *Sacramento 3,* ☎ *95/414–3556. AE, DC, MC, V. Closed Mon. and Aug. No dinner Sun.*

$$$ ✕▦ **Alcázar de la Reina.** Stylish and contemporary, this hotel, opened in 1999, is a welcome addition to Carmona's lodging scene. The public areas, which incorporate three courtyards, are bright and airy, with marble floors and pastel walls. Guest rooms are spacious and comfortable. The hotel's large and elegant restaurant, Ferrara, serves tasty Spanish dishes. Aside from à la carte choices, there is a menú de degustación featuring four courses plus dessert for €20. ☒ *Plaza de Lasso 2, 41410,* ☎ *95/419–6200,* 𝖥𝖠𝖷 *95/414–0113,* 𝖶𝖤𝖡 *www.alcazar-reina. es. 66 rooms, 2 suites. Restaurant, in-room safes, pool, bar, meeting room, parking (fee), some pets allowed. AE, DC, MC, V.*

$$$$ ▦ **Casa de Carmona.** Set in the historic Palacio Lasso de la Vega, the Casa de Carmona is one of the most distinctive hotels in Spain. The public rooms are decorated with antiques, rich fabrics, and museum-quality rugs, and the guest rooms are luxuriously furnished. They are all different in tone, some are split-level, and they vary in size from the tiny, intimate Room 21 to the enormous Suite Azul. Between jaunts you can relax in the Arabian-style garden, with orange trees and fountain. There have been problems in the past with the plumbing: the old-fashioned English bathroom fixtures originally installed were hopelessly impractical and are gradually being replaced with standard-issue faucets. ☒ *Plaza de Lasso, 41410,* ☎ *95/414–3300,* 𝖥𝖠𝖷 *95/419–0189,*

WEB *www.casadecarmona.com. 30 rooms, 3 suites. Restaurant, mini-bars, cable TV, pool, health club, sauna, library, bar, laundry service, concierge, some pets allowed. AE, DC, MC, V.*

$$$ ▣ **Parador Alcázar del Rey Don Pedro.** This delightful parador has su-
★ perb views from its hilltop position among the ruins of Pedro the Cruel's summer palace. The public rooms open off a central, Moorish-style patio, and the vaulted dining hall and adjacent bar open onto a terrace that overlooks the sloping garden, where even the pool is tiled in Moorish patterns. The spacious rooms have traditional decor, with rugs and dark furniture. All but six, which look onto the front courtyard, face south over the valley; the best rooms are on the top floor. ✉ *Alcázar, 41410,* ☎ *95/414–1010,* FAX *95/414–1712. 63 rooms. Restaurant, minibars, cable TV, pool, bar. AE, DC, MC, V.*

## Écija

⑥⑧ *48 km (30 mi) northeast of Carmona, 51 km (31 mi) southwest of Córdoba, 92 km (55 mi) northeast of Seville.*

Écija is alternately dubbed the "the frying pan," "furnace," and "oven" of Andalusia for midsummer temperatures often reaching 100°F/37°C. It has more ceramic-tiled baroque church towers per capita (11) than any other town in Spain. Écija's most famous ornamented church is the **Iglesia de Santa María** in the palm tree–shaded Plaza de España, an important meeting point on infernally hot summer evenings. The **Iglesia de San Juan** has an intricate and harmoniously crafted Mudéjar bell tower. The **Iglesia de Santiago** assembles Mudéjar windows from an earlier structure with an 18th-century patio and 17th-century nave and side aisles. Important civil structures in Écija begin with the baroque **Palacio de Peñaflor** (✉ C. Emilio Castelar 26, ☎ 95/483–0273; 🎫 free; ⊙ patio only: weekdays 10–1, 4:30–7:30, weekends 11–1) with its concave facade and its *trampantojo* (trompe l'oeil) faux-relief paintings. Note the presentation of the stable windows below the false wrought-iron balcony, which is the noblest feature in the facade. The Renaissance **Vallehermoso Palace** near the Iglesia de San Juan is an elegant and aristocratic structure. The **Palacio de Benamejí** with its two watchtowers is another of Écija's finest houses. The **Palacio del Conde de Aguilar** has a lovely baroque portal and a wrought-iron gallery.

Near Écija, the lovely village of **Puente Genil** is famous for its Holy Week processions during which villagers act the parts of biblical figures.

### Dining and Lodging

$–$$ ✕▣ **Platería.** This little hideaway in the old silversmiths' quarter has breezy rooms with plenty of space and a good restaurant that serves regional and national dishes. The building is a modern structure, and the rooms are decorated in sleek, spare lines and tones that exert a cooling influence (along with the air-conditioning) in this hottest of Andalusian towns. ✉ *C. Platería 4, 41400,* ☎ *95/590–2754,* FAX *95/590–4553. 18 rooms. Restaurant, bar. AE, DC, MC, V.*

## Osuna

⑥⑨ *80 km (48 mi) east of Seville, 35 km (21 mi) south of Écija.*

From Écija, C430 runs south to Osuna, an important Roman garrison that lost strategic significance throughout the Visigothic and Moorish regimes. In the 16th century the dukes of Osuna, then among the wealthiest people in Spain, endowed the now-sleepy town with its impressive Renaissance palaces. A walk around town will reveal a rich concentration of baroque facades and mammoth wooden doorways usually left partly open so passersby can admire the wrought-iron grillwork and the refreshing patios within. Look especially for the Cabildo Colegial (Chapterhouse), the Antigua Audiencia (former courthouse), the Palacio de la Marquesa de Gomera, and the churches of Santo Domingo and San Agustín. The **Colegiata de Santa María church,** built in the 1530s, is Osuna's main architectural attraction; with its churrigueresque altar and four Jose de Ribera paintings.

### Dining and Lodging

$$–$$$  ✕⊞ **Palacio del Marqués de la Gomera.** This elegant mansion, on the
   ★    street with the most minipalaces in Europe, is one of Osuna's finest dining and lodging opportunities. The palace itself is a dazzling example of 18th-century baroque architecture. Franco Zeffirelli filmed *Callas Forever* here. The suites, two with balconies, have Jacuzzis. The gourmet restaurant, La Casa del Marqués, is one of La Campiña's best, featuring fine Andalusian cooking interpreted in original ways. ⊠ *C. San Pedro 20,* ☎ *95/481–2223,* FAX *95/481–0200. 20 rooms. Restaurant, cafeteria, minibars, cable TV, bar. AE, MC, V.*

$  ⊞ **El Caballo Blanco.** This stately mansion built in 1511 offers a chance to become part of Osuna's history. Rooms are on the small side and are simply furnished but have air-conditioning and modern plumbing. The elegant stairway and the profusion of Moorish azulejos are dazzling. ⊠ *C. Granada 1, 41640,* ☎ FAX *95/481–0184. 13 rooms. Restaurant, bar. AE, DC, MC, V.*

## Marchena

⑦  *60 km (36 mi) east of Seville, 35 km (21 mi) northwest of Osuna, 182 km (109 mi) west of Granada.*

This wealthy Campiña town boasts innumerable noble mansions and eight notable churches and convents. Surrounded by fertile farmland and thriving ever since the Bronze Age, Marchena was settled by the Romans and later by the Moors, who called the town *Marssen'ah.* Near the Plaza de la Constitución, the **Arco de Rosa,** a lovely Moorish horseshoe arch, is the keyhole-shaped way to enter what was once the walled part of Marchena. The 15th-century Mudéjar **Iglesia de San Juan Bautista** and its **Zurbarán Museum** contain nine canvases by Seville's great baroque chiaroscuro master Francisco de Zurbarán (1598–1664). The tower and castle of **Santa María de la Mota** is an architectural treasure, as are the **Iglesia de San Agustín** and the noble town house known as **La Casa del Escudo** (The House of the Shield).

## Estepa

⑦  *105 km (63 mi) southeast of Seville, 25 km (15 mi) east of Osuna, 145 km (87 mi) west of Granada.*

Estepa is known for the legendary mass suicide committed in 206 BC to avoid defeat and capture by the Roman army of Lucio Marcio. This dark and unusual saga and the town's long history as a refuge for both Moorish and Spanish bandoleros (chronicled by Washington Irving) contrast with the Estepa of today and the picturesque strolls through narrow streets dominated by elegant mansions and palaces. **La Iglesia de Nuestra Señora del Carmen** is the foremost architectural gem of Estepa, with its rich black-and-white baroque doorway and facade, and the **Iglesia de San Sebastián** and the **Palacio de los Marqueses de Cerverales** are also splendid. The view from the Cerro de San Cristóbal is a panorama of Estepa's towers and the rolling Campiña beyond.

### Dining and Lodging

$  ✕⊞ **El Balcón de Andalucía.** Overlooking the mountains and the Campiña as well, this comfortable little haven is well known as the spot to stay in this part of the Sierra Sur. Rooms are small but bright, the staff is cheery and helpful, and the restaurant's local mountain cooking ($$) is simple, fresh, and carefully prepared. ⊠ *Av. Andalucía 23, 41640,* ☎ ℻ *95/591–2680. 18 rooms. Restaurant, bar, pool. AE, DC, MC, V.*

# SIERRA NORTE

This northern spur of the province of Seville in the Sierra Morena serves as both border and barrier between Andalusia and the plains of La Mancha and Extremadura to the north. This Andalusian highland is cool in summer and a favorite retreat for Sevillanos escaping the stifling summer heat along the all-but-boiling Guadalquivir. In the fall and winter, the Sierra Norte is one of Andalusia's prime hunting reserves. Hiking the ancient livestock trails and the backwoods paths between mountain farms and towns is increasingly popular here, and the conversion of mountain mills and dwellings to inns and refuges is making this natural resource more and more a part of life in and near Seville. Cazalla de la Sierra and Constantina are the main towns in the Sierra Norte, the former a somewhat overgentrified and cosmopolitan weekend favorite, and the latter a peaceful Arcadian refuge from the sprawl and bustle of the metropolis.

## Cazalla de la Sierra

🕖 *95 km (57 mi) north of Seville 102 km (61 mi) northwest of Écija.*

Cazalla de la Sierra was an important way station on the route to the Roman Vía de Plata (Silver Road) that connected Hispania Ulterior's western Roman outposts at Seville, Mérida, Salamanca, León, and Santiago de Compostela. It was also an important Moorish stronghold, as the two horseshoe arches in the nearby Moorish fortress testify. Known for its anise liqueur and another brand of easily avoidable firewater called *licor de guindas* (hot pepper liqueur), Cazalla has become a nightlife favorite for Seville's young and not-so-young off on a highland fling.

Cazalla's main architectural treasure is the Gothic-Mudéjar **Iglesia de Nuestra Señora de Consolación.** Built into an entryway in the ancient Almohad walls, the earliest part of the church was begun in 1350. Later construction in 1533 tore down part of the original church and converted the structure into a rectangular, three-naved space. The third and final phase in the evolution of the church was the 18th-century sculpting of the baroque main altar.

The **Monasterio de la Cartuja** is a peaceful and graceful enclave. The central square, **Plaza Mayor** is a timeworn yet elegant hub. **La Ermita del Virgen del Monte** is one of Cazalla's most beloved gems. Cazalla's four convents, **Los Conventos de San Francisco, Madre de Dios, Santa Clara,** and **San Agustin** (now the town hall) are emblematic of the town and pretty spots to track down.

### Dining and Lodging

$ ✕▥ **Posada del Moro.** It can be difficult to book a room in this little mountain inn when the summer crowds pile in during July and August. In a modern building at the entrance to town, the rooms are decorated in light and airy tones. The mountain cooking is excellent—there are barbecues in the terrace in summer—and the owners are happy to recommend excursions in the Sierra. ⊠ *Paseo del Moro s/n, 41370,* ☎ *95/488–4858,* ℻ *95/488–4858. 14 rooms. Restaurant, pool, bar. AE, DC, MC, V.*

$$ \text{\$\$} \quad \text{🏠 \textbf{Hospedería La Cartuja.}} $$

**$$** 🏠 **Hospedería La Cartuja.** This onetime Carthusian monastery has be-
★ come a popular retreat for artists in search of peace and quiet. The four
suites are in converted monastic cells. The restaurant, exclusively for
guests, serves creditable renditions of Andalusian mountain fare. ✉
*Crtra. A–455 Cazalla–Constantina Km 2.5. 41370,* ☎ *95/488–4516,*
FAX *95/488–4707. 8 rooms, 4 suites. Restaurant, pool, bar. AE, DC, V.*

## Constantina

🚍 *95 km (57 mi) north of Seville; 82 km (49 mi) northwest of Écija.*

This quiet mountain village just southeast of Cazalla de la Sierra is the
peaceful alternative to Cazalla's more robust and cosmopolitan char-
acter. The ruins of the Moorish castle at the top of the village lend a
timeless and romantic touch to a town known more for its views over
the surrounding countryside than for anything that actually happens
there.

**$** ✗ **Cambio de Tercio.** A simple highland refuge and bar decorated with
taurine themes, this is the best of Constantinas's three restaurants. *Cam-
bio de tercio* means a "change of acts" in a bullfight (as from the pi-
cador to the banderilleros), or a change of theme in a conversation, an
appropriate name for a place in Constantina. The menu here features
partridge, wild boar, and venison in season. ✉ *Virgen del Robledo 53,*
☎ *95/588–1080. AE, DC, MC, V. Closed Tues. and 1 wk during June
and Sept.*

**$** ✗🏠 **San Blas.** This cozy mountain inn offers great sleeping in chilly
air during Seville's torrid summer. A simple and rustic spot with no
frills, no restaurant (the bar serves cheeses, hams, and the odd tapa),
and usually only a handful of guests, the San Blas is the classic desti-
nation to get away from it all. ✉ *Miraflores 4, 41450,* ☎ *95/588–0077,*
FAX *95/588–1900. 15 rooms. Dining room, pool, bar. AE, DC, MC, V.*

# SIERRA SUR

Southeast from Seville, the Sierra Sur and the Cordillera Penibética begin
to rise up from the flatlands around Morón de la Frontera. Hideout
and refuge for the Robin Hood–esque José María El Tempranillo and
the bandits of the 19th century, the Sierra Sur and the unspoiled vil-
lages and landscapes of this onetime border area with Muslim-held An-
dalusia are a pristine mountain stronghold. Morón is the doorway to
mountain villages with names such as Montellano, Coripe, Pruna, Al-
gámitas, El Saucejo, Los Corrales, Pedrera, Casariche, and Badolatosa
that stretch east to the three-way corner with Córdoba and Málaga
and the road to Granada.

## Morón de la Frontera

🚍 *68 km (41 mi) southeast of Seville, 25 km (15 mi) south of Marchena.*

Morón, on the edge of La Campiña at the threshold of the sierra, is
the gateway to Seville's Sierra Sur. It has numerous notable structures:
the Pequeña Catedral de la Sierra Sur (Little Cathedral of the South-
ern Sierra), the Gothic San Miguel church, several 16th- and 17th-cen-
tury palaces (such as the Palacio de Marques de Pilares), the 17th-century
Iglesia de la Merced, el Convento de Santa Clara, and the 16th-cen-
tury Iglesia de Nuestra Señora de la Victoria. The well-known castillo,
built over the ruins of a Roman fortress, has elements dating back to
the 11th century.

OFF THE
BEATEN PATH

**VÍAVERDE –** The name, which translates as "greenway," is fitting for one of the many of Spain's 7,000 km of abandoned railway lines that have been converted into grassy hiking, biking, and equestrian trails. The route begins at Morón de la Frontera and follows through spectacular riverbeds, canyons, and landscapes populated with a wide variety of fauna, flora, and dramatic terrain features. Villages on the route include Villanueva de San Juan, El Coronil, Montellano, Coripe, Pruna, and la Puebla de Cazalla.

# SEVILLE PROVINCE A TO Z

*To research prices, get advice from other travelers, and book travel arrangements, visit www.fodors.com.*

## AIR TRAVEL

CARRIERS

International flights arrive in Seville from Amsterdam, Brussels, Frankfurt, London, and Paris. Domestic flights connect the Andalusian capital with Madrid, Barcelona, Valencia, and other major cities.

➤ CONTACTS: **Air Europa** (☎ 95/444–9179). **Air Nostrum** (✉ Aeropuerto de Sevilla, ☎ 902/400500). **Iberia** (☎ 902/400500 or 95/422–9345). **Spanair** (☎ 902/121415).

## AIRPORTS

Seville Airport is 12 km (7 mi) east of the city on the N-IV to Córdoba. There is a bus from the airport to the center of Seville every half hour on weekdays (between 6:30 AM and 8 PM), less often on weekends.

➤ AIRPORT INFORMATION: **Aeropuerto de Sevilla** (☎ 95/444–9000).

## BUS TRAVEL

Alsa/Enatcar long-distance buses connect Seville with Madrid; with Cáceres, Mérida, and Badajoz in Extremadura; and with Córdoba, Granada, Málaga, Ronda, and Huelva in Andalusia. Regional buses connect all of the towns and villages in this region—indeed, buses within Andalusia (and between Seville and Extremadura) tend to be more frequent and convenient than trains. The coastal route links Granada, Málaga, and Marbella to Cádiz. From Ronda, buses run to Arcos, Jerez, and Cádiz.

Seville has two bus stations. The older one is the Estación del Prado de San Sebastián, just off Plaza de San Sebastián between Manuel Vázquez Sagastizabal and José María Osborne; buses from here serve points west and northwest. The second station, a glittering modern terminal on the banks of the Guadalquivir River downtown, next to the east end of Cachorro Bridge, is called Estación Plaza de Armas and serves central and eastern Spain. The tourist office can confirm which station you need.

➤ BUS COMPANIES: **Alsa/Enatcar** (Spain: ☎ 902/422242, WEB www.alsa.es).

➤ BUS STATIONS: **Seville–Estación del Prado de San Sebastián** (✉ Prado de San Sebastián s/n, ☎ 95/441–7111 or 95/441–7118). **Seville–Estación Plaza de Armas** (✉ Cristo de la Expiración, ☎ 95/490–7737).

## BUS TRAVEL WITHIN SEVILLE

Seville's urban bus service is efficient and covers the greater city area. Buses do not run within the Moorish Santa Cruz area, the most popular with tourists, because the streets are too narrow.

FARES AND SCHEDULES

Seville's urban bus services cover the whole city and operate a limited night service between midnight and 2 AM, with no service between 2 and 4 AM. Single rides cost 90 centimos, but it is more economical to buy a ticket for 10 rides, which costs 4.50 euros for use on any bus and 3.80 euros for use on only the city's urban bus service. There is also a ticket valid for any ride during 30 days, which costs 26 euros and is transferable between anyone. Tickets are on sale at newspaper kiosks and at the main bus station between 8 and 3 weekdays. It also handles lost property inquiries.

➤ CONTACT INFORMATION: (⊠ Prado de San Sebastian, ☎ 954/557200).

## CAR RENTAL

➤ LOCAL AGENCIES: **Avis** (⊠ Aeropuerto de Sevilla, ☎ 95/451–4315; ⊠ Estación de Santa Justa, ☎ 95/453–7861). **Budget** (⊠ Aeropuerto de Sevilla, ☎ 95/499–3137). **Europcar** (⊠ Aeropuerto de Sevilla, ☎ 95/425–4298; ⊠ Estació de Santa Justa, ☎ 95/453–3914). **Hertz** (⊠ Aeropuerto de Sevilla, ☎ 95/451–4720; ⊠ Estación de Santa Justa, ☎ 95/442–6156). **National/Atesa** (⊠ Aeropuerto de Sevilla, ☎ 95/451–4735; ⊠ Avda. Kansas City 3, ☎ 95/457–3131).

## CAR TRAVEL

The main road from Madrid is the N-IV through Córdoba, a four-lane *autovía* (highway), but it's one of Spain's busiest roads, and trucks can cause delays. From Granada or Málaga, head for Antequera; then take A39 autovía by way of Osuna to Seville. Road trips from Seville to Córdoba, Granada, and the Costa del Sol (by way of Ronda) are reasonably quick and pleasant. From the Costa del Sol, the coastal N340 highway is rarely very busy west of Algeciras except in July and August.

Driving within western Andalusia is easy—the terrain is mostly flat land or gently rolling hills, and the roads are straight. From Seville to Jerez and Cádiz, you can choose between the N-IV and the faster A4 toll road. The only way to access Doñana National Park by road is to take the A49 Seville–Huelva highway, exit for Almonte/Bollullos par del Condado, then follow the signs for El Rocío and Matalascañas. The A49 west of Seville will also lead you to the freeway to Portugal and the Algarve. Getting into and out of Seville is not unduly difficult thanks to the SE30 ring road, but getting around the city by car is still trying. Try to avoid the 7:15–8:30 PM rush hour, and be wary of the lunchtime rush hour, around 2–3 PM. Don't try to bring a car to Seville during Holy Week or the April Fair—processions close most of the streets to traffic.

## CONSULATES

➤ AUSTRALIA: **Seville** (⊠ Federico Rubio 14, Santa Cruz, ☎ 954/220971 or 954/220240).
➤ CANADA: **Seville** (⊠ Avda. de los Pinos 34, Casa 4 41927 Mairena del Aljarafe, ☎ 954/229413).
➤ UNITED KINGDOM: **Seville** (⊠ Plaza Nueva 8, ☎ 954/228874 or 954/228875).
➤ UNITED STATES: **Seville** (⊠ Paseo de las Delicias 7, Arenal, ☎ 95/423–1885).

## EMERGENCIES

In case of emergency, the first resort is to call 112—there's a good chance you'll reach someone who speaks English, though it's not a given. For a list of pharmacies and their opening hours, consult local newspapers. Pharmacies have a flashing green cross outside their premises.

➤ EMERGENCIES: Fire, Police, Ambulance (☎ 112). Guardia Civil (☎ 062). Información Toxicológica (poisoning: ☎ 91/562–0420). Insalud (public health service: ☎ 061). Policía Local (☎ 092). Policía Nacional (☎ 091). Servicio Marítimo (air-sea rescue: ☎ 90/220–2202).

## ENGLISH-LANGUAGE MEDIA

There are no local English-language papers in the area. British papers and the *Herald Tribune* (which includes a supplement in English of Spanish news from *El País*, the main national newspaper) are available at main news outlets.

➤ ENGLISH-LANGUAGE BOOKSTORES: International House (⊠ Mendez Nuñez 13, Centro, Seville, ☎ 95/450–2792).

## MAIL AND SHIPPING

➤ POST OFFICE: Correos–main post office (⊠ Avda. de la Constitución 32, El Arenal, ☎ 95/421–6476; ☼ weekdays 8:30–8:30, Sat. 9:30–2).
➤ INTERNET CAFÉS: Cibercenter (⊠ Julio César 8, Centro, Seville, ☎ 95/422–8899; ☼ weekdays 9–9, Sat. 10–2). Downtown New York (⊠ Pérez galdós 1, La Alfalfa, Seville, ☎ 95/450–1046). Internet Pumarejo (⊠ San Luis 91, Alameda, Seville, ☎ 95/490–8175, ᵂᴱᴮ www.sol.com/internet/pumarejo).

## SAFETY

Seville has long been notorious for petty crime. Tourists continue to be thieves' favored victims, so take commonsense precautions. Drive with your car doors locked; lock all your luggage out of sight in the trunk; never leave *anything* in a parked car; and keep a wary eye on scooter riders, who have been known to snatch purses or even smash the windows of moving cars. Take only a small amount of cash and one credit card out with you. Leave your passport, traveler's checks, and other credit cards in the hotel safe, if possible, and avoid carrying purses and expensive cameras or wearing valuable jewelry.

## SIGHTSEEING TOURS

In Seville, any of the three organizations listed below (A.P.I.T., Guidetour, and I.T.A.) can hook you up with a qualified English-speaking guide. The tourist office has information on open-bus city tours run by Servirama, Hispalense de Tranvias, and others; buses leave every half hour from the Torre del Oro, with stops at Parque María Luisa and the Isla Mágica theme park. You can hop on and off at any stop; the complete tour lasts about 90 minutes.

➤ CONTACTS: Asociación Provincial de Informadores Turísticos (⊠ Glorieta de Palacio de Congresos, Parque de María Luisa, ☎ 95/425–5957). Guidetour (⊠ Lope de Rueda 13, Barrio de Santa Cruz, ☎ 95/422–2374 or 95/422–2375). ITA (⊠ Santa Teresa 1, Barrio de Santa Cruz, ☎ 95/422–4641).

## TAXIS

➤ TAXI SERVICES: Radio Taxi (☎ 95/458–0000 or 95/457–1111). Tele Taxi (☎ 95/462–2222 or 95/462–1461). Radio Teléfono Giralda (☎ 954/675555).

## TRAIN TRAVEL

Seville, Jerez, and Cádiz all lie on the main rail line from Madrid to southwestern Spain. Trains leave from Madrid for Seville (via Córdoba) almost hourly, most of them high-speed AVE trains that reach Seville in 2½ hours. Two of the non-AVE trains continue on to Jerez and Cádiz; travel time from Seville to Cádiz is 1½ to 2 hours. From Granada, Málaga, Ronda, and Algeciras, trains go to Seville by way of Bobadilla, where, more often than not, you have to change.

A dozen or more local trains each day connect Cádiz with Seville, Puerto de Santa María, and Jerez. There are no trains to Doñana National Park, Sanlúcar de Barrameda, or Arcos de la Frontera or between Cádiz and the Costa del Sol.

In Seville, the sprawling Santa Justa station is on Avenida Kansas City.

*Al Andalus* is a vintage 1920s luxury train that makes a weekly six-day trip in season from Seville to Córdoba, Granada, and Antequera, with side trips to Carmona and Jerez.

➤ Train Information: **RENFE** (☎ 902/240202, WEB www.renfe.es).
➤ Train Stations: **Seville–Estación Santa Justa** (☎ 95/454–0202).

### TRAVEL AGENCIES

Seville has more than 40 travel agency offices, and all other major towns in the region have agencies.

➤ Agencies: **Halcón Viajes** (⊠ Avda. San Francisco Javier 22, Centro, Seville, ☎ 95/492–6245). **Marsans Viajes** (⊠ Avda. de la Constitución 13, Centro, Seville, ☎ 95/421–8302, WEB www.marsans.es). **Nouvelles Frontieres** (⊠ Cuesta del Rosario 6, Centro, Seville, ☎ 95/422–0700, WEB www.nouvelles-frontieres.es). **Ultramar Express** (⊠ Virgen del Aguila 2, Centro, Seville, ☎ 95/499–1629).

### VISITOR INFORMATION

➤ Local Tourist Offices: **Carmona** (⊠ Arco de la Puerta de Sevilla, ☎ 954/190955, WEB www.turismo.carmona.org). **Cazalla de la Sierra** (⊠ El Robledo, ☎ 95/488–4236, WEB www.turismo.cazalla.org). **Constantina** (⊠ Ayuntamiento, ☎ 95/588–0700, WEB www.turismo. constantina.org). **Écija** (⊠ Canovas del Castillo 4 [Palacio de Benamejí], ☎ 95/590–2933, WEB www.turismo.ecija.org). **Estepa** (⊠ Casa de Cultura, Calle Saladillo 12, ☎ 95/591–2771, WEB www.turismo.estepa. org). **Itálica** (⊠ Oficina de Turismo, ☎ 95/599–7376, WEB www. turismo.italica.org).**Marchena** (⊠ Torreon árabe, Calle San Francisco s/n, ☎ 95/584–6167, WEB www.turismo.marchena.org). **Morón de la Frontera** (⊠ Plaza del Ayuntamiento 1, ☎ 95/485–1008, WEB www. turismo.moron.org). **Osuna** (⊠ Plaza Mayor s/n, ☎ 95/582–1400, WEB www.turismo.osuna.org). **Seville** (⊠ Arjona 28, Arenal, ☎ 95/450–5667, WEB www.sevilla.org; ⊠ Costurero de la Reina, Paseo de las Delicias 9, Arenal, ☎ 95/423–4465).
➤ Provincial Tourist Office: **Seville** (⊠ Plaza de Triunfo 1–3 (by cathedral), Santa Cruz, ☎ 95/421–0005, WEB www.turismosevilla.org).
➤ Regional Tourist Office: **Seville** (⊠ Avda. de la Constitución 21, Centro, ☎ 95/422–1404, 954/218157, or 95/444–9128, WEB www. andalucia.org).

# 3 HUELVA PROVINCE

Tucked in at the junction of Spain, Portugal, and the Atlantic Ocean, in the Iberian Peninsula's southwest corner, Huelva's mountains, beaches, and wetlands offer spectacular natural resources to travelers who have had their fill of civilization and culture. Whether hiking in the Sierra de Aracena, ranging the silver strands of the Costa de la Luz, or exploring Europe's wildest wetlands at Doñana National Park, Huelva is a breath of fresh air in the wake of Andalusia's human, architectural, and artistic urban treasures.

A NDALUSIA'S DIZZYING COSMOPOLITAN DELIGHTS and cultural plenty are not easy to leave behind, but the untamed nature of the province of Huelva seems all the wilder and more beautiful for its proximity to the shimmering memories of the Mezquitas, Alcázares, and Alhambras of Córdoba, Seville, and Granada. The Sierra de Aracena in the northern highlands; the Parque Nacional de Doñana, one of the largest and richest wildlife refuges in Europe; and the pristine beaches along the Costa de la Luz are each about an hour's drive from Seville.

By George
Semler

Founded by the Phoenicians as Onuba more than 3,000 years ago, the port of Huelva was an important commercial and fishing center before the Carthaginians and Romans began exploiting the copper mining resources of the upper Rio Tinto valley. The suspected site of the city of Tartessus (also known as Tarsish), a prehistoric metropolis of uncertain location mentioned in the Bible (Kings 10:22), Huelva languished and lost luster under the Visigoths and Moors until Alfonso X el Sabio conquered the city for Christian Spain in 1257. Steel mining and fishing have been the mainstays of Huelva's economy throughout the modern era, with tourism, agriculture (especially strawberries), and the porcine industry emerging as the main breadwinners of today. The city of Huelva was largely destroyed by the so-called Lisbon earthquake of 1755, and is today almost completely lacking in charm.

Huelva's Ruta Colombina (Route of Columbus), a narrow strip of marshland rich in history, traces the beginnings of Columbus's voyage to the New World, which was launched from the monastery of La Rábida and from the port of Palos de la Frontera. For Doñana, turn off the Seville–Huelva highway, drive through Almonte and El Rocío—scene of the Whitsuntide pilgrimage to the hermitage of La Virgen del Rocío (the Virgin of the Dew)—and you'll come to the Doñana National Park visitor center at La Rocina.

## Pleasures and Pastimes

### Beaches

Huelva's Costa de la Luz is an almost uninterrupted beach that stretches from the Portuguese border on the river Guadiana in the west to the border with the province of Cádiz on the Guadalquivir river in the east. The Playa de Isla Canela is the westernmost beach on the Costa de la Luz. Isla Cristina is a fishing village with splendid beaches and sportfishing in the *ría* (inland lagoon), off the beach, and in the open sea. Islantilla is a modern tourist complex with everything from a 27-hole golf course to a yacht marina. La Antilla, just east of Islantilla, has a nudist beach. The Playa de Nueva Umbría stretches along the Atlantic south of the town of El Rompido. Punta Umbría is one of the most complete and comprehensive tourist complexes on the coast with a yacht club, sport marina, and all manner of aquatic sport facilities. The Playa de Punta Umbría extends southeast into the Atlantic as if pointing the way (more or less) for Christopher Columbus's caravels. The Playa de Mazagón extends all the way to Matalascañas, and the town itself has a parador and a 516-mooring yacht marina. Matalsacañas, wedged between the Atlantic Ocean and the Doñana wetlands, is the top beach resort in western Andalusia, with the greatest hotel capacity, infrastructure, and general services, as well as miles of fine, white-sand beaches.

### Dining

Huelva's gastronomical offerings logically encompass the best of *mar y montaña*, or surf 'n turf. Whereas the coast and wetlands are rich in seafood, the Huelva uplands, especially around the village of Jabugo, are famous for cured ham from the free-ranging, wild Iberian pig along with many kinds of sausages and products derived from this acorn-fattened national treasure. But Huelva's mountain fare goes much further than ham. Soups and *guisos serranos* (mountain stews) such as the *sopa de ajo gañán* (farmworker's garlic soup), or the herb-rich *sopa de olores* (garlic, cumin, and vegetable "soup of fragrances" simmered with a ham bone) join *migas de pastor* (shepherd's bread crumbs with garlic, peppers, and Jabugo ham); the *salchichón en aguardiente de Cortegana* (Cortegana sausage in brandy); and *revoltillo de callos de cabrito* (goat tripe in scrambled eggs) to complete a sturdy assortment of country and mountain fare. Around Jabugo, keep your eyes peeled for *guarrito frito,* chunks of caramelized, melt-in-your-mouth suckling piglet. Also known for sweets, a Moorish legacy, the Sierra de Aracena has *tarta de castañas de Fuenteheridos* (chestnut tart from Fuenteheridos), *melocotones en aguardiente de Aracena* (peaches in brandy from Aracena), and *tarta de bellotas y flores de miel* (acorn and honey tart). Cortegana is also known for *gazpacho de culantros* (sweet coriander gazpacho) and *torta de chicharrones* (pork crisp pie). The town of Almonaster holds an annual Arab and Moorish cooking workshop that explores and restores medieval recipes.

| CATEGORY | COST* |
|---|---|
| $$$$ | over €18 |
| $$$ | €13–€18 |
| $$ | €8–€13 |
| $ | under €8 |

*per person for a main course at dinner*

## Fiestas

Huelva province's most famous festival takes place in May, when worshipers make a multitudinous horseback, horsedrawn cart, covered wagon, and pedestrian Whitsuntide pilgrimage to the shrine of the **Virgen del Rocío** (Virgin of the Dew) in the village of Almonte. Huelva's **Fiestas Colombinas,** held in late July and early August to commemorate Christopher Columbus's August 3, 1492, departure for the Americas, are a solid week of bullfights, concerts, street dances, and general carousing. Aracena's **Romería de Nuestra Señora de los Angeles** takes place September 7–9. In Cortegana, the **Romería de San Antonio de Padua** fills the streets with revelers on the 15th and 16th of June. Almonaster la Real celebrates its **Feria de Agosto** on and around August 15. Mazagón celebrates **La Virgen del Carmen** during the first week of May.

## Hiking and Trekking

The Sierra de Aracena is crisscrossed with more than 700 km (420 mi) of both long- and short-range equestrian and pedestrian trails covering dozens of routes between the main villages of the region. For fitness and for building appetites powerful enough to take full advantage of the hearty highland cuisine, getting out of the car and off the road is indispensable. One of the best and most famous walks is from the town of Aracena through Alájar, Santa Ana la Real, Almonaster la Real, and Cortegana, to Aroche; it's a good 30-km (18-mi) hike, best executed over two or even three days. Local tourist offices will provide maps, guides, and equestrian recommendations.

## Lodging

The province of Huelva has two paradors: a modern installation in Ayamonte with panoramic views over the Guadiana river, and a sleek and comfortable modern hotel at Mazagón on the Atlantic coast. Upland country inns and *fincas* (ranches) such as La Silladilla, near Jabugo, offer the chance to stay in a house on an Iberian pig range and listen to the acorns that make this ham so delicious bouncing off the roof. For beachside comfort, Punta Umbría and Matalascañas have top luxury hotels with sunset views and sandy expanses.

| CATEGORY | COST* |
|---|---|
| $$$$ | over €140 |
| $$$ | €100–€140 |
| $$ | €60–€100 |
| $ | under €60 |

*All prices are for a standard double room, excluding tax.*

# Exploring Huelva Province

The Guadiana River, the border with Portugal, flows along Huelva's western periphery, and the Guadalquivir River marks its eastern border. The rivers Odiel and Tinto drain the province's central highlands, the Sierra de Aracena, and the Picos de Aroche. Huelva's three main geographical entities—mountain ranges, beaches, and wetlands—can be explored with relative ease in a few days, although exploring the area in greater detail has its rewards.

## Great Itineraries

Huelva has several different routes or itineraries through its inland, upland, and coastal zones, though the basic choices are three: mountains, wetlands, or beaches. The Sierra de Aracena is surprisingly green and forested, a nearly pre-Alpine pocket of Atlantic freshness that seems out of place so close to North Africa. The Doñana and Odiel *marismas* (wetlands) are filled with wildlife and are always fascinating to explore at any time of year. The Ruta Colombina combines history and marshlands. The beaches of the Costa de la Luz offer aquatic sports, sailing, and deep gulps of air and iodine from the Atlantic Ocean.

### IF YOU HAVE 3 DAYS

If you are limited to a three-day run through Huelva, and you are coming from Seville and points north, spend the first day touring the Sierra de Aracena, with stops at **Aracena** ② and the Gruta de las Maravillas. Continue along the A-470 route through Linares de la Sierra and Alájar on the way to **Jabugo** ③ and the famous Cinco Jotas (5 J's) Iberian ham processing center. Find your way to **Almonaster la Real** ④ for a look through the stunningly miniaturesque Moorish *mezquita* (mosque), the tiny bullring, and the town itself. Spend the night in the village promontory of ⛰ **Cortegana** ⑤, with its Moorish lookout fortress and its Mudéjar church, the Divino Salvador, or continue to Los Romeros for a night at an Iberian pig ranch at the Finca de la Silladilla. On Day 2, see the village of Aroche before driving around the western edge of Huelva to the Parador Nacional on the border of Portugal at **Ayamonte** ⑥. Spend time on the beaches of Isla Cristina or La Antilla before exploring **Las Marismas de Odiel** ⑦ on your way to ⛰ **Punta Umbría** ⑧ for the night. While in Punta Umbría, have a look at the city of **Huelva** ⑨. On Day 3, swing around the Rio Tinto wetlands and explore the Ruta Colombina, stopping at **Niebla** ⑩, **Moguer** ⑪, **Palos de la Frontera** ⑫, and **La Rábida** ⑬ on your way to **Mazagón** ⑭, **Matalascañas** ⑮, and the **Doñana National Park** ⑯.

### IF YOU HAVE 5 DAYS

In five days you can visit **Ríotinto** ① on your way into the Sierra de Aracena. Spend more time in the Sierra and the Picos de Aroche before moving down to the coast, with an extra half day on the beach. Spend another day visiting **Niebla** ⑩, Almonte, and El Rocío on your way to

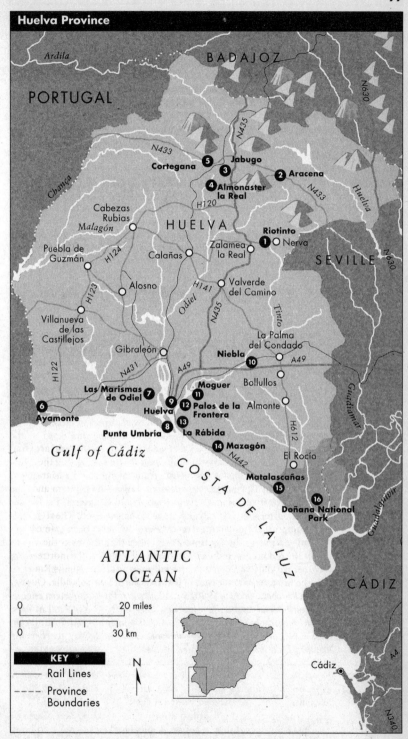

**Huelva Province**

Ardila

BADAJOZ

PORTUGAL

N630

Chança

N433

Cortegana ⑤ ③ Jabugo

② Aracena

④ Almonaster
la Real

N435

N433

Huelva

H120

Cabezas
Rubias

Malagón

HUELVA

Zalamea
la Real

Riotinto ①  ○ Nerva

SEVILLE

N630

Puebla de
Guzmán

H124

Calañas ○

○ Valverde
del Camino

H123

Alosno ○

H141

Odiel

N435

Tinto

Villanueva
de las
Castillejos

La Palma
del Condado ○

H122

Gibraleón ○

N431

A49

Niebla ⑩

A49

Guadiamar

Las Marismas
de Odiel ⑦

Moguer ⑪

Bollullos ○

⑨ ⑫ Palos de la
Frontera

Almonte ○

⑥
Ayamonte

Huelva ⑧ ⑬
Punta Umbría    La Rábida

El Rocío ○

H612

Gulf of Cádiz

⑭ Mazagón

N442

Matalascañas
⑮

⑯ Doñana National
Park

C O S T A   D E   L A   L U Z

Guadalquivir

ATLANTIC
OCEAN

CÁDIZ

0 _____ 20 miles
0 _____ 30 km

**KEY**
— Rail Lines
--- Province
    Boundaries

N

Cádiz ◉

A4

N340

more thoroughly explore the **Doñana National Park** ⑯ on foot, horseback, or by boat.

### When to Tour

Summertime, as well as being blistering hot in this southwestern corner of Spain, is also crowded with local vacationers. Winter is an off-peak time, when reservations are more easily available and there is greater ease of movement. The crisp highland air of the Sierra de Aracena is ideal between December and March. Spring and fall (October–November and April–May) are ideal for temperate weather and also have fewer visitors, with the exception of Easter Week, for which advance reservations are indispensable.

# SIERRA DE ARACENA AND THE NORTH

## Riotinto

❶  *74 km (46 mi) northeast of Huelva.*

Heading north from Seville on the N433, at Km 53 you'll reach the turnoff into the A476 to Nerva and Minas de Riotinto, the mining town near the source of the Riotinto (literally, "Red River"). The river's waters are the color of blood because of the minerals leached from the surrounding mountains: this area contains some of the richest copper deposits in the world, as well as gold and silver. It has been mined since antiquity, as the many Iberian, Tartessian, and Roman artifacts found here attest. In 1873 the mines were taken over by the British Rio Tinto Company Ltd., which started to dig a massive open-pit mine and build a 64-km (40-mi) railway to the port of Huelva to transport mineral ore. The British left in 1954, but mining activity continues today, albeit on a smaller scale.

Riotinto's multicolor landscape, scarred by centuries of intensive mining, makes for an unusual and well-organized **tour** conducted by the Fundación Riotinto. The tour's first stop, the **Museo Minero** (Museum of Mining), has archaeological finds, exhibits on the area's mining history, and a collection of historical steam engines and rail coaches. Next comes the **Corta Atalaya**, one of the largest open-pit mines in the world (4,000 ft across and 1,100 ft deep), and **Bellavista**, the elegant English quarter where the British mine managers lived. The tour ends with an optional ride on the **Tren Minero** (Miners' Train), which follows the course of the Riotinto along more than 24 restored km (15 mi) of the old mining railway. On the first Sunday of the month, from October to May, you can take the full tour by steam engine. You can take the full tour as described, or just visit the individual sights. ⊠ *Fundación Riotinto,* ☎ *959/590025.* ☞ *Full tour: €14 with steam engine, €17 with diesel engine.* ☉ *Museum daily 10:30–3 and 4–7; Miners' Train mid-July–mid-Sept., daily 1:30 PM; mid-June–mid-Sept., weekends 4 PM; mid-Apr.–mid-May and mid-Sept.–mid-Oct., weekends 5 PM; mid-Oct.–mid-Apr., weekends 4 PM.*

## Aracena

❷  *105 km (65 mi) northeast of Huelva, 100 km (62 mi) northwest of Seville.*

Stretching north of the Riotinto mines is the 460,000-acre Sierra de Aracena nature park, an expanse of hills cloaked in cork and holm oak. This region is known for its cured hams, which come from the prized free-ranging Iberian pigs that gorge on acorns in the autumn months prior to slaughter; the hams are buried in salt and then hung in cellars to dry-cure for at least two years. The finest hams come from the village of Jabugo. The best driving tour of the Sierra de Aracena is along the A-470 road from Aracena, through Linares de la Sierra, Alájar, Santa Ana la Real, Almonaster la Real, and Arroyo, to Cortegana. The capital of the region is Aracena, a town of handsome noble houses clustered at the foot of a 14th-century Templar castle that has a tower, two wells, and a section of ramparts. Prior to its tenure as a Christian fortress, the structure was a Moorish mosque, as were most of the castles and churches in the region. The churches of Santa Lucía, San Jerónimo, and La Asunción complete Aracena's architectural sights, and the Museo de Arte Contemporáneo de Escultura al Aire Libre (Contemporary Art Museum of Outdoor Sculpture) has a brilliant collection of works in bronze, marble, wood, and wrought iron. Aracena's main attraction is the spectacular cave known as the **Gruta de las Maravillas** (Cave of Marvels). The 12 caverns hide long corridors, stalactites and stalagmites arranged in wonderful patterns, and stunning underground lakes. Note that guided tours are given only if there are a sufficient number of visitors. ⊠ *Plaza Pozo de Nieves, Pozo de Nieves,* ☎ *959/128355.* ⌕ *€7.* ⊙ *Guided tours daily at 10:30, 11:30, 12:30, 1:30, 3, 4, 5, and 6.*

## Dining and Lodging

$$–$$$ ✕ **José Vicente.** Diners come from Seville and beyond for the food at this small restaurant near the Seville exit from Aracena. The menu is short but tempting. This is an ideal place to try dishes made with fresh pork (as opposed to the more commonly available cured ham) from the free-ranging Iberian pig. Appetizers always include a few vegetable dishes and soups. If the main dining room is full, and it often is, you can dine at one of four tables in the adjoining Despensa de José Vicente, which doubles as a bar and a shop selling local produce. ⊠ *Avda. de Andalucía 51–3, Aracena,* ☎ *959/128455. AE, DC, MC, V. Closed June 15–30. No lunch Fri.*

$$ ✕ **Mesón Arrieros.** Take the A-470 road 6 km (4 mi) to Linares de la Sierra for one of the prettiest towns and restaurants in the area. Handmade cobblestone streets twist through this country village, leading you to one of the top area specialists in wild Iberian pork and ham products. This rustic restaurant is the real thing; try the *paté de la casa* (homemade paté). Dinner is arranged by reservation only. ⊠ *C/Arrieros 2, Linares de la Sierra,* ☎ *959/463717. AE, DC, MC, V. Closed Wed.*

$$$ ⌂ **Finca Buenvino.** Six kilometers from Aracena, this lovely country house nestles in 150 acres of woods and is run like a small, beautifully furnished, stately home by a charming British couple, Sam and Jeannie Chesterton. Jeannie runs Andalusian, Mediterranean, and North African cooking courses. The room price includes a big breakfast and an excellent dinner with tapas beforehand. Barbecues can also be served by the large pool. There are three woodland self-catering cottages to let, each with its own pool. Reservations are essential. ⊠ *Crtra. N433 Km 95, 21293 Los Marines,* ☎ *959/124034,* ℻ *959/501029,* WEB *www.buenvino.com. 5 rooms, 3 cottages. Restaurant, some kitchens, 3 pools, bar, Internet; no a/c, no room phones, no in-room TVs. Closed mid-July–mid-Sept. MC, V.*

$ ⌂ **Los Castãnos.** This hotel offers basic but comfortable accommodations in small, simple rooms. Some face the street, others an interior patio; upstairs rooms have balconies. ⊠ *Avenida de Huelva 5, 21200,* ☎ *959/126300,* ℻ *959/126287. 33 rooms. Restaurant, café, parking (fee), some pets allowed; no a/c in some rooms. AE, DC, MC, V.*

# Jabugo

❸   *112 km (67 mi) northeast of Huelva, 106 km (64 mi) northwest of Seville.*

Synonymous with Spain's finest mountain-cured, acorn-fed, free-range, wild Iberian hams (though Salamanca's Guijuelo ham is preferred by many gourmet palates), Jabugo is best known for its Cinco Jotas (5 J's) label denoting the highest level of produce. At the **Sanchez Romero Carvajal–Cinco Jotas,** the factory where the famous Iberian ham is produced, you can see exactly how this exquisite product is bred, fed, slaughtered, and processed. ✉ *Crtra. San Juan del Puerto s/n,* ☎ *959/121194.* 🎫 *€5.* ☉ *Guided tours 9–1, 4–7.*

## Dining and Lodging

$$–$$$   ✕ **Mesón Cinco Jotas.** This central spot serves some of the top ham products in Andalusia, as well as Sierra de Aracena specialties such as *migas* and *castañetas* (glands of Iberian pig). *Tentullos con garbanzos* (wild mushrooms with garbanzo beans) is another dish to look for. ✉ *Ctra. de San Juan del Puerto s/n,* ☎ *959/121071. AE, DC, MC, V. Closed Wed.*

$–$$   ✕ **El Molino de Jabugo.** Built around an immense and ancient olive press last used in the 1950s, this former oil mill serves guarrito frito you won't forget. *Carrillada en salsa* (pig cheek in sauce) is another favorite. ✉ *Plaza de la Constitución 8,* ☎ *959/121059. AE, DC, MC, V. Closed Mon.*

$$–$$$   🏠 **Finca de la Silladilla.** This pretty ranch, in a wild Iberian pig–infested live oak and cork oak forest, is a chance to see Spain's most prized products priming themselves for your palate. The rooms and small stone houses are all impeccably decorated in heavy slabs of beautifully finished wood. One has a bathroom with an oak tree growing through the roof. The staff is helpful with organizing tours of the Sierra de Aracena, equestrian outings, or visits to nearby Jabugo, *bellota* (acorn-fed) ham capital of Spain. ✉ *Crtra. Los Romeros 21290 Los Romeros* ☎ *959/501350,* FAX *959/501184. 2 rooms, 2 suites, 4 houses. Kitchens, horseback riding. AE, DC, MC, V.*

$   🏠 **Galaroza Sierra.** On the outskirts of the village of Galaroza, this whitewashed hotel is 3 km (2 mi) from Jabugo. The common areas and rooms are modern rustic, with light wood and woven blankets. Rooms have small balconies and views of the mountains, and the four bungalows face the swimming pool. Noise from the nearby road can be a problem. The restaurant specializes in preparations of fresh pork from the black-hooved Iberian pig. ✉ *Carretera Sevilla–Lisboa, Km 69.5, 21291 Galaroza,* ☎ *959/123237,* FAX *959/123236,* WEB *www. hotelgalaroza.com. 22 rooms, 7 bungalows. Restaurant, pool, some pets allowed; no a/c in some rooms. DC, MC, V.*

# Almonaster la Real

❹   *105 km (64 mi) northeast of Huelva, 7 km (4 mi) southwest of Jabugo.*

This little village has some of the best architectural treasures of the Sierra de Aracena. The intimate fortified **mezquita** (mosque) sits on the hill overlooking the village to the north, and to the south are the hills of Huelva's Andévalo region, the transitional piedmont leading out to the flatlands. Built at the beginning of the 10th century using materials recycled from earlier Roman and Visigothic structures, the mosque is a miniature Mezquita de Cordoba, with five naves of horseshoe arches supported by pillars of various different configurations and sizes. Complete with east-facing mihrab, a patio for ablutions, an *aljibe* or watering trough with water flowing in from the fountain, and a minaret for the call to prayer, all elements of the mosque are present. Don't

## Close-Up

# JAMÓN IBÉRICO DE BELLOTA

**H**UELVA HAS LONG BEEN SPAIN'S uncontested ham capital. *Jamón Ibérico* means wild, free-range Iberian pig (also known as *pata negra,* black hoof, for its characteristic black feet. *De bellota* (of acorn) means that these pigs have been fed only acorns. Jamón Ibérico de bellota is one of Spain's great culinary treasures; if your Spanish host wants to splurge, he will insist that you have a taste of Jabugo ham from Huelva's famous Iberian ham-producing town in the Sierra de Aracena. True "bellota," as it is called, is filled with "good cholesterol" or the polyunsaturated oils from the acorns. Acorns, like olives, are a wild fruit and are filled with cholesterol that actually breaks down the fatty deposits that clog arteries. Spanish ham comes in confusing qualities, prices, and nomenclature. *Jamón York* is boiled ham from a white pig fed on feed pellets. *Jamón Serrano* covers all varieties of ham dried in the mountains *(la sierra),* but usually refers to pellet-fed, white pig, the cheapest and least-prized product of the genre. *Jamón Ibérico de recebo* is wild Iberian pig fattened on pellets. *De recebo y bellota* is ham from a pig fattened on a mixture of pellets and acorns. *Jamón Ibérico de bellota* touches all the bases and assures you are getting the top of the line, blue-chip Iberian ham.

miss the powerful scent of rosemary that pervades this 2,500-year-old place of meeting and worship first used by Romans and Visigoths in the 4th and 5th centuries.

The tiny **bullring** just outside the mosque was built in the early 19th century in what was the Patio de Armas of the fortress that replaced the mosque after the Christian Reconquest. Bullfights are held here in August. Inside the village, look for the Gothic–Mudéjar **Iglesia de San Martín,** built between the 14th and the 18th centuries. The three naves, the vaulted ceiling over the choir, the 16th-century Puerta del Perdón, and a *portada manuelina*—a doorway in the style typical of the reign of Manuel I of Portugal (1469–1521)—are the church's most interesting architectural features.

### Dining and Lodging

$ ✕🏨 **Casa García.** On the main road into town, this busy spot appears to be the nerve center of Almonaster la Real. Rooms are on the small side but comfortable. The restaurant serves excellent mountain home cooking and Iberian pig. Try the *revuelto de gurumelos* (eggs scrambled with wild mushrooms) during mushroom season. ⊠ *Avda. de San Martín 2, 21350,* ☎ *959/143109,* FAX *959/143143. 22 rooms. Restaurant, minibars, cable TV, bar. AE, DC, MC, V.*

## Cortegana

**⑤** *114 km (68 mi) northeast of Huelva, 30 km (18 mi) west of Aracena.*

Visible for miles around, especially at night when it's illuminated, Cortegana's onetime **Moorish lookout fortress** and later Christian palace is the main architectural treasure here. The **Iglesia del Divino Salvador** is the town's other gem, a Mudéjar church known for its medieval look and the harmony of its design.

### Lodging

$$    🏠 **La Posada de Cortegana.** With a series of Nordic-style wooden cabins that have a full set of modern comforts, from air-conditioning to cable TV, this rural complex is a pleasant base camp from which to explore the Sierra de Aracena. ⊠ *Crtra. Repilado–La Corte Km 2.5, 21230,* ☎ *959/503301,* FAX *959/503302. 40 rooms. Restaurant, minibars, cable TV, pool, bar. AE, DC, MC, V.*

# LA COSTA DE LA LUZ AND DOÑANA NATIONAL PARK

On either side of the capital city of Huelva, the Costa de la Luz (Coast of Light) extends from the border with Portugal at the Guadiana River to the Guadalquivir River to the east. Doñana National Park is the greatest natural resource and wildlife refuge in Europe. The Marismas del Odiel (Odiel Wetlands) west of Huelva and the Ruta Colombina (route of Columbus) east of the capital are two of the best destinations to explore within these areas, the first for its flora and fauna, and the second for its historical connections with the Discovery of the New World.

## Ayamonte

**6** *52 km (31 mi) west of Huelva.*

With one foot in Portugal's Algarve region, Ayamonte has a bustling fishing and commercial port and a few sights and monuments of its own to seek out. The 15th-century Iglesia del Salvador, the 16th-century Iglesia de Nuestra Señora de las Angustias, and the convents of San Francisco and Santa Clara give evidence of the town's long and splendid history, and the nearby beach and leisure resorts keep visitors busy during high season (mostly summer).

### Dining and Lodging

$$–$$$    ✕🏠 **Parador de Ayamonte.** Overlooking the estuary of the Guadiana River and the border with Portugal, this sleek, modern structure is known more for its stupendous views than for its inherent charm. The beaches of Isla Canela and Isla Cristina are close by, and the parador will take very good care of you between sessions on the beaches. ⊠ *El Castillito, 21400,* ☎ *959/320700,* FAX *959/320700,* WEB *www.parador.es. 52 rooms. Restaurant, minibars, cable TV, pool, hot tub, sauna, bar, meeting room, free parking. AE, DC, MC, V.*

## Las Marismas de Odiel

**7** *10 km (6 mi) west of Huelva.*

The Odiel marshes, one of Andalusia's eight protected wetlands, can be explored using Huelva or Punta Umbría as a base camp. A natural preserve of 7,100 hectares lying between Huelva, Gibraleón, Aljaraque, and Punta Umbría, the Odiel marshlands form the estuary at the mouths of the Odiel and Tinto rivers. They reveal a plethora of migrating or reproducing waterfowl. Spoonbills are the star performers here, wading birds related to the ibis. In high spoonbill season it is thought that one-third of the European population is in residence here. Other common Odiel species are the grey heron, the purple heron, and the marsh harrier.

# Punta Umbría

**8** *21 km (12 mi) south of Huelva.*

One of the most comprehensive tourist complexes on the Costa de la Luz, Punta Umbría has a port, a yacht club, and a dozen hotels, including the four-star Barceló, which is arguably the top hotel in the province. Sailing, windsurfing, fishing, and every aquatic and maritime sport imaginable is available on this slender peninsula of pleasure.

## Dining and Lodging

**$$$** ✕⊡ **Barceló Punta Umbría.** This is the top choice for exploring beaches on the Costa de la Luz and having an occasional glance through the city of Huelva. A gleaming glass-and-steel oasis of comfort with miles of wild beach and Atlantic waters at its feet, the Barceló is completely equipped and impeccably modern. It is one of the province's top tourist resorts. ✉ *Avda. del Oceano s/n, 21100,* ☎ *959/495400,* ⅢAX *959/ 310244,* ⊞ *www.barcelo.com. 300 rooms. Restaurant, minibars, cable TV, 2 pools (1 indoor), gym, hot tub, sauna, bar, meeting room, free parking. AE, DC, MC, V.*

# Huelva

**9** *92 km (55 mi) west of Seville; 105 km (63 mi) east of Faro (Portugal).*

Once a thriving Roman port, Huelva was largely destroyed by the 1755 Lisbon earthquake and, as a result, claims the dubious honor of being the least distinguished city in Andalusia. If you didn't visit Huelva at all you would have gained a few hours and avoided an unnecessary urban hassle. If you do visit Huelva, take a walk around the Plaza de las Monjas, the city nerve center, before diving into the pedestrianized streets just one block south where there are abundant shops and watering holes. Sites to seek out include the Catedral de la Merced and its Virgen de Cinta by Martínez Montañés, the Iglesia de San Pedro on Plaza San Pedro, the city's oldest surviving church, and the Santuario de Nuestra Señora de Cinta off Avenida de Manuel Siurot, a chapel that Columbus visited before setting sail for what he thought might be the West Indies. A ceramic-tile portrait of the event by artist Daniel Zuloaga commemorates the event.

## Dining

**$$$** ✕ **Taberna el Condado.** For a sure-bet tavern for tapas and a beer, this is a place to keep in mind. It is just a few steps southeast of Plaza de las Monjas. ✉ *Sor Angela de la Cruz 3, 21000,* ☎ *959/261123. AE, DC, MC, V.*

# Niebla

**10** *20 km (12 mi) west of Huelva.*

The first stop on the so-called Ruta Colombina that begins at Niebla and ends at La Rábida, this monumental town on the Río Tinto is filled with memorable architecture. The Moorish ramparts, nearly 2 km (1 mi) long, are the longest and best-preserved Moorish defensive walls in Spain. Built between the 11th and 13th centuries by the Almoravid and Almohad dynasties, the walls are defended by some 50 fortified towers. Five of the towers cover the gates to the city. La Puerta del Socorro leads in to the Iglesia de San Martín, formerly a mosque and synagogue. The street actually splits the structure in two, so that the bell tower, apse, and chapel are on one side of the street, and the main doorway is on the other. The bridge over the Río Tinto is a long, massive bulwark of notable grace and power. The **Castillo de Niebla** is a 12th-century marvel that once belonged to the powerful Guzman family that

owned most of the Guadalquivir valley. ✉ *Plaza de Santa María s/n,*
☎ *959/362270,* WEB *www.castillodeniebla.com.* 🎫 *€4.* ⊙ *Daily 9–1:30,*
*4:30–7:30.*

## Moguer

⓫ *12 km (7 mi) northeast of Palos de la Frontera.*

The inhabitants of this old port town now spend more time growing
strawberries than they do seafaring, as you'll see from the surrounding fields. The **Convento de Santa Clara** dates from 1337. ✉ *Plaza de*
*los Monjes s/n,* ☎ *959/370107.* 🎫 *€2.* ⊙ *Guided tours Tues.–Sat. 11,*
*12, 1, 5, 6, 7.*

While in Moguer, see the **Casa-Museo Juan Ramón Jiménez,** former
home of the Nobel Prize–winning poet who penned the much-loved
*Platero y Yo.* At press time the Casa-Museo building was undergoing
renovations and the exhibition (same price and hours) had been moved
to **Casa Natal** (✉ Ribera 2), the house where he was born. ✉ *C. Juan*
*Ramón Jiménez,* ☎ *959/372148.* 🎫 *€2.* ⊙ *Tues.–Sat. 10:15–1:15 and*
*5:15–7:15, Sun. 10:15–1:15.*

## Palos de la Frontera

⓬ *4 km (2½ mi) northwest of La Rábida, 12 km (7 mi) northeast of*
*Mazagón.*

Did you learn *this* detail in school? On August 2, 1492, Columbus's
three famous caravels, the *Niña,* the *Pinta,* and the *Santa María,* set
sail from Palos de la Frontera. Most of the crew were men from Palos
and neighboring Moguer. At the door of the church of **San Jorge**
(1473), the royal letter ordering the levy of the ships' crew and equipment was read aloud, and the voyagers took their water supplies from
the Fontanilla (fountain) at the town's entrance.

## La Rábida

★ ⓭ *30 km (19 mi) northwest of Doñana, 8 km (5 mi) northwest of*
*Mazagón.*

You may want to extend your Doñana tour to see the monastery of
**Santa María de la Rábida,** "the birthplace of America." In 1485
Columbus came from Portugal with his son Diego to stay in this Mudéjar-style Franciscan monastery. Here he discussed his theories with friars Antonio de Marchena and Juan Pérez, who interceded on his behalf
with Queen Isabella. The early 15th-century church holds a much-ven-
erated 14th-century statue of the **Virgen de los Milagros** (Virgin of Mir-
acles). The **frescoes** in the gatehouse were painted by Daniel Vázquez
Díaz in 1930. ☎ *959/350411.* 🎫 *€3.* ⊙ *Tues.–Sun. 10–1 and 4–6:15*
*(4–7 Mar.–Oct.; 4:45–8 Aug.).*

Two kilometers (one mile) from the monastery, on the seashore, is the
**Muelle de las Carabelas** (Caravels' Wharf), a reproduction of a 15th-
century port. The star exhibits here are the full-size reproductions of
Columbus's flotilla, the *Niña, Pinta,* and *Santa María,* which were built
using the same techniques as in Columbus's day. You can climb aboard
each one and learn more (or refresh your memory) about discovery of
the New World in the adjoining museum. ✉ *Paraje de la Rábida,* ☎
*959/530597 or 959/530312.* 🎫 *€3.* ⊙ *Oct.–Mar., Tues.–Sun. 10–7;*
*Apr.–Sept., Tues.–Fri. 10–2 and 5–9, weekends 11–8.*

## Close-Up

# LA ROMERÍA DEL ROCÍO

**T**HE ANNUAL PENTECOST (seventh Sunday after Easter) pilgrimage to the Ermita del Rocío (Hermitage of Our Lady of the Dew), also known as La Blanca Paloma (the White Dove) near Almonte is one of Andalusia's wildest and most beloved events. In a perfect amalgam of pagan, religious, and Gypsy fervor, some 1 million *rocieros* (devotees of La Virgn del Rocío) converge on Almonte to pay homage to El Rocío. On foot, horseback, oxen-hauled covered wagons, or by horse and carriage, gaily attired in flamenco dresses and Andalusian mayoral suits, the advancing revelers camp en route, sing and dance flamenco, and generally party their way across the Guadalquivir marshlands toward the hermitage. From the east they ford the Guadalquivir by boat and continue through Doñana; from Seville they come by horse; from Huelva they cross the Río Tinto wetlands; and from points north pilgrims descend from the Sierra de Aracena. Beginning with the Saturday presentations of the 100-odd rociera brotherhoods and ending in the predawn hours of Monday when members of the Almonte brotherhood scale the famous iron grillwork and carry La Blanca Paloma out into the streets, the emotion grows into a near-delirium of wine- and music-induced ecstasy. A three-day flamenco *juerga* (binge) with Gypsy and liturgical overtones, this celebration is not for the faint of heart, but, like many things Andalusian, its passion and joy are larger than life.

---

OFF THE BEATEN PATH

**EL ROCÍO AND ALMONTE** – Both places are good visits whether it's Pentecost (Whitsuntide) or not. The road between Matalascañas and Bollullos del Condado runs through both of these key *rociera* destinations (of special interest to devotees of La Virgen del Rocío, Our Lady of the Dew). Even out of season these towns seem to be glowing with pre- or post-Rocío excitement.

---

# Mazagón

⑭ *22 km (14 mi) northwest of Matalascañas.*

True, there isn't much to see or do in this coastal town, but its parador makes a nice base for touring La Rábida, Palos de la Frontera, and Moguer. Mazagón's beautiful beach is among the nicest in the region.

### Dining and Lodging

$$$ ✕🏨 **Parador Cristóbal Colón.** This peaceful, modern parador stands on a cliff surrounded by pine groves, overlooking a sandy beach 3 km (2 mi) southeast of Mazagón. Most rooms have balconies overlooking the garden. The restaurant serves traditional Andalusian dishes and local seafood specialties, such as stuffed baby squid and hake medallions. ⊠ *Ctra. San Juan del Puerto–Matalascañas Km 30, 21130,* ☎ *959/536300,* FAX *959/536228,* WEB *www.parador.es. 63 rooms. Restaurant, cable TV, 18-hole golf course, 2 tennis courts, 2 pools (1 indoor), hot tub, sauna, windsurfing, fishing, bicycles, horseback riding, bar, meeting room, free parking. AE, DC, MC, V.*

# Matalascañas

**⑮** *3 km (2 mi) south of Acebuche; 85 km (53 mi) southwest of Seville.*

Its proximity to Acebuche, the main reception center at Doñana National Park, makes Matalascañas a convenient lodging base for park visitors. Otherwise, it's a rather incongruous and ugly sprawl of hotels and vacation homes, very crowded at Easter and in summer, and eerily deserted the rest of the year (most hotels are closed from November to March). There are some nice beaches for those who just want to relax, and the ocean waters draw windsurfers and other water athletes.

### Lodging

**$** ☒ **Tierra Mar.** Check into this large beachfront hotel if you want to combine Doñana with the seashore. The hotel is large, modern, and somewhat lacking in intimacy and character, but the wide open spaces around it make up for its shortcomings. Rooms are bright and sparsely decorated. ☒ *Matalascañas Parcela 120 Sector M, 21760,* ☎ *959/440300,* FAX *959/440720,* WEB *www.hoteltierramar.com. 250 rooms. Restaurant, café, pool, sauna. AE, DC, MC, V.*

# Doñana National Park

**⑯** *100 km (62 mi) southwest of Seville.*

One of Europe's last true wilderness redoubts, these marshy bogs and swamps flanking the Guadalquivir estuary form Spain's most extensive protected wetlands and national parks. Long a favorite hunting grounds for the Spanish royal family, the site was named for Doña Ana de Mendoza, wife of the seventh Duke of Medina Sidonia. Doña Ana retired to the *coto* (game preserve) in 1585, and the Palacio de Doñana was built for Doña Ana by her husband in the late 16th century. The park covers 188,000 acres (an area 64 km by 15 km [40 mi by 9 mi]) and is a paradise for nature lovers, especially bird-watchers: it sits on the migratory route from Africa to Europe and is the winter home and breeding ground for as many as 150 species of rare birds. The park's habitats range from beaches and shifting sand dunes to marshes, dense brushwood, and sandy hillsides of pine and cork oak. Two of Europe's most endangered species, the imperial eagle and the Iberian lynx, make their homes here, and kestrels, kites, buzzards, egrets, storks, and spoonbills breed among the cork oaks.

A good base of exploration is the hamlet of **El Rocío,** on the park's northern fringe. In spring, during the famous Romería del Rocío pilgrimage, up to a million people converge on the local *santuario* (shrine) to worship the Virgen del Rocío (June 9 in 2003, May 31 in 2004). The rest of the year, most of El Rocío's pilgrim-brotherhood houses are empty, but there are some pleasant hotels and restaurants. Most of the streets are unpaved—not for want of civic enterprise, but to make them more comfortable for horses.

At the Doñana visitor center at **La Rocina** (☎ 959/442340; ☉ daily 9–2 and 3–sundown), less than 2 km (1 mi) from El Rocío, you can peer at the park's many bird species from a 3½-km (2-mi) footpath. Five kilometers (three miles) away, an exhibit at the **Palacio de Acebrón** (☎ no phone; ☉ daily 8–3 and 4–sundown; last entrance one hour before closing) explains the park's ecosystems. Two kilometers (one mile) before Matalascañas, you'll find **Acebuche,** the park's main interpretation center and the departure point for jeep tours, which must be reserved in advance (☎ 959/430432 for jeep tours; ☉ center open daily June–Sept. 8–9, Oct.–May 9–7). Tours leave at 8:30 and 5 June–September and 8:30 and 3 October–May, and last four hours, cost €18.20, and cover a 70-km (43-mi) route across beaches, sand dunes, marshes, and scrub. Off-season, from November to February, you can usually book a tour with just a day's notice; at other times, book as far in advance as possible.

### Lodging

$$$  ⊞ **Cortijo Los Mimbrales.** This convivial, one-story Andalusian farm-hacienda on the Rocío–Matalascañas road is the perfect base for exploring Doñana: it's perched on the park's edge, a mere 1 km (½ mi) from the visitor center at La Rocina. The large common lounge with comfy chairs and fireplace makes for relaxed evening chitchat with fellow nature lovers. Accommodations are in colorfully decorated rooms or in bungalows sleeping two to four, with kitchenettes and small private gardens. Some rooms and bungalows have fireplaces. There are stables on the premises, and the hotel can arrange horseback rides on the fringes of the park. ⊠ *Carretera del Rocío (A483) Km 30,* ☎ *959/ 442237,* FAX *959/442443,* WEB *www.cortijomimbrales.com. 20 rooms, 6 bungalows. Restaurant, pool, horseback riding, some pets allowed; no a/c. AE, DC, MC, V.*

$$  ⊞ **Toruño.** Despite its location behind the famous Rocío shrine, the theme at this simple, friendly hotel is nature: it's run by the same cooperative that leads official park tours, and has become a favorite of birdwatchers. Each room is named after a different species of local bird, and some have priceless views over the marshes. ⊠ *Plaza del Acebuchal 22,* ☎ *959/442323,* FAX *959/442338. 30 rooms. Restaurant. MC, V.*

# HUELVA PROVINCE A TO Z

*To research prices, get advice from other travelers, and book travel arrangements, visit www.fodors.com.*

#### AIR TRAVEL

The nearest airport to Huelva is Seville's San Pablo, 12 km (7½ mi) east of the city on the N-IV to Córdoba. The airport at Faro, Portugal, 105 km (63 mi) west, is nearly equidistant from Huelva. The region's other airport is Jerez de la Frontera's Aeropuerto de la Parra, 7 km (4 mi) from Jerez on the road to Seville.
➤ AIRLINE CONTACTS: Iberia (⊠ Almirante Lobo 2, Seville, ☎ 95/422-8901 or 902/400500).
➤ AIRPORT INFORMATION: **Aeropuerto de la Parra** (☎ 956/150000). **San Pablo** (☎ 95/444–9000).

#### BUS TRAVEL

Buses connect all of the towns and villages in this region. Long-distance buses connect Huelva with Seville and Madrid; with Cáceres, Mérida, and Badajoz in Extremadura; and with Córdoba, Granada, Málaga, and Ronda in Andalusia. Regional buses take the coastal route from Granada, Málaga, and Marbella to Cádiz. Buses from Ronda run to Arcos, Jerez, and Cádiz. Buses throughout Andalusia, and between Extremadura and Seville, tend to be more frequent and convenient than trains.
➤ BUS INFORMATION: Huelva: **Damas** (⊠ Doctor Rubio, s/n, ☎ 959/ 256900). Aracena: **Casal** (☎ 959/128196). Ayamonte: **Damas** (☎ 959/128196). Isla Cristina: **Damas** (⊠ Manuel Siurot s/n, ☎ 959/ 331652). Lepe: **Lepe Bus** (⊠ Polg. El Chorrillo, nave 43, ☎ 959/ 382068). Mazagón: **Damas** (⊠ Plaza Mayor s/n, ☎ 959/256900). Punta Umbría: **Damas** (⊠ Avda. de Portugal 9, ☎ 959/256900).

### CAR TRAVEL

The main road connecting Huelva with Seville is the A49/E1, continuing as the N-IV through Córdoba to Madrid. This is a four-lane *autovía* and one of Spain's busiest roads; note that trucks can cause delays. The A49/E1 continues west from Huelva through Ayamonte into Portugal. The N435 north from Huelva is the main highway through Jabugo and Zafra to Mérida. The N442 east to Doñana National Park does *not* get you across the Guadalquivir river to Sanlúcar de Barrameda. Plan on backtracking to Seville (there is also a slight shortcut through Colinas and La Puebla del Río, though this route is more scenic than timesaving).

Driving in Huelva is easy enough in the flatlands, though the Sierra de Aracena can be more challenging. The main difficulty is keeping your eyes on the road with so much tempting scenery all around you. The only way to access Doñana National Park by road is to take the A49/E1 Seville–Huelva highway, exit for Almonte/Bollullos par del Condado, then follow the signs for El Rocío and Matalascañas.

➤ UNITED STATES: (✉ Paseo de las Delicias 7, Seville, ☎ 95/423–1883).

### EMERGENCIES

➤ CONTACTS: **Police** (☎ 091). **Ambulance** (☎ 061).

### SAFETY

Southern Spain has always been notorious for rampant petty crime. Commonsense precautions are fundamental, as foreign visitors continue to be the favored victims of pickpockets and bag snatchers. Drive with your car doors locked; lock all your luggage out of sight in the trunk; *never* leave *anything* in a parked car; and keep a wary eye on scooter riders, who have been known to snatch purses or even smash the windows of moving cars. Take only a small amount of cash and one credit card out with you. Leave your passport, traveler's checks, and other credit cards in the hotel safe, if possible, and avoid carrying purses and expensive cameras or wearing valuable jewelry.

### TOURS

➤ CONTACTS: **Asociación Provincial de Informadores Turísticos** (✉ Glorieta de Palacio de Congresos, Seville, ☎ 95/425–5957). **Guidetour** (✉ Lope de Rueda 13, ☎ 95/422–2374 or 95/422–2375). **ITA** (✉ Santa Teresa 1, ☎ 95/422–4641).

### DOÑANA NATIONAL PARK

Jeep tours of the reserve depart twice daily (Tuesday–Sunday 8:30 and 3) from the park's reception center, 2 km (1 mi) from Matalascañas. Tours are limited to 125 people and should be booked well in advance. Passengers can often be collected from hotels in Matalascañas. Write or call the Parque Nacional de Doñana.

➤ FEES AND SCHEDULES: **Parque Nacional de Doñana** (✉ Cooperativa Marisma del Rocío, Centro de Recepción, 21760 Matalascañas, Huelva, ☎ 959/430432).

### TRAIN TRAVEL

Huelva's railroad links are limited to the capital city itself and Niebla on the line to Seville, and the line north through Jabugo to Extremadura.

➤ TRAIN INFORMATION: **RENFE** (☎ 902/240202, WEB www.renfe.es). **Huelva, Estación de FFCC** (✉ Avda. de Italia s/n, Huelva, ☎ 959/245614). **Niebla, Estación de FFCC** (✉ Estación de Ferrocarril s/n, Niebla, ☎ 959/36334).

## VISITOR INFORMATION

➤ TOURIST INFORMATION: **Western Andalusia regional tourist office** (⊠ Avda. de la Constitución 21, Seville, ☎ 95/422–1404 or 95/421–8157, FAX 95/422–9753). **Huelva, Oficina de Turismo de la Junta de Andalucía** (⊠ Avda. de Alemania 12, ☎ 959/257403). **Huelva, Patronato Provincial de Turismo** (⊠ Fernando el Católico 18, ☎ 959/257467). Local tourist offices: **Almonte** (⊠ Calle Alonso Perez 1, ☎ 959/450419). **Aracena** (⊠ Plaza San Pedro s/n, ☎ 959/128206). **Ayamonte** (⊠ Avda. Ramón y Cajal s/n, ☎ 959/470988). **El Rocío** (⊠ Avda. de la Canaliega s/n, ☎ 959/443808). **Gibraleón** (⊠ Plaza Mayor s/n, ☎ 959/300211). **Isla Cristina** (⊠ Gran Vía 33, ☎ 959/332694). **Islantilla** (⊠ Paseo de las Delicias 9, ☎ 959/646013). **La Antilla** (⊠ Avda. Castilla s/n, ☎ 959/481479). **La Rábida** (⊠ Paraje de la Rábida, ☎ 959/531137). **Lepe** (⊠ Plaza de España s/n, ☎ 959/445079). **Matalascañas** (⊠ Avda. de las Adelfas s/n, ☎ 959/430086). **Mazagón** (⊠ Ed. Mancomunidad Moguer-Palos, ☎ 959/376300). **Moguer** (⊠ San Francisco s/n, ☎ 959/371898). **Niebla** (⊠ Plaza de Santa Maria s/n, ☎ 959/362270). **Nerva** (⊠ Avda. Francisco López Real s/n, ☎ 959/580073). **Punta Umbría** (⊠ Avda. Ciudad de Huelva s/n, ☎ 959/495160). **Zalamea la Real** (⊠ Ctra. Nacional, Km 345, ☎ 959/562284).

# 4 CÁDIZ PROVINCE

Cádiz may be overshadowed by Andalusia's more famous regions, but it's rich in cultural treasures. The sherry, horse, tapa, wind, and flamenco capital of Spain, with three millennia of history and architecture and the "white villages" and natural bounty of the Sierra de Grazalema, Spain's southernmost province is a destination in its own right. Jerez de la Frontera, Sanlúcar de Barrameda, Puerto de Santa María, and Arcos de la Frontera all vie with the capital for favorite town status, and Tarifa is a world windsurfing magnet.

THE PROVINCE OF CÁDIZ is a surprisingly comprehensive micro-cosm of sierra, sand, and civilization. In Jerez, you can savor the town's internationally known sherry or delight in the acrobatic skills and graceful forms of purebred Carthusian horses. The Costa de la Luz offers fine beaches, from Cádiz's Playa Victoria through Chiclana de la Frontera's La Barrosa to Tarifa's wind-buffeted shores. In the province's upper reaches are *los pueblos blancos* (the white villages) climbing hillsides green with the flora endemic to the Sierra de Grazalema. Arcos de la Frontera perches precariously on a sheer cliff overlooking the gorge of the Guadalete River. Meanwhile, the city of Cádiz offers an opportunity to absorb the culinary and cultural resources of the oldest continuously inhabited city in the Western world.

By George
Semler

## Pleasures and Pastimes

### Dining

The great tapas triangle of Sanlúcar de Barrameda, Jerez de la Frontera and the city of Cádiz (with Puerto de Santa María in the middle) is known throughout Spain. Food enthusiasts come from all over the peninsula to sample the giant shrimp and succulent seafood of Puerto de Santa María and Sanlúcar de Barrameda, and to sip *fino* (a light, dry sherry from Jerez) and *Manzanilla* (a delicate Sanlúcar sherry with a hint of saltiness). Cádiz is a seafood cornucopia with fresh fish, crustaceans, and shellfish all but beaching themselves from the surrounding waters of the Mediterranean, the Atlantic, and the rich Guadalquivir estuary. The classic seafood tapa in the province of Cádiz is known for its purity and simplicity: no bread, no sauce, no puddings or pastes—just freshly captured and perfectly cooked. Cádiz's inland and highland cheeses, meats, and *guisos* (stews) are also distinguished for their upcountry integrity and natural power.

| CATEGORY | COST* |
|---|---|
| $$$$ | over €18 |
| $$$ | €13–€18 |
| $$ | €8–€13 |
| $ | under €8 |

*per person for a main course at dinner

### Fiestas

The February **Carnival** in Cádiz is one of the best in the land. Crowds also flock to the revelries of Jerez's May **Feria del Caballo** (Horse Fair) and September **harvest festival**. Jerez's April **flamenco festival** is a chance to see the top stars in this uniquely Andalusian musical genre performing for each other, not for tourists. If you prefer to travel crowd-free, avoid these dates, but if you're ready to party, don't miss them.

Jerez and Cádiz have major **Semana Santa** (Holy Week) processions. **Corpus Christi** (the second Thursday after Whitsunday) is celebrated with processions in Cádiz and Jerez; the celebration in the mountain town of Zahara de la Sierra is one of the most beautiful. In September, all wine-producing towns in the province of Cádiz celebrate the **Fiesta de la Vendimia** (Grape Harvest Festival). Jerez's **Fiesta de Otoño** (Autumn Festival) is particularly spectacular. Cádiz commemorates its patron, the **Virgen del Rosario** (Virgin of the Rosary), in October.

### Flamenco

Jerez and Seville are widely acknowledged to be Spain's flamenco headquarters. Jerez's Centro Andaluz de Flamenco is dedicated to the history of this quintessentially Andalusian art form. Jerez's annual spring flamenco festival offers a chance to see the best of the genre in song, dance, and guitar, whereas the *tablaos* (flamenco nightspots) and *peñas* (flamenco clubs) offer different kinds and qualities of flamenco.

## Golf

Cádiz has a series of golf courses widely considered to be among the world's best, especially for year-round play. The Valderrama course at Sotogrande is officially ranked No. 1 in Europe, and the Sotogrande and San Roque courses are not far behind. Spain's all-time top golf hero, Severiano Ballesteros, designed the course at Chiclana de la Frontera, and Jerez's Montecastillo course hosted the Volvo Masters in 1997. El Puerto de Santa María's seaside Vista Hermosa course is another favorite, and Rota's Costa Ballena (Whale Coast) course was designed by the heir to Severiano's crown, José María Olazabal.

## Horses

Jerez's purebred Carthusian horses are shown off in the annual Feria del Caballo, in May. These handsome animals perform every Thursday throughout the year at Jerez's Royal Andalusian School of Equestrian Art. Horse races are held on the beach in Sanlúcar de Barrameda on two weekends in August (the dates depend on the tides), a tradition dating back to 1845.

## Lodging

Charming hotels are found throughout Cádiz, though maximum luxury (and maximum cost) establishments are rare. Arcos de la Frontera has a spectacular parador, among other fine lodging options. The Parador Hotel Atlántico, in Cádiz, is a modern installation with terrific views. You can also stay at a converted monastery in Puerto de Santa María, or on a private luxury ranch near Arcos de la Frontera.

If you want to see Jerez's Horse Fair or Harvest Festival while living grandly, you should book early—four to eight months in advance. To see Cádiz during Carnival, try to reserve at least a month ahead. All hotel prices rise steeply—by at least half—during the May and September *ferias* in Jerez.

| CATEGORY | COST |
|---|---|
| **$$$$** | over €140 |
| **$$$** | €100–€140 |
| **$$** | €60–€100 |
| **$** | under €60 |

*All prices are for a standard double room, excluding tax.*

## Exploring Cádiz Province

The Province of Cádiz is composed of six very different routes, interests, and worlds. For food and wine, the triangle with points at Cádiz, Jerez de la Frontera, and Sanlúcar de Barrameda encompasses Andalusia's sherry country, as well as, along the way, some of the finest tapas masters anywhere in Spain. A pueblos blancos itinerary takes you through the Sierra de Grazalema nature preserve as well as the upland architecture and landscapes. The coastal route along the Costa de la Luz from Cádiz to Tarifa offers pristine strands, Roman ruins, and windsurfing madness. The inland route midway between the coast and the mountains traverses pastures and ranges where fighting bulls are bred. Cádiz's equine world revolves around Jerez's Real Escuela Andaluza del Arte Ecuestre and the August horse races at Sanlúcar de Barrameda. Last but not least, the golf courses perched on the province's easternmost edge are among the best in the world, with those around Jerez, Chiclana de la Frontera, and Puerto de Santa María not far behind.

## Great Itineraries

The 3,000-year old city of Cádiz, sherry country, and the Sierra de Grazalema's whitewashed villages are the essence of the province. Golf courses and beaches, although excellent, are more generic. Gibraltar and Algeciras are of only moderate interest, and Tarifa is Andalusia's Big Sur with a flamenco timbre.

IF YOU HAVE 3 DAYS

Starting at **Cádiz** ①–⑭, explore the city for at least a half day and drive (or take the ferry) to 🗷 **Puerto de Santa María** ⑮ for the evening. Spend Day 2 exploring **Jerez de la Frontera** ⑯, a sherry bodega, and, if you can find time, the Real Escuela Andaluza del Arte Ecuestre, before catching the sunset at 🗷 **Sanlúcar de Barrameda** ⑰ from the Bajo de Guía beach over jumbo shrimp and Manzanilla. After an evening carouse through the Plaza del Cabildo and a night in Sanlúcar, drive up to 🗷 **Arcos de la Frontera** ⑱ on the third day for a walk around town and a night in a hotel room perched on the cliffs over the Guadalete River.

IF YOU HAVE 5 DAYS

After completing the three-day tour continue east into the Sierra de Grazalema and visit 🗷 **Grazalema** ⑲, **Ubrique** ⑳, and **Zahara de la Sierra** ㉑ with a night in the mountains. On Day 5 drive down through the farmlands and pastures of the provincial heartland, passing through Alcalá de los Gazules and Medina Sidonia on your way to the Costa de la Luz and **Chiclana de la Frontera** ㉒ or **Tarifa** ㉓. With more time, visit **Gibraltar** ㉕–㊳, or the golf paradise at **San Roque** ㉔ and Sotogrande.

## When to Tour Cádiz

May and October are the best times to visit Cádiz, with April and November close on their heels. Moderate temperatures, off-season tranquility, and general ease of movement are the main advantages of this recommended timetable.

# CÁDIZ AND THE SHERRY TRIANGLE

A trip through Cádiz is a trip back in time. Winding roads take you through scenes ranging from flat and barren plains to seemingly endless vineyards, and the rolling countryside is carpeted with blindingly white soil known as *albariza*—unique to this area, and the secret to the grapes used in sherry. In Jerez, you can taste sherry or admire the purebred Carthusian horses at the Real Escuela Andaluza de Arte Ecuestre. Finally, in the city of Cádiz, absorb about 3,000 years of history in this oldest of Western metropolises.

## Cádiz

*32 km (20 mi) southwest of Jerez, 149 km (93 mi) southwest of Seville.*

Spaniards flock here in February for Cádiz's unique Carnival celebration, but few foreigners have discovered the real charm of this city. Surrounded by the Atlantic Ocean on three sides, Cádiz was founded as Gadir by Phoenician traders in 1100 BC. Hannibal lived here for a time, and this is where Julius Caesar first held public office. Roman poet and chronicler Martial (40–104) praised the "fiery eroticism of the gaditana women with their upraised arms" dancing what must have been a precursor of flamenco, and the production of *garum*, a salty, black olive and fish paste was a staple export to Rome.

After centuries of decline under Moorish rule, Cádiz regained its commercial importance after the discovery of the Americas. Columbus set out from here on his second voyage, and Cádiz later became the home base of the Spanish fleet, competing fiercely with Seville. When the

**Cádiz Province**

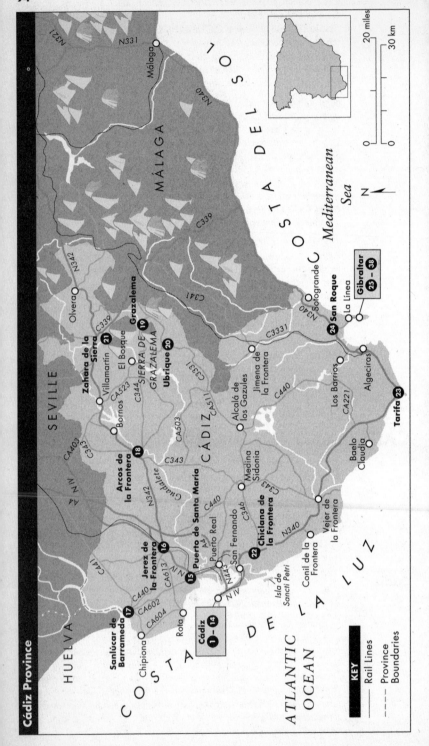

KEY

— Rail Lines
- - - Province Boundaries

Guadalquivir silted up in the 18th century, Cádiz monopolized New World trade and became the wealthiest port in Western Europe. Most of its buildings date from this period, including the cathedral, which was built in part with gold and silver from the New World. This period gave Cádiz its era of great cultural flourishing, when the city orchestra attracted the best musicians in Europe and Spain's first progressive middle class produced the liberal Constitution of 1812, unwittingly setting the stage for nearly two centuries of bloody strife between liberals and conservatives, a conflict that was not truly resolved until the death of Franco in 1975.

Often compared, not too surprisingly, in form and feel to Havana, the old city is a cluster of smallish houses in dazzling whites and ocher hues that would become typical of the colonial architecture of New World. Cadíz's narrow streets open onto small, charming squares. The golden cupola of the cathedral looms above ranks of low buildings, and the whole place has a comfortable, at once timeless and ephemeral atmosphere, as if sailors and fishermen had set up temporary landlocked quarters here that just happened to endure for 3,000 years. In a few hours' walk around the headlands, you'll see the entire old town and pass through lush and leafy parks with centenary ficus trees, shady corners, and fine views out over the bay.

## A Good Walk

Begin in the **Plaza de Mina** ①, a large square lined with palm trees and plenty of benches. The ornamental facade of the Colegio de Arquitectos (College of Architects) on the western side is especially beautiful. In the northwestern corner of the square is the tourist office. On the east side, you'll find the **Museo de Cádiz** ② with works by Murillo and Alonso Cano, and the *Four Evangelists* and a set of saints by Zurbarán. **Plaza de San Francisco** ③, just east, is a pretty square filled with orange trees and elegant street lamps and surrounded by Cádiz's signature snowy white and rich yellow houses. Two blocks farther east, next to the Iglesia del Rosario, is the **Oratorio de la Santa Cueva** ④. Backtrack to Plaza de Mina and head down Calle Zorilla to the **Oratorio de San Felipe Neri** ⑤, where Spain's first liberal constitution was declared in 1812. Next door, the small but pleasant **Museo Histórico Municipal** ⑥ has a 19th-century mural depicting the establishment of the constitution. Four blocks west is the Plaza Manuel de Falla, overlooked by a neo-Mudéjar redbrick building, the **Gran Teatro Manuel de Falla** ⑦. Taking Calle Sacramento back toward the city center, you'll come to **Torre Tavira** ⑧. A block and a half south is the **Hospital de Mujeres** ⑨, which is just west of the Mercado Central and **Plaza de Topete** ⑩. A four-minute walk through Calle de la Compañia opens out under the gold dome and neoclassical facade of the **Catedral de Cádiz** ⑪, begun in 1722 when the city was at the height of its power. Next door is the Iglesia de Santa Cruz, next to the remains of a 1st-century BC **Teatro Romano** ⑫ discovered by chance in 1982. The impressive **ayuntamiento** ⑬ overlooks the Plaza San Juan de Diós, one of Cádiz's liveliest hubs. A five-minute walk east brings you to the **Cárcel Real** ⑭, with its ornate 18th-century baroque facade.

TIMING

Not counting stops for tapas, coffee, meals, and museums, this could be a four-hour walk.

## Sights to See

⑬ **Ayuntamiento** (Town Hall). Overlooking Plaza San Juan de Diós, this is one of Cádiz's liveliest nerve centers. Built in two parts, in 1799 and 1861, in late neoclassical and 19th-century belle epoque splendor, the building is impressively illuminated at night. The rough and tumble

**96**

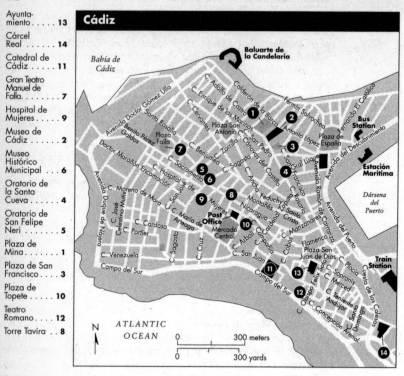

Cádiz

Barrio del Pópulo, Cádiz's medieval nucleus, spreads out in all its
seedy pungency around this formal explosion of elegance. ⊠ *Plaza San
Juan de Dios 11,* ☎ *956/241001.* ☉ *Group visits only by prior arrangement.*

**14** **Cárcel Real** (Royal Jail). A short walk east of Plaza San Juan de Dios,
this former prison's best feature is its richly ornamented baroque facade. Now the municipal courtroom building, the jailhouse is set into
the medieval walls that defended the narrow neck connecting Cádiz
to the mainland. ⊠ *C. Concepción Arenal, s/n.*

**11** **Catedral de Cádiz.** Begun in 1722 when the city was at the height of
its power, the Cádiz cathedral is one of Andalusia's finest baroque structures (neoclassical elements notwithstanding). The golden ceramic
**cupola** shimmers richly across Playa Victoria and is one of Cádiz's most
striking landmarks. The neoclassical facade faces northeast over the
Plaza de la Catedral, though the baroque vaulting within is more representative of the reigning sensibility of the cathedral and the city itself. Cádiz-born composer Manuel de Falla (1876–1946) is buried in
the **crypt.** The cathedral **museum,** on Calle Acero, overflows with
gold, silver, and precious jewels from the New World; one of its priceless possessions is Enrique de Arfe's processional cross, which is carried in the annual Corpus Christi parades. The cathedral is known as
the Catedral Nueva (New Cathedral) because it supplanted the original 13th-century structure next door, which was destroyed by the
British in 1592, later rebuilt and renamed **Iglesia de Santa Cruz** when
the Catedral Nueva was constructed. ⊠ *Plaza de la Catedral,* ☎ *956/
259812 for museum.* ☒ *Museum €3.* ☉ *Cathedral and museum
Tues.–Fri. 10–2, 4:30–7:30, Sat. 10–1; cathedral mass Sun. noon.*

❼ **Gran Teatro Manuel de Falla.** The imposing neo-Mudéjar redbrick building four blocks west of Santa Inés in Plaza Manuel de Falla is Cádiz's traditional theatrical venue. The classic interior is as impressive as the facade; try to attend a performance. ✉ *Plaza Manuel de Falla,* ☎ *956/ 220828.* ☉ *Tues.–Fri. 10–2, 4:30–7:30, Sat. 10–1.*

❾ **Hospital de Mujeres** (Women's Hospital). Once an 18th-century hospital for women, this handsome, rambling building is visited primarily for its elaborately decorated chapel. Built during Cádiz's 18th-century golden age, it has a profusion of baroque elements on the main altar and Goya's *Éxtasis de San Francisco,* in which the saint is portrayed dressed in a flowing cloak in the midst of an ecstatic mystical vision. ✉ *C. Hospital de Mujeres s/n,* ☎ *956/808187.* ☜ €*1.* ☉ *Weekdays 10–1:30.*

❷ **Museo de Cádiz** (Provincial Museum). Featured works in the collection here are by Murillo and Alonso Cano, along with the *Four Evangelists* and the series of saints by Zurbarán. The saints have much in common with his masterpieces at Guadalupe, in Extremadura. The archaeological section contains Phoenician sarcophagi from the time of this ancient city's birth. ✉ *Plaza de Mina,* ☎ *956/212281.* ☜ €*1.80; EU citizens free.* ☉ *Tues. 2:30–8, Wed.–Sat. 9–8, Sun. 9–2.*

❻ **Museo Histórico Municipal.** The Municipal History Museum has a 19th-century mural depicting the establishment of the Constitution of 1812. Its real showpiece, however, is a fascinating 1779 ivory and mahogany model of Cádiz, which reproduces all of the city's streets and buildings in minute detail, looking, in fact, much as they do today. ✉ *Santa Inés 9,* ☎ *956/221788.* ☜ *Free.* ☉ *Tues.–Fri. 9–1 and 4–7 (5– 8 June–Sept.), weekends 9–1.*

❹ **Oratorio de la Santa Cueva.** Built in the late 18th century in the neoclassical style, this double chapel next to the Iglesia del Rosario has a lower section, the Santa Cueva (Holy Cave) or Capilla Baja (Lower Chapel), in a somber underground space, and an ornate ovaloid Capilla Alta (Upper Chapel). Three of the eight arched spaces in the Capilla Alta contain Goya frescoes: *The Miracle of the Loaves and Fishes, The Wedding Guest,* and *The Last Supper.* ✉ *C. Rosario 10,* ☎ *956/ 222262.* ☜ €*1.50.* ☉ *Tues.–Fri. 10–1, 4:30–7:30, weekends 10–1.*

❺ **Oratorio de San Felipe Neri.** One of Cádiz's best baroque churches, this was where Spain's first liberal (democratic) constitution was declared in 1812. The Cortes (Parliament) of Cádiz met here when the rest of Spain was subjected to the rule of Napoléon's brother, Joseph Bonaparte (more popularly known as Pepe Botella, for his love of the bottle). On the main altar is an *Immaculate Conception* by Murillo, the great Seville artist who in 1682 fell to his death from a scaffold while working on his *Mystic Marriage of St. Catherine* in Cádiz's Chapel of Santa Catalina. ✉ *Santa Inés 38,* ☎ *956/211612.* ☜ €*1.20.* ☉ *Mon.–Sat. 10–1.*

❶ **Plaza de Mina.** This large, leafy square with palm trees and plenty of benches is a hub of activity in the heart of Cádiz's historic center. On the square's western flank is the rich facade of the **Colegio de Arquitectos** (Architects' College). In the northwestern corner of the square is the tourist office. Calle Zorrilla, leading out past a series of popular taverns and restaurants to the Alameda and the sea wall looking across to El Puerto de Santa María, fills on Sunday and holidays for the midday aperitif, preprandial tapa, and Manzanilla, with crowds spilling congenially out into the street from one end to the other.

❸ **Plaza de San Francisco.** This pretty square, surrounded by typical Cádiz houses and populated with orange trees and ornate street lamps, is a lively evening hangout for *gaditanos* (Cádiz residents, from the Phoenician name, Gadir, for the city).

❿ **Plaza de Topete.** Next to the always exciting Mercado Central, Cádiz's central food supply point (and therefore most vital forum), this busy square is often called by its old name, Plaza de las Flores. Flower markets and birds in cages fill the square, which is well served by numerous cafés and outdoor terraces.

⓬ **Teatro Romano.** This remarkably well-preserved 2nd-century Roman theater was discovered while excavating an underground parking lot. The archaeological exhibit here brings to life Cádiz's three millennia of history, and paintings are also on temporary display. ⊠ *San Juan de Dios s/n,* ☎ *956/212281.* ▣ *Free.* ⊙ *Tues.–Sun. 11–1:30.*

❽ **Torre Tavira.** At 150 ft, this tower is the highest point in the old city, one of more than 100 such watchtowers used by Cádiz ship owners to spot their arriving fleets. The 18th-century palace below the tower is now Cádiz's music conservatory. A camera obscura reflects, via a convex lens, panoramic overviews of the city and its monuments. The last visit begins half an hour before closing time. ⊠ *Marqués del Real Tesoro 10,* ☎ *956/212910.* ▣ *€3.* ⊙ *Mid-June–mid-Sept., daily 10– 8; mid-Sept.–mid-June, daily 10–6.*

## Dining and Lodging

$$–$$$ ✕ **El Faro.** Gonzalo Córdoba's fishing-quarter restaurant deserves its
★       fame as the best restaurant in the province. Outside, it's one of many low white houses decorated with bright-blue flowerpots; the interior is warm and inviting, with half-tile walls, glass lanterns, oil paintings, and photos of old Cádiz. Seafood dominate the menu, but there are plenty of alternatives, such as *cebón al queso de cabrales* (filet mignon in blue-cheese sauce). ⊠ *San Félix 15,* ☎ *956/211068. AE, DC, MC, V.*

$$ ✕ **Casa Manteca.** Cádiz's most quintessentially Andalusian tavern is just down the street from El Faro restaurant and a little deeper into La Viña barrio (named for the vineyard that once grew here). *Chacina* (Iberian ham or sausage) served on waxed paper and Manzanilla (sherry from Sanlúcar de Barrameda) are standard fare at this low wooden counter that has served bullfighters and flamenco singers as well as dignitaries from around the world. ⊠ *Corralón de los Carros 66,* ☎ *956/213603. AE, DC, MC, V. No lunch Sun.*

$$ ✕ **La Perola & Cia.** This semisecret spot serves gourmet tapas and small dishes in ever-surprising and original ways. Owner and culinary ideologue Francisco Leal restores lost recipes discovered in Andalusian convents and Moroccan mountain villages, adding his own touches and contemporary nuances. ⊠ *Canovas del Castillo 34,* ☎ *956/211430. AE, DC, MC, V. Closed Sun. July–Aug.*

$–$$ ✕ **El Ventorrillo del Chato.** Standing on its own on the sandy isthmus
★     connecting Cádiz to the mainland, this former inn was founded in 1780 by a man ironically nicknamed "El Chato" (pug nose) for his prominent proboscis. Run by a scion of El Faro's Gonzalo Córdoba, the restaurant serves tasty regional specialties in charming Andalusian surroundings. Seafood is a specialty, but meat, stews, and rice dishes are also well represented on the menu, and the wine list is very good. ⊠ *Vía Augusta Julia (rte. N-IV) s/n,* ☎ *956/250025. AE, DC, MC, V. Closed Sun.*

$$$–$$$$ ▥ **Parador Atlántico.** Cádiz's modern parador commands a privileged position on the headland overlooking the bay, and is the only hotel in its class in the old part of Cádiz. The spacious indoor public rooms

have gleaming marble floors, and tables and chairs surround a fountain on the small patio. The cheerful, bright-green bar, decorated with ceramic tiles and bullfighting posters, is a popular meeting place for Cádiz society. Most rooms have small balconies facing the sea. ✉ *Duque de Nájera 9, 11002,* ☎ *956/226905,* FAX *956/214582,* WEB *www. parador.es. 143 rooms, 6 suites. Restaurant, pool, cable TV, sauna, gym, bar, Internet, free parking, some pets allowed. AE, DC, MC, V.*

$$$-$$$$ 🏨 **Playa Victoria.** This massive modern structure overlooking the spotless Playa Victoria has rooms with lovely views out over the Atlantic. Creature comforts are flawless here, and Cádiz's old quarter is just a 15-minute walk away. ✉ *Glorieta Ingeniero La Cierva 4, 11010,* ☎ *956/205100,* FAX *956/263300,* WEB *www.hpv.es. 184 rooms. Restaurant, pool, cable TV, gym, sauna, beach, bar, Internet, parking (fee). AE, DC, MC, V.*

$$ 🏨 **Francia y Paris.** The advantage here is the central location, on a pretty pedestrian square in the heart of the old town. The rather dull modern interior includes a vast lobby, a large sitting room, and a small bar and breakfast room. Guest rooms are simple; some have small balconies facing the square. ✉ *Plaza San Francisco 2, 11004,* ☎ *956/222348,* FAX *956/222431. 57 rooms. Cable TV, bar, Internet, meeting rooms. AE, DC, MC, V.*

### Nightlife and the Arts

The most popular spot for cultural events in Cádiz is the **Gran Teatro Manuel de Falla** (✉ Plaza Manuel de Falla, ☎ 956/220828). The tourist office has performance schedules.

### Shopping

Traditional Andalusian handicrafts such as ceramics and wicker are specialties here. Just off the Plaza de la Mina, **Belle Epoque** (✉ Antonio Lopez 2, ☎ 956/226810) is one of Cádiz's better—and more reasonably priced—antiques stores, specializing in furniture.

## Puerto de Santa María

⑮ *12 km (7 mi) southwest of Jerez, 17 km (11 mi) north of Cádiz.*

Source of the name of Columbus's caravel, this little fishing port on the northern shore of the Bay of Cádiz is a jumble of white houses with peeling facades and floor-length green grilles covering the doors and windows. The town is dominated by the Terry and Osborne sherry and brandy bodegas. Christopher Columbus lived in a house on the square that bears his name (Cristóbal Colón), and Washington Irving spent the autumn of 1828 at Calle Palacios 57. The town's chief monuments are its castle and bullring.

The *marisco* bars along the Ribera del Marisco (Seafood Shore) are Puerto de Santa María's current claim to fame. Casa Luis, Romerijo, La Guachi, and Paco Ceballos are among the most popular as well as Er Beti at Misericordia 7. If you want to really binge, the tourist office has a list of six tapa routes taking in 39 tapa bars, listing their specialties.

The **Castillo de San Marcos** was built in the 13th century on the site of a mosque. Created by Alfonso X, it was later home to the duke of Medinaceli. Among those who stayed here were Christopher Columbus (who tried unsuccessfully to persuade the duke to finance his voyage west) and Juan de la Cosa, who, within these walls, drew up the first map ever to include the New World. The red lettering on the walls is a 19th-century addition. ✉ *Plaza del Castillo,* ☎ *956/851751.* 🏛 *€3, Tues. free.* ☉ *Tues., Thurs., and Sat. 10–2.*

The neo-Mudéjar **Plaza de Toros,** one of the most attractive bullrings in Andalusia, was built in 1880 thanks to a donation from the wine maker Thomas Osborne. It originally had seating for exactly 12,816 people, the population of Puerto at that time. ⊠ *Los Moros.* ☜ *Free.* ⏱ *Apr.–Oct., Thurs.–Tues. 11–1:30 and 6–7:30; Nov.–Mar., Thurs.–Tues. 11–1:30 and 5:30–7. Closed day prior to, day of, and day after bullfights.*

## Dining and Lodging

$–$$$   ✕ **El Faro de El Puerto.** Set in a villa just outside town, the "Lighthouse in the Port" is run by the same family that established the classic El Faro in Cádiz. Like the original, it serves excellent fish dishes, but you can also browse the meat department for such delicacies as veal rolls filled with foie gras in a sweet sherry sauce. ⊠ *Carretera Fuenterabia–Rota, Km 0.5,* ☎ *956/858003 or 956/870952. AE, DC, MC, V. No dinner Sun.*

$–$$   ✕ **Casa Flores.** A bit more upmarket than the neighboring Ribera del Marisco haunts, Flores serves the same fresh seafood. You approach the two dining rooms, decorated with tiles and wood paneling, through a long bar hung with hams. Specialties include *filete de urta al camarón* (fillet of bream in shrimp sauce) and *fritos de la bahía* (assorted fried fish from the Bay of Cádiz). ⊠ *Ribera del Río 9,* ☎ *956/543512. AE, DC, MC, V.*

$–$$   ✕ **Los Portales.** A Ribera del Marisco favorite, this comfortable dining room is decorated with a marine motif. At the large, very popular bar, you can sample such unusual sea creatures as *ortiguillas* (fried sea anemones, a local favorite) plus the more standard fish and shellfish, grilled or fried. ⊠ *Ribera del Río 13,* ☎ *956/542116. AE, DC, MC, V.*

$$$$   🏨 **Monasterio de San Miguel.** Dating from 1733, this onetime monastery
★    is in the heart of town a few blocks from the harbor. There's nothing spartan about the former cells; they're now air-conditioned rooms with all the trappings, though you might need a map just to find yours along the interminable corridors. The restaurant is in a large, vaulted hall, the baroque church is now a concert hall, and the cloister's gardens provide a peaceful refuge. Beamed ceilings, polished marble floors, and huge brass lamps elegantly enhance the 18th-century feel. ⊠ *Larga 27, 11500,* ☎ *956/540440,* FAX *956/542604,* WEB *www.jale. com/monasterio. 140 rooms, 10 suites. Restaurant, cable TV, pool, paddle tennis, squash, bar, Internet, meeting rooms, parking (fee). AE, DC, MC, V.*

## Nightlife

The **Casino Bahía de Cádiz,** on the road between Jerez and Puerto de Santa María, is the only casino in this part of Andalusia. You can play the usual games, and there's a restaurant. You must present your passport to enter. On the weekend there's a disco, and in summer there are live shows. ⊠ *N-IV, Km 649,* ☎ *956/871042.* ☜ *€3; free for first-time visitors, also free entry vouchers at tourist office.* ⏱ *Sun.–Wed. 5 PM–3 AM, Thurs. 5 PM–4 AM, weekends and daily in Aug. 5 PM–6 AM.*

# Jerez de la Frontera

★ ⑯   *35 km (21 mi) northeast of Cádiz; 97 km (60 mi) south of Seville.*

World sherry headquarters, Jerez is surrounded by sprawling vineyards growing in rich limestone soil and filled with Palomino grapes that have funded a host of churches and noble mansions. Names such as González Byass, Domecq, Harvey, and Sandeman are inextricably linked with Jerez. The word *sherry,* first used in Great Britain in 1608, is actually an English corruption of the town's old Moorish name, Xeres. Both sherry and horses have been central to Jerez's Anglo-Spanish aristocracy ever since their Catholic ancestors came here from England two or three centuries ago.

At any given time, more than half a million barrels of sherry are maturing in Jerez's vast aboveground wine cellars. If you visit a bodega (winery), your guide will explain the *solera* method of blending old wine with new (the term is from the word *suelo* for ground or floor, referring to the blending of the younger and older vintages into the lower barrels), and the importance of the *flor* (a sort of yeast that forms on the surface of the wine as it ages) in determining the kind of sherry. Most bodegas welcome visitors, but it's always advisable to phone ahead for an appointment, if only to make sure you join a group that speaks your language. Cellars usually charge an admission fee of €3–€6, and some close for the month of August. Tours last between 40 minutes and an hour and usually start with an audiovisual program or short film about sherry and the history of that particular winery. You'll then tour the aging cellars, with their endless rows of casks. (You won't see the actual fermenting and bottling, which take place in more modern, less romantic plants outside town.) Finally, you'll be invited to sample generous amounts of pale, dry fino; nutty *amontillado;* or rich, deep *oloroso*—and, of course, to purchase a few bottles at interesting prices in the winery shop.

For the other attractions, an hour's stroll around the city center is all you'll need. May and September are the most exciting times to visit Jerez, as their spectacular fiestas transform the town. For the Feria del Caballo (Horse Fair), in early May, carriages and riders fill the streets, and purebreds from the School of Equestrian Art compete in races and dressage displays. September brings the Fiesta de Otoño (Autumn Festival), when the first of the grape harvest is blessed on the steps of the cathedral.

For visits to bodegas in the "wine triangle" of Jerez, El Puerto, and Sanlúcar, the listings here are the main options. If you have time for only one bodega, tour the prestigious **González Byass** (☎ 956/357000), home of the famous Tío Pepe. This tour is well organized and includes La Concha, an open-air aging cellar designed by Gustave Eiffel. Jerez's oldest bodega is **Domecq** (⊠ San Ildefonso 3, ☎ 956/151500), founded in 1730. Aside from sherry, Domecq makes the world's best-selling brandy, Fundador. Sanlúcar de Barrameda's **Barbadillo** (⊠ Luis de Eguilaz 11, ☎ 956/360894) is the number one brewery for Manzanilla, the supreme sherrylike product of the province. Both the Cava del Toro and the high-ceilinged La Arboledilla, known as "the cathedral of Manzanilla," are cool and fragrant visits. Puerto de Santa María's **Osborne** (⊠ Fernán Caballero 3, ☎ 956/855211) offers a memorable tour of their winery. Jerez's **John Harvey** (⊠ Arcos s/n, ☎ 956/346004) is the source of Harvey's Bristol Cream. **Sandeman** (⊠ Pizarro 10, ☎ 956/151700) is known for its man-in-a-cape logo.

Housed in a 19th-century bodega, the **Museo de Vino,** a sherry museum, is due to open in Jerez by spring of 2003. The museum will include a multimedia show and exhibits, a bar, a restaurant, and a shop. ⊠ *Cervantes 3, La Atalaya,* ☎ *956/182100.*

The 12th-century **Alcázar** was once the residence of the caliph of Seville. Its small, octagonal **mosque,** with an outstanding cupola, and **baths** were built for the Moorish governor's private use. The baths are among the best-preserved in Spain and have three sections: the *sala fria* (cold room), the larger *sala templada* (warm room), and the *sala caliente* (hot room), for steam baths. In the midst of it all is the 17th-

## Close-Up

# FINO OR MANZANILLA?

I N CÁDIZ, the rivalry between dry sherry (fino) and Manzanilla is serious. Both are made from the standard palomino grape that grows in the chalky white soil of northwest Cádiz; Manzanilla comes from the vineyards of Sanlúcar de Barrameda, whereas sherry comes from Jerez (from which it got its name). The sherry *denominación de origen* (with guarantee of geographical exclusivity and certificate of origin) includes El Puerto de Santa María, Chiclana de la Frontera, Puerto Real, Rota, Chipiona, and Trebujena. Manzanilla has a slightly tangy, salty taste from the sea air of the vineyards and bodegas of Sanlúcar. Traditionally believed to taste better on Bajo de Guía beach than in upper Sanlúcar, pure Manzanilla travels poorly. Because its bodegas are closer to sea level than those of Jerez, Manzanilla develops and retains a thicker layer of yeast, known as the *flor*, containing abundant anti-hangover vitamin B. Taken well chilled, Manzanilla is generally the beverage of choice to accompany tapas in Andalusia. A visit to a sherry bodega will reveal the *solera* system used to mix and age sherries in American oak barrels, always taking the sherry to be bottled from the lower barrel, or solera, so-called because it's at floor (*suelo*) level. The *cata*, or tasting ritual, features the *venencia*, a slender, long-handled dipper used to extract sherry from the barrel and pour a thin amber stream from overhead into a sherry glass held at waist level.

century **Palacio de Villavicencio,** built on the site of the original Moorish palace. A camera obscura, a lens-and-mirrors device that projects the outdoors onto a large indoor screen, offers a 360-degree view of Jerez and its principal monuments from the palace's highest tower—a perfect introduction to the town. If you have a mobile phone, dial 650/800100 and you can access an English language audio guide to the Alcázar that costs about €0.30 per minute. ⊠ *Alameda Vieja,* ☎ *956/319798.* ☜ *€1.29; €3.25 including camera obscura.* ☉ *Mid-Sept.–Apr., daily 10–6; May–mid-Sept., daily 10–8.*

NEED A
BREAK?
Faustino Rodríguez and his family serve a total of 50 different tapas, *raciones* (small portions), and other morsels near the Alcázar at **Bar Juanito** (⊠ Pescadería Vieja 8 and 10, ☎ 956/334838). This excellent and ancient bar with a pretty patio is a winner of the national Tapas Prize.

Across from the Alcázar and around the corner from the González Byass winery, the **cathedral** (⊠ Plaza del Arroyo), which is open for Mass only, has an octagonal cupola and a separate bell tower.

One block from the Plaza del Arenal, near the Alcázar, **San Miguel** is the only church in Jerez that opens during the day for sightseers. Built over the 15th and 16th centuries, the interior is an interesting illustration of the evolution of Gothic architecture, with various styles mixed into the design. ⊠ *Plaza de San Miguel,* ☎ *956/343347.* ☜ *€1.80.* ☉ *Tues.–Fri. 10:30–1:30, weekends for Mass only.*

On the **Plaza de la Asunción,** one of Jerez's most intimate squares, you'll find the Mudéjar church of **San Dionisio** and the ornate **cabildo municipal** (city hall), whose lovely plateresque facade dates from 1575.

The unusual and interesting **Museo de los Relojes** is a museum devoted entirely to clocks, with 300 timepieces on display. ⊠ *C. Cervantes 3,* ☎ *956/182100.* ☒ *€4.50.* ⊘ *Tues.–Sat. 10–2 and 5–7, Sun. 10–2. Closed Jan. 10–31.*

The **Centro Andaluz de Flamenco** (Flamenco Center of Andalusia) is a modern facility, complete with library and multimedia show. The location is in the Iglesia de Santiago area. Gypsies may not have invented flamenco, but there is little debate that they are now most identified with this musical genre, and Gypsies have lived in this part of town since the 17th century, making it famous for its flamenco musical tradition. For an overview of this quintessentially Andalusian musical art form, this is a good place to start. ⊠ *Palacio Pemartín, Plaza San Juan 1,* ☎ *956/321127,* WEB *www.caf.cica.es.* ☒ *Free.* ⊘ *Weekdays 9–2.*

Diving into the maze of streets that form the scruffy San Mateo neighborhood east of the town center, you'll come to the **Museo Arqueológico,** one of Andalusia's best archaeological museums. The collection is strongest on the pre-Roman period, and the neatly displayed artifacts are enhanced by photographs and information on archaeological digs. The star item, discovered near Jerez, is a Greek helmet dating from the 7th century BC. ⊠ *Plaza del Mercado s/n,* ☎ *956/341350,* WEB *www. ctv.es/users/jerezmuseoarq/home.htm.* ☒ *€2.* ⊘ *Sept.–mid-June, Tues.– Fri. 10–2 and 4–7, weekends 10–2:30; mid-June–Aug., Tues.–Sun. 10–2:30.*

★ ⛭ The **Real Escuela Andaluza del Arte Ecuestre** (Royal Andalusian School of Equestrian Art) operates on the grounds of the Recreo de las Cadenas, a splendid 19th-century palace. This prestigious school was masterminded by Alvaro Domecq in the 1970s. Every Thursday the Cartujana horses—a breed created from a cross between the native Andalusian workhorse and the Arabian—and skilled riders in 18th-century costume demonstrate intricate dressage techniques and jumping in the spectacular show "Cómo Bailan los Caballos Andaluces" (roughly, "The Dancing Horses of Andalusia"). Reservations are essential. Admission price depends on how close to the action you sit; the first two rows are the priciest. ⊠ *Avda. Duque de Abrantes s/n,* ☎ *956/319635,* WEB *www.realescuela.org.* ☒ *€18, €15, or €12.* ⊘ *Nov.–Feb., Thurs. noon; Mar.–Oct., Tues. and Thurs. noon; July 15– Oct. 31, Tues., Thurs., and Fri. noon; during March fair 10:30 nightly.*

At other times during the week, you can visit the stables and tack room, watch the horses being schooled, and witness **rehearsals** for the show. ☒ *€6.* ⊘ *Mon. and Wed. 11–1.*

Just outside Jerez de la Frontera is **Yeguada de la Cartuja,** the largest state-run stud farm in Spain for Carthusian horses. In the 15th century, a Carthusian monastery on this site started the breed for which Jerez and the rest of Spain are now famous. Every Saturday at 11 AM you can take a full tour and see a show. ⊠ *Finca Fuente El Suero, Ctra. Medina–El Portal Km 6.5,* ☎ *956/162809,* WEB *www.yeguadacartuja. com.* ☒ *€9.02.* ⊘ *Sat. 11 AM.*

## Dining and Lodging

$$–$$$ ✕ **El Bosque.** Set in a pleasant modern villa decorated with contemporary paintings of bullfighting themes, El Bosque is one of the most stylish dining spots in town. Most of the tables are round (a sure sign of civilization) and seat four; the smaller of the two dining rooms has picture windows overlooking a park. The food is contemporary Spanish. *Sopa de galeras* (soup of mantis shrimp) makes a rich appetizer; follow up with *confit de pato de laguna* (leg of wild duck) or *perdiz estofado con castañas* (stewed partridge with chestnuts). ⊠ *Avda. Al-*

*calde Alvaro Domecq 26,* ☎ *956/307030. AE, DC, MC, V. Closed Sun. No dinner Aug.*

**$$–$$$** ✕ **Gaitán.** Within walking distance of the riding school, this restaurant has white walls and brick arches decorated with colorful ceramic plates and photos of famous guests. It's crowded with businesspeople at lunchtime. The menu is Andalusian, with a few Basque dishes thrown in. *Setas* (wild mushrooms) make a delicious starter in season; follow them with *cordero asado* (roast lamb) in a sauce of honey and Jerez brandy. ⊠ *Gaitán 3,* ☎ *956/345859. AE, DC, MC, V. No dinner Sun.*

**$$–$$$** ✕ **La Posada.** This place is strange in that its two small dining rooms, both enlivened by bullfight-red tablecloths, are on opposite sides of the street. Waiters dash back and forth to attend to their customers. The menu strikes another unusual note: it offers only grilled meat and grilled fish, according to what's best at the market, plus salad. Each course can be ordered in a full or half portion. ⊠ *Arboledilla 1 and 2,* ☎ *956/348165 or 607/515797. AE, MC, V. Closed Sun. and Aug. No dinner Sat.*

**$–$$** ✕ **Venta Antonio.** Crowds come to this roadside inn from far and wide to dine on superb, fresh seafood cooked in top-quality olive oil. You enter through the busy bar, where fresh fish bask and lobsters await their demise in a tank. Try the specialties of the Bay of Cádiz, such as *sopa de mariscos* (shellfish soup) followed by *bogavantes de Sanlúcar* (succulent local lobster). ⊠ *Carretera de Jerez–Sanlúcar, Km 5,* ☎ *956/140535. AE, DC, MC, V.*

**$** ✕ **La Mesa Redonda.** Owner José Antonio Valdespino spent years re-
★ searching the classic recipes once served in aristocratic Jerez homes, and now his son José presents them in this small, friendly restaurant off Avenida Alvaro Domecq, around the corner from the Hotel Avenida Jerez. It feels like a family dining room: the eight tables are surrounded by shelves lined with cookbooks. (The round table at one end of the room gives the restaurant its name.) The menu changes constantly; your best bet is to take the advice of the chef's mother, Margarita, who also has an encyclopedic knowledge of Spanish wines. ⊠ *Manuel de la Quintana 3,* ☎ *956/340069. AE, DC, MC, V. Closed Sun. and mid-June–mid-Aug.*

**$** ✕ **Tendido 6.** The name gives you this restaurant's location: near the bullring, opposite Gate 6. The two dining rooms, the larger of which occupies a covered patio, are enlivened with bright-red tablecloths and decorated with bullfight posters. The menu has all the Spanish standbys: *jamón serrano* (cured ham), *gambas al ajillo* (garlic shrimp), and *tarta de almendra* (almond tart). ⊠ *Circo 10,* ☎ *956/344835. AE, DC, MC, V. Closed Sun.*

**$$$$** ▣ **Montecastillo Hotel and Golf Resort.** Situated outside Jerez near the racetrack, the sprawling, modern Montecastillo adjoins a golf course designed by Jack Nicklaus. The spacious common areas have marble floors. Rooms are cheerfully decorated, with off-white walls, bright floral bedspreads, and rustic clay tiles. Ask for a room with a terrace overlooking the golf course. ⊠ *Carretera de Arcos, Km 9, 11406,* ☎ *956/151200,* FAX *956/151209,* WEB *www.montecastillo.com. 119 rooms, 2 suites, 20 villas. Restaurant, 18-hole golf course, 2 pools (1 indoor), health club, sauna, spa, soccer, Internet. AE, DC, MC, V.*

**$$$** ▣ **Jerez.** This luxury hotel occupies a low, white, three-story building in the residential neighborhood north of town. The bar and the elegant restaurant, El Cartujano, overlook the sun terrace, large pool, and big, leafy garden. Public rooms get lots of natural light through picture windows. The best guest rooms overlook the pool and garden; those in back face the tennis courts and parking lot. ⊠ *Avda. Alvaro Domecq 35, 11405,* ☎ *956/300600,* FAX *956/305001,* WEB *www.*

*jerezhotel.com. 129 rooms. Restaurant, 2 tennis courts, 2 pools (1 indoor), gym, hair salon, jacuzzi, massage, sauna, bar, Internet, free parking. AE, DC, MC, V.*

**$$$** ☷ **Royal Sherry Park.** Set back from the road in an unusually large,
★ tree-filled garden, the modern Royal Sherry Park is designed around
several patios filled with exotic foliage. The sunny hallways are hung
with contemporary paintings. Rooms are bright and airy, and most have
balconies overlooking the garden. ⊠ *Avda. Alvaro Domecq 11 Bis,
11405,* ☎ *956/317614,* FAX *956/311300,* WEB *www.sherryparkhotel.com.
173 rooms. Restaurant, coffee shop, 2 pools (1 indoor), gym, sauna,
hair salon, bar, meeting room. AE, DC, MC, V.*

**$$** ☷ **NH Avenida Jerez.** Opposite the Royal Sherry Park, this modern hotel
has bright, sunny beige-and-blue rooms with hardwood floors. All rooms
have VCRs. Ask for one at the back; rooms in front are close to the
road and can be noisy, despite double glazing. Weekends bring discounts:
inquire when you book. ⊠ *Avda. Alvaro Domecq 10, 11405,* ☎ *956/
347411,* FAX *956/337296.* WEB *www.nh-hoteles.es. 95 rooms. Restaurant, coffee shop, bar. AE, DC, MC, V.*

**$–$$** ☷ **Ávila.** This friendly hostelry on a side street off Calle Arcos offers
affordable central lodgings. The rooms have basic furnishings and tile
floors; beds are European twin-size. A TV lounge and a small bar and
breakfast room adjoin the lobby. ⊠ *Ávila 3, 11401,* ☎ *956/334808,*
FAX *956/336807. 32 rooms. Bar. AE, DC, MC, V.*

## Spectator Sports

### AUTO RACING

Formula One Grand Prix races—along with the Spanish motorcycle
Gran Prix on the first weekend in May—are held at Jerez's racetrack,
the **Circuito Permanente de Velocidad** (⊠ Ctra. Arcos Km 10, ☎ 956/
151100, WEB www.circuitojerez.com). Call the track or check with the
tourist office for event information.

### BULLFIGHTING

Jerez's **bullring** is on Calle Circo, northeast of the city center. Tickets
are sold at the official ticket office on Calle Porvera, though only
about five bullfights are held each year, in May and October.

Six blocks from the bullring is the **Museo Restaurante Taurino,** a museum of bullfighting where admission includes a drink. ⊠ *Pozo del Olivar 6,* ☎ 956/323000. ⊡ €2.40. ⊙ *Weekdays 9–1.*

## Shopping

You can browse for wicker and ceramic items along Calle Corredera
and Calle Bodegas. **Duarte** (⊠ Lancería 15, ☎ 956/342751) is the best-
known saddle shop in this horse town, sending beautifully wrought
leather all over the world, including to the British royal family. It's worth
a visit; you can choose from all kinds of smaller but beautifully worked
leather items.

# Sanlúcar de Barrameda

★ ⓱ *24 km (15 mi) northwest of Jerez.*

Columbus sailed from here on his third voyage to the Americas, in 1498.
Twenty years later, Magellan steered his ships out of the same harbor
to begin his circumnavigation of the planet. Today this unspoiled fishing town is known primarily for its *langostinos* (giant shrimp) and Manzanilla, an exceptionally dry sherry. The most popular restaurants are
along the **Bajo de Guía** beach bordering the Guadalquivir. Here, too,
is the Fábrica de Hielo, which serves as a visitor center for **Doñana
National Park** in Huelva.

Boat trips can take you up the river, stopping at various points in the park; the *Real Fernando* makes a four-hour cruise, with bar and café, up the Guadalquivir to the Coto de Doñana. ⊠ *Bajo de Guí,* ☎ *956/ 363813.* ☎ *€14.* ⊙ *Cruise times: 10 AM Oct.–Dec. and Feb.; 10 AM and 4 PM in March; 10 AM and 5 PM June–Sept.*

**Los Cristóbal** is a riverboat service with a three-hour cruise, a café, and binoculars for hire. Call to check the timetable and prices. ⊠ *Avda. Bajo de Guía,* ☎ *956/960766.*

From the *puerto pesquero* (fishing port) of **Bonanza,** 4 km (2½ mi) up-river from Sanlúcar, there's a fine view of fishing boats and the pine trees of Doñana on the opposite bank. Sandy beaches extend along Sanlúcar's southern promontory to Chipiona, where the Roman general Scipio Africanus built a beacon tower.

### Dining and Lodging

**\$\$–\$\$\$**   ✕ **Bigote.** The Bajo de Guía is renowned for its seafood, and this colorful, informal fish restaurant sits right on the beach. The kitchen is known for its fried *acedias* (a type of small sole) and langostinos, which come from these very waters—if you want them any fresher, you'll have to catch them yourself. The seafood paella is also good. Reservations are essential in summer. ⊠ *Bajo de Guía,* ☎ *956/362696. AE, DC, MC, V. Closed Sun.*

**\$\$–\$\$\$**   ✕ **Mirador de Doñana.** A Bajo de Guía landmark, the Mirador de Doñana serves superfresh sole, shrimp, and *puntillas* (baby squid). The dining area overlooks the large bar, which is always busy. ⊠ *Bajo de Guía,* ☎ *956/364205. MC, V.*

**\$–\$\$**   ✕ **Casa Balbino.** After the sunset at Bajo de Guía beach, the serious
★   tapas and tippling begins in Sanlúcar's local party nerve center in the Plaza del Cabildo. Balbino is the best of these taverns—though the *patatas aliñá* (potatoes dressed in an olive oil vinaigrette) at Bar Barbiana are noteworthy as well. ⊠ *Plaza del Cabildo 14,* ☎ *956/362647. AE, DC, MC, V.*

**\$–\$\$**   🏠 **Posada de Palacio.** Across the street from the luxuriant gardens of the Palacio de los Infantes de Orleans—now the Sanlúcar town hall—this restored 18th-century palace houses a friendly family-run hotel, with rooms grouped around a cool patio adorned with potted plants. There is also a swimming pool. ⊠ *Caballeros 11, 11540,* ☎ *956/364840,* FAX *956/365060. 16 rooms. Restaurant, pool, some pets allowed; no a/c, no room TVs. AE, DC, MC, V.*

**\$**   🏠 **Los Helechos.** Named for the ferns *(los helechos)* that dominate the
★   patio and entryway, this breezy place with a lovely rooftop terrace has the distinct advantage of being out of earshot but within crawling distance of the Plaza del Cabildo. ⊠ *Plaza Madre de Dios 9, 11540,* ☎ *956/361349,* FAX *956/369650. 56 rooms. Restaurant, cable TV, bar, parking (fee). AE, DC, MC, V.*

# NORTHEASTERN CÁDIZ AND THE PUEBLOS BLANCOS

Cádiz's famous pueblos blancos (white villages) rank among Andalusia's most striking tours. Beginning at Arcos de la Frontera, the largest and most splendid of mountain villages, an exploration, including a probe up to Ubrique and a trip out to Zahara de la Sierra, is a pretty drive through rugged scenery and flower-covered, whitewashed clusters of low-roofed houses of unmistakable North African parentage.

Originally established in the mountains for defensive reasons during the centuries of border skirmishes between Moorish and Christian forces, these agricultural communities, some 21 towns in all, are surrounded by the Parque Natural de la Sierra de Grazalema in the north and, farther to the south, the Parque Natural de Los Alcornocales.

Along with the scenery, mountain cooking is one of the attractions of this upland exploration, with powerful dishes such as *cocido con tagarninas* (a soup or stew with sausage and vegetables, including wild asparaguslike *tagarninas*), *quemones* (a *salmorejo*, or coarse gazpacho with parsley, onion, and egg), a wide selection of mountain *chacina* (hams and sausages), and specialties such as *migas* (bread crumbs with garlic and ham).

## Arcos de la Frontera

★ **⓲** *31 km (19 mi) east of Jerez.*

With its narrow and steep cobblestone streets, whitewashed houses, and finely crafted wrought-iron window grilles, Arcos is the quintessence of the Andalusian pueblo blanco. Make your way to the main square, the **Plaza de España,** the highest point in the village: one side of the square is open, and a balcony at the edge of the cliff offers views of the Guadalete valley. On the opposite end is the church of **Santa María,** a fascinating blend of architectural styles: Romanesque, Gothic, and Mudéjar, with a plateresque doorway, a Renaissance *retablo,* and a 17th-century baroque choir. The **ayuntamiento** stands at the foot of the old castle walls on the northern side of the square; across from here is the **Casa del Corregidor,** onetime residence of the governor and now a parador.

### Dining and Lodging

$$–$$$ ✕📷 **Parador Casa del Corregidor.** Perched over the cliffs at the upper
★ northeastern corner of Arcos, this spectacular parador has unbeatable views over the *vega,* the fertile flatlands rolling out across the valley of the Guadalete River. Public rooms include a popular bar and a panoramic restaurant that open onto the terrace, as well as an enclosed patio. The spacious rooms are furnished in traditional parador style, with dark Castilian furniture, *esparto* (grass) rugs, and abundant tiles. The best rooms are Nos. 15–18, which overlook the valley. The restaurant's local dishes include *berenjenas arcenses* (spicy eggplant with ham and chorizo), or you can ask for the *menu gastronómico,* featuring 10 different regional specialties. ✉ *Plaza del Cabildo, 11630,* ☎ *956/ 700500,* FAX *956/701116,* WEB *www.parador.es. 24 rooms. Restaurant, café, bar. AE, DC, MC, V.*

$$ 📷 **La Casa Grande.** Built in 1729, this extraordinary town house is as-
★ sembled around a lushly vegetated central patio and perched on the edge of the 400-ft cliff to which Arcos de la Frontera clings. Each room has been lovingly redesigned and restored by owners and consummate aesthetes Elena Posa and Ferran Grau. The artwork, the casually elegant design of the living quarters, and the inventive bathrooms are all a delight. The breakfast terrace allows you to look down on kestrels circling hundreds of feet above the riverbed below. The rooftop rooms *El Palomar* (the pigeon roost) and *El Soberao* (the attic) are the best. ✉ *Calle Maldonado 10 11630,* ☎ *956/703930,* FAX *956/703930,* WEB *www.lacasagrande.net. 4 rooms, 2 suites. Library. AE, DC, MC, V.*

$–$$ 📷 **Cortijo Fain.** This intimate resort hotel is in a 17th-century farmhouse on a ranch 3 km (2 mi) southeast of Arcos. The old *cortijo* (farm estate) is surrounded by olive groves and enclosed in high, white walls covered in bougainvillea. Aim for one of the two suites that have their own fireplaces. Reservations are essential. ✉ *Carretera de Algar, Km 3, 11630,* ☎ *956/231396,* FAX *956/231961. 3 rooms, 5 suites. Restau-*

*rant, pool, horseback riding, library, meeting room, some pets allowed; no room TVs. AE, DC, MC, V. Closed Jan.–mid-Feb.*

**$–$$** 🏨 **El Convento.** Perched on top of the cliff right behind the parador, this tiny hotel shares the parador's amazing view, though the rooms are much smaller, more simply furnished, and cheaper (about half the price, in fact). The building is a former convent. ⊠ *Calle Maldonado 2, 11630,* ☎ *956/702333,* 🆁🆇 *956/704128,* 🆆🅴🅱 *www.webdearcos. com/elconvento. 11 rooms. Cafeteria. AE, DC, MC, V.*

**$–$$** 🏨 **Marqués de Torresoto.** The hotel is in a restored 17th-century palace with a large courtyard, a mesón-style restaurant, and an ornate baroque chapel of its own. Each guest room is different; most are spacious. Those on the uppermost of the three floors are the nicest, and some look over the village rooftops, but you'll have to walk up, as there is no elevator, and rooms that face the street can be noisy. ⊠ *Marqués de Torresoto, 11630,* ☎ *956/700717,* 🆁🆇 *956/704205,* 🆆🅴🅱 *www.tugasa.com. 15 rooms. Restaurant, bar, some pets allowed. AE, DC, MC, V.*

## Sierra de Grazalema

*28 km (17 mi) northwest of Ronda, 23 km (14 mi) northeast of Ubrique.*

Protected as a nature park, the 323-square-km (200-square-mi) Sierra de Grazalema straddles the provinces of Málaga and Cádiz. These mountains trap the rain clouds that roll in from the Atlantic and thus have the distinction of being the wettest place in Spain, with an average annual rainfall of 88 inches. Thanks to the park's altitude and prevailing humidity, it's one of the last habitats for the rare fir tree *abies pinsapo* and is home to ibex, vultures, and numerous birds of prey. The pinsapo, known throughout Europe as the Spanish fir, is a living fossil from the Tertiary Era native to the Sierra de Grazalema and grows only at altitudes higher than 3,000 feet. Other Sierra de Grazalema vegetation includes cork oak, holm oak, live oak, and olive. Mountain goats, roe deer, foxes, otters, and weasels populate the forests, reservoirs, and riverbeds and Royal Eagle, kestrels, and various types of hawks patrol the skies. Parts of the park are restricted, accessible only on foot and accompanied by an official guide.

★ ⑲ Standing dramatically at the entrance to the Sierra de Grazalema, the village of **Grazalema** is the prettiest of the pueblos blancos. Its cobbled streets of houses with pink-and-ocher roofs wind up the hillside; red geraniums splash white walls; and black wrought-iron lanterns and grilles cling to the house fronts.

⑳ From Grazalema, the winding C3331 takes you to **Ubrique,** spread on the slopes of the Saltadero Mountains and known for its leather tanning and embossing industry. Look for the **Convento de los Capuchinos** (Capuchin Convent) and the churches of **San Pedro** and **Nuestra Señora de la O.**

An excursion from Grazalema takes you through the heart of the nature park: follow the A344 west through dramatic mountain scenery, past the village of Benamahoma, to **El Bosque,** home of the main park-information center and a trout stream.

㉑ **Zahara de la Sierra,** north of Grazalema, is a cluster of whitewashed houses in the shadow of a Moorish castle, and is especially known for its mid-June Corpus Christi celebration. For the event the streets of town are lushly paved with green grass, and balconies and facades of houses are lined with vegetation set up in the early morning. Just hours later, incense-burning processions file through the streets prior to an all-night celebration.

## Dining and Lodging

**$–$$** ✕ **Cádiz el Chico.** Serving Andalusian cooking with a highland flair, this little tavern and restaurant in the heart of the town of Grazalema is a solid choice for a meal in the most prototypical of the pueblos blancos. Try the partridge stew during the winter and the salmorejo in summer. ✉ *Plaza de España 8,* ☎ *956/132027. AE, DC, MC, V.*

**$** ✕🛏 **Casa de las Piedras.** Home mountain cooking based on local products and game is the rule here. Rooms are small but perfect for a highland hideout. ✉ *Las Piedras 32, 11610 Grazalema,* ☎ *956/132041,* 𝖥𝖠𝖷 *956/132238. 16 rooms. Restaurant, bar; no a/c, no room TVs. AE, DC, MC, V.*

**$–$$** 🛏 **Villa Turística de Grazalema.** Across the valley from the village of Grazalema, this complex consists of a hotel proper and a village of 38 semidetached apartments sleeping two to six. Most have splendid views of the village and the mountains beyond. It's popular with families, so the noise level can rise during school holidays; at other times, it offers excellent value and a fine base for exploring the Grazalema park. ✉ *El Olivar (exit just before village), 11610 Grazalema,* ☎ *956/ 132136,* 𝖥𝖠𝖷 *956/132213. 24 rooms, 38 apartments. Restaurant, pool. MC, V.*

**$** 🛏 **Arco de la Villa.** In the middle of Zahara de la Sierra with views over the reservoir, the sierra, and neighboring villages, this is the coziest and most panoramic place to be in this mountain retreat. ✉ *Camino Nazarí s/n, 11688 Zahara de la Sierra,* ☎ *956/123254,* 𝖥𝖠𝖷 *956/ 123244. 17 rooms. Restaurant, bar. AE, DC, MC, V.*

**$** 🛏 **Marqués de Zahara.** This noble 17th-century mansion in the center of Zahara de la Sierra is decorated in typical rustic Castilian style, with rooms simply and tastefully appointed. The mountain soups and *guisos* (stews) are a delight as well. ✉ *San Juan 3, 11688 Zahara de la Sierra,* ☎ *956/123061,* 𝖥𝖠𝖷 *956/123268. 10 rooms. Restaurant, bar; no a/c, no room TVs. AE, DC, MC, V.*

# COSTA DE LA LUZ AND THE SOUTHEAST

Cádiz's Costa de la Luz, so called for the bright sunlight that bathes this windswept southernmost coast of the Iberian Peninsula, runs from the capital to Tarifa, windsurfing mecca of Spain. Algeciras is just around the corner to the east, followed by the British enclave at Gibraltar and, farther east, the golf courses of San Roque and Sotogrande.

## Chiclana de la Frontera

**㉒** *24 km (14 mi) east of Cádiz, 102 km (61 mi) west of Algeciras.*

Between beaches, salt flats, and pine forests, this quintessential Andalusian town of narrow streets and flower-choked patios is known for its wildlife-rich Marismas de Sancti Petri wetlands, the excellent La Barrosa beach, and the offshore Isla de Sancti Petri, 7 km (4 mi) southwest of town, with its 18th-century fortress. From La Loma el Puerco, a natural lookout point, spectators watched the October 21, 1805, Battle of Trafalgar, in which the British fleet under Admiral Nelson defeated a combined French and Spanish force, though Nelson himself was killed in the battle.

## Lodging

**$$$$** 🛏 **Melia Sancti Petri.** This dazzling behemoth offers comforts and facilities of every description, though the setting is anything but intimate. The glass and steel structure is a graceful and sweeping promontory over the expanse of sand, while the various bars and restaurants are cozy corners to relax in. The miles of fine sand seem doubly wild around this oasis of comfort, while the sheer size of the hotel promises a handy combination of activity and anonymity. The views out over the Atlantic are nonpareil. ⊠ *Playa de la Barrosa, 11130,* ☎ *956/491200,* FAX *956/ 497053,* WEB *www.solmelia.com. 223 rooms. 3 restaurants, minibars, cable TV, golf, tennis, 2 pools (1 indoor), horseback riding, bar, meeting rooms, parking (fee). AE, MC, V.*

# Tarifa

**㉓** *35 km (21 mi) west of San Roque.*

Standing on the Strait of Gibraltar at the southernmost tip of mainland Europe—where the Mediterranean and the Atlantic meet and the Rif Mountains of Africa seem so close you can almost touch them—Tarifa was one of the earliest Moorish settlements in Spain. Strong prevailing winds kept Tarifa off the tourist maps for years, but they have ultimately proven a source of wealth. Aeolic power is generated on the vast wind farm occupying the surrounding hills, and the wide, white-sand beaches stretching north of the town have become Europe's biggest windsurfing center.

Tarifa's 10th-century **castle** is famous for its siege of 1292, when the defender Guzmán el Bueno refused to surrender even though the attacking Moors threatened to kill his captive son. In defiance, he flung his own dagger down to them, shouting "Here, use this"—or something to that effect. The Spanish military turned the castle over to the town in the mid-1990s, and it now contains a **museum** devoted to Guzmán and the sacrifice of his son. *Plaza de Santa María s/n,* ☎ *956/ 680993.* ⊡ *€1.50.* ☉ *Tues.–Sun. 10–2 and 4–6.*

Twenty-one kilometers (twelve miles) northwest of Tarifa on the Atlantic coast are the Roman ruins of **Baelo Claudia.** This settlement was a thriving production center of garum, a salty fish paste much appreciated in Rome. The forum, the thermal baths, and the tuna salting factory are the main attractions in this well preserved 2,000-year-old site. ⊠ *Bolonia s/n,* ☎ *956/688530.* ⊡ *€1.50.* ☉ *Mon.–Sat. 10–8, Sun. 10–2.*

## Lodging

**$$$** 🏨 **Hurricane Hotel.** This laid-back, palm-kissed hotel next to the beach is a favorite hangout of the windsurfing set. The atmosphere is fun and informal, the rooms simple but adequate. The staff can organize horse-back-riding trips along the beach or inland. ⊠ *Carretera Cádiz–Málaga, Km 77, 11380,* ☎ *956/684919,* FAX *956/684329. 28 rooms, 5 suites. Restaurant, pool, horseback riding. AE, MC, V.*

## Windsurfing

Tarifa windsurfing and Sierra Nevada snowboarding cultures have merged into Spain's Big Sur with an added Alpine and flamenco flair. Atlantic gales blowing across flat Mediterranean seas make this patch of ocean and beach in the Strait of Gibraltar ideal for Aeolic acrobatics. The beaches of Los Lances, Valdevaqueros, and Punta Paloma are the main theaters for windsurfing. For lessons and equipment report to **Spin Out Surf Base** (⊠ Casa del Porro. Crtra. N 340/E5, ☎ 956/ 236352). **Patanegra** (⊠ Hostal el Millón, Playa de los Lances, ☎ 639/113867) provides windsurfing equipment, orientation, and expertise.

# San Roque

**㉔** *92 km (57 mi) southwest of Ronda, 64 km (40 mi) west of Marbella.*

The town of San Roque was founded within sight of Gibraltar by Spaniards fleeing the Rock after the British capture of it in 1704.

Three hundred years later, San Roque's inhabitants still see themselves as the only genuine Gibraltarians. While the town is of only moderate interest, the surrounding golf courses are some of the best in the world. Fourteen kilometers (ten miles) east of San Roque is the luxury **Sotogrande** complex, a gated community with sprawling millionaires' villas, a yacht marina, and four golf courses, including the legendary Valderrama, which once hosted the Ryder Cup.

## Dining and Lodging

**$$–$$$** ✕ **Los Remos.** The dining room in this gracious colonial villa has peach-colored walls with quasi-baroque adornments: gilt rococo mirrors, swirling cherubs, friezes of grapes, and crystal lamps. It overlooks a formal, leafy garden full of palms, cedars, and trailing ivy. Entrées include *urta del estrecho en salsa de erizos marinos* (perch from the Strait of Gibraltar in sea-urchin sauce). All seafood comes from the Bay of Algeciras area, and the wine cellar has some 20,000 bottles. ⊠ *Villa Victoria, Campo de Gibraltar (between San Roque and Campamento)*, ☎ *956/698412. AE, DC, MC, V. Closed Sun.*

**$$$$** 🏨 **Almenara.** This deluxe resort 6 km (4 mi) from the coast in the Sotogrande development is a complex of semidetached, Andalusian-style houses clustered around a main building on the edge of an 18-hole golf course. Reached via golf cart, each house is surrounded by gardens and has a private terrace. The best views—over the golf course with the Mediterranean in the distance—are from rooms numbered in the 600s. ⊠ *Avda. Almenara, 11310 Sotogrande*, ☎ *956/582000,* FAX *956/582001,* WEB *www.sotogrande.com. 136 rooms, 12 suites. Restaurant, snack bar, 18-hole and 9-hole golf courses, pool, spa, bar. AE, DC, MC, V.*

**$$$$** 🏨 **The Suites.** Next to the San Roque golf course, halfway between the village and Sotogrande, is this sumptuous, Moorish-Andalusian–style pueblo. The ocher main building houses the reception area, golf clubhouse, and two restaurants, one specializing in Japanese food. The rooms and suites are in white houses scattered around a luxuriant garden with fountains and exotic plants. Each room has a little garden patio, and each suite has an enclosed courtyard as well. ⊠ *San Roque Club, Carretera N340, Km 127, 11360,* ☎ *956/613030,* FAX *956/613013,* WEB *www.sanroqueclub.com. 50 rooms, 50 suites. 2 restaurants, cable TV with movies, 18-hole golf course, 4 tennis courts, pool, horseback riding, some pets allowed. AE, DC, MC, V.*

## Nightlife

The **Casino de San Roque** (⊠ Carretera N340, Km 124, ☎ 956/780100), open 8 PM (9 in winter) to 5 AM, has a gaming room with roulette and blackjack tables, and a less formal slot-machine area. Jacket and tie (for men) and a passport are required.

## Golf

Cádiz, for all its Gypsy and flamenco culture, is also the golf capital of the Iberian Peninsula. The excellent golf courses in and around San Roque are well worth the €100–€250 greens fees they cost, as well as the occasional inconvenience getting on them may entail. Valderrama, for example, requires proof of membership in a hometown club and a handicap of 24 or under. While other courses accept golfers of lower skill level, they do require proof of golf club membership. **Valderrama** (⊠ Urb. Sotogrande [4 km /2.4 mi southeast], ☎ 956/791200, FAX 956/796028). **Sotogrande** (⊠ Paseo del Parque, ☎ 956/785014, FAX 956/795029). **San Roque** (⊠ Crtra. de Málaga [8 km/5 mi northeast], ☎ 956/613030, FAX 956/613013). **Alcaidesa Links** (⊠ Crtra. de Málaga, ☎ 956/7951040, FAX 956/791041).

# GIBRALTAR

*144 km (86 mi) east of Cádiz, 20 km (12 mi) east of Algeciras, 7 km (4 mi) west of San Roque.*

Just east of Algeciras, the tiny British colony of Gibraltar—nicknamed Gib, or simply the Rock—looms over the strait between Spain and Morocco. It's actually a rock 6 km (4 mi) long, 1 km (½ mi) wide, and 1,369 ft high. It was once one of the two Pillars of Hercules marking the western limits of the known world (the other was the mountain Djebel Musa, between the Moroccan cities of Ceuta and Tangier). Gibraltar's prime position commanding the narrow entrance to the Mediterranean inspired the Moors to seize it in 711 as a preliminary step in the conquest of Spain. They held Gibraltar longer than either the Spaniards or the British, as is reflected in its name: it was originally Djebel Tariq (Mountain of Tariq), for the Moorish commander who built the first fort here.

After the Moors had ruled for 750 years, the Spaniards recaptured Tariq's Rock in 1462, on the feast day of St. Bernard (now the colony's co–patron saint along with Our Lady of Europe, whose shrine stands at the Rock's southernmost tip). The English, heading an Anglo-Dutch fleet in the War of the Spanish Succession, seized the Rock in 1704 after three days of fighting, and after several years of local skirmishes, Gibraltar was ceded to Great Britain in the 1713 Treaty of Utrecht. Spain has been trying to get it back ever since. In 1779 a combined French and Spanish force laid siege to the Rock for three years, to no avail. In the Napoléonic Wars, Gibraltar was Admiral Nelson's base for the decisive naval Battle of Trafalgar, and during the two World Wars, it served the Allies as a naval and air base. In 1967, Franco closed the border with Spain to strengthen his claims over the colony, and it remained closed until 1985.

Today, much of Gibraltar has the air of a faded garrison town. The number of British troops stationed here has been cut back, and millions of dollars are being invested in developing the Rock's tourist potential. The Costa del Sol's 100,000-plus expatriate Britons have given the economy of this tiny colony another boost: many take advantage of Gibraltar's status as an offshore financial center.

Few places in the world are entered by walking or driving across an airport runway, but that's what happens in Gibraltar. First, show your passport; then make your way out onto the narrow strip of land linking Spain's La Linea with Britain's Rock. Unless you have a good reason to take your car—such as loading up on cheap gas or duty-free goodies—you're better off leaving it in a guarded parking area in La Linea, the Spanish border town, and relying on buses and taxis in Gibraltar, whose streets are narrow and congested. The Official Rock Tour—conducted either by minibus or, at a greater cost, taxi—takes about 90 minutes and includes all the major sights, allowing you to choose which places to come back to and linger at later.

Although the British pound is Gibraltar's official currency, the Euro is universally accepted. The Rock's handful of hotels cost considerably more than similar lodgings in Spain. When dialing Gibraltar from Spain, the area code is 9567; when dialing from other countries, the code is 350.

## Exploring Gibraltar

*Numbers in the margin correspond to points of interest on the Gibraltar map.*

### A Good Walk

Beginning on the Rock's eastern side, turn left down Devil's Tower Road as you enter Gibraltar. Here, on the eastern shore, is **Catalan Bay** ㉕,

# Gibraltar

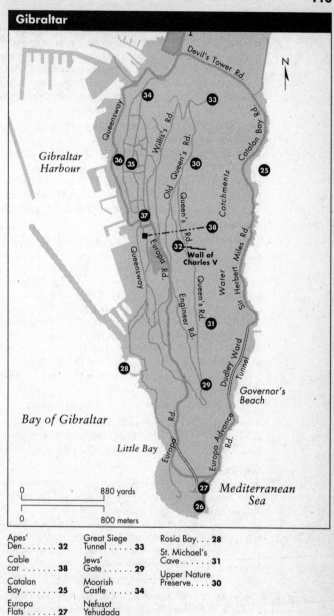

a fishing village founded by Genoese settlers, now a picturesque resort. You'll see the massive water catchments that once supplied the colony's drinking water. The road beyond here is closed, so head back west through the town of Gibraltar (which you'll explore later) and out to the Rock's southern tip, **Punta Grande de Europa** ㉖ for the view across the straits to Morocco, 23 km (14 mi) away. Near the lighthouse is **Europa Flats** ㉗, where you can see Nun's Well, a medieval Moorish cistern, and the Shrine of Our Lady of Europe.

From Europa Flats, follow Europa Road back along the Rock's western slopes, high above **Rosia Bay** ㉘, famous as the final port of call for the British dead after the Battle of Trafalgar in 1805. From Rosia Bay, continue on Europa Road as far as the casino, above the Alameda Gardens. Make a sharp right here up Engineer Road to **Jews' Gate** ㉙ lookout point. Here you can access the **Upper Nature Preserve** ㉚, with **St. Michael's Cave** ㉛, the **Apes' Den** ㉜, the **Great Siege Tunnel** ㉝, and the **Moorish Castle** ㉞.

Willis Road leads steeply down to the colorful, congested town of **Gibraltar** ㉟. Apart from the shops, restaurants, and pubs on busy Main Street, you'll want to visit the Governor's Residence for the Changing of the Guard and Ceremony of the Keys. (The Changing of the Guard takes place daily, every 80 minutes between 9 AM and 5 PM, while the Ceremony of the Keys is held twice annually.) Other sights include the two cathedrals, one Protestant, one Catholic, the **Gibraltar Museum** ㊱, and the **Nefusot Yehudada Synagogue** ㊲. The Koehler Gun in Casemates Square at the northern end of Main Street, is an impressive example of the type of gun developed during the Great Siege. Finally, take a ride to the top of the Rock on the **cable car** ㊳ for superb views over Gibraltar and the Straits.

TIMING

With allowance for stops and museums, this could be a three-hour to full-day tour with lunch at one of the Rock's many taverns and restaurants. Walking straight through would take about two hours.

## Sights to See

㉜ **Apes' Den.** The famous Barbary Apes are a breed of cinnamon-color, tailless monkeys native to Morocco's Atlas Mountains. Legend holds that as long as the apes remain, the British will keep the Rock; Winston Churchill went so far as to issue an order for their preservation when the apes' numbers began to dwindle during World War II. Today they are publicly fed twice daily, at 8 and 4. Among their mischievous talents are purse and camera snatching. The den is down Old Queens Road from St. Michael's Cave, near the Wall of Charles V.

★ ㊳ **Cable car.** The ride to the top of the Rock on the famous cable car offers splendid views. Reminiscent of a ski gondola, the car doesn't go very far from the ground, but the views of Spain and Africa from the Rock's pinnacle are superb. It leaves every 20 minutes between 9:30 AM and 5:30 PM from a station on Grand Parade, at the southern end of Main Street. ⌧ *Grand Parade*, ☎ *9567/77826*. ⌧ *€4.90 roundtrip (includes cable car, Michael's Cave, and Apes' Den).* ☉ *Daily 9:30–5:15*

㉕ **Catalan Bay.** This eastern shore resort was originally settled in the 14th century by the Genoese shipwrights who followed the British fleet, repairing ships whenever necessary. Their descendants still live in this tiny fishing village. The minuscule beach is excellent. The town retains a maritime flavor and is a favorite local outing for relaxed seafood dining along the shore.

**㉗ Europa Flats.** Near the lighthouse, Europa Flats is the home of an ancient Moorish cistern known as the **Nun's Well.** Nearby is the **Shrine of Our Lady of Europe,** venerated by seafarers since 1462.

**㉟ Gibraltar.** The village of Gilbraltar tumbles down the steep flanks of the Rock below Willis Road, a jumble of smallish houses with dignified Regency-style architecture typical of early 19th-century London blending oddly with the balconies and patios of southern Spain. The tourist offices are on Cathedral Square and in Casemates Square. Main Street's boutiques and taverns provide the Rock's urban hustle and bustle. Look for the **Law Courts,** where the famous case of the sailing ship *Mary Celeste* was heard in 1872. The Anglican **Cathedral of the Holy Trinity;** and the Catholic **Cathedral of St. Mary the Crowned** are Gibraltar's most important liturgical structures, along with four synagogues, two mosques, a Hindu temple, and more than a dozen Catholic and Protestant churches.

**㊱ Gibraltar Museum.** Exhibits here detail the history of the Rock throughout the ages. The well-presented displays include a beautiful 14th-century Moorish bathhouse, evocations of the Great Siege and of the Battle of Trafalgar, and an 1865 model of the Rock. There's also a reproduction of the "Gibraltar Woman," the Neanderthal skull discovered here in 1848. ⊠ *Bomb House Lane,* ☎ *9567/74289.* ▱ *€2.* ☉ *Weekdays 10–6, Sat. 10–2.*

**㉝ Great Siege Tunnel.** Formerly known as the Upper Galleries, this tunnel was carved out at the northern end of the Rock during the Great Siege of 1779–82. Governor Lord Napier of Magdala entertained former U.S. president Ulysses S. Grant here in 1878, with a banquet in St. George's Hall. The Holyland Tunnel leads to a vantage point on the east side of the Rock, high above Catalan Bay.

**㉙ Jews' Gate.** This unbeatable lookout point over the docks and Bay of Gibraltar to Algeciras is called Jew's gate for the Jewish Cemetery hidden away here after the 1713 Treaty of Utrecht outlawed Gibraltar's Sephardic community. After living as ostensible Christians, Jews were buried in this cemetery overlooking Tetuan and the coast of North Africa.

**㉞ Moorish Castle.** This castle on Willis Road was originally built by the descendants of Tariq, who conquered the Rock in 711. The present Tower of Homage dates from 1333, and its walls bear the scars of sieges in which stones from medieval catapults (and, later, cannonballs) were hurled against it. Admiral Rooke hoisted the British flag from its summit when he captured the Rock in 1704, and it has flown here ever since. ⊠ *Upper Nature Preserve,* ☎ *9567/54242.* ☉ *Daily 9:30–sunset.*

**㊲ Nefusot Yehudada Synagogue.** Constructed in the 18th century, the synagogue is one of four in this British enclave suspended between Spain and North Africa. On Line Wall Road near the Gibraltar tourist office and museum, this is the Flemish synagogue, dedicated to Jewish worshippers from the Lowlands. ⊠ *Line Wall Road s/n,* ☎ *9567/54143.* ☉ *Daily 10–2, 4–7.*

**㉖ Punta Grande de Europa.** One of the two ancient Pillars of Hercules, the Europa Point lighthouse has dominated the meeting place of the Atlantic and the Mediterranean since 1841; sailors can see its light from a distance of 27 km (17 mi). (The other Pillar of Hercules is Morocco's Jbel Musa at the southern side of the Strait of Gibraltar.)

**㉘ Rosia Bay.** This was the inlet to which Nelson's flagship, HMS *Victory,* was towed after the Battle of Trafalgar in 1805. On board were the dead, who were buried in Trafalgar Cemetery on the southern edge of town—except, of course, for Admiral Nelson, whose body went home to England preserved in a barrel of rum.

**③ St. Michael's Cave.** The largest of Gibraltar's 150 caves is a series of underground chambers hung with stalactites and stalagmites, situated at the end of Old Queens Road. It provides a dramatic setting for concerts, ballet, and theater. Sound-and-light shows are held here most days at 11 and 4. The skull of a Neanderthal woman (now in the British Museum) was found at nearby Forbes Quarry eight years *before* the world-famous discovery in Germany's Neander Valley in 1856; nobody paid much attention to it at the time, which is why we call this prehistoric race Neanderthals rather than *homo calpensis* (literally, "Gibraltar Man"—after the Romans' name for the Rock, *Calpe*). ⊠ *Upper Nature Preserve,* ☎ 9567/74975. ⊙ *Daily 9:30–sunset.*

**③ Upper Nature Reserve.** This upper section of the Rock of Gibraltar was stripped of nearly all vegetation by the British fortress and herds of hungry goats during the 18th and 19th centuries. Concerted efforts to restore the Rock's natural assets have resulted in some 650 plant species thriving there today. The Upper Nature Reserve's attractions begin with the Pillars of Hercules monument overlooking Europa Point, the mosque, and the lighthouse just inside the control post. Other visits include the Apes' Den, Saint Michael's Cave, the Great Siege Tunnel, the Military Heritage Centre, the Gibraltar, a City Under Siege Exhibition, and the Moorish Castle, the remnants of the Tower of Homage built in 1333.

## Dining and Lodging

**$$$ ✕ Raffles.** This restaurant opens onto the yacht harbor at Queensway Quay, Gibraltar's most fashionable marina. The outdoor terrace is very pleasant; the dining room inside is more cramped. The extensive menu incorporates international dishes, including some Spanish specialties. ⊠ *Queensway Quay,* ☎ 9567/40362. MC, V.

**$–$$ ✕ La Bayuca.** One of the Rock's oldest restaurants, La Bayuca is renowned for its onion soup and Mediterranean dishes. Prince Charles and Prince Andrew both dined here while on naval service. For the main course, try the lamb casserole or kebab. ⊠ *21 Turnbull's Lane,* ☎ 9567/ 75119. *MC, V. Closed Tues. No lunch Sat. or Sun.*

**$$$$ ▥ The Eliott.** This is the most modern of the Rock's hotels, in the center of the town in what used to be the Gibraltar Holiday Inn. The rooms are functional and comfortable. Ask for one at the top of the hotel with a view over the Bay of Gibraltar. ⊠ *2 Governor's Parade,* ☎ 9567/ 70500, ℻ 9567/70243. *114 rooms, 2 suites. Pool, sauna. AE, DC, MC, V.*

**$$$$ ▥ The Rock.** Overlooking Gibraltar, this Rock first opened in 1932. Furnishings in the rooms and restaurant can compete with those in good international hotels anywhere, yet they manage to preserve something of the English colonial style, with bamboo, ceiling fans, and a fine terrace bar. ⊠ *3 Europa Rd.,* ☎ 9567/73000, ℻ 9567/73513. *112 rooms, 8 suites. Restaurant, pool, hair salon, bar. AE, DC, MC, V.*

**$$ ▥ Bristol.** This colonial-style hotel is in the heart of town, with splendid views of the bay and the cathedral. Rooms are spacious but basic. The tropical garden is a real haven, and the wood-panel lounge has two pool tables. ⊠ *10 Cathedral Sq.,* ☎ 9567/76800, ℻ 9567/77613. *60 rooms. Dining room, pool, bar, free parking. AE, DC, MC, V.*

## Nightlife

The **Ladbroke International Casino** (⊠ 7 Europa Rd., ☎ 9567/76666) is open from 7:30 PM (cocktail bar) and 9 (gaming room) until 4 AM; dress in the gaming room is smart casual. No passport is required.

# CÁDIZ PROVINCE A TO Z

*To research prices, get advice from other travelers, and book travel arrangements, visit www.fodors.com.*

### AIR TRAVEL

Cádiz's airport is Jerez de la Frontera's Aeropuerto de la Parra, 7 km (4 mi) from Jerez on the road to Seville. Iberia flies from here to Madrid, Barcelona, Valencia–Palma de Mallorca, and Zaragoza.

➤ AIRLINES AND CONTACTS: **Iberia** (⌗ Almirante Lobo 2, Seville, ☎ 95/422–8901 or 902/400500).

➤ AIRPORT INFORMATION: **Aeropuerto de la Parra** (☎ 956/150000). **Gibraltar Airport** (☎ 9567/73026).

### BUS TRAVEL

Buses throughout Andalusia, and between Extremadura and Seville, tend to be more frequent and convenient than trains. Buses connect all of the towns and villages in this region. Cádiz has two bus depots: Comes, which serves most destinations in Andalusia, and Los Amarillos, serving Jerez, Seville, Córdoba, Puerto de Santa María, Sanlúcar de Barrameda, and Chipiona. The bus station in Jerez, on the Plaza Madre de Dios, is served by two companies: La Valenciana and Los Amarillos.

➤ BUS INFORMATION: Cádiz: **Comes** (⌗ Plaza Hispanidad, Cádiz, ☎ 956/224271). **Los Amarillos** (⌗ Diego Fernández Herreras 34, Cádiz, ☎ 956/285852). Jerez: **La Valenciana** (☎ 956/341063). **Los Amarillos** (☎ 956/329347).

### CAR TRAVEL

The mountain roads along the pueblos blancos route are slow and scenic. Plan on averaging no more than 50–60 km an hour. Along the coastal N-340/E05 you can cruise quickly from Cádiz to Algeciras (124 km) in less than an hour.

### EMERGENCIES

➤ CONTACTS: **Police** (☎ 091). **Ambulance** (☎ 061).

### SAFETY

*Never* leave *anything* in a parked car. Take only a small amount of cash and one credit card out with you. Leave your passport, traveler's checks, and other credit cards in the hotel safe, if possible, and avoid carrying purses and expensive cameras or wearing valuable jewelry.

### TOURS

For English-speaking local guides in Cádiz or Jerez, contact the local tourist office.

➤ CONTACTS: **Asociación Provincial de Informadores Turísticos** (⌗ Glorieta de Palacio de Congresos, Seville, ☎ 95/425–5957). **Guidetour** (⌗ Lope de Rueda 13, ☎ 95/422–2374 or 95/422–2375). **ITA** (⌗ Santa Teresa 1, ☎ 95/422–4641).

#### AL ANDALUS

*Al Andalus* is a vintage 1920s luxury train that makes a weekly six-day trip in season from Seville to Córdoba, Granada, and Antequera, with side trips to Carmona and Jerez. For details, *see* Train Travel *in* Smart Travel Tips A to Z.

#### SHERRY BODEGAS

Tours of sherry bodegas can be arranged from Seville and Cádiz. In Jerez, most bodegas are open to visitors except during August. Tours, which include a tasting of brandy and sherry, should be reserved in advance; English-speaking guides are usually available. Call the bodega and ask for Public Relations. Domecq charges €3 weekdays, €4.50 weekends; González Byass has a tour in English every hour and charges €6. Harvey charges €2.70 weekdays, €4.50 weekends for its winery tour. The Sandeman winery charges €3 on weekdays and €3.60 on weekends for its tour; and Williams and Humbert charges €2.40 to tour its winery. For schedules, call the winery or check with the Jerez tourist office.

To visit bodegas in Puerto de Santa María, contact Osborne or Terry. In Sanlúcar de Barrameda contact Barbadillo. If possible, reserve a tour one day in advance; otherwise, call before noon.

➤ FEES AND SCHEDULES: **Barbadillo** (⊠ Calle Luis de Eguilaz, ☎ 956/360894). **Domecq** (☎ 956/151500). **González Byass** (☎ 956/357000). **Harvey** (☎ 956/346004). **Osborne** (⊠ Fernán Caballero 3, ☎ 956/855211) **Sandeman** (☎ 956/301100). **Terry** (⊠ Santa Trinidad, ☎ 956/857700). **Williams and Humbert** (☎ 956/353406).

### TRAIN TRAVEL

Jerez and Cádiz are on the main railroad line from Madrid to southwestern Spain. From Madrid, some six trains run to Seville daily, via Córdoba; three of these continue on to Jerez and Cádiz. RENFE also operates the high-speed AVE train between Madrid and Seville; it costs more than regular trains, but it makes the journey in 2½ hours and has become the most popular mode of travel between the two cities.

A dozen or more local trains each day connect Cádiz with Puerto de Santa María, Jerez, and Seville. Journey time from Cádiz to Seville is 1½ to 2 hours. There are no trains to Doñana National Park, Sanlúcar de Barrameda, or Arcos de la Frontera, or between Cádiz and the Costa del Sol.

Cádiz's station is on Plaza de Sevilla near the docks. Jerez's station is on Plaza de la Estación, off Diego Fernández Herrera, in the eastern part of town. For general train information, call the national RENFE information line.

➤ TRAIN INFORMATION: **RENFE** (☎ 902/240202, WEB www.renfe.es). **Cádiz** (☎ 956/254301). **Algeciras** (☎ 956/630202).

### VISITOR INFORMATION

➤ TOURIST INFORMATION: **Western Andalusia regional tourist office** (⊠ Avda. de la Constitución 21, Seville, ☎ 95/422–1404 or 95/421–8157, FAX 95/422–9753). Local tourist offices: **Algeciras** (⊠ C. Juan de la Cierva s/n, ☎ 956/572636). **Arcos de la Frontera** (⊠ Plaza del Cabildo s/n, ☎ 956/702264). **Cádiz** (⊠ Calderón de la Barca 1, ☎ 956/211313). **Conil de la Frontera** (⊠ C. Carretera 1, ☎ 956/440501). **Chiclana de la Frontera** (⊠ Alameda del Río s/n, ☎ 956/535969). **El Puerto de Santa María** (⊠ C. Luna 22, ☎ 956/542475). **Grazalema** (⊠ Plaza de España 11, ☎ 956/132225). **Jerez de la Frontera** (⊠ Larga 39, ☎ 956/331150 or 956/331162). **Sanlúcar de Barrameda** (⊠ Calzada del Ejército s/n, ☎ 956/366110). **San Roque** (⊠ Crtra. N-340, Km 135, Torreguadiaro, ☎ 956/616307). **Setenil de las Bodegas** (⊠ Calle Villa 2, ☎ 956/134261). **Tarifa** (⊠ Paseo de la Alameda s/n, ☎ 956/680993). **Ubrique** (⊠ Calle Morena de Mora 19-A, ☎ 956/464900). **Vejer de la Frontera** (⊠ C. Marqués de Tamarón 10, ☎ 956/450191). **Villamartín** (⊠ Plaza Ayuntamiento 10, ☎ 956/715015).

# 5 MÁLAGA PROVINCE

The allure of sun and sand is never to be underestimated—and Málaga's Costa del Sol, a touristy, fun-in-the-sun tour-de-force, is perhaps the ultimate proof. Head inland and the contrast could not be more vivid. Sprinkled around the splendid town of Ronda—itself perched above a plunging gorge—are the famed pueblos blancos, whitewashed mountaintop villages splashed with red and pink geraniums. The capital city of Málaga, birthplace of Picasso, buzzes with the energy of its half a million inhabitants.

By Annelise
Sorensen

F ROM A GLITTERING, skyscraper-studded shoreline that unfolds brashly across southern Andalusia to rustic upland villages ensconced in lush valleys to craggy cliffs and gaping caves where dagger-wielding *bandoleros* once used to hide from the law, Málaga is a kaleidoscope of contrasts, at once blatantly tourist-savvy and quietly traditional.

Hogging the limelight is the Costa del Sol, an over-the-top orgy of highrises, self-catering apartments, cruise ships disgorging sunburned passengers, water parks, casinos—and miles of sandy beaches, lined with row upon row of identical beach parasols. Sunseekers from bleaker climes seem to be crammed into every corner of the coast, particularly in the mega-resort towns of Torremolinos and Benalmádena-Costa. This might not be the Andalusia of the independent traveler's dreams, but it does have its attractions. The Costa averages some 320 days of sunshine a year, and balmy days are not unknown even in January or February. And, despite the hubbub, you *can* unwind here, basking or strolling on clean, sunny beaches and enjoying a full range of land and water sports. In some places, mountains roll right down to the Mediterranean; in others, hillsides of olive groves, cork oaks, and terraced vineyards unfold toward vistas of the sea glinting in the distance.

Inland Málaga beckons with its quiet villages where black-shawled women go about their daily routine much as they did half a century ago, and where donkeys and mules are still used for farmwork. Throughout the hills and valleys of the interior, the Moorish legacy is a unifying visual theme, connecting the tiny streets honeycombing the steamy depths of the villages, the rocky cliffs and gorges between Alora, Archidona, and the Axarquía, the layout of the farms, and the crops themselves, including oranges and lemons. Straddling the spectacular El Tajo gorge, the romantic town of Ronda is speckled with handsome plazas and colorful Mudéjar architecture. Steeped in medieval lore—and the scene of many a reconquest battle—the perched *pueblos blancos* (white villages) around Ronda form one of Andalusia's most scenic and emblematic travel routes. The capital of Málaga is a thriving city with a host of museums, churches, and Moorish fortifications.

## Pleasures and Pastimes

### Beaches

The beaches of the Costa del Sol range from shingle and pebbles at worst (Almuñecar, Nerja, Málaga) to a fine, gray, gritty sand (from Torremolinos westward). Pebbles and pollution can make swimming in the sea unpleasant. Look for beaches flying the blue EU flag, which indicates that the facilities conform to European Union standards. All beaches are packed in July and August, when Spanish families take their annual vacations, and on Sundays from May to October, when they become picnic sites.

All beaches in Spain are free. Changing facilities are usually not available, though you'll find free, cold showers on the major beaches. It's quite acceptable for women to go topless here; if you want to take it *all* off, you'll have to drive to one of the more isolated beaches designated *playa naturista*. The most popular nude beaches are in Maro (near Nerja) and between Benalmádena-Costa and Fuengirola. Costa Natura, 3 km (2 mi) west of Estepona, is the region's official nudist colony.

The best—and most crowded—beaches are El Bajondillo and La Carihuela, in Torremolinos; the long stretch between Carvajal, Los Boliches, and Fuengirola; and those on either side of Marbella. You may find the odd secluded beach west of Estepona. For wide beaches of fine sand, you'll have to head west past Gibraltar, around the southern tip of Spain to Tarifa and the Cádiz coast, though strong winds are often a deterrent there.

## Dining

Spain's southern coast is known for fresh seafood, breaded with fine flour and exquisitely fried. Sardines roasted on skewers at beachside restaurants are another popular and unforgettable treat. Gazpacho shows up in the Andalusian culinary canon as both complement and antidote. Málaga is best for traditional Spanish cooking, with a wealth of bars and seafood restaurants serving *fritura malagueña,* the city's famous fried fish. Torremolinos's Carihuela district is also a paradise for lovers of Spanish seafood. The resorts serve every conceivable foreign cuisine as well, from Thai to the Scandinavian smorgasbord; Marbella has internationally renowned restaurants. At the other end of the scale, and perhaps even more enjoyable, are the Costa's traditional *chiringuitos* and *merenderos*; strung out along the beaches, these rough-and-ready, summer-only shack restaurants serve seafood fresh off the boats.

Because of the international clientele, meals on the coast itself are served earlier than elsewhere in Andalusia, with restaurants opening at 1 or 1:30 for lunch and 7 or 8 for dinner. Reservations are advisable for all Marbella restaurants listed as $$$–$$$$ and for the better restaurants in Málaga; elsewhere, they're rarely necessary. Expect beach restaurants, such as Málaga's Casa Pedro and all those on the Carihuela seafront in Torremolinos, to be packed after 3 PM on Sunday.

| CATEGORY | COST* |
| --- | --- |
| $$$$ | over €18 |
| $$$ | €13–€18 |
| $$ | €8–€13 |
| $ | under €8 |

*per person for a main course at dinner*

## Fiestas

Málaga holds a colorful parade on January 5, the eve of the **Día de los Tres Reyes** (Feast of the Three Kings, or Epiphany), and the city's **Semana Santa** (Holy Week) processions are among the most dramatic in Andalusia. Nerja and Estepona celebrate **San Isidro** (May 15) with typically Andalusian *ferias* (fairs). Midsummer, or the feast of **San Juan** (June 23–24), is marked by midnight bonfires on beaches all along the coast. The **Virgen del Carmen** is the patron saint of fishermen, so fishing communities all along the coast honor her feast day (July 16) with seaborne processions of fishing boats. Málaga and Fuengirola throw popular annual **city festivals**, Málaga's at the beginning of August and Fuengirola's in the fall, October 6–12.

## Golf

With nearly 40 golf courses between Rincón de la Victoria (east of Málaga) and Gibraltar, the Costa del Sol has the highest concentration of courses in Europe. Some are quite hilly, making them both spectacular to look at and challenging to play. The best season for golf is October through June; greens fees are lower during the hot summer months.

Certain hotels cater almost exclusively to golfers, and some offer guests reduced greens fees: these include the Parador de Golf, near the Málaga airport; the Byblos and La Cala Resort, near Fuengirola; Los Monteros, near Marbella; the Hotel Atalaya Park and El Paraíso, between San Pedro and Estepona; and Almenara and The Suites, near San Roque.

Indispensable for anyone trying to make independent golf arrangements is a copy of *Sun Golf,* a free magazine available at hotels and golf clubs. The *Andalucía Golf Guide,* published by Andalusia's regional tourist office, details all the courses on the Costa del Sol; it's available at any Tourist Office of Spain.

## Lodging

Most hotels on the more highly developed stretch, between Torremolinos and Fuengirola, offer large, functional rooms near the sea at competitive rates. The area's ongoing popularity as a budget destination means that most such hotels are booked in high season by foreign package-tour operators. Finding a room at Easter, in July and August, or around the October 12 holiday weekend can be difficult if you haven't reserved in advance.

Málaga has a handful of top-end hotels, but not enough for a city of its size, so it's imperative to book early if you're traveling here in the high season. Marbella, conversely, packs more than its fair share of grand hotels, including some of Spain's most expensive accommodations. Málaga has an excellent but small parador that is often full. Elsewhere, there are paradors in Ronda and Archidona.

The province of Málaga also has plentiful *casas rurales,* accommodations in farmhouses and country homes, particularly in the Axarquía in eastern Málaga. Tourist offices can provide up-to-date lists of available casas rurales in the province. **Turismo Rural en la Axarquía** (⊠ Las Arenas 1, 29740 Torre del Mar, ☎ 952/540914, WEB www.axarquia-rural. com), based in Torre del Mar, just south of Vélez-Málaga, provides bookings and info on casas rurales in the Axarquía.

| CATEGORY | COST |
|----------|------|
| **$$$$** | over €140 |
| **$$$** | €100–€140 |
| **$$** | €60–€100 |
| **$** | under €60 |

*All prices are for a standard double room, excluding tax.*

# Exploring Málaga Province

The capital city of Málaga, with its nearby airport and clutch of high-end hotels, makes for a good base to exploring the province, with both the Costa del Sol and the inland villages no more than a couple of hours away by car or bus. If you're keen on exploring the vast outdoors, then head for the city of Ronda—with plenty of both budget and more expensive, classy accommodations, conveniently surrounded by the province's three natural parks, easily accessible by car or public transportation. Well worth a detour is the lush, hilly Axarquíla, in eastern Málaga, strewn with vineyards, quiet villages, and casas rurales. For a bit of both worlds—sunny beaches and rustic inland—you can opt to stay in the coastal town of Nerja, which lies just south of the Axarquíla. Finally, although the Costa del Sol is understood as the area's prime resource, much of it is lined with skyscrapers and crowded with tourists, which may not be what you had in mind. The shore is, however, well endowed with hotels and restaurants, making it another fine base, as inland Málaga, including Ronda and the pueblos blancos, are just a few hours away. Keep in mind, too, that the sights of Granada, Córdoba, and Seville are all within easy access from Málaga.

*Numbers in the text correspond to numbers in the margin and on the Málaga province and city maps.*

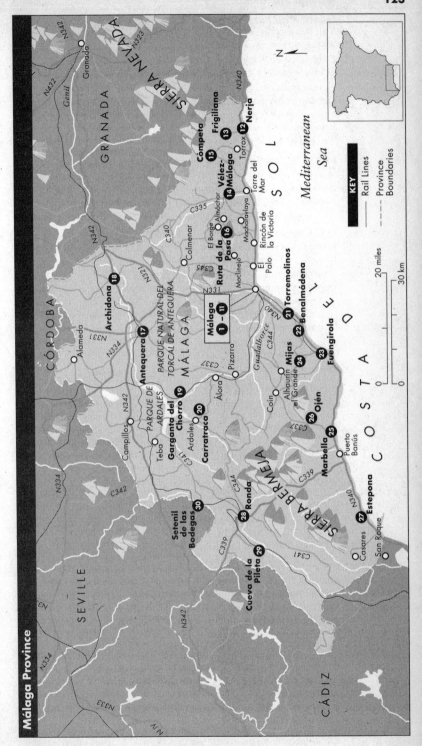

Málaga Province

KEY
— Rail Lines
----- Province Boundaries

Mediterranean Sea

N

GRANADA

SIERRA NEVADA

CÓRDOBA

SEVILLE

CÁDIZ

MÁLAGA

PARQUE NATURAL DEL TORCAL DE ANTEQUERA

PARQUE DE ARDALES

SIERRA BERMEJA

COSTA DEL SOL

Granada

Genil

Cómpeta **15**

Frigiliana **13**

Nerja **12**

Torrox

Vélez-Málaga **14**

Torre del Mar

Almáchar

El Borge

Ruta de la Pasa **16**

Machaviaya

El Rincón de la Victoria

El Palo

Colmenar

Moclinejo

Torremolinos **21**

Benalmádena **22**

Fuengirola **23**

Mijas **24**

Alhaurín el Grande

Coín

Ojén **26**

Puerto Banús

Marbella **25**

Estepona **27**

Casares

San Roque

Ronda **28**

Setenil de las Bodegas **30**

Cueva de la Pileta **29**

Archidona **18**

Antequera **17**

Álora

Pizarra

Garganta del Chorro **19**

Carratraca **20**

Ardales

Teba

Campillos

Alameda

Málaga **1 – 11**

Guadalhorce

C335

C340

C345

C337

C344

C339

C341

C342

N331

N340

N342

N323

N432

N331

N334

N333

N334

N334

20 miles

30 km

## Great Itineraries

This drive takes in Málaga from east to west, along the coastal highway N340. It starts in eastern Málaga, then heads west along the Costa Tropical. (If you arrive at the coast from Cádiz, follow the drive in reverse order.) The main towns en route are Nerja, Málaga (the region's capital and only major city), Torremolinos, Fuengirola, Marbella, and Estepona; detours inland bring you to mountain villages, the historical town of Antequera, and the dramatic scenery of the Chorro gorge. Ronda makes a particularly inspiring excursion, high in the mountains 49 km (30 mi) from the coast.

In 7 to 10 days you can see the major beaches and cities, venture inland, and even hop across to Morocco. Five days is really the minimum if you want to do anything other than drive or lie on the beach. Three days gives you a taste of the major sights and a look at the coast.

IF YOU HAVE 3 DAYS

Explore eastern Málaga, starting out in **Nerja** ⑫, with its Balcón de Europa over the sea. Have lunch at one of the sea-view restaurants near the square. Visit the villages of **Frigiliana** ⑬ and **Cómpeta** ⑮ in the lush Axarquía before proceeding to ⊡ **Málaga** ①–⑪ for the night. The next morning, explore Málaga before moving up into the hills for lunch in **Antequera** ⑰ or **Archidona** ⑱. From Antequera, make the 100-km (62-mi) drive over to ⊡ **Ronda** ㉘ for your second night. Explore Ronda in the early morning and drive to coastal **Marbella** ㉕ for lunch at the beach. From Marbella you can either move west to Sotogrande and San Roque in Cádiz or back east to tumultuous ⊡ **Torremolinos** ㉑ for a night on the town.

IF YOU HAVE 5 DAYS

Follow the itinerary above for your first day, settling down in ⊡ **Málaga** ①–⑪ for the night. Devote your second day to exploring Málaga before moving up into the hills for the sunset and a night in the parador in ⊡ **Antequera** ⑰. On Day 3, drive from Antequera up to the village of **Archidona** ⑱. From here, follow a small road north to the **Garganta del Chorro** ⑲. Continue on to ⊡ **Torremolinos** ㉑, where the Carihuela beach district provides a radical change of scenery. On your fourth day, explore the picturesque village of **Mijas** ㉔ before moving on to **Marbella** ㉕ for an afternoon among the glitterati. If this scene is too manicured for your taste, hop up to the village of **Ojén** ㉖ for a complete change of pace. Spend the early evening driving to ⊡ **Ronda** ㉘ for a look at one of Andalusia's most stunning mountain enclaves. Day 5 is a chance to see more of Ronda before touring **Setenil de las Bodegas** ㉚, the Roman settlement of Acinipo.

## When to Tour

Winter is a good time to be on this coast; the temperatures are moderate, and there are fewer tourists. Fall and spring are also good. Avoid July and August, when it's too hot and crowded. May and June have the longest days and the fewest travelers. Holy Week brings memorable ceremonies and processions.

# MÁLAGA

The capital city of Málaga has long been relegated to the sidelines, a mere afterthought in visitors' minds as they troop toward the Costa del Sol and then pop up to Ronda. In fact, the closest most sunseekers get to Málaga is its airport—spending just long enough to collect their baggage and a tube or two of tanning oil. At first glance, this might not seem such a bad idea—approaching the city, you'll be greeted by grimy suburbs and huge 1970s high-rises that march determinedly toward Torremolinos. But don't despair: in its center and its eastern suburbs, Málaga is a pleasant port city, with ancient streets and lovely villas amid exotic foliage. Cutting a leafy swath through Málaga is the Paseo del Parque, a handsome pedestrian promenade lined with palm trees.

Málaga's roots go back to the Phoenicians, who settled here and dubbed the city Malaka. The Moors moved in during the 8th century, when Málaga's formidable port was bringing prosperity and population to the city. Impressive reminders of Málaga's Moorish past loom about town, including the 14th-century Gibralfaro, a grand 14th-century defense fortification built by the Moors, which failed to protect them against the armies of the Christian reconquest, who conquered Málaga in 1487.

A word of warning: Málaga has one of the highest unemployment rates in Spain, and poverty and crime are rife (though drug peddling, once fairly common, has declined). Numerous muggings have been reported; it's best not to carry a purse or any valuables in the streets or on the way up to Gibralfaro. If you arrive by car, you'll have to contend with *gorrillas*, volunteer parking attendants who demand money to "watch" your car. Stick to areas with meters or uniformed attendants.

## Exploring Málaga

Málaga is an eminently walkable and compact city, and you can cover most of the main sights on foot. In fact, the old town, with its web of narrow, cobbled streets and clutch of churches, is best negotiated—and enjoyed—by a leisurely stroll, the better to explore its atmospheric nooks and crannies. The Paseo del Parque, flanked by lush gardens, leads from the city center toward the Plaza de Toros and the beach. The city's sights are also well linked by frequent buses, most of which depart from and/or stop at the Paseo del Parque. A helpful geographical landmark is the dried-up Guadalmedina River, which runs north through the center of town. The train and bus stations lie to the west of the river.

### A Good Walk

Embark on your stroll through Málaga in the city center, starting at the Plaza de la Marina, with cafés and an illuminated fountain overlooking the port. From here, stroll through the shady, palm-lined gardens of the **Paseo del Parque** ① or browse on Calle Marqués de Larios, the main shopping street. The narrow streets and alleys on each side of Calle Marqués de Larios have charms of their own. Wander the warren of passageways around Pasaje Chinitas, off Plaza de la Constitución, and peep into the dark, vaulted bodegas where old men down glasses of *seco añejo* or *Málaga Virgen*, local wines made from Málaga's muscatel grapes. Across Larios, in the streets leading to Calle Nueva, you'll see shoe-shine boys, lottery-ticket vendors, carnation-sporting Gypsies, beggars, and a wealth of tapas bars dispensing wine from huge barrels. From the Plaza Felix Saenz, at the southern end of Calle Nueva, turn onto Sagasta to reach the **Mercado de Atarazanas** ②, one of Andalusia's most colorful markets.

Just a few blocks north of the market, up Calle Moreno Carbonero, is the **Museo de Artes Populares** ③, housed in a 17th-century inn, where you can view Malagueño folk costumes, ceramics, and sculptures. From here, head back toward the city center along Calle Cisneros. Just off this street, on Calle San Juan, is Iglesia de San Juan, with a baroque, 18th-century interior. Cross Calle Marqués de Larios and continue your exploration of Málaga's old town with a visit to the **cathedral** ④, with a spectacular enclosed choir, the work of the renowned

17th-century artist Pedro de Mena. The **Palacio Episcopal** ⑤, facing the main entrance of the cathedral, displays changing art exhibits.

Saunter through the old town along nearby San Agustin, one of Málaga's best-conserved historical streets, until you reach **Palacio de Buenavista** ⑥, home of the future Picasso Museum. From here, it's a short walk to the bustling Plaza de la Merced, surrounded by restaurants and cafés. Overlooking the plaza is Pablo Picasso's childhood home, which today houses the **Fundación Picasso** ⑦, with exhibits of Picasso's engravings and sculptures. From Plaza de la Merced, head along Calle Alcazabilla, where just beyond the ruins of a Roman theater is the splendid 8th-century Moorish **Alcazaba** ⑧. Looming above the Alcazaba is the **Gibralfaro** ⑨, Moorish fortifications built in the 14th century. Magnificent vistas of the city and coastline beckon.

Head toward the Plaza del General Torrijos; nearby stands Málaga's impressive bullring, La Malagueta, built in 1874. At sunset, walk along the Paseo de la Farola, where you can gaze out at Málaga's formidable port, where huge cruise ships glide through the waters to dock, and watch the lighthouse start its nightly vigil. Move on to the seafront promenade, the Paseo Marítimo, and saunter along the beach, taking in the last rays of sun disappearing behind the sea. Pause for a drink at one of the string of outdoor terraces that line the paseo. If you continue along the Paseo Marítimo, you'll come to the suburbs of El Palo and **Pedregalejo** ⑩, once traditional fishing villages in their own right, where you can eat wonderfully fresh fish in the numerous crusty chiringuitos on the beach.

If you have a second day in Málaga, use it to take a relaxing stroll in the lush botanical garden, **La Concepción** ⑪, north of the city. Afterward, head toward Paseo Marítimo and Málaga's beaches, where the sun and sand beckon; doze and soak up the rays before dining on fresh fish at a waterfront restaurant.

TIMING

This walk takes a full day; note that some sights, including the Fundación Picasso, close between 2 and 5. In the summer, the hot Málaga sun can be relentless, so it's best to tackle the sights in the morning, and then, Spanish style, take a break from the heat in the early afternoon—perhaps in the shaded terrace of a restaurant or ice-creamery—and continue your sightseeing after 5 when the air starts to cool. Alternately, you may want to do this walk over two days, thus allowing time for some sunning on the beach.

## Sights to See

❽ **Alcazaba.** This impressive Moorish fortress is one of Málaga's greatest monuments. It was begun in the 8th century, when Málaga was the principal port of the Moorish kingdom, though most of the current structure dates from the 11th century. The inner palace was built between 1057 and 1063, when the Moorish emirs took up residence; Ferdinand and Isabella lived here for a time after conquering Málaga in 1487. The ruins are dappled with orange trees and bougainvillea, and their heights afford views of the park and port. ⊠ *Entrance on Alcazabilla,* ☎ *952/216005.* ⊡ *€3.* ☉ *Oct.–Mar., Tues.–Sun. 9–8; Apr.–Sept., Tues.–Sun. 9:30–8.*

❹ **Cathedral.** Built between 1528 and 1782, the cathedral is not one of the greatest in Spain, having been left unfinished when the funds ran out. Because it lacks one of its two towers, the building has been called La Manquita (the One-Armed Lady). The lovely enclosed choir, which miraculously survived the burnings of the civil war, is the work of the great 17th-century artist Pedro de Mena, who carved the wood wafer-

thin in some places to express the fold of a robe or shape of a finger. The choir also has a pair of massive 18th-century pipe organs, one of which is still used for the occasional concert. Adjoining the cathedral is a small museum of religious art and artifacts, and a walk around the cathedral on Calle Cister will take you to the late-Gothic Puerta del Sagrario. The back of the cathedral is hemmed in by a small, leafy garden, with a pond where lilies sprout out of the mossy depths. ⊠ *Calle de Molina Larios,* ☎ *952/215917.* 🎟 *€1.80 for both cathedral and museum.* ☼ *Mon.–Sat. 10–6:45.*

**7** **Fundación Picasso.** On Plaza de la Merced, No. 15 was the childhood home of Málaga's most famous native son, Pablo Picasso, born here in 1881. It now houses a foundation and library for art historians. The interior has been entirely remodeled, with no trace of its original furnishings. The second floor, where Picasso's family lived, has a permanent exhibition with engravings and a few pieces of sculpture and ceramics; temporary exhibits of assorted art and memorabilia fill the ground floor. ⊠ *Plaza de la Merced 15,* ☎ *952/600215.* 🎟 *Free.* ☼ *Mon.–Sat. 11–2 and 5–8, Sun. 11–2.*

**9** **Gibralfaro.** Magnificent vistas beckon at these Moorish fortifications built for Yusuf I in the 14th century. The Moors called them Jebel-faro, from the Arab word for "mount" and the Greek word for "lighthouse," after a beacon that stood here to guide ships into the harbor and warn of invading pirates. The beacon has been succeeded by a small parador. Thieves have been said to hover here, so avoid going alone, and don't carry valuables. You can drive here by way of Calle Victoria or take a minibus that leaves 10 times a day between 11 and 7, or roughly every hour, from the bus stop in the park near the Plaza de la Marina. Also, Bus 35 travels here, departing from the Paseo del

Parque. ✉ *Gibralfaro Mountain,* ☎ *9952/220043.* 🎫 *Free.* ⊙ *Castle daily 9–6.*

**⑪ La Concepción.** Providing a relaxing respite from the bustle and bleating horns of the city, this 150-year-old botanical garden might better be described as a luxuriant green jungle. It was created by the daughter of the British consul, who married a Spanish shipping magnate—the captains of the Spaniard's fleet had standing orders to bring back seedlings and cuttings from every "exotic" country they called at. The garden was abandoned for many years, the tropical plants left to their own devices, but La Concepción has been carefully and lovingly restored. The garden is just off the exit road to Granada—too far to walk, but well worth the cab fare from the city center. Bus 2 (Ciudad Jardin) heads to La Concepción from the Alameda Principal in the city center. ✉ *Carretera de las Pedrizas, Km 166,* ☎ *952/252148.* 🎫 *€3.* ⊙ *Tues.–Sun. 10 AM–sundown.*

**❷ Mercado de Atarazanas.** The stalls at this lively market sell an amazing assortment of fresh fish, spices, and vegetables. The typical 19th-century iron structure incorporates the original Puerta de Atarazanas, the attractive 14th-century Moorish gate that once connected the city with the port. ✉ *Calle Atarazanas s/n.* ⊙ *Mon.–Sat. 9–2.*

NEED A BREAK?
The **Antigua Casa de la Guardia** (✉ Alameda 18, ☎ no phone), around the corner from the Mercado de Atarazanas, is Málaga's oldest bar, founded in 1840. Andalusian wines flow straight from the barrel, and the floor is ankle-deep in discarded shrimp shells.

**❸ Museo de Artes Populares.** Málaga's Arts and Crafts Museum is housed in the the old Mesón de la Victoria, a 17th-century inn. On display are horse-drawn carriages and carts, old agricultural implements, folk costumes, a forge, a bakery, an ancient grape press, and Malagueño ceramics and sculptures. ✉ *Pasillo de Santa Isabel 10,* ☎ *952/217137.* 🎫 *€2.* ⊙ *Weekdays 10–1:30 and 4–7 (5–8 June–Aug.), Sat. 10–1:30.*

**❻ Palacio de Buenavista.** The future Picasso Museum—which is sure to become, judging from the growing excitement, the pride and joy of Málaga—will be housed in the regal, 16th-century Buenavista Palace, once home to the Counts of Buenavista. The museum will have a core collection donated by Picasso's daughter-in-law Christine and grandson Bernard. The museum is scheduled to open with much fanfare on October 25 (Picasso's birthday) in 2003. (The opening date has been routinely delayed, most recently by the discovery of archaeological remains.) Although Picasso's family moved to the north of Spain when he was 10, and he spent the last three decades of his life in exile after the Spanish Civil War, the artist always considered himself first and foremost an Andalusian. ✉ *Calle de San Agustín.*

**❺ Palacio Episcopal.** The Bishop's Palace, facing the cathedral, is used for art and cultural exhibits. ✉ *Plaza Obispo 6,* ☎ *952/602722.* 🎫 *Free.* ⊙ *Tues.–Sun. 10–2 and 6–9.*

**❶ Paseo del Parque.** Lined with palm trees and a botanical garden, this pedestrian promenade unfolds as the "lungs of Málaga," where you can relax amid verdant nooks, shaded benches, and quiet paths. Constructed in 1897, the Paseo is punctuated along the way with a spate of impressive buildings, including the stylish, turn-of-the-20th-century *ayuntamiento* (town hall) and the grand Oficina Central de Correos, the city's old central post office. The Paseo runs from the Plaza de la Marina to the bullring.

**⑩ Pedregalejo.** At the eastern end of the Paseo Marítimo you'll find this beach suburb, once a traditional fishing village. Here you can dine on *fritura malagueña*, Málaga's ubiquitous fried fish, in the chiringuitos on the beach and stroll seafront promenade or the tree-lined streets of El Limonar. Note that the walk to Pedregalejo can take up to an hour, so if you want to give your feet a rest, hop on Bus 11, which travels to Pedregalejo from Avenida de Cervantes (near the Paseo del Parque). The bus route follows Paseo de Reding and Paseo de Sancha, which run parallel to Paseo Marítimo, but a few blocks inland.

---

NEED A BREAK?

When the sweat starts trickling down your back—and you find that you're not so much strolling as plodding down Paseo Marítimo—escape is around the corner at one of Málaga's oldest ice-creameries, **Helados Cremades** (⊠ Paseo Marítimo Pedregalejo, ☎ 952/2298170; ⊠ Paseo Marítimo El Palo, Playa Virginia 23), where you can rejuvenate under a shaded blue-and-white terrace and relieve your parched throat with a blessedly cool *granizado* (crushed ice drink) in such flavors as lemon, orange, and the *blanco y negro* (black and white—coffee-flavored granizado topped with whipped cream). For more elaborate concoctions, go for the plethora of ice-cream dishes, including the *Copa Sol,* mounds of fresh peaches and peach ice cream topped with whipped cream drizzled in caramel.

---

# Dining and Lodging

**$$$** ✗ **Adolfo.** On Málaga's Paseo Marítimo, this small restaurant has a solid reputation for Spanish cuisine with a contemporary touch. The dining room is inviting, with a wood floor and exposed-brick walls, service is smooth and professional, and there's a good wine list. Entrées include *vieiras con setas* (scallops with wild mushrooms) and *cabrito lechal a la miel de romero* (roast baby kid in rosemary-honey sauce). ⊠ *Paseo Marítimo Pablo Ruiz Picasso 12,* ☎ *952/601914. AE, D, MC, V. Closed Sun.*

**$$$** ✗ **Café de Paris.** The owner of this elegant Paseo Marítimo restaurant ★ was once a chef at Madrid's Horcher. The red-and-mahogany interior is warm and intimate. Sophisticated diners come from far afield for dishes prepared with creative flair from the freshest of ingredients. The menu changes daily, but there's always a good selection of appetizers, meat, and fish. *Rodaballo* (turbot) and *lubina* (sea bass) are usually present in one form or another, as is *solomillo de buy café de Paris* (beef fillet with herb-butter sauce). The *menú de degustación* lets you try a bit of everything. ⊠ *Vélez Málaga 8,* ☎ *952/225043. Reservations essential. AE, DC, MC, V. Closed Sun. No dinner Mon.*

**$$–$$$** ✗ **Antonio Martín.** Once a humble snack shack, this beachfront institution is now a sprawling restaurant, with a large sea-view terrace that's covered with glass in winter. Variations on local dishes mark the culinary theme, with specialties including *zarzuela de pescado y mariscos de la Bahía* (seafood stew) and *solomillo de cerdo estilo Montes de Málaga* (Málaga-style pork fillet). ⊠ *Plaza la Malagueta,* ☎ *952/ 227382. AE, DC, MC, V. Closed Oct.–Mar. No dinner Sun.*

**$$–$$$** ✗ **El Chinitas.** At one end of Pasaje Chinitas, Málaga's most *típico* street, you'll find this tile-bedecked place. The tapas bar is popular, especially for its cured ham. The second floor has two private dining rooms—groups of 12–20 can and do reserve the Sala Antequera, with a Camelot-style round table—and a third that's a banquet hall. Try the *sopa viña AB,* a fish soup flavored with sherry and thickened with mayonnaise, or *solomillo al vino de Málaga,* fillet steak in Málaga wine sauce. ⊠ *Moreno Monroy 4,* ☎ *952/210972. DC, MC, V.*

$$–$$$  ✕ **Escuela de Hostelería.** For a memorable lunch, it's well worth going
  ★     out of your way to Málaga's hotel and catering school, in a 19th-cen-
        tury mansion 8 km (5 mi) outside town on the Churriana road. The
        dining room is in a light, airy building of striking modern design, ad-
        joining the La Cónsula mansion and its luxuriant garden. The delicious,
        exquisitely presented seasonal dishes include *solomillo de cerdo ibérico
        relleno de jamón con salsa de vino de Málaga* (pork fillet enveloped
        with ham and topped with Málaga wine sauce). ⊠ *Finca La Cónsula,
        Churriana,* ☎ *952/622562. Reservations essential. AE, DC, MC, V.
        Closed weekends and Aug. No dinner.*

$$–$$$  ✕ **Rincón Catedral.** Tucked into a bright *rincón* (corner) next to the
        cathedral, this is an intimate nook, with only six tables and a rustic
        decor. On the menu are simple yet flavorful fish and meat dishes, such
        as fritura malagueña, *brocheta de solomillo Iberico* (Iberian sirloin bro-
        chette), and a hearty starter of *revuelto de patatas y espinacas* (scram-
        bled eggs with potato and spinach). The friendly couple at the
        helm—Paco cooks, and Emilia attends to the customers—will also likely
        give you a taste of chatty Malagueño hospitality. ⊠ *Calle Cañón 7,*
        ☎ *952/2600518. AE, MC, V. Closed Sun. June–Sept.*

$$      ✕ **Rincón del Trillo.** Of the many restaurants in the pedestrian shop-
        ping area between Calle Marqués de Larios and Calle Nueva, this is
        one of the best. You enter through a small bar; the somewhat cramped
        but pleasant dining room is upstairs. The menu is more interesting than
        most, with several dishes from northern Spain. *Bacalao* (salt cod) is
        served up half a dozen different ways, and there's a good selection of
        grilled meats. There are tables on the sidewalk in summer. ⊠ *Es-
        parteros 6,* ☎ *952/213135. AE, DC, MC, V.*

$–$$    ✕ **Cortijo de Pepe.** The bar may be sticky, the floor littered with nap-
        kins, and the waiters a tad brusque—but that's how good tapas bars
        usually are. At this former *cortijo* (country estate), it's best to do like
        the locals: pull up a stool, order a *caña* (a glass of beer) or a *vino tinto
        de la casa* (house red wine), and point to whatever tapa looks good—
        anything from garlic shrimp to citrus-scented salad with avocado and
        tuna to an asparagus omelette. The other specialty is *carnes a la brasa*
        (grilled meats), which you can order at the bar or in the more formal
        restaurant upstairs. ⊠ *Plaza de la Merced 2,* ☎ *952/224071. No
        credit cards. Closed Tues.*

$–$$    ✕ **El Jardín.** This comfortably cluttered bar and restaurant overlooks
        the sculpted cathedral garden from its corner perch on cheery Calle
        Cañón. The central location means that in summer it's thronged with
        more visitors than locals, but it manages to maintain an authentic ap-
        peal. You can dig into a range of local dishes, including *cordero con
        piñones* (lamb with pine nuts) and *revuelto El Jardín* (a hefty plate of
        scrambled eggs with ham, shrimp, and asparagus). On Friday and Sat-
        urday nights in the summer, you can hear Andalusian piano music per-
        formed live. ⊠ *Calle Cañón 1,* ☎ *952/220419. AE, DC, MC, V.*

$–$$    ✕ **El Tintero.** This sprawling seafood restaurant, with a massive ter-
  ★     race overlooking the beach boardwalk, is a Málaga institution, famous
        for its fresh fish—and the way that it's ordered. No menus here. In-
        stead, waiters fan out among the tables, bearing large silver trays of
        seafood and singing out what's on offer: *"Yo llevo pulpo!"* ("I have
        octopus!") and *"Llevo calamares!"* ("I have squid!"). Diners choose
        from the passing platters and eat off paper plates (albeit sturdy ones),
        which are counted to determine the bill. At meal's end waiters come
        along shouting *"Yo cobro!"* (literally, "I charge!" or "Pay your bill
        here!"). ⊠ *Playa de Dedo,* ☎ *952/204464. MC, V.*

$–$$    ✕ **La Cancela.** In an alley off Calle Granada, at the top of Molina Lar-
        ios (one block from the Palacio Episcopal), this pretty bistro serves stan-
        dard Spanish fare, such as *riñones al jerez* (kidneys sautéed with sherry)

and *cerdo al vino de Málaga* (pork with Málaga wine sauce). It's ideal for lunch after a morning of shopping. The two dining rooms (one upstairs, one down) are filled with curious objects: iron grilles, birdcages, potted plants, plastic flowers. In summer, tables appear on the sidewalk for outdoor dining. ⊠ *Denís Belgrano 5*, ☎ *952/223125. AE, DC, MC, V. Closed Wed. No dinner Mon.*

$$$$ ✕🏨 **AC Málaga Palacio.** This luxury hotel looms over Málaga's bustling heart—the cathedral sits one block away, and a 10-minute stroll along the Paseo del Parque brings you to the city's *playas* (beaches). The ample rooms have blond-wood furnishings that contrast nicely with the blue-and-white decor. There's an elegant lobby lounge, and the large, airy restaurant ($$$) serves top-notch regional fare, including *presa de ibérico con setas* (wild boar with mushrooms) and *albóndigas con salsa de Jabugo* (meatballs in ham sauce). The *tarta de chocolate al aroma de naranja* (orange-scented chocolate cake) is mouthwatering. ⊠ *Cortina del Muelle 1, 29015,* ☎ *952/215185,* FAX *952/225100,* WEB *www. ac-hoteles.com. 214 rooms. Restaurant, pool, gym, sauna, bar, meeting rooms. AE, DC, MC, V.*

$$$ ✕🏨 **Euromar Málaga Centro.** From the gleaming marble lobby to the equally impressive marble bathrooms, this hotel—opened in 2001 along the Guadalmedina riverbed—radiates a certain old-fashioned elegance. Rooms are warmly decorated with dark blue upholstery and floral bedspreads and curtains. The bright restaurant, adorned with red-and-white tablecloths, serves a fine array of fish dishes. ⊠ *Calle Mármoles 6, 29007,* ☎ *952/070216,* FAX *952/283360,* WEB *www.euro-mar.com. 113 rooms, 5 suites. Restaurant, pool, bar, meeting rooms. AE, DC, MC, V.*

$$$ ✕🏨 **Parador de Málaga–Gibralfaro.** Surrounded by pine trees on top
★ of Gibralfaro, 3 km (2 mi) above the city, this cozy, gray-stone parador has spectacular views of the bay. The attractive rooms—blue curtains and bedspreads, woven rugs on tile floors—are the best in Málaga. Reserve well in advance. The restaurant has fabulous views and fine food, including both regional and international dishes. ⊠ *Monte de Gibralfaro, 29016,* ☎ *952/221902,* FAX *952/221904,* WEB *www.parador.es. 38 rooms. Restaurant, cafeteria, pool, bar, meeting room. AE, DC, MC, V.*

$$$$ 🏨 **Larios.** This small hotel is in an elegantly restored 19th-century building on the central Plaza de la Constitución. Black-and-white tile floors lend subdued elegance to the second-floor lobby; the rooms are furnished with light wood and cream-color fabrics and accented with artsy black-and-white photographs. ⊠ *Marqués de Larios 2, 29005,* ☎ *952/222200,* FAX *952/222407,* WEB *www.hotel-larios.com. 34 rooms, 6 suites. Restaurant, cable TV with movies, meeting room. AE, DC, MC, V.*

$$$–$$$$ 🏨 **NH Málaga.** You'll find this sleek modern building next to the (usually dry) Guadalmedina River. Guest rooms offer streamlined comfort, with beige curtains and bedspreads and wood floors; there are nine conference rooms, making it popular with business guests. ⊠ *Avda. Río Guadalmedina, 29007,* ☎ *952/071323,* FAX *952/393862.* WEB *www.nh-hoteles.com. 129 rooms, 4 suites. Restaurant, sauna, bar, meeting rooms, some pets allowed. AE, DC, MC, V.*

$$$ 🏨 **Los Naranjos.** Named after the orange trees that flourish throughout Andalusia, this small, family-owned hotel is popular with business travelers who favor more subdued settings. It's tucked away in a quiet residential neighborhood, and yet is just a few blocks from Málaga's beaches—rooms on the top floors have sea views. The hotel's cheerful, whitewashed Andalusian façade gives way, unfortunately, to a drab lobby, but the rooms are brightly decorated in a green-and-white decor, with crisp white bedspreads. ⊠ *Paseo de Sancha 35, 290016,* ☎ *952/224316,* FAX *952/225975,* WEB *www.hotel-losnaranjos.com. 41 rooms. Restaurant, bar. AE, DC, MC, V.*

$$$  ⊡ **Don Curro.** Just around the corner from the cathedral, this family classic is going through continual renovations, but an old-fashioned air permeates the wood-paneled common rooms, the fireplace lounge, and the somewhat stodgy, wood-floored guest rooms. The best rooms are in the new wing, at the back of the building. ⊠ *Sancha de Lara 7, 29015,* ☎ *952/227200,* ℻ *952/215946.* ⓌⒺⒷ *www.infonegocio. com/doncurro. 112 rooms, 6 suites. Restaurant, some pets allowed. AE, DC, MC, V.*

$$  ⊡ **Las Vegas.** Though the name suggests casinos, there's nothing of the sort at this long-established hotel in a pleasant section of town east of the center, a five-minute stroll to the beach. Some parts show their age, but ongoing renovations have kept most of the hotel reasonably up-to-date. Guest rooms are light and bright, most with balconies; for the best view, ask for one in the new wing or on the top two floors of the old wing. Many of the friendly staff have been around since the hotel's opening in 1964. The simple dining room, with a fine sea view over the Paseo Marítimo, is refreshingly inexpensive. ⊠ *Paseo de Sancha 22, 29016,* ☎ *952/217712,* ℻ *952/224889. 107 rooms, 10 suites. Restaurant, pool, bar. AE, DC, MC, V.*

$$  ⊡ **Venecia.** A good budget option, this four-story hotel has a central location on the Alameda Principal, next to the Plaza de la Marina. The rooms are simply furnished but spacious. ⊠ *Alameda Principal 9, 29001,* ☎ *952/213636,* ℻ *952/213637. 40 rooms. AE, DC, MC, V.*

# Nightlife and the Arts

Start with Málaga's year-round balmy weather and its plethora of outdoor *terrazas,* add the city's sizeable population of half a million people, the Málagan penchant for socializing, and the region's popular muscatel wines, and it's no surprise that Málaga's *la marcha* (night "scene") is as hip and happening as anywhere in Andalusia. The foreign-student contingent—Málaga is one of Spain's most popular cities for Spanish-language studies—adds to the lively nighttime atmosphere, particularly in the city center plazas. In summer, rock concerts are staged in the bullring.

## Bars and Clubs

Málaga's main nightlife districts are the Maestranza, between the bullring and Playa de la Malagueta, and the beachfront in the suburb of Pedregalejos. The Paseo Marítimo is also dotted with bars, many with terrazas that spill over with revelers—locals and sunburned visitors alike—in the summer months. **El Navegante** (⊠ Paseo Marítimo 19, ☎ 952/228835) is a lively pub with pool table and bar inside, and a large, breezy terrace with wicker tables and chairs outside.

Central Málaga, particularly around Plaza Uncibay and Plaza de la Merced, has a bustling bar scene. **El Pimpi** (⊠ Calle Granada 62, ☎ no phone), just off Plaza de la Constitución, is a dark bodega-style bar that transforms into a club later in the evening, with dance tunes that keep the crowd moving until the wee hours.

## Theater, Film, and Concerts

The region's main theater is the **Teatro Cervantes** (⊠ Calle Ramos Marín, ☎ 952/224100 or 952/220237 for information; 901/246246 for tickets, ⓌⒺⒷ www.teatrocervantes.com). Programs include Spanish-language plays, concerts, ballet, and flamenco.

The **Festival Cine de Málaga** (Málaga Film Festival, ☎ 952/228242) usually takes place in early June. It showcases new Spanish-language films, including documentaries, and draws film and video buyers from around Europe. Most showings are at the Teatro Cervantes.

The **Málaga Symphony Orchestra** (☏ 952/224109 or 952/220237) has a winter season of orchestral concerts and chamber music, with most performances in the Teatro Cervantes.

## Spectator Sports

### Bullfighting

Most Andalusian cities have a prominent bullring, and Málaga is no exception. **La Malagueta** rises between the central Plaza del General Torrijos and the nearby strip of La Malagueta beaches (named after the ring). Bullfights generally occur twice a year, during Semana Santa (Holy Week), and during the raucous, weeklong Feria de Málaga in early to mid-August. Ticket prices vary because of a number of factors, including distance from the bullring and whether you choose to sit in *sol* (sun) or *sombra* (shade). They're available at the ring's box office; usually getting tickets the day of the event isn't a problem.

### Soccer

**C. F. Málaga** (Club de Futbol Málaga) is a formidable contender in the fiercely competitive world of Spanish soccer. Fans will get a kick out of seeing C. F. Málaga play at **La Rosaleda,** the city's soccer stadium, particularly when they're pitted against another big-name team. Just watching the passionate fans erupt into cheers and chants might be entertainment enough. La Rosaleda sits north of the city. Bus 2 or 17 from Alameda Principal near the center of town head to the stadium. Buy tickets at the box office, open 11 to 2 and 6 to 9; there are usually seats available the day of the game, unless the opponent is Barcelona or Madrid, in which case a sellout is likely two weeks in advance or more.

## Shopping

Málaga's main shopping thoroughfare is Calle Marqués de Larios, lined with clothing, shoes, and accessories shops—and plenty of cafés and ice-creameries to sustain you along the way. Wander the web of old, narrow streets around Calle Marqués de Larios to find silversmiths and vendors of religious books and statues working from shops that have changed little in a century.

Near the train and bus stations, the **El Corte Inglés** department store (✉ Avda. de Andalucía 4–6, ☏ 95/230-0000; closed Sun.)—part of the ubiquitous Spanish chain—has English interpreters, shipping, VAT refunds, and currency exchange.

**Larios Centro** (✉ Avda. de la Aurora 25, ☏ 95/369393; closed Sun.), a shopping mall near the train and bus stations, has the stock lineup of Spanish clothing stores, including Zara (the perennially popular women's casual-wear store), Mango (ditto), a range of shoe stores, plus a multiplex movie theater.

Málaga has several bustling markets where you can browse for bargains—and soak up the local color. On Sunday from 9 until about 3, you can check out the biggest of them, **Rastro Martiricos** (✉ Paseo de Martiricos s/n), near the La Rosaleda soccer stadium north of the center. This sprawling open-air flea market is packed with makeshift stalls, presided over by their barker-owners selling everything from cheap T-shirts to costume jewelry to pirated CDs to lingerie. Whatever you buy probably won't last out the year, but it's hard to complain when you're paying rock-bottom prices like €1 for two halter tops. It's roughly a 25-minute walk from the center of town to the flea market; an alternative is to hop on Bus 2 or 17 from Alameda Principal.

From glistening pyramids of oranges and kiwis to oversized bins of pungent spices to slimy mounds of fresh squid and octopus, the **Mercado de Atarazanas** (✉ Calle Atarazanas s/n), housed in an eye-catching 19th-century metal building near Plaza Felix Saenz, is a foodie's fantasy. It's open Monday to Saturday, 9 to 2.

# THE AXARQUÍA

The Axarquía occupies the eastern third of Málaga's province, stretching from Málaga to Nerja. Its coast consists of narrow, pebbly beaches and a string of drab fishing villages on either side of the ugly high-rise resort town Torre del Mar. The area's largest town is the burgeoning beach resort of Nerja, which has managed to maintain a modicum of authenticity in the face of the run-away resort development that plagues so much of Málaga's coast. Nerja's claim to fame is its nearby caves, where you'll find the world's largest stalactite. Axarquía's capital is the Vélez-Málaga, a relaxed town with white houses, small churches, and Moorish ruins.

The region's charm lies in its mountainous interior, peppered with picturesque white pueblos—31 in all—vineyards, and tiny farms. The four-lane E-15 highway speeds across the region a few miles in from the coast; traffic on the old coastal road (N340) is slower. If you have a car and an up-to-date road map, explore the Axarquía's inland villages, where you can follow a wine and raisin route through flourishing vineyards. The Ruta de los Tajos (Route of Gorges) winds among the plunging gorges of western Axarquía, through the white village of Comares and Colmenar.

## Nerja

**⑫** *52 km (32 mi) east of Málaga.*

Nerja—the name comes from the Moorish word *narixa,* meaning "abundant springs"—is a developing resort. Much of its growth has been confined to *urbanizaciones* ("village" developments) outside town. The old village is on a headland above small beaches and rocky coves, which offer reasonable bathing despite the gray, gritty sand. In high season, the beaches are packed with northern Europeans, and parts of Nerja are bogged down with its share of overpriced tourist restaurants and blocky hotels. However, Nerja also has a pleasant old town with a web of narrow streets and a relaxed atmosphere of locals going about their day that has all but been obliterated in the larger resort towns on the Costa del Sol. The **Balcón de Europa,** a lookout high above the sea, on a promontory just off the central square, is the highlight of Nerja.

The **Cuevas de Nerja** (Nerja Caves) lie between Almuñecar and Nerja on a road surrounded by giant cliffs and dramatic seascapes. Signs point to the cave entrance above the village of Maro, 4 km (2½ mi) east of Nerja. The caves were discovered in 1959 by children playing on the hillside; they're now floodlit for better views of the spires and turrets created by millenniums of dripping water. One suspended pinnacle is 200 ft long, making it the world's largest stalactite. The awesome subterranean chambers make an impressive setting for concerts and ballets during July's Nerja Caves Festival. ✉ *Carretera N-340, 4 km north of Nerja,* ☎ *952/529520.* 💷 *€5.* ⊙ *Daily 10–2 and 4–6:30 (4–8 in summer).*

## Dining and Lodging

**$$$–$$$$** ✕ **Udo Heimer.** Your host and the restaurant's namesake, a genial German, welcomes you warmly to this stylish art deco villa in a development to the east of Nerja. The visual flair extends to the presentation of the food, which mixes German and Spanish flavors. Favorites include a warm salad of prawns and avocado mousse and an entrée of stuffed quail with Armagnac sauce and sauerkraut. The excellent wine list features rarities from all over Spain. The servers are a bit listless, perhaps overshadowed by their ebullient boss. ⊠ *Pueblo Andaluz 27,* ☎ *952/520032. MC, V. Closed Wed. No lunch in summer.*

**$$–$$$** ✕ **Casa Luque.** One of Nerja's most authentic Spanish restaurants, Casa Luque is in an old Andalusian house behind the Balcón de Europa church. The menu has dishes from northern Spain, often of Basque or Navarrese origin, with an emphasis on meat and game; good fresh fish is also on offer. The lovely patio is a perfect setting in summer. ⊠ *Plaza Cavana 2,* ☎ *952/521004. AE, DC, MC, V. Closed Sun.*

**$$–$$$** ✕🏨 **Parador de Nerja.** This modern parador is on a cliff's edge, with rooms whose balconies overlook a garden and the sea. Rooms in the newer, single-story wing open onto their own patios. An elevator takes you down to the rocky beach. The restaurant serves primarily local cuisine and is known for its fish; the menu changes daily. It might include *pez espada a la naranja* (swordfish in orange sauce) or giant *langostino* (shrimp). ⊠ *Almuñecar 8, 29780,* ☎ *952/520050,* ℻ *952/521997,* 🖳 *www.parador.es. 73 rooms. Restaurant, pool. AE, DC, MC, V.*

**$$** 🏨 **Paraiso del Mar.** An erstwhile private villa was expanded to form this small hotel, perched on the edge of a cliff overlooking the sea east of the Balcón de Europa. Decor is bright and cheerful, with light-blue and yellow fabrics, lots of potted plants, and sunlight pouring in through picture windows. Some rooms have terraces, four have hot tubs, and most have sea views. ⊠ *Prolongación del Carabeo 22, 29780,* ☎ *952/521621,* ℻ *952/522309. 9 rooms, 3 suites. Pool. AE, DC, MC, V. Closed mid-Nov.–mid-Dec.*

## Nightlife and the Arts

**El Colono** (⊠ Granada 6, ☎ 952/521826) is a flamenco club in a typical Andalusian house in the town center. Dinner shows begin at 9 on Wednesday in winter, and at 9:30 or 10 Wednesday and Friday in summer. You can choose from three prix-fixe menus.

# Frigiliana

**⑬** *6 km (4 mi) north of Nerja, 58 km (36 mi) east of Málaga.*

The village of Frigiliana sits on a mountain ridge overlooking the sea. One of the last battles between the Christians and the Moors was waged here in 1567. The short drive off the highway rewards you with spectacular views and an old quarter full of cobbled streets and ancient houses. If you don't have a car, take a bus here from Nerja; six buses depart daily.

# Vélez-Málaga

**⑭** *25 km (16 mi) west of Nerja, 36 km (22 mi) east of Málaga, 4 km (2.5 mi) north of Torre del Mar.*

The capital of the Axarquía, Vélez-Málaga is a pleasant agricultural town of white houses and a center for strawberry fields and vineyards. The Thursday market, near the Plaza del Trabajo, is a bustling affair, with stalls selling everything from fresh produce to cut-price T-shirts and sandals. Perched above Vélez-Málaga are the ruins of a Moorish **castillo** (castle), with views of the village rooftops and the sea.

The church of **Santa María la Mayor** was built in Mudéjar style on the site of a mosque that was destroyed when the town fell to the Christians in 1487. At this writing the church is closed for renovations; open hours vary, but are usually daily from 9 AM to 8 PM.

## Dining and Lodging

Vélez-Málaga is light on lodgings, so one option—if you are not averse to masses of Spanish and Northern European sunseekers—is to stay in nearby Torre del Mar, a tacky resort town, but one with several high-end hotels and a string of seafood restaurants. Torre del Mar is just 4 km (2.5 mi) south of Vélez-Málaga, and numerous buses link the two towns.

$  ✕ **La Cueva.** It's food over fanciness at this busy restaurant on Paseo de Larios, the main pedestrian thoroughfare in Torre del Mar. The long stainless steel bar and paper tablecloths won't win any awards, but the fresh seafood draws crowds of happy diners. And for a resort town, where marked-up mediocrity is the norm, the fantastically low prices are a breath of fresh air. Noteworthy dishes include *pulpo frito* (fried octopus), *pimientos en su jugo* (peppers fried in their own juice), and the aptly named *patatas pobres* ("poor potatoes," wedges of potatoes fried in olive oil). ✉ *Paseo de Larios 1, Torre del Mar,* ☎ *952/540223. MC, V. Closed Tues.*

$$$  🏨 **Husa Mainake.** A short stroll from Torre del Mar's beach and Paseo Marítimo, this four-star hotel has ample rooms with sunny terraces and a roof pool where you can enjoy the *sol* away from beach crowds. Munch on simple yet tasty fare at the outdoor terrace and bar set on a busy, sun-speckled corner facing the beach. ✉ *Prolongación Calle Copo at Avenida Toré Toré, 29740 Torre del Mar,* ☎ *952/547246,* FAX *952/541543.* WEB *www.husa.es. 40 rooms. Restaurant, pool, bar, meeting rooms. AE, DC, MC, V.*

# Cómpeta

🔟 *28 km (17 mi) northeast of Vélez-Málaga, 30 km (19 mi) north of Nerja (via Torrox and Frigiliana).*

The **Ruta del Vino** (Wine Route) winds its way through the Axarquía 22 km (14 mi) inland from the coast, stopping at villages that produce the sweet, earthy local wine. Cómpeta is of particular note—it's a white-washed hill village encircled by lush vineyards. Here, you can wine-taste to your heart's content at various bodegas and bars, including the Museo del Vino, a bustling bodega, wine store, and restaurant all rolled into one. The village of Cómpeta erupts with the sounds of popping corks on August 15 for its annual **Noche de Vino** (Wine Night) when 1,500 liters of wine are guzzled down in the streets, plazas, and bars by a merry crowd of locals and visitors. In the central Plaza de la Vendimia, villagers engage in the age-old ritual of stomping grapes to make wine that is bottled for consumption the following year.

## Dining

$–$$  ✕ **Museo del Vino.** Barrels and bottles of muscatel wine line the bodega of this rustic restaurant with brick walls and a wood-beamed ceiling. Start out the evening wine-tasting and sampling a variety of tasty tapas, including pungent Manchego cheese, cured hams, and olives. Then, if you're still hungry, settle in for a full meal, featuring grilled meats, the house specialty. ✉ *Calle Constitución s/n,* ☎ *952/553314. MC, V. Closed Mon.*

## Ruta de la Pasa

**⑯** *Almáchar: 54 km (34 mi) west of Cómpeta (via Vélez-Málaga), 26 km (16 mi) northwest of Vélez-Málaga; El Borge: 2 km (1 mi) northwest of Almáchar.*

The Ruta de la Pasa (Raisin Route) passes through the sleepy villages of Moclinejo, Almáchar, and El Borge, and is especially spectacular during the late-summer grape-harvest season and in late autumn, when the leaves of the vines turn gold. The white pueblo of **Almáchar** is crisscrossed with winding streets flanked by whitewashed houses adorned with bright geraniums. In the center of town is the **Iglesia de San Mateo,** a 16th-century church with a Mudéjar bell tower. Almáchar splashes out on September 1 for its **Fiesta de Ajoblanco,** when folks down bowl upon bowl of *ajoblanco,* a gazpacholike soup made with almonds and garlic, and, special to this region, flavored with muscatel wine and then sprinkled liberally with raisins. **El Borge,** the "raisin capital" of the region, throws its annual **Fiesta de la Pasa** (Raisin Festival) on September 16, when thousands of bags of raisins are passed out amid music and merriment.

*En Route* History buffs should make a short detour to **Macharaviaya** (7 km [4 mi] north of Rincón de la Victoria) and ponder the past glory of this now sleepy village: in 1776 one of its sons, Bernardo de Gálvez, became Spanish governor of Louisiana, and later he fought in the American Revolution. (Galveston, Texas, takes its name from him.) Macharaviaya prospered under his heirs, and for many years enjoyed a lucrative monopoly on the manufacture of playing cards for South America.

# ANTEQUERA AND NORTHERN MÁLAGA

The contrast between inland and the coast is nowhere more keenly felt than in northern Málaga. While development of Costa del Sol continues on unchecked, here, deep in the interior, there are craggy cliffs, quiet vineyards, sloping farm fields, dusty roads—and, refreshingly, not much else. Rugged plains—where farmers break the red earth with a hoe, dwarfed against a backdrop of towering mountain ranges—and sun-strewn orchards are dotted with unspoiled, geranium-filled villages. Penetrate this northern interior, and time seems to reverse itself, like a wind peeling back the pages of a calendar. Gossiping with the *vecinos* (neighbors) still means heading for the local *panadería* (bakery), black-clad widows return from the market with live chickens in their baskets, and on Sunday mornings, tolling church bells pierce the silence of ancient, winding streets. Antequera is northern Málaga's hub, a spirited town with an impressive clutch of churches and convents. The whitewashed village of Archidona has one of the province's only octagonal squares, the splendid Plaza Ochavada. Natural treasures abound: meander through the otherworldly limestone landscape of the Parque Natural del Torcal; commune with flamingos on the banks of Andalusia's largest lake, the Fuente de Piedra; and gape at the daunting Garganta del Chorro, a breathtaking gorge above the Guadalhorce River.

## Antequera

**⑰** *64 km (40 mi) northwest of Málaga, 100 km (62 mi) northwest of Vélez-Málaga (via Málaga), 108 km (67 mi) northeast of Ronda (via Pizarra).*

Antequera became one of the great strongholds of the Moors after their defeat at Córdoba and Seville in the 13th century. Its fall to the Christians in 1410 paved the way for the reconquest of Granada—the Moors retreated, leaving a **fortress** on the town heights. Next door is the former church of **Santa María la Mayor,** one of 27 churches, convents, and monasteries in Antequera. Built of sandstone in the 16th century, it has a fine ribbed vault and is now a concert hall. Another landmark is the church of **San Sebastián,** whose brick baroque Mudéjar tower is topped by a winged figure called the Angelote ("big angel"), the symbol of Antequera. The church of **Nuestra Señora del Carmen** (Our Lady of Carmen) has an extraordinary baroque altarpiece that towers to the ceiling.

The dramatic silhouette of the **Peña de los Enamorados** (Lovers' Rock), east of Antequera along N342, is an Andalusian landmark. Legend has it that a Moorish princess and a Christian shepherd boy eloped here one night and cast themselves to their deaths from the peak the next morning. The rock's outline is often likened to the profile of the Córdoban bullfighter Manolete.

Antequera's pride and joy is Efebo, a beautiful bronze statue of a boy that dates back to Roman times. Standing almost 5 ft high, it's on display in the **Museo Municipal,** which also houses an array of Roman artifacts excavated from throughout the region, and religious paintings from nearby churches. ⊠ *Palacio de Nájera, Coso Viejo,* ☎ *952/ 704051.* ⊠ *€1.20.* ☉ *Tues.–Fri. 10–1:30 and 4–6, Sat. 10–1:30, Sun. 11–1:30.*

The mysterious prehistoric **Dolmens** are megalithic burial chambers, built some 4,000 years ago out of massive slabs of stone weighing more than 100 tons each. The best-preserved dolmen is La Menga. They're just outside Antequera. ⊠ *Off the Málaga exit road.* ⊠ *Free.* ☉ *Tues. 9–3:30, Wed.–Sat. 9–6, Sun. 9:30–2:30.*

Europe's major nesting area for the greater flamingo is **Fuente de Piedra,** a shallow, eliptical saltwater lagoon. In February and March, the birds arrive from Africa by the thousands to spend the summer here. The visitor center has wildlife information available in English. ⊠ *10 km (6 mi) northwest of Antequera, off the A92 highway to Seville,* ☎ *952/111715.* ⊠ *Free.* ☉ *June–Aug., Wed.–Sun. 10–2 and 4–6; Sept.– May, Wed.–Sun. 10–2 and 6–8.*

Well-marked walking trails guide you at the **Parque Natural del Torcal de Antequera** (El Torcal Nature Park). You'll walk among eerie pillars of pink limestone sculpted by eons of wind and rain. The park is also home to an impressive bird population, including the imperial eagle and peregrine falcon, many of which nest in the large clefts of the towering rocks, as well as several species of owls. Wear sturdy shoes and be careful not to wander from the marked paths, as it's easy to get lost in the maze of rock formations. ⊠ *10 km (6 mi) south of Antequera on C3310,* ☎ *952/031389.* ⊠ *Free.* ☉ *Visitor center daily 10–5, park open 24 hours.*

## Dining and Lodging

$$–$$$    ✕ **Casa Fox.** This cozy, family-owned restaurant is just west of the city center in a pleasant residential neighborhood. Casa Fox's highlight is its sunny patio, with potted geraniums hung on whitewashed walls and a lemon tree shading the tables. Flickering candles light the patio in the evening. The owners are from Antequera and the chef Catalan, resulting in a creative mix of cuisines. Dishes include *bacalao a la cerveza* (cod in a beer sauce) and flavorful salad combinations such as avocado with white asparagus and smoked salmon with seasonal vegetables in a vinaigrette. ⊠ *Calle Estrella 8,* ☎ *952/706445. MC, V.*

$$–$$$ ✕ **El Angelote.** Right across the square from the Museo Municipal, the two wood-beam dining rooms here are usually packed. The menu features some fine local cuisine, including *porrilla de setas* (wild mushrooms with thyme and rosemary) and *perdiz hortelana* (stewed partridge). For dessert, there's the regional specialty *bienmesabe* (sponge cake with almonds dusted with sugar and cinnamon). ✉ *Plaza Coso Viejo,* ☎ *952/703465. DC, MC, V. Closed Mon. No dinner Sun.*

$$–$$$ ✕ **La Espuela.** Tucked behind the San Agustín church, this handsome, rose-colored restaurant sits on a cobbled alley shaded by the church's high walls. On the menu is Andalusian fare with a light, modern twist. A highlight among starters is *espárragos con almejas* (asparagus with clams). Among the main courses, look for *rabo de toro* (oxtail stew), flavored with a honey-rosemary sauce, and the ubiquitous—and fortifying—*porra Antequerana,* a version of gazpacho thickened with bread and hard-boiled eggs. The regional desserts shine, including Antequera's typical dessert, the bienmesabe. ✉ *Calle San Agustín,* ☎ *952/ 703031. MC, V.*

$–$$ ✕ **Caserío San Benito.** If it weren't for the cell-phone transmission tower looming next to this country restaurant 11 km (7 mi) north of Antequera, you might think you'd been transported back to the 18th century. In fact, the building was constructed by its current owner, a history buff and collector of memorabilia. The food includes popular local dishes such as porra Antequerana, *migas* (fried bread with bits of sausage), and *conejo con arroz* (rabbit with rice). ✉ *Carretera Málaga-Córdoba, Km 108,* ☎ *952/111103. MC, V. Closed Mon. and first half of July. No dinner Tues.–Thurs.*

$$ ✕⌂ **Parador de Antequera.** Overlooking the *vega,* Antequera's fertile valley, is this modern white parador on a hill. Common rooms are simple but tasteful, with antique carpets on tile floors and taurine prints on the walls. The comfortable guest rooms have twin beds covered with woven rugs and spacious tiled bathrooms. The dining room, with a lofty wood ceiling, serves good local dishes, such as *pío antequerano* (a salad of orange, cod, and olives) and oxtail in a sauce made with the sweet regional wine. The terrace next to the pool has a view of the Peña de los Enamorados. ✉ *García del Olmo, 29200,* ☎ *952/840261,* FAX *952/841312,* WEB *www.parador.es. 55 rooms. Restaurant, pool, bar. AE, DC, MC, V.*

$–$$ ⌂ **Hotel Papabellotas.** Peer out of any of the windows at this comfortable, intimate hotel and you're rewarded with views of the Papabellotas tower, rising over the stone walls of Antequera's *alcazaba* (fortress) ruins. Rustic touches, such as hand-painted iron headboards, wooden furniture, and colorful bathroom tiles, enliven the guest rooms. It's hard to get more central: the hotel sits mere paces from Antequera's main square, Plaza de San Sebastián. ✉ *Calle Encarnación 5, 29200,* ☎ *952/ 705045,* FAX *952/846410. 8 rooms. Restaurant. AE, DC, MC, V.*

$ ⌂ **Hotel Castilla.** This simple hotel overlooking Antequera's main thoroughfare has basic, clean rooms with blue-and-white tiled floors. For views of the Antequera action, ask for a room *con balcón* (with balcony), where you can gaze down over the bustling Calle Infante Don Fernando. The long-running downstairs bar is often packed with locals. ✉ *Calle Infante Don Fernando 40, 29200,* ☎ FAX *952/843090,* WEB *www.hotelcastilladeantequera.com. 22 rooms. Restaurant, bar. AE, DC, MC, V.*

## Nightlife

Antequera's nightlife is centered on and around Calle Calzada, where you'll find a string of lively bars. **La Madriguera** (✉ Calle Calzada 16, ☎ 952/841028) draws a crowd on the weekends. The impressive CD collection behind the bar is a good hint of what awaits later in the evening, when dance tunes fill the air and a large screen showing music videos is lowered from the ceiling. **Bar Calzada** (⊠ Calle Calzada 13, ☎ 952/700084), with a long bar and a few tables, fills with twentysomething revelers who chat over beers and pop music. In July and August, the hippest club in town—and, in fact, in the entire *comarca* (county)—is **Discoteca Caracho** (⊠ Carretera Valle de Abdalajaís 1, ☎ no phone), a large disco with a roof that can be opened in good weather—which means virtually all the time. There's also an outdoor terrace garden planted with palm trees where you can sip cocktails under the night sky.

## Shopping

The bustling pedestrian street **Calle Duranes,** which cuts through the heart of Antequera's old town, is peppered with shoe and clothing shops. The **Alameda de Andalucía** has a string of clothing and gift shops, *heladerís* (ice-cream parlors), and the ubiquitous Spanish versions of five-and-dime stores, here called "Everything under a Euro." For Antequeran souvenirs, try **Bazar Lobe** (⊠ Alameda de Andalucía 18, ☎ 952/703869), which sells everything from Andalusian ceramics to miniature reproductions of the *dolmens* (megalithic burial chambers found outside Antequera).

# Archidona

**⑱** *23 km (14 mi) northeast of Antequera, 87 km (54 mi) northeast of Málaga, 131 km (82 mi) northeast of Ronda (via Pizarra).*

The amiable village of Archidona, with its flower-filled squares and narrow, cobbled streets, seems to have changed hardly at all since American writer Washington Irving passed through in 1829 and described it as "in the breast of a high hill, with a three-pointed mountain above it and the ruins of a Moorish fortress." It was called Arcis Domina (Lady on the Height) by the Romans, and the name evolved into Archiduna with the arrival of the Moors in the 8th century. Thanks to its strategic elevated location along the *camino* (way) between Granada and Seville, Archidona rose to great prominence under the Moors, and served as official residence for a string of noteworthy Moorish rulers and as capital of the Málaga province until the 11th century.

★ Dominating the center of the old town is Archidona's highlight, the **Plaza Ochavada,** a magnificent, octagonal 18th-century square resplendent with contrasting red and ocher stone. Ringing the square are arches topped by whitewashed buildings with bright green doors that open onto wrought-iron balconies spilling over with red and pink geraniums. Created in the image of a French square, Plaza Ochavada is the bustling heart of the village. Until 1954, bullfights were staged here—the audience seated in the balconies—and today the square fills with concerts and celebrations in the summer months, particularly during Archidona's festival from August 14 to 18. Dog lovers may want to come for Archidona's well-known **Feria del Pero** (Dog Festival). On the first weekend of June, dogs and their owners from all over Spain descend upon Archidona for two days of beauty and grooming contests, races, and plenty of shop talk.

Looming above Archidona are the ruins of a **Moorish fortress,** originally built in the 9th century and expanded in the 13th and 15th centuries. Underneath an adjoining patio—now overgrown with weeds—is a large well where rainwater deposits were stored for the village population. Enjoy sweeping vistas of the Antequeran countryside, a dusky patchwork of red-dirt and green fields, behind which rises the signature shape of the Peña de los Enamorados (Lovers' Rock). Archidona's huddle of bright houses with tiled rooftops stand out like a dab of white paint on a canvas of a rugged, earthy landscape that stretches toward the horizon. ⊠ *Camino del Santuario s/n.* ☎ *Free.*

The **Ermita de la Virgen de Gracia,** a lovely parish church and hermitage next to Archidona's fortress, was built within the area's only remaining mosque, originally constructed in the 9th century. After the Christian reconquest, the mosque was converted into a church, but its walls and pillars were preserved and incorporated into the church structure. The layout of the church reveals this unusual commingling of religions: as you face the front, you look onto the Christian altar; turn to the right, and you're looking at what was once the front of the mosque, facing Mecca. It's a 2-km (1.2-mi) steep trek to the fortress and church; if you want to skip the hike, you can hail a taxi in the center of town, though the five-minute trip is pricy at about €6. ⊠ *Camino del Santuario s/n.* ☎ *Free.* ☉ *May–Aug., daily 7–2 and 5–10; Sept.–Oct. and Feb.–Apr., daily 8–2 and 4–8; Nov.–Jan., daily 9–2 and 3–7.*

Visible from all over Archidona is the brick Mudéjar tower—topped with green, white, and pale pink tiles—that rises alongside the **Convento de Monjas Mínimas,** a church and convent of *monjas en clausura* (cloistered nuns). The convent is not open to the public, but if you'd like to taste a regional treat, then you've come to the right spot. The nuns make a delectable range of Andalusian *dulces* (sweets), including *mantecados* (shortbread) and *yemas* (sugared egg yolks). A cloistered nun sells the sweets through a *torno,* a type of "turning" window that allows you to collect your purchases while the nun keeps her face shielded. ⊠ *Calle Nueva 30,* ☎ *952/714184.* ☉ *Sweets sold weekdays 10–1 and 5–7.*

## Dining and Lodging

$–$$    ✕ **Restaurante Central.** Aptly named, this family restaurant sits in the center of Archidona, just steps from Plaza Ochavada. The front room is dominated by a dark-wood-and-brick bar hung with haunches of ham; here you can munch on tasty tapas while gazing out the swinging front doors onto the lovely street scene. In the plant-filled dining room, fronted by a stained-glass arch and with a partially open rooftop, you can sample from a *menu de degustación* (tasting menu) that includes the typical *porra Antequerana,* a type of thick gazpacho blended with bread. ⊠ *Calle Nueva 49,* ☎ *952/714811. MC, V. Closed Thurs.*

$    ✕🏨 **Hotel Escua.** Just west of Archidona's center you'll find this whitewashed, wooden-shuttered hotel of 15 rooms. The comfortable beds are on wrought-iron frames, and half the rooms have terraces and views of the Peña de los Enamorados. The adjoining restaurant has an octagonal roof and skylight that showers sun over the dining room. Lamb and other meats are roasted in a wood oven; regional fare includes *conejo al ajillo* (rabbit in garlic sauce) and stuffed quail, and, for dessert, yogurtlike *cuajada.* The hotel offers tours through the countryside on ATVs and balloon rides for groups of four or more. ⊠ *Carretera Jerez-Cartagena, Km 176, 29200,* ☎ *952/705045,* FAX *952/ 846410. 15 rooms. Restaurant, bar, some pets allowed. MC, V.*

## Shopping

A number of artists and ceramicists have workshops in Archidona where you can pick up local crafts. Overlooking Plaza Ochavada is **El Testero** (⊠ Plaza Ochavada 9, ☎ 654/909270), a small crafts store and workshop where two young artists, both Archidona natives, create and sell their pieces, which include ceramic porra Antequerana bowls, clay reproductions of Plaza Ochavada and the facades of Archidona's churches, and colorful jewelry. For handmade Moorish-style marquetry (varnished tables and boxes inlaid with colorful pieces of wood) head to the **Casa de la Artesanía** (⊠ Carretera Salinas-Villanueva de Tapia, Km 0.5, ☎ 952/716391), 9 km (6 mi) north of Archidona.

## Garganta del Chorro

**⑲** *63 km (39 mi) southwest of Archidona, 40 km (25 mi) southwest of Antequera, 50 km (31 mi) northeast of Málaga.*

The awe-inspiring Garganta del Chorro (Gorge of the Stream) is a deep limestone chasm where the Guadalhorce River churns and snakes its way some 600 ft below the road. The railroad track that worms in and out of tunnels in the cleft is, amazingly, the main line heading north from Málaga for Bobadilla junction and, eventually, Madrid. Clinging to the cliffside is the **Caminito del Rey** (King's Walk), a suspended catwalk built for a visit from King Alfonso XIII at the beginning of the 19th century. Do *not* attempt to walk it: the structure is seriously damaged, and travelers have gotten into a number of accidents here, some of them fatal. You can pick up information on the Garganta del Chorro in the small whitewashed village of Álora, which lies 13 km (8 mi) to the south, at its *ayuntamiento* (town hall, ⊠ Avenida de la Constitución 102, ☎ 952/498380; ◷ weekdays 9–2). To reach El Chorro from Antequera, depart Antequera via the El Torcal exit, turn right onto the A343, and when you reach Álora head north.

*En Route*    North of the gorge, the Guadalhorce has been dammed to form a series of scenic reservoirs surrounded by pine-clad hills, which constitute the **Parque de Ardales** nature area. Informal, open-air restaurants overlook the lakes and a number of picnic spots. The village of Ardales, with its lively Plaza de la Constitucín, is a good spot to get more information about the park, available at the ayuntamiento (⊠ Plaza de la Constitucín 1, ☎ 952/458087; ◷ weekdays 9–2).

## Carratraca

**⑳** *5 km (3 mi) southeast of Ardales, 55 km (34 mi) northwest of Málaga.*

The old spa town of Carratraca was once a favorite with both Spanish and foreign aristocracy. It has a Moorish-style ayuntamiento and an unusual polygonal bullring. Carratraca's old hotel, the **Hostal del Príncipe,** once sheltered Empress Eugénie, wife of Napoleon III; Lord Byron also came seeking the cure. The splendid Roman-style marble-and-tile bathhouse is being restored.

OFF THE
BEATEN PATH     **PIZARRA** – From Carratraca, head south 15 km (10 mi) along the A357 toward Málaga until you reach the turnoff to this quiet village. The highlight of Pizarra is the **Museo Municipal de Pizarra** (formerly the Hollander Museum) in a renovated farmhouse just south of the village. Over their two decades in Pizarra, American artist Gino Hollander and his wife, Barbara, built up this exceptional collection of paintings, objets d'art, furniture, and archaeological finds. One section displays Moorish and Roman archaeological objects; the other is devoted to rustic Andalusian furniture and farm implements. ⊠ *Cortijo Casablanca 29,* ☎ *952/483237.* ⌑ €1.95. ◷ *Tues.–Sun. 10–2 and 4–8 (4–7 in winter).*

# THE COSTA DEL SOL

The sprawling outskirts of Torremolinos signal that you're leaving the "real" Spain—and entering the "real" Costa del Sol, with its beaches, high-rise hotels, and intense tourist activity. Technically, the stretch of Andalusian shore known as the Costa del Sol runs west from the Costa

Tropical, near Granada, to the tip of Tarifa, past Gibraltar. For most of the Europeans who have flocked here over the past 40 years, though, the Sun Coast has been largely restricted to the 70-km (43-mi) sprawl of hotels, holiday villas, golf courses, marinas, and nightclubs between Torremolinos, which lies just west of Málaga, and Estepona, down toward Gibraltar. Since the late 1950s this area has mushroomed from a group of impoverished fishing villages afflicted with malaria and near-starvation into an overdeveloped seaside playground and retirement haven.

The Costa's transformation went into high gear in the 1960s and early '70s, when hundreds of high-rises shot up in Torremolinos and Fuengirola, and luxury hotels and leafy villas erupted on the shore of Marbella, pushing the former village to the forefront of high-end European resorts. The late 1980s saw a second boom, bringing new golf courses, luxury marinas, villa developments, and yet more world-class hotels. These days, the coast's audacious appetite for tourist dollars continues to be evident no matter where you turn. What with its quadri-lingual menus, Ye Olde English pubs, and "Oktoberfest Night" German beer gardens, you could easily forget that you're in Spain. Nevertheless, the Costa does have its draws, particularly if you just want to kick back and soak up the rays for a few days. The climate is terrific, with around 320 days of sun a year, and the sandy beaches, despite the crowds, are well maintained and offer unparalleled vistas of the glittering Mediterranean lapping the shores.

Torremolinos is a budget destination catering almost exclusively to the mass market; it appeals very much to singles and to those who come purely to lie in the sun and dance the night away. Fuengirola is quieter, and geared more toward family vacations; farther west, the Marbella–San Pedro de Alcántara area is more exclusive and, of course, more expensive.

# Torremolinos

🟤 *11 km (7 mi) west of Málaga, 16 km (10 mi) northeast of Fuengirola, 43 km (27 mi) east of Marbella.*

Torremolinos is all about fun in the sun. Its wildest days may be over, its atmosphere more subdued than in the roaring '60s and '70s, but swarms of northern Europeans—young and not so young, scantily attired and fair in hue—still throng its streets in season. They shop for bargains on Calle San Miguel, down sangría in the bars of La Nogalera, and dance the night away in discotheques. By day, the sunseekers flock to the beaches of El Bajondillo and La Carihuela, where the sand is a fine, gray grit; in high summer it's hard to find a patch of your own.

Torremolinos has two sections. The first, simply called **Torremolinos** (and known to expats as "Central T-town"), is built around the Plaza Costa del Sol; Calle San Miguel, the main shopping street; and the brash Nogalera Plaza, full of overpriced bars and international restaurants. The Pueblo Blanco area, off Calle Casablanca, is more pleasant, and the Cuesta del Tajo, at the far end of San Miguel, winds down a steep slope to the Bajondillo beach. Here, crumbling walls, bougainvillea-clad patios, and old cottages hint at the quiet fishing village this once was.

The second, much nicer section is **La Carihuela.** To find it, head west on Avenida Carlota Alessandri and turn left by the Hotel La Paloma. Far more authentically Spanish, the Carihuela retains many old fishermen's cottages and excellent fish restaurants. The traffic-free esplanade makes for an enjoyable stroll, especially on a summer evening or Sunday at lunchtime, when it's packed with Spanish families.

The **Aquapark,** off the bypass, near the Palacio de Congresos convention center, has water chutes, artificial waves, water mountains, and pools. ☎ 952/388888. ⊡ €14.50. ☉ *May–June and Sept., daily 10–6; July–Aug., daily 10–7.*

## Dining and Lodging

$$$ ✕ **Juan.** With a sunny outdoor patio facing the sea, this hot spot in the Carihuela neighborhood is a good place for seafood in summer. House specialties include the great Costa del Sol standbys—*sopa de mariscos* (shellfish soup), *dorada al horno* (oven-roasted giltheads), and *fritura malagueña.* ⊠ *Paseo Marítimo 29,* ☎ *952/385656. AE, DC, MC, V.*

$$–$$$ ✕ **Casa Guaquin.** On a seaside patio in La Carihuela, Casa Guaquin is the best seafood restaurant in the area. Ever-changing daily catches are served alongside such stalwarts as *coquinas* (wedge-shell clams) and *boquerones fritos* (fried anchovies). ⊠ *Paseo Marítimo 63,* ☎ *952/384530. AE, MC, V. Closed Mon. and mid-Dec.–mid-Jan.*

$$–$$$ ✕ **El Roqueo.** Owned by a former fisherman, El Roqueo is one of the locals' favorite Carihuela fish joints. The room is spacious, bright, and airy, with a large terrace over the seafront promenade. *Pescadito frito* (fried small fish) and *dorada a la sal* (sea bream baked in coarse salt) are popular choices. The ingredients are always fresh, and prices are very reasonable. ⊠ *Carmen 35,* ☎ *952/384946. AE, DC, MC, V. Closed Tues. and Dec.–mid-Jan.*

$$$–$$$$ 🏨 **Tropicana.** This relaxing resort hotel with its own beach club is at the far end of the Carihuela, in one of the most pleasant parts of Torremolinos. A tropical theme is carried throughout, from the leafy gardens and kidney-shape pool to the common areas, with exotic plants, raffia floor mats, and bamboo furniture. The guest rooms are distinguished by ceiling fans and marble floors. From here you're a five-minute walk to a range of good restaurants. ⊠ *Trópico 6, 29620,* ☎ *952/386600,* 🖷 *952/380568,* 🌐 *www.hotel-tropicana.net. 84 rooms. Pool, beach. AE, DC, MC, V.*

$$$ 🏨 **Cervantes.** A busy, cosmopolitan hotel—one of the better lodgings in the heart of Torremolinos—Cervantes is ideal for those who want to be in the middle of things. It's not by the beach, but there's a pool, and the rooms are well furnished and comfortable. Service is good, and the panoramic dining room on the top floor is popular with locals. Drawbacks: package tours often alight here, rooms on the bottom floors can be noisy, and parking can be a problem. ⊠ *Las Mercedes, 29620,* ☎ *952/384033,* 🖷 *952/384857,* 🌐 *www.hotelcervantestorremolinos. com. 397 rooms. Dining room, 2 pools, hair salon, sauna, nightclub. AE, DC, MC, V.*

$$$ 🏨 **Meliá Costa del Sol.** Located in the Bajondillo (eastern beach) section of town, the Meliá looks somewhat boxy from the outside, with the assembly-line architecture typical of 1970s Torremolinos. Inside, however, it's modern and well run. Every room has a sea-view balcony and gets lots of light; before you book, decide whether you prefer direct sun in the morning or evening. ⊠ *Paseo Marítimo 11, Playa del Bajondillo, 29620,* ☎ *952/386677,* 🖷 *952/386417,* 🌐 *www.solmelia. com. 517 rooms, 18 suites. Restaurant, pool, health club, bar, meeting rooms. AE, DC, MC, V.*

$$ 🏨 **Sidi Lago Rojo.** In the heart of old Carihuela, this modern, four-story building is just two blocks from the seafront. The rooms are well maintained, and all have balconies; some overlook the pool and small, tree-filled garden. There's no great view, but prices are moderate, and you're close to the town's best bars and restaurants. ⊠ *C. Miami 5, 29620,* ☎ *952/387666,* 🖷 *952/380891,* 🌐 *www.hotelessidi.es. 144 rooms. Restaurant, pool, bar. AE, DC, MC, V.*

$ ⊞ **Miami.** Set in an old Andalusian villa in a shady garden west of the Carihuela, Miami is something of a find amid the ocean of concrete towers. Staying here is like visiting a private Spanish home; the rooms are individually furnished, and there's a sitting room with a cozy fireplace. It's very popular, so reserve ahead. ⊠ *Aladino 14, at C. Miami, 29620,* ☎ *952/385255. 26 rooms. Pool, bar, some pets allowed; no a/c, no room TVs. No credit cards.*

### Nightlife and the Arts

Most nightlife is in the center of town and along the Montemar strip heading west. Some bars have live music, but Torremolinos is best known for its discos. As the gay capital of the Costa del Sol, Torremolinos also has numerous bars and clubs catering to an almost exclusively gay clientele.

The trends are in constant flux, but one of the longest-running clubs is **Paladium** (⊠ Avda. Palma de Mallorca 36, ☎ 952/384289), which has two floors and a covered swimming pool. For flamenco, your best bet in Torremolinos is **Taberna Flamenca Pepe López** (⊠ Plaza de la Gamba Alegre, ☎ 952/381284).

## Benalmádena

㉒ *9 km (5½ mi) west of Torremolinos, 9 km (5½ mi) east of Mijas.*

**Benalmádena-Costa** is practically an extension of Torremolinos, run almost exclusively by package-tour operators. It has little for the independent traveler, but there's a pleasant-enough marina, which draws Málaga's youth at night. **Benalmádena-Pueblo** is on the mountainside 7 km (4 mi) from the coast and is surprisingly unspoiled, offering a glimpse of the old, pretourist Andalusia.

In Benalmádena-Costa's marina, **Sea Life Benalmadena** aquarium displays varied examples of fish from local waters, including rays, sharks, and sunfish. ⊠ *Puerto Marina Benalmádena,* ☎ *952/560150,* ⓌⒺⒷ *www.sealife.es.* ⊡ *€6.60.* ⊙ *June–Sept., daily 10 AM–midnight; Oct.–May, daily 10–6.*

𝒞 The Costa del Sol's leading amusement park is **Tivoli World,** which has a 4,000-seat, open-air auditorium that often showcases international stars alongside cancan, flamenco, or Spanish ballet performances. The park also has roller coasters, a Ferris wheel, illuminated fountains, a Chinese pagoda, Wild West shows, and 40-odd restaurants and snack bars. ⊠ *Arroyo de la Miel,* ☎ *952/442848.* ⊡ *€3.60; €.60 Sun. 11 AM–3 PM.* ⊙ *Summer, daily 1 PM–1 AM; winter, Sat. 1–10, Sun. 11–10.*

### Dining and Lodging

$$$–$$$$ ✕ **Mar de Alborán.** Right next to the Benalmádena yacht harbor, this restaurant has a touch more class than most of its peers, having earned its reputation as one of the finest restaurants on the coast. The dining room is cheerful, with picture windows that fill the space with light at lunchtime. Unusual fish dishes such as the Basque-inspired *lomo de merluza con kokotxas y almejas* (hake with cheek morsels and clams) are a welcome switch from standard Costa fare. Meat and fowl are also well represented. ⊠ *Avda. de Alay 5,* ☎ *952/446427. AE, MC, V. Closed Mon. No dinner Sun.*

$$$ ✕ **Ventorillo de la Perra.** If you've been scouring the coast for something typically Spanish, try this old inn, which dates from 1785. Outside, there's a leafy patio; inside, a cozy, rustic atmosphere prevails in the dining room and at the bar, where the ceiling is hung with hams. Choose between local malagueño cooking, including *gazpacuelo malagueño* (warm gazpacho of potatoes, rice, and shrimp), and gen-

eral Spanish fare, such as *conejo en salsa de almendras* (rabbit in al-mond sauce). The *ajo blanco* (a cold, garlicky almond-based soup) makes a particularly good appetizer. ✉ *Avda. Constitución 115, Km 13, Arroyo de la Miel,* ☎ *952/441966. AE, DC, MC, V. Closed Mon. and Nov.*

$$ ✕ **Casa Fidel.** Heavy beams and a large fireplace give a rustic feel to this Benalmádena-Pueblo restaurant. The menu combines international and Spanish dishes, all well prepared. For an interesting starter, try *cecina de León* (dried beef from León) or *queso de cabra a la plancha* (grilled goat cheese). Main courses include old favorites such as grilled sole, more exotic options such as *perdiz en salsa de vino de Málaga* (partridge in Málaga wine sauce), and a celebrated house specialty, English-style roast lamb. ✉ *Maestra Ayala 1,* ☎ *952/449165. AE, DC, MC, V. Closed Tues. and mid-Nov.–mid-Dec. No lunch Wed.*

$$ ▥ **La Fonda.** At the edge of the village Benalmádena-Pueblo, this small hotel grants a true taste of Andalusia. Rooms have white walls, marble floors, and floral fabrics. Some enjoy peerless views of the coast and the Mediterranean; others look onto the cool interior patio or the village street. The pool is heated in winter. In the same building, under different management, is a restaurant run by Málaga's official hotel school; it's open for lunch on weekdays. ✉ *Santo Domingo 7, 29639,* ☎ ℻ *952/568273. 26 rooms. Pool. AE, DC, MC, V.*

### Nightlife

The Fortuna Nightclub in the **Casino Torrequebrada** (✉ N340, Km 220, Benalmádena-Costa, ☎ 952/446000; ⏱ 9 PM–4 AM) has flamenco and an international dance show with a live orchestra, beginning at 9:30. Passport, jacket, and tie are required in the casino.

## Fuengirola

㉓  *16 km (10 mi) west of Torremolinos, 27 km (17 mi) east of Marbella.*

Fuengirola is less frenetic than Torremolinos. Many of its waterfront high-rises are holiday apartments catering to budget-minded sunseekers from northern Europe and, in summer, a large contingent from Córdoba and other parts of Spain. The town is also a haven for British retirees (with plenty of English and Irish pubs to serve them) and a shopping and business center for the rest of the Costa del Sol. Its Tuesday market is the largest on the coast and a major tourist attraction.

The most prominent landmark in Fuengirola is **Castillo de Sohail,** whose partly Arabic name means "Castle of the Star." The original structure dates from the 12th century, but the castle served as a military fortress until the early 19th century, and there were many additions made over the years. The castle is west of town on a hilltop. ✉ *Carretera N-340, Km 207, 3 km from Fuengirola.* ▦ €1.20. ⏱ *Tues.–Sun. 10–2:30 and 4–6.*

### Dining and Lodging

$$$–$$$$ ✕ **La Langosta.** This tiny restaurant, two blocks from the water on a side street in Los Boliches beach area, has been a favorite for 40 years. Needless to say, the specialty is *langosta* (lobster), prepared in a variety of ways, including *al champán* (in champagne sauce). The *mejillones a la crema de azafrán* (mussels in saffron sauce) are a savory alternative. ✉ *Francisco Cano 1,* ☎ *952/475049. AE, MC, V. Closed Sun. No lunch.*

$$$ ✕ **Portofino.** You'll find this lively restaurant, one of the best in Fuengirola, camouflaged amid the brassy souvenir shops and fast-food joints on the promenade, just east of the port. The menu is international, with a few nods to the owner's Italian origins. The carpaccio

is a popular appetizer; for the main course, try the veal scallops in lemon sauce or the roast lamb. Service is fast, friendly, and professional. ⊠ *Paseo Marítimo 29,* ☎ *952/470643. AE, DC, MC, V. Closed Mon. No lunch July 1–Sept. 15.*

**$$–$$$** ✕ **Mesón Castellano.** True to its name, this *mesón* (tavern) next to the town hall is a little bit of Castile in Fuengirola. The large tapas bar adjoins a pleasant dining room decorated like a central-Spanish tavern. The specialty is roast *lechazo* (baby lamb), shipped in from Burgos. If you're up to it, try the *cabeza de lechazo* (roast head of lamb: brains, tongue, cheeks, eyes, the works) or *oreja de cerdo con tomate* (pigs' ears in tomato sauce). ⊠ *Camino de Coín 5,* ☎ *952/462736. AE, DC, MC, V. Closed Wed.*

**$$** ☷ **Florida.** Inland from the port, this simple but comfortable hotel is set back from the sea behind a shady, semitropical garden where you can sunbathe and sip a drink at the poolside bar. One of Fuengirola's oldest lodgings, it dates back to the years before the land boom and is still managed by its original owners. Rooms are on the small side, but are nicely decorated in orange and light-brown tones. ⊠ *Paseo Marítimo s/n, 29640,* ☎ *952/476100,* 🖷 *952/581529,* 🌐 *www.costadelsol.spa.es/hotel/ florida. 110 rooms. Restaurant, pool, bar. AE, DC, MC, V.*

**$$** ☷ **Villa de Laredo.** With a prime location on the seaside promenade, one block east of the port, this is the place to stay if you want to be in the midst of the Fuengirola's waterfront activity. Rooms are decorated in cream and navy blue; some have terraces and sea views. The pool is on the roof. ⊠ *Paseo Marítimo 42, 29640,* ☎ *952/477689,* 🖷 *952/ 477950. 50 rooms. Restaurant, pool. AE, DC, MC, V.*

### Nightlife and the Arts

Amateur local troupes sometimes stage plays in English at the **Salón de Variétés Theater** (⊠ Emancipación 30, ☎ 952/474542). For concerts—from classical to rock to jazz—check out the modern **Palacio de la Paz** near the city center (⊠ Recinto Ferial, Avda. Jesus Santo Rein, ☎ 952/589349).

## Mijas

★ ❷   *8 km (5 mi) north of Fuengirola, 18 km (11 mi) west of Torremolinos.*

The picturesque village of Mijas is nestled in the foothills of the sierra just north of the coast. Buses leave Fuengirola every half hour for the 20-minute drive through hills peppered with whitewashed villas. If you have a car and don't mind a mildly hair-raising drive, take the more dramatic approach from Benalmádena-Pueblo, a winding mountain road with some great views.

Mijas was discovered long ago by foreign retirees, and the large, touristy square where you arrive may look like an extension of the Costa, yet beyond this are hilly streets of whitewashed houses and a somewhat authentic village atmosphere. Try to come here late in the afternoon, when the tour buses have left and you have the town to yourself. Park in the Plaza Virgen de la Peña, where you should take a quick look at the chapel of Mijas's patron, the Virgen de la Peña, and hire a "*burro taxi*" (guided donkey) to explore the village.

If miniature curiosities are your thing, explore **Carromato de Max**, a museum that has a rendition of the Last Supper on a grain of rice, Abraham Lincoln painted on a pinhead, and fleas wearing clothes. ⊠ *Avda. del Compás,* ☎ *952/489500.* 🎟 *€3.* ☉ *Daily 10–7.*

Bullfights take place throughout the year, usually on Sunday at 4:30, at Mijas's tiny **bullring.** It's one of the few square bullrings in Spain. It's off the Plaza Constitución—Mijas's old village square—and up the slope beside the Mirlo Blanco restaurant. ⊠ *Plaza Constitución,* ☎ *952/485248.* 🎟 *€3.* ⊙ *June–Sept., daily 10–10; Oct.–Feb., daily 9:30–6:30; Mar., daily 10–7:30; Apr.–May, daily 10–8:30.*

Worth a visit is the delightful village **Iglesia Parroquial de la Inmaculada Concepción** (Church of the Immaculate Conception). It's impeccably decorated, especially at Easter, and its terrace and spacious gardens afford a splendid panorama. The church is just up the hill from the Mijas bullring. ⊠ *Plaza Constitución.*

NEED A
BREAK?
The **Bar Menguíñez** (⊠ Calle San Sebastián 4, ☎ no phone) also known as Casa de los Jamones, has a ceiling strung with row after row of hams. Inexpensive meals are served at a handful of tables.

Mijas extends down to the coast, and the coastal strip between Fuengirola and Marbella is officially called **Mijas-Costa.** This area holds a range of hotels, restaurants, and golf courses.

### Dining and Lodging

$$$–$$$$ ✕ **El Padrastro.** Perched on a cliff above the Plaza Virgen de la Peña, "The Stepfather" is accessible by an elevator from the square or, if you're energetic, by stairs. Views over Fuengirola and the coast are the restaurant's main attraction. The menu features international and Spanish dishes such as *medallones de cerdo con pasa y piñones* (pork medallions with raisins and pine nuts, in a Málaga wine sauce) and, in the unconventional department, *avestruz con higos y ciruelas*—ostrich with figs and plums. A large terrace adds alfresco ambience. ⊠ *Avda. del Compás,* ☎ *952/485000. AE, DC, MC, V.*

$$$–$$$$ ✕ **Mirlo Blanco.** In an old house on the pleasant Plaza de la Constitución, with a terrace for outdoor dining in warm weather, this place is run by the second generation of a Basque family that has been in the Costa del Sol restaurant business for decades. Try Basque specialties such as *txangurro* (crab) and *merluza a la vasca* (hake with asparagus, eggs, and clam sauce). ⊠ *Plaza de la Constitución 13,* ☎ *952/485700. AE, MC, V. Closed Jan.*

$$–$$$ ✕ **Valparaíso.** Halfway up the road from Fuengirola to Mijas, this restaurant is all about setting: the sprawling villa stands in its own garden, complete with swimming pool. In summer, you can dine outdoors on the terrace and dance the night away to live music. Valparaíso is a favorite among local (mainly British) expatriates, who come here in full evening dress to celebrate their birthdays. In winter, logs burn in a cozy fireplace. The *pato a la naranja* (duck in orange sauce) is typical of the continental cuisine here. ⊠ *Carretera de Mijas–Fuengirola, Km 4,* ☎ *952/485996. AE, DC, MC, V. Closed Sun. Oct.–June.*

$$$$ ✕🛏 **Byblos Andaluz.** This luxury hotel on the edge of Mijas's golf course
★ (closer to Fuengirola than to Mijas) is the most expensive on the entire Costa del Sol. Set in a huge garden of palms, cypresses, and fountains, it is first and foremost a spa and is known particularly for its *thalasso* therapy, a skin treatment that uses seawater and seaweed—applied here in a Roman temple of cool, white marble and blue tiles. Both of the outstanding restaurants serve regional dishes as well as highly sophisticated international cuisine. ⊠ *Urbanización Mijas-Golf, 29640 Mijas-Costa,* ☎ *952/473050,* 🖷 *952/476783,* 🌐 *www.byblos-andaluz. com. 109 rooms, 35 suites. 2 restaurants, cable TV with movies, 2 18-hole golf courses, 5 tennis courts, 3 pools (1 indoor), health club, hair salon, spa, some pets allowed. AE, DC, MC, V.*

$$$$ 🛏 **La Cala Resort.** Set amid its own two golf courses a few miles inland, this stylish modern resort is a world unto itself. The already pleasing cosmopolitan atmosphere is enhanced by contemporary Andalusian architecture. All rooms have large balconies with unspoiled views over

the fairways and greens and the countryside beyond. La Cala appeals primarily to golfers, but nongolfers will find plenty to keep themselves amused as well. ⊠ *La Cala de Mijas, 29649 Mijas-Costa,* ☎ *952/ 669000,* FAX *952/669039,* WEB *www.lacala.com. 96 rooms, 5 suites. 2 restaurants, cafeteria, 2 18-hole golf courses, 2 tennis courts, 2 pools (1 indoor), sauna, squash, bar, meeting rooms. AE, DC, MC, V.*

$$ ⊞ **Mijas.** At the entrance to Mijas, this beautifully situated hotel has a poolside restaurant and bar, gardens with views of the hillsides stretching down to Fuengirola and the sea, marble floors throughout, wrought-iron window grilles, and Moorish shutters. The lobby is large and airy, and there's a delightful glass-roof terrace. All rooms are well furnished in modern Andalusian style, with wood fittings and marble floors, but only some enjoy the sweeping view of the coast. ⊠ *Urbanización Tamisa, 29650,* ☎ *952/485800,* FAX *952/485825. 101 rooms, 2 suites. Restaurant, coffee shop, tennis court, pool, health club, hair salon. AE, DC, MC, V.*

# Marbella

**㉕** *27 km (17 mi) west of Fuengirola, 28 km (17 mi) east of Estepona, 50 km (31 mi) southeast of Ronda.*

Playground of the rich and home of movie stars, rock musicians, and dispossessed royal families, Marbella has attained the top rung on Europe's social ladder. Dip into any Spanish gossip magazine, and chances are the glittering parties that fill its pages are set in Marbella.

Much of this action takes place on the fringes, for grand hotels and luxury restaurants line the waterfront for 20 km (12 mi) on each side of the town center. In the town itself, you may well wonder how Marbella became so famous. The main thoroughfare, Avenida Ricardo Soriano, is distinctly lacking in charm, and the Paseo Marítimo, though pleasant enough, with an array of seafood restaurants and pizzerias overlooking an ordinary beach, is far from spectacular.

Marbella's appeal lies in the heart of the **old village,** which remains miraculously intact. Here, a block or two back from the main highway, narrow alleys of whitewashed houses cluster around the central **Plaza de los Naranjos** (Orange Square), where colorful restaurants vie for space under the orange trees. You can climb onto what remains of the old fortifications and stroll along the quaint Calle Virgen de los Dolores to the Plaza de Santo Cristo, wander the maze of lanes, and enjoy the geranium-speckled windows and splashing fountains.

Punctuating the opulence of Marbella is the road to Puerto Banús, which has been called the **Golden Mile.** Here, a mosque, Arab banks, and the onetime residence of Saudi Arabia's King Fahd betray the influence of petro-dollars in this wealthy enclave. Seven kilometers (4½ mi) west of central Marbella (between Km 175 and Km 174), a sign indicates the turnoff leading down to Puerto Banús. Though now hemmed in by a belt of brand-new high-rises, Marbella's plush marina, with 915 berths, is a gem of ostentatious wealth, a kind of Spanish answer to St. Tropez. Huge and flashy yachts, beautiful people, and countless expensive stores and restaurants make up the glittering parade that marches long into the night. The backdrop is an Andalusian pueblo—built in the 1980s in imitation of the fishing villages that once lined this coast.

The **Museo del Grabado Español Contemporáneo** (Museum of Contemporary Spanish Engraving), in a restored 16th-century building, has an outstanding collection of modern Spanish etchings. The museum is in the old village. ⊠ *Hospital Bazán,* ☎ *952/825035,* WEB *www.*

*museodelgrabado.com.* ✉ *€2.50.* ⊙ *Tues.–Sat. 10–2 and 5:30–8:30, Sun. 10:30–2.*

Stop for a glass of wine and a platter of fried fish at the popular **La Pesquera** (✉ Plaza de la Victoria, ☎ 952/765170), at the western entrance to the old village.

In a modern building just east of Marbella's old quarter, the **Museo de Bonsai** has one of the most extensive collections of bonsai trees in Europe. ✉ *Parque Arroyo de la Repesa, Avda. Dr. Maiz Viñal,* ☎ *952/ 862926.* ✉ *€3.* ⊙ *Daily 10:30–1:30 and 5–8:30 in summer; daily 10:30–1:30 and 4–7 in winter.*

On the outskirts of Marbella, a spacious, elegant 18th-century *cortijo* (country estate) houses the **Museo Cortijo Miraflores,** where you can peruse art and cultural exhibits. There's also a **Museo del Aceite** (Olive Oil Museum), which traces the olive oil–making process through photos, colorful panels, and a collection of traditional machines and tools, including wooden and hydraulic oil presses. ✉ *Calle José Luis Morales y Marín s/n,* ☎ *952/902714.* ✉ *Free.* ⊙ *Tues.–Sat. 10–2 and 5:30– 8:30; in July–Aug., Tues.–Sat. 11-2 and 6–8.*

## Dining and Lodging

$$$$ ✕ **La Meridiana.** The local jet set favors La Meridiana, 100 yards inland from the mosque west of town. The striking modern architecture has a Moorish flavor, and the enclosed terrace allows "outdoor" dining year-round. The Mediterranean cuisine is famous for its overall quality and freshness of its ingredients; both characteristics are evident on the menú de degustación. The à la carte menu changes seasonally but always includes favorites such as *lubina grillé al tomillo fresco* (sea bass grilled with fresh thyme). In summer, sample the restaurant's upmarket version of ajo blanco, a garlicky gazpacho featuring almonds instead of tomatoes. ✉ *Camino de la Cruz,* ☎ *952/776190. AE, DC, MC, V. Closed Jan. No lunch.*

$$$$ ✕ **El Portalón.** This attractive restaurant, with a light, glassed-in dining room, combines two extremes of the culinary spectrum: on the one hand, substantial Castilian roasts; on the other, innovative *cocina de mercado,* based on whatever's freshest at the market. Unless you're determined to tuck into a roast suckling pig, go for one of a dozen or so *sugerencias del día* (suggestions of the day). The restaurant prides itself on its wine list, and wine is sold by the glass in the adjoining *vinoteca* (wine cellar). ✉ *Carretera de Cádiz, Km 178 (across from Marbella Club hotel),* ☎ *952/861075. AE, DC, MC, V.*

$$$–$$$$ ✕ **La Hacienda.** Set in a large, pleasant villa 12 km (7 mi) east of Marbella, the Hacienda was founded in the early '70s by the late Belgian chef Paul Schiff, who played a key role in transforming the Costa del Sol culinary scene with his modern approach and judicious use of local ingredients. His legacy lives on here, as his family serves creative fare from a changing menu. Schiff's signature dish, *pintada con pasas al vino de Málaga* (guinea fowl with raisins, in Málaga wine sauce) is often available. ✉ *Urbanización Las Chapas, N340 Km 193,* ☎ *952/831267. AE, MC, V. Mid-Nov.–mid-Dec. closed Mon., Tues. No lunch July–Aug.*

$$$–$$$$ ✕ **Santiago.** Marbella's most esteemed fish restaurant is appropriately located facing the seafront promenade. Try the *ensalada de langosta* (lobster salad), followed by *besugo al horno* (baked red bream). The menu also features roasts, such as *cochinillo* (suckling pig) and *cordero* (lamb) of the owner's native Castile. Around the corner from the restaurant (and sharing the same phone number) is Santiago's popular tapas bar. ✉ *Paseo Marítimo 5,* ☎ *952/770078. AE, DC, MC, V. Closed Nov.*

**$$–$$$$** ✕ **Antonio.** Perched on the front line in the Puerto Banús, Antonio is one of the oldest of the many restaurants in Marbella's famous yacht harbor. The accent is on fresh fish and shellfish, including *brocheta de rape* (monkfish kebab) and large fish such as bream or sea bass baked in salt. A number of rice dishes are also featured. Dine on the terrace to observe the port's parade of Rolls-Royces, luxury yachts, and beautiful people. ✉ *Muella de Ribera, Puerto Banús,* ☎ 952/813536. AE, D, MC, V.

**$$$$** 🏨 **Los Monteros.** Five kilometers (three miles) east of Marbella, on the road to Málaga, this exclusive hotel stands surrounded by tropical gardens on the sea side of the highway. The extensive facilities and perks include easy access to an uncrowded beach, golf privileges on the adjoining courses, and gourmet dining in the famous El Corzo Grill. The rooms are formally decorated, and service is impeccable. ✉ *Urbanización Los Monteros, Carretera N340, Km 187, 29600,* ☎ 952/ 771700, 𝙵𝙰𝚇 952/825846, 𝚆𝙴𝙱 *www.monteros.com. 161 rooms, 10 suites. 3 restaurants, 10 tennis courts, 2 pools, gym, hair salon, sauna, nightclub, meeting room.* AE, DC, MC, V.

**$$$$** 🏨 **Marbella Club.** The grande dame of Marbella hotels was a creation
★ of Alfonso von Hohenlohe, the man who "founded" Marbella. The Club has long attracted an international clientele as well as local patricians. The bungalow-style rooms, some with private pools, come in various sizes, and the decor varies from regional to modern. The grounds are exquisite; breakfast is served on a patio where songbirds flit through the vegetation. ✉ *Blvd. Alfonso von Hohenlohe, Carretera de Cádiz, Km 178 (3 km [2 mi] west of Marbella), 29600,* ☎ 952/822211, 𝙵𝙰𝚇 952/829884, 𝚆𝙴𝙱 *www.marbellaclub.com. 84 rooms, 37 suites, 16 bungalows. 2 restaurants, 3 pools, gym, sauna.* AE, DC, MC, V.

**$$$$** 🏨 **Puente Romano.** This spectacular, deluxe modern hotel and apart-
★ ment complex is made up of low, white stucco buildings between the Marbella Club and Puerto Banús west of Marbella. As the name suggests, there's a genuine Roman bridge on the beautifully landscaped grounds, which run right down to the beach. The large, renovated rooms are brightly colored in blues, yellows, and reds. Among the three restaurants is the outstanding La Plaza, serving Mediterranean cuisine including seafood and salads. The hotel's nightclub is open only in July and August. ✉ *Carretera Cádiz, Km 177, 29600,* ☎ 952/820900, 𝙵𝙰𝚇 952/775766, 𝚆𝙴𝙱 *www.puenteromano.com. 149 rooms, 77 suites. 3 restaurants, 10 tennis courts, 2 pools, nightclub, meeting room.* AE, DC, MC, V.

**$$$–$$$$** 🏨 **El Fuerte.** The building here is vintage 1950s, and the decor is still a bit gloomy for the sunny South, with lots of dark wood, but everything is well maintained. El Fuerte is still the top all-around choice for a hotel near the old town. Most rooms have balconies overlooking the sea. The hotel stands at the end of the Paseo Marítimo, separated from the beach by a palm-filled garden with a pool. ✉ *Avda. El Fuerte, 29600,* ☎ 952/861500, 𝙵𝙰𝚇 952/824411, 𝚆𝙴𝙱 *www.fuertehoteles.com. 261 rooms, 2 suites. Restaurant, 2 pools (1 indoor), health club, meeting room.* AE, DC, MC, V.

**$–$$** 🏨 **Hotel Central.** This intimate hotel is decorated with 19th-century French antiques and black-and-white tiled floors. Bright rooms open onto balconies festooned with flowers. The location is the sunny pedestrian street of Calle San Ramón, within strolling distance of the beach and the Plaza de los Naranjos. ✉ *Calle San Ramón 15, 29600,* ☎ 952/ 902442, 𝙵𝙰𝚇 952/902556. *15 rooms.* AE, DC, MC, V.

**$–$$** 🏨 **Lima.** Here's a good midrange option in downtown Marbella, two blocks from the beach. Decor is simple, with dark-wood furniture, but all rooms have small balconies. The corner rooms are the largest.

✉ *Avda. Belón 2, 29600,* ☎ *952/770500,* FAX *952/863091. 64 rooms. AE, DC, MC, V.*

### Nightlife and the Arts

Much of the nighttime action revolves around the Puerto Banús, in bars such as Sinatra's, Joe's, and La Comedia. Art exhibits are held in private galleries and several of Marbella's leading hotels, notably the Puente Romano. The tourist office publishes a free monthly calendar of exhibits and other events. The **Teatro Ciudad de Marbella** (✉ Plaza Ramón Martínez s/n, ☎ 952/903159) offers a varied lineup of theater, concerts, ballet, and flamenco.

Marbella's most famous nightspot is the **Olivia Valere** disco (✉ Carretera de Istán, Km 0.8, ☎ 952/828845), an Arab fantasy club near the mosque. The trendy **La Notte** (✉ Camino de la Cruz, ☎ 952/776190) is an art deco bar with live music, next to La Meridiana. The **Casino Nueva Andalucía** (✉ Bajos Hotel Andalucía Plaza, N340, ☎ 952/814000) is a chic gambling spot in the Hotel Andalucía Plaza, just east of Puerto Banús. Jacket and tie are required for men, passports for all. **Ana María** (✉ Plaza de Santo Cristo 5, ☎ 952/775646) is a popular flamenco venue in the center of Marbella.

Marbella's "tapas alley" is Calle San Lázaro, near Plaza de los Naranjos. Here you can nibble on tapas along with a glass of house red at a string of small, buzzing bars, each with its own specialty. **La Marejadilla** (✉ Calle San Lázaro s/n, ☎ 952/2829597) serves up minishrimp omelets, and on Sunday there's often a flamenco shows upstairs. **El Estrecho** (✉ Calle San Lázaro 12, ☎ 952/2829597) makes tasty croquettes and fried peppers.

## Ojén

❷❻  *10 km (6 mi) north of Marbella.*

For a contrast to the glamour of the coast, drive up to Ojén, in the hills above Marbella. This ancient village is another world. Look for the beautiful pottery sold here. The **Refugio del Juanar,** a former hunting lodge in the heart of the Sierra Blanca, is 4 km (2½ mi) from Ojén at the southern edge of the Serranía de Ronda, a mountainous wilderness. Not far from the Refugio, you might spot the herd of wild ibex that dwell among the rocky crags; the best times to watch are dawn and dusk, when they descend from their hiding places. A bumpy trail takes you a mile from the Refugio to the Mirador (lookout), which has a sweeping view of the Costa del Sol and the coast of northern Africa.

### Dining and Lodging

$$  ✕▨ **Refugio del Juanar.** Once an aristocratic hunting lodge, counting King Alfonso XIII among its guests, this secluded hotel and restaurant ($$$) later became part of the parador chain. The hunting theme prevails, both in the common areas—where a log fire roars in winter—and on the restaurant menu, where game dishes get pride of place. The rooms are simply decorated in a rustic style, and six (including the three suites) have their own fireplaces. ✉ *Sierra Blanca, 29610,* ☎ *952/881000,* FAX *952/881001,* WEB *www.juanar.com. 23 rooms, 3 suites. Restaurant, tennis court, pool, meeting room. AE, DC, MC, V.*

$$$  ▨ **Castillo de Monda.** Designed to resemble a castle, this paradorlike hotel incorporates the ruins of a Moorish fortress, some of which date back to the 8th century. Rooms are decorated with authentic Andalusian tiles and antique fittings. The bar, with walls covered in Alhambra-style carvings, and the light-flooded restaurant are on the top floor of this seven-story building, providing the best views of the surrounding countryside. From its hilltop location, the building presides over the

village of Monda, 7 km (4 mi) from Ojén. ⊠ *Calle Castillo de Monda s/n, 29110 Monda,* ☎ *952/457142,* FAX *952/457336. 17 rooms, 6 suites. Restaurant, pool. AE, MC, V.*

## Estepona

**㉗** *17 km (11 mi) west of San Pedro de Alcántara.*

Estepona used to mark the tail end of the Costa del Sol's urban sprawl, but today—thanks largely to the increasing importance of Gibraltar's airport—it's fast becoming the biggest boomtown on the coast. Still, the old fishing village hangs on; back from the main Avenida de España, it's surprisingly unspoiled. The beach, more than 1 km (⅔ mi) long, is lined with fishing boats, and the promenade passes well-kept, aromatic flower gardens. The gleaming white **Puerto Deportivo** is lively and packed with restaurants, serving everything from fresh fish to pizza to Chinese food.

### Dining and Lodging

$$–$$$ ✕ **Alcaría de Ramos.** José Ramos, a winner of Spain's National Gastronomy Prize, opened this restaurant in the El Paraíso complex, between Estepona and San Pedro de Alcántara, and has watched it develop a large and enthusiastic following. Try the *ensalada de lentejas con salmón ahumado* (lentil and smoked salmon salad), followed by *cordero asado* (roast lamb) and Ramos's deservedly famous fried ice cream. ⊠ *Urbanización El Paraíso, Carretera N340, Km 167,* ☎ *952/886178. MC, V. Closed Sun. No lunch.*

$–$$ ✕ **La Rada.** Locals flock to this bright, busy establishment for excellent value and an amazing variety of freshly caught fish and shellfish. Service is brisk—waiters dash among the tables in the two dining rooms. Ask about the daily specials or dig into the house specialty, *arroz a la marinera* (seafood rice). ⊠ *Avda. España 16,* ☎ *952/791036. AE, MC, V. Closed Tues.*

$$$$ ▥ **Atalaya Park.** Closer to San Pedro de Alcántara than to Estepona, this comfortable resort hotel is set in subtropical gardens beside the sea and has extensive sports facilities. Rooms overlook either the Mediterranean or the mountains; some have such nice touches as exposed brick, dark carpets, and picture windows. ⊠ *Carretera N340, Km 168, 29688,* ☎ *952/889000,* FAX *952/889022,* WEB *www.atalaya-park.es. 454 rooms, 33 suites, 14 bungalows. 7 restaurants, 2 18-hole golf courses, 9 tennis courts, 6 pools (2 indoor), hair salon, massage, sauna, 3 bars. AE, DC, MC, V.*

$$$$ ▥ **Kempinski.** From the outside, this ocher-colored luxury resort between the coastal highway and the beach looks like a cross between a Moroccan Casbah and the Hanging Gardens of Babylon. Tropical gardens and a succession of large swimming pools lead down to the beach. Dressed in cream colors, the rooms are spacious, modern, and luxurious, with faux–North African decor and balconies overlooking the Mediterranean. The Sunday-afternoon jazz brunch, with a live band and lavish buffet, is something of a social occasion for locals. ⊠ *Playa El Padrón, Carretera N340, Km 159, 29680,* ☎ *952/809500,* FAX *952/ 809550,* WEB *www.kempinski-spain.com. 133 rooms, 16 suites. Restaurant, 4 pools (1 indoor), gym, hair salon, shop, some pets allowed. AE, DC, MC, V.*

$$$$ ▥ **Las Dunas.** Rising like a multicolor apparition next to the beach, this spectacular hotel is halfway between Estepona and Marbella. The setting is palatial, with trickling fountains and copious exotic plants, and the large guest rooms are bright and airy, with easy chairs, hemp carpets, and light-green furniture. Sea views command a premium. The restaurant serves first-class international food, and the health center

offers a range of therapies. ⊠ *La Boladilla Baja, Carretera de Cádiz,
Km 163, 29689,* ☏ *952/794345,* ℻ *952/794825,* 🌐 *www.las-dunas.
com. 33 rooms, 39 suites, 33 apartments. 2 restaurants, pool, health
club, massage, sauna. AE, DC, MC, V.*

OFF THE
BEATEN PATH
**CASARES –** This mountain village lies high above Estepona in the Sierra
Bermeja. Streets of ancient white houses piled one on top of the other
perch on the slopes beneath a ruined but impressive Moorish castle. The
heights afford stunning views over orchards, olive groves, and cork
woods to the Mediterranean, sparkling in the distance.

# RONDA AND THE PUEBLOS BLANCOS

It's been suggested that Picasso was inspired to create cubism by the
pueblos blancos of his youth. The story may or may not be apocryphal,
but it's nonetheless easy to imagine—there *is* something wondrous and
inspiring about Andalusia's whitewashed villages, with their dwellings
that seem to tumble down the mountain slopes like giant dice. Perhaps
it's the contrast in color: the bright white against the pine green. Or
perhaps the mountaintop isolation: at these altitudes, the morning
light breaks silently over the slopes, the only movement a far-off shepherd guiding his flock.

Each village has its own personality, drawn from its unique relationship to the wilderness surrounding it. In Setenil de las Bodegas, villagers
long ago built their dwellings into the very cliffs that loom above
them. The sparkling village of Grazalema, across the border in Cádiz
province (*see* Chapter 4) seems determinedly perched above it all. The
undisputed queen bee of the region is Ronda, a gorgeous town set in
a prime location and steeped in history. Rising over the impressive El
Tajo gorge, Ronda is richly endowed with Mudéjar architecture, Christian churches, and a famed bullring, where some of Spain's greatest
*toreros* have brandished their capes. Surrounding Ronda are three nature parks, where outdoor activities abound—from hiking to mountain climbing to hang gliding.

## Ronda

★ ㉘   *61 km (38 mi) northwest of Marbella, 108 km (67 mi) southwest of
Antequera (via Pizarra).*

Ronda is one of the oldest towns in Spain and is suitably picturesque
and dramatic. Secure in its mountain fastness on a rock high over the
River Guadalevín, the town is 49 km (30 mi) inland. The most attractive
approach is from the south: take the first turnoff to Ronda on the winding but well-maintained A473 from San Pedro de Alcántara, and the
town looms before you in all its medieval splendor. Tour buses roll in
daily with sightseers from the coast, and on weekends affluent Sevillanos flock to their second homes here; an overnight stay in midweek
is the best way to see this noble town's true colors.

Entering the lowest part of Ronda, known as El Barrio, you'll see parts
of the old walls, including the 13th-century **Puerta de Almocobar** and
the 16th-century **Puerta de Carlos V** gates. The road climbs past the
**Iglesia del Espíritu Santo** (Church of the Holy Spirit) and up into the
heart of town. Begin your visit in the **Plaza de España**, where the
tourist office can supply you with a map.

Ronda's most dramatic feature is **El Tajo** (the gorge, 360 ft deep and
210 ft across), which divides La Ciudad, the old Moorish town, from
El Mercadillo, the "new town," which sprang up after the Christian

reconquest of 1485. The **Puente Nuevo** (New Bridge), crossing the ravine immediately south from the Plaza de España, is an architectural marvel built between 1755 and 1793. The bridge's lantern-lit parapet offers dizzying views of the river far below. The architect of the Puente Nuevo fell to his death while inspecting work on the bridge, and just how many other people have met their end here nobody knows. During the civil war, hundreds of victims on both sides were hurled from it. Once you've crossed the Puente Nuevo into **La Ciudad,** the old Moorish town, you can wander through twisting streets of white houses with birdcage balconies, punctuated by stately Renaissance mansions.

The so-called House of the Moorish King, **Casa del Rey Moro,** was actually built in 1709 on the site of an earlier Moorish residence. Despite the name and the *azulejo* (painted tile) plaque depicting a Moor on the facade, it's unlikely that Moorish rulers ever lived here. The garden has a great view of the gorge, and from here a stairway of some 365 steps (known as La Mina) descends to the river. The house, across the Puente Nuevo in La Ciudad on Santo Domingo, is being converted into a luxury hotel and is closed to the public, but you can visit the gardens and La Mina. ⊠ *Cuesta de Santo Domingo 9,* ☎ *952/187200.* 🎫 *€4.* ☉ *Daily 10–8 in summer, 10–7 in winter.*

Note the strange figures carved on the facade of the **Palacio del Marqués de Salvatierra,** a Renaissance mansion with wrought-iron balconies and an impressive portal. The house is occupied by descendants of the original family. The palace is just down the street from the Casa del Rey Moro. ⊠ *Cuesta de Santo Domingo.* ☉ *Mon.–Wed., Fri., Sat. 11–2 and 4 to 7 PM; Sun. 11–2.*

The excavated remains of the **Baños Arabes** (Arab Baths) date from Ronda's tenure as capital of a Moorish *taifa* (kingdom). The star-shape vents in the roof are an inferior imitation of the ceiling of the beautiful bathhouse in Granada's Alhambra. Gangs of youths have been known to threaten tourists for money here, so be on guard. The baths are beneath the Puente Arabe (Arab Bridge) in a ravine below the Palacio del Marqués de Salvatierra. 🎫 *Free.* ☉ *Tues. 9–1:30 and 4–6; Wed.– Sat. 9:30–3:30.*

The collegiate church of **Santa María la Mayor,** which serves as Ronda's cathedral, has roots in Moorish times; originally the Great Mosque of Moorish Ronda, it was rebuilt as a Christian church and dedicated to the Virgen de la Encarnación after the reconquest. Its flamboyant mixture of styles reflects Ronda's heterogeneous past: the naves are late Gothic, the main altar is heavy with baroque gold leaf. The church is around the corner from the remains of a mosque, Minarete Árabe (Moorish minaret), at the end of the Marqués de Salvatierra. ⊠ *Plaza Duquesa de Parcent.* 🎫 *€2.* ☉ *Daily 10–8 in summer; 10–5 in winter.*

A stone palace with twin Mudéjar towers is known as the **Casa de Mondragón** (Plaza de Mondragón). Appropriated by Ferdinand and Isabella after their victory in 1485, it had probably been the residence of Ronda's Moorish kings. Today you can wander through the patios, with their brick arches and delicate, Mudéjar stucco tracery, and admire the mosaics and *artesonado* (coffered) ceiling. The second floor holds a small museum with archaeological items found near Ronda, plus the reproduction of a dolmen. ⊠ *Ronda de Gameros,* ☎ *952/878450.* 🎫 *€1.80.* ☉ *Weekdays 10–6 (10–7 in summer), weekends 10–3.*

The main sight in Ronda's commercial center, El Mercadillo, is the **Plaza de Toros,** one of the oldest and most handsome bullrings in Spain. Pedro Romero (1754–1839), the father of modern bullfighting and Ronda's most famous native son, is said to have killed 5,600 bulls here during his long career. In the museum beneath the plaza you can see posters for Ronda's very first fights, held here in 1785. The plaza is owned by the famous, now-retired bullfighter Antonio Ordóñez (on whose nearby ranch Orson Welles's ashes were scattered, in accordance with the director's will). Every September, the bullring is the scene of Ronda's *corridas goyescas,* named after Goya, whose bullfight sketches (*tauromaquias*) were inspired by the skill and art of Pedro Romero. Seats for these fights cost a small fortune and are booked far in advance, and both the participants and the dignitaries in the audience don the costumes of Goya's time for the occasion. Other than that, the plaza is rarely used for fights except during Ronda's May festival and sometimes in September. ☎ 952/874132. ☒ €4. ☉ *Mid-Apr.–Oct., daily 10–8; Nov.–Feb., daily 10–6; Mar.–mid-Apr., daily 10–7.*

The shady **Alameda del Tajo** gardens, beyond the bullring, are one of the loveliest spots in Ronda. At gardens' end, a balcony protrudes from the face of the cliff, offering a vertigo-inducing view of the valley below. Stroll along the clifftop walk to the Old World Reina Victoria hotel, built by British settlers from Gibraltar at the turn of the 20th century as a fashionable rest stop on their Algeciras–Bobadilla railroad line.

The lives and dirty deeds of Andalusia's mythologized *bandoleros,* the ruthless and dashing bandits who galloped across the Andalusian plains, are laid bare at the **Museo del Bandolero** (The Bandit Museum). Here you can discover the men behind the legends—including the famed José Maria Hinojosa ("El Tempranillo") and José Ulloa ("El Tragabuches")—via their birth and death certificates, arrest warrants, and the like. ☒ *Calle Armiñan 65,* ☎ *952/877785.* ☒ *€2.70.* ☉ *Daily 10–8.*

## Dining and Lodging

**$$$–$$$$**   ✕ **Tragabuches.** Around the corner from Ronda's parador and the tourist
   ★ office, this stylish restaurant has taken the Spanish culinary scene by storm. The urbane decor combines traditional and modern materials in two dining rooms (one with a picture window), and the food has earned Ronda-born Sergio López a national award as Best Young Chef in Spain. The menú de degustación, consisting of five courses and two desserts, is ample proof of his talent for imaginative treatment of classic ingredients. Where else would you find *rabo de toro* (oxtail stew) accompanied by a sweet chestnut puree, or thyme ice cream for dessert? ☒ *José Aparicio 1,* ☎ *952/190291. AE, DC, MC, V. Closed Mon. No dinner Sun.*

**$$–$$$**   ✕ **Mesón Santiago.** Lunching at this tavern is like dining in the home of your extended Spanish family. Always packed, the several dining rooms are decorated with Sevillian tiles and ceramic plates. In summer, you can lunch outdoors on the patio. The cuisine is simple Spanish fare, including tongue, partridge, quail, and the rib-sticking *cocido de la casa,* a savory stew of chard, potatoes, and chickpeas. ☒ *Marina 3,* ☎ *952/871559. AE, DC, MC, V. No dinner. Closed Dec.–Feb.*

**$$–$$$**   ✕ **Pedro Romero.** Named after the father of modern bullfighting, this restaurant opposite the bullring is filled with colorful taurine decor. Sad-eyed bulls peer down at you as you sample the *sopa del mesón* (house soup), rabo de toro, or *perdiz estofada con salsa de vino blanco y hierbas* (stewed partridge with white wine and herb sauce). For dessert, try the *tocinillo del cielo al coco* (caramel custard flavored with coconut). ☒ *Virgen de la Paz 18,* ☎ *952/871110. AE, DC, MC, V.*

$$$ ✕🏨 **Parador de Ronda.** The exterior of this parador is the old town
★    hall, perched at the edge of the Tajo gorge, but only the shell of the
building remains—inside, the design is daringly modern. The combi-
nation of old and new is spectacular from the moment you step into
the glass-enclosed courtyard. The large guest rooms, in cream tones,
are comfortable, with enormous bathrooms. The restaurant is famous
in its own right: try the green-pepper gazpacho, and, for dessert, *helado
de aceite de oliva* (olive oil ice cream), the chef's invention. Note that
this parador fills up quickly—book well in advance. ⊠ *Plaza de Es-
paña, 29400,* ☎ *952/877500,* 🅵🅰🆇 *952/878188,* 🆆🅴🅱 *www.parador.es.
70 rooms, 8 suites. Restaurant, pool, meeting room. AE, DC, MC, V.*

$$ ✕🏨 **Don Miguel.** This refurbished Ronda institution, perched on the
edge of the Tajo next to the Puente Nuevo, has comfortable and mod-
ern, though rather plain, rooms, some with views of the gorge and bridge.
In the popular restaurant, which has spacious terraces with equally attractive views, you can enjoy old favorites such as *codornices a la ser-
rana* (mountain-style quail) and *trucha almendrada* (trout with almonds).
⊠ *Villanueva 4, 29400,* ☎ *952/877722,* 🅵🅰🆇 *952/878377,* 🆆🅴🅱 *www.
dmiguel.com. 30 rooms. Restaurant, cafeteria. AE, D, MC, V.*

$$$ 🏨 **Reina Victoria.** Built in 1906 by the Gibraltar British as a weekend
stop for passengers on the new rail line between Algeciras and Bobadilla,
this classic Spanish hotel rose to fame in 1912, when the ailing Ger-
man poet Rainer Maria Rilke came here to convalesce. (His room has
been preserved as a museum.) Today the Queen Victoria maintains a
mood of faded glory and has a somewhat neglected, tumbledown air,
though the majority of the rooms have been refurbished. The pre-
dominance of tour groups detracts from the hotel's charm, but the views
from its garden are still unbeatable. ⊠ *Jerez 25, 29400,* ☎ *952/
871240,* 🅵🅰🆇 *952/871075. 89 rooms. Restaurant, pool, parking (fee),
some pets allowed. AE, DC, MC, V.*

$$ 🏨 **El Molino del Santo.** In a converted mill (the name means "the
saint's mill") next to a rushing stream near Benaoján, 10 km (7 mi)
from Ronda, this British-run establishment was one of Andalusia's first
country hotels and has served as a model for the rest. Guest rooms are
arranged around a pleasant patio and come in various sizes, some with
terraces. This is a good base for walks in the mountains, and the hotel
rents mountain bikes as well. The restaurant is justifiably popular. ⊠
*Estación de Benaoján, 29370 Benaoján,* ☎ *952/167151,* 🅵🅰🆇 *952/
167327. 15 rooms. Restaurant, pool. AE, DC, MC, V.*

$$ 🏨 **Maestranza.** Occupying the site of the house where the legendary
bullfighter Pedro Romero once lived (only one facade remains of the
original), this bright and elegant modern hotel is across the street from
the Ronda bullring. The carpeted rooms are of good size, with dark-
wood furniture contrasting with cream-color walls and light, pastel fab-
rics. Some have views of the *plaza de toros.* The large Sol y Sombra
restaurant serves regional dishes such as *conejo a la rondeña* (rabbit
in herb sauce). ⊠ *Virgen de la Paz, 29400,* ☎ *952/190170,* 🅵🅰🆇 *952/
875723,* 🆆🅴🅱 *www.hotelmaestranza.com. 52 rooms, 2 suites. Restau-
rant, cafeteria, parking (fee). AE, D, MC, V.*

$$ 🏨 **Polo.** Cozy, old-fashioned, and centrally located, the Polo offers comfortably furnished rooms and a good, reasonably priced restaurant. The
common areas are spacious, with black and white tiles and huge white
settees. Guest rooms have blue carpets and beds dressed in white. ⊠
*Mariano Souvirón 8, 29400,* ☎ *952/872447,* 🅵🅰🆇 *952/872449. 36
rooms. Restaurant, cafeteria. AE, DC, MC, V.*

$$ 🏨 **San Gabriel.** In the oldest part of Ronda, this hotel is run by a fam-
ily who converted their 18th-century home into an elegant yet infor-
mal hostelry. (Part of the building is still the family residence.) The
common areas, furnished with antiques, are warm and cozy and in-

clude a video screening room adorned with autographed photos of actors. (John Lithgow, Isabella Rossellini, and Bob Hoskins, in town to film *Don Quixote,* were among the hotel's first guests.) Rooms vary in size; some have small sitting rooms, all are stylishly furnished with antiques. ⊠ *Marqués de Moctezuma, 19, 29400,* ☎ *952/190392,* ⨂ *952/190117. 15 rooms, 1 suite. Cafeteria, minibars, parking (fee). AE, MC, V.*

**$–$$** ▥ **Alavera de los Baños.** Charm takes precedence over functionality at this dollhouse of a hotel right next door to Ronda's Moorish baths. The tasteful decor evokes a Moorish theme with ocher and pastel tones. The two rooms on the first floor have their own terraces, opening up onto the garden. The rooms upstairs have sloping, wood-beam ceilings. The whole place, including the large restaurant, has a warm, friendly feel. ⊠ *San Miguel, 29400,* ☎ ⨂ *952/879143,* ⊞ *www. andalucia.com/alavera. 10 rooms. Restaurant; no a/c, no room phones, no room TVs. MC, V.*

### Outdoor Activities

Ronda is surrounded by no fewer than three nature parks—the Parque Natural de Sierra de Grazalema (*see* Chapter 4), the Parque Natural de Sierra de las Nieves, and the Parque Natural de los Acornocales—where outdoor enthusiasts will find a slew of activities. Numerous hiking trails fan out from Ronda into the surrounding wilderness, some along flat terrain past oak forests and others through flourishing valleys wedged between limestone peaks. The tourist office publishes an excellent hiking guide, *Ronda: Naturaleza y Cultura, 10 Rutas para Senderistas Exigentes,* with detailed directions and maps, researched and written by two local hiking experts. It details 10 hiking routes around Ronda, including one that follows an old road once used by foot messengers who carried news between Ronda and the surrounding villages, and another that encircles the Tajo gorge and explores the surrounding rock formations, prime bird-watching territory. Ronda, with its numerous outdoor sports organizations and clubs, is an excellent place to pick up information or hook up with guided groups before heading off to explore the great outdoors. **Pangea Active Nature** (⊠ Calle Dolores Ibarruri 4 29400, ☎ 952/873496) offers a range of outdoor guided tours for all levels, including exploring the nearby valleys, gorges, and rivers by foot or by bike, meandering through the pueblos blancos on mountain bike, and even "descending from the top of the Sierra de las Nieves to the Mediterranean Sea." To rent bicycles, try **Acobis** (⊠ Plaza del Ahorro 1, ☎ 952/870221); the cost is €10 per bike for a day.

## Cueva de la Pileta

**㉙** *22 km (14 mi) southwest of Ronda.*

Magnificent caves are dotted around Ronda, many of which were once the cavernous hiding spots of *bandoleros* (bandits) who roamed the Andalusian countryside. One of the most impressive is the prehistoric Cueva de la Pileta, deep in a lush valley south of Ronda. The cave walls are graced with Paleolithic cave paintings depicting symbols and animals, some of them in particularly vivid black and red. In the Sala del Castillo (Castle Chamber), enormous stalagmites rise from the cave floor, creating the impression of being in an eerie castle. Wear comfortable shoes and clothes, because there are some narrow, low passages, and the ground can be uneven. You can enter only with a guide, who is posted at the entrance. Guides speak Spanish (with a smidgen of English) on the 50-minute tour, but the paintings—some dating as early as 25,000 BC—speak for themselves. To get here, leave Ronda on the Carretera A376 to Seville; 3 km out of Ronda, take the exit for Benoján. From Benoján, the caves are clearly signposted. ☎ 952/167343. 🎫 €6.50. ☉ Mid-May–Aug., daily 10–1 and 4–6; Sept.–mid-May, daily 10–1 and 4–5.

## Setenil de las Bodegas

③⓪ *18 km (mi) north of Ronda, 120 km (75 mi) northwest of Málaga.*

Sprinkled atop—and within—a rugged mountainside in the wilderness north of Ronda is this eye-catching *pueblo blanco*. Its distinguishing characteristic is the curious and clever way that villagers took advantage of their rocky surroundings. Along the village's steep, narrow streets slicing into the rock face are whitewashed dwellings that have been built into the cliff's craggy crevices, with the roof and sometimes a wall of the house formed completely from a mossy overhang or cliffside. The contrast of the whitewashed houses brightly reflecting the noonday sun from their cliffside cubbyholes is a vivid sight. That Setenil's plethora of caves were once used as bodegas explains its name.

The 16th-century **ayuntamiento** (town hall), near Plaza de la Andalucía, has a splendid Mudéjar ceiling and an inscription marking the Christian reconquest of Setenil on September 21, 1484. Just outside the village is the simple, whitewashed **Ermita de San Sebastián,** a hermitage that was the first Christian building constructed during the reconquest, supposedly to commemorate the birth of Queen Isabella's premature son, named Sebastian, who died shortly after birth.

Five kilometers (three miles) southwest of Setenil are the Roman ruins of **Acinipo**, with remains of an ampitheater. The site's earliest findings date back to the Neolithic era, and later the Phoenicians settled here before the Romans arrived in the first century. Excavations are often under way at the site, in which case it's closed to the public. Call or visit the tourist office in Setenil (✉ Calle Villa 2, ☎ 956/134261) before visiting to get an update. To get here, head east 2 km out of Setenil and take the exit marked "Ronda 23 km"; shortly thereafter you'll see signs to Acinipo. ✉ *Carretera El Gastor,* ☎ *no phone.* 🎫 *Free.* ☉ *Wed.–Sat. 9–3:30, Sun. 10–4:30.*

# MÁLAGA PROVINCE A TO Z

*To research prices, get advice from other travelers, and book travel arrangements, visit www.fodors.com.*

### AIR TRAVEL

From the United States, you'll have to connect in Madrid for Málaga. Iberia and British Airways fly once daily from London, and numerous British charter companies link London with Málaga. Most major European cities have direct flights to Málaga on Iberia or their own national airlines. Iberia has up to eight flights daily from Madrid (flying time one hour), three flights a day from Barcelona (1½ hours), and regular flights from other Spanish cities.

➤ CONTACTS: **Iberia** (✉ Molina Lario 13, Málaga, ☎ 952/136147; 952/136166 at airport; 902/400500 for general information).

### AIRPORTS AND TRANSFERS

Málaga's airport lies 10 km (6 mi) west of town. If you're coming from Britain and heading for the coast west of Marbella, consider flying into Gibraltar instead: the airport is right next to the frontier, and once you've crossed into Spain you can catch buses in La Linea for all coastal resorts.

Trains connect Málaga's airport with several nearby cities, and an Iberia bus leaves every 20 minutes for downtown Málaga (6:30 AM–midnight) at a fare of €.90. Taxis are plentiful, and official fares to Málaga, Torremolinos, and other resorts are posted inside the terminal. The trip from the airport to Torremolinos costs about €12.

➤ AIRPORTS: **Aeropuerto de Málaga** (☎ 952/048804). **Gibraltar Airport** (☎ 9567/73026).

### BIKE TRAVEL

The Costa del Sol is famous for its sun and sand, but increasingly visitors are supplementing their beach time with mountain bike forays into the hilly interior, particularly around Ojén, near Marbella, and also along the mountain roads around Ronda. A popular route, which affords sweeping vistas, is via the mountain road from Ojén west to Istán. The Costa del Sol's warm climate is ideal for biking, although it can be unpleasant—and a health risk—to overexert yourself in June, July, and August, when the soaring temperatures hit. There are numerous bike rental shops around the Costa del Sol, particularly in Marbella, Ronda, and Ojén, many of which can also arrange bike excursions. The cost to rent a mountain bike for the day ranges between €12 and €18. Guided bike excursions, which include the bikes and support staff with cars, generally start at about €54 a day.

➤ BIKE RENTALS: **Antonio Ortiz Bicicletas** (⊠ Avda. Arias de Velasco 28, Marbella, ☎ 952/770490). **Monte Aventura** (⊠ Plaza de Andalucía 1, Ojén, ☎ 952/881519). **Spanish Cycling Federation** (⊠ Ferraz 16, Madrid, 28008, ☎ 91/24294334).

### BOAT AND FERRY TRAVEL

Trasmediterránea, Spain's major car-ferry line, operates from Málaga to the Spanish city of Melilla on the north African coast once a day for most of the year; from late June to August, there are usually two or three daily ferries.

➤ CONTACT: **Trasmediterránea** (☎ 902/454645).

### BUS TRAVEL

Buses are the best means of public transit for reaching Málaga from Seville or Granada, and the best way to get around once you're here. Long-distance buses connect Málaga with Madrid, Cartagena, Almería, Granada, Úbeda, Córdoba, Seville, and Badajoz. You can also reach Marbella directly from Madrid or Seville; another useful route is Seville–Fuengirola. Within Málaga, buses fan out to all corners of the region. If you want to get off the beaten track and you're relying on public transportation, buses are your only option. The Costa del Sol is well linked to the rest of the region, and particularly to the city of Málaga. Buses depart from Málaga to Torremolinos and Benalmádena Costa every 15 minutes from 6:15 AM until 1 AM. On Saturday, an *autobus nocturna* (night bus) operates all night. Buses also travel to Antequera, the Axarquía, and Ronda and the pueblos blancos. Note that on Sunday and holidays, buses operate on limited schedules.

The Portillo bus company serves most of the Costa del Sol; Alsina Graells Sur serves Granada, Córdoba, Seville, and Nerja. Málaga's and Ronda's tourist offices have details on other bus lines. Los Amarillos travels from Ronda to several of the pueblos blancos.

➤ BUS COMPANIES: **Alsina Graells Sur** (☎ 952/318295). **Los Amarillos** (⊠ Málaga bus station, ☎ 952/363024; ⊠ Ronda bus station, ☎ 952/187061). **Portillo** (⊠ Málaga bus station, ☎ 952/360191; ⊠ Ronda bus station, ☎ 952/872262).

➤ Bus Stations: **Málaga** (✉ Paseo de los Tilos, ☎ 952/350061). **Marbella** (✉ Avda. Trapiche, ☎ 952/764400). **Ronda** (✉ Plaza Concepción García Redondo, ☎ 952/872262).

## CAR TRAVEL

Málaga is 580 km (360 mi) from Madrid via the N-IV to Córdoba, then the N331 to Antequera and N321; 182 km (114 mi) from Córdoba via Antequera; 214 km (134 mi) from Seville; and 129 km (81 mi) from Granada by the shortest route of N342 to Loja, then N321 to Málaga.

A car gives you the freedom to explore Andalusia's mountain villages. Mountain driving can be an adventure—hair-raising curves, precipices, and mediocre road services are common—but it's getting more manageable as highways are resurfaced, widened, and in some cases completely rebuilt.

➤ Car Rental Agencies: **Autopro** (✉ Carril de Montañez 49, Málaga, ☎ 952/176030, WEB www.autopro.es). **Caramba Car** (✉ Ramal Hoyo 7 Torremolinos, ☎ 952/376517, WEB www.carambacar.com). **Hertz** (✉ Málaga airport, ☎ 952/233086, WEB www.hertz.com).

## CONSULATES

➤ Canada: **Canadian Consulate** (✉ Plaza de la Malagueta 3, Málaga, ☎ 952/223346).

➤ United Kingdom: **British Consulate** (✉ Mauricio Moro 2, Málaga, ☎ 952/352300).

➤ United States: **U.S. Consulate** (✉ Centro Comercial Las Rampas, Fuengirola, ☎ 952/474891).

## EMERGENCIES

In case of an emergency, call one of the Spain-wide emergency numbers, for either police, ambulance, or fire services. The local Red Cross (*Cruz Roja*) can also dispatch an ambulance in case of an emergency. For nonemergencies, you'll find private medical clinics throughout the Costa del Sol, where the staff can often speak some English. Every town has at least one pharmacy that is on-duty for 24 hours; the address of the on-duty pharmacy is generally posted on the front door of all pharmacies. You can also dial Spain's general information number for the location of a doctor's office or the pharmacy that's open nearest you.

➤ Contacts: **General emergency number** (☎ 112). **Hospital Carlos de Haya** (✉ Avda. Carlos de Haya at Avda. Santa Rosa de Lima, Málaga, ☎ 952/390400). **Fire Department** (☎ 080). **Local Police** (✉ ☎ 092). **Medical Emergencies** (☎ 061). **National Information Line** (☎ 1003). **National Police** (☎ 091). **Red Cross** (☎ 952/443545).

## ENGLISH-LANGUAGE MEDIA

The Costa del Sol's longtime popularity as a travel destination—particularly among non-Spanish speakers—means that there is plenty of English reading material available. Many newspaper stands, particularly in the more touristed areas, sell international newspapers and magazines (such as the *International Herald Tribune* and *Time*), and beach paperbacks in English. Additionally, there is a sizeable lineup of local English-language magazines and newspapers. The glossy, monthly magazines *Essential* and *Absolute Marbella* are filled with chatty articles on entertainment, culture, travel, and restaurants around the Costa del Sol, along with local celebrity interviews. The monthly magazine the *Reporter* covers news and entertainment along the Costa del Sol. All these magazines are free and can be picked up at various stores, restaurants, and occasionally tourist offices in the larger towns, including Málaga and Marbella. The weekly newspaper *Costa del Sol News* reports local and international news, and has TV and entertainment listings. Once a week, an English version of the Spanish daily *Sur* comes out, with local news and a large classifieds section. Another weekly newspaper is *Entertainer,* with local news, financial articles, and a sizeable classifieds section.

### RADIO

There are a number of English-language radio stations on the dial in the Costa del Sol, all of which offer a mix of tunes and talk. Many also broadcast the BBC news at various times of the day, usually in the evenings and on weekends. Central FM (98.6 FM), Spectrum FM (107.9 and 105.5 FM), and Global (96.5 FM) are the three main English-language stations.

## LODGING

### APARTMENT AND VILLA RENTALS

The Costa del Sol caters to those in search of some uninterrupted R&R and, accordingly, there is no shortage of apartments and villas— from basic to luxury—for both short- and long-term stays. The rural interior is peppered with *casas rurales,* accommodations in everything from traditional Andalusian farmhouses to self-catering rustic cottages. Note that an excellent source for apartment and villa rentals is www.andalucia.com, where you can peruse a varied list of accommodations. For those with an eye to buy, you'll find a host of magazines, in English, that cover the Costa del Sol's real estate market, including *Real(i)ty News.*

➤ LOCAL AGENTS: **Golden Mile Residences** (✉ Guadelmina Alta, Marbella, 29670, ☎ 952/880086, WEB www.goldenmile.es). **La Posada del Torcal's Rural Retreats** (✉ Partido de Jeva, Villanueva de la Concepción, 29230, ☎ 952/031177). **Turismo Rural en la Axarquía** (✉ Las Arenas 1, Torre del Mar, 29740, ☎ 952/540914, WEB www. axarquia-rural.com).

## TOURS

Numerous one- and two-day excursions from Costa del Sol resorts are run by the national company Pullmantur and various smaller firms. All local travel agents and most hotels have leaflets on hand and can book you a tour; excursions leave from Málaga, Torremolinos, Fuengirola, Marbella, and Estepona, with prices varying by departure point. Most tours last half a day, and in most cases you can be picked up at your hotel.

Popular tours include Málaga, the Cuevas de Nerja, Mijas, Marbella, and Puerto Banús; a burro safari in Coín; and a countryside tour of Alhaurín de la Torre, Alhaurín el Grande, Coín, Ojén, and Ronda. Night tours include a barbecue evening, a bullfighting evening with dinner, and a night at the Casino Torrequebrada.

If you're on a tight schedule, the colorful, open-topped Málaga Tour City Sightseeing Bus is a good way to view the city's sights within a day. The bus travels to all the main attractions, including Gibralfaro, and you can "hop on and hop off" as many times as you'd like.
➤ CONTACTS: **Málaga Tour City Sightseeing Bus** (✉ Málaga, ☎ 952/ 363133, WEB www.citysightseeing-spain.com). **Pullmantur** (✉ Avda. Imperial, Torremolinos, ☎ 952/384400).

## TRAIN TRAVEL

Málaga is the main rail terminus, with eight trains a day from Madrid and two from Barcelona and Valencia. Most Málaga-bound trains leave from Madrid's Atocha station, though some leave from Chamartín. Travel time varies between 4½ and 10 hours; the best and fastest train is the daytime *Talgo 200* from Atocha. All Madrid–Málaga trains stop at Córdoba. From both Seville (4 hours) and Granada (3–3½ hours) to Málaga, you have to change at Bobadilla, making buses a more efficient mode of travel from those cities. In fact, aside from the direct Madrid–Córdoba–Málaga line, trains in Andalusia can be slow because of the hilly terrain. Buses are generally more convenient.

Málaga's train station is a 15-minute walk from the city center, across the river. Call RENFE for schedules and fares.

A useful suburban train service connects Málaga, Torremolinos, and Fuengirola, calling at the airport and all resorts along the way. The train leaves Málaga every half hour between 6 AM and 10:30 PM and Fuengirola every half hour from 6:35 AM to 11:35 PM. Its terminus in Málaga is the Guadalmedina station, near the Corte Inglés department store, but it also stops at Málaga's RENFE station. The Fuengirola terminus is across from the bus station, where you can catch buses for Mijas, Marbella, Estepona, and Algeciras.

Two trains a day connect Málaga and Ronda via the dramatic Chorro gorge, with a change at Bobadilla. Travel time is around three hours. Three trains a day make the direct two-hour trip between Ronda and Algeciras on a spectacular mountain track.

➤ TRAIN INFORMATION: **Málaga train station** (✉ Explanada de la Estación, ☎ 952/360202). **RENFE** (☎ 902/240202, WEB www.renfe.es).

### TRAVEL AGENCIES

American Express has an office in Marbella. Wagons-Lits Viajes is the major agency in Málaga.

➤ CONTACTS: **American Express** (✉ Avda. Duque de Ahumada, Marbella, ☎ 952/821494). **Wagons-Lits Viajes** (✉ Strachan 10, Málaga, ☎ 952/217695).

### VISITOR INFORMATION

➤ LOCAL TOURIST OFFICES: **Almuñecar** (✉ Palacete de La Najarra, Avda. Europa, ☎ 958/631125). **Antequera** (✉ Palacio de Najera, Coso Viejo, ☎ 952/702505). **Archidona** (✉ Plaza Ochavada 1, ☎ 952/2716479). **Benalmádena Costa** (✉ Avda. Antonio Machado 14, ☎ 952/442494). **Estepona** (✉ Paseo Marítimo, ☎ 952/800913). **Fuengirola** (✉ Avda. Jesús Santos Rein 6, ☎ 952/467457). **Málaga** (✉ Avda. Cervantes 1, Paseo del Parque, ☎ 952/604410). **Marbella** (✉ Glorieta de la Fontanilla, ☎ 952/822818). **Nerja** (✉ Puerta del Mar 2, ☎ 952/521531). **Ronda** (✉ Plaza de España 1, ☎ 952/871272). **Torremolinos** (✉ Ayuntamiento, Plaza Blas Infante, ☎ 952/379511).

➤ REGIONAL TOURIST OFFICES: **Málaga** (✉ Pasaje de Chinitas 4, ☎ 952/213445).

# 6 CÓRDOBA PROVINCE

Córdoba's labyrinthine Mezquita (a mosque-turned-cathedral), Roman bridge, Moorish ramparts, and former synagogue make visitors feel tiny in time and space, a headshrinking process fundamental to the experience of travel. The idea that Roman philosopher Seneca and the Hispano-Arabic thinker Averroës, both Córdobans, were separated by a millennium from each other and by another thousand years from the present, eloquently illustrates the sweep of Andalusian history, while Córdoba's Mudéjar churches and the paintings of Julio Romero de Torres intrigue the eye and mind.

By George
Semler

T HE CITY OF THREE CULTURES" (Muslim, Jewish, and Christian), Córdoba of the present is an ongoing exploration and celebration of its rich past. Strategically located beside the Guadalquivir River, it was first inhabited by Iberian tribes, then Phoenician and Greek traders, Carthaginian conquerors, and, more enduringly, Romans, who established the city as capital of Hispania Ulterior and of Bética, the southern region of Spain that the Moors would call Al-Andalus. Visigoths followed the Romans in the 6th century and dominated until the arrival of Moorish troops in 715. The Ummayyad dynasty under the leadership of Abd ar-Rahman I, a refugee from the Caliphate of Damascus, founded the Independent Emirate of Córdoba in the mid-8th century, which was succeeded by the caliphate established by Abd ar-Rahman III in 929. Abd ar-Rahman III declared himself caliph, or "Prince of the Believers," and proceeded to make Córdoba the greatest city in the west of its time. Córdoba reached its zenith during the time of the caliphate, declined after internecine strife caused the fall of the Umayyads in the 11th century, and finally fell to King Fernando III, the Christian saint, in 1236.

Córdoba today, with its modest population of just over 300,000, offers a cultural depth and intensity—a direct legacy from the great emirs, caliphs, philosophers, physicians, poets, and engineers of the days of the caliphate—that far outstrips the city's current commercial and political power. The *mezquita-catedral* (mosque-cathedral), as it is ever-more-frequently called; the winding, whitewashed streets of the Judería (the medieval Jewish quarter); the jasmine-, geranium-, and orange blossom–filled patios; the Renaissance palaces; and the two dozen churches, convents, and hermitages, nearly all of them Mudéjar (built by Moorish artisans) or built directly over former mosques—these are all major historical and artistic treasures.

The province of Córdoba outside of the capital city stretches from the Sierra Moreno and the northernmost Pedroches region through the Guadiato region to the northwest along the valley of the Guadiato River, the upper Guadalquivir valley east and west of the city of Córdoba, into the vineyard- and olive-rich Campiña to the south, and the mountainous Subbética bordering Málaga and Granada provinces. Each of these provincial subdivisions has architectural and natural gems to explore, whether you're en route to Seville, Granada, or Jaén.

## Pleasures and Pastimes

### Churches and Taverns

Some of the most characteristic and rewarding places to explore in Córdoba are the parish churches and the taverns that inevitably accompany them. The *iglesias fernandinas* (so-called for their construction after Saint-King Fernando III's conquest of Córdoba) are nearly always built over mosques with stunning horseshoe arch doorways and Mudéjar towers. Taverns tended to spring up around these populous hubs of city life. Examples are the Taberna de San Miguel (aka Casa el Pisto) next to the church of the same name, and the Bar Santa Marina (aka Casa Obispo) next to the Santa Marina church. Most neighborhoods are built around their parish churches and have a well-known tavern, if not several, nearby, providing an excellent way to explore neighborhoods, see churches, and taste *finos* (montilla-moriles sherry) and *tentempies* (tapas—literally, "keep you on your feet").

## Dining

Although Córdoba has a number of good restaurants and taverns, some of the most prestigious dining establishments seem somewhat tourist-weary: the fare is listless and the service mediocre. Generally speaking, the farther away from the Mezquita you get, the better and more authentic dining you find. Córdoba's specialties are gazpacho, *salmorejo* (a thick version of gazpacho) and *rabo de toro* (oxtail stew). Many Córdoban restaurants are creating inventive new dishes based on old Arab recipes. *Fino de Montilla,* a dry, sherrylike wine from the local Montilla-Moriles district, makes a good aperitif or bar drink, and dinner wines from La Rioja or Ribera de Duero remain superior to any local offerings.

| CATEGORY | COST* |
| --- | --- |
| $$$$ | over €18 |
| $$$ | €13–€18 |
| $$ | €8–€13 |
| $ | under €8 |

*per person for a main course at dinner

## Fiestas

Córdoba parties hard during **Carnival,** on the days leading up to Ash Wednesday, and **Semana Santa** (Holy Week) is always intensely celebrated with dramatic religious processions. May brings **Las Cruces de Mayo** (The Crosses of May) during the first week of the month, the **Festival de los Patios** (Patio Festival) during the second, and the **Concurso Nacional de Flamenco** (National Flamenco competition) during the second week of May every third year. Córdoba's annual **Feria de Mayo** is the city's main street party, held during the last week of May. The **International Guitar Festival** brings major artists to Córdoba in early July. Córdoba celebrates **Nuestra Señora de Fuensanta** on the last Sunday in September and the **Romería de San Miguel** (Procession of St. Michael) on September 29.

## Lodging

Córdoba has accommodations for all tastes and budgets, from simple bed-and-breakfasts, hostals, and pensions to luxurious hotels and paradors. There are also rooms in houses in the old quarter close to the mosque. Air-conditioning is a key factor for comfortable sleeping from June through September, and most places, even budget choices, have it. Finding a room in Córdoba is generally never a problem except during Holy Week and the May Patio Festival. Since parking can be difficult and an extra expense in the area immediately around the mosque-cathedral, the hotels farther out along the periphery of the Moorish walls or near the center of town (Plaza de las Tendillas) offer advantages over the classic mosque-view spots. In addition, the area around the mosque-cathedral is so intensely touristic and commercial that it's not the most interesting part of town to spend time in, except for touring through and around the Mezquita itself.

In the countryside, look for *cortijos* (ranches), *almazaras* (olive oil mills), *eras* (threshing floors), and *posadas* (inns) that have been converted into rural lodging establishments. These can range wildly in both cost and comfort, so check carefully when making your plans.

| CATEGORY | COST |
| --- | --- |
| $$$$ | over €140 |
| $$$ | €100–€140 |
| $$ | €60–€100 |
| $ | under €60 |

*All prices are for a standard double room, excluding tax.

## May Flowers: Crosses and Patios

In the first half of May Córdoba is an avalanche of flowers, beginning with the Cruces de Mayo (Crosses of May), when the city's most characteristic corners fill with elaborate cruciform flower arrangements, and continuing through the Fiesta de los Patios (Patio Festival), when more than 150 courtyards compete in a best-patio competition. Córdoba's patio tradition, dating back to Roman times, reached its greatest splendor under Moorish rule, when patios with gleaming whitewashed walls, geometrically patterned floor tiles, tiny stairways leading to upper levels, and often fountains, springs, or wells became a city trademark. The patio competition offers a wonderful way to see Córdoba beyond the Mezquita and the Judería, with *verbenas* (garden parties) lasting late into the cool early summer evenings.

# Exploring Córdoba and Córdoba Province

The city of Córdoba is densely packed with beautiful patios, doorways, streets, rooftops, windows bursting with flowers, and twisting alleyways with surprises around every corner. Neighborhoods are known by the parish churches at their center, but the main city subdivisions are the **Judería,** including the Mezquita, the Barrio de San Basilio behind the Jardines de los Reales Alcázares, and the Torre de la Calahorra across the river; the **Plaza de la Corredera,** from the Paseo de la Ribera along the Guadalquivir to the ruins of the Roman Temple; and the **Centro,** from Plaza de las Tendillas to the Iglesia de Santa Marina and the Torre de la Malmuerta.

Beyond the city, the archaeological site at Madinat al-Zahra, the northern Pedroches area, the Guadiato River valley to the northwest, the vineyards of Montilla-Moriles, the olive plantations of Baena in the Campiña, and the towns of Zuheros and Priego de Córdoba in the mountainous Subbética region to the south toward Granada provide a plethora of options.

## Great Itineraries

With a half day devoted to the Mezquita, a tour of the Judería can easily take a full day in itself. The Torre de la Calahorra offers insight into the Córdoba *de las tres culturas* and deserves 90 minutes. Leaving Córdoba without a good eyeful of sensual hometown painter Julio Romero de Torres is a mistake, and while you're at the Museo Provincial de Bellas Artes you can't miss the Posada del Potro across the square. The Palacio de Viana would be the last unmissable visit. The Barrio de San Basilio is an evening tavern tour, and the Plaza de la Corredora comes to life after dinner.

Driving through the province of Córdoba toward your next destination, be it Seville, Granada, Jaén, or points beyond, offers a choice of destinations, though Madinat al-Zahra, 8 km (5 mi) from downtown Córdoba fits any plan.

IF YOU HAVE 3 DAYS

On your tour of ⌧ **Córdoba** ①–㊺, start with a walk of the Puente Romano, see the museum at the **Torre de la Calahorra** ⑥, and tour the outside of the **Mezquita** ① and the **Calleja de las Flores** ③. In the afternoon, see the Judería, the **Sinagoga** ⑬, the **Museo Taurino** ⑯, the **Casa Andalusí** ⑫, and the **Monumento a Seneca** ⑪ just outside the Puerta de Almodóvar. Walk down through the gardens along the Moorish ramparts and enter the Judería again by the **Monumento a Averroës** ⑩. In the evening wander the **Barrio de San Basilio** ⑧ to the **Monumento a Ibn Hazm** ⑨ at the Puerta de Sevilla before heading for a restaurant for a late dinner. On Day 2, walk through the **Plaza de la Corredera** ⑳

# Córdoba Province

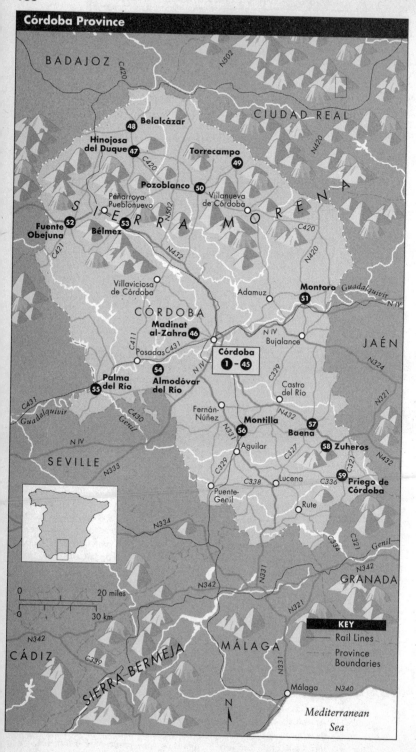

BADAJOZ

CIUDAD REAL

C420

N502

Belalcázar **48**

Hinojosa **47**
del Duque

C420

Torrecampo **49**

Pozoblanco **50**

Peñarroya-
Pueblonuevo

N502

Villanueva
de Córdoba

C420

S I E R R A        M O R E N A

Fuente **52**
Obejuna

**53**

Bélmez

C421

N432

N420

Villaviciosa
de Córdoba

Adamuz

Montoro **51**

Guadalquivir

N IV

CÓRDOBA

JAÉN

Madinat **46**
al-Zahra

N IV

Bujalance

C411

Posadas

C431

N324

Córdoba
**1 - 45**

C329

Palma **55**
del Río

Almodóvar **54**
del Río

N IV

Castro
del Río

N432

Guadalquivir

C431

C430

Genil

Fernán-
Núñez

N321

N IV

Montilla **56**

Baena **57**

C327

Zuheros **58**

C321

N333

Aguilar

C329

C338

Lucena

C336

Priego de **59**
Córdoba

N432

Puente-
Genil

Rute

C321

N334

C336

Genil

GRANADA

SEVILLE

0        20 miles

0        30 km

N334

N342

N331

N321

N342

N342

CÁDIZ

C339

MÁLAGA

N331

**KEY**
Rail Lines
Province
Boundaries

S I E R R A   B E R M E J A

Málaga

N340

N

Mediterranean
Sea

and down into Plaza del Potro for a look at the **Posada del Potro** ㉖, the **Museo Provincial de Bellas Artes** ㉔, and the **Museo Julio Romero de Torres** ㉕ facing one another in the top part of the square. If you can make it to the **Palacio de los Marqueses de Viana** ㊴ by 2, you can have the 13 patios all to yourself. Try El Rincón de las Beatillas around the corner. Devote the afternoon of the second day to the Mezquita. Try for an early dinner followed by a flamenco performance. On Day 3 walk the Centro area, starting at the ruins of the **Roman Temple** ⑱ and ending at the **Iglesia de Santa Marina** ㊶ next to the Manolete monument, where the Bar Santa Marina with its icy air and icier *fino* (Montilla-Moriles sherry) will restore you. In the afternoon drive or take a taxi or bus out to **Madinat al-Zahra** ㊻ for a visit to a royal summer palace that, had it not been pillaged in the 11th century, would rival the Alhambra.

IF YOU HAVE 5 DAYS

Five days in Córdoba will allow you to complete the three-day visit above as well as explore a few of the farther-flung churches and squares such as the **Iglesia de San Lorenzo** ㊺ or the **Iglesia de San Agustín** ㊵. Even better, you can travel out to towns and villages in the Campiña. **Almodóvar del Río** ㊴ with its castle, **Montilla** ㊶ with its vineyards and bodegas, and **Baena** ㊷ with its Nuñez de Prado olive oil artisans are prime candidates, with **Fuente Obejuna** ㊾ and Parque Natural Sierra de Hornachuelos close behind. The northern Valle de los Pedroches and the southern Subbética Cordobesa sierra with the perched village of **Zuheros** ㊹ and the gemlike baroque town of **Priego de Córdoba** ㊿ are rewarding visits.

## When to Tour

Córdoba booms in May when one fiesta follows another: Cruces de Mayo, patios, flamenco, and feria. March, April, and May are all high season in Córdoba; hotel prices rise and bookings must be made well in advance. June through September are tour group months and oppressively hot. October may be the best month to visit, as the weather is ideal, the tourist pressure reduced, and the prices lower. November through February are also fine months to have the place to yourself, with brisk temperatures that stimulate both hiking around the city and taking on your fair share of the local cuisine.

# CÓRDOBA

*166 km (103 mi) northwest of Granada, 407 km (250 mi) southwest of Madrid.*

The city of Córdoba is known for its Moorish Mezquita (mosque), now a mosque-cathedral, constructed between the 8th and the 10th centuries. The city's old neighborhoods, and particularly the medieval Jewish quarter, lend themselves to quiet exploration: they're characterized by narrow, whitewashed alleys, tiled patios with effusions of flowers, and the only synagogue in Andalusia to survive the 1492 expulsion of the Jews. All of Córdoba is explorable on foot, and the archaeological treasures at Madinat al-Zahra 8 km (5 mi) south are easily reached by bus or taxi. Córdoba's so close to Madrid (less than two hours by the high-speed railroad, the AVE) that it makes sense to go by train and rent a car in Córdoba for the next leg of your journey—unless you're going on to Seville, another 45 minutes away by AVE, where you won't need a car either.

Perched on the east bank of the Guadalquivir, Córdoba is chilly in winter, hot in summer, and so small you'll see the same fellow travelers over and over again. It has been little more than a minor provincial capital for the last seven centuries, but the city is of immense importance to the cultural history of the Iberian Peninsula. Córdoba was both the Roman and Moorish capital of Spain, and its old quarter, clustered around its famous Mezquita, remains one of the country's grandest examples of its Moorish heritage. The Moorish emirs and caliphs of the West held court here from the 8th to the 11th centuries, when Córdoba's opulence was legendary. Under the Moors, Córdoba became one of the greatest centers of art, culture, and learning in the Western world; the library of Caliph al-Hakam II had more than 400,000 volumes by the year 961, a staggering number at the time. Moors, Christians, and Jews lived in harmony in what chroniclers of the day reported was Europe's largest city, with a population of more than half a million. Today there are 310,500 Cordobeses.

Córdoba remained in Moorish hands until it was conquered by Saint-King Ferdinand III in 1236, after which the Catholic Monarchs used the city as a base from which to plan the conquest of Granada. In Columbus's time, the Guadalquivir was navigable as far upstream as Córdoba, and great galleons sailed its waters. Today, the river's muddy flow and marshy banks evoke little of Córdoba's glorious past, but the city's impressive bridge—of Roman origin, though much restored by the Arabs and successive generations—and the old Arab *noria* (waterwheel) are vestiges of a far grander era.

## La Judería

This tour encompasses the city's most characteristic spots, including the Mezquita and Córdoba's medieval Jewish quarter. It concentrates on the area around the mosque, the Roman bridge, the Moorish ramparts, the streets surrounding the synagogue, and the Judería itself just northwest of the mosque.

### A Good Walk

Allot half a day for the rambling **Mezquita** ① at the start or finish (preferably the start) of this tour. From there, situate yourself on Calle Torrijos on the west side of the mosque. In the sacristy of the former hospital at Calle Torrijos 10 is the regional tourist office where you can examine a scale model of the mosque and pick up maps and tours of taverns, patios, and historic sites. Next door is the **Museo Diocesano** ②. Along the back wall of the Mezquita's Patio de los Naranjos, near the bell tower, walk up Calle Velázquez Bosco to the **Calleja de las Flores** ③, famous for its hanging flower baskets and the view back to the bell tower. Up Calle de la Encarnación is the **Museo Arqueológico** ④. Back on Cardenal Herrero, continue around the mosque to Calle Martinez Rücker. In Plaza de la Concha at No. 40 there are marvelous tiles in the patio. The tiny Calleja del Panuelo on the north side of this diminutive square is reputed to be the slenderest street in Spain, the late Queen Mother (of King Juan Carlos I) having measured it with a *pañuelo* (handkerchief). Farther down Calle Martinez Rücker, look up into the spectacular corner tower with a wooden mesh ceiling, ancient ceramic tiling, and grass growing out of the roof. Past the lush courtyard of the Huéspedes Martinez Rücker hostal (a bargain bed, though hot in summer), at the next corner is a stunning horseshoe arch, its circle completed by the top of the iron gate below. Plaza de Abades to the right, with its tiny 18th-century Ermita de la Concepción, leads through to Calle de la Portería de Santa Clara and the **Mezquita de Santa Clara** ⑤ at the corner of Calle Rey Heredia. From here, Calle de las Cabezas leads to the plaque at No. 18 explaining that in the year 974, while their father was held captive in the house, the heads of his seven sons, the Infantes de Lara, were displayed on the arches covering the Calleja de los Arquillos. Walk back through Calle del Corregidor Luis de la Cerda to the Mezquita, continuing across the southeast end to the Puerta del Puente and the nearby Triunfo de San Rafael monument dedicated to Córdoba's *santo custodio* (guardian saint). Across the Puente Romano is the **Torre de la Calahorra** ⑥ with an excellent exhibit on Córdoba's most brilliant period. Below the bridge are the mills and the *noria* (waterwheel) that supplied water from the Guadalquivir into the nearby **Alcázar de los Reyes Cristianos** ⑦. Behind the gardens of the Alcázar is the **Barrio de San Basilio** ⑧, a picturesque micro-neighborhood to explore. Moving up Avenida de Doctor Fleming from the Alcázar through Campo Santo de los Mártires, past the **Monumento a Ibn Hazm** ⑨ and the Baños Califales (Moorish baths), the Moorish walls lead along Calle Cairuán past the **Monumento a Averroës** ⑩ and **Monumento a Seneca** ⑪ to the Puerta de Almodóvar, where a quick right into Calle Judíos leads down past the **Casa Andalusí** ⑫ to Córdoba's (and Andalusia's) only **Sinagoga** ⑬. Continue along Calle Judíos to the **Zoco** ⑭, on the left, and go through the arch to the courtyard, where a former Arab *souk* (market) hosts working artisans by day and flamenco music on summer evenings. A little farther down Calle Judíos is the tiny Plaza Tiberiades and the **Monumento a Maimónides** ⑮, just above Plaza Maimónides and the **Museo Taurino** ⑯. Calle Salazar leads over to the **Antiguo Hospital del Cardenal Salazar** ⑰. From here, Calle Romero leads across Calle Deanes into Calle de la Judería, and the southwest corner of the Mezquita.

TIMING

This walk may look intimidating on the map, but you will be surprised, if you have walked Seville or Madrid, at what a small town Córdoba is. The walk around the Mezquita and through the heart of the Judería could be achieved in two hours of forced march, but it would be better to spend three or four and carefully visit the Torre de la Calahorra's excellent exhibit. The Barrio de San Basilio can be more carefully explored in an evening tavern crawl. Check closing times for the synagogue and the Museo Taurino to make sure you arrive in time to see them. Set aside a full morning or afternoon for the Mezquita.

## Sights to See

**❼ Alcázar de los Reyes Cristianos** (Fortress of the Christian Monarchs). Built by Alfonso XI in 1328, the Alcázar is a Moorish-style palace with splendid gardens. (The original Moorish Alcázar stood beside the Mezquita, on the site of the present Bishop's Palace.) This is where, in the 15th century, the Catholic Monarchs held court and launched their conquest of Granada. Boabdil, Granada's final Nasrid Sultan, was imprisoned here for a time in 1483, and for nearly 300 years the Alcázar served as a base for the Inquisition. ⌧ *Plaza Campo Santo de los Mártires, Barrio de San Basilio,* ☎ *957/420151.* ⌸ *€1.87; free Fri.* ☉ *Apr.–Sept., Tues.–Sat. 10–2 and 5:30–7:30, Sun. 9:30–3; Oct.– Mar., Tues.–Sat. 10–2 and 4:30–6:30, Sun. 10–2.*

**❼ Antiguo Hospital del Cardenal Salazar.** This building originally founded by Cardinal Salazar as a choir school became a hospital during a 17th-century epidemic. Now home to the University of Córdoba arts and letters faculty, this outstanding example of Andalusian baroque architecture is filled with lovely patios, vaulted staircases, and chapels. The early 15th-century San Bartolomé chapel is one of Córdoba's Gothic-Mudéjar gems. The cubic chapel has inner walls decorated with intricate plaster carving and colorful ceramics. The tile floors are original, as is the atrium over the entryway. In the square outside are the **Iglesia de San Pedro de Alcántara** and a monument to **Al-Gafequi**, famous 11th-century Arab oculist and source of the Spanish word for

# Córdoba

Avda. de América

Avda. de Cervantes

C. Reyes Católicos

43 44

Plaz
de Cc

Ronda de los Tejares

Avda. del Gran Capitán

José Cruz Conde

Osario

Conde

36

Pl. Aguilar
Galindo

33

C. de Rubledo

Ob

Góngora

Pl. San
34
Miguel Capuc
Pl

José Zorrilla

32

Concepción

Gondomar

27 Pl. de
las
Tendillas

JARDINES DE LA VICTORIA

31

San Felipe

Perez de Castro

Pl.Emilio
Luque
Sevilla

Valdés Real

Jesús María

Juan de Mena

Paseo de la Victoria

Pl. R. y
Cajal

L. de Hoces

R. Sánchez

30

Com

Pl. S.
Juan

Valladares

C. Barroso

Gran
Viera

29

Pl.
Trinidad

11

Almanzor

Blanco Belmonte

Rey Heredia

A. Crist

Pl.
Pae

12

Pl.
Benavente

3

Encarnación

Avda. del Conde de Vallellano

13

14 17

16 Pl.
Maimónides

Salazar

15

Cairuán

Pl. Judá
Leví

Deanes

Cardenal
Herrero

Tomás Manríquez

Torrijos

Hospital Glez. Francés

M. Rucker

Avda. Dr.
Fleming

10

2

1

Cardenal

Pl. Campo
Santo de
los Mártires

Amador de
los Ríos

Pl.
Vallinas

Ronda de

7

Puente

8 9

C. Reales

Avda. del Alcázar

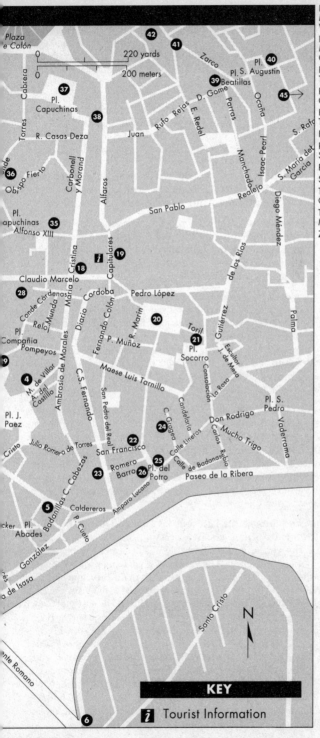

**KEY**

*i* Tourist Information

eyeglasses, *gafas.* ⊠ *Plaza del Cardenal Salazar s/n, Judería,* ☎ 957/ 218826. ☉ *Daily 9–9.*

**❽ Barrio de San Basilio.** This miniaturesque wedge of houses, also known as the Barrio del Alcázar Viejo (old fortress) for the earliest walled fortifications constructed here by the Moorish Umayyad dynasty, consists of three streets paralleling the Guadalquivir River: Calle San Basilio, Calle Enmedio, and Calle Postrera (literally, San Basilio, Middle, and Back streets). The entrance to the barrio is through the archway at the Torre de Belén, which houses a chapel. The **Iglesia de San Basilio,** also known as Nuestra Señora de la Paz, was founded in 1590 but underwent alterations during the 18th century; thus the simple facade conceals a baroque interior. The Barrio de San Basilio offers several cozy taverns along Calle San Basilio, and some superb flower-filled patios (such as the one at No. 50 Calle San Basilio) complete with wells, staircases, ceramic tiles, and gas-lamp-type lanterns.

**❸ Calleja de las Flores.** Some of Córdoba's prettiest patios are on this tiny street, with their ceramic tiles, lush foliage, and wrought-iron grilles. Patios are the key to Córdoba's architecture, at least in the old Moorish quarter, where sturdy, outer walls guarded the sanctity of the home and shut out the fierce summer sun.

**⓬ Casa Andalusí.** This charming little refuge under the Moorish walls in the Jewish quarter is filled with art, flowers, guitar music, books, gifts, and CDs. The basement has a collection of archaeological finds. The fountain in the inner patio, the quiet resonance of the guitar, and the fresh coolness of this hideaway all define the intimacy of the medieval Moorish home of 9th- to 12th-century Córdoba, which was said to number as many as 100,000 houses. ⊠ *Calle de los Judíos, 12, La Judería,* ☎ 957/290642. ☑ €2.50. ☉ *Daily 10:30–6 (8:30 in summer).*

**★ ❶ Mezquita.** A sprawling mosque so spacious that the 16th-century cathedral dropped in the middle of it is all but lost in the forest of columns and arches, Córdoba's Mezquita is one of the earliest and most transportingly beautiful examples of Spanish Muslim architecture. Built by four different emirs over five generations from 780 to 987, its rough, crenellated walls around the outside do little to prepare you for the sublime beauty and gradually encroaching sense of peace that overtakes you within.

As you enter through the **Puerta de las Palmas** (Door of the Palms), so-called for the Palm Sunday procession that traditionally passes through this entrance, some 850 columns of jasper, marble, granite, and onyx rise before you. The variety of pillars and ornate capitals in this earliest part of the structure is the result of the recycling of Roman materials, some of which were already being used in the Visigothic Basilica de San Vicente that was razed to make way for the mosque. Crowning the pillars, an endless array of red-and-white-striped arches curves into the dimness. Horseshoe arches in alternating colors of white limestone and red brick support a series of midpoint arches above, a technique Moorish architects learned from studying the Roman aqueducts built 500 years earlier. The ceiling is carved of delicately tinted cedar. The indirect lighting in use here now is meant to reproduce the Moors' own illumination of the mosque, though at their time the building's side arches would have been open to the outdoors, making the interior much brighter.

Exploring the Mezquita without a guide or at least a clear idea of what to look for can be a bewildering, though aesthetically exciting, exercise. The mosque and cathedral come to life in the search for the clues to the six phases of its construction, from the initial Abd ar-Rahman

I section through those of Abd-ar Rahman II, Al Hakam II, Al Mansur, and, in the Christian era, the 13th-century Villaviciosa chapel and the 16th-century cathedral.

The Mezquita was begun in 780 by Abd ar-Rahman I (756–788) on a site he initially shared with and ultimately bought from the Christian Visigoths. He pulled down their church and replaced it with a mosque, one-third the size of the current structure, composed of the first series of naves you encounter upon entering.

Abd ar-Rahman II (822–852) added the next, relatively small, section of the mosque, continuing out for several more naves. In this section recycled elements become scarcer, and pillars and capitals specifically created for the mosque (the ones with the uniformly leafed ornamentation) appear. Abd ar-Rahman II, poet-emir, vigorously promoted agriculture and industry as well as arts and sciences. It was this enlightened ruler, in fact, who brought to Córdoba the famous Ziryâb—Baghdadian musician, chef, stylist, and general aesthetic adviser and commissar for the city's cultural life. During this era the Mezquita boasted an original copy of the Koran and a bone from the arm of the prophet Mohammed; it became a Muslim pilgrimage site second only to Mecca in importance.

Al Hakam II (961–976), son of the illustrious first caliph Abd ar-Rahman III (891–961), presided over the Second Caliphate and inherited Córdoba at its pinnacle of power as the intellectual center of the known world. Al Hakam II started the second enlargement of the Mezquita in 962. In this section of the mosque there are no recycled materials, and its dazzling **mihrab**, a sacred prayer niche, is the Mezquita's greatest jewel. Make your way over to the **qiblah**, the south-facing wall in which the mihrab was hollowed out. To the right-hand (southeastern) end of this wall is the **Museo Visigodo de San Vicente**, where archaeological discoveries and remnants of the original Christian basilica are displayed. Unmarked, at the corner of the mosque, is a door leading to a bathroom, a water fountain, and a view over the river from a small window, which, as well as a breath of fresh air, helps with general orientation. A look at a map shows that this window faces east-southeast, contrary to Muslim law, which decrees that a mihrab face directly east, toward Mecca, and that worshipers do likewise when they pray. Al Hakam II reportedly agonized over a means of correcting such a serious mistake, though in the end he was persuaded by wise architects not to raze and rebuild the mosque. In front of the mihrab is the **maksoureh**, an anteroom for the caliph and his court, a masterpiece of Islamic art with exquisite mosaics and plasterwork.

The last addition to the mosque, basically the entire far (northeastern) side of the structure, was completed around 987 by Al Mansur ("The Victorious"), first minister of Caliph Hixem II, so-called for his military triumphs all over the Iberian Peninsula. (Al Mansur conquered Santiago de Compostela and had the bell from the Santiago cathedral carried back to Córdoba by Christian slaves.) Al Mansur more than doubled the size of the Mezquita he inherited, while widening the Patio de los Naranjos to the rectangular shape of today. Note that the red sections of the arches in Al Mansur's part of the mosque are painted to match the previous brick and limestone counterpoint, his exclusive use of stone an unequivocal sign of wealth and power. Archaeological research has confirmed that Al Mansur commandeered an entire street of houses for his enlargement, though legend has it that one stubborn little old lady refused to sell out and required that he rebuild her house stone by stone *and* replant her orange tree.

After the reconquest, the Christians initially left the Mezquita largely undisturbed; they simply dedicated it to the Virgin Mary and set about using it as a place of Christian worship. The clerics did erect a wall closing off the mosque from its courtyard, which helped dim the interior and thus separate the house of worship from the world outside. In the 13th century, Christians had the **Villaviciosa Chapel** built by Moorish craftsmen, its Mudéjar architecture blending harmoniously with the lines of the mosque. Not so the heavy, incongruous baroque structure of the **cathedral**, sanctioned in the very heart of the mosque by Charles V in the 1520s. To the emperor's credit, he was allegedly horrified when he saw the new construction, exclaiming to the architects, "If I had known what this was, I would never have allowed it; to build something you can find anywhere, you have destroyed something that was unique." (This sentiment did not, however, stop him from erecting the circular bastionlike Palacio Carlos V in Granada's Alhambra, or from adding new elements to Seville's Alcázar.) Surprisingly, the cathedral occupies a small percentage (less than 10%) of the entire area of the mosque. The most important parts of this building within a building are the **crucero** (transept), and the **capilla mayor** (main chapel). Built by the famous Renaissance architect Hernan Ruiz and continued by his son and grandson, the cathedral was under construction from the 16th to the 18th century and contains Gothic, Renaissance, and baroque elements. The red marble altarpiece and the Cuban mahogany choir stalls sculpted with biblical scenes carved by Pedro Duque Cornejo around 1750 are among the most impressive elements. The stone on the floor just outside the choir marks the sculptor's final resting place. **La Capilla del Sagrario** (Chapel of the Sanctuary) occupying three naves in the Almansur section at the eastern corner of the Mezquita is covered with rich 16th-century frescoes by Italian Renaissance painter Cesar Arbasia. The finest treasure in **El Tesoro** (treasury) is the giant 16th-century silver and gold *custodia* (monstrance) by Enrique de Arfe, which is taken through the streets in the Corpus Christi procession on the Thursday after Trinity Sunday.

The more time you spend in the Mezquita, the more rewarding it becomes. The labyrinthine repetitions in form and light and perhaps the leftover energy of so many devout, of many faiths, in search of life's meaning create an exhilarating, mystical sense of peace. More than 50 chapels are distributed around the periphery of the mosque. Chapel No. 13, the **Capilla de San Esteban y San Bartolomé,** holds the remains of D. Luis de Gongora, Spain's greatest baroque poet. Chapel No. 44, near the exit on the Patio de los Naranjos end of the mosque, has a small iron cage over a cross said to have been carved into the pillar by the fingernail of a Christian slave. Nearby is a grate where you can drop a coin for good luck.

The **Patio de los Naranjos** (Orange Court), perfumed in springtime by orange blossoms, centers on a fountain said to possess magical properties: if you drink from the one under the olive tree, you will marry. The patio is a popular space for Cordobeses and visitors alike to read, converse, and meditate. The **Puerta del Perdón** (Gate of Forgiveness), on the north wall, serves as the formal entrance to the mosque. The **Virgen de los Faroles** (Virgin of the Lanterns), a small statue in a niche along the north wall of the mosque, on Cardenal Herrero, stands behind a lantern-hung grille, rather like a lady awaiting a serenade. The painting of the Virgin is by Julio Romero de Torres, a favorite son of Córdoba from the early 20th century. The **Torre del Alminar,** the minaret once used to summon the faithful to prayer, was built directly over and made into a baroque belfry in the 17th century. From inside the tower, stairways and elements of the original alminar are still visible. At midday, from the top of the tower, you can hear the muezzin from a present-day Córdoban mosque hauntingly singing, as if from the past, the call to prayer. ⊠ *Torrijos and Cardenal Herrero, La Judería,* ☎ *957/470512.* ⊡ *€6.50.* ☉ *Oct.–May, Mon.–Sat. 10–5, Sun. morning mass and 2–5; June–Sept., Mon.–Sat. 10–7, Sun. morning mass and 2–7.*

**⑤ Mezquita de Santa Clara.** The Antiguo Convento de Santa Clara on the corner of Calle Santa Clara and Calle Rey Heredia contains the remains of a 10th-century alminar thought to be one of the earliest in Córdoba. The convent was founded in 1265 and closed in 1846. The lower part of the tower is Moorish, and the upper part was built over during the early Christian era. ⊠ *Calle Rey Heredia s/n, La Judería.*

**⑩ Monumento a Averroës.** Along the Moorish ramparts on the Calle Cairuán, just outside the portal leading into Calle Villaceballos, the monument to Averroës (1126–1198) commemorates the great Hispano-Arabian philosopher and contemporary of Maimónides, his fellow physician and lawyer. More influential in Jewish and Christian thought than in Islam, Averroës's greatest work was his interpretation of Aristotle. Averroës defines a just society as one in which ". . . every woman, every child, and every man is given the means of developing the possibilities God has given them" and in which ". . . no one says: this is mine." ⊠ *Calle Cairuán, La Judería.*

**⑨ Monumento a Ibn Hazm.** Author of *El Collar de la Paloma* (The Ring of the Dove), Ibn Hazm (994–1064) is considered one of the earliest analysts of the phenomenon of romantic love. An independent poet and philosopher who remained aloof from the official court, his support of the Umayyad dynasty nevertheless eventually won him early exile to his family's estates near Niebla. Though he wrote on theology, philosophy, and jurisprudence, his most famous treatise on love—part prose, part poetry—was written in his early 30s and addresses the immense human capacity for self-deceit triggered by romantic love, which he sees as, in any case, a quest for oneness: "God is unity. The unity of love, of the lover, and the beloved. Every love is a wish for union. Every love consciously or unconsciously is a love for God." ⊠ *Puerta de Sevilla s/n, La Judería.*

**⑮ Monumento a Maimónides.** Just off Calle de los Judíos, the bronze likeness of Maimónides sits in a reflective pose, thumb marking a passage in the Torah, as if about to illuminate some thousand-year-old point we still haven't grasped. Córdoban-born Maimónides (1135–1204) was a rabbi, physician, and philosopher and one of the foremost Hebrew scholars of all time. Nicknamed Rambam (for the initials of Rabbi Moses ben Maimon), his *Guide for the Perplexed* addresses biblical esoterica, proves the existence of God, debates the principle of creation, and discusses metaphysical and religious notions. Reflecting his profound knowledge of Aristotelian thought, the *Guide* dominated Jewish thinking and greatly influenced Christian thinkers. Maimónides's most important scholarship is dedicated to Jewish law, the Mishna. Examples of Maimónides's thought include, on the Koran and the Torah: "These are two manifestations of the same truth; there is only a contradiction when one is faithful to a literal reading of the scriptures, overlooking their eternal meaning"; on a healthy society: "The purpose of every society faithful to God is the growth of men and not wealth." ⊠ *Plaza de Tiberiades, La Judería.*

**⑪ Monumento a Seneca.** Outside the Moorish ramparts at the Puerta de Almodóvar is the monument to the Córdoban-born Lucius Annaeus Seneca (3 BC–AD 65), philosopher, orator, essayist, playwright, and poet.

Known chiefly for embracing the philosophy of Stoicism, and for stoically slashing his veins when ordered to dispose of himself by Nero, whom he had tutored as a boy, Seneca's *Dialogi* include essays on anger, divine providence, Stoic impassivity, and the peace of the soul. Though he spent nearly all of his life in Rome, Seneca has been much treasured as a Spanish thinker and even as a proto-Christian as a result of his thoughts on the subject of the Supreme Being: "Live with men as if God saw you; converse with God as if men heard you." The main body of his writing addresses the ethics of the virtuous man in a just society ("that government is ill conducted when the mob rules its leaders") and the theme of personal courage in the face of adversity ("fire tries gold, misery tries brave men"; "the fear of war is worse than war itself"; "life, if you know how to use it, is long enough"). ⊠ *Puerta de Almodóvar, La Judería.*

**❹ Museo Arqueológico.** In the heart of the old quarter (to the northeast of the mosque), this museum displays finds from Córdoba's varied cultural past. On the ground floor are Roman statues, mosaics, and artifacts and a collection of pre-Roman Iberian statuary. The second floor is devoted to Moorish art. Ruins of a Roman theater were discovered in 2000, and can be glimpsed just inside the museum entrance. The alleys and steps along Alta de Santa Ana are among Córdoba's most picturesque. ⊠ *Plaza Jerónimo Páez, La Judería,* ☎ *957/471076.* ⊞ *€1.50; EU citizens free.* ☉ *Tues. 3–8, Wed.–Sat. 9–8, Sun. 9–3.*

**❷ Museo Diocesano.** Housed in the former Bishop's Palace next to the mosque, the Diocesan Museum displays religious art, illustrated prayer books, tapestries, paintings (including some of Julio Romero de Torres's tamer works), and sculpture. The medieval wood sculptures are superb. ⊠ *Torrijos 12, La Judería,* ☎ *957/479375.* ⊞ *€1.50 (free with Mezquita ticket).* ☉ *Oct.–May, weekdays 9:30–1:30 and 3:30–5:30, Sat. 9:30–1:30; June–Sept., weekdays 9:30–3, Sat. 9:30–1:30.*

**❶❻ Museo Taurino** (Museum of Bullfighting). This impressive museum on the Plaza Maimónides is housed in two adjoining mansions. The restored structure itself, as well as antique posters, art nouveau paintings, and memorabilia of famous Córdoban bullfighters recommend a visit. The reproduction of the tomb of Spain's all-time taurine martyr, Manolete, and the head of the bull, Islero, who killed him in the Linares bullring in 1947, are among the most treasured items here. ⊠ *Plaza Maimónides, La Judería,* ☎ *957/201056.* ⊞ *€2.95; free Fri.* ☉ *Tues.–Sat. 10–2 and 4:30–6:30 (6–8 June–Sept.), Sun. 10–2.*

**❶❸ Sinagoga.** Córdoba's synagogue is the only Jewish temple in Andalusia to survive the 1492 expulsion of the Jews and one of only three ancient synagogues left in Spain (the other two are in Toledo). Though no longer in use as a place of worship, it has become a treasured symbol for Spain's modern Jewish communities. The outside is plain, but inside you'll find exquisite Mudéjar stucco tracery—look for the plant motifs and the Hebrew inscription saying that the synagogue was built in 1315. The women's gallery still stands, and in the east wall you can see the arch where the sacred scrolls of the law were kept. ⊠ *C. Judíos 20, La Judería,* ☎ *957/202928.* ⊞ *€0.30.* ☉ *Tues.–Sat. 10–1:30 and 3:30–5:30, Sun. 10–1:30.*

**❻ Torre de la Calahorra.** The tower on the far side of the Puente Romano (Roman Bridge) was built in 1369 to guard the entrance to Córdoba. It now houses the **Museo Vivo de Al-Andalus** (Museum of Al-Andalus), where audiovisual guides (in English) walk you through Córdoba's history, particularly its tricultural period, the time of the Moorish caliphate.

The scale models of Granada's Alhambra and of Córdoba's own Mezquita are superb, as is the presentation of extracts from the Islamic, Judaic, and Christian philosophies of, respectively, Averroës, Maimónides, and Alfonso X el Sabio. The scale models showing irrigation and agricultural techniques are also an excellent study of the Moorish expertise that turned much of Spain's arid tableland into fertile plantations between the 8th and the 15th centuries (only to have the Catholic Monarchs and their successors return much of it to grazing lands for sheep and cattle). The narrow staircase to the top of the tower offers nonpareil views over the Roman Bridge and the Mezquita across the river. ✉ *Puente Romano s/n, La Ribera*, ☎ *957/293929.* 💳 *€4, €5 with audiovisual show.* ⊙ *May–Sept., daily 10–2 and 4:30–8:30; Oct.–Apr., daily 10–6. Last tour one hour before closing.*

🞶 **Zoco.** *Zoco* is the Spanish word for the Arab *souk* (market), the one-time function of this courtyard near the synagogue. It now hosts a daily crafts market, where you can see artisans at work, and evening flamenco in summer. ✉ *Judíos s/n, La Judería*, ☎ *957/204033.* 💳 *Free.* ⊙ *Daily 9–9.*

# Plaza de la Corredera and Plaza del Potro

La Corredera, one of Córdoba's historic gathering places for everything from horse races to bullfights, is at the center of this tour through the southeastern part of Córdoba's historic section. The walk ends at the Plaza del Potro, famous for the inn, La Posada del Potro, where Miguel de Cervantes spent a few nights in the late 16th century. Filled with some of the city's oldest and most authentic corners, this is *real* Córdoba, minus the souvenir merchants clustered around the Mezquita.

## A Good Walk

Beginning at the ruins of the **Roman Temple** ⑱ at Calle Capitulares next to the ayuntamiento (town hall), cross to the **Convento de San Pablo** ⑲ before walking back toward the Guadalquivir along Calle Espartería, so named for the rope makers who once worked here. Now a social hub lined with terraces and taverns, **Plaza de la Corredera** ⑳ (officially Plaza de la Constitución) has been the setting for horse races, Inquisitional autos-da-fé, bullfights, and theatrical performances. Exiting through Calle Toril on the square's east side (so-named because it was the point where the bulls once entered), turn right to Plaza del Socorro and the **Ermita de Nuestra Señora del Socorro** ㉑. Moving right (southwest) through Plaza de las Cañas and Calle Maese Luis Tarnillo will take you to Galle San Fernando. Turn left for the **Iglesia de San Francisco** ㉒ and the baroque portal, the Compás de San Francisco. Back on Calle de San Fernando, pass the Moorish ramparts and gateway into the **Palacio de los Marqueses del Carpio** ㉓. Down Calle San Francisco is Plaza del Potro and the **Museo Provincial de Bellas Artes** ㉔, the **Museo Julio Romero de Torres** ㉕, and the **Posada del Potro** ㉖, three of Córdoba's finest compendiums of art, architecture, and history.

TIMING

This walk from the ruins of the Roman Temple through Plaza de la Corredera to the Iglesia de San Francisco and Plaza del Potro can be done in an hour without stops, but stops are essential, so plan for three hours at least, with a fourth for a careful look through the Museo Provincial de Bellas Artes and the Museo Julio Romero de Torres. This sensual painter of Córdoba's spirit and subconscious is so important that, in the event of any timing conflict, you might be wise to do this area first (while you're fresh) and then jump by five-minute taxi to the Roman Temple for the walk back.

## Sights to See

**⑲ Convento de San Pablo.** Through the baroque 18th-century *compás* (gate) with its spiraling columns and scrolled facade, the late 13th–early 14th-century church and convent of San Pablo combines styles and epochs. The antechamber of the sacristy is thought to have been a private oratory, part of a palace from the Berber Muslim Almohad dynasty that ruled Spain in the 12th and early 13th centuries just prior to Córdoba's 1236 fall to Saint-King Fernando III. The coffered Mudéjar ceiling over the main nave and the sculpture of *La Virgen de las Angustias* by Juan de Mena (his last work, finished in 1627, the year of his death) are San Pablo's finest treasures. ⊠ *Calle Capitulares s/n, La Corredera,* ☎ *957/471200.* 🎫 *Free.* ☉ *Open for mass: weekdays 10, 11, 12, 1:30, 6, 7, 8; weekends 10, 7, 8.*

**㉑ Ermita de Nuestra Señora del Socorro.** This tiny hermitage just off Plaza de la Corredera next to Calle del Toril was built in 1685 and became the seat of La Hermandad del Socorro (Brotherhood of the Rescue) after an early 16th-century playboy, Don Clemente de Cáceres, was cornered against the door of the church by a mob of angry swordsmen he had offended by seducing their wives, sisters, and mothers. With a desperate scream of "Madre mía, ven en mi socorro" (Mother mine, come to my rescue) the young rakehell fell through the heavy wooden door, which closed behind him just as eight swords struck home. Don Clemente went on to lead an exemplary life in payment for his rescue by La Señora de los Ángeles. The interior of the chapel is in the shape of a Latin cross, with an oval cupola covering an image of the Virgin, with St. Acisclo and St. Victoria, Córdoba's patrons, on either side. ⊠ *Plaza del Socorro, La Corredera,* ☎ *957/330310.* 🎫 € *1.20.* ☉ *Mon.–Sat. 10–1:30, 4:30–7:45; Sun. 11–1:30, 4:30–7:45.*

**㉒ Iglesia de San Francisco.** The Compás (gate or entryway) into the Iglesia de San Francisco was once the opening into the Moorish city, or *medina,* from the walled medieval neighborhood of San Nicolas de la Axerquía. The entryway itself, on Calle de San Fernando, is a magnificent baroque-scrolled free-standing portal with an empty scallop shell–vaulted niche, once inhabited by an image of Sant Francis of Assisi; it was toppled during anticlerical violence at the outbreak of the Spanish Civil War in 1936. The church behind the portal was initially built in 1246, though what is visible now was constructed over the original structures in the 17th and 18th centuries. Inside, the cloister and the baroque paintings are the best parts of this antique and somewhat disheveled church and convent. From No. 23 Calle de San Francisco there is a lovely view of the lateral facade of the church, with a tiny cupola and lush gardens. Note that the hours of the church are irregular. ⊠ *Compás de San Francisco s/n, La Corredera,* ☎ *957/475867.*

**★ ㉕ Museo Julio Romero de Torres.** On the right side as you enter the Hospital de la Caridad courtyard is the museum dedicated to Córdoba's greatest and most emblematic painter. Trained by his father, Rafael, professor of fine arts and first curator of the Museo Provincial de Bellas Artes, Julio Romero de Torres (1874–1930) became one of Córdoba's most beloved figures during his short life. Romero de Torres fully embraced Gypsy, flamenco, and folklore themes with his tragic visions of love, death, nostalgia, and eroticism. Credited with capturing nothing less than the soul of Córdoba, his dark, symbol-filled paintings nearly always feature beautiful, bare-breasted women with tortured and tear-filled eyes. His reputation has grown from a *costumbrista* (folklorist) to a symbolist analyst of Andalusia's popular roots; today Romero de Torres is recognized as the modern painter who best sythesized the epic elements in Andalusian life, death, and passion. The

# When you pack your MCI Calling Card, it's like packing your loved ones along too.

Your MCI Calling Card is the easy way to stay in touch when you travel. Use it to call to and from over 125 countries. Plus, every time you call, you can earn frequent flier miles. So wherever your travels take you, call home with your MCI Calling Card. It's even easy to get one. Just visit **www.mci.com/worldphone** or **www.mci.com/partners**.

## EASY TO CALL WORLDWIDE

1. Just enter the WorldPhone® access number of the country you're calling from.
2. Enter or give the operator your MCI Calling Card number.
3. Enter or give the number you're calling.

| | |
|---|---|
| Austria ◆ | 0800-200-235 |
| Belgium ◆ | 0800-10012 |
| Czech Republic ◆ | 00-42-000112 |
| Denmark ◆ | 8001-0022 |
| Estonia ★ | 0800-1122 |
| Finland ◆ | 08001-102-80 |
| France ◆ | 0-800-99-0019 |
| Germany | 0800-888-8000 |
| Greece ◆ | 00-800-1211 |

| | |
|---|---|
| Hungary ◆ | 06▼800-01411 |
| Ireland | 1-800-55-1001 |
| Italy ◆ | 800-17-2401 |
| Luxembourg | 8002-0112 |
| Netherlands ◆ | 0800-022-91-22 |
| Norway ◆ | 800-19912 |
| Poland ⋇ | 00-800-111-21-22 |
| Portugal ⋇ | 800-800-123 |
| Romania ⋇ | 01-800-1800 |
| Russia ◆ ⋇ | 747-3322 |
| Spain | 900-99-0014 |
| Sweden ◆ | 020-795-922 |
| Switzerland ◆ | 0800-89-0222 |
| Ukraine ⋇ | 8▼10-013 |
| United Kingdom | 0800-89-0222 |
| Vatican City | 172-1022 |

◆ Public phones may require deposit of coin or phone card for dial tone.  ★ Not available from public pay phones.
▼ Wait for second dial tone.  ⋇ Limited availability.

## EARN FREQUENT FLIER MILES

# Find America *with a Compass*

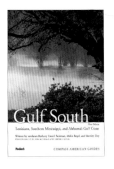

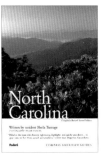

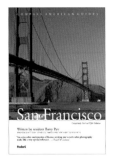

Written by local authors and illustrated throughout
with spectacular color images, Compass American
Guides reveal the character and culture of more than
40 of America's most fascinating destinations. Perfect
for residents who want to explore their own backyards
and for visitors who want an insider's perspective
on the history, heritage, and all there is to see and do.

**Fodor's** COMPASS AMERICAN GUIDES

*At bookstores everywhere.*

macabre *Cante Jondo* (Flamenco Song, 1930), the tragically allegori-
cal *La nieta de la Trini* (La Trini's Granddaughter, 1930), or the hu-
morously titled *Naranjas y limones* (Oranges and Lemons, 1928) are
among the best of the 75 paintings on display here, in addition to the
photographs, letters, and other memorabilia from the life of the painter.
⊠ *Plaza del Potro 1, La Corredera*, ☎ *957/491909.* 🎫 *€3, Fri. free;
EU citizens free.* 🕙 *Tues.–Sat. 10–2, 4:30–6:30 (Oct.–Apr. 5:30–7:30);
Sun. 9:30–2.*

**㉔ Museo Provincial de Bellas Artes** (Museum of Fine Arts). Behind a lovely
Gothic facade in a small courtyard just off the top of Plaza del Potro,
this museum was once the Hospital de la Caridad (Charity Hospice)
founded in the 15th century by the Catholic Monarchs, Ferdinand and
Isabella, who twice received Columbus here. The collection includes,
on the lower floor, Córdoban paintings from the medieval, Renaissance,
and mannerist periods, with works by Adriano de León, Pedro de Córdoba, Pablo de Céspedes, and Francisco Pacheco. Also on the lower
floor is the baroque collection, with prominent works of José Ruiz de
Sarabia, Francisco de Zurbarán, Juan de Valdés Leal, Acisclo Antonio
Palomino, and Jose Ignacio de Cobo y Guzmán. Antonio del Castillo
Saavedra's *San Pablo* is a standout. Juan de Mesa's *Niño Jesús* is the
most important sculpture from this period. The upper floor, with mod-
ern and contemporary Córdoban art, modern Spanish art, and a col-
lection of sketches and engravings, features the works of Rafael Romero
Barros (1832–95), the father of the painters Rafael, Enrique, and Julio
Romero de Torres, all also represented here. Look for the Rafael
Romero de Barros painting *Chicos jugando a los carros* (Young Boys
Playing with Carts) and you will easily recognize the young Julio
Romero de Torres on the right. Mateo Inurria Lainosa's sensual sculptures of the female form, particularly *Deseo* (Desire) and *Las tres
edades de la mujer* (The Three Ages of Woman), are worthy of note,
as are the paintings of Zuloaga, Sorolla, Casas, and Fortuny. ⊠ *Plaza
del Potro, 1, La Corredera,* ☎ *957/473345.* 🎫 *€1.50; EU citizens free.*
🕙 *Tues. 3–8; Wed.–Sat. 9–8, Sun. 9–3.*

**㉓ Palacio de los Marqueses del Carpio.** This spectacular little verdant corner, with tower, walls, and crenellated battlements, was originally a gift
of Saint-King Fernando III to the Méndez de Sotomayor family after
the city was conquered from the Moors in 1236. Next to the ramparts,
the 15th-century tower contains a lush Moorish-style patio and the remains of a Roman house. ⊠ *Calle San Fernando, 70, La Corredera.*

**㉒ Plaza de la Corredera.** Modeled after the Castilian *plazas mayores* (main
squares), such as Spain's most famous ones in Madrid and Salamanca,
this is the only square of its kind in Andalusia. Built between 1683 and
1687 on a spot designated in medieval times as *"un lugar destinado
para correr caballos"* (a place destined for running horses), the Corredera, or "running place," has been used for bullfights, autos-da-fé, theatrical presentations, and town fiestas, for which the balconies were
rented out as box seats. The Calle del Toril at the eastern end of the
square was the chute through which bulls were released into the square.
The medieval prison and the house of the *corregidor* (mayor) stand on
the south side of the square, and the southeastern side was a 16th-cen-
tury mansion. The square, now a key social hub filled with taverns and
terraces, is flanked by the Sanchez Peña market on the eastern side occupying the former jailhouse; markets fill the main area of the square
on Sunday and holidays. ⊠ *Plaza de la Constitución, La Corredera.*

**㉖ Posada del Potro.** A lovely flower-filled, whitewashed *corrala* (corral
with space for animals below and tiers of galleries for lodging above),
this slender slot with wooden balconies and ancient wagon wheels from

the 16th-century stagecoach inn known as *El Mesón de la Pastora* once numbered Miguel de Cervantes as a client. A *posada* (inn) since the 14th century, the space was later also used for theatrical productions during the 15th and 16th centuries. The square outside was named Plaza del Potro (colt) for the medieval horse and mule trading exchange traditionally held there; the Renaissance fountain at the upper end of the square with a rearing horse holding Córdoba's coat of arms between its raised hooves commemorates this equestrian market. It's now an exhibition gallery and concert venue; keep your eye out for listings of early music and guitar performances. ⊠ *Plaza del Potro 10, La Corredera,* ☎ *957/485001.* 🎟 *Free.* ⊗ *Weekdays 9–9.*

**⓲ Roman Temple.** At the corner of Calles Capitulares and Claudio Marcelo, Córdoba's 1st-century Roman temple towered over the surrounding city and was visible for miles around the municipal outskirts. Only its ruins remain. The open-air altar was 15 ft high, and the construction materials included marble, limestone, and concrete. Visible now are eight fluted Corinthian columns that surrounded the images of Roman emperors worshipped as divine figures. ⊠ *Calle Claudio Marcelo s/n, La Corredera.*

## Centro

Córdoba's so-called *centro comercial* is much more than a succession of shops and stores. The town's real life, the everyday hustle and bustle, takes place here, and the general ambience is very different from that of the tourist center around the Mezquita. Some of the city's finest Mudéjar churches and best taverns, as well as the Palacio de los Marqueses de Viana, are in this pivotal part of town well back from the Guadalquivir waterfront.

### A Good Walk

Begin at the **Plaza de las Tendillas** ㉗, the center of the city's shopping district. Move southeast down Calle Duque de Hornachuelos to the **Iglesia de San Salvador y Santo Domingo de Silos** ㉘. Nearby is the **Iglesia y Colegio de Santa Victoria** ㉙, with its neoclassical circular nave. Down Calle Juan de Mena is the **Antigua Casa de Rodrigo Méndez de Sotomayor** ㉚, now the Conservatorio Superior de Música. To the left off Calle Jesús María, Calle Rodriguez Sanchez leads through Plaza Emilio Luque past the 16th-century Casa de los Venegas de Henestrosa, now the seat of the Gobierno Civil (Civil Government). Head north on Calle San Felipe to the **Iglesia de San Nicolás de la Villa** ㉛, with its Mudéjar tower, then head north on Calle José Zorrilla past the **Gran Teatro** ㉜ to the **Real Colegiata de San Hipólito** ㉝. Calle Gongora leads over to the **Iglesia de San Miguel** ㉞, one of Córdoba's best early churches. Take Calle Zoilo to the first corner, where a hard right leads to Plaza de Capuchinos and the monument to Obispo Osio (Bishop Hosius) on the lateral facade of the **Círculo de la Amistad** ㉟. After a look in, cut back to the intersection with Calle Zoilo and continue right through Plaza de las Capuchinas to Calle Conde Torres Cabrera and the **Palacio de Torres Cabrera** ㊱, an elegant 17th-century town house. From here a right turn into Calle Capuchinos reveals the curious **Cristo de los Faroles** ㊲. Continue through the square to the **Cuesta del Bailío** ㊳, a lovely stairway leading down to Calle Alfaros. Two steps up Alfaros to the left is the Puerta del Rincón (corner portal), the cylindrical corner watchtower for the Moorish ramparts. Straight across Calle Alfaros at the bottom of the stairs, Calle Mateo Inurria leads to Zamorano, where a left and quick right on Jurado Aguilar takes you to the **Palacio de los Marqueses de Viana** ㊴ (where you must arrive by 1:55 to make it in). After seeing the Palacio de Viana, walk two blocks north to the **Iglesia de San Agustín** ⑳, then cut west over to Plaza Santa Marina de las Aguas Santas, on the edge of the Barrio de los Toreros. Here you will find the **Iglesia de Santa Marina** ㊶, and just up the street, the **Monumento a Manolete** ㊷. From here, walk up Calle Mayor de Santa Marina past the excellent Cabello Armería (hunting and gun shop) and left on Avenida de las Ollerías to the **Torre de la Malmuerta** ㊸ and, across the top of Plaza de Colón, the **Antiguo Convento de la Merced** ㊹. Finally, for a look at one of Córdoba's loveliest off-the-beaten-track churches, consider a probe north to the **Iglesia de San Lorenzo** ㊺.

TIMING

This is a good hike. Allow four hours and try to cut it up into before and after the Palacio de los Marqueses de Viana, which is the longest single visit on this tour. Many of the churches are open only for mass and vespers services, and thus are likely to be closed when you pass, but a view from the outside is generally sufficient.

## Sights to See

⑳ **Antigua Casa de Rodrigo Méndez de Sotomayor.** The Conservatorio Superior de Música is housed in one of Córdoba's best civil Renaissance buildings. The plateresque facade, built in 1551, is designed in a honeycombed pattern known in Spanish as *de galleta,* or "biscuit-like." Note the reddish earth tones, the fluted columns, and the family shields and mythological themes carved into the window over the entryway. Concerts are held Sunday evenings at 8. ⊠ *Calle Angel de Saavedra 1, Centro,* ☎ *957/476661.* 🎫 *Free.* ☉ *Weekdays 9–9.*

㊹ **Antiguo Convento de la Merced.** Built by San Pedro Nolasco, co-founder of the Mercedarios (Order of Mercy) in the mid-13th century, the medieval structure has been entirely replaced by the 18th-century baroque convent now visible here. The porticoed patio centered around its black marble fountain, the imperial staircase in polychromatic marble, the chapel with its 14th-century Cristo de la Merced woodcarving, and the helicoidal columns in the richly textured baroque entry are the most striking elements in this elegant building, now home of the Diputación Provincial de Córdoba. ⊠ *Plaza Colon s/n, Centro,* ☎ *957/211100.* 🎫 *Free.* ☉ *Daily 9–2, 5–8.*

㉟ **Círculo de la Amistad.** This private club founded in 1854 as the Círculo de la Amistad-Liceo Artístico y Literario de Córdoba has lovely ceramic-tiled, horseshoe-arched porticoes around its patio and a sumptuous banquet hall with mural paintings. The 1904 Julio Romero de Torres painting is the best piece of art in the gallery, and the reading room's allegories of the five senses and the library's 10,000 volumes are the Círculo's treasures. Built over the 14th-century Convento de Agustinas Recoletas de Nuestra Señora de las Nieves, the Círculo de Amistad is the venue for the city's most important receptions and celebrations. Note that visitors (men and women) wearing shorts will not be admitted. ⊠ *Alfonso XIII 14, Centro,* ☎ *957/479000,* WEB *www. circuloamistad.com/pincipa.htm.* 🎫 *Free.* ☉ *Daily 9–9.*

㊲ **Cristo de los Faroles.** The singular statue of *El Cristo de los Faroles* (Christ of the Lanterns) is a crucifix surrounded by eight lanterns hanging from twisted, wrought-iron brackets. It's tucked away in the intimate Plaza de los Dolores, also known as the Plaza de los Capuchinos, a small square north of Plaza San Miguel surrounded by the 17th-century Convento de los Capuchinos. The oblong square is a quiet redoubt where you can feel the city's languid pace. Since its creation in 1794, the Cristo de los Faroles has been one of Córdoba's most beloved icons. ⊠ *Plaza de los Capuchinos, Centro.* 🎫 *Free.*

**➌➑ Cuesta del Bailío.** This graceful expanse of stairs leading down to Calle Alfaros is often compared to Rome's Spanish Steps. It was the passageway between the medieval Moorish medina and the walled eastern section of town known as the *Axerquía*. This doorway between the two parts of Córdoba became known as the *Portillo de Bailío* (Doorway of the Bailiff) when a member of the powerful Fernández de Córdoba family, owners of the Palacio de Torres Cabrera at the head of the stairs, became chief magistrate. ⊠ *Cuesta del Bailío s/n, Centro.*

**➌➋ Gran Teatro.** Córdoba's most traditional theatrical venue, inaugurated in 1873, faces Calle de la Alegría. The Avenida Gran Capitán lateral facade of the theater is adorned with busts of Spain's most prolific playwright, Félix Lope de Vega (1562–1635); Córdoban-born playwright Angel de Saavedra, better known as the Duque de Rivas (1791–1865); Seneca; and Beethoven. ⊠ *Av. Gran Capitán, 3, Centro,* ☎ 957/480644, WEB *www.teatrocordoba.com.*

**➍➓ Iglesia de San Agustín.** This 16th-century church and convent is distinguished by its 17th-century murals. The ornate main altar is surrounded by paintings of St. John the Baptist, St. John the Evangelist, and the Conversion of St. Augustine, all by Cristóbal Vela (1634–76), from Jaén. You need to call ahead to arrange a visit here—ask for Padre Rafael Cantueso. ⊠ *Plaza de San Agustín s/n, Centro.* ☎ 957/484625. ☉ *By appointment.*

**➍➎ Iglesia de San Lorenzo.** One of Córdoba's loveliest *iglesias fernandinas* (so-called for their construction after Saint-King Fernando III's conquest of Córdoba), this former 10th-century mosque converted between 1244 and 1300 is known for its immense Mudéjar rose window in a stalwart sandstone facade. Over this bulk towers a slim Renaissance bell tower designed by Hernan Ruiz II and considered an ancestor of Sevilla's Giralda. ⊠ *Plaza de San Lorenzo s/n, Centro,* ☎ 957/483479. ☉ *Mass daily 8 PM, or call for appointment.*

**➌➍ Iglesia de San Miguel.** One of Córdoba's 14 iglesias fernandinas, this is one of Córdoba's best late-13th-century Mudéjar churches. The golden sandstone blocks, the tufts of grass growing out of cracks and crevices in the chaotic jumble of roofs, the tightly closed Moorish horseshoe arch on the north side clearly part of an earlier mosque, the minuscule dormer window with its tiny chimney on the roof, and the full 360-degree circumference of the facade all seem all the more medieval for being in this modern part of town. The neighboring Taberna de San Miguel (aka Casa el Pisto) is one of the top tapas specialists. ⊠ *Plaza de San Miguel s/n, Centro,* ☎ 957/476635. ☉ *Mass daily 8:30, noon, and 6:30.*

**➌➊ Iglesia de San Nicolás de la Villa.** An iglesia fernandina, San Nicolás de Villa, not begun until 1276, combines Moorish, Renaissance, and baroque elements. The former Islamic alminar, the tower used for the call to prayer, now a bell tower, is the oldest and best feature. ⊠ *Plaza San Felipe, Centro,* ☎ 957/476832. ☉ *Mass daily 9, 10, 11:30.*

**➋➑ Iglesia de San Salvador y Santo Domingo de Silos.** This was originally the church of the Jesuit school (aka La Compañía), closed in 1767 when the Jesuit order, in constant conflict with ecclesiastical and monarchical powers, was suppressed in Spain. Begun in 1564 under the direction of Córdoba's principal Renaissance architect, Hernan Ruiz II, the church is distinguished by the ornamentation of the main doorway, the baroque marble stairway, and the mannerist cupola with its slender skylight. The richly carved wooden altarpiece and the helicoidal columns in the side chapels are plateresque masterpieces. ⊠ *Plaza de la Compañía, Centro.* ☉ *Mass daily 8:30 PM.*

**41** **Iglesia de Santa Marina.** At the edge of the Barrio de los Toreros, in the Plaza de Santa Marina de las Aguas Santas, this Mudéjar church has been the home parish for many of Córdoba's bullfighters. Santa Marina combines late Romanesque, Gothic, and Mudéjar elements with a Renaissance tower and an 18th-century baroque tabernacle. The door on the west side is especially interesting, a haunting and archaic melange of Moorish and Romanesque elements facing the excellent Bar Santa Marina on the corner. ⊠ *Plaza de los Condes de Priego, Centro,* ☎ *957/483667.* ☉ *Mass 8:30 PM, or call for appointment.*

**29** **Iglesia y Colegio de Santa Victoria.** This neoclassical church and school, one of the only examples of this 18th-century architectural style in Córdoba, was begun in 1761 and consists of a circular church attached to the corner of the rectangular school building. The immense cupola is the most arresting feature of this church dedicated to the Córdoban St. Victoria, martyred at the hands of the Romans in the 4th century. ⊠ *Calle Juan Valera, Centro.* ☎ *957/273444.* ☉ *Mass daily 8 PM.*

**42** **Monumento a Manolete.** This sculpture dedicated to Spain's most legendary torero, killed in the bullring in 1947, is a bizarre and wonderful jumble of rearing horses restrained by boys, infants reclining around the head of a bull, and, of course, Manolete (1917–47). Son and grandson of toreros, both of whom also fought under the nickname of Manolete, Manuel Rodríguez y Sánchez remains Córdoba's most sacrosanct bullfighting figure. The haunting symbolism of painter Julio Romero de Torres reverberates in this 1956 monument by Luis Moya and Manuel Álvarez Laviada. ⊠ *Plaza de los Condes de Priego, Centro.*

**39** **Palacio de los Marqueses de Viana.** This 17th-century palace is Córdoba's most splendid aristocratic home. It is known as the Museum of Patios for its 12 patios, each one different. Inside are a carriage museum, a library, embossed leather wall hangings, filigree silver, and grand galleries. The patios and gardens are planted with cypresses, orange trees, and myrtles. ⊠ *Plaza Don Gomé 2, Centro,* ☎ *957/480134.* 🖃 *Patios €3; tour of patios and apartments €6.* ☉ *June–Sept., Thurs.–Tues. 9–2; Oct.–May, weekdays 10–1 and 4–6, Sat. 10–1.*

**36** **Palacio de Torres Cabrera.** This splendid town house was the property of an illustrious Córdoban, Ricardo Martel Fernández de Córdoba, Conde de Torres Cabrera, named senator for life and Grandee of Spain by King Alfonso XII (who stayed here during Easter in 1877). The private house, not open for visits, is a massive neoclassical facade that communicates a sense of symmetry, serenity, and power. Designed by Hernan Ruiz II in the 16th-century Renaissance style, the plateresque facade is intensely decorated with mythological themes. ⊠ *Calle Conde de Torres Cabrera s/n, Centro,* ☎ *957/485334.*

**27** **Plaza de las Tendillas.** Here is the city's commercial hub, surrounded by banks and stores. At its center is an equestrian statue of General Gonzalo Fernández de Córdoba (1453–1515), called *el Gran Capitán* (the Great Captain) for his exploits in Spain and Italy. An innovator in infantry weapons specialization, he was relieved of his governorship of Naples in 1507 by a jealous King Ferdinand II and placed under house arrest at Loja, west of Granada. The statue has the peculiarity of being bronze except for the head, which is white marble. Café Boston and Café Siena are the best of the terrace cafés.

**33** **Real Colegiata de San Hipólito.** The Royal Collegiate Church of San Hipólito was founded by King Alfonso XI (1311–1350) as a royal pantheon and a place for holding religious services in memory of deceased monarchs—one of which he was soon to be. Construction of the church was not completed until some 400 years after Alfonso's death, whereupon his remains were moved here from the Capilla Real (Royal Chapel) of the cathedral. The church, with its Mudéjar bell tower and baroque nave, transept, sacristy, and facade, is an example of the superimposition of architectural styles over the centuries. ⊠ *Plaza Ignacio de Loyola, Centro.* ☎ *Free.* ⊙ *Mass hours irregular.*

**㊸** **Torre de la Malmuerta.** This massive octagonal lookout and defensive tower on the northeast corner of the city walls was constructed in 1408. Connected to the walls by an arch, the tower was occasionally used as a prison over the centuries. Many legends have arisen over the tower's name, Malmuerta, which means, literally, "she who died badly." ⊠ *Plaza de Moreno s/n, Centro.* ☎ *Free.* ⊙ *Daily, 24 hours.*

## Dining

$$$ ✕ **El Blasón.** Under the same ownership as El Caballo Rojo, this restaurant has earned itself a name for fine food and unbeatable ambience. It's tucked away in an old inn one block west of Avenida Gran Capitán; a Moorish-style entrance bar leads onto a patio enclosed by ivy-covered walls. Upstairs are two elegant dining rooms where blue walls, aquamarine silk curtains, and candelabras evoke early 19th-century luxury. The innovative menu includes *salmón con naranjas de la mezquita* (salmon in oranges from the mosque) and *musclo de oca al vino afrutado* (leg of goose in fruited wine). ⊠ *José Zorrilla 11, Centro,* ☎ *957/480625. AE, DC, MC, V.*

$$$ ✕ **El Caballo Rojo.** The Red Horse, on the north side of the mosque, is a Córdoba institution. The interior resembles a cool, leafy Andalusian patio, and the menu mixes traditional specialties, such as *rabo de toro* (oxtail stew) and *salmorejo* (cold, tomato-based soup), with exotic dishes inspired by Córdoba's Moorish and Jewish heritage, such as *alboronia* (stewed vegetables with honey, saffron, and aniseed) and the popular *cordero a la miel* (lamb roasted with honey). ⊠ *Cardenal Herrero 28, La Judería,* ☎ *957/478001. AE, DC, MC, V.*

$$–$$$ ✕ **Bodegas Campos.** One block east from the Plaza del Potro, this maze-
★ like restaurant in a converted wine cellar offers the complete Andalusian experience in a warren of barrel-heavy dining rooms and leafy courtyards. Regional dishes prepared with flair include *ensalada de bacalao y naranja* (salad of salt cod and orange with olive oil) and *manitas de cerdo relleno com jamón iberico* (pork knuckles with Iberian ham). The menu also has dishes from elsewhere in Spain, such as Basque *cogote de merluza* (hake's neck with prawns). ⊠ *Los Lineros 32, Corredera,* ☎ *957/497500. AE, MC, V. No dinner Sun.*

$$–$$$ ✕ **Casa Matías.** Off the beaten track near La Diputación north of Ronda
★ de los Tejares, Casa Matías is known for simple and carefully prepared Córdoban cuisine. The bar offers such tapas as *patatas con jamón y gambas* (potatoes with ham and shrimp) and *revuelta de espárragos y jamón ibérico* (eggs scrambled with Iberian ham and asparagus). *Arroz caldoso de perdiz* (partridge and rice stew) and the *salmorejo cordobés* (a rough Córdoban gazpacho) are just two of the winners among the main courses. ⊠ *Calle del Nogal 16, Centro,* ☎ *957/277653. AE, DC, MC, V. July–Aug., closed Sun.*

$$–$$$ ✕ **Ciro's.** You can expect serious service and an exciting selection of
★ Córdoban dishes at this local favorite. It's hidden on the edge of the central commercial area, a short walk up the gardens along the outside of the Moorish walls near the church of San Nicolás de la Villa. Menu highlights include *conejo de monte escabechado* (wild rabbit marinade), *guisos* (stews), and *revueltos* (eggs scrambled with anything from

mushrooms to shrimp). ⊠ *Paseo de la Victoria 19–21, Centro,* ☎ *957/ 290464. AE, DC, MC, V. July–Aug., closed Sun.*

$$–$$$ ✕ **El Churrasco.** This outstanding restaurant, in the heart of the Jud-
★ ería just two minutes' walk from the mosque, serves the best steak in town. The bar is ideal tapas habitat, the grilled fish is very fresh, and the picturesque environment includes alfresco dining in the inner patio. In a separate house, two doors down the street, is the restaurant's formidable wine cellar, which is also a small museum. ⊠ *Romero 16, La Judería,* ☎ *957/290819. AE, DC, MC, V. Closed Aug.*

$$–$$$ ✕ **La Almudaina.** This 15th-century house across the square from the Alcázar gardens has both an Andalusian patio topped with a stained-glass cupola and a *mesón bodega* (wine cellar). Fresh market produce is the rule: try *calabacín con salsa de carabineros* (squash with prawn sauce), *lubina al hinojo* (sea bass in fennel), or *lomo de venado en salsa de setas* (venison in wild-mushroom sauce). ⊠ *Jardines de Los Santos Mártires 1, La Judería,* ☎ *957/474342. AE, DC, MC, V. June–Sept. closed Sun. Oct.–May no dinner Sun.*

$$ ✕ **Casa Pepe de la Judería.** This three-floor labyrinth of neat rooms, just around the corner from the mosque toward the Judería, serves a full selection of tapas and house specialties such as rabo de toro. There is live Spanish guitar music most nights, and in summer the rooftop opens for barbecues. ⊠ *Romero 1, off Deanes, La Judería,* ☎ *957/ 200744. AE, DC, MC, V.*

$–$$ ✕ **Puerta de Sevilla.** This cozy tavern at the southern end of the Bar-rio de San Basilio is a fine place for a meal, a tapa, or a *caña* (draft beer). The nearby monument to Ibn Hazm, baths of the caliph, and Alcázar de los Reyes Cristianos all contribute to making this spot feel alive. The cuisine is typically Andalusian, ranging from *rape con puerros y zana-horias* (monkfish with leeks and carrots) to *pato a la crema de caramelo con pasas y piñones* (duck in candied cream with raisins and pine nuts) to *solomillo al perfume de albahaca* (filet mignon with basil). ⊠ *Calle Postrera 51, San Basilio,* ☎ *957/297380. AE, DC, MC, V.*

$ ✕ **Federación de Peñas Cordobesas.** You'll find this popular budget restaurant on one of the main thoroughfares of the old quarter, halfway between the mosque and the Plaza Tendillas. You can eat inside or at one of several tables around the fountain in the spacious courtyard, surrounded by horseshoe arches. The food is traditional Spanish fare, and there are several fixed menus at attractive prices. ⊠ *Conde y Duque 8, La Judería,* ☎ *957/475427. MC, V.*

## Tapas Bars and Taverns

Córdoba's best tastes and aromas—better than in the city's formal, sit-down restaurants—are found in its tapas bars and taverns, where itin-erant diners seem to take as long as they need to. Look for Manual María López Alejandre's book *De Tabernas por Córdoba* (available in Spanish only), in which the author, a lifelong local tavernologist, dis-cusses the origins, owners, and philosophies of some 85 Córdoban tav-erns. For starters, López Alejandre debunks the "lid" theory (according to which the term *tapa*—"lid" or "cover"—refers to cheese or ham cov-ering a glass of wine), in favor of the finger-in-the-dike theory (according to which the name *tapa* comes from its role to *tapar*—close, quell, cover—hunger). The Tourist Office distributes *Ruta de las Tabernas de Cór-doba,* a map with 66 recommendations.

**Bar Santa Marina (Casa Obispo).** This cool and shadowy oasis is a rest for the eye and spirit on a hot day and serves some of the best and ici-est finos you'll find in town. Try the *boquerones* (pickled anchovies) and *cogollos* (lettuce hearts) for a refreshing jump-starter. ⊠ *Calle Mayor de Santa Marina 1, Centro,* ☎ *957/473056.*

**188**

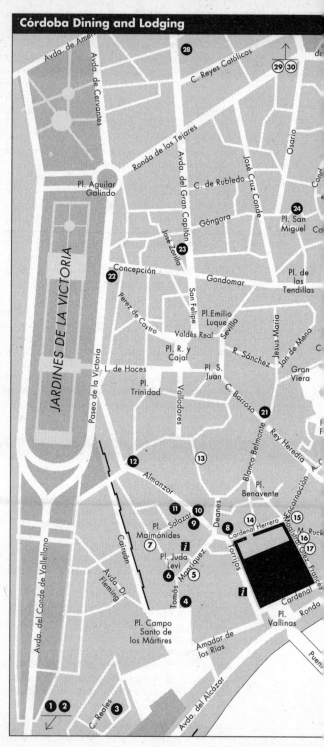

## Córdoba Dining and Lodging

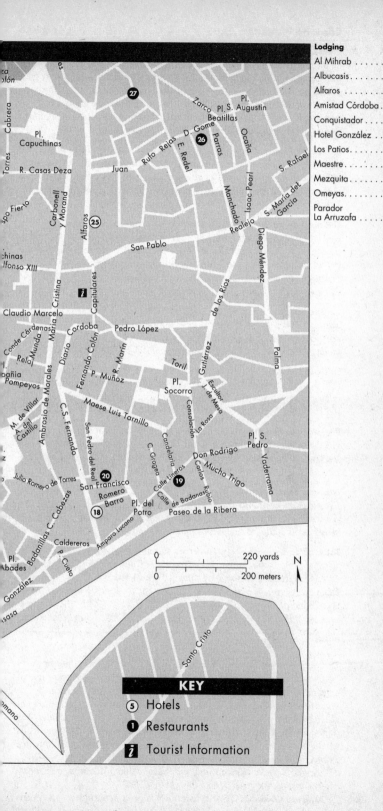

**KEY**

⑤ Hotels

❶ Restaurants

𝒊 Tourist Information

★ **Casa el Pisto.** Founded in 1880, this booming spot next to the Iglesia de San Miguel (it is also known as Taberna de San Miguel) is an original and a Córdoba landmark. The feeding frenzy and general joy generated here, at table or at the lovely oaken bar, is contagious. Salmorejo, *jabugo* (free-range) ham, *lechuga con ajo* (lettuce with garlic), *zanahorias en adobo* (carrots in vinaigrette dressing): it's all good. ⊠ *Plaza San Miguel 1, Centro,* ☎ *957/478328. Closed Wed.*

**El Novillo Precoz.** Tucked away at the far corner of the funky Barrio de San Basilio, this little tavern built into what was once the royal stables is worth seeking out. Try the rabo de toro, a Córdoban specialty, with a freezing fino of Montilla-Moriles. ⊠ *Caballerizas Reales 10, San Basilio,* ☎ *957/201828. No dinner Sun., Mon.*

**El Rincón de las Beatillas.** Just a step or two behind the Palacio de Viana, this is the place to sate yourself after visiting the 13 patios. The *ancas de rana* (frogs' legs) are the most exotic (for Andalusia) offering, but everything they propose here is good, from *crianzas* (aged wines) to finos, cheese to *chacina* (sausages and cuts of ham). ⊠ *Calle Ocaña 2, Centro,* ☎ *957/483336. Closed Wed.*

**La Bacalá.** Not surprisingly, *bacalao* (salt cod) is the top draw here, although beer, finos, plates of *bellota* (acorn-fed) ham and *espinacas con garbanzos* (spinach with garbanzos) are all exquisitely done. ⊠ *Calle Medina y Corella 3, La Judería,* ☎ *957/472643. Closed Sun.*

**La Galga.** A well-known stop in the Barrio de San Basilio (also known as "el Alcázar Viejo" for the emplacement there of the original Moorish fortress), this is a usually boisterous spot with fine tapas and freezing finos. ⊠ *Calle San Basilio 25,* ☎ *957/299033. Closed Sun.*

**Plateros de San Francisco.** Though there are several Plateros around Córdoba, this friendly spot is the best, for its relaxed courtyard and Vienna coffeehouse "together but alone" feeling. ⊠ *Calle San Francisco 8, La Corredera,* ☎ *957/470042. Closed Sun.*

**Taberna Casa Salinas.** One of Córdoba's *de toda la vida* (perennial) taverns, this cool and shady refuge decorated with intricate Moorish tiles offers fine dining and good wines in a gastronomically erudite environment. ⊠ *Puerta del Almodóvar s/n, La Judería,* ☎ *957/290–846.*

**Taberna la Lechuga.** Named for its star offering, lettuce hearts filled with hot oil, garlic, and a drop of vinegar (they call this *lechuga frita*, or fried lettuce, but don't be alarmed: the lettuce itself is not fried), this little tavern is just in from Campo Santo de los Mártires on the river edge of the Jewish quarter. ⊠ *Calle Tomás Conde 12, La Judería,* ☎ *957/203585 (owner's separate café). Closed Sun.*

## Lodging

$$$$ 🏨 **Conquistador.** Located right next to the mosque, this contemporary hotel is decorated in Andalusian-Moorish style, making good use of ceramic tiles and inlaid marquetry in the bar and public rooms. The reception area overlooks a colonnaded patio, fountain, and small enclosed garden. Rooms are comfortable, elegant, and classically Andalusian; those at the front have small balconies overlooking the walls of the mosque, which are floodlit at night. ⊠ *Magistral González Francés 15–17, La Judería, 14003,* ☎ *957/481102,* 🖷 *957/474677. 99 rooms, 3 suites. Restaurant, minibars, cable TV, sauna, bar, meeting rooms, parking (fee). AE, DC, MC, V.*

$$$ 🏨 **Amistad Córdoba.** This stylish hotel is built around two 18th-cen-
★ tury mansions that look out upon the Plaza de Maimónides in the heart of the Judería. (You can also enter through the old Moorish walls on

Calle Cairuan.) It features a Mudéjar courtyard, carved-wood ceilings, and a plush lounge area. The rooms are large and comfortable. The newer wing has a more modern look, with blues and grays and Norwegian wood. ⊠ *Plaza de Maimónides 3, La Judería, 14004,* ☎ *957/420335,* FAX *957/420365,* WEB *www.nh-hoteles.com. 84 rooms. Restaurant, minibars, bar, meeting rooms, parking (fee). AE, DC, MC, V.*

$$$ 🏨 **Parador La Arruzafa.** Five kilometers (three miles) north of town, this modern parador is set in a leafy garden on the slopes of the Sierra de Córdoba. Rooms are sunny, with wood or wicker furnishings; many have balconies over the garden or looking toward Córdoba. ⊠ *Avda. de la Arruzafa, Av. del Brillante, 14012,* ☎ *957/275900,* FAX *957/280409,* WEB *www.parador.es. 90 rooms, 4 suites. Restaurant, minibars, cable TV, tennis courts, pool, bar, meeting rooms, parking (fee). AE, DC, MC, V.*

$$–$$$ 🏨 **Alfaros.** This modern establishment built on the site of a medieval
★ Moorish *alminar* (tower used for the call to Islamic prayer) is so-named for the lantern traditionally placed there, which led to the Spanish word *faro,* for lighthouse. The lantern theme appears throughout this sleek and rambling hotel overlooking the churches of Santa Marta and San Andrés. Rooms are impeccably furnished and well equipped. ⊠ *Calle Alfaros 18, Centro, 14001,* ☎ *957/491920,* FAX *957/492210,* WEB *www.maciahoteles.com. 131 rooms, 2 suites. Restaurant, minibars, cable TV, pool, bar, parking (fee). AE, DC, MC, V.*

$$ 🏨 **Al Mihrab.** Outside town, past the parador, this three-story, dark-ochre building is set among trees in the tranquil foothills of the Sierra de Córdoba. Rooms are large, with white marble floors and colorful, patterned bedspreads and curtains. Most have good mountain or city views, and the view of Córdoba from the greenhouse restaurant (open to hotel guests only) is spectacular. ⊠ *Avda. del Brillante, Km 5, Av. del Brillante, 14012,* ☎ FAX *957/272198,* WEB *www.hotel-al-mihrab.com. 58 rooms. Restaurant, pool, outdoor hot tub, sauna. MC, V.*

$–$$ 🏨 **Albucasis.** Tucked away in the heart of the old quarter is the friendly, family-run Albucasis. The rooms are spotless, with marble-tile floors and green-tile bathrooms. Doubles overlook the pretty patio and have a limited view of the Torre del Alminar. Breakfast and drinks are served in the attractive reception area. ⊠ *Buen Pastor 11, La Judería, 14003,* ☎ FAX *957/478625. 15 rooms. Bar. MC, V. Closed Jan.*

$–$$ 🏨 **Hotel González.** A mere 40 meters from the Mezquita on a quiet back street and square, this graceful 16th-century town house was once a residence of the family of Julio Romero de Torres, Córdoba's most emblematic painter. The restaurant serves excellent Andalusian cuisine in a typical patio, and the ambience here is refined, personal, and un-hotel-like. ⊠ *Calle Manriquez 3, La Judería, 14003,* ☎ *957/479819,* FAX *957/486187. 16 rooms. Restaurant, bar. AE, DC, MC, V.*

$–$$ 🏨 **Omeyas.** Just one block north of the mosque, this small hotel has rooms on two floors around an arcaded central patio. The lobby is decorated in garish neo-Moorish motifs, complete with horseshoe arches echoing those in the mosque. Rooms are comfortably appointed and, despite the central location, quiet enough so that you can hear the nearby muezzin calling the faithful to prayer at Córdoba's only functioning mosque. The staff couldn't be more helpful and friendly, and the toast and butter breakfasts are served quickly and pleasantly. ⊠ *Encarnación 17, La Judería, 14003,* ☎ *957/492267,* FAX *957/491659. 29 rooms. Cafeteria. AE, DC, MC, V.*

$ 🏨 **Los Patios.** Just behind the Patio de los Naranjos and the Mezquita, this relatively new establishment manages to avoid the shortcomings common to places too close to the city's tourist hub. Built around three characteristic Córdoban patios, it's a carefully tended hostelry also known for its fine restaurant, Los Patios, one of the best spots to try the local cuisine in this part of town. ⊠ *Calle Cardenal Herrero 14, La Judería, 41003,* ☎ *957/478340.* [FAX] *957/486966,* [WEB] *www.lospatios.net. 23 rooms. Restaurant. AE, DC, MC, V.*

$ 🏨 **Maestre.** This small hotel around the corner from the Plaza del Potro is one of the best lodging values in Córdoba. Room decor is simple but modern, and there is a pleasant patio. The management also runs an even cheaper lodging, the Hostal Maestre, and self-catered apartments down the street. ⊠ *Romero Barros 4, La Corredera, 14003,* ☎ *957/472410,* [FAX] *957/475395,* [WEB] *www.hotelmaestre.com. 26 rooms. Parking (fee). AE, MC, V.*

$ 🏨 **Mezquita.** Ideally located next to the mosque, this hotel occupies a restored 16th-century home. The public areas are dappled with bronze sculptures on Andalusian themes that reflect the owner's penchant for collecting antiques. The best rooms face the interior patio; their decor is on the plain side. The only real drawback is the lack of parking. ⊠ *Plaza Santa Catalina 1, La Judería, 41003,* ☎ *957/475585.* [FAX] *957/476219. 21 rooms. Dining room. AE, DC, MC, V.*

## Nightlife and the Arts

Concerts, ballets, and plays are performed in the **Gran Teatro** (⊠ Avda. del Gran Capitán 3, Centro, ☎ 957/480237). The **International Guitar Festival** attracts top Spanish and international guitarists for more than two weeks of great music in July. Contact the tourist office for schedules and ticket information. Orchestras perform in the garden of the **Alcázar** (⊠ Plaza Campo Santo de los Mártires, Barrio de San Basilio, ☎ 957/420151) on Sundays throughout the summer. **Galería Cobalto** (⊠ Calle Jose Maria Martorell 28, Centro, ☎ 957/238570) is a leading art gallery.

Flamenco is performed (mainly for tourists) in the **Zoco** (⊠ Judíos s/n, La Judería, ☎ 957/204033) on summer evenings. **Tablao Cardenal** (⊠ Torrijos 10, facing the Mezquita, La Judería, ☎ 957/483112), Córdoba's most popular flamenco club, merits a visit just for the setting, the courtyard of a 16th-century building that was Córdoba's first hospital. **Mesón la Bulería** (⊠ Pedro López 3, La Judería, ☎ 957/483839), open Easter through September, stages flamenco song and dance shows. For an authentic flamenco experience, seek out a *peña* (a club or association in a semiprivate bar), where, if you're patient, you just might witness a spontaneous performance. **La Peña Flamenca de Córdoba** (⊠ Campo Madre de Dios), **La Pena El Rincón del Cante** (⊠ Calleja del Niño Perdido), and the **Círculo Flamenco Cordobés** (⊠ Plaza de la Teja) are three likely spots, but ask around: there are others.

## Outdoor Activities and Sports

The top golf course near Córdoba is the 18-hole **Club de Campo y Deportivo de Córdoba** (⊠ Crta. Antigua de Córdoba–Obejo Km 9, Av. del Brillante, ☎ 957/350208). For swimming, try the **Piscina Municipal** (⊠ Av. del Brillante, Polideportivo Ciudad Jardín, Alcalde Sanz Noguer s/n, Av. del Brillante, ☎ 957/484846).

## Shopping

Córdoba's main shopping district is around Plaza de las Tendillas, the commercial center of the city. Avenida Gran Capitán, Ronda de los Tejares, Calle Cruz Conde, and Plaza de Colón also offer a wide range of shopping options. **Al-Andalus** (⊠ Calle Manriquez, 1, Centro, ☎ 957/483815) sells books, crafts, and diverse gift items. **Art–Andalus** (⊠ Corregidor Luis de la Cerda 43, Centro, ☎ 957/484828) offers crafts and jewelry. The **Association of Córdoban Artisans** (⊠ C. Judíos s/n, opposite synagogue, La Judería, ☎ 957/200934) sells crafts in the Zoco; note that many stalls are open May–September only. **Carlos López-Obrero (Meryam)** (⊠ Calleja de las Flores 2, La Judería) is one of Córdoba's best workshops for embossed leather. **El Caballo** (⊠ Calle Manuel Sandoval 10, Centro, ☎ 957/487356) specializes in leathers and equestrian-related products. **Juan Isidro** (⊠ Plaza del las Tendillas s/n, Centro, ☎ 957/474852) is the place for Mudéjar jewelry (or any other kind from Piaget to Cartier to Rolex). **Julia** (⊠ Plaza de las Tendillas 3, La Corredera, ☎ 957/472725) offers an interesting selection of travel bags, briefcases, and handbags. **Librería Luque** (⊠ Calle Cruz Conde 19, Centro, ☎ 957/473034) is one of the town's leading bookstores, especially for titles relating to Córdoba.

**Amaltea** (⊠ Ronda de Isasa 10, Centro, ☎ 957/491968) is a combination ecological produce store, tapas bar, and art gallery specializing in Córdoban crafts and food products. **El Piamonte** (⊠ Calle Molinos Alta 1, Plaza Flor del Olivo, La Judería, ☎ 957/484920) is among Córdoba's top ice cream parlors, serving homemade ice cream, yogurt, custard, and pudding. **Ibéricos Covap** (⊠ Calle Barqueros 2, La Judería, ☎ 957/498505 ) specializes in the very best free-range Iberian acorn-fed hams and sausages. **La Tienda del Olivo** (⊠ Calle Corregidor Luis de la Cerda [corner of Calle san Fernando], La Judería, ☎ 957/474495) has everything an olive tree can produce, from handmade wooden utensils and containers to olive pâté to recipes and guides to olive oil–related culture. **Serrano** (⊠ Calle Concepción 3, Centro, ☎ 957/498780), with additional locations at Avda. Jesús Rescatado 7 and at Avda. Ronda de los Tejares 38, is a top pastry artisan and a specialist in the traditional *pastel Cordobés* (Córdoban cake). **Tienda Pepito** (⊠ Calle Romero 10, Centro, ☎ 957/473012) has a wide selection of cheeses, wines, and other products from Córdoba.

## Side Trip from Córdoba

### Madinat al-Zahra

㊻ *8 km (5 mi) west of Córdoba on the C431.*

The ruins and partial reconstruction of the fabulous Muslim palace Madinat al-Zahra (sometimes spelled Medina Azahara) are well worth a detour. Begun in 936, the palace was built by Abd ar-Rahman III for his favorite concubine, az-Zahra. According to contemporary chroniclers, it took 10,000 men, 2,600 mules, and 400 camels 25 years to erect this fantasy of 4,300 columns in dazzling pink, green, and white marble and jasper brought from Carthage. Here, on three terraces, stood a palace, a mosque, luxurious baths, fragrant gardens, fishponds, even an aviary and a zoo. In 1013 the place was sacked and destroyed by Berber mercenaries. In 1944 the royal apartments were rediscovered and the throne room was carefully reconstructed. The outline of the mosque has also been excavated. The only covered part of the site is the Salon de Abd Al Rahman III; the rest is a sprawl of foundations, defense walls, and arches that hint at the splendor of the original city-palace. ⊠ *Crta. de Palma del Río Km 8, off C431 (follow signs en route to Almodóvar del Río),* ☎ *957/329130,* WEB *www.junta-andalucia. es/cultura.* 🎫 *€1.50; EU citizens free.* ☉ *May–Sept. 15, Tues.–Sat. 10–8:30, Sun. 10–2; Sept. 16.–Apr., Tues.–Sat. 10–6:30, Sun. 10–2.*

# LOS PEDROCHES

The valley of Los Pedroches, an easy one-day excursion from Córdoba, provides a look at the high, flat, pre-*meseta* rangeland called La Dehesa, where thousands of live oaks punctuate miles and miles of open meadowland and free-range Iberian pigs gather acorns. Hinojosa del Duque, Belalcázar, and Pozoblanco are the main towns, and storks are the most frequent residents of the bell towers and rooftops.

## Hinojosa del Duque

**47** *97 km (58 mi) north of Córdoba.*

Famed for its 15th-century Renaissance Gothic **Iglesia de San Juan Bautista,** known as "La Catedral de La Sierra" for its size and artistic quality, Hinojosa del Duque, sitting astride the intersection of no fewer than six country roads, is the hub of Córdoba's northern rangeland.

## Belalcázar

**48** *106 km (63 mi) north of Córdoba.*

This northernmost Pedroches town has an immense tower, the **Castillo de Sotomayor,** now in ruins, which was built as a fortress in 1466 to guard the access to the route north to the Christian capital at Toledo.

## Torrecampo

**49** *97 km (58 mi) north of Córdoba.*

Torrecampo is the home of the renowned **Posada del Moro,** a 14th-century inn (now a museum) that has remained largely intact over six centuries since its founding. Its medieval pig slaughtering kitchen is a virtual museum of the typical Valle de los Pedroches pig butchering and artisanal ham producing tradition.

## Pozoblanco

**50** *67 km (58 mi) north of Córdoba.*

Pozoblanco became known throughout Spain when popular matador Paquirri was killed in the bullring here in 1984. It's also known for its cheese industry, its Easter Week celebration featuring the Roman *Prendimiento de Jesus Nazareno* (a reenactment of the rest of the Nazarene Christ), and the February Virgen de la Luna Pilgrimage.

# ALTO GUADALQUIVIR

Córdoba's Alto Guadalquivir is at the eastern end of the province and covers parts of the Sierra Morena, the Guadalquivir river basin, and the farmland around Bujalance and Cañete de las Torres. The Parque Natural de la Sierra de Cardeña y Montoro in Córdoba's far northeastern corner offers striking landscapes over and around the river Yeguas as well as a wide variety of flora and fauna.

## Montoro

**51** *43 km (25 mi) northeast of Córdoba.*

Montoro's monumental 15th-century **Puente de las Donadas** is its best-known landmark; it took more than 50 years to finish. Built on five hills over a bend in the Gudalquivir, the town's steep and narrow streets are its most distinctive and charming feature. The plateresque facade of the town hall is its finest architectural gem, and the leather products, such as bags and saddles, produced here are known for their high quality.

# GUADIATO Y SIERRA

The Valle del Guadiato occupies Córdoba's northwestern corner and is made up of 11 towns offering a wide range of architecture and cuisine and some of the most famous and well-populated game preserves on the Iberian Peninsula. Wild boar, deer, mountain goat, hare, and redleg partridge are abundant throughout this wild border region of Andalusia.

## Fuente Obejuna

**52** *86 km (52 mi) northwest of Córdoba.*

Fray Félix Lope de Vega Carpio (1562–1635), better known as Lope de Vega, Spain's Shakespeare, set his most famous play, *Fuenteovejuna,* in this town, describing a women-instigated peasant uprising in which the hated local governor is hurled from a window and torn apart in the square below. When the judge demanded to know who was responsible for the lynching, the entire town answered, "Fuenteovejuna, señor." In Lope's play, sometimes performed in the town's central square, no one is punished. The 15th-century church of **Nuestra Señora del Castillo** is one of Fuente Obejuna's top architectural assets. The unusual art nouveau **Casa Cardona** is the best (and nearly the only) modernist structure in all of Andalusia. Built in the early 20th century by a wealthy and capricious landowner, it looks as if it fell through a looking glass along Barcelona's Paseo de Gràcia.

## Bélmez

**53** *61 km (37 mi) northwest of Córdoba.*

The 13th-century castle occupying a promontory overlooking this pretty town offers stunning views over the Upper Guadiato. The six cylindrical towers and the expanse of mottled rock are reminders of the area's embattled past. The town's churches, from the medieval **La Anunciación** with its redbrick Mudéjar tower to the baroque hermitage of **La Virgen de los Remedios** to the medieval sanctuary of **Nuestra Senora del Castillo**, are gems.

# BAJO GUADALQUIVIR

Downriver west of Córdoba, this fertile crease includes the river basin towns of Almodóvar del Río and Palma del Río as well as Córdoba's largest nature preserve, the Parque Natural Sierra de Hornachuelos in the highlands north of the river.

## Almodóvar del Río

**54** *18 km (11 mi) southwest of Córdoba.*

The little town of Almodóvar del Río looks up at one of Córdoba's most stunning sights, a **Moorish castle** and fortress originally built in the 8th century. Though Pedro I el Cruel reconstructed the castle in the 14th century, elements of the earlier structure are still visible.

## Palma del Río

**55** *55 km (33 mi) southwest of Córdoba.*

The 12th-century Almohad walls here invite you to imagine battles of a thousand years ago along this Moorish and Christian frontier. Roman remains are also visible along the roadway that connected Córdoba and Itálica, and the baroque **Iglesia de la Asunción** is the town's most interesting church. The Monasterio de San Francisco's 15th-century cloister merits a visit whether or not you choose to stay in its all-but-irresistible inn. The town is perhaps best known as the birthplace of El Cordobés, the rock 'n' roll bullfighter of 1960s fame.

### Dining and Lodging

**$$**   ✕ 🏨 **Hospederia de San Francisco.** Once a Franciscan monastery, this
★   simple but lovely spot serves excellent cuisine in a rustic and peaceful setting. The rooms occupy what were once monastic cells. ✉ *Av. Pio XII 35, 14700,* ☎ *957/710183,* 🖷 *957/710236,* 🕸 *www.casasypalacios. com. 21 rooms. Restaurant. AE, DC, MC, V.*

OFF THE     **PARQUE NATURAL SIERRA DE HORNACHUELOS –** The mountain wilderness
BEATEN PATH   and highland villages north of Palma del Río have some of Córdoba's most pristine forests, peaks, and wetlands. The route up to San Calixto through the town of Hornachuelos takes you through grassy uplands and a network of reservoirs and rivers, the most important of which is the Bembézar. Live oak, cork oak, carob, arbutus, and reforested pines are among the vegetation, and fauna include imperial and golden eagles, black storks, vultures, deer, mouflon, and wild boar.

# LA CAMPIÑA

The fertile and undulating spaces south of Córdoba are known as La Campiña, roughly translatable as "the countryside," stretching down past the Montilla wine country and olive oil–rich Baena to the foothills of La Subbética, Córdoba's southern mountainous zone and frontier with Granada. Whether taking the low road (N331) through Montilla and cutting north to Baena via Zuheros or taking the high road (N432) through Espejo and Baena and cutting south through Cabra, all of these towns merit a visit.

## Montilla

**56**   *46 km (28 mi) south of Córdoba.*

Heading south from Córdoba to Málaga through rolling hills, ablaze with sunflowers in early summer, you reach the Montilla-Morilés vineyards. Every fall, 47,000 acres' worth of Pedro Ximénez grapes are crushed here to produce the region's rich Montilla wines, not unlike sherry except that, because the local grapes contain so much sugar (transformed into alcohol during fermentation), they are not fortified with the addition of extra alcohol. For this reason—or so the locals claim—Montilla wines do not give you a hangover. On the outskirts of Montilla, coopers' shops produce barrels of various sizes, some small enough to serve as creative souvenirs.

The oldest of the area wineries, in the town of Montilla itself, is **Alvear,** founded in 1729 (✉ Avda. María Auxiliadora 1, ☎ 957/650100). It sells to the public, but you can visit the facilities by appointment only. At Aguilar de Frontera, 8 km (5 mi) south of Montilla, you can visit **Bodegas Toro Albala** (✉ Crta. Málaga–Córdoba s/n, ☎ 957/689044; phone first to make an appointment), an interesting winery museum where you can buy highly regarded Pedro Ximénez dessert wine.

### Dining and Lodging

**$$**   ✕ **Las Camachas.** The best-known restaurant in southern Córdoba province, Las Camachas occupies an Andalusian-style hacienda outside Montilla near the main Málaga–Córdoba road. Start with tapas in the lively tiled bar, then make yourself comfortable in one of the four dining rooms. Regional dishes include *alcachofas al Montilla* (artichokes braised in Montilla wine), salmorejo, *perdiz campiña* (country-style partridge), and *cordero a la miel de Jara* (lamb with Jara honey). You can also buy local wines here. ⊠ *Avda. de Europa 3 (Antigua Carretera Córdoba–Málaga),* ☎ *957/650004. AE, DC, MC, V.*

**$–$$** 🏨 **Don Gonzalo.** Just 2 km (1 mi) south of Montilla, the Don Gonzalo is one of Andalusia's better roadside hostelries. The wood-beamed common areas have an eclectic mix of decor elements (note the elephant tusks flanking the TV in the lounge). The clay-tiled rooms are large and comfortable; some look onto the road, others onto the garden and pool. Be sure to visit the wine cellar. ⊠ *Carretera Córdoba–Málaga, Km 47, 14550,* ☎ *957/650658,* FAX *957/650666. 29 rooms. Restaurant, tennis court, pool, dance club, meeting rooms. AE, MC, V.*

## Baena

**57** *66 km (43 mi) southeast of Córdoba, 105 km (69 mi) northwest of Granada.*

This is an old town of narrow streets, whitewashed houses, ancient mansions, and churches clustered beneath Moorish battlements, all surrounded by chalk fields producing top-quality olive oil. Baena is home to one of Spain's best-known olive oil producers, the family-owned **Nuñez del Prado** label. The oil mill and processing facility are open to the public and especially interesting during harvest season (November–December). The visit includes a cellar containing the old clay storage jars, each holding 525 gallons and dating from 1795. ⊠ *Avda. de Cervantes 15, Baena,* ☎ *957/670141.* 🎟 *Free.* ☉ *Weekdays 9–1:30 and 4–6, Sat. 9–1.*

### Dining and Lodging

**$** ✕ **El Primero de la Mañana.** The best thing about this friendly truck stop on the main drag through town—so-named because it's Baena's first place open in the morning (around 5)—is the frozen beer mug that comes with every draft beer. ⊠ *Plaza Llano del Rincón 13,* ☎ *957/ 671523. AE, DC, MC, V.*

**$$–$$$** 🏨 **La Casa Grande.** Do not hesitate to spend a night in this graceful
**★** hotel, the best place in Baena (and for miles around). Rooms are regally outfitted and liberally endowed with bronze sculptures from the fine arts studio and foundry at the hotel's branch in Torrejon de Ardoz, just outside of Madrid. The pervading sense of wealth and comfort stands as a reminder that wealth derived from oil vastly predates the internal combustion engine. ⊠ *Av. de Cervantes 35, 14850,* ☎ *957/671905,* FAX *957/692189,* WEB *www.lacasagrande.es. 19 rooms. Restaurant, minibars, bar. AE, DC, MC, V.*

# LA SUBBÉTICA CORDOBESA

La Subbética lies in the southeastern corner of Córdoba's province, a largely undiscovered cluster of villages and small towns protected as a nature park. You'll need a car to explore this area, and in some places you'll find the roads bumpy and rather rough. The **Mancomunidad de la Subbética** (⊠ C. Pilarejo, Carcabuey, ☎ 957/704106) can provide general information and hiking advice.

At the southern tip of the province, southeast of Lucena, C334 crosses the **Embalse de Iznájar** (Iznájar Reservoir) amid spectacular scenery. On C334 halfway between Lucena and the reservoir, in **Rute,** you can sample the *anís* liqueur for which this small, whitewashed town is famous. In **Lucena** you can see the Torre del Moral, where Boabdil was imprisoned in 1483 after launching an unsuccessful attack on the Christians. Today the town makes furniture and brass and copper pots.

## Zuheros

**⑤⑧** *81 km (49 mi) southeast of Córdoba, 103 km (62 mi) northwest of Granada.*

Zuheros, at the northern edge of the Subbética, is a jewel of a mountain village. Within the rocky mountain face that towers over the town is the **Cueva de los Murciélagos** (Cave of the Bats), which contains good stalactites and stalagmites as well as interesting Neolithic remains. You can explore on weekends or during the week if a group is visiting—call ahead to check. ☎ *957/694545.* 🎟 *€4.* ⊙ *Tours weekends, 11, 12:30, 2, 6, 7:30.*

### Lodging

**$** 🏨 **Zuhayra.** This simple but comfortable hotel on a narrow street in picturesque Zuheros makes a good base for exploring. The large rooms have splendid views over the village rooftops to the valley below. ⊠ *C. Mirador 10, 14870,* ☎ *957/694693,* FAX *957/694702,* WEB *www.zuheros.com. 18 rooms. Restaurant. AE, DC, MC, V.*

## Priego de Córdoba

★ **⑤⑨** *103 km (64 mi) southeast of Córdoba, 79 km (47 mi) northwest of Granada.*

This baroque festival of a town, called Baguh during its 9th-century Moorish era, lies at the foot of Mt. Tinosa—from Lucena, head north 9 km (5½ mi) on C327 to Cabra, where you'll turn east on C336; after 32 km (20 mi), you'll reach Priego. Wander down Calle del Río opposite the *ayuntamiento* (town hall) to see fine 18th-century mansions, once the homes of silk merchants. At the end of the street is the Fuente del Rey (King's Fountain), with some 130 water jets, built in 1803. Don't miss the lavish baroque churches of La Asunción and La Aurora or the Barrio de la Villa, an old Moorish quarter. El Adarve, the promenade running around the Moorish ramparts to the Fuente de la Salud, offers panoramic views as it circles around the Villa neighborhood's tiny streets lined with flower-bedecked whitewashed villas.

### Lodging

**$–$$** 🏨 **Villa Turística de Priego.** Near the hamlet of Zagrilla, 6 km (4 mi) from Priego de Córdoba, this gleaming-white complex is in the heart of the Subbética nature park. Accommodation is in semidetached units, clustered like an Andalusian pueblo. The units, rather plainly decorated, sleep between two and six guests, most have a balcony or terrace, and all but five have kitchenettes. ⊠ *Aldea de Zagrilla, 14816,* ☎ *957/703503,* FAX *957/703573,* WEB *www.villaturisticadepriego.com. 52 units. Restaurant, kitchenettes, pool, meeting rooms. AE, DC, MC, V. Closed Jan.*

# CÓRDOBA PROVINCE A TO Z

*To research prices, get advice from other travelers, and book travel arrangements, visit www.fodors.com.*

### AIR TRAVEL

Sevilla-San Pablo Airport is the closest commercial airport to Córdoba, an hour away, 126 km (75 mi) southwest on the N-IV freeway. There are several daily flights to and from Madrid and Barcelona.

➤ AIRPORT INFORMATION: **Sevilla-San Pablo Airport** (☎ 95/444–9000).

## BUS TRAVEL

If you're not driving, buses are the best method of transportation in this region. They run to most of the outlying towns and villages, and their connections between major cities are generally faster and more frequent than those of the trains.

Buses connect Córdoba with several Spanish cities. For information, go to the bus station, next to the AVE (high-speed train) station, and inquire with the following bus companies: Alsina Gräells runs services from Córdoba to Badajoz, Cádiz, Granada, Seville, and Málaga; Ureña links Córdoba to Seville and Jaén; Secorbus serves Madrid and Andújar; and López runs services to Ciudad Real and Madrid (via Ciudad Real). Ramírez serves small towns near Córdoba.

➤ BUS INFORMATION: **Bus station** (⊠ Plaza de las Tres Culturas, Centro, Córdoba, ☎ 957/404040, WEB www.infonegocio.com/estaciondecordoba). **Alsina Gräells** (⊠ Glorieta de las Tres Culturas, Centro, Córdoba, ☎ 957/278100, WEB www.alsinagraells.net). **López** (⊠ Glorieta de las Tres Culturas, Centro, Córdoba, ☎ 957/767077). **Secorbus** (⊠ Glorieta de las Tres Culturas, Centro, Córdoba, ☎ 902/229292, WEB www.secorbus.es). **Ureña** (⊠ Glorieta de las Tres Culturas, Centro, Córdoba, ☎ 957/404558).

## CAR RENTAL

Córdoba's RENFE station is the place to pick up a car from Europcar or Hertz; Avis and National-Atesa have offices in the Centro area.

➤ LOCAL AGENCIES: **Avis** (⊠ Plaza Colón 35, Centro, ☎ 957/476862, WEB www.avis.es). **Europcar** (⊠ RENFE Station, Av. de América s/n, La Paz, ☎ 957/402396 or 957/403480, WEB www.europcar.es). **Hertz** (⊠ RENFE Station, Av. de América s/n, La Paz, ☎ 957/402061 or 902/204300, WEB www.hertz.es). **National-Atesa** (⊠ Avda de Cervantes 20, Centro, ☎ 957/475979, WEB www.atesa.es).

## CAR TRAVEL

Be prepared for—but by no means daunted by—parking problems. The layout of smaller towns dates from Moorish times and is hardly suited to modern-day traffic. In Córdoba, added to parking problems is the ever-present threat of break-ins. It is best to use an underground parking garage. Most of Córdoba's hotels are in a labyrinth of narrow streets that can be a nightmare to negotiate, even with a small car. In Córdoba, all sights are within walking distance of one another.

## EMERGENCIES

➤ CONTACTS: **Fire, Police, or Ambulance** (☎ 112). **Ambulance** (☎ 061 or 957/217903). **Fire Department** (☎ 080). **Guardia Civil** (☎ 062 or 957/414111). **General Information** (☎ 902/197197). **National Police** (☎ 092 or 091).

## MAIL AND SHIPPING

➤ INTERNET ACCESS: **Cibermanía** (⊠ Plaza de Colón 34, Centro, ☎ 957/488058).
➤ POST OFFICE: **Córdoba** (⊠ José Cruz Conde 15, Centro, ☎ 957/479196).

## TAXIS

➤ TAXI COMPANIES: **Aguilar de la Frontera** (☎ 957/661050). **Baena** (☎ 957/670043). **Cabra** (☎ 957/521302). **Castro** (☎ 957/370888). **Lucena** (☎ 957/500356). **Montilla** (☎ 957/654444). **Montoro** (☎ 957/160349). **Palma del Río** (☎ 957/710416). **Peñarroya-Pueblonuevo** (☎ 957/560026). **Priego de Córdoba** (☎ 957/541046). **Puente Genil** (☎ 957/601674). **Radio Taxi Córdoba** (☎ 957/764444).

## TOURS

### BIKING TOURS

Córdoba La Llana organizes five-hour cycling tours of Córdoba city as well as bike tours to Madinat al-Zahra.
➤ FEES AND SCHEDULES: **Córdoba La Llana** (✉ Calle Lucano 20, Centro, Córdoba, ☎ 639/425884).

### BUS TOURS

Pullmantur runs numerous tours to this region, which you can book through most travel agents, many hotels, or through the company's Madrid office. Córdoba Vision offers both daytime and nighttime tours, among them trips to Madinat al-Zahra.
➤ FEES AND SCHEDULES: **Córdoba Vision** (✉ Avda. Dr. Fleming 10, Centro, ☎ 957/760241, FAX 957/200368). **Pullmantur** (✉ Plaza de Oriente 8, Madrid, ☎ 91/541–1805).

### WALKING TOURS

In Córdoba, you can hire English-speaking guides for the mosque and synagogue through the Asociación Profesional de Informadores Turísticos.
➤ FEES AND SCHEDULES: **Asociación Profesional de Informadores Turísticos** (✉ Museo Diocesano, Torrijos 12, La Judería, Córdoba, ☎ 957/486997).

## TRAIN TRAVEL

The high-speed AVE connects Madrid with Córdoba in less than two hours. Seville is another 40 minutes south on this sleek and panoramic train. Overnight trains connect Seville, Córdoba, Málaga, Granada, and Algeciras with Madrid and Barcelona. For transport within Andalusia, only the Córdoba–Seville connection is useful. Although Córdoba, Úbeda, Almería, Granada, Málaga, Seville, Algeciras, Huelva, and Cádiz are connected by train, nearly all connections are irregular and require changes.
➤ TRAIN INFORMATION: **RENFE** (☎ 902/240202, WEB www.renfe.es). **Estacion del AVE** (✉ Av. de América s/n, La Paz, Córdoba, ☎ 957/400202).

## TRAVEL AGENCIES

➤ CONTACTS: **Halcón Viajes** (✉ Calle José Cruz Conde 6, Centro, Córdoba, ☎ 957/483000 or 902/433000, WEB www.halconviajes.com). **Viajes Ecuador (WagonsLits Cook)** (✉ José Cruz Conde 28, Centro, Córdoba, ☎ 957/478534, WEB www.viajesecuador.com). **Viajes Marsans** (✉ José Cruz Conde 19, Centro, Córdoba, ☎ 957/478125 or 902/306090, WEB www.marsans.es).

## VISITOR INFORMATION

Córdoba also has a regional tourist office for Andalusia, at the Palacio de Exposiciones, next to the mosque.
➤ REGIONAL TOURIST OFFICES: **Córdoba Municipal Tourist Office** (✉ Plaza de Juda Levi s/n, La Judería, ☎ 957/201040 or 957/200522, FAX 957/200522, WEB www.turiscordoba.es). **Andalusian Regional Tourist Office** (✉ Torrijos 10, La Judería, Córdoba, ☎ 957/471235, WEB www.andalucia.org). **Córdoba Hotels and Restaurants Information Point** (✉ Estación del Ave-RENFE, Avda. de América s/n, La Paz, Córdoba, ☎ 957/279964).

➤ LOCAL TOURIST OFFICES: **Almodóvar del Río** (✉ Vicente Aleixandre 3, ☎ 957/635014. **Baena** (✉ Plaza de La Constitución, ☎ 957/671946). **Bélmez** (✉ Córdoba 1, ☎ 957/580012). **Bujalance** (✉ Plaza Mayor 1, ☎ 957/171289). **Fuente Obejuna** (✉ Luis Rodríguez 27, ☎ 957/584900). **Hinojosa del Duque** (✉ Plaza San Juan 1, ☎ FAX 957/

141831). **Lucena** (⊠ Plaza Nueva 1, ☎ 957/513282). **Montilla** (⊠ Capitan Alonso de Vargas 3, ☎ 957/652462, WEB www.turismomontilla. com). **Montoro** (⊠ Plaza de España 8, ☎ 957/160089). **Palma del Río** (⊠ Cardenal Portocarraro s/n, ☎ 957/644370, WEB www.interbook. net/ayuntamiento/palmadelrio). **Priego de Córdoba** (⊠ Pl. de la Constitución 3, ☎ 957/708420, WEB www.aytopriegodecordoba.es). **Rute** (⊠ Parque Nuestra Señora del Carmen, near Calle Toledo, ☎ 957/ 532929). **Subbética Region** (⊠ Mancomunidad de la Subbética Carta. Carcabuey–Zagrilla, Km 5.75, ☎ 957/704106, WEB www.subbetica. org). **Torrecampo** (⊠ Plaza Jesús 19, ☎ 957/155001). **Zuheros** (⊠ Plaza de la Paz s/n, near Castle, ☎ 957/694545).

# 7  JAÉN PROVINCE

In Andalusia's northeastern province you're away from the coastline and instead awash in a sea of olive trees, for this is the greatest olive-producing region in all of Spain. Amid the groves are attractive towns—most notably Údeba—highlighted by masterworks of Renaissance architecture. Spain's largest park dominates the mountainous eastern part of the province, drawing outdoor adventurers of all levels.

By Edward
Owen

**T**HE THREE MAIN ATTRACTIONS OF JAÉN PROVINCE are the superb Renaissance city of Úbeda; the huge Cazorla, Segura, and La Villa Nature Park; and the world's largest olive grove, covering most of the province's 5,211 square mi. From Madrid it takes about two and a half hours to drive to the spectacular Despeñaperros Pass, the gateway to Andalusia where the province of Jaén starts. The mountains of Despeñaperros form a natural barrier between Spain's great central *meseta* (plateau) and the Guadalquivir valley. The 350-mi-long river starts in the mountains of the Cazorla Nature Park, northeast of Jaén province, and eventually flows westward between the olive trees to Andújar and the cities of Córdoba and Seville.

Jaén city is dominated by a magnificent parador-castle that looks down on the Moorish-Gypsy quarter with its Arab baths and 16th-century churches and convents. Baeza and Úbeda are packed with lovely Renaissance buildings, one of which is now the parador in Úbeda. The Cazorla Nature Park is the largest reserve in Spain (826 square mi) with hikes and drives in four-wheel-drive vehicles through pine forests on mountains soaring to 6,910 ft. It is dotted with plunging waterfalls, and there are opportunities to see eagles, vultures, deer, mountain goats, wild boar, and a rich tapestry of flora, including indigenous orchids and carnivorous plants. Linares has a fascinating museum to the great guitarist Andrés Segovia. Bailen and Úbeda make and sell fine ceramics. In Andújar's nature park is a shrine to a shepherd's apparition that draws an annual pilgrimage of half a million people.

The mountains of Cazorla were thrown up about 22 million years ago by the collision between the European and African tectonic plates of the earth's crust. The sedimentary rock at Cazorla has been eroded to form spectacular river gorges and numerous caves. Fossils abound here and in the Sierra Magina, near Jaén city, and the Sierras de Andújar and Despeñaperros.

The earliest traces of humans in Jaén date from 25,000 years ago. You can still see an irrigation system from the Magdalena spring in Jaén city that dates to 2500 BC. The Carthaginians were followed by the Romans in AD 229 under Lucio Scipio, who called the area Auringis and the capital Giennium. "Gien" in Arabic means fertility.

After the Visigoth era the Moors conquered Jaén in 711. The main Arab towns included Yayyan (Jaén), Andújar, Baeza, and Úbeda. The retreat of the Moors started with the Christian victory at the Battle of Navas de Tolosa in Despeñaperros in 1212. Jaén province has the remains of some 200 castles, and still today the Moorish influence is extraordinarily strong, especially in architecture and cuisine.

## Pleasures and Pastimes

### Dining

Typical Jiennense dishes include starters such as *pipirrana* (a salad made with garlic, green pepper, peeled tomato, bread crumbs, and olive oil) and *espinacas al estilo de Jaén* (lightly boiled spinach with sausage, herbs, and spices). Main courses include *cordero estilo Mozárabe* (lamb with sweet and sour sauce), *lomo de cerdo en adobo* (pork loin fillets in an herb marinade), *bacalao a la baezana* (fried cod with a sauce of tomato, onion, pine nuts, and red pepper), and rich stews known as *andrajos*. Game dishes abound, and partridge is served everywhere, in salads, as a pate, stewed, and as *escabeche* (pickled). For a typical dessert try *papajotes* (cookies) or *Almendros de Bailén* (almond meringues).

| CATEGORY | COST* |
| --- | --- |
| $$$$ | over €18 |
| $$$ | €13–€18 |
| $$ | €8–€13 |
| $ | under €8 |

*per person for a main course at dinner

## Fiestas

On the night of January 6, Jaén marks the **Fiesta de las Lumbres de San Antón** with bonfires. **Semana Santa** (Holy Week), in April or May, and **Corpus Christi,** usually in the beginning of June, are major occasions. The pilgrimage to the **Cristo del Arroz** takes place on the second Sunday in May. The summer fiestas of **Nuestra Señora de la Capilla** are held around June 10–14, with June 11 the biggest day. The **Feria de San Lucas** is in mid-October. The exhausting pilgrimage to the **Castillo de Santa Catalina** is held on November 25.

In Andújar, as throughout Spain, **Semana Santa** (Holy Week) is filled with dramatic religious processions. The shrine of the **Virgen de la Cabeza,** near Andújar, is the scene of one of Spain's biggest *romerías* (pilgrimages), on the last weekend in April. The **local fiestas** in Andújar are held in early September.

In Baeza, **Corpus Christi** is marked by the parade of a giant silver monstrance. Also there are the **Fiestas de la Patrona Virgen del Alcázar** in mid-August and the **Romería del Cristo de la Yedra y la Virgen del Rosel** on September 7.

In Úbeda, **Semana Santa** has been declared of National Touristic Interest. The **Festival Internacional de Música y Danza** is held during May. The town fiesta of **San Miguel Arcángel** takes place in late September and early October. The **Fiesta de Nuestra Señora de Guadalupe** is held on September 8.

## Hiking and Walking

Thanks to a number of well-run outdoor clubs and a general interest in preserving the wilderness, Jaén is well endowed with parks for both recreation and camping. The village of Cazorla leads to the pine-clad slopes of the Cazorla Nature Park. Here there are numerous marked trails for hikes ranging from one hour to several days. It is also possible to hire four-wheel-drive vehicles, with or without a guide. The large nature parks of Sierra de Andújar and Despeñaperros also have many trails, rivers, and reservoirs. Hiking boots should be worn rather than sneakers, and beware of sunburn.

Tourist offices have maps with the main hiking trails and campsites in the parks. For those who expect to spend several days hiking, there are several books in Spanish with full trail details. Among the best are those in the series **Colección Guís Verdes GV,** published by Susaeta Ediciones SA (⊠ Calle Capezo s/n, 28022 Madrid, ☎ 913/009100, ℻ 913/009118) and **Senderos de Pequeño Recorrido** by Justo Robles Alvarez, distributed by El Olivo SLL (⊠ Calle Cazorla s/n, Aptdo. 238, 23400 Úbeda, ☎ 953/796123, ℻ 953/796475, ⓌⒺⒷ www.biblioandalucia.com).

## Lodging

Two of Andalusia's best historical paradors, one in the heart of the historic Úbeda and the other in the castle overlooking Jaén, offer a truly atmospheric touch to any visit. The former is in a wonderful old palace with a fine patio, and the latter is a restored castle with exposed stone walls and high wooden ceilings. But it is the parador nestled on the pine-clad slopes of the Cazorla Nature Park that's most heavily booked.

If you want to get a bedroom with mountain views, you must reserve far in advance.

Please note that in Cazorla Nature Park no hotels offer air-conditioning—it's not usually necessary in summer because of the cool altitude. In winter most places have central heating and often a log fire in a public room. Both Baeza and Úbeda have several hotels in refurbished palaces that are good alternatives if the paradors are full.

| CATEGORY | COST* |
| --- | --- |
| $$$$ | over €140 |
| $$$ | €100–€140 |
| $$ | €60–€100 |
| $ | under €60 |

*All prices are for a standard double room, excluding tax.*

# Exploring Jaén Province

Jaén province looks like a map of the United States without Florida. The Sierra Morena with the nature parks of Andújar and Despeñaperros are to the north, the Sierra de Cazorla with the largest nature park in Spain is to the east, and the Sierra Magina is in the southeast.

The province is far enough inland to be a watershed between the Mediterranean and the Atlantic. The river Segura flows out of Segura Nature Park to near Alicante, and the mighty Guadalquivir flows north from the Sierra de Cazorla, then changes its mind and flows westward across the entire province, fed by other rivers flowing from the Sierra Morena and the Sierra Magina.

## Great Itineraries

If you are fortunate enough to have secured rooms at the paradors of Jaén, Úbeda, and in the Cazorla Nature Park, then you have chosen a perfect route through the province. There are many other places to stay, especially if you're on a budget, but few are so well located.

Another route, which can be undertaken fairly rapidly since it borders the A–4 *autovía* (freeway), would be to visit Andújar and its shrine in the adjacent Sierra de Andújar Nature Park, browse for ceramics outside Bailén, see the Andrés Segovia Museum in Linares, and stop for some partridge in La Carolina. Rejoining the autovía northward, get a good view of the Despeñaperros Park from its twisting pass (take care—the road surface is very slippery even in summer). You could also venture off to see La Cascada de la Cimbarra waterfall near Aldeaquemada.

IF YOU HAVE 3 DAYS

One day should be sufficient to visit ⊠ **Jaén** ① with priority given to the cathedral, the Arab baths at the Palacio de Villardompardo, and the Museo Provincial. A few tapas and a meal in the tiny old quarter near the cathedral should complete a good day.

Next drive to **Baeza** ⑦, stopping en route to buy some fine olive oil at an *almazara* (olive oil mill), and visiting the Olive Oil Museum near Puente del Obispo. In Baeza, save up energy to clamber up the cathedral tower, admire the lovely Romanesque church of Santa Cruz, and enjoy an outdoor refreshment gazing up at the Torre de los Aliatores. End the afternoon in ⊠ **Úbeda** ⑧–㉒; the old part of the town will overwhelm you with its large plazas and superb Renaissance buildings, many with ornate plateresque facades. Try to find time in the afternoon and the following morning to take in the Hospital de Santiago, the private church of the Sacra Capilla Funerária del Salvador, the Casa Museo

Andalusi, the Museo de San Juan de La Cruz, and the Calle Valencia to see the potters at work.

You can dedicate Day 3 to Úbeda, but you'd miss the opportunity to head to the mountains for some cool air. It is about an hour's drive to **Cazorla** ㉓, from which the road narrows and climbs up to a mountain pass. Here you get your first view of the largest nature park in Spain, a stunning vista of deep valleys between pine-clad slopes and craggy mountain peaks. The road plunges into the park, and the nearby parador is well signed.

### IF·YOU HAVE 6 DAYS

Spend Day 1 in 🏨 **Jaén** ①. On Day 2, head north early to **Andújar** ②, see the park and sanctuary, then spend the night in 🏨 **Baeza** ⑦. Explore Baeza and spend that afternoon and the morning of Day 4 in 🏨 **Úbeda** ⑧–㉒. On the afternoon of Day 4 or early morning of Day 5, drive to 🏨 **Cazorla** ㉓ and dedicate the rest of your time to the park. You could spend many days walking and exploring here. Deer, mountain goats, and wild boar abound, and eagles and vultures glide above. If you have a license, you can even do a little fishing.

## When to Tour

May, June, and October are the best months to visit the province of Jaén. The summer heat is oppressive, although it's cooler in the higher altitudes of the nature parks. Spring is the best time for the parks because of the huge variety of flowers on display. Check to see if your visit coincides with any local fiestas. They're fun to attend, but you will have to fight for accommodations. Try to avoid traveling on the autovía (especially through Despeñaperros) at the end of July (heading south) and the end of August (heading north), because they can be clogged with vacationers, including a million Moroccans taking their annual leave from jobs in Europe.

# JAÉN AND THE NORTH

The rugged, dramatic Despeñaperros Pass in northern Jaén has been for centuries the quintessential gateway to Andalusia for travelers from the north.Today the Autovía de Andalucía passes through it, leading down past Andújar and to the regional capital.

## Jaén

① *93 km (58 mi) north of Granada; 335 km (209 mi) south of Madrid.*

The city of Jaén nestles below and partly around the steep pine-covered slopes of the Cerro de Santa Catalina, which rises to 2,690 ft and is crowned by the castle-parador. Stretching in front of the small city are rolling, olive-clad hills. In the southwest rise the peaks of the Sierra Magina, and behind the city to the southeast is Mt. Jabalcuz, at 5,293 ft. The main reason for Jaén's location is the abundance of fresh spring water and the protection offered by the Santa Catalina castle. The water was vital for the Arab baths, one of the city's main tourist sights.

The Moors called it Yayyan (Route of the Caravans) because it formed a crossroad between Castile and Andalusia. In 1246, the Moorish ruler of the city surrendered to Fernando III after a long siege; the Moors were forced to convert to Christianity and destroy their mosque, which had stood on what was to become the site of the cathedral since 825.

In 1460 Miguel Lucas de Iranzo was sent as governor to Jaén by Henry IV. He found the city in decay and initiated a program of urban renewal, building the pleasant Plaza de Ildefonso and Calle Millán de

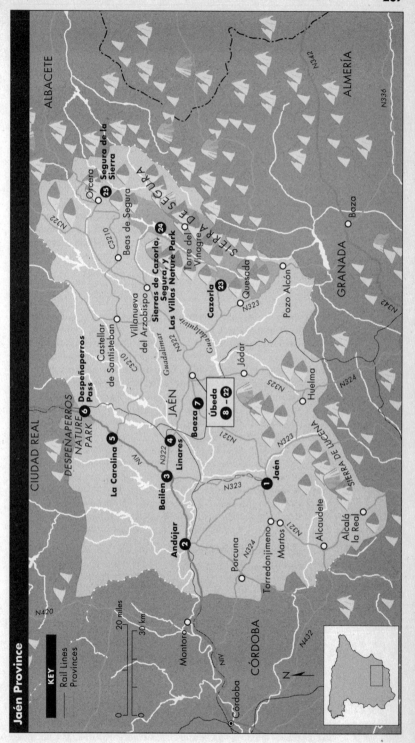

**207**

**Jaén Province**

KEY
— Rail Lines
— Provinces

0   20 miles
0   30 km

N

ALBACETE

Segura de la Sierra **25**

Orcera

C3210

Beas de Segura

Castellar de Santisteban

Villanueva del Arzobispo

Sierras de Cazorla, Segura, y Las Villas Nature Park **24**

SIERRA DE SEGURA

N322

Torre del Vinagre

Cazorla **23**

Quesada

N323

Pozo Alcón

Baza

GRANADA

ALMERÍA

N342

N336

N342

Guadalimar

Guadalquivir

Jódar

Huelma

N325

N323

N324

SIERRA DE LUCENA

DESPEÑAPERROS NATURE PARK

Despeñaperros Pass **6**

CIUDAD REAL

La Carolina **5**

Bailén **3**

Linares **4**

N322

NIV

Andújar **2**

JAÉN

Baeza **7**

Úbeda **8 – 22**

N321

Jaén **1**

N323

Porcuna

Torredonjimeno

Martos

N324

N321

Alcaudete

Alcalá la Real

N420

Montoro

NIV

Córdoba

CÓRDOBA

N432

Priego. However, the locals considered him a tyrant, and he was murdered in the cathedral in 1473.

For centuries Jaén survived mainly on passing trade and agriculture. At the start of the 20th century, the city had 26,000 inhabitants and was dominated by a few wealthy landowners. The population had doubled by the start of the Spanish Civil War in 1936, in which the locals took up arms with the Republicans. After Franco bombed the impoverished city in April 1937, revenge was rapid: 128 Nationalist prisoners were executed. The 1940s were difficult, but by the 1960s a new prosperity had arrived, with more people and more efficient agriculture.

Today Jaén still has the feel of a somewhat sleepy country town with a strong Moorish influence. The university is a focal point for the young, and large industrial estates provide jobs, though employment remains a problem. Underground parking lots have been built in the city center, but the system of one-way streets is poorly signposted. As you tour the city, you'll see how the narrow Moorish streets continue through the districts of San Juan and La Magdalena, which have a large Gypsy population. Older women shuffle by in black, the eyes in their wrinkled walnut-shell faces squinting against whitewashed walls reflecting a fierce sun. You press yourself to a wall to let a shiny pickup truck pass by, its speakers blaring out flamenco. Jaén is still at its crossroads.

★ The **Castillo de Santa Catalina,** perched on a rocky crag 5 km (3 mi) from the center of Jaén, is the city's star monument. The castle may have originated as a tower erected by Hannibal; in any case the site was fortified continuously over the centuries. The Nasrid king Alhamar, builder of Granada's Alhambra, constructed an *alcázar* (fortress) here, but King Ferdinand III captured it from him in 1246 on the feast day of Santa Catalina (St. Catherine). Catalina consequently became Jaén's patron saint, and when the Christians built a new castle and chapel here, they dedicated both to her. The castle ruins make a dramatic setting for the parador set in their midst—the main salon and the bar are a lesson in castle restoration. After undergoing repairs, the castle is scheduled to reopen to the public in 2003, with a new museum and plans to use an open area for concerts. But even when the castle is closed, the path from the parador to the large cross on the edge of the escarpment provides wonderful views of Jaén below, the neighboring sierra, and the endless olive groves. ⊠ *Castillo de Santa Catalina.* 🖭 *Free.* ☉ *Summer, Thurs.–Tues. 10:30–1:30; winter, Thurs.–Tues. 10–2.*

The imposing **cathedral** in the center of the city looms above the modest buildings around it. Begun around 1540 on the site of a 825 mosque, it wasn't finished until the end of the 18th century. Its chief architect was the brilliant Andrés de Vandelvira (1509–75), many more of whose buildings can be seen in Úbeda and Baeza. The ornate baroque facade was sculpted by Pedro Roldán, and the figures on top of the columns include San Fernando (King Ferdinand III) surrounded by the four evangelists. The cathedral's most treasured relic is the Santo Rostro (Holy Face), the cloth with which, according to tradition, St. Veronica cleansed Christ's face on the way to Calvary, leaving his image imprinted on the fabric. The *rostro* is displayed every Friday in the underground museum, to the right of the cathedral entrance. Also look for the *Immaculate Conception* by Alonso Cano, *San Lorenzo* by Martínez Montañés, and a Calvary scene by Jácobo Florentino. ⊠ *Plaza Santa María.* 🖭 *Cathedral free, €1.80 to see Santo Rostro only, €3 for museum.* ☉ *Cathedral Mon.–Sat. 8:30–1 and 4:30–7 (5–8 in summer), Sun. 9–1:30, 6–8; museum Tues.–Sun. 10:30–1.*

The **Conservatorio Oficial de Música** is worth taking a peek into to see the magnificent original patio-cloister of what was a 16th-century Jesuit college. ⊠ *Calle Campañía 1,* ☎ *953/232314.*

At the **Arco de San Lorenzo,** what looks like an old city wall gate is actually all that remains of the former 13th- to 14th-century San Lorenzo church. Closed to the public, the interior has fine Moorish tiles and plasterwork. ⊠ *Calle Almendros s/n.*

★ Built in the 16th century by Fernando de Torres y Portugal, Count of Villardompardo and a viceroy of Peru, **Palacio de Villardompardo** sits atop the ruins of the 11th-century **Baños Árabes** (Arab baths), some of the finest in Spain. These have been painstakingly restored. The baths were known as the Baños del Niño and were connected by an underground passage, more than a quarter mile long, to the palace of the Moorish kings that later became the Convent of Santa Domingo and now houses the Provincial Archives. After the conquest of Jaén in 1246 the baths fell into decline and were used partly as a tannery. They were filled in during the construction of the palace and not rediscovered until 1913. Under the barrel vaulting you enter the marble-flagged Cold Room and then the small Warm Room, walking on glass above the stone remains, and continue into the narrow Hot Room. Next is a second Warm Room, impressive for its size with a central pool surrounded by eight horseshoe arches. In the ceilings are lovely star-shape holes that originally let in natural light. Wine jars, figurines, and coins found during the excavations are on display.

The route through the baths leads to the extensive **Museo de Artes Populares,** which includes an ancient threshing machine, olive cultivation artifacts, and three magnificent 19th-century carts. Also in the palace is the **Museo de Arte Naïf,** a fun collection of brightly colored art of the region depicting serried ranks of olive trees, bullfights, and religious processions. Look for the amazing wood sculpture of the 20 members of the Moral family. Outside the building is a pleasant square with mature trees and a duck fountain. ⊠ *Plaza Luisa de Marillac,* ☎ *953/ 236292.* 🎫 *Free.* ☉ *Tues.–Fri. 9–8, weekends 9:30–2:30.*

In use since Roman times, **Raudal de la Magdalena** is a curious spring that incorporates a column beside a large lizard, emblematic of Jaén because of the old town's lizardlike shape (with the Plaza de Santa María as its head). ⊠ *Calle Zumbajarros, near the Iglesia de Magdalena.*

The **Museo Provincial** is some way from other sights, halfway to the station from the Plaza de Constitución. It's a delightful museum, with one of the best collections of Iberian (pre-Roman) artifacts in Spain. Two 16th-century doorways were moved to the patio of the converted 1547 mansion: the Pósito doorway by Francisco del Castillo and one from the old San Miguel church attributed to Andrés de Vandelvira. Sala 1 displays local finds from the Palaeolithic until about 1000 BC, including an idol carved in bone from about 2000 BC. Salas 2–5 house the huge Iberian collection, with items dating from 6 BC; some highlights are 20 life-size sculptures discovered near the village of Porcuna in 1975, a collection of 4 BC Greek glasses, and a stone engraved with the silhouettes of seven Iberian men and women dancing. Roman, Visigoth, and Moorish items are also on display. Don't miss the famous AD 4 sarcophagus depicting the seven parables from the life of Jesus. The large fine-arts section, dominated by Spanish Romantic works, includes a roomful of Goya lithographs. ⊠ *Paseo de la Estación 27,* ☎ *953/250600.* 🎫 *Free.* ☉ *Tues. 3–8, Wed.–Sat. 9–8, Sun. 9–3.*

Jaén's second church, **Iglesia de San Idelfonso,** to the east of the city center, was begun in the 13th century after Fernando III's conquest and is notable for its three facades. The eastern side is Gothic-Isabeline; the northern side has a Renaissance doorway by Francisco del Castillo and a tower built in various stages; and the western facade and tower were finished at the end of the 18th century by Francisco Calvo. Inside, note the elegant arches and a 12th-century statue of Virgin and Child, normally in the ornate Virgen de la Capilla chapel at the end on the right with frescoes of the apostles. Legend has it that the Virgin appeared here on June 10, 1430. The golden altar piece of the church shows the event. By the chapel is a small museum dedicated to the Virgin's appearance. ✉ *Plaza Santa María,* ☎ *953/190346.* 🎫 *Free.* ⏲ *Church daily 8:30–noon, 6–9; museum Tues.–Fri. 6 PM–8 PM.*

## Dining and Lodging

$$ ✕ **Casa Vicente.** Locals pack this stylish restaurant filled with Andalusian charm around the corner from the cathedral. You can have tapas at the small bar, then move on to the dining room in an old columned patio with lots of plants and bullfight posters. The traditional Jaén dishes—such as game casseroles, spinach with egg and pine nuts, and *cordero estilo Mozárabe* (roast lamb with a sweet-and-sour sauce)—are especially good. ✉ *Francisco Martín Mora 1,* ☎ *953/232222 or 953/232816. DC, MC, V. Closed Aug., Sun. June–Sept. No dinner Sun. Oct.–May.*

$$$ ★ ✕🏨 **Parador de Santa Catalina.** Built on a mountain amid the towers of the Moorish castle, Jaén's parador is one of the showpieces of the parador chain—the bar and main salon are superb—and a reason in itself to visit Jaén. Lofty ceilings, tapestries, baronial shields, and suits of armor add to the castle atmosphere. The comfortable bedrooms have wooden balconies overlooking the mountains. The local cuisine at the restaurant ($$) is well prepared, and there is a large pool in a walled garden. ✉ *Castillo de Santa Catalina, 23001,* ☎ *953/230000,* FAX *953/230930,* WEB *www.parador.es. 45 rooms. Restaurant, in-room safes, minibars, cable TV, pool, bar. AE, DC, MC, V.*

$ 🏨 **Hostal La Española.** Right in the heart of the lively old quarter near the cathedral, this aging, eccentric hostal has clean, spartan, bargain-rate rooms. The two elderly ladies who run the old place fuss over the massive assortment of plastic and real flowers in the large tiled patio entrance. Make sure you get an outside window in summer. ✉ *Bernardo Lóez 9,* ☎ *953/230254. 18 rooms. No a/c, no room phones. No credit cards.*

$ 🏨 **Hotel Hotusa Xauen.** This friendly three-star hotel is in the city center right beside the Plaza de la Constitución (where it is advisable to park). The rooms (triples are available) are painted white, with dark-wood trim and furniture. Breakfast is served daily from mid-June to September. *Xauen,* in case you were wondering, means passing caravans (of camels) in Arabic. ✉ *Plaza Deán Mazas 3, 23001,* ☎ *953/240789,* FAX *953/190312,* WEB *www.hotelxauenjaen.com. 35 rooms. Café, cable TV, meeting rooms, some pets allowed. AE, DC, MC, V.*

TAPAS BARS

There are some interesting tapas bars in the old area beside the cathedral between Calles Maestra and La Parra. Many more are near the Plaza de la Constitución, especially in Calle Nuevo. Many have restaurant tables in addition to bar service, but remember, the latter is the better bargain.

**El Gorrion** (✉ Arco de Consuelo 7, ☎ 953/232000; closed Mon. and July 7–Aug. 7), in a narrow alley near the cathedral, claims to be the oldest bar in town, and certainly looks it, with walls and wine barrels encrusted with age and dirt. Excellent cheese is served as a free tapa with drinks, and matadors and flamenco types pop in to be insulted by the somewhat obtuse barman. **La Manchega** (✉ Calle Bernardo López 8, Arco de Consuelo s/n, ☎ 953/232192; closed Tues. and Aug.) has a long bar on the ground floor festooned with ironmongery, knickknacks, and paintings; downstairs is a low-ceiling bodega restaurant. **Bar del Pósito** (✉ Plaza del Pósito s/n, ☎ 953/190023) fills the plaza near the Diputación, the provincial government building. It serves cafés and *copas* (drinks) at nice tables outside near the orange trees. **Cervecería Daniel's** (✉ Calle Nueva 2, ☎ 953/242041; closed Sun. and Aug.) is a modern bar with tables and a good choice of beers and tapas. Recommended are *revuelto de habas* (scrambled eggs with broad beans) and *solomillo al Jerez* (steak in sherry sauce). **Mesón Museo del Vino** (✉ Calle Doctor Sagaz Zubelzu 4, ☎ 953/242688; closed Sun. and Aug.) has hundreds of bottles of wine on its walls and a large bar. There's a good menu of the day served at the tables. The small **El Hortelano** (✉ Calle Teodoro Calvache 25, ☎ 953/242940; closed Sun. and Aug. 15–Sept. 7) has a good selection of tapas, some vegetarian, and a lively crowd.

## Shopping

The main shopping street is Paseo de la Estación with probably the smallest branch in Spain of the ubiquitous department store **El Corte Inglés** at the top (✉ Calle Roldán y Marín 2, ☎ 953/247880). The **mercado** weekly market is held in the Recinto Ferial near the bullring. For small souvenirs, visit **Arte y Costumbres** (✉ Maestra 8, Bajo Derecha, ☎ 650/380115; ⊙ weekdays 9:30–2, 5:30–9; weekends 10–2:30) near the cathedral. For olive oil, go to **La Tienda de Aceite de Jaén** (✉ Calle Millá de Priego 76 [just east of La Magdalena neighborhood], ☎ 953/252912; ⊙ Mon.–Sat. 9:30–1:30, 6–9).

# Andújar

❷ *64 km (40 mi) northwest of Jaén; 323 km (202 mi) south of Madrid.*

Just off the Autovía de Andalucía A–4 highway that connects Seville and Córdoba to northern Spain, Andújar is best known for two things: its huge sunflower oil factory (with its countless pigeons attracted by the windblown seeds) and its patroness, the Virgen de la Cabeza, whose shrine is the object of the oldest, and one of the region's largest, annual pilgrimages. The city's long history includes being beseiged by the Carthaginians and rescued by the Roman Scipio (the 13-arch bridge across the Guadalquivir was left by the Romans), and a long term of Moorish rule, which ended in 1224 after 70 years of fighting.

The sunflower oil factory may not be appealing, but the center of Andújar is a pleasant place. The Mudéjar-style **Torre de Reloj**, a clock tower erected in 1535 as homage to King Charles I, is the site of Andújar's accommodating tourist office, and thus a logical first stop when visiting the town. ✉ *Plaza de Santa María,* ☎ *953/504959.* 🎟 *Free.* ⊙ *Mon.–Sat. 10–2, 5–8.*

The star attraction at the central **Iglesia de Santa María** is a painting by El Greco, *La Oració en el Huerto,* which is kept in the chapel of Don Luis de Valdivia. The church was built between 1467 and 1624. The Renaissance-style door facing Calle Feria, and the tower, made of brick with Mudéjar decorations, were 16th-century additions. The cupola of the Mayor chapel has some fine 17th-century frescoes. ✉ *Plaza de Santa María 1,* ☎ *953/500139.* 🎟 *Free.* ⊙ *Hours irregular; service times posted outside church.*

The **Museo Profesor Sotomayor,** in the Palacio de los Niños de Don Gome, exhibits artifacts spanning the area's rich history, dating from the Paleolithic era through the times of the Romans and Moors to the city's golden age in the 16th century. The palace itself was constructed

in the 16th and the 17th centuries and has a finely decorated facade.
⌧ *Calle Maestras s/n,* ☎ *953/500603.* 🎟 *Free.* ☉ *Tues.–Fri. 7 PM–9
PM, weekends 11–1.*

The **Santuario de la Virgen de la Cabeza** marks the spot where, in 1227,
on a mountaintop 32 km (20 mi) from the Andújar, a shepherd named
Juan de Rivas had a vision of the virgin. A shrine was erected, word
spread of the miracle, and an annual pilgrimage followed. Now every
April, more than half a million people converge on the shrine, in the
heart of the rugged Sierra de Andújar Nature Park. It is a somewhat
gloomy construction, rebuilt after the 16th-century hermitage was
mostly destroyed in 1937. To one side of the building is the **Museo Mariano,** devoted to religious artifacts, but more intriguing is the small chapel
on the other side, the oldest part of the building, where the faithful
leave ex-votos, tokens of thanks for favors granted. The collection includes everything from orthopedic devices to wedding dresses. Car keys
indicate the gratitude of a survivor of an automobile accident, crutches
the recovery from an injury, hundreds of cigarette butts the determi-
nation to quit smoking. ⌧ *Ctra. J-501, past Las Viñas, 32 km north
of Andújar,* ☎ *953/549015.* 🎟 *Free.* ☉ *Weekdays, groups by prior
appointment; Sat. 11–1, 4–8; Sun. 1–2, 4–6.*

<table>
<tr><td>OFF THE<br>BEATEN PATH</td><td>**PARQUE NATURAL DE LA SIERRA ANDÚJAR –** This nature park covers 152,000 acres in the Sierra Morena, which divides the central meseta from the Guadalquivir valley. It's home to some of Europe's last surviving colonies of black vultures and wolves. Some of the area is meadowland with grazing fighting bulls (safely fenced in) shaded by holm oaks, gall oaks, and cork oaks; higher up are ash and pine. The park is bisected by the J-501 Andújar–Solana del Pino road, with a few roads and tracks leading off. In the hunting season, licenses are dispensed for fallow deer, rabbit, hare, partridge, and wild boar. Fishing is popular in the rivers Jándula and Yeguas, with water sports on the reservoirs of La Lancha, El Encinarejo, and El Rumblar. The tourist office in Andújar has specifics about activities in the park, which is open all hours and doesn't charge admission.</td></tr>
</table>

## Dining and Lodging

$$–$$$   ✕ **Mesón Asador El Churrasco.** You get a good value on barbecued and
roast meat and fish at this pleasant spot on a main street parallel to
the entrance to town from the autovía. The Castillian-style long bar
serves tapas, and the large dining room, divided by cane screens and
dressed with yellow and green tablecloths, has the atmosphere of a serious eatery. T-bone steak, a huge chunk of prime beef for two, and
sea bream roasted in sea salt are good choices from the extensive
menu. ⌧ *Crr. Capuchinos 24,* ☎ *953/502120. AE, MC, V.*

$   🏨 **Hotel Don Pedro.** You reach this two-star hotel close to the town
center through a courtyard from the street. You'll find basic accommodations here: the rooms are clean but small and sparsely furnished.
From September to March the courtyard is also the entrance to a
weekend disco and flamenco show. The restaurant has an €8 set lunch
and a reasonably priced à la carte menu. ⌧ *Calle Gabriel Zamora 5,
23740,* ☎ *953/501274,* FAX *953/504785. 79 rooms. Restaurant, café,
cable TV, bar, some pets allowed. AE, DC, MC, V.*

# Bailén

❸ *39 km (24 mi) north of Jaén.*

Bailén is known as the crossroads of Andalusia, for here the main highway from Madrid and northern Spain splits after squeezing through

the Despeñaperros Pass, one branch heading west to Córdoba and Seville, the other south to Jaén, Granada, and Málaga. It has many ceramics shops to tempt passing motorists, and until 1995 its roadside parador (now under private management) provided food and lodging to weary travelers, but otherwise this industrious but rather drab town makes few concessions to tourism.

The redbrick **Iglesia de Nuestra Señora de la Encarnación** in the center of Bailén was built in the 15th century in Gothic Isabellist style, but its interior obviously suffered terribly in the civil war. Concrete angels now adorn the walls behind the altar, and elsewhere hang truly ghastly religious paintings. ✉ *Calle Iglesia,* ☎ *953/671168.* 💲 *Free.* ⏰ *Hours irregular; service times posted outside church.*

OFF THE BEATEN PATH

**EL CASTILLO DE BURGALIMAR** – This enormous Moorish castle, visible for miles, is in Baños de la Encina, 11 km (7 mi) north of Bailén in the Sierra Morena. An inscription, preserved in the National Archaeological Museum in Madrid, shows that the Caliph Al-Haken II ordered its construction and that it was finished in 968. In medieval times it was known as Bury Al-Hamma and was used to garrison Berber troops for the annual battles against the Christians. The small town has various 16th-century buildings and shops selling honey, olive oil, and capers.

## Shopping

This is a great place to buy bricks, but probably of more interest are the local ceramics. You won't find delicate stuff here, but it's fine for planters, ashtrays, and cookware. There are more than 50 shops selling everything from tiles to casseroles to enormous *tinajas* (jars used in the old days for storing olive oil, but now commonly garden ornaments). The best area to browse is along the old Madrid–Cádiz dual carriageway on the outskirts of Bailén from Km 292 to 297, rather than on the new autovía.

# Linares

④ *50 km (31 mi) northeast of Jaén.*

Linares is known as the town where the great Spanish guitarist Andrés Segovia was born and the great bullfighter Manolete died, and more recently as the locale of an annual late-winter international chess tournament. The area has been mined, mainly for lead, copper, and silver, since as far back as 1000 BC. The town had a surge of prosperity with the arrival of British mining engineers with modern technology in the 19th and 20th centuries; there is still a British Club, and you can see pitshaft wheels in the countryside north of town toward the A-4 autovía.

When visiting the town, follow the signs indicating "Ayuntamiento—Parking," and after negotiating the narrow streets you'll reach an underground garage below a tasteless modern plaza. From here it's an easy walk (facing the town hall, turn right and right again before the start of the pedestrian shopping street) to both the Segovia and archaeological museums, taking in a tapa or two along the way.

The **Casa Museo Andrés Segovia** is five minutes' walk from the Plaza Ayuntamiento (although it is not signposted). Andrés Segovia (1893–1987), Marqués de Salobreña, one of the world's greatest classical guitarists, was born to a humble family in Linares, and it was his wish to be buried in this fascinating, intimate museum dedicated to his life. In 2002 his coffin was moved from Madrid and buried in the vaulted brick cellar, now a simple chapel, of the 17th-century palace. On the ground floor is a display of posters and concert programs, including the one from his first public concert in Granada in 1913. On the first floor is a room crammed with items from Segovia's life, including his photographs, books, guitars, and furniture from his studio in Madrid and house in Granada. Another room displays Segovia stamps and letters. The foundation plans to add a music archive for researchers. ⊠ *Cánovas del Castillo 59,* ☎ *953/651390,* WEB *www.segoviamuseo.com.* ✉ *€2.* ☉ *Tues. and Thurs. 10–1:30, 4–7; weekends 10–1:30.*

The **Museo Arqueológico** displays artifacts from one of Europe's most important archaeological sites, Cástulo, 7 km (5 mi) from Linares. This fortified city was occupied from Neolithic times. Its most important era was during its Iberian and Roman phases; now all that remains are a hill and two excavations. The most important piece in the museum is a perfume burner, in the form of a bronze cup with figures of lions and deer, from the 7th or 6th century BC. ⊠ *Calle General Echagüe 2,* ☎ *953/692463.* ✉ *€1.50, EU citizens free.* ☉ *Winter, Tues.– Sun. 10–2; summer, Tues.–Sat. 10-2.*

The **Plaza de Toros** bullring, dating from 1866, is one of the most famous in Spain, because it was here on the afternoon of August 28, 1947, that one of the country's greatest bullfighters was fatally gored. Manuel Rodríguez Sánchez, known as Manolete, was 30 when he met his death on the horns of a Miura bull. Manolete was famed for his poker face in the ring and the way he would fight bulls close, with a daring economy of movement. Outside the ring there's a ceramic version of the bullfight poster for his last afternoon, and in the adjacent gardens is a memorial statue. ⊠ *Plaza de Santa Margarita s/n,* ☎ *953/690849.*

| | |
|---|---|
| OFF THE BEATEN PATH | **CÁSTULO** – Seven kilometers (five miles) from Linares on the road to Torreblascopedro is one of the most important archaeological sites in Europe. This ancient settlement was a fortified city with remains found from the Neolithic to medieval times. It was of particular importance during the Iberian and Roman epochs. There's not much to see here now except some Roman remains, but the archaeological museum in Linares has a good selection of the finds from the site. |

## Tapas Bars

Generous tapas are usually served free with drinks in Linares, but if you want something more substantial, ask for the list of *raciones* (portions). **Cafetería Rosario** (⊠ Calle General Echagüe 11, ☎ 953/694785), opposite the Archaeological Museum, is a smart pastry shop with a bar at the back serving teas, coffee, and drinks. There are also tables where you can relax with your refreshments. **Bar Rhin** (⊠ Pasaje del Comercio 2, ☎ 953/699628) near the Plaza Ayuntamiento parking garage, has an old-fashion long bar. It serves fresh orange juice, coffee, and drinks and offers a variety of tapas such as *mojama* (dried tuna).

# La Carolina

**⑤** *67 km (42 mi) northeast of Jaén.*

La Carolina, named in honor of 18th-century King Charles III, is one of the best examples of urban planning of its time, with wide streets and airy plazas. Today it's a pleasure to enter from the autovía—it is easy to find anything and easy to park. The area is best known in Spanish history for the decisive battle at Navas de Tolosa, on July 16, 1212, when King Alfonso VIII's army of 110,000, reinforced by 70,000 crusaders from elsewhere in Europe, defeated a force of 250,000 Moors led by the feared Almohad commander Al-Nasir. The battle, in which

60,000 Moors were killed, according to contemporary reports, marked the beginning of the end of Moorish rule in Spain: within four decades Seville and Córdoba had been conquered, leaving only the Kingdom of Granada under rule of the Moors. Today a ruined Moorish watchtower standing behind the La Perdiz restaurant on the highway near Navas de Tolosa remains as a lone relic from the wars.

### Dining and Lodging

This is great partridge country, thus the two hotels called Perdiz. Both are signed with different exits from the Madrid–Sevilla autovía, with the Orellana Perdiz north of the Hotel NH La Perdiz.

**$$–$$$** ✕ **Restaurante La Toja.** Easy to reach off the highway, this is a great stop on the drive between Madrid and Seville, with an excellent, comfortable tapas bar and an elegant restaurant. The rich partridge paté has become so popular that the owner now has a local factory that produces venison and ostrich patés as well. Another restaurant specialty is *lomos de venado con salsa grosella* (venison with red currant sauce). There are two set menus, one for €16.50, the other a gastronomic blowout at €30. ⊠ *Avda. Juan Carlos 1,* ☎ *953/661018 or 953/ 682322. AE, MC, V.*

**$$** ✕🏨 **Hotel NH La Perdiz.** An unusual feature at this hotel, part of the NH chain, is that 28 rooms have en suite garages—providing added peace of mind if you have valuables packed in your car. These rooms also have little stone terraces overlooking a shady, mature garden. All rooms have rough-hewn wood beams, yellow walls, green bedspreads, functional furniture, and modern baths. The cafeteria-bar has a sunny terrace, and the good restaurant ($$$) serves national dishes plus local game such as venison, wild boar, and, of course, partridge. ⊠ *Autovía de Andalucía salida 268 (south and north), 23200,* ☎ *953/660300,* FAX *953/681362,* WEB *www.nh-hoteles.es. 84 rooms. Restaurant, café, minibars, cable TV, pool, bicycles, bar, Internet, meeting rooms, some pets allowed. AE, DC, MC, V.*

**$** ✕🏨 **Orellana Perdiz.** Since about 1920 the restaurant here has been a landmark on the road between Madrid and Seville. It still serves as a good pit stop, with small, inexpensive hotel rooms. The mesón-style restaurant is famous for its partridge, which you can have soused in too much mayonnaise as a salad, as an *encebollada* (stew—a much better option), or *escabeche* (pickled in vinegar—an acquired taste). Other game, including pheasant, is available in season. The Orellana Perdiz also offers various weekend excursions, by bus and on foot to the Parques Natural de Despeñaperros and Cazorla. ⊠ *Autovía de Andalucía salida 265 south and 266 north, 23200,* ☎ *953/661830,* FAX *953/ 662170,* WEB *www.orellanaperdiz.com. 18 rooms. Restaurant, café, bar, meeting rooms, some pets allowed. AE, DC, MC, V.*

## Despeñaperros Pass

**⑥** *85 km (53 mi) north of Jaén, 252 km (158 mi) south of Madrid.*

For those arriving by car from northern Spain, Despeñaperros is familiar as the dramatic gateway to Andalusia. Flanked by towering rock faces, the twisting Despeñaperros Pass in the Sierra Morena slices through the 19,292-acre Despeñaperros Nature Park.

Despeñaperros translates roughly as "the place where the dogs fall off rocks." The origin of the name is something of a mystery, but it is a graphic illustration of the area's rugged landscape, with sheer cliffs plunging hundreds of feet. The sparsely populated region is home to deer and wild boar, eagles and vultures.

Apart from the autovía, entry into the park is from Santa Elena at the higher southern end of the park. From here you can walk down the Arroya del Rey valley or take the road to Aldea de Miranda del Rey, the only village in the park, which is walking distance from two caves, La Granja and del Santo, both of which contain Stone Age paintings. There is a visitor center at Casa Forestal de Valdeazores. ☒ *Ctra. Nacional IV Km 245, Santa Elena,* ☏ *953/125018 or 953/105018.*

OFF THE          **LA CASCADA DE LA CIMBARRA –** Plunging 130 ft, this waterfall is one of
BEATEN PATH    Andalusia's most striking natural wonders, an especially spectacular
                 sight during winter and spring. To see it, you have to leave the main
                 highway and travel 15 mi along a mountain road to the tiny village of
                 **Aldeaquemada.** From here, guides take you to La Cimbarra, which is
                 easily accessible on foot. Other, equally dramatic waterfalls in the vicin-
                 ity can be visited by more serious hikers.

# EASTERN JAÉN

As it spreads east, Jaén province's sea of olive groves touches on two of Spain's most impressive collections of hilltop monuments, at Baeza and Úbeda. For two and a half centuries after their conquest from the Moors by King Ferdinand "the Saint" in 1227, both towns lived an uneasy existence on the border between Christendom and the Moorish kingdom of Granada. The final defeat of the Moors and a boom in farming and the textile trade brought prosperity to the two towns, or, more precisely, to the handful of noble families who ruled them. In the 16th century, at the time when Renaissance style was all the rage, the local aristocrats embarked on a feverish palace-building spree, each one striving to erect a home more impressive than his neighbor's. At the same time they funded the construction of churches and convents, hoping by doing so to jump the queue to paradise in the afterlife. Many of the buildings are the work of the brilliant 16th-century Renaissance architect Andrés de Vandelvira, said to have been of Flemish extraction, who was commissioned to build the cathedral in Jaén and spent the rest of his lucrative but hectic life designing palaces and convents in the province.

## Baeza

★ ❼ *48 km (30 mi) northeast of Jaén on the N321.*

The historic town of Baeza sits atop a hill with a commanding view of its major industry: the surrounding olive groves. Founded by the Romans as Biatia or Vivatia, it later housed the Visigoths and as Bayyasa it became the capital of a *taifa* (kingdom) under the Moors. The Saint King, Ferdinand III, captured Baeza in 1227, and for the next 200 years it stood on the frontier of the Moorish kingdom of Granada. In the 16th and 17th centuries, Baeza's nobles gave the city a wealth of splendid Renaissance palaces. But feuding between two local aristocratic families, the Benavides and the Carvajales, led to loss of favors and to royal decrees to demolish the city gates (some were later rebuilt) and walls. Unemployment is a serious problem, since half the population of 16,000 depends on the highly seasonal olive oil industry. But the profusion of young civil guards all over town in their sage-green uniforms is not because of unrest but because their academy is in the town.

The **Casa del Pópulo,** in the central *paseo*—where the Plaza del Pópulo (or Plaza de los Leones) and Plaza del Mercado Viejo merge to form a delightful cobbled square—is a beautiful plateresque structure from 1535. The first mass of the reconquest was reputedly celebrated on the balcony on the right in 1227. The three coats of arms are of, from left to right, Baeza, the imperial shield, and Governor Guevara. You'll find the tourist office here. ✉ *Plaza de Pópulo s/n,* ☎ *953/740444.* ⊙ *Tues.– Fri. 9:30–2:30, 5–7; Sat. 10–1, 5–7; Sun. 10–1, 4–6.*

The **Puerta de Jaén & Arco de Villalar** are two arches in the corner of Plaza de Pópulo. The Puerta de Jaén, on the left with the same three coats of arms as on the adjoining building, was a city gate but was demolished on the orders of Queen Isabel because of feuding between two Baeza families. It was rebuilt in 1526 to commemorate Charles V's visit to Baeza. The Villalar arch was erected in 1522 to commemorate Charles V's victory the year before against the Comuneros. ✉ *Plaza del Pópulo s/n.*

The **Antiguas Carnicerías** (Old Butchers) building was moved to the Plaza de Pópulo in 1962–63 from the nearby Calle Atarazanas, where it was built in 1547. It has been used as a tannery and an archive and is now home of the law courts. ✉ *Plaza de Pópulo s/n.*

The **Fuente de los Leones** (Fountain of the Lions) was erected in the center of Plaza de Pópulo after being brought from the nearby Roman city of Cástulo at the beginning of the 16th century. The ancient Iberian-Roman statue is thought to depict Iberian princess Imilce, wife of Hannibal; the head was destroyed during the civil war and was replaced by a work of local sculptor Gávez Mata.

The golden-stone **Palacio de Jabalquinto,** on the Cuesta (Slope) de San Felipe, was built by Juan Alonso Benavides, second cousin of Ferdinand of Aragón. Its facade is a masterpiece of the late-15th-century Isabelline Gothic. At press time the building was closed for restoration, but you can see the palace's interesting courtyard with palms, olives, and oleander from the street. ⊙ *Wed.–Sun. 10–1 and 4–6.*

Baeza's **cathedral** was begun by Ferdinand III on the site of a former mosque, but it has undergone many a transformation since his day. The original structure collapsed and was largely rebuilt by Andrés de Vandelvira, architect of Jaén's cathedral, between 1570 and 1593, though the west side of the front has earlier architectural features. The tower was damaged by lightning in 1832; it fell down in 1862 and was not fully rebuilt until 1959. A fine 14th-century rose window crowns the 13th-century Puerta de la Luna (Moon Door). Don't miss the three-tiered baroque 1714 silver monstrance, which is carried in Baeza's Corpus Christi processions; it's kept in a concealed niche behind a painting by the rear door that leads to the tower. To see the piece in all its flamboyant splendor, put a €1 coin in a slot to reveal its hiding place and light it up (money well spent). Entrance to the clock tower requires a small donation (€0.60) and a 176-step climb up a narrow spiral staircase, but your reward is one of the best views of Baeza. The remains of the original mosque are in the cathedral's Gothic cloisters. ✉ *Plaza de Santa María s/n,* ☎ *953/744157.* ⊙ *Daily 10:30–1 and 4–6 (5–7 in summer); Sun. mass 7 PM.*

At the seminary of **San Felipe Neri,** built in 1660 opposite the cathedral entrance, you can visit only the patio. The ancient student custom of inscribing names and graduation dates in bull's blood on the walls is still in practice. ✉ *Plaza de Santa María s/n,* ☎ *953/742775,* FAX *953/742975,* WEB *www.uia.es.*

In the lovely little 13th-century Romanesque **Iglesia de Santa Cruz,** the 15th-century frescoes in the half cupola behind the altar and the adjacent chapel on the left were discovered below a layer of white paint. The altar fresco shows, from left to right, the Last Supper, Mary Magdalen, and St. John. In the chapel you can see the Martyrdom of St. Catherine, and in the facing archway is St. Sebastian. ⊠ *Plaza Santa Cruz s/n,* ☎ *953/744157 (cathedral).* ☉ *Mon.–Sat. 11–3, 4–8; Sun. noon–2 and 4–6.*

There are good views of the town and surrounding countryside to be had if you mount the steel stairs of the stone **Puerta de Úbeda** and enter the tower, which includes a souvenir shop with a coin-operated telescope. ⊠ *Corner Calle Barreras and Calle Julio Burrel.* ☎ *€1.* ☉ *Tues.– Sun. 10–2, 4–7.*

Along the Paseo de la Constitución is the 12th-century **Torre de los Aliatares,** named after a Moorish tribe that occupied it before the reconquest. It's been rebuilt several times and now has a 19th-century clock. ⊠ *Plaza de España.*

The **ayuntamiento** (town hall), on the Plaza Cardenal Benavides, just north of the Plaza del Pópulo, was designed by Andrés de Vandelvira and finished in 1523. Look up at the ornate plateresque facade between the balconies and you'll see the coats of arms of Philip II, the city of Baeza, and the magistrate Juan de Borja. The door on the left was the entrance to the prison; the two figures represent Justice and Charity. By appointment you can visit the council chamber, which has a highly decorated Renaissance ceiling and pictures of local notables and the Battle of Navas de Tolosa. ⊠ *Pasaje del Cardenal Benavides s/n,* ☎ *953/740150.* ☎ *Free.* ☉ *By appointment.*

Baeza is one of the world's olive oil capitals, and it's well worth a visit to the **Museo de la Cultura del Olivo,** a 15-minute drive out of town on the road to Jaén. The location is a 19th-century *almazara* (olive oil mill), the main feature of which is a basement bodega with 10 huge stone vats. Other rooms show the stages in the production of oil with some huge old presses and giant jars. Most fascinating is the *prensa de Alorí,* driven by a donkey—the stuffed one on display looks too healthy to have been the original—which simultaneously crushed the olives and squeezed the oil out of them in two separate operations. Different types of olive trees grow in the entrance courtyard. A stumbling block here is that there are no guides or useful leaflets, and the brief descriptions are only in Spanish. The museum adjoins the Escuela de Hostelería, a good spot for lunch. ⊠ *Puente del Obispo, 8 km (5 mi) outside Baeza off N321 to Jaén,* ☎ *953/765084.* ☎ *Free if no attendant.* ☉ *Tues.–Sun. 9:30–1:30, 2–6.*

### Dining and Lodging

$$$ ×☷ **Hotel Juanito.** This mesón-style restaurant is the epicenter of fine olive oil and traditional Jiennense cooking. For years Jaunito and his wife, Luisa, have produced truly superb dishes, mostly using the best local olive oil. He still fusses over the tables and gives out extra dishes such as braised artichokes with oil and partridge paté on oiled toast (superb). The *salmorejo* (gazpacho garnished with chopped boiled egg) is light and creamy, and the *bacalao estilo Baeza* (cod fillets with a light oil and herbed tomato sauce) is a lesson in balancing tastes. There's an olive oil shop, and upstairs are cozy, inexpensive lodgings ($). Juanito is on the eastern edge of town, beside the municipal sports center. ⊠ *Paseo Arca del Agua s/n 23440,* ☎ *953/740040,* 𝖥𝖠𝖷 *953/742324,* 𝖶𝖤𝖡 *www.juanitobaeza.com. 34 rooms, 2 suites. Restaurant, pool, bar, some pets allowed. MC, V. No dinner Sun., Mon.*

$$ ×☷ **Hotel Palacete Santa Ana.** Basque Ramón Cueto, a nuclear scientist, has turned this lovely two-story 16th-century palace with three patios into a boutique hotel with reproduction furniture as well as gen-

uine antiques and paintings. The rooms are large and comfortable, with exceptional bathrooms, some with hydro-massage baths. Though rooms aren't equipped with air-conditioners, portable units are available. In an adjoining building you'll find a rustic bar (an over-the-top exercise in pueblo sensibility), a large, formal restaurant upstairs serving local and Basque dishes, and a rooftop terrace for summer barbecues. The location is a few minutes walk from the town center. ⊠ *Santa Ana Vieja 9, 23440,* ☎ FAX *953/741657,* WEB *www.palacetesantana.com. 13 rooms. Restaurant, cable TV, bar, Internet, meeting rooms, some pets allowed. AE, DC, MC, V.*

$$ ⊞ **Confortel Baeza.** Tacked on to a 16th-century convent in the town center, this is a large, modern hotel with spacious public areas and cozy, rustic bedrooms with good-size baths. You can dine outside on the patio from a set menu. ⊠ *Calle Concepción 3, 23440,* ☎ *953/748130,* FAX *953/742519,* WEB *www.confortelbaeza.com. 81 rooms, 3 suites. Restaurant, café, bar, Internet, meeting rooms. AE, DC, MC, V. Closed mid-Dec.–Jan.*

$ ⊞ **Hostal El Patio.** Ideal for both the budget-minded and the footsore, this basic hostal with surprisingly large rooms is right in the historic center next to all the sights and the Plaza de la Constitución bars. You enter the 16th-century palace past twin coats of arms and through a shadowy patio that has seen better days and is watched over by the stuffed heads of a tatty bull and a bearded goat. The location is in the street behind the Plaza de Pópulo tourist office. ⊠ *Calle Conde Romanones 13, 23440,* ☎ *953/740200,* FAX *953/748260. 15 rooms. No a/c, no room phones, no room TV. No credit cards.*

TAPAS BARS

You can obtain a small, free booklet from the tourist office, *Ruta para Tapear, Comer y Divertirse,* with information about local tapas haunts, including a handy map. Be aware that in Baeza whole families have been known to occupy tapas bars, loudly, late into the evening. One of the best tapas spots is the narrow **Arcediano** (⊠ Calle Barbacana s/n, entry beside La Torre de los Aliatares, ☎ 953/748184), where specialties include *flamenquines* (ham rolled around cheese and fried in bread crumbs) and *revuelto de espárragos* (scrambled eggs with diced asparagus). If you want to buy a late-night snack, go to **Croissantería San Pablo** (⊠ Calle San Pablo 39, the pedestrian street at the clock tower end of the Plaza de la Constitución) which sells pizza, croissants with fillings, bread, cold drinks, and ice cream. **El Nuevo Casino** (⊠ Calle San Pablo 24, ☎ 953/748218) is really the locals' club, but the public is allowed up the steps from the street to take sensibly priced drinks and tapas in the charming, open-air 16th-century patio. Do not enter areas marked *"Socios."*

## Shopping

Given that Baeza is the unofficial olive oil capital of Spain, it's surprising that there's only one serious retail oil shop apart from Hotel Juanito, but it's a good one. **La Casa del Aceite** (⊠ Paseo de la Constitución 9, near Plaza del Pópulo, ☎ 953/748081) sells olive oil, serving jugs, local canned foods, cookbooks, and olive-wood knickknacks. To buy top-quality oil at factory prices, trave 1 km off the Jaén–Baeza road to visit **Valle Magina** (⊠ Cortijo Virgen de los Milagros, Ctra. Jaén–Baeza Km 30, Mancha Real, ☎ 953/350178), the oil mill voted the best in the region and supplier for the European Commission dining room. A local **mercadillo** (market) is held every Friday and Sunday morning in a field at Ciudad Salaría, near Hipermueble, by the road between Úbeda and Baeza. There's a smaller market on Tuesday, 9–2, near the bullring.

# Úbeda

★ *9 km (5½ mi) northeast of Baeza.*

The Casco Antiguo (Old Town) of Úbeda is a superbly pure example of a Renaissance town and one of the most outstanding enclaves of 16th-century architecture in Spain. It is an oasis of good taste and tranquility compared with the busy modern part of the town, which has little sightseeing interest. Follow the signs to the Zona Monumental, where you'll pass countless Renaissance palaces and stately mansions, some converted into hotels, and each with its own distinctive features—an unusual balcony or a fine sculptured facade. Most of the private residences are closed to the public, but you can wander into many of the old churches and the several museums.

Why Úbeda has more appeal than neighboring—and far from unattractive—Baeza is difficult to pinpoint; perhaps it's that all the historic buildings are congregated around one another. It helps that the area is rich in building materials, a fact not lost on the Romans and the Moors, though sadly, Moorish Úbeda was razed to the ground by Alfonso VIII eight days after his victory at Navas de Tolosa. Francisco de los Cobos, the secretary of the Emperor Charles V, had a significant hand in the town's rebirth, for he was the one who commissioned the architect Andrés de Vandelvira and a host of other talent to create an Italian Renaissance vision in sunny Andalusia.

## A Good Walk

This daylong walk falls into segments, one beginning in the morning and the other in the evening. Start the first segment at 10 AM in the **Plaza Váquez de Molina** ⑧ and head for its southern portion to visit the **Palacio del Marqués de Mancera** ⑨, which is open only from 10 to 11. Note the front of the **Palacio de las Cadenas** ⑩ (the ayuntamiento) before exiting the square, turning left onto Calle Corazón de Jesús, and right onto Calle Baja del Marqués for a stop at the tourist office on the left. Head back to the rear of the Palacio de las Cadenas to see its patio. Reenter the Plaza de Váquez de Molina and walk eastward to the **Sacra Capilla del Salvador** ⑪ and then pop into the Parador Condestable Dávalos. Next walk up Calle Horno Contado, on the right of the parador, to the large **Plaza del Primero de Mayo** ⑫ and turn right down Calle San Juan de la Cruz to visit the **Oratorio y Museo de San Juan de la Cruz** ⑬. Retrace your steps to the Plaza del Primero de Mayo and cross it to the left, passing the **Ayuntamiento Antiguo** ⑭ as you enter Calle María de Molina on its left. Head right onto Calle Real and turn left down Calle Juan Pascual and left onto Calle Narvaez to reach the **Casa Museo Arte Andalusi** ⑮. Continue on Narvaez and turn right down Calle Luna y Sol, turning left to reach the **Casa de las Torres** ⑯. Stroll across Plaza San Lorenzo and past the ivy-clad, 16th-century Iglesia de San Lorenzo to the **Miradores de San Lorenzo** ⑰ for a great view southward.

For the evening portion of the walk, start about 6:30 PM at the **Museo Arqueológico de Úbeda** ⑱ on Calle Cervantes, off Plaza Primero de Mayo, followed by a visit to the **Iglesia de San Pablo** ⑲, on the corner of Cervantes and the plaza (note that it doesn't open until 7 PM). Then walk past the church to Calle Losal and down to and through the Múdejar **Puerta de Losal** ⑳. Turn left up Fuente Seca, veer left onto Calle Cruz de Hierro, and then walk along Corredera de San Francisco to reach the Plaza de Andalucía, where you can see the **Torre del Reloj** ㉑. Finally, end your day of touring on Calle Obispo Cobos at the **Hospital de Santiago** ㉒.

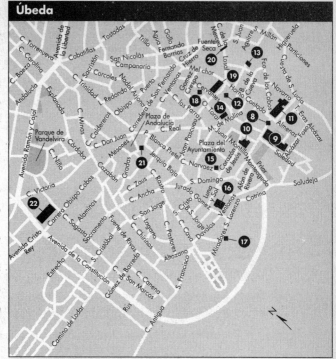

## Sights to See

**14 Ayuntamiento Antiguo.** The Plaza Primero de Mayo, by way of the Calle Horno Cantador, leads you to the old town hall, begun in the early 16th century but restored as a beautiful arcaded baroque palace in 1680. It's now a conservatory of music. The figures in the upper niches are Michael the Archangel and San Juan, patron and co-patron of the city. From the hall's upper balcony, the town council watched celebrations and autos-da-fé ("acts of faith," or executions of heretics sentenced by the Inquisition) in the square below. ⊠ *Plaza Primero de Mayo.*

**16 Casa de las Torres.** The first Renaissance mansion in Úbeda, named for its twin towers, still has a medieval look—note, for example, the evil gargoyles above the patio, poised threateningly over virtuous but somewhat undressed maidens. It was built for a former governor of Castille and given a part plateresque facade. Legend has it that a beautiful girl was murdered and buried in the basement walls by a past owner and that she haunts the building—doubtless inspiration for the art students who now study here. ⊠ *Plaza de San Lorenzo s/n.* 🎟 *Free.* ⊙ *Daily 8–2:30 and 3:30–6.*

**15 Casa Museo Arte Andalusi.** For a chance to sample bygone and current domestic life in historic Úbeda, visit this private 15th- to 16th-century palace, which displays the antiques collection of Francisco Castro and adjoins his home and lovely garden. There is a charming if not decadent atmosphere around the patio, with its tinkling fountain where Don Francisco sells refreshments and CDs of old Sephardic music by the Spanish musicologist Carlos Cruz. The owner and his family have restored parts of the palace; you'll find a collection of Mudéjar pieces, ceramics, utensils, woodwork, doors, stone fonts, and a vaulted bodega. ⊠ *Calle Narvaez 11,* ☎ *619/076132.* 🎟 *€2.* ⊙ *Oct.–May, daily 11–2:30 and 4–9; June–Sept., daily 11–2:30 and 6–9:30.*

**㉒ Hospital de Santiago.** Often jokingly called the Escorial of Andalusia, this huge, angular building is Vandelvira's 1575 masterpiece and was built as a charitable hospital, pantheon, and palace. Its generally plain facade is decorated with ceramic medallions, and over the main entrance is a relief of St. James as a warrior on horseback. Inside are a fine arcaded patio and a grand staircase. The frescoes above the stairs and in the sacristy are unusual given the otherwise restrained Renaissance style. The building is on the eastern end of Avenida Cristo Rey in the modern section of town, a short walk from the bus depot and the main drag, Ramón y Cajal. It's now used as a cultural center. ⊠ *Calle Obispo Cobos s/n.* 🔁 *Free.* ⊗ *Weekdays 8–3 and 3:30–10 (7 in winter); weekends 11–3 and 6–9:30.*

★ **⑲ Iglesia de San Pablo.** This is one of the oldest churches in Úbeda, with records indicating that part of it was burned in 1368. The majority of the construction is Gothic, with later changes. Most notable are the 14th-century Carpenters' Door onto Calle Cervantes and the main 1511 Isabelline-Gothic doorway facing the plaza. ⊠ *Plaza del Primero de Mayo.* 🔁 *Free.* ⊗ *Daily 7 PM–9 PM.*

**⑰ Miradores de San Lorenzo.** From here you get a magnificent view of the Guadalquivir valley with the serried rows of olive trees marching toward the distant Sierra Mágina. ⊠ *Miradores de San Lorenzo.*

**⑱ Museo Arqueológico de Úbeda.** A lovely 14th-century Mudéjar-style palace houses this rather sad collection of artifacts. Donated by the founder in 1973, they look as though they haven't been touched since, even though the small building has a staff of three. There are few labels and no translations, not even from Arabic to Spanish. You can see Stone and Bronze Age implements; Roman remains, including an olive mill stone; early ceramics; and a medieval model in stone of a castle. ⊠ *Calle Cervantes 6,* ☎ 953/753702, WEB *www.junta-andalucia. es/cultura.* 🔁 €1.50. ⊗ *Tues. 3–8, Wed.–Sat. 9–8, Sun. 9–3.*

**⑬ Oratorio y Museo de San Juan de la Cruz.** The mystic San Juan de la Cruz (1542–1591) died in Úbeda, and two years after his death his body was secretly moved by night (*see* Chapter 19 of Don Quixote) to Segovia. Subsequent litigation by angry Úbeda residents resulted in the grisly return in 1609 of a part of his body, which is now venerated as a holy relic in the ornate 1627 oratorio. The 11-room museum includes the cell where he died, displays telling the story of his life and philosophy, and a library. ⊠ *Calle del Carmen 13,* ☎ 953/750615. 🔁 €1.20. ⊗ *Tues.–Sun. 11–3 and 5–7.*

**⑩ Palacio de las Cadenas.** The "House of Chains," so called because decorative iron chains were once affixed to the columns of its main doorway, is more formally known as Palacio Juan Vázquez de Molina, and it's the work of Vandelvira. It currently houses the city government and, when not being refurbished, the Ceramics Museum. You can visit the patio with its classic arches and central fountain. ⊠ *Plaza de Váquez de Molina s/n,* ☎ 953/750440. 🔁 *Free.* ⊗ *Daily 10–2 and 5–9.*

**⑨ Palacio del Marqués de Mancera.** This palace was built in the 16th and 17th centuries for Pedro de Toledo, the viceroy of Peru, and is distinctly influenced by Valdevira. The neomedieval tower, like other such towers in the city, has an open gallery on top. The patio has timber touches intended to evoke buildings of the same era in South America. ⊠ *Plaza de Váquez de Molina s/n.* 🔁 *Free.* ⊗ *Daily 10 AM–11 AM.*

**⑫ Plaza del Primero de Mayo.** Flanked by the old town hall and the church of San Pablo, this square was the medieval hub of life in Úbeda, witnessing markets, executions, bullfights, elections, and celebrations. In the 19th century it was turned into a quiet garden plaza with a bandstand, palms, and acacias. In the center is a 1969 statue of San Juan de la Cruz, and on the south side is a line of houses where you're likely to see brightly colored flowers bursting from window boxes.

**⑧ Plaza Váquez de Molina.** Here's one of the best examples of Renaissance planning in Spain. It combines various spaces—open plazas, a square with trees, and two esplanades—that link churches, government buildings, and private palaces. A ban on parking, enforced by an on-the-spot police station, helps preserve the feeling of the place. A statue to the main architect of Úbeda, Andrés de Vandelvira, stands in front of the Palacio del Marqué de Mancera.

**⑳ Puerta de Losal.** This 14th-century Mudéjar city gate has a fine double arch, the smaller in the classic horseshoe shape. Beside it is a shrine to the Virgen de la Soledad. ⊠ *Between Calles Losal and Fuente Seca.*

★ **⑪ Sacra Capilla del Salvador.** The Plaza Vázquez de Molina, in the heart of the old town, is home to this most ornate of Úbeda's churches, built in 1559. It was designed by Vandelvira for Francisco de los Cobos, the secretary of Charles V, to serve as Cobos's burial place, and it's one of the few remaining privately owned churches in Spain. Vandelvira based his design on some 1536 plans by Diego de Siloé, architect of Granada's cathedral. The chapel was sacked in the frenzy of church burnings at the outbreak of the civil war but retains its ornate west facade and its altarpiece, which holds a rare Berruguete sculpture. Sacra Capilla del Salvador is photographed so often that it has become the city's unofficial symbol. Next door is the Renaissance palace that now serves as Úbeda's parador. ⊠ *Plaza Vázquez de Molina.* €2. ☉ *Oct.–Mar., Mon.–Sat. 10–2 and 4:30–7, Sun. 10:45–2 and 4–7; Apr.–Sept., Mon.–Sat. 10–2 and 5–7:30, Sun. 10:45–2 and 5–7:30.*

**㉑ Torre del Reloj.** This was originally a defensive tower in the town's medieval walls; the clock and bells were added in the 16th century. In an arched window is a copy of a painting (the original is in the town hall) of Nuestra Señora de los Remedios, a town favorite, before which (so the plaque says) Charles V, Philip II, and other kings have sworn respect to the local council. ⊠ *Plaza de la Constitución s/n.*

## Dining and Lodging

$$–$$$ ✕ **Mesón Gabína.** In 1977 the Expósito brothers turned this cave in the city's walls—once an Arab water reservoir—into an atmospheric mesón with a large menu, and today brother Nicolás is still the enthusiastic host. Good free tapas come with the strong but smooth house wine at the bar. A great starter is *habas con jamon* (broad beans with diced ham), and main courses include *lomo de cerdo al Jerez* (pork loin in sherry) and *chuleton a la brasa* (barbecued T-bone steak). ⊠ *Fuente Seca s/n,* ☎ *953/754207 or 953/757553. AE, DC, MC, V. No dinner Mon.*

$$$ ✕🏨 **Parador Condestable Dávalos.** This splendid parador occupies a
★ 16th-century ducal palace next to the Capilla del Salvador on the Plaza Vázquez de Molina. From the interior patio a slender grand stairway, decked with tapestries and suits of armor, leads up to the guest rooms, which have tiled floors, lofty wood ceilings, dark, Castilian-style furniture, and large bathtubs. Some rooms (such as 105) are huge, with mega-bathrooms. The candlelit dining room serves perhaps the best food in Úbeda, specializing in regional dishes. The *pimientos rellenos con perdiz* (green peppers stuffed with partridge in an almond and orange sauce) is both unique and exceptionally good. There's an atmospheric bar offering tapas in the vaulted basement. ⊠ *Plaza Vázquez de Molina 1, 23400,* ☎ *953/750345,* FAX *953/751259,* WEB *www.parador.es. 34 rooms, 2 suites. Restaurant, in-room safes, minibars, cable TV, bar, Internet, meeting rooms. AE, DC, MC, V.*

**$$$**   🏨 **Hotel Palacio de la Rambla.** This wonderful 1545 mansion in old Úbeda has been in the same family since it was built, and it still hosts the marquesa de la Rambla when she's in town. Eight of the rooms are open to guests. Each is different, but all are large and furnished with huge beds, antiques, tapestries, and works of art; some have chandeliers. The palace is arranged on two levels around a cool, ivy-covered patio with a magnificent salon and a small garden. ✉ *Plaza del Marqués 1, 23400,* ☎ *953/750196,* FAX *953/750267. 7 rooms, 1 suite. Café, minibars, meeting rooms. AE, MC, V. Closed June 15–Aug. 15.*

**$$**   🏨 **Hotel Husa Rosaleda de Don Pedro.** Part of the Husa chain, this comfortable, modern hotel with classic touches is in the historic center. The rooms, finished in pastel shades, have long beds and good baths. A feature is the huge, high-ceilinged library, and there is an outdoor terrace for eating near the small pool. The hotel will organize guided local visits and activities in the Cazorla Natural Park, including trips in four-wheel-drive vehicles. ✉ *Calle Obispo Toral 2, 23400,* ☎ *953/795147,* FAX *953/795149,* WEB *www.rosaledadedonpedro.com. 30 rooms, 4 suites. Restaurant, café, in-room safes, minibars, cable TV, pool, bar, Internet, meeting rooms. AE, DC, MC, V.*

**$**   🏨 **La Paz.** This homey hostel on a busy street in modern Úbeda is a good budget alternative. The rooms are simply furnished but well maintained, mostly with plain white walls and traditional dark-wood furniture. Some rooms (133, 114, 456, 458) have big bathrooms. ✉ *Calle Andalucía 1, 23400,* ☎ *953/750848,* FAX *953/752140,* WEB *www.hotel-lapaz.com. 45 rooms. Café, cable TV, bar, meeting rooms, some pets allowed. MC, V.*

### Nightlife

**Bar Siglo XV** (✉ Prior Blanca 7, ☎ 953/793199) is a disco-pub in an interesting 16th-century building with ivy-clad patio near Plaza de Andalucía. The ground-floor bar serves the three-story complex, which includes a vaulted cellar and upper galleries. Don't be put off by the uniformed civil guards who drop in early: they're students from the nearby academy in Baeza, bent on extracurricular activities. Unfortunately the owners pay more attention to the bar and the music than the state of the bathrooms.

### Shopping

Úbeda is the crafts capital of Andalusia, with some two dozen workshops devoted to carpentry, basket making, wrought iron, stone carving, stained glass, and, especially, pottery. The city's most famous potter was Pablo Tito, whose craft is carried on at three different workshops, run by two of his sons, Paco and Juan, and a son-in-law, Melchor, all of whom claim to be the sole true heir to the art. **Calle Valencia** is Úbeda's traditional potters' quarter, running from the bottom of town to the city's general crafts center, northwest of the old quarter; follow signs to Calle Valencia or Barrio de Alfareros. The extroverted **Juan Tito** (✉ Plaza del Ayuntamiento 12, ☎ 953/751302) can often be found at the wheel in his rambling shop packed with objects of every size and shape, behind Úbeda's town hall. **Paco Tito** (✉ C. Valencia 22, ☎ 953/751496 or 953/751496) sells excellent ceramics made by his son Pablo while he devotes himself to major creations such as clay sculptures of characters from *Don Quixote,* fired in a huge old Moorish-style kiln. His shop has a small museum above the studio area. **Melchor Tito** (✉ C. Valencia 44, ☎ 953/753365; ✉ C. Fuente Seco 17, ☎ 953/753365) is a purist, producing classic green-glazed pottery. All kinds of ceramics are sold at **Alfarería Góngora** (✉ Cuesta de la Merced 32, ☎ 953/754605).

Metalworking has been an art in Úbeda for centuries. **Forja Santa María** (✉ Jurado Gómez 15, ☎ 953/751281) has its forge alongside the art school in the Casa de las Torres and has intricate objects for sale in its shop; most pieces are made to order. For handmade *esparto* grassware, such as rugs, mats, and baskets, check out **Artesanía Blanco** (✉ Real 47, ☎ 953/750456), which is supplied by its own local factory.

OFF THE BEATEN PATH

**SABIOTE** – It's well worth the side trip to this charming medieval hilltop village above the Guadalimar River 8 km (5 mi) northeast of Úbeda. Declared a national historic site in 1972, it's surrounded by 14th- and 15th-century fortified walls, from which numerous lookout towers have great views, and the narrow streets are lined with 16th- and 17th-century palaces. The alcázar was renovated by Andrés de Vandelvira in 1543. You'll find a number of tapas bars and mesónes for refueling. The Úbeda tourist office has a useful booklet about the village.

# Cazorla

**❷** *48 km (35 mi) southeast of Úbeda.*

The remote and unspoiled Andalusian village of Cazorla, at the east end of the province of Jaén, is one of the gateways to the Cazorla Nature Park. Its location is spectacular: the pine-clad slopes and towering peaks of the Cazorla and Segura sierras rise above the village, and below it stretch miles of olive groves. The town's character is defined by its rural surroundings, but its shops and bars are often bustling. In spring, purple Judas trees blossom in the picturesque plazas. Good walking routes up the mountainside to hermitages and to the cliffs of El Chorro, where many vultures nest, start from here.

If you're traveling by car, park near the Plaza de la Constitución and do not drive into town unless you absolutely must. Some streets, without warning, become too narrow for vehicles, and others are very steep.

The large **Iglesia Mayor de Santa María** was mostly destroyed by the French during the War of Independence. It was originally built by master stonemasons Diego de Alcaráz and Gabriel Ruiz Tauste in the 16th century, probably under architect Andrés de Vandelvira. All that remains is the largest chapel, a wall with a doorway, and a tower with a niche and Mannerist window.

Soaring above Cazorla is the Moorish **Castillo de la Yedra,** reached by a steep road and from a small parking lot. The castle is the site of the **Museo de Artes y Costumbres Populares del Alto Guadalquivir.** It was considerably remodeled after the Moors were vanquished. Above the door is the coat of arms of the Archbishop Sandoval (1606), and the chapel has a fine Romanesque-Byzantine crucifix from the 17th century. On the second floor are displayed various weapons used by the Moors and Christians as well as 15th- to 17th-century furniture. The third floor shows three fine 17th-century Flemish tapestries. There are great views from the medieval tower, adjoining which is an annex with three rooms showing artifacts of rural domestic life in the Cazorla region. ✉ *Castillo de la Yedra,* ☎ *953/710039,* WEB *www.junta-andalucia.es/cultura.* ☞ *€1.50, free for EU citizens.* ☉ *Tues. 3–8, Wed.–Sat. 9–8, Sun. 9–2.*

About 2 km (1 mi) from Cazorla on the road up to the park is the little village of La Iruela with its **Castillo de La Iruela** perched perilously on top of a towering crag. It is said to have been built by the Knights Templar but is now mostly in ruins. ✉ *La Iruela, near Cazorla.*

## Dining and Lodging

**$–$$** ✕ **Restaurante La Sarga.** This surprisingly elegant restaurant has won numerous awards, probably because the owners were trained and worked in paradors. Starters include *sopa de la huerta con albondiguillos,* (vegetable soup with meatballs) and broad beans with diced ham, and main courses feature great local game such as *chuletas de jabalí en adobo* (wild-boar chops in bread crumbs) and trout in almond sauce. There's also a good six-course tasting menu. ⊠ *Plaza del Mercado s/n, opposite the market,* ☎ *953/721507. DC, MC, V. Closed Tues. and Sept.*

**$$** ✕️☲ **Villa Turística de Cazorla.** Here you'll find semidetached apartments sleeping one to six, on a hillside with superb views of the village of Cazorla. Each apartment has a kitchenette, fireplace, and balcony or terrace. The restaurant, dressed in cheerful yellow tones, specializes in trout, lamb, and game dishes. The management will organize excursions for you on bike, horse, or four-wheel-drive. The road entrance is on the right just before reaching Cazorla from the direction of Úbeda. ⊠ *Ladera de San Isicio s/n, 23470,* ☎ *953/710100,* 𝔽𝔸𝕏 *953/710152,* 𝖂𝖤𝖡 *www.villacazorla.com. 32 apartments. Restaurant, kitchenettes, refrigerators, pool, meeting rooms. MC, V.*

**$$** ☲ **Sierra de Cazorla.** Most rooms have stunning views at this low-slung hotel in La Iruela, nestled in a bend in the road leading up into the mountains 2 km (1 mi) above Cazorla. Rooms in the two-story modern section are functional but comfortable, and larger than those in the older building. From June to September a monitor is available to help arrange excursions and activities in the park. The restaurant dishes include cold cuts of game and fried rabbit with garlic. ⊠ *Carretera Sierra de Cazorla, Km 2, 23476 La Iruela,* ☎ *953/720015,* 𝔽𝔸𝕏 *953/720017,* 𝖂𝖤𝖡 *www.hotelsierradecazorla.com. 60 rooms, 4 suites. Restaurant, café, in-room safes, pool, bicycles, bar, meeting rooms, some pets allowed. AE, DC, MC, V.*

**$** ☲ **Hotel La Finca Mercedes.** This small hotel and restaurant is on the edge of La Iruela on the road from Cazorla to the nature park. Rooms are modern, with good bathrooms, and three have terraces overlooking the garden and pool, with a great view of endless olive groves beyond. Mercedes runs a cheerful house with a small, rustic bar and a comfortable restaurant, popular with locals. On the menu are regional dishes such as wild boar stew and fresh trout. ⊠ *Carretera Sierra de Cazorla, Km 1, 23476 La Iruela,* ☎ *953/721087,* 𝖂𝖤𝖡 *www.lafincamercedes.com. 9 rooms. Restaurant, pool, bar. No credit cards.*

TAPAS BARS

On one corner of the Plaza de la Constitución is the tiny, friendly **Cafe Bar Sola** (⊠ Calle Dr. Muñoz 30, ☎ 953/72058), which has good tapas, especially slightly picante venison sausage on a roll. **Las Vegas** (⊠ Plaza de la Corredera 17, ☎ 953/720277) offers a great plate of mixed tapas called *plato olimpico* as well as game dishes. **La Montería** (⊠ Plaza de la Corredera 18, ☎ 953/720542) has a good selection of *raciones*.

# Sierras de Cazorla, Segura, y Las Villas Nature Park

**㉔** *Torre del Vinagre Visitor Center 56 km (35 mi) from Cazorla.*

The Sierras de Cazorla, Segura, and Las Villas together make up the largest nature park in Spain and second largest in Europe, covering 535,000 acres. The park is a watershed between the Mediterranean and the Atlantic, with the Segura flowing into the former and the Guadalquivir into the latter. At the point where the three mountain ranges meet, the Guadalquivir has been dammed up to create El Tranco reservoir. The mountains—El Cerro de la Empanadas is the highest at 6,910 ft—were formed by the collision of the European and African tectonic plates, and the sedimentary nature of their rock explains the extensive water erosion, with numerous gorges and a proliferation of fossils. For hunting (allowed only for culling of specific beats) or fishing permits, apply to the Jaén office of the **Environmental Agency** (⊠ Calle Fuente del Servo 3, Las Fuentezuelas, 23071 Jaén, ☎ 953/012400) well in advance. Deer, wild boar, and mountain goats roam the slopes of this carefully protected patch of mountain wilderness, and hawks, eagles, and vultures soar overhead.

The park boasts 2,170 different species of flora and fauna, 34 of which are unique to the area, such as fuchsia-colored violets (*viola cazorlensis*). There are 52 orchid varieties as well as carnivorous plants (*atrapamoscas*) that trap flies and insects with their sticky leaves. Within the park, at Cañada de las Fuentes (Fountains Ravine), is the source of the Guadalquivir. The asphalt road from Cazorla village climbs up to 3,880 feet before dropping into the park, with a signed side road to the parador, and follows a section of the Guadalquivir River to the shores of **Lago Tranco de Beas** and continues northward. Rocky mountains, alpine meadows, pine forests, springs, waterfalls, caves, and gorges all make Cazorla a rewarding place to hike.

Past the Lago Tranco and the village of Hornos, the road takes you northeast into the Sierra de Segura, the least crowded section of the park. This mountain region was designated in 1748 as a "maritime province," even though the sea is 90 mi away, because tall pines felled on the slopes of the Sierra de Segura were floated down the Guadalquivir as far as Seville, where the wood was used to construct ships for the Spanish armada's galleons and the excursions to the Americas. Segura timber also went into building Seville's Royal Tobacco Factory and, a bit later, Spanish railroads. Although the mountains were replanted with introduced pine species, much of the original forest survives. The **Bosque de las Acebeas** is a shaded valley where giant holly bushes (*acebo* in Spanish) flourish along with pines and wild hazelnut trees.

The best source for information on the park, with route maps for walking, bicycling, or four-wheel-drive trips, is the **Cazorla tourist office** (✉ Paseo de Santo Cristo 17 bajo, 23470, ☎ 953/710102, WEB www.ayto-cazorla.es). The commercially run **visitor center** at Torre de Vinagre (✉ Ctra. de Tranco, ☎ no phone), open daily 11–2 and 4—6 (June 4–7, July–mid-Sept. 5–8) has seen better days, but a useful model of the park and displays explaining area flora, fauna, fossils, and geology are there. The staff can advise you on camping, fishing, and hiking. The park has seven well-equipped campsites, open June–October.

## Dining and Lodging

$$ ✕🏠 **Parador El Adelantado.** This modern, whitewashed parador with a red-tile roof stands peacefully isolated on the slopes of a valley at the edge of Cazorla Nature Park, 30 minutes' drive from Cazorla on a twisting road. It's a quiet place, popular with hikers, hunters, and anglers, and the few rooms with a lovely view, over the garden and across wooded valleys to distant peaks, are booked well in advance. The fine restaurant ($$$) specializes in regional cooking, such as *ajo blanco* (almond soup with garlic), delicious local trout with ham, and, in season, game dishes. The parador organizes half- or full-day four-wheel-drive excursions with excellent guide-drivers. ✉ *Sierra de Cazorla, 23470,* ☎ *953/727075,* FAX *953/727077,* WEB *www.parador.es. 32 rooms, 1 suite. Restaurant, café, minibars, cable TV, pool, bicycles, Ping-Pong, bar, meeting rooms. AE, DC, MC, V.*

## Outdoor Activities and Sports

### MOUNTAIN BIKING

The numerous trails offer all sorts of possibilities for mountain bikers. Bicycles can be rented at many hotels and places hiring out horses and four-wheel-drive vehicles. The Jaén Tourist Board produces a free leaflet with details of six routes in the park. **Excursiones Bujarkay** (✉

Calle Martínez Falero 28, Cazorla, ☎ 953/721111, WEB www.
guiasnativos.com) rents bikes in addition to providing for a full range
of excursions.

#### 4X4 EXCURSIONS

A number of companies offer excursions in the park in four-wheel-drive
vehicles, many with safari-style roofs that open at the back so you can
stand up and enjoy views and take photographs. Hotels can organize
these trips, which last either a half or a full day. The advantages are that
the trained driver-guides know where to go and can impart a wealth of
information, and you don't have to run your car through rough terrain
and miss the action because you are driving. **Excursiones Cazorla** (⊠ Ctra.
de la Sierra s/n, La Iruela, ☎ 639/993545, WEB www.cazorlaexcursiones.
com) conducts excursions for the parador and has excellent guides.

#### HIKING

There are many marked trails throughout the park; for easy hikes, your
hotel is likely to have all the information you need, and the Cazorla
tourist office is a useful resource. For guided hikes, consult one of the
area excursion companies.

#### HORSEBACK RIDING

This a perfect area for horseback riding. Practically every village seems
to have stables with waiting mounts—hotels can make arrangements.
**Quercus** (⊠ Cale Juan Domingo 2, Cazorla, ☎ 953/720115 or 953/
710068 or 606/686171, WEB www.excursionesquercus.com), one of the
area's long-established excursion companies, can arrange horseback
rides as well as four-wheel-drive excursions and other park activities.

*En Route*   You can leave the Cazorla Park by an alternate route to take in a spectacular gorge carved by the river Guadalquivir, here a rushing torrent
favored by kayaking enthusiasts. At the El Tranco dam, follow signs
to Villanueva del Arzobispo, where the N322 road takes you back to
Úbeda, Baeza, and Jaén.

## Segura de la Sierra

★ ㉕   *42 km (26 mi) from Torre de Vinagre.*

At 1,100 m (3,600 ft), the spectacular village of Segura de la Sierra is
crowned by an almost perfect castle. Impressive defense walls, a Moorish bath, and a square bullring are among its other landmarks.

A short trek from the village, the hilltop **Castillo de Segura** was originally Moorish but was remodeled by the Christians in the 13th century after the reconquest. It suffered damage during the French invasion
and underwent extensive rebuilding. Inside you can see the Patio de
Armas (weapons), the Santa Ana chapel, and the three-story Homage
Tower. ⊠ *Castillo de Segura,* ☎ *953/480280.* ☉ *Call for appointment
and obtain keys from town hall.*

The town's **murallas** (walls) were built by the Moors and have four
gates. The best preserved is Catena; the other three were re-erected in
the 16th century.

**Iglesia de Nuestra Señora del Collado** was built on Romanesque ruins.
Inside is an interesting Gothic-style sculpture of the Virgen de la Peña
in alabaster and a recumbant Christ, attributed to Gregorio Hernández. ☎ *953/480280.* ☉ *Open during church services; hours irregular.*

The **Baños Arabes** (Arab baths) are below street level and consist of
three long sections for the cold, warm, and hot rooms. Bathers lolled
under the horseshoe arches and barrel vaults with skylights. ☎ *953/
480280.* ☉ *Obtain keys from town hall.*

# JAÉN PROVINCE A TO Z

*To research prices, get advice from other travelers, and book travel arrangements, visit www.fodors.com.*

### AIR TRAVEL

Granada Airport is 100 km (63 mi) south of Jaén. Iberia and Air Europa have daily flights to and from Madrid, Barcelona, Palma de Mallorca, Melilla, and, in summer only, Tenerife.

➤ AIRPORT INFORMATION: **Granada Airport** (☎ 958/245200).

➤ TAXIS AND SHUTTLES: **J. González** (☎ 958/131309).

### BUS TRAVEL

If you're not driving, buses are the best method of transportation in this region. They run to most of the outlying towns and villages, and their connections between major cities are generally faster and more frequent than those of the few trains.

➤ BUS STATIONS: **Andújar** (✉ Calle Sevilla 27, ☎ 953/513072). **Baeza** (✉ Avda. Puche Pardo 1 ☎ 953/740468). **Bailén** (✉ Avda. de Málaga s/n, ☎ 953/670072). **Jaén** (✉ Plaza Coca de la Piñera s/n, ☎ 953/250106). **La Carolina** (✉ Plaza de la Delicias s/n, ☎ 953/660335 or 953/660023). **Linares** (✉ Avda. de María Auxiladora s/n , ☎ 953/693607). **Úbeda** (✉ San José 6, ☎ 953/752157).

### CAR RENTAL

Rent four-wheel-drive vehicles with route maps for Cazorla Nature Park from €45 a day from Cazorla Cars.

➤ LOCAL AGENCIES: **Avis** (✉ Avda. de Madrid s/n, near Cuétara, Jaén, ☎ 953/280937, 902/135531 throughout Spain, WEB www.avis.com). **Cazorla Cars** (✉ Cazorla and Arroyo Frío, ☎ 953/721992). **Europcar** (✉ Plaza Jaén por la Paz s/n, Jaén, ☎ 953/266011, 902/105030 throughout Spain, WEB www.europcar.com). **Hertz** (✉ Ctra. de Madrid 11, bajo 1, Jaén, ☎ 953/250701, 902/402405 throughout Spain, FAX 953/295597, WEB www2.hertz.com). **National Atesa** (✉ Estación RENFE, Plaza de Jaépor la Paz s/n, Jaén, ☎ 953/255963; ✉ Avda. Ciudad de Linares s/n, Úbeda, ☎ 953/791544; ☎ 902/100101 throughout Spain, WEB www.atesa.es).

### CAR TRAVEL

Be prepared for parking problems, especially in smaller towns where the street layouts date from Moorish times.

The province is bisected north–south by the A–4/N–323 freeways (Madrid–Granada) and east–west by the A–4/N–322 route (Córdoba–Albacete). These roads cross at Bailén. There are generally good, hassle-free roads between Jaén, Baeza, and Úbeda, but from there to Cazorla the roads have more curves. In the nature park roads are narrow, with occasional hairpin bends. Generally, though, driving is one of the most pleasant ways to see the countryside.

### EMERGENCIES

➤ CONTACTS: **Fire, Police, or Ambulance** (☎ 112).

### MAIL AND SHIPPING

➤ INTERNET CAFÉS: **Jaén** (Cyber Net Jaén, ✉ Cale Melchor C. Medina 11, ☎ 953/233083). **Andújar** (Cibercafé Badulake, ✉ Calle Las Monjas 5 bajo). **Baeza** (Cibercafé ✉ Calle San Pedro s/n, ☎ 953/744391). **Bailén** (Mundo Cyber, ✉ Calle Cristobal Colón 23). **Cazorla** (Interguías SL, ✉ Calle Martínez Falero 30, ☎ 953/710531).

➤ Post Offices: **Andújar** (✉ Plaza de la Constitución s/n, ☎ 953/500983). **Baeza** (✉ Calle Julio Burell 19, ☎ 953/740839). **Bailén** (✉ Plaza Reding 1, ☎ 953/670242). **Cazorla** (✉ Calle Mariano Extremera 2, ☎ 953/720261). **Jaén** (✉ Plaza de los Jardinillos, ☎ 953/247800). **Linares** (✉ Plaza San Francisco 1, ☎ 953/690614). **La Carolina** (✉ Calle Ondeanos 1, ☎ 953/660068). **Segura de la Sierra** (✉ Calle Wenceslao de la Cruz 4, ☎ 953/480079. **Úbeda** (✉ Calle Trinidad 4, ☎ 953/750031).

## TAXIS

➤ Contacts: **Andújar** (☎ 608/659721 or 630/141414). **Baeza** (☎ 619/222881). **Bailén** (☎ 658/840893 or 627/570702). **Cazorla** (☎ 953/720837). **Jaén** (☎ 953/222222). **La Carolina** (☎ 953/681462 or 953/662178). **La Iruela** (☎ 639/686915). **Linares** (☎ 953/691787). **Úbeda** (☎ 953/751490, 600/405579, 639/682912, or 667/733935).

## TOURS

### WALKING TOURS

Guided tours of Úbeda are offered by Artificis. Populo offers guided tours, lasting two hours, of the main sights in Baeza as well as a half-hour road-train trip. APIT can provide professional guides in Jaén.

➤ Tour Operators: **APIT** (Associació Provincial de Informadores Turísticos, ✉ Avda. de Madrid 2–4, Jaén, ☎ 953/254442). **Artificis** (✉ Juan Ruiz Gonzalez 19, next to parador, Úbeda, ☎ 953/758150). **Populo** (✉ Plaza de los Leones 1, Baeza, ☎ FAX 953/744370).

## TRAIN TRAVEL

The wonderful, high-speed AVE connects Madrid with Córdoba in less than two hours. Train service from Córdoba to Jaén, however, is poor, and there is no service at all between Granada and Jaén. Both Córdoba and Jaén have trains to Linares-Baeza, but from there you must take a bus into Baeza, Úbeda, or Cazorla. Andújar also has a station, and La Carolina is near the village of Vilches, which has daily trains at 11:50 AM and 9:40 PM to Jaén.

➤ Train Information: **Andújar station** (✉ Estació de Ferrocarril s/n, ☎ 957/769224). **Jaén station** (✉ Paseo de la Estación s/n, ☎ 953/251756). **Linares-Baeza station** (✉ off the N-322 at Barriada del Puente, ☎ 953/650202). **RENFE** (☎ 902/240202, WEB www.renfe.es). **Vilches station** (☎ 953/630279).

## TRAVEL AGENCIES

➤ Contacts: **Halcón Viajes** (✉ Calle Navas de Tolosa 9, Jaén, ☎ 953/259600; ✉ Calle Vientidos de Julio 4, Andújar, ☎ 953/522214; ✉ Calle Isaac Peral 8, Linares, ☎ 953/603048; ✉ Calle Rastro 13, Úbeda, ☎ 953/757557; ☎ 902/433000 throughout Spain, WEB www.halconviajes.com). **Viajes Marsans** (✉ Calle San Clemente 34, Jaén, ☎ 953/241400).

## VISITOR INFORMATION

➤ Tourist Information: **Andalusian Regional Tourist Offices: Baeza** (✉ Plaza de Pópulo s/n, ☎ FAX 953/740444, WEB www.adalucia.org). **Jaén** (✉ Maestra 13, ☎ 953/242624 or 953/190455, FAX 953/242624, WEB www.andalucia.org or www.promojaen.es). **Úbeda** (✉ Cale Baja del Marqués 4, ☎ 953/750897, FAX 953/792670). **Municipal Tourist Offices: Alcalá la Real** (✉ Calle Casa Pineda s/n, ☎ 953/582217). **Andújar** (✉ Torre de Reloj, Plaza de Santa María s/n, ☎ 953/504959). **Cazorla** (✉ Paseo de Santo Cristo 17 bajo, near Plaza de la Constitución, ☎ 953/710102, WEB www.ayto-cazorla.es). **La Carolina** (✉ Plaza Ayuntamiento s/n, ☎ 953/680882). **Martos** (✉ Avda. Oierre Cibié 14, ☎ 953/700139). **Segura de la Sierra** (✉ Calle Regidor Juan de Isla, ☎ 953/480280).

# 8 GRANADA PROVINCE

Granada shimmers red-gold and amber in the mind's eye, an indelibly romantic reverie. The Alhambra, suspended between the darkened river gorge of the Darro and the snowcapped Sierra Nevada, is every bit as mysterious and inspiring as Washington Irving found it nearly two centuries ago. The cobblestoned and bougainvillea-scented Albayzín hillside, Sacromonte and its Gypsy caves, and the city center bustling beneath: Granada is visually voluptuous, a dreamlike place you will not easily forget.

By George
Semler

**H**ELD BY THE MOORS for two and a half centuries longer than her Andalusian sister cities, Granada is arguably Spain's most romantic and exotic metropolis. Its dual heritage—part Islamic and Eastern, part Christian and European—gives Granada a diversity that dazzles and bewitches. Washington Irving and the 19th-century romantics found the Alhambra, the medieval Moorish quarter known as the Albayzín, and the Gypsy-inhabited hillside of Sacromonte to be paradigms of Spain's East-meets-West fascination. Add to this the Renaissance and baroque architecture of Granada's 500-year Christian tenure, and the result is a visual feast, attested to by well-worn Granada sayings such as *Dale una limosna, mujer, que no hay nada como ser ciego en Granada* (Give him alms, woman, for there is nothing like being blind in Granada) and *Quien no haya visto Granada no ha visto nada* (Whoever has not seen Granada has not seen anything).

In the 13th century, King Ferdinand III, the greatest champion of the Christian reconquest, captured Baeza, Úbeda, Córdoba, Jaén, and, in 1246, Seville. The Moors fled south to Granada, at the junction of the rivers Darro and Genil, where they remained for no less than 250 years. The 14th and 15th centuries were filled with constant battles and skirmishes between Moors and Christians, until Ferdinand of Aragón and Isabella of Castile, known jointly as the Catholic Monarchs, scored the ultimate victory of the reconquest. Split by internal squabbles, Granada's Moorish Nasrid dynasty presented Ferdinand of Aragón with the chance he needed in 1491. Spurred by Isabella's religious fanaticism, Ferdinand laid siege to the city for seven months, and on January 2, 1492, Boabdil, the "Rey Chico" (Boy King), was forced to surrender the keys of the city. As Boabdil fled the Alhambra by the Puerta de los Siete Suelos, he asked that the gate be sealed forever. He took to the Alpujarra mountains east of Granada for another decade of purgatory after his defeat.

The Moors left their mark here, but so did the Christian conquerors and their descendants. Granada today is rich in Gothic chapels, a Renaissance cathedral, and baroque monasteries and churches. Elsewhere in the province, sturdy, stone mansions and baroque churches of noble towns such as Guadix, Baza, and Huéscar contrast dramatically with the humble, whitewashed village houses of the Alpujarra.

The province of Granada offers a variety of geography as well as architecture. From snowcapped peaks, an hour's drive will take you through subtropical valleys to the coast of the Mediterranean. Granada's fertile plain (known as *la vega*), covered with lush orchards and tobacco and poplar groves, stretches up to the mountains of the majestic Sierra Nevada. Snow-clad most of the year, this range has the highest peaks on mainland Spain, the 11,427-ft Mulhacén (named for Muley Hacen, father of Boabdil) and the 11,215-ft Veleta. The Alpujarra, the mountains running east to west on the south side of the Sierra Nevada peaks, are a treasury of tiny villages and alpine valleys, and the Altiplano (literally, high plain) in the province's northeast corner combines parched lunar expanses with the clear rivers and wooded hillsides of the Sierra de Castril.

## Pleasures and Pastimes

### Dining

As with all things Granadan, the Moorish culinary influence is stronger here than anywhere else in Andalusia. The use of almonds and the combinations of sweet and salt are strongly redolent of North African cuisine, as are the bitter oranges and the widespread use of Granada's emblematic fig. Sugar mills were one of the chief sources of Granada's wealth until well into the 19th century, and as a result pastries made of syrups, almonds, and flour became specialties, particularly in convents, all over the province.

*Habas con jamón de Trevélez* (broad beans with ham from the Alpujarran village of Trevélez) is Granada's most famous regional dish, with *tortilla de Sacromonte* (an omelet traditionally made of calf's brains, sweetbreads, diced ham, potatoes, and peas) just behind. *Sopa sevillana* (tasty fish and seafood soup made with mayonnaise), surprisingly named for Granada's most direct rival city, is another staple, and *choto albaicinero* (braised kid with garlic, also known simply as *choto al ajillo*) is also a specialty. Moorish dishes such as *bstella* (from the Moorish *bastilla,* a salty-sweet puff pastry with pigeon or other meat, pine nuts, and almonds) and spicy *crema de almendras* (almond cream soup) are not uncommon on Granada menus.

Worth a try is the earthy local *vino de la costa* from the Alpujarras region served in many taverns and restaurants, though better wines from the Rioja and Ribera de Duero are advisable.

Lunch is the main meal here. Restaurants start serving around 2, but most tables don't fill up until at least 3, and many diners are still at the table at 5. After such a long, late lunch, few Andalusians dine out in the evening; instead, they make the rounds of the bars, dipping into tapas and plates of ham, shellfish, and cheese. If you go for lunch around 2, you won't need a reservation; wait until 3 and you may have trouble finding a table. Similarly, in the evening, you shouldn't have a problem if you dine early—at, say, 9 or 10; 10:30 to 11:30 is the peak time.

| CATEGORY | COST* |
|---|---|
| **$$$$** | over €18 |
| **$$$** | €13–€18 |
| **$$** | €8–€13 |
| **$** | under €8 |

*per person for a main course at dinner*

## Fiestas

Granada celebrates **La Toma** (the Capture), the 1492 surrender to the Catholic Monarchs, on January 2. On January 5, the eve of the **Día de los Reyes** (Feast of the Three Kings), every city and village holds processions of the three Wise Men. On February 1, Granada organizes a **romería** (pilgrimage) to the Monastery of San Cecilio, on Sacromonte. Granada is wild during **Carnival,** on the days leading up to Ash Wednesday, and celebrates **Semana Santa** (Holy Week) with dramatic religious processions of pointy-hatted penitents and floral floats bearing Christ on the cross and the Virgin Mary. Granada's **Día de la Cruz** (Day of the Cross) is celebrated the first Sunday in May, **San Isidro** on May 15, and **Mariana Pineda** (a 19th-century political heroine) on May 26. June is marked by **Corpus Christi** and **San Pedro** (June 29); the **International Festival of Music and Dance,** with some events in the Alhambra, begins in late June and runs into July. Granada honors **Nuestra Señora de las Angustias** (Our Lady of Distress) on the last Sunday in September and celebrates the **Romería de San Miguel** (Procession of St. Michael) on September 29.

## Hiking and Walking

South of Granada, the Sierra Nevada and the Alpujarra have some of the most impressive walking routes and panoramic vistas in all of Spain. The towns of Capileira and Trevélez are important jumping-off points for treks to the La Veleta and Mulhacén, Spain's highest peaks.

The GR-7 walking trail across the Alpujarra is one of Spain's most famous and picturesque long-distance hiking routes, and the local routes around the central Alpujarra between Bérchules and Yegen offer three circular day trips and a fourth jaunt connecting the villages of Mecina Bombarón and Yegen. The short, three-hour *Sendero de Gerald Brenan* (Gerald Brenan trail) honors the famous British Hispanist and author of *The Spanish Labyrinth* in a tour around Yegen, the town where Brenan lived for more than half a century, and the *Sendero de las Acequias* follows the ancient Moorish irrigation canals (*acequias*) up and down the gorges north of Mecina Bombarón. The *Sendero de la Salud* begins and ends at Yegen after climbing up through fields and gorges to Los Alamos and descending through chestnut forests. Finally, the trail connecting Mecina Bombarón and Yegen crosses a Roman bridge, an oak forest, and an ancient mill before descending to Yegen, where the excellent Rincón de Yegen will put you back on the map with its fine traditional yet creative cuisine.

## Lodging

Granada and its province have accommodations for all budgets, from simple bed-and-breakfasts and *agroturismos* (farm stays) to luxurious paradors. At the high end, the Parador de San Francisco, nestled beside the Alhambra, is a magnificent way to enjoy both Granada and the storied past of southern Spain, though many visitors prefer to stay in the restored Moorish palaces of the Albayzín and have the Alhambra across the way to admire and visit. Bed-and-breakfast lodgings, available in many villages, give you access to the countryside and its rich folk traditions.

Finding lodging in Granada during high season can be difficult: the Alhambra is the most popular monument in Spain. The city has plenty of hotels, but the high season runs long, from Easter to late October. Hotels on the Alhambra hill must be reserved well in advance, and those in the city center, around the Puerta Real and Acera del Darro, are unbelievably noisy—ask for rooms at the back. Reserve well ahead for Holy Week and the International Festival of Music and Dance (mid-June–mid-July). If you're traveling by car, inquire with hotels about parking.

| CATEGORY | COST* |
|---|---|
| $$$$ | over €140 |
| $$$ | €100–€140 |
| $$ | €60–€100 |
| $ | under €60 |

*All prices are for a standard double room, excluding tax.*

## Skiing

Morocco's Rif mountain range continues, after a brief interruption by the Strait of Gibraltar, into Andalusia's Sierra Nevada, site of the 1996 World Alpine Ski Championships; at the Pradollano and Borreguiles stations there's good skiing from December through May. These are the only ski stations in the world with a cultural center of Granada's scope and quality less than half an hour from the snow. And, when the light is right, morning views from the 3,398-ft Veleta peak over the Alpujarra and across the Mediterranean to Africa give you a powerful geographical rush.

Both the Pradollano and the higher Borreguiles stations have a special snowboarding circuit, floodlit night slopes, a children's ski school, and après-ski sun and swimming in the Mediterranean less than an hour (33 km/20 mi) away. The Sierra Nevada has become an international rendezvous point for snowboarding culture, with a school, access to all runs, and a special "snow park" for snowboarders. Just as nearby Tarifa is a world windsurfing capital, Sierra Nevada, with its preponderantly spring snow and sunny climate, is now touted as a snowboarder's paradise. Combination ski and golfing trips are also popular, with mornings in powder snow followed by afternoons on some of the world's top golf courses.

# Exploring Granada and Granada Province

About a square mile in its roughly circular area (using La Cartuja, the Huerta de San Vicente's Federico García Lorca museum, Campo del Príncipe, the Alhambra, and Sacromonte as outer limits), the city center of Granada can be thoroughly walked in three days, though five would be more comfortable. To save wear and tear on your feet, taxis are useful for reaching the more peripheral points, though the four areas to explore carefully—the Alhambra, the Albayzín, el Realejo (around Campo del Príncipe), and el Centro (around the cathedral)—are too small and densely packed to require transport.

The province of Granada outside of the capital is divided into six regions ranging from the fertile western Poniente Granadino to the parched eastern Altiplano, a *meseta* (high plateau) 1,000–1,500 ft above sea level at the provincial border with Murcia. In between are the Sierra Nevada, with the Iberian Peninsula's tallest mountains; the Alpujarra, rough foothills and valleys on the southern slopes of the Sierra Nevada; the Costa Tropical beaches along the Mediterranean coast; and the Guadix y Marquesada flatland north of the Sierra Nevada, west of the Sierra de Baza, and south of the Sierra de Castril. Granada has the most extreme geographical variety of any Spanish province, ranging from alpine glaciers to tropical littoral in less than 30 km (18 mi) of horizontal distance between the 11,427-ft Mulhacén peak and the beach at Playa La Mamola.

## Great Itineraries

One day in Granada should be spent at the Alhambra in the morning and exploring the Albayzín in the afternoon and evening. If you're here longer, spend the first morning exploring the center of Granada. This way you can go by the tourist office at Plaza de Mariana Pineda 10 and pick up maps, lists of taverns, and well-explained cultural routes while getting the general lay of the land. Trips out to the edge of town to see La Cartuja and the Federico García Lorca museum at Huerta de San Vicente are walkable, depending on your energy level and the time available. It is advisable to get these outlying visits and Christian Granada in early before the Alhambra and the Albayzín completely hijack your imagination.

The province of Granada's most interesting road trip is the drive through the valleys and villages of the Alpujarra range, an 85-km (51-mi) tour ideally accomplished with an overnight stay at Bérchules or Yegen. The 6,500-ft mountain pass at Puerto de la Ragua leads north past Lacalahorra to Guadix and on into the Altiplano and the Sierra de Castril. Granada's Costa Tropical is yet another option—you can explore beach towns such as Salobreña, Almuñécar, Marina del Este, and La Herradura.

IF YOU HAVE 3 DAYS

Visit central Christian monuments of **Granada** ①–㉟ around the **cathedral** ㉙ on the first morning. A trip out to the **Monasterio de la Cartuja** ㉝ and the **Casa-Museo Federico García Lorca** ㉞ at Huerta de San Vicente can be followed by a tour of the upper part of the Albayzín in the afternoon and evening. Sunset should find you at the **Mirador de**

**San Nicolás** ⑪ (along with everyone else, young and old, local and otherwise). Dinner overlooking the Alhambra is a must, at one of the terrace restaurants in the Albayzín. On Day 2, explore the lower part of the Albayzín, starting along the River Darro and working your way into the heart of this labyrinthine hillside Moorish quarter. In the afternoon, taxi up to **Cármen de los Mártires** ⑱ and work your way down the hillside past the **Torres Bermejas** ㉑ through the Realejo district to the **Campo del Príncipe** ㉕. Dedicate Day 3 to the **Alhambra** ① for as long as possible, followed by an early evening drive up into the Alpujarra for a night at ⛺ **Bérchules** ㊼ or ⛺ **Yegen** ㊽.

IF YOU HAVE 5 DAYS

Follow the above itinerary for the first three days, dedicating all of the third day to the Alhambra, with time in late afternoon and evening for further exploring in the Albayzín and another dinner overlooking the palace and the Sierra Nevada behind. On Day 4 drive up into the Alpujarra, stopping along the way at **Capileira** ㊺ and **Trevélez** ㊻ and spending a night at ⛺ **Bérchules** ㊼ or ⛺ **Yegen** ㊽. On Day 5 drive through the Puerta de la Ragua, take a glimpse at the Renaissance castle at Lacalahorra, and continue to **Guadix** ㊿ for a look at the area's caves or, alternately, head for the coast and a night on the beach at ⛺ **Almuñécar** ㊾.

IF YOU HAVE 7 DAYS

With seven days to spend in and around Granada, you can complete the five-day recommendations at a more leisurely pace and fit in a day skiing in winter, or hiking up to Spain's highest peak in the Sierra Nevada or on the beach in spring or summer. **Pradollano** ㊷ is the winter sport destination. Beach towns such as **Salobreña** ㊾ and **Almuñécar** ㊿ have much to offer, and the northeastern Altiplano and the Sierra de Castril have rugged and unspoiled streams and forests to explore.

## When to Tour

Granada and its province are so stunning when the bougainvillea, jasmine, jacaranda, morning glories, roses, hibiscus, geraniums, and a thousand other flowers cascade down from medieval walls, balconies, and dormer windows that it's hard to advise coming anytime but spring and early summer. Granada's high season begins at Easter and continues until the middle or end of October. With reservations and advance tickets to the Alhambra, you should be able to get along fine during this period despite the crowds. The heat is oppressive from June through September, but air-conditioning is becoming standard in even the simplest bars, taverns, pensiones, and *hostales*; from the standpoint of weather, May and October are the best months. The Spanish *Puente de la Constitución* (long weekend of the Constitution) makes the end of the first week of December a hard time to find a bed in Granada. In winter, temperatures can drop to the 30s, and the wind off the Sierra Nevada can be as chilling as any in New England. The period from December through April brings skiers to the city for the slopes of the Sierra Nevada 40 km (24 mi) away. November's probably the flattest (and thus most intimate) month, but the floral display is less eye-popping, even though there are perennials (such as the *jazmin solanum*) that bloom year-round.

# GRANADA

*430 km (265 mi) south of Madrid, 261 km (162 mi) east of Córdoba.*

Granada rises lightly and majestically from a plain onto three hills, dwarfed—on a clear day—by the mighty snowcapped peaks of the Sierra Nevada. Atop one of these hills languishes the red-gold Alhambra palace, at once splendidly imposing and infinitely delicate. The stunning view from its heights takes in the sprawling ancient Moorish quarter, the Albayzín, the caves of the Sacromonte hill, and the fertile vega beyond with its orchards, tobacco fields, and poplar groves. The Realejo hill and neighborhood, once the medieval Jewish quarter, descend from the Alhambra's southern side, whereas the city center around the cathedral occupies the basin below.

## The Albayzín and the Alhambra

Much of Granada's dramatic scenery is the result of the city's steep hills, river gorges, and the views back and forth across them. The Albayzín, so-named for the Moors from Baeza (*"Baez-ines"*) who originally settled here, is the city's most picturesque and surprising area to explore, with its steep cobblestone streets and flower-covered villas. Covering a hill of its own, across the Darro ravine from the Alhambra, this ancient Moorish neighborhood is a fascinating mix of dilapidated white houses, elegant Moorish palaces, and immaculate *cármenes* (private villas in walled gardens). Founded in 1228 after Baeza was captured by Saint King Ferdinand III, the Albayzín guards its old Moorish atmosphere jealously, though its 30 mosques were long since converted to Mudéjar or baroque churches. A 500-yard stretch of original Moorish ramparts runs beside the Cuesta de la Alhacaba, and farther out, another section, nearly three times as long, defends the city's northern edge.

The Albayzín can be entered from either the Cuesta de Elvira or the Plaza Nueva. (On Cuesta de Elvira and the adjoining Calderería, be sure to try one of the delightful tea shops; thanks to its Moorish heritage, Granada serves some of the best mint tea in all of Spain.) But the classic way into the Albayzín begins in the Plaza Santa Ana and follows the Carrera del Darro, Paseo Padre Manjón (Paseo del los Tristes), and Cuesta del Chapiz. Once inside the Albayzín, allow your eyes and instincts to guide you freely from one irresistible spot to another.

### A Good Walk

It's best to save at least a half to a full day for the **Alhambra** ① and the neighboring sites on the Alhambra hill: the Alcazaba, Generalife, Alhambra Museum, and Museo de Bellas Artes in the Palacio de Carlos V. The following walk covers the hillside across from the Alhambra, the winding, flower-choked, cobblestone alleys of the Albayzín, Granada's most magical and romantic neighborhood.

Begin from Plaza Nueva, overlooked by the 16th-century Real Cancillería (Royal Chancery), which now houses the Tribunal Superior de Justicia (High Court). Artisans have set up shops in the surrounding area. At the north end of the plaza is the adjacent Plaza Santa Ana, where you'll find the Mudéjar **Iglesia de San Gil y Santa Ana** ② designed by Diego de Siloé. After a look through the church, make a short probe up the left bank (to your right, looking upstream) of the River Darro on Calle Santa Ana. At No. 16 is the Hammam, an excellent, fully functioning Moorish bathhouse, tearoom, and restaurant. Back down on Carrera del Darro on the other side of the river is the **Casa de los Pisa** ③, with the perfectly conserved room where San Juan de Dios expired in 1550. North of Plaza Santa Ana on the Carrera del Darro you'll reach the 11th-century Arab baths, **El Bañuelo** ④. Just up Carrera del Darro is the 16th-century **Casa de Castril** ⑤, which houses Granada's Archaeological Museum. The church across the street over the Darro is another Mudéjar gem, the **Iglesia de San Pedro y San Pablo** ⑥. Follow the river along the Paseo del Padre Manjón—also known as the Paseo de los Tristes—to the end, and have a look at the

## Granada

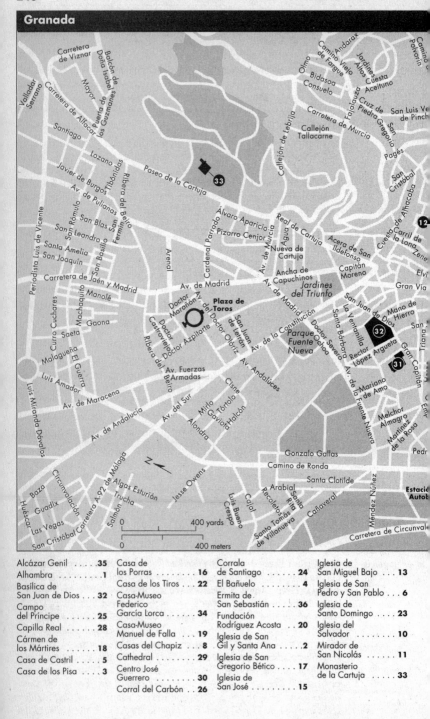

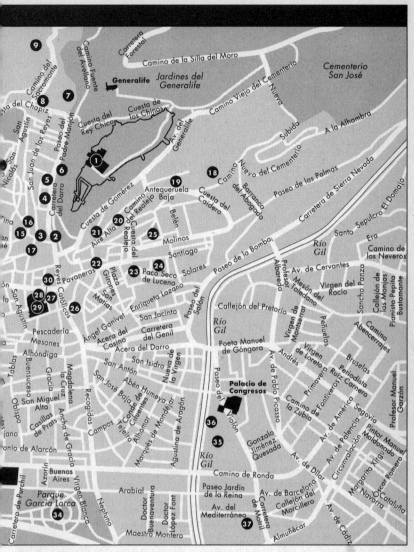

**Palacio de los Córdoba** ⑦. Head north up the Cuesta del Chapíz to the Morisco **Casas del Chapiz** ⑧. East of here are the caves of the **Sacromonte** ⑨, which require a special expedition on foot or by minibus. Continue up La Cuesta del Chapiz to the Plaza del Salvador, center of the Albayzín alto (upper Albayzín) where the **Iglesia del Salvador** ⑩ occupies the spot on which the Mezquita Mayor (main mosque) once stood.

The **Mirador de San Nicolás** ⑪, the best-known belvedere for sunset views of the Alhambra, and the 16th-century Iglesia de San Nicolás are just a five-minute walk from the Iglesia del Salvador through Callejón Horno de San Agustín. From here, walk west through Calle de San Nicolás to Calle Nuevo de San Nicolás and take a right on Calle Pilar Seco to Calle de los Monjes, where a left leads inside the section of Moorish walls to the corner of Callejón del Gallo. Just around the corner is one of the gems of the Albayzín, the painstakingly restored **Palacio Dar-al-Horra** ⑫, an exquisite Moorish palace built for Aixa, mother of Boabdil, the last Moorish king. Continue through Callejón del Gallo into Plaza de San Miguel Bajo, a pretty little space with terraces and cafés under the Mudéjar **Iglesia de San Miguel Bajo** ⑬. Just past the church on Calle Nuevo de San Nicolás is the **Monasterio de Santa Isabel la Real** ⑭ with its flamboyant Gothic doorway next to a Mudéjar *alminar* (call-to-prayer minaret), transformed into a bell tower. From here, walk down the Calle de San Jose past the **Iglesia de San José** ⑮ (also with alminar–turned–bell tower), and through Placeta de las Porras and the beautifully restored cultural center at the **Casa de los Porras** ⑯. Cuesta de San Gregorio leads past the **Iglesia de San Gregorio Bético** ⑰ into Calle Calderería Nueva, which drops down through a cluster of shops to the edge of the Albayzín on Calle Elvira, nearly underneath the cathedral. Calderería Vieja, which forks left, will return you to Plaza Nueva, where you started a few light-years ago.

TIMING

Set aside a half day at minimum for the Alhambra and the same for the Albayzín. Both could be happily explored for days on end.

## Sights to See

★ ❶   **The Alhambra.** Walking *to* the Alhambra can be as inspiring as walking *around* it. If you're up to a long, scenic approach, start in the Plaza Nueva and climb the Cuesta de Gomerez—through the slopes of green elms planted by the Duke of Wellington—to reach the **Puerta de las Granadas** (Pomegranate Gate), a Renaissance gateway built by Charles V and topped by three pomegranates, symbols of Granada. Just past the gate, take the path branching off to the left to the **Puerta de la Justicia** (Gate of Justice), one of the Alhambra's entrances. Yusuf I built the gate in 1348; on its two arches are carved a key and a hand, with the five fingers representing the five laws of the Koran.

Unless you've already bought a ticket (see *below*), continue up the hill along the Alhambra's outer walls to the parking lot and the adjacent ticket office. If you're driving, you'll approach the Alhambra from the opposite direction; just be warned that parking here is expensive, and the lot has virtually no shade. It's more convenient to take a taxi or the minibus that runs from the Plaza Nueva every 15 minutes. For walking down, don't miss the sylvan solitude of the Cuesta de los Chinos that winds from the top of the River Darro and enters the palace grounds between the Alhambra and the Generalife. (At the entrance, don't hesitate to rent the excellent earphone guide to the Alhambra, a cleverly produced tour of the palace with none other than Washington Irving himself to guide you.)

The Alhambra, whose name derives from the Arabic *qa'lat al-hamra* (red castle), was begun in 1238 by Ibn el-Ahmar, or Alhamar, the first king of the Nasrids. The location on the Sabica hill, one of seven hills around Granada, was chosen less for defensive purposes than for dramatic ones: it was the optimum point for being seen and admired by every citizen. The great citadel once comprised an entire complex of houses, schools, baths, barracks, and gardens surrounded by defense towers and seemingly impregnable walls. Today, only the Alcazaba fortress and the Nasrid Royal Palace, built chiefly by Yusuf I (1334–54) and his son Mohammed V (1354–91), remain. The palace is an endless, intricate fantasy of patios, pools, arches, and cupolas fashioned from wood, plaster, marble, and tile, lavishly colored and adorned with marquetry and ceramics in geometric patterns, surmounted by delicate, frothy profusions of lacelike stucco and *mocárabes* (ornamental stalactites). Built of perishable materials, it was never intended to last, but to be forever replaced and replenished by succeeding generations.

By the early 17th century, ruin and decay had set in, and the Alhambra was abandoned by all but tramps and stray dogs. Napoléon's troops commandeered it in 1812, but their attempts to blow it up were foiled by a disabled French soldier who removed the fuses. In 1814, the Alhambra's fortunes rose with the arrival of the Duke of Wellington, who came here to escape the pressures of the Peninsular War. Soon afterward, in 1829, Washington Irving came to live on the premises and helped revive interest in the crumbling palace, in part through his 1832 book *Tales of the Alhambra*. In 1862, Granada finally launched a complete restoration program that has been carried on ever since.

Across from the main entrance is the original fortress, the **Alcazaba.** Its ruins are dominated by the **Torre de la Vela** (Watchtower), whose summit offers superlative views of the city—to the north, the Albayzín; to the northeast, the Sacromonte; and to the west, the cathedral. The tower's great bell was once used by both the Moors and the Christians to announce the opening and closing of the irrigation system on Granada's great plain, but on January 2, 1492, the bell forever replaced the haunting call to prayer of the Islamic muezzin.

The Renaissance **Palacio de Carlos V** (Palace of Charles V), with its perfectly square exterior enclosing a circular interior courtyard, stands imposingly and incongruously on what was originally the site of the sultans' private apartments. A perfect metaphor for the imposition of European Renaissance values onto the refined Arabic and Andalusian culture, the palace was designed in 1526 by Michelangelo pupil Pedro Machuca. Once used for bullfights and mock tournaments, today the structure's perfect acoustics make it a fine setting for summer symphony concerts during Granada's International Festival of Music and Dance (about which there's an excellent retrospective on the ground floor of the palace). Part of the building houses the **Museo de la Alhambra,** devoted to Islamic art, open Tuesday through Saturday 9–2:30. Upstairs is the **Museo de Bellas Artes** (Museum of Fine Arts), with an interesting collection of paintings by, among others, Fray Juan Sanchez Cotan (1560–1627) and the Granada painter and collector José María Rodríguez Acosta (1878–1941). The museum is open Wednesday through Saturday 9–6, Sunday 9–2:30, and Tuesday 2:30–6. The Palace of Charles V and the museums can be visited independently of the Alhambra.

A wisteria-covered walkway leads to the heart of the Alhambra, the **Palacios Nazaries** (Nasrid Royal Palace), sometimes called the Casa Real (Royal Palace). Here, delicate apartments, lazy fountains, and tranquil pools contrast vividly with the hulking fortifications outside. The interior walls are decorated with elaborately carved inscriptions from

244

# The Alhambra

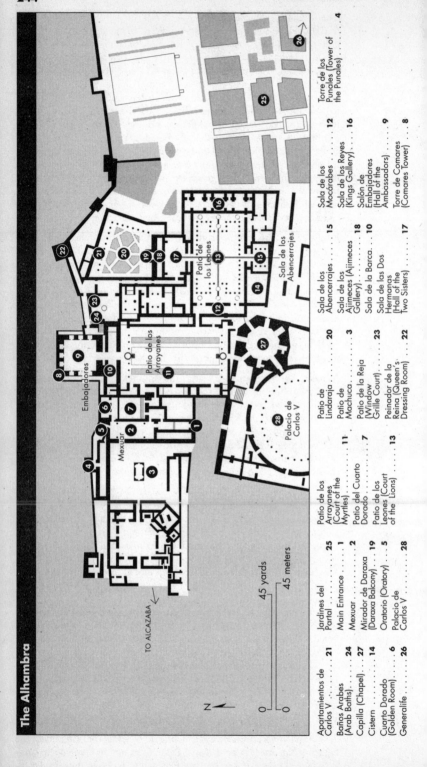

TO ALCAZABA

N

0   45 yards
0   45 meters

Mexuar

Embajadores

Patio de los Arrayanes

Patio de los Leones

Sala de los Abencerrajes

Palacio de Carlos V

Apartamientos de
Carlos V . . . . . . . . **21**

Baños Arabes
(Arab Baths) . . . . **24**

Capilla (Chapel) . . . **27**

Cistern . . . . . . . . . **14**

Cuarto Dorado
(Golden Room) . . . **6**

Generalife . . . . . . . **26**

Jardines del
Partal . . . . . . . . . **25**

Main Entrance . . . . **1**

Mexuar . . . . . . . . **2**

Mirador de Daraxa
(Daraxa Balcony) . . **19**

Oratorio (Oratory) . . **5**

Palacio de
Carlos V . . . . . . . **28**

Patio de los
Arrayanes
(Court of the
Myrtles) . . . . . . . . **11**

Patio del Cuarto
Dorado . . . . . . . . **7**

Patio de los
Leones (Court
of the Lions) . . . . . **13**

Patio de
Lindaraja . . . . . . . **20**

Patio de
Machuca . . . . . . . **3**

Patio de la Reja
(Window
Grille Court) . . . . . **13**

Peinador de la
Reina (Queen's
Dressing Room) . . . **22**

Sala de los
Abencerrajes . . . . . **15**

Sala de los
Ajimeces (Ajimeces
Gallery) . . . . . . . . **18**

Sala de la Barca . . . **10**

Sala de las Dos
Hermanas
(Hall of the
Two Sisters) . . . . . **22**

Sala de los
Mocárabes . . . . . . **12**

Sala de los Reyes
(Kings Gallery) . . . **16**

Salón de
Embajadores
(Hall of the
Ambassadors) . . . . **9**

Torre de Comares
(Comares Tower) . . **8**

Torre de los
Punales (Tower of
the Punales) . . . . . **4**

the Koran in Kufic script, the most repeated being "There is no Conqueror but God," Mohammed V's standard response when hailed as *Mansur* (Conqueror).

The Royal Palace is divided into three sections: the **Mexuar,** where business, government, and palace administration were headquartered; the **Serrallo,** or **Hall of Comares,** used for state events, receptions, and other formal occasions; and the **harem,** the private residence of the sultan's family. Connected by subtle, off-center entryways and porticoes, the Royal Palace communicates a palpable sense of being drawn into an increasingly fantastic labyrinth progressing from routine elegance through formal splendor to interior or spiritual ecstasy.

The Mexuar (administrative office) was converted to a chapel by the Catholic Monarchs, as the crowns over the door and the inscription *non plus ultra* attest. Its windows overlook the formal Jardines de Machuca, named for the architect of the Palacio de Carlos V, who lived in these rooms during his time in the Alhambra. These chambers include a prayer niche, the **Oratorio,** suspended over the northern edge of the palace with bird's-eye views of the Albayzín and Sacromonte. The Mexuar leads into the **Cuarto Dorado** and the **Patio del Cuarto Dorado** with a marble basin in the center, intricate gold lettering and ornamentation on the carved wood ceiling of the covered area, and a richly decorated facade with polychrome wood friezes, arabesques, and latticed jalousies on the overlooking balconies designed to permit discreet observation of visitors from above. The reiterated four over four, eight-pointed star design (based on the Pythagorean theorem) alludes to the four rivers (milk, honey, oil, and wine) and the four trees (cypress, cedar, olive, and fig) of Islamic paradise.

The Serrallo, the second section of the Nasrid palace, is a series of state rooms where the sultans held court and entertained ambassadors and dignitaries. In the heart of the Serrallo is the **Patio de los Arrayanes** (Court of the Myrtles), with a long goldfish pool surrounded by myrtle bushes, an evergreen (the official color of Islam) held sacred as a symbol of love, fertility, and peace. This patio is, along with the Patio de los Leones, the most spectacular use of water in the palace, a constant theme in the Alhambra and in all Moorish architecture and engineering. (That Granada received fresh water from the snows of the Sierra Nevada made it the definiton of earthly paradise for the Moors, descendants of desert tribes, and the Alhambra clearly intends to suggest this.) The reflections in the dark pool, occasionally set to movement by the fins of a goldfish, show in endlessly changing ways the reddish ramparts above and the flights of pigeons, swallows, sparrows, and larks that live in and around the Alhambra. Granada's summer International Festival of Music and Dance holds classical concerts here, with chairs set up around the pool, an event to start reserving tickets for months, if not years, in advance.

At the northern end of the patio is the **Sala de la Barca** (Hall of the Boat), often thought to have been named for the coffered ceiling's similarity to the hull of an upturned boat, though in fact the name derives from the Arabic word *baraka* (divine blessing, or luck). The **Torre de Comares,** at 45 meters the tallest tower in the Alhambra, is named for the stained-glass windows (*comarías*) that once separated the Throne Room or **Salón de Embajadores** (Hall of the Ambassadors) from the patio. Behind the magnificent cedar door of this hall, Boabdil, the last Nasrid sultan, signed the terms of his surrender to the Catholic Monarchs. Soon afterward, Queen Isabella received Christopher Columbus here prior to his first voyage to the New World, pledging to sell her jewels to help finance the navigator's plan. The ceiling, richly adorned with *mocárabe* (stalactite vaulting patterns), is the grandest of the Alhambra. It represents the seven heavens of Islamic paradise, topped by the eighth level, which is reserved for Allah and inscribed with verses from the 67th chapter of the Koran, most importantly, "Allah, omnipotent creator of heaven and earth and the only source of power." Look for the geometrically varied points of light penetrating through the upper jalousies onto the floor of the hall, in continual movement with the changing angle of the sun.

The final section of the Nasrid palace is the harem, the area around the **Patio de los Leones** (Court of the Lions), originally entered only by the sultan, his family, and their trusted servants, most of them eunuchs. To reach it, you'll pass through the **Sala de los Mocárabes** (Hall of the Mocárabes, or ornamental stalactites): note the splendid, though damaged, ceiling, followed by your first glimpse of stalactite carving in the arches above. Surrounded by a forest of 124 columns, the stately Patio de los Leones is the heart of the harem. From the fountain in the center, 12 puppylike lions, which may represent the months or signs of the zodiac, stare out stonily. Four streams flow to the surrounding state apartments and, symbolically, to the four corners of the earth. They're also taken to represent the four rivers of Islamic paradise or the cardinal points of the compass. The moving water, in contrast to the static pool in the Patio de los Arrayanes, creates an upbeat mood, designed for leisure time and possibly for children to play in. The verses by Moorish poet Ibn Zamrak in Kufic script around the edge of the fountain refer to the magic of the water as "pearls of translucent clarity with borders adorned with a necklace of dewdrops/liquid silver flowing among the pearls/water and marble fused into one so we cannot tell which is in motion." (The lions are currently being restored after suffering centuries of Granada's summer-to-winter temperature changes, and, more recently, the effects of acid rain. Some of the lions are temporary replacements and the water may not be flowing when you visit.)

The **Sala de los Abencerrajes** (Hall of the Abencerrajes), on the south side of the palace, may be the Alhambra's most beautiful gallery, with a stunning stalactite ceiling and a star-shaped *muquarna* (honeycombed) skylight and cupola reflected in the pool below. The 16 tracery windows in the eight-sided cupola, another geometrical demonstration of the Pythagorean theorem, throw a diffused light into the dome. Here Boabdil's father, Muley Hacen, is alleged to have massacred 16 members of the Abencerraj family—whose chief was the lover of his own favorite, the Christian captive Isabel de Solís, called Zoraya—and piled their bloodstained heads in this font, as the rusty stain on the marble floor seems to attest. This story, part of the popular post–Al-Andalus tendency to portray the vanquished Moors as bloodthirsty heathen, has been proven apocryphal. The stains were caused by oxidation of the marble. In any case, the idea that the sultan would slaughter an entire family in his intimate private quarters is difficult to reconcile with the tenor of this beautiful place and should probably be eliminated from the repertory of romantic but untrue tales that have taken root here.

The **Sala de los Reyes** (Kings' Hall), also known as La Sala de Justicia (Hall of Justice), is on the patio's east side, decorated with ceiling frescoes that were almost certainly painted by Christians in the last days of the Moors' tenure. The name of the hall probably stems from the 10 portraits of Nasrid kings on the ceiling. To the north of the fountain is the **Sala de las Dos Hermanas** (Hall of the Two Sisters), the abode of the king's favorite wife. Its name comes from the two white-marble slabs in its floor, and its ceiling is resplendent with some of the Alhambra's most superb stucco work, an intricate pattern of honeycomb cells. Note the symmetrically placed pomegranates on the walls. The adjoining **Mirador de Daraxa** (Sultan's Lookout) overlooks the cypress-filled **Jardin de Lindaraja**. The two small windows on the far side of the garden open into the rooms Washington Irving inhabited during his 1829 stay in the Alhambra, and even farther out, perched on the northern edge of the palace, is the **La Torre del Peinador de le Reina** (The Tower of the Queen's Dressing Room), which is not open to the public.

The **Baños Arabes,** the Alhambra's semi-subterranean bathhouse, is where the sultan's favorite wives luxuriated in baths of brightly tiled mosaic and performed their ablutions lit by star-shaped pinpoints of light from the ceiling above. The baths are closed to the public, but you can catch a glimpse of them through the door.

Leaving the Casas Reales (Royal Houses) by the Puerta de la Rawda (cemetery) at the eastern end of the Sala de los Reyes, you enter the **Jardines del Partal** (Partal Gardens), which stretch out along the Alhambra walls and watchtowers toward the Generalife gardens beyond. The Palacio del Partal, so named for the five-arched *partal,* or porticoes reflected in the pool, is also known as **La Torre de las Damas** (Tower of the Ladies), for no known reason other than the hint of mystery and romance suggested by the tower's three small upper windows. Various other towers on the ramparts to the east include the **Torre del Mihrab** (Tower of the Prayer Niche), a Nasrid oratory, and the **Torre de la Cautiva** (Tower of the Captive), associated with the story of Isabel de Solís, known as Zoraya, the Christian captive said to have been the favorite of King Muley Hacen. The way to the Generalife gardens passes above the Cuesta de los Chinos, the path up from the upper Albayzín.

The **Generalife** was the summer palace of the Nasrid kings. It stands on the Cerro del Sol (Hill of the Sun), and its name comes from the Arabic *Yannat al-Arif*—Garden of the Architect. Designed as places of rest and withdrawal, the terraces and promenades here grant incomparable views of the city, stretching away to the distant vega. The different uses of water in the Generalife gardens represent its most interesting architectural feature, and the dead cypress in the inner garden is the spot where the captive Princess Zoraya is said to have met her Abcencerraje lover. During summer's International Festival of Music and Dance, these stately cypresses are the backdrop for evening ballets in the Generalife amphitheater. Between the Generalife and the Alhambra is the 16th-century convent of San Francisco, now one of the most luxurious paradors in Spain.

With nearly 2 million visitors a year, the Alhambra is Spain's most popular attraction. In an effort to contain the crowds, the monument restricts admission to the Nasrid Royal Palace to 350 people every half hour and sometimes closes rooms or sections for restoration. You can buy tickets when you arrive if they're available, but you're better off reserving them in advance through the Banco Bilbao Vizcaya (BBV) for a €1 surcharge. Same-day tickets are sold at the BBV branch on Plaza Isabel Católica 1, or you can reserve by phone or at any BBV branch up to a year in advance. (By phone, you pay with Visa or MasterCard, then pick up your tickets at any BBV branch when you arrive in Spain.) Purchasing tickets on-line, at www.alhambratickets.com, is another option. Your ticket will show the half-hour time slot for your entry; once inside, you can stay as long as you like. On busy days, you may have several hours to spare before your visit to the interior palaces, in which case you can spend the interim visiting the Generalife, the Alcazaba, the Alhambra Museum, and the Fine Arts Museum. There might even be enough time to walk to the Cármen de los Mártires and to have lunch at one of the restaurants on the Alhambra hill.

For an entirely different (and calmer) perspective, come back for a flood-lit tour of the Alhambra at night. ⊠ *Cuesta de Gomérez,* ☎ *958/220912; 902/224460 within Spain for advance ticket sales (BBVA); 91/374–5420 from outside Spain,* WEB *www.alhambra-patronato.es; advance ticket sales: www.alhambratickets.com.* 🎫 *Alhambra and Generalife* €7.80. ☉ *Mar.–Oct., Mon.–Sat. 9–8, Sun. 9–7; floodlit visits Tues., Thurs., and Sat. 10 PM–midnight. Nov.–Feb., daily 8:30–6; floodlit visits Fri. and Sat. 8 PM–9:30 PM. Ticket office opens 30 min before opening and closes 1 hr before closing.*

**❺ Casa de Castril.** A richly decorated 16th-century palace in the plateresque (silversmithlike) style, this noble town house once belonged to Bernardo Zafra, secretary to Queen Isabella. Before you enter, notice the exquisite portal and the facade carved with scallop shells and a phoenix. Inside is the **Museo Arqueológico** (Archaeological Museum), where you'll find Moorish curios and artifacts; Phoenician burial urns from Almuñécar, on Granada's coast; a full-size copy of the Dama de Baza, a large Iberian sculpture discovered in the north of the province in 1971 (the original is in Madrid), and various finds from provincial caves. ⊠ *Carrera del Darro 41, El Albayzín,* ☎ *958/225640.* 🎫 €1.50, *EU citizens free.* ☉ *Wed.–Sat. 9–8, Sun. 9–2:30, Tues. 3–8.*

NEED A BREAK? The park at **Paseo Padre Manjón,** along the Darro River—also known as the Paseo de los Tristes (Promenade of the Sad, so called because funeral processions would pass here on the way to the cemetery)—is a handy place for a coffee break. Dappled with fountains and stone walkways, the park has a stunning view up to the Alhambra's northern side.

**❸ Casa de los Pisa.** This 16th-century house, once property of the Pisa family, is kept as a museum dedicated to San Juan de Dios (1495–1550), who died here in a room kept exactly as it was when the saint expired on March 8, 1550. A tireless worker for the poor, San Juan de Dios was born in Portugal, came to Granada in 1538, and dedicated his life to the founding of hospitals (which is why many Spanish hospitals bear his name). The Pisa house is a treasury of religious art. The Gothic stone portal leads into a patio centered around a fountain with white marble columns supporting a gallery and a richly coffered ceiling. ⊠ *Calle de la Convalecencia 1, El Albayzín,* ☎ *958/222144,* WEB *www.sanjuandedios-oh.es.* 🎫 €2.40. ☉ *Mon.–Sat. 10–1.*

**⑯ Casa de los Porras.** There are clear signs of Mudéjar design in this 16th-century Renaissance palace—making it one of Granada's finest examples of this combination of architectural styles. The entryway leads diagonally (a typical characteristic of Granada palaces) to a four-tiered patio centered on a well and fountain, a classic Moorish town house arrangement. A splendid stairway leads up to the first level, where a carved wooden balustrade supports wooden columns. The house, long abandoned, was declared a ruin in 1968 and acquired by the University of Granada, which now uses the space for art exhibits, concerts, dance classes, lectures, and workshops. ⊠ *Plaza de Porras s/n, El Albayzín,* ☎ *958/224425.* 🎫 *Free.* ☉ *Mon.–Sat. 10–2, 4–8.*

**❽ Casas del Chapiz.** This fine 16th-century Morisco palace, not generally open to the public, houses both the School of Arabic Studies and the Centro Superior de Investigaciones Científicas. As potential researchers, of course, all visitors are welcome, and, if you're lucky, the caretaker might even show you around. The garden and its rectangular

pool, a modest miniature replica of the Alhambra's Patio de los Arrayanes, overlooks the narrow valley of the Darro River. ⊠ *Cuesta del
Chapiz 22, El Albayzín.* ☎ *958/222290.* ⊠ *Free.* ⊙ *Weekdays 8–8.*

**④ El Bañuelo** (Little Bathhouse). They may seem a little dark and dank
now, but try to imagine these 11th-century Arab steam baths 900
years ago filled with Moorish beauties, backed by bright ceramic tiles,
tapestries, and rugs on the dull brick walls. Light comes in through
star-shaped vents in the ceiling, reminiscent of those in the Alhambra.
The columns are crowned with Visigothic, Christian, and Arabic capitals. Keep in mind that the baths close at 2; this is a morning visit. ⊠
*Carrera del Darro 31, El Albayzín,* ☎ *958/027800.* ⊠ *Free.* ⊙ *Tues.–
Sat. 10–2.*

**② Iglesia de San Gil y Santa Ana.** The intricately carved plateresque portal and the coffered ribbon-work of the carved and painted ceiling are
the best features in this 16th-century Mudéjar church facing over Plaza
Nueva at the entrance to the Carrera del Darro. The church was built
between 1537 and 1548 on plans drawn up by Diego de Siloé, sculptor and architect of the cathedrals of Granada and Seville. Built over
the site of the small Almanzora mosque that preceded the Christian
conquest of the city, the slender minaret–turned–bell tower with its midpoint arches and ceramic tilework in the spandrels (the areas over the
arches) gracefully balances the compact riverside bulk of the church
itself. Interred here are Juan Latino, the famous 16th-century Ethiopian
humanist, scholar, and University of Granada professor, and Mariana
Pineda (1804–1831), the liberal heroine executed for sewing a banner
to be used by a liberal movement during Fernando VII's absolutist reactionary purge. Federico García Lorca, who was, somewhat ironically,
executed by the same totalitarian movement 105 years later, wrote an
eerily premonitory play, *Mariana Pineda,* based on the heroine's dramatic story 10 years before his own death in 1936. ⊠ *Plaza Santa Ana
s/n, El Albayzín,* ☎ *958/225004.* ⊠ *Free.* ⊙ *Open for masses only:
June–Sept., Mon.–Sat. 7* PM*, Sun 11* AM*; Oct.–May, Mon.–Sat. 6* PM*,
Sun. 11* AM*.*

**⑰ Iglesia de San Gregorio Bético.** This little church at the top of Calle
Calderería Nueva occupies the point of convergence of the Calles de
San Gregorio and San Juan de los Reyes, the high and low roads, respectively, across the Albayzín. The church was constructed by order
of the Catholic kings on the spot where many Christian martyrs were
buried, notably Saints Peter and John of the Friars Minor, reportedly
dragged to their deaths by horses from the Alhambra to this point. The
facade of the church features a simple stone portal with columns
topped by ionic capitals. Pomegranates, symbolic of Granada, are
sculpted over the archway, and San Gregorio, Bishop of Iliberis, occupies the vaulted niche above. ⊠ *Placeta de San Gregorio s/n, El Albayzín,* ☎ *958/125650.* ⊠ *Free.* ⊙ *Mon.–Sat. 10–1, 4–7; Sun. 10–2.*

**⑮ Iglesia de San José.** This 16th-century Mudéjar church on the Albayzín
hillside has a 10th-century alminar–cum–bell tower that was once
part of the mosque that stood here through the 15th century. Look for
the horseshoe arch at the first level and note where the bell tower was
added over the Moorish exposed redbrick surface. ⊠ *Plaza de San José
s/n, El Albayzín,* ☎ *958/227671.* ⊠ *Free.* ⊙ *Open for masses only:
June–Sept., Mon.–Sat. 7* PM*, Sun 11* AM*; Oct.–May, Mon.–Sat. 6* PM*,
Sun. 11* AM*.*

**⑬ Iglesia de San Miguel Bajo.** Built, like almost all Albayzín churches,
on the site of an earlier mosque, this church overlooks the Plaza de
San Miguel Bajo and is undergoing restoration that should be com-

pleted in 2004. Finished in 1556, the portal is thought to have been designed by Diego de Siloé (1498–1563). The portal's midpoint or semicircular arch is set between Corinthian pilasters below a niche containing the image the archangel San Miguel. On the side of the church facing the square is part of the earlier mosque, a horseshoe arch resting on Roman columns. The square itself is a bustling agglomeration of taverns and terraces. (Check El Rincón de Aurora for the tavern's ancient photographs of the San Miguel neighborhood.) The far end of the square is known as *Las Vistillas* (heights or views) *de San Miguel,* for its panorama over Granada and over the flat farmland, the vega, stretching out to the southwest. ⊠ *Plaza de San Miguel Bajo s/n, El Albayzín.* ⊘ *Closed for repair.*

**➏ Iglesia de San Pedro y San Pablo.** Don't miss a chance to have a look at the Renaissance coffered wooden ceiling in this little church perched over a bend in the Darro River across from the Casa Castril. Once the site of La Mezquita de los Baños (the Mosque of the Baths, so-named for the nearby Moorish bathhouse), the church was completed in 1563. The most important work of art is the *Scourging at the Pillar,* attributed to the Flemish school, in the first chapel inside to the left. Look for the arched remains of the aqueduct on the far side of the river and the Alhambra hanging almost directly overhead. Every May this church is the departure point for Granada's *rocieros,* pilgrims to Huelva's village of Almonte, where Nuestra Señora del Rocío (Our Lady of the Dew) is venerated. ⊠ *Carrera del Darro 2, El Albayzín,* ☎ 958/223233. 🎟 *Free* ⊘ *Open for masses only: June–Sept., Mon.–Sat. 7 PM, Sun 11 AM; Oct.–May, Mon.–Sat. 6 PM, Sun. 11 AM.*

**➓ Iglesia del Salvador.** Built in the 16th century over what was once the Mezquita Mayor del Albayzín (Main Mosque of the Albayzín), the church's polychrome stone portal is its most important artistic feature. The patio is unchanged from the structure's days as a mosque. ⊠ *Plaza del Abad 2, El Albayzín,* ☎ 958/278644. 🎟 *Free.* ⊘ *Mon.–Sat. 10–1 and 4–8:30, Sun. 11–2.*

**⓫ Mirador de San Nicolás.** This leafy square looking across the valley of the Darro River to the illuminated tawny-hued walls of the Alhambra is one of the most frequented spots in Granada, for both visitors and Granadinos. The views, not only of the Alhambra but of the snow-capped Sierra Nevada looming up behind it, the city below, and the flat expanse of the vega beyond, all add up to one of the most spectacular and romantic vantage points in the Albayzín. The San Nicolás church flanking the square, originally constructed in 1525, was burned during anticlerical violence in the Spanish Civil War in 1932. The restored church is of little artistic interest. ⊠ *Plaza de San Nicolás, El Albayzín.*

**⓮ Monasterio de Santa Isabel la Real.** Founded in 1501 by Isabel la Católica, this Clarist convent is best known for its ogival portal (in to the left) complete with a Florentine arch and an unusually full range of flamboyant Gothic details, from elaborate traceries to crockets, pinnacles, and canopied niches. With a Mudéjar bell tower–alminar standing next to it, the effect is unique. The right side of the building (straight in from the entryway) is also unusual, with its porticoed loggia and timbered columns. Don't miss the ceramic tribute to Santa Clara de Asis, the founder of the order. Inside, the exquisitely painted Mudéjar wooden ceiling is the star feature, along with a rich endowment of paintings, sculptures, and friezes. ⊠ *Camino Nuevo de San Nicolás 15, El Albayzín,* ☎ 958/277836. 🎟 €2. ⊘ *Portada always open. Mass: June–Sept., Mon.–Sat. 7:45 PM, Sun 10 AM; Oct.–May, Mon.–Sat. 7 PM, Sun. 10 AM.*

⑫ **Palacio Dar-al-Horra.** Tucked between the Moorish ramparts and the Monastery of Santa Isabel la Real, Dar al-Horra (the Queen's House) was originally built in the last third of the 15th century as a residence for Aixa, mother of Boabdil, the last Moorish king of Granada. Later part of the convent and, for a time, inhabited by Queen Isabella herself, the palace was abandoned for many years, became a ruin, and was nearly demolished before the Granada municipal government took it over and architect Leopoldo Torres Balbás began a lengthy restoration. The building is remarkably intact and graceful, with many decorative themes and techniques, not surprisingly, in common with the Alhambra. The room to the right of the entrance was used as a Christian chapel by Queen Isabella and, as a result, has distinctive ornamentation around the edges of the coffered cedar ceiling. The small central pool and the patio connect the entrance with a *mirador* (viewpoint) north over the Moorish battlements. The stairway leads up to a tower from which, through small horseshoe-arched windows, you can see the Clarist nuns at the adjoining convent hanging laundry in their light-blue cassocks. Be sure to have a close look at the painted and carved coffered ceilings overhead and the small, kidney-shaped, red and black forms reiterated throughout the palace. ⊠ *Callejón de las Monjas s/n, El Albayzín,* ☎ *Fundación del Albayzín: 958/200688.* ⊠ €2. ⊗ *Gardens only: Easter–Oct., Thurs.–Sat. 10–2; Nov.–Easter, Sat. 10–2. Other visits by arrangement with the Fundación del Albayzín.*

❼ **Palacio de los Córdoba.** This palace, at the end of the Paseo Padre Manjón, was constructed in 1969 using the plans and materials from the 16th-century noble house built here by Don Luis Fernández de Córdoba. Today it houses Granada's municipal archives and is used for municipal functions and art exhibits. You're free to wander the large garden. ⊠ *Cuesta del Chapiz s/n, El Albayzín,* ☎ *958/226371.* ⊠ *Free.* ⊗ *Daily 10–8.*

❾ **Sacromonte.** The third of Granada's three hills, the Sacromonte rises behind the Albayzín, dotted with prickly pear cacti and riddled with caverns. These caves may have sheltered early Christians; 15th-century treasure hunters found a collection of bones inside and assumed they belonged to San Cecilio, the city's patron saint. Thus the hill was sanctified—*sacro monte* means holy mountain—and an abbey built on its summit. The **Abadía de Sacromonte** (⊠ Camino del Sacromonte, ☎ 958/221445) is open Tuesday through Saturday 11–1 and 4–6, Sunday noon–1 and 4–6; guided tours are every half hour; admission is €2.

Sacromonte has long been notorious as a lawless Gypsy stronghold and a den of pickpockets and thieves, but its poor reputation is largely undeserved. The quarter's ambience is more evocative of a quiet Andalusian whitewashed pueblo than of a rough no-go area. Few Gypsy families live in the quarter's colorful cave-homes, many of which have been restored as middle-class residences. Some of the old spirit lives on in the handful of *zambras*, flamenco performances in caves garishly decorated with a profusion of brass plates and cooking utensils. They differ from the more formally staged *tablaos flamencos* (flamenco shows) in that the performers mingle with the guests, and usually drag one or two of them onto the floor for an improvised flamenco dancing lesson. Flamenco purists frown on such displays as touristy malarkey, but the shows are certainly colorful, and they do provide a chance to venture inside the famous *cuevas* (caves). A good idea is to take a tour, which usually includes a walk through the neighboring Albayzín and a drink at a tapas bar in addition to the zambra performance, bookable through most hotels. Not to be missed in Sacromonte is **La Chumbera,** the restaurant, cultural forum, and Centro Internacional de Estudios Gitanos (International Gypsy Studies Center) that on Saturday offers free flamenco performances with up-and-coming flamenco artists.

OFF THE BEATEN PATH

**UPPER ALBAYZÍN –** For a tour of the Upper Albayzín, start at the top of the *Cerro del Aceituno* (hill of the olive tree) and the Ermita de San Miguel. Walk west on Calle San Luis to the Placeta de la Cruz de Piedra, from which you can see the Puerta de Fajalauza (Bib-Fagg-Allauz in Arabic, meaning "potters' gate"), the portal through the Moorish walls used by the ceramic artisans and for which the famous green-and-blue pottery typical of Granada is named. Callejón de San Gregorio leads down to the Convento de San Gregorio Magno. From there, the Calle del Blanqueo Viejo leads to the Callejón del Conde, where a left turn takes you to Plaza Del Conde and a right turn takes you into the Placeta de las Tres Estrellas with its gorgeous Cármen de las Tres Estrellas (Cottage of the Three Stars). In Calle Pagés is the extraordinary Casa de los Mascarones (House of the Masks), and up at the top of Callejón del Materillo where it joins Calle Larga de San Cristóbal is the Mirador de San Cristóbal (San Cristóbal Lookout), offering a nonpareil panoramic view over Granada. Across the Carretera de Murcia is the Iglesia de San Cristóbal going down Calle Larga de San Cristóbal and Calle Panaderos to Plaza Aljibe de Polo leads around the Iglesia del Salvador to Placeta del Abad and the Convento de Santo Tomás de Villanueva. Look for the Moorish fountain here and the double towers of an early fortified doorway.

# El Realejo

Much of the Realejo district was included in the steep labyrinth of streets that made up the city's medieval Jewish quarter, called *Garnata al-Yahud* (Garnata of the Jew), which eventually became the name of the city as a result of the decisive role of the Jews in the 8th-century Moorish capture of Granada from the Visigoths. (Both the Jewish Garnata and the Moorish Garnattha referred to the pomegranate, *granada*, in Spanish.) Today El Realejo includes the Mauror hillside, the area around and including Campo del Príncipe, and the streets between Plaza de Santo Domingo and Plaza del Padre Suarez.

## A Good Walk

Beginning on the Alhambra hill at the **Cármen de los Mártires** ⑱, find your way downhill to the Centro Cultural Manuel de Falla just down to the left. Next is the **Casa-Museo Manuel de Falla** ⑲ and the luxurious Hotel Alhambra Palace, before starting down the steep Mauror hill into the Callejón Niño del Rollo, which leads to the **Fundación Rodríguez Acosta** ⑳, a fascinating repository of design, art, and architecture. The **Torres Bermejas** ㉑ are another 50 meters down, near the excellent Cármen de San Miguel restaurant. Continuing down Calle Cruz de Piedra, a hard left takes you into Placeta Puerta del Sol with its ancient *lavadero* (clothes-washing place). The nearby Placeta del Hospicio Viejo now houses the Modern Language Center of the University of Granada. From here, go down to the **Casa de los Tiros** ㉒ on Calle Pavaneros, cut through Plaza del Padre Suarez, past the excellent and charming La Alacena restaurant to Calle Jesus y María, where a left turn takes you past the Palacio Condes de Gabia and the Casa Girones before reaching the Plaza de Santo Domingo. After exploring the **Iglesia de Santo Domingo** ㉓ and the Colegio Santa Cruz la Real next to it, cut around to the left, passing through the tunnel-like alleyway to the left of the church, and walk up past the Convento de las Comendadoras de Santiago to Calle Santiago, where a left turn will take you to the lovely **Corrala de Santiago** ㉔. From here continue through

Plaza del Realejo up to Calle Cocheras, where a right turn will take you into **Campo del Príncipe** ㉕.

This walk takes three to four hours, depending on how much time you spend in the Fundación Rodríguez Acosta and the Instituto Gómez Moreno. Campo del Príncipe, with its terrace restaurants and cafés, makes a fitting finale for this twisting (though nearly always descending) hike.

## Sights to See

㉕ **Campo del Príncipe.** This hub of activity is the most populous part of the Realejo district and a repository of bars, taverns, terraces, and restaurants for all tastes. The square was cleared and set aside for the 1497 wedding of Príncipe Juan, son of the Catholic Monarchs. In the early 16th century it was used as a venue for jousts and bullfights, and for this reason perhaps, the Campo del Príncipe still exerts a powerfully magnetic attraction throughout Granada. ⊠ *Campo del Príncipe s/n, El Realejo.*

⑱ **Cármen de los Mártires.** Located just up the hill from the Hotel Alhambra Palace, this elegant turn-of-the-century Granada *cármen* (villa) and its gardens are like a Generalife in miniature. Temporary painting or photography exhibits are usually on display inside, but even if you arrive when the building is closed, the gardens and the views down over the Realejo from the *Balcón del Paraíso* (Balcony of Paradise), as the gardens are called, are stunning. It was constructed on a site once used for underground dungeons for Christian captives (hence *mártires*, martyrs) used as slave labor in the construction of the Alhambra palace and the Generalife gardens; Queen Isabella was the first to erect a shrine here in their honor. German traveler and chronicler Hieronymous Münzer visited Granada in 1494 and records witnessing 14 large dungeons, each with a capacity of 200 captives. Entered through a small hole at ground level, the 25-ft-in-diameter chambers opened out at a depth of 20 ft and contained radiating sections for brick bunks with brick headrests. Water jars were distributed at intervals, and a circular channel drained into a central sump. Site of a 16th-century Carmelite convent presided over by the great Spanish mystic San Juan de la Cruz (St. John of the Cross), the present-day gardens—combining French formal symmetry with the spontaneous disorder of the English Romantic tradition—are a far cry from the catacombs of living captives for which the cármen is named. ⊠ *Paseo de los Mártires s/n, Alhambra,* ☎ *958/227953.* ⊠ *Free.* ☉ *Apr.–Sept., weekdays 10–2 and 5–7, weekends 10–7; Oct.–Mar., weekdays 4–6, weekends 10–6.*

⑲ **Casa-Museo Manuel de Falla.** In this villa Manuel de Falla (1876–1946), one of Spain's greatest composers, lived and wrote his music from 1921 until 1939, when he went to Argentina in self-imposed exile after Franco's victory. Falla was born in Cádiz, studied piano in Madrid, and later spent time in Paris, where he became friends with Debussy, Dukas, Ravel, and Albéniz. His first triumph was his 1913 *La Vida Breve* (The Short Life). After moving to Granada he composed the ballet *El Amor Brujo* (Love Bewitched) and *El Sombrero de los Tres Picos* (The Three-Cornered Hat) while organizing much-celebrated *cante jondo* (Gypsy flamenco song) festivals with Federico García Lorca, a fellow pianist and Andalusian folk music enthusiast. Later works include *Noches en los Jardines de España* (Nights in the Gardens of Spain), *Fantasía Bética* (Andalusian Fantasy) and *Soneto a Córdoba* (Cordoba Sonnet). Falla's cármen, next to the auditorium and cultural center named for him, contains personal mementos, furniture, the Pleyel piano, on which he composed, and the desk where he created much of his music.

Items to look for include the origami bird made by Spanish philosopher, novelist, and academic Miguel de Unamuno, Picasso sketches for *El Sombrero de los Tres Picos,* an oil painting by Vázquez Díaz, and a stone bust of Falla by the Granada sculptor Bernardo Olmedo. ✉ *C. Antequeruela Alta 11, Alhambra,* ☎ *958/229421.* 🎫 *€2.* ⊙ *Tues.– Sat. 10–3.*

NEED A
BREAK?

The booming taverns and cafés around **Campo del Príncipe** are always hopping with groups from all over the world as well as hometown Granada students during the school year. From terrace tables to balcony perches high over the square to cozy saloons, this is a standard Granada hangout for young and old.

**㉒ Casa de los Tiros.** The name of this 16th-century palace, which translates as "House of the Shots," comes from the musket barrels that protrude from the upper part of its singular facade. The theme throughout is that of Christian combat, from the uppermost crenellated battlements (partly disfigured by a roof added in the 19th century) to the sword over the door with a heart at its point and the motto *el mande* (may he command), allusive to the authority of God over the human heart in time of war. The human figures on the facade represent Hercules, Theseus, Jason, and Hector in Roman battle dress, surrounding Mercury, dressed as a herald with the house arms emblazoned on his tabard. The small museum is on the second floor, reached by a flight of stairs flanked by portraits of Spanish royals from Ferdinand and Isabella to Phillip IV (none of them look very happy). The highlight is the intricately carved wood ceiling in the Cuadra Dorada room, adorned with portraits of royals and knights distinguished through heroism during the Christian reconquest of Spain from the Moors. This coffered ceiling, nearly surreal in its complexity, is one of the gems of the Realejo. Of the exhibits, the historical lithographs, engravings, and photographs showing life in Granada in times gone by are especially noteworthy. Check listings (in the excellent monthly *Guía de Granada*) for cultural events in this extraordinary space. ✉ *Pavaneras 19, El Realejo,* ☎ *958/221072.* 🎫 *Free.* ⊙ *Weekdays 2:30–8.*

**㉔ Corrala de Santiago.** Built in the 16th century, this residence for visiting professors to the University of Granada is a perfect example of the communal *patio de vecinos* (courtyard of neighbors) style of apartment house based on the North African *caravanserai* (lodging house) layout prevalent in southern Spain. Three levels of wood-balustrade balconies surround a large central patio with a quiet fountain, plants, and ancient, rough-hewn stone pillars supporting the galleries. The close and sometimes tumultuous relationships between working-class families in the *corralas* (another term for patios de vecinos) was a legendary part of urban life in early Spain. Getting rooms here is possible if you can establish some link with the University of Granada (researching a book, for example) and procure an invitation. ✉ *Calle de Santiago 5, El Realejo.* ☎ *958/220527.* 🎫 *Free.* ⊙ *Open all hours.*

**㉒⁰ Fundación Rodríguez Acosta.** One of Granada's finest 20th-century pieces of architecture and landscape gardening, this quirky amalgam of more than a thousand years of building techniques and design was created by the Granada artist and collector José María Rodríguez-Acosta (1878–1941). A painter himself—with some excellent work hanging in the Museo de Bellas Artes in the Alhambra's Palacio de Carlos V— Rodriguez-Acosta began painting late in life. The quality of the works he encountered on a visit to Paris is said to have so impressed (and depressed) him that he determined never again to pick up a paintbrush— thus ending his brief artistic career. The "cármen" housing the

Rodriguez-Acosta foundation, in reality an immense mansion, was designed by its owner, who took complete control over construction. The collection of pieces of decorative art, archaeological treasures, and works by Rodriguez-Acosta provide an eclectic vision of the tastes and talents of this extraordinary Granadino, whose intent, as expressed in his will, was to "extend awareness of this miracle which is life, which we have the joyful obligation to make ever more noble, beautiful and happy." ✉ *Callejón del Niño del Royo 8, El Realejo,* ☎ *958/227497.* ✉ *€3.* ☉ *Tues.–Sat. 10–1:30, by appointment.*

**㉓ Iglesia de Santo Domingo.** Begun in 1512, this somewhat gloomy, predominantly Gothic church has a triple-arched stone portico over trompe l'oeil baroque paintings on the facade. Fray Luis de Granada is the serene and sober figure caught in a meditative moment in front of the portico. Look for the initials of Ferdinand and Isabella in the spandrels (flat surfaces between arches), and the royal motto *tanto monta* (roughly, "the one rides as much as the other," indicating the equally shared power) in the coat of arms of Carlos V in the center. ✉ *Plaza de Santo Domingo 1, El Realejo,* ☎ *958/227331.* ☉ *Mon.–Sat. 10:30– 1:30 and 3:30–6:30, Sun. 3:30–6.*

**㉑ Torres Bermejas** (Crimson Towers). These towers constituted the forward bastion of the Alcazaba fortress at the tip of the Alhambra palace. Dating as far back as the late 8th century, the walls (some sections of which are now missing) linked up with the ones now interrupted by the Puerta de las Granadas and continue north to the Alcazaba and to the southwest down the Mauror hill to the city center. ✉ *Callejón del Niño del Rollo s/n, El Realejo.*

# El Centro

Granada's central area around the cathedral is flatter and less dramatic than the Albayzín or Realejo hillsides, though the monumental Christian churches, nearly all built over earlier mosques, graphically tell the story of the city's past. Likewise, the Plaza Bib-Rambla, the Madraza, the Alcaicería shop area, and the former Moroccan caravanserai at the Corral del Carbón all reinforce Granada's Moorish heritage. The Federico García Lorca museum at Huerta de San Vicente and the Monasterio de la Cartuja at Granada's northern edge are not-to-miss side trips.

## A Good Walk

Begin at the Plaza Isabel La Católica (at the junction of the Gran Vía and Calle Reyes Católicos), with its statue of Columbus presenting Queen Isabella with his maps of the New World. Walk down Calle Reyes Católicos and turn left into the **Corral del Carbón** ㉖. The tourist office here has maps and brochures. Cross back over Calle Reyes Católicos: directly ahead is the Alcaicería, once the Arabs' silk market and now a maze of alleys packed with souvenir shops and restaurants. Turn left from the Alcaicería to reach the relaxed Plaza Bib-Rambla, with its flower stalls and the colorful Gran Café Bib-Rambla, the perfect place to grab an ice cream or a coffee. From the northeast corner of the square, Calle Oficios takes you to the **Palacio Madraza** ㉗, the old Arab University, and the **Capilla Real** ㉘, next to which is the **cathedral** ㉙. Look for the **Centro José Guerrero** ㉚ art gallery just across from the Capilla Real for an even better view of the cathedral. Outside the cathedral's west front is the 16th-century Escuela de las Niñas Nobles, with its plateresque facade. Next to the cathedral, along the Plaza de Alonso Cano, are the impressive Curia Eclesiástica, used as an Imperial College until 1769; the Palacio del Arzobispo; and the 18th-century Iglesia de Sagrario, with splendid Corinthian columns. Behind the cathedral is the Gran Vía de Colón, one of Granada's main thoroughfares. This artery was built in the late 19th century in an effort to modernize cross-town transportation; unfortunately, several wonderful old palaces were destroyed in the process. Circling the cathedral, look for the spice market (only if it's Saturday) on Calle Cárcel Baja on the northwest facade. Make the short walk down Calle de San Jerónimo to Plaza de la Universidad and check out the statue of Carlos V before continuing to the **Monasterio e Iglesia de San Jerónimo** ㉛. The **Basílica de San Juan de Dios** ㉜ is two blocks north, and the historic 9th-century Moorish triumphal arch, the Puerta de Elvira, is at Plaza del Triunfo.

Granada's other major sights are on the edge of town and best reached by car or taxi: 2 km (1 mi) north of the city center, off Calle Real de Cartuja, is the 16th-century baroque **Monasterio de la Cartuja** ㉝. To the south are the **Casa-Museo Federico García Lorca** ㉞, and across the river Genil, the Nasrid palace known as the **Alcázar Genil** ㉟; **Ermita de San Sebastián** ㊱, the last Moorish oratory in Granada; and the **Parque de las Ciencias** ㊲, an interactive science museum.

TIMING

This walk takes from four to five hours, including two of the outlying visits at the edge of the city.

## Sights to See

㉟ **Alcázar Genil.** This lovely palace and fortress was the property of Boabdil's mother, Aixa, who used it as a rural retreat. The tower with its intensely decorated inner chamber is surrounded by lateral walls and sleeping alcoves. Friezes in Kufic and italic script glorify the reigning sultan, probably in allusion to Yussuf I. ⊠ *Rey Abu Said s/n, Centro,* ☎ *958/130018.* ⊡ *Free.* ☉ *Weekdays 10–2.*

㉜ **Basílica de San Juan de Dios.** Completed in a mere 22 years (1737–59), this baroque masterpiece shows exceptional unity of design. The cruciform floor plan is surrounded by four smaller chapels and covered by a lofty cupola over the central intersection. A tabernacle behind the brilliant gilt altar contains the remains of San Juan de Dios, born Juan Ciudad Duarte in Portugal in 1495. He was at various times a shepherd, soldier, cattle herder, bookseller, and founder of the Bothers of the Basket of St. John of God. His order was known for the crook and basket unfailingly carried by its members. ⊠ *San Juan de Dios 23, Centro,* ☎ *958/275700.* ⊡ *Free.* ☉ *Daily 8–11, 6–9.*

★ ㉘ **Capilla Real** (Royal Chapel). The chapel is a shrine of local history second only to the Alhambra, because it is the burial place of the momentous Catholic Monarchs, Isabella of Castile and Ferdinand of Aragón. The couple originally planned to be buried in Toledo's San Juan de los Reyes, but Isabella changed her mind when the pair conquered Granada in 1492. When she died, in 1504, her body was first laid to rest in the Convent of San Francisco (now the parador), on the Alhambra hill. The architect Enrique Egas began work on the Royal Chapel in 1506 and completed it 15 years later; it is a masterpiece of the ornate Gothic style now known in Spain as Isabelline. In 1521 Isabella's body was brought to a simple lead coffin in the Royal Chapel crypt, where it was joined by that of her husband, Ferdinand, and later her unfortunate daughter, Juana la Loca (Joan the Mad), and son-in-law, Felipe el Hermoso (Philip the Handsome). Felipe died young, and Juana had his casket borne about the peninsula with her for years, opening the lid each night to kiss her embalmed spouse good night. A small coffin to the right contains the remains of Prince Felipe of Asturias, a grandson of the Catholic Monarchs and Juana la Loca's nephew, who died in his infancy. (Had he lived longer, he would have inherited the throne.) The underground crypt containing the five lead coffins is quite simple, but above it are the elaborate marble tombs showing Ferdinand and Isabella lying side by side; these were commissioned by their grandson Charles V and fashioned by the sculptor Domenico Fancelli. The altarpiece, by Felipe Vigarini (1522), consists of 34 carved panels depicting religious and historical scenes. The bottom row shows Boabdil surrendering the keys of the city to its conquerors and the forced baptism of the defeated Moors. In the sacristy are Ferdinand's sword, Isabella's crown and scepter, and a fine collection of Flemish paintings once owned by Isabella. ⊠ *Oficios 3, Centro,* ☎ *958/227848.* 🎟 *€2.10* ☉ *Mar.–Oct., Mon.–Sat. 10:30–1 and 4–7, Sun. 11–1, 4–7; Nov.–Feb., Mon.–Sat. 10:30–1 and 3:30–6:30, Sun. 11–1.*

NEED A BREAK?

**Plaza Bib-Rambla** and its cafés and terraces are famous gathering spots for people-watching and passing time in the shadow of the cathedral. Bib-Rambla's three terraces—Bocadillería Centro, Restaurante Gallo, and Gran-Café Bib-Rambla—are all fine spots for a breather, surrounded by the Zacatín, the Moorish clothing market, and the Alcaicería, the former silk market. The plaza's name derives from the Arabic *bab* for gate or portal and *rmel* for dry watercourse or arroyo.

**34 Casa-Museo Federico García Lorca.** Granada's most famous native son, poet Federico García Lorca, gets his due here, in the middle of a park on the southern fringe of the city. The García Lorca family's summer home was once a remote corner of the fertile vega, surrounded by cornfields and the sounds of water rushing through the area's complex irrigation system. **La Huerta de San Vicente** is now a museum—run by the poet's niece, Laura García Lorca—with such artifacts as the poet's beloved piano and temporary exhibits on specific aspects of García Lorca's life. Look for the portraits and photographs of him with his three brothers and sisters, a Dalí sketch of a woman smoking a pipe, García Lorca's desk in his upstairs bedroom, and designs for the sets and costumes of the Barraca theater performances he directed as part of the Spanish Second Republic's program to bring classical theater to the masses. The bookstore sells (for about €6) a perfect facsimile of the poet's first publication, *Romancero Gitano,* a gem sure to enhance any bibliophile's collection. ⊠ *C. Virgen Blanca s/n (Parque García Lorca), Huerta de San Vicente,* ☎ *958/258466.* 🎟 *€2.* ☉ *Oct.–Apr., Tues.–Sun. 10–1 and 4–7; May–July and Sept., Tues.–Sun. 10–1 and 5–8; Aug., Tues.–Sun. 10–2. Mandatory guided tours every 45 mins, from 15 mins after opening until 30 mins before closing.*

**29 Cathedral.** Granada's cathedral was commissioned in 1521 by Charles V, who considered the Royal Chapel "too small for so much glory" and decided to house his illustrious late grandparents someplace more worthy. Charles undoubtedly had great designs, as the cathedral was created by some of the finest architects of its time: Enrique Egas, Diego de Siloé, Alonso Cano, and sculptor Juan de Mena. But his ambitions came to little, for the cathedral is a grandiose and gloomy monument, not completed until 1714 and never used as the crypt of his parents *or* grandparents. You enter through a small door at the back, off the Gran Vía. The cathedral has an interesting collection of old hymnals, displayed throughout, and there is a small museum, the star exhibit of which is an impressive 14th-century gold and silver monstrance donated to the city by Queen Isabella. ⊠ *Gran Vía 5, Centro,* ☎ *958/ 222959.* 🎟 *€2.10.* ☉ *Mar.–Sept., Mon.–Sat. 10:30–1.30 and 4–7, Sun. 4–7; Oct.–Feb., Mon.–Sat. 10:30–1:30 and 3:30–6:30, Sun. 3:30–6.*

**30 Centro José Guerrero.** This excellent space is as interesting for its bird's-eye views over the cathedral and the Capilla Real as for its content, a permanent collection of works by Granada's greatest 20th-century painter, the dramatic colorist José Guerrero (1914–91). The 10 superb rooms over four floors, with abundant chairs and benches perched just inside the glass walls overlooking the rooftops and towers of the cathedral, are a fresh and economical exercise in wood, glass, and steel. The Center is one of Granada's most impressive examples of how contemporary design can actually enhance neighboring medieval architecture. ✉ *Oficios 8, Centro,* ☎ *958/225185,* WEB *www.centroguerrero.org.* 🎫 *Free.* ⏲ *Tues.–Sat. 11–2 and 5–9, Sun. 11–2. Guided tours by arrangement.*

26 **Corral del Carbón** (Corral of the Coal). The lovely Moorish horseshoe arch opening out onto Calle Mariana Pineda leads into one of Granada's most interesting spaces. Used to store coal in the 19th century, the Corral del Carbón is in fact one of the earliest Moorish buildings in the city, dating from the 14th century, when itinerant merchants used it as a caravanserai, or lodging house. Animals were kept on the ground floor, and goods and chattel were stored on the upper levels, along with their owners. Thought to be the only North African–style inn of its kind in Spain, the space was later used by Christians as a semi-outdoor theater, called a *corrala,* similar to the Elizabethan theater-in-the-round with the audience arranged on the ground floor surrounded by balconies. Expertly restored with a marble fountain and watering trough in the center and grapevines climbing the walls, the Corral del Carbón now houses the regional tourist office as well as an excellent bookstore and a furniture and crafts shop. Check for the Wednesday and Thursday flamenco performances, Friday and Saturday theater productions, and for musical events during Granada's summer music and dance festival. ✉ *C. Mariana Pineda 12, Centro,* ☎ *(Iglesia de San José) 958/130522.* 🎫 *Free.* ⏲ *Weekdays 9–7, weekends 10–2.*

36 **Ermita de San Sebastián.** This hermitage chapel was site of the January 2, 1492, meeting of Muley Boabdil and the Catholic Monarchs, Ferdinand and Isabella, when the Moorish king, having surrendered the city, was beginning his journey into exile in the Alpujarra. As a Muslim shrine or oratory, the chapel is the only surviving building of its kind in Granada. Composed of 16 lobes or segments with ribs forming a star at their junction, the pointed horseshoe-arched brickwork portal is one of the chapel's oldest and most aesthetically pleasing features. ✉ *Ribera el Violón s/n, Centro,* ☎ *958/216913.* 🎫 *Free* ⏲ *Mon.–Sat. 10–1 and 4–8, Sun. 10–noon and 4–8.*

★ 33 **Monasterio de la Cartuja.** This Carthusian monastery in northern Granada (2 km [1 mi] from the center) was begun in 1506 and moved to its current site in 1516, though construction continued intermittently for the next 300 years. In time, it became one of the most outstanding baroque buildings in Andalusia. The exterior is somewhat sober and monolithic, but when you enter the church and see its twisted, multicolor marble columns; profusion of gold, silver, tortoiseshell, and ivory; intricate stucco; and extravagant churrigueresque sacristy, you'll see why Cartuja has been called the Christian response to the Alhambra. Of particular note are the trompe l'oeil nails in the cross (look closely—birds have been seen attempting to alight on these faux spikes) painted by Fray Juan Sanchez Cotan on the wall above the Last Supper in the refectory. The gory series of paintings around the room, also by Sanchez Cotan, depict the martyrization of Carthusian monks and priors by Henry the VII during the 16th-century English Protestant reform. ✉ *Paseo de la Cartuja s/n (Crtra. de Alfacar), Centro,* ☎ *958/161932.* 🎫 *€2.10.* ⏲ *Apr.–Oct., Mon.–Sat. 10–1 and 4–8; Nov.–Mar., daily 10–1 and 3:30–6:30.*

31 **Monasterio e Iglesia de San Jerónimo.** One of the major works of the Spanish Renaissance, this colossal church and monastery was begun

in 1496 and finished in the early 16th century. Architect Diego de Siloé is credited with much of the work, consisting of two courtyards, one Gothic and the other Renaissance. Isabel of Portugal, wife of Emperor Carlos V, spent most of her time in Granada here after her husband's departure during her pregnancy in the cold winter of 1526. Flanking the altar are the tombs of Spanish general Gonzalo Fernández de Córdoba (1453–1515) and his wife María Fernández de Córdoba. ⊠ *Rector López Argueta 9, Centro,* ☎ *958/279337.* ⊑ *€2.10.* ☉ *Apr.–Sept., daily 10–1.30, 3–7.30; Oct.–Mar., Mon.–Sat. 10–1:30, 3–7:30, Sun. 11–1:30.*

**㉗** **Palacio Madraza.** This building conceals what was once a Moorish Koranic university built in 1349 by Yusuf I. The word *madraza* is, in fact, a corruption of the Arabic *medersa* used for student residential colleges. The baroque facade is dark and intriguing; inside, across from the entrance, an octagonal room is crowned by a Moorish dome over a perfectly preserved Islamic *mihrab* (prayer niche). The building is now an exhibition and cultural center. ⊠ *Oficios 14, Centro,* ☎ *958/223447.* ⊑ *€2.10.* ☉ *Oct.–Apr., weekdays 8–2; May–Sept., Mon.–Sat. 10–1, 4–8, Sun. 10–12, 4–8.*

**㋛ ㊲** **Parque de las Ciencias** (Science Park). Across from Granada's convention center, this hands-on museum has interactive exhibits, scientific experiments, a planetarium, and a 165-ft tower with observation deck. Light, sound, magnifying glasses, and mirrors; animal and plant life; video cameras, computers, multimedia programs, and an observatory—all of the features here encourage your participation. ⊠ *Avda. del Mediterráneo, Centro,* ☎ *958/131900,* ⓦⒺⒷ *www.parqueciencias. com.* ⊑ *€3; planetarium €2.* ☉ *Tues.–Sat. 10–7, Sun. 10–3.*

## Dining

**$$$–$$$$** ✕ **Cármen de San Miguel.** Hidden down a lane a short distance from the Alhambra Palace hotel, in a villa on the Mauror hill above the Realejo, this restaurant has a spacious dining room and Andalusian-style terrace that would merit a visit just for the view over the city. The food—a mixture of Andalusian traditional and creative cuisine by chef David Reyes—also merits the highest marks. Try the *habas a la granadina* (broad beans with mint and prawns) or the *pichón asado con anís estellado y puré de castãnas* (roast squab with aniseed and chestnut sauce). ⊠ *Paseo de Torres Bermejas 3, El Realejo,* ☎ *958/226723. AE, MC, V. Closed Sun.*

**$$$–$$$$** ✕ **Terraza Las Tomasas.** Serving 18 tables, all outside on the terrace, this relatively new Albayzín spot provides an ample choice of light dishes such as gazpacho and salmorejo in summer and international specialties from *magret de pato* (duck breast) to foie gras in fall and winter. Look for *revuelta de morcilla* (scrambled eggs with black sausage) and *lubina a la sal* (sea wolf cooked in salt). It's advisable to call ahead for special *guisos* (stews) in winter. The long stairway down to the restaurant leads to a panoramic perch over the Alhambra and simple but impeccable dining and service. ⊠ *Carril de San Agustín s/n (across from the Tomasas convent), El Albayzín,* ☎ *958/224108. AE, DC, MC, V. Closed Mon. No lunch May–Sept.*

**$$$** ✕ **El Huerto de Juan Ranas.** Gastronomically a cut above most Albayzín terrace restaurants, this intimate spot has only two or three difficult-to-secure outside tables. Views of the Alhambra from inside are still excellent, though temperatures can soar in summer. The cuisine is both Moorish and Spanish, ranging from *pastilla* (sweet and salty meat in puff pastry) to *croquetas de perdiz y jamón ibérico* (partridge and ham croquettes). The cármen itself, two steps below the Mirador

**260**

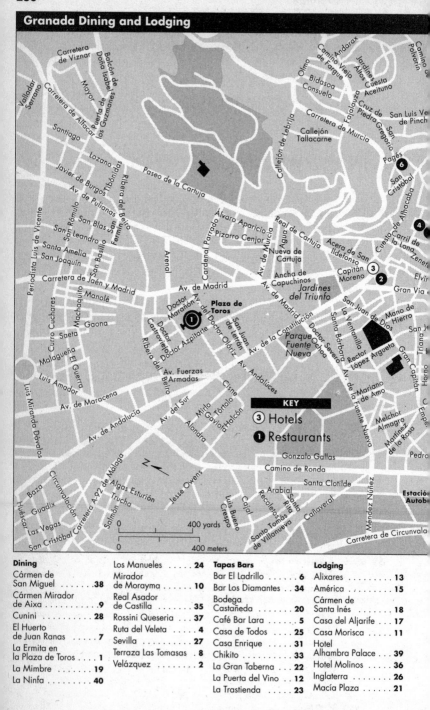

**Dining**

Cármen de
San Miguel . . . . . . **38**
Cármen Mirador
de Aixa . . . . . . . . . **9**
Cunini . . . . . . . . . **28**
El Huerto
de Juan Ranas . . **7**
La Ermita en
la Plaza de Toros . **1**
La Mimbre . . . . . . **19**
La Ninfa . . . . . . . . **40**

Los Manueles . . . . **24**
Mirador
de Morayma . . . . **10**
Real Asador
de Castilla . . . . . . **35**
Rossini Queseria . . **37**
Ruta del Veleta . . . **4**
Sevilla . . . . . . . . . **27**
Terraza Las Tomasas . **8**
Velázquez . . . . . . . **2**

**Tapas Bars**

Bar El Ladrillo . . . . . **6**
Bar Los Diamantes . . **34**
Bodega
Castañeda . . . . . . **20**
Café Bar Lara . . . . . **5**
Casa de Todos . . . . **25**
Casa Enrique . . . . **31**
Chikito . . . . . . . . . **33**
La Gran Taberna . . **22**
La Puerta del Vino . **12**
La Trastienda . . . . **23**

**Lodging**

Alixares . . . . . . . . **13**
América . . . . . . . . **15**
Cármen de
Santa Inés . . . . . **18**
Casa del Aljarife . . . **17**
Casa Morisca . . . . **11**
Hotel
Alhambra Palace . . **39**
Hotel Molinos . . . . **36**
Inglaterra . . . . . . . **26**
Macía Plaza . . . . . **21**

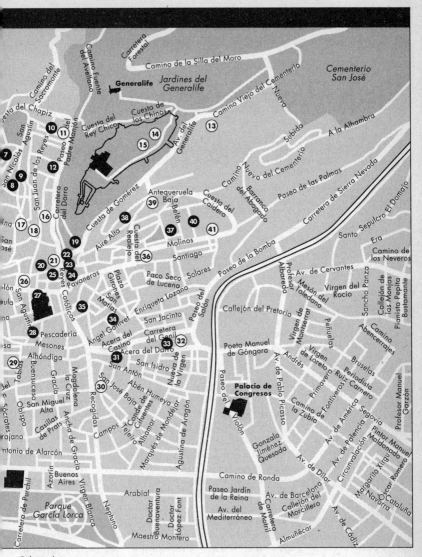

de San Nicolás, is spectacularly restored and decorated with taste and elegance. Reservations are essential between Easter and October. ⊠ *Atarazana Vieja 6-8, El Albayzín,* ☎ *958/286925. AE, MC, V. Closed Mon.*

**$$$**   ✕ **Real Asador de Castilla.** Just behind the *ayuntamiento* (town hall), this traditional Castilian restaurant specializes in roasted and grilled meats, from *chuleta de buey* (beef) to *cochinillo asado* (roast suckling pig) to *cordero lechal* (suckling lamb). The rack of lamb is also excellent, as are the stews and soups, from *sopa de ajo* (garlic soup) to the typical Castilian *cocido* (garbanzo bean and meat stew). This is winter cuisine, best when Granada is lashed by the frigid winds of the Sierra Nevada. ⊠ *Escudo del Cármen 17, Centro,* ☎ *958/222910. AE, DC, MC, V. Closed Mon.*

**$$$**   ✕ **Ruta del Veleta.** Just over 5 km (3 mi) out of town, in Cenes de la
  ★  Vega, this traditionally decorated restaurant serves some of Granada's best cuisine. The many house specialties include *carnes a la brasa* (succulent grilled meats) and fish dishes cooked in rock salt, as well as regional dishes such as *jabalí estilo mozárabe* (wild boar cooked with apples). Dessert might be *puding de manzanas en salsa de moras* (apple pudding in blackberry sauce). ⊠ *Carretera Sierra Nevada, Km 5.4, Cenes de la Vega,* ☎ *958/486134. AE, DC, MC, V. No dinner Sun.*

**$$–$$$**   ✕ **Cármen Mirador de Aixa.** This ample terrace on the way up to the Mirador de San Nicolas is one of the Albayzín dining spots with panoramic views of the Alhambra. Menu choices range from *guisos* (stews) in winter to summer salmorejos and light vegetable specialties such as *aguacates con gambas* (avocado with shrimp). ⊠ *Carril de San Agustín 2, El Albayzín,* ☎ *958/223616. AE, DC, MC, V. Closed Mon. and Nov.–Apr.*

**$$–$$$**   ✕ **La Ermita en la Plaza de Toros.** This graceful restaurant and terrace built in under the vaults supporting the Granada bullring is a little out of the way, but the decor is exotic and the food excellent. The specialty, appropriately, is meat—the *jamón ibérico "Sanchez Romero 5-Jotas"* is top-of-the-line Iberian ham, and the *solomillo de buey sobre salsa de hongos y espuma de foie* (filet mignon with wild mushrooms and goose liver foam) is exquisite. Whether for tapas or a full meal, this is a place for carnivores to consider, especially after a late-afternoon *corrida* (bullfight). ⊠ *Avda. Doctor Olóriz 25, Centro,* ☎ *958/290257. AE, DC, MC, V. Closed Mon.*

**$$–$$$**   ✕ **Mirador de Morayma.** It may be difficult to find this spot on the
  ★  northeastern end of the Albayzín, and it might appear closed (ring the doorbell), but your efforts will be rewarded with a romantic setting in Granada's most classic cármen. Terrace views of the Alhambra are magic; if weather dictates indoor dining, try for one of the three tables in the smaller dining room. The food is mediocre and the service disorganized, but the value, considering the location, is excellent. Beware the "crab" salad and the *vinos de la costa.* Stick with *sopa de cuchara de habichuelas y morcilla* (broad bean and sausage soup), green salad, red meat, and wines from La Rioja and La Ribera de Duero. Reserve well in advance. To dine outside, you must insist vigorously. (Try for confirmation by fax.) ⊠ *Pianista García Carrillo 2, El Albayzín,* ☎ *958/ 228290,* ℻ *958/228125. Reservations required. AE, DC, MC, V. Closed Sun.*

**$$**   ✕ **Cunini.** Around the corner from the cathedral is one of Granada's best seafood restaurants. Fresh fish are displayed in the window, at the end of the long tapas bar, and the menu is an anthology of fish recipes from all over Spain, including some Basque specialties. Both the *pescadito frito* (deep-fried whitebait) and the *parrillada* (grilled fish) are good choices, and if it's chilly you can warm up with *zarzuela* (fish stew).

There are tables outdoors in warm weather. ⊠ *Pescadería 14, Centro,* ☎ *958/250777. AE, DC, MC, V. Closed Mon.*

**$$** ✕ **La Mimbre.** Location, location, location: this small, slightly cramped lunch spot is tucked right under the walls of the Alhambra, next to the Generalife. Inside, you sit on chairs upholstered with typical Alpujarran fabric; outside, the spacious patio is shady, romantic, and delightful in warm weather. The food is classically Granadino: *habas con jamón* (broad beans and ham) and *choto al ajillo* (braised kid with garlic). ⊠ *Avda. del Generalife s/n, Alhambra,* ☎ *958/222276. AE, MC, V. Nov.–Mar. closed Sat.*

**$$** ✕ **Rossini Queseria.** This gorgeously decorated, living-room–style bar and salon is a good choice for light grazing on a hot night in the Realejo. Specialists in cheeses, patés, smoked fish, hams, and sausages, the savvy proprietors here can create for you a satisfying potpourri of Spain's and Andalusia's finest artisanal food products. ⊠ *Campo del Príncipe 15, Campo del Príncipe,* ☎ *958/227276. AE, DC, MC, V. Closed Sun.*

**$$** ✕ **Sevilla.** This colorful, central, two-story restaurant has been going
★ strong since 1930 and has fed the likes of composer Manuel de Falla and poet Federico García Lorca over the years. There are a small but superb tapas bar and four picturesque dining rooms; you can also dine on an outdoor terrace overlooking the Royal Chapel. The menu features such Granadino favorites as *sopa sevillana* (a white soup with hake and shrimp) and *tortilla al Sacromonte* (omelette with brains and testicles of pork or lamb). ⊠ *Oficios 12 (beside cathedral), Centro,* ☎ *958/ 221223. AE, DC, MC, V. Closed Mon. No dinner Sun. Jan. 7–Feb. 7.*

**$$** ✕ **Velázquez.** Locals have long been enthusiastic about this cozy, very Spanish restaurant on a side street one block west of the Puerta de Elvira and Plaza del Triunfo. At street level is a brick-wall bar hung with hams; an intimate, wood-beamed dining room is upstairs. Specialties include *zancarrón cordero a la miel* (lamb with honey) and *lomitos de rape* (braised monkfish medallions). ⊠ *Profesor Emilio Orozco 1, Centro,* ☎ *958/289109. MC, V. Closed Sun. and Aug.*

**$–$$** ✕ **La Ninfa.** This singular and slender tower decorated with ceramic platters on its whitewashed facade is a cardinal vantage point over Campo del Príncipe, especially from the fourth-floor roof garden. Offering a balanced menu of meat and seafood of all kinds, La Ninfa is a reliable choice among the many taverns and restaurants that line this uproarious Realejo nightlife hub. ⊠ *Campo del Príncipe 14, Campo del Príncipe,* ☎ *958/229630. AE, DC, MC, V. Closed Tues. and 15 days in Nov.*

**$–$$** ✕ **Los Manueles.** This ancient tavern is usually packed. The food is not remarkable—tortilla *al Sacromonte* (omelet with kid's brains, ham, and vegetables) and other local fare—but the decor, atmosphere, and friendly waiters make this inn off Reyes Católicos popular with both Granadinos and travelers. Alpujarran rugs, ceramic plates, and other knickknacks cover the walls, and a plaque commemorates a visit from Spain's royal family in 1982. Gigantic hams adorn the bar. ⊠ *Zaragoza 2 and 4, Centro,* ☎ *958/223413. AE, DC, MC, V.*

## Tapas Bars and Taverns

For the most colorful bars and tapas emporiums, look around the Albayzín, Campo del Príncipe, the Plaza del Cármen–Calle Navas area, and the Pedro de Alarcón–Martínez de la Rosa zone out toward the University of Granada campus in the city's southwest corner. There are also popular terraces and taverns stacked in under the bullring. **Bar Los Diamantes** (⊠ Calle Navas 26, Centro, ☎ 958/212006) is a booming success, with fried fish in several varieties the staple. **La Trastienda** (⊠ Plaza de Cuchilleros 11, Centro, ☎ 958/220307) is a lively saloon with fine tapas and a cozy ambience. **Bar El Ladrillo** (⊠ Plaza de Fátima, El Albayzín) is a tiny but popular tapas bar with outdoor tables in summer. **Café Bar Lara** (⊠ Plaza de San Miguel Bajo 4, El Albayzín) is a small, busy tapas bar in one of the Albayzín's most characteristic squares. **Casa de Todos** (⊠ Calle Elvira [corner of Plaza Nueva], El Albayzín) is a *bocadillo* (sandwich) specialist just off Plaza Nueva. For a splendid array of regional wines with your morsels, try **La Puerta del Vino** (⊠ Paseo Padre Manjón 5, El Albayzín, ☎ 958/210026), a 10-table bar hung with old paintings. **Chikito** (⊠ Plaza del Campillo 9, El Realejo, ☎ 958/223364) is best known for its tasty sit-down meals, but the bar offers excellent tapas-grazing as well. The place is usually packed, even in summer, when additional tables are set up in the plaza. The popular **Bodegas Castañeda** (⊠ Elvira 6, El Albayzín, ☎ 958/226362) draws a local crowd. On the Plaza Nueva, **La Gran Taberna** (⊠ Plaza Nueva 12, El Albayzín, ☎ 958/228846), a bi-level bar with wooden gallery upstairs, is famous for its *montaditos,* little open-face sandwiches made with the ingredients of your choice. Favored by intellectuals, **Casa Enrique** (⊠ Acera del Darro 8, El Albayzín, ☎ 958/255008), known to locals as "El Elefante," is a dark little hole-in-the-wall founded in 1870 and specializing in Iberian ham, anchovies, and fine wine.

## Lodging

**$$$$**  🏠 **Parador de San Francisco.** Magnificently set within the Alhambra precincts, Spain's most popular (and expensive) parador occupies an old Franciscan convent built by the Catholic Monarchs after they captured Granada. The rooms in the old section are furnished with antiques, woven curtains, and bedspreads; those in the new wing are simpler. Reserve four to six months in advance. ⊠ *Alhambra, 18009,* ☎ *958/221440,* FAX *958/222264,* WEB *www.parador.es. 36 rooms. Restaurant, bar, meeting rooms, parking (fee). AE, DC, MC, V.*

**$$$–$$$$**  🏠 **Cármen de Santa Inés.** This slightly smaller sister ship of the Palacio de Santa Inés just down the hill is a charming Albayzín hideaway. With a breakfast terrace in the garden overlooking the Alhambra, the painstakingly restored wood and tile work, the private chapel, and the overall elegance and taste of the place, you'll feel right at home by the time you get to the Nasrid palace across the Darro. ⊠ *Placeta de Porras 7/San Juan de los Reyes 15, El Albayzín, 18018,* ☎ *958/226380,* FAX *958/224404. 9 rooms. Minibars. AE, DC, MC, V.*

**$$$–$$$$**  🏠 **Casa Morisca.** Just off the Paseo de los Tristes at the upper end of
    ★   the Carrera del Darro, this exquisitely restored 15th-century Moorish town house offers absolute comfort in an aesthetic tour de force. Each room is unique, but the tower room, with views out three sides, the blue room overlooking the Alhambra, and the astounding bridal suite with its original, hand-painted cedar ceiling are the standouts. ⊠ *Cuesta de la Victoria 9, El Albayzín, 18010,* ☎ *958/221100,* FAX *958/215796,* WEB *www.hotelcasamorisca.com. 14 rooms. Dining room, minibars, free parking. AE, DC, MC, V.*

**$$$–$$$$**  🏠 **Hotel Alhambra Palace.** A flamboyant, ocher-red, neo-Moorish
    ★   pile, this 1910 hotel commands a superb position on leafy grounds at the back of the Alhambra hill. The interior is exotic, very Arabian Nights, with orange and brown overtones, multicolor tiles, and Moorish arches and pillars. Even the bar is incongruously decorated as a mosque. The rooms overlooking the town have incredible views, as does the terrace, a perfect place to watch the sun set on the city of Granada and its fertile vega. ⊠ *Peña Partida 2, Alhambra, 18009,* ☎ *958/221468,* FAX *958/226404,* WEB *www.h-alhambrapalace.es. 122 rooms, 13 suites. Restaurant, 2 bars, some pets allowed. AE, DC, MC, V.*

**$$$–$$$$** ☆ 🏨 **Palacio de Santa Inés.** The chief attraction of this small lodging is its special location in the heart of the Albayzín. The setting is a converted 16th-century palace surrounding a frescoed courtyard. The rooms occupy the two upper floors, and each is uniquely decorated with tasteful antiques and low-key modern art. Some of the suites have balconies with Alhambra views. ✉ *Cuesta de Santa Inés 9, El Albayzín, 18010,* ☎ *958/222362,* 🖷 *958/222465. 9 rooms, 2 suites. Minibars, bar, some pets allowed AE, DC, MC, V.*

**$$$–$$$$** 🏨 **Tryp Albayzin.** Located on the tree-lined Carrera del Genil, the Tryp is next to El Corte Inglés department store and well placed for general downtown shopping. Decor in the common areas and the large, air-conditioned guest rooms is a tasteful modern-Moorish, light and airy. The inner patio comes complete with an Alhambra-style trickling fountain. ✉ *Carrera del Genil 46, Centro, 18005,* ☎ *958/220002,* 🖷 *958/220181,* 🌐 *www.somelia.es. 108 rooms. Restaurant, sauna, meeting rooms, parking (fee). AE, DC, MC, V.*

**$$–$$$$** 🏨 **Inglaterra.** Two blocks east of the Gran Vía de Colón, in the heart of town, this hotel combines the best of three worlds: a central location, a 19th-century house with an old-world facade, and a modern, comfortable interior. The lounges have polished wood floors; guest rooms are carpeted and painted a pleasing salmon color, with contemporary blond-wood furniture. ✉ *Cetti Meriem 4, Centro, 18010,* ☎ *958/221558,* 🖷 *958/227100. 36 rooms. Restaurant, meeting room, parking (fee). AE, DC, MC, V.*

**$$–$$$** 🏨 **América.** This simple but charming hotel within the Alhambra precinct is very popular, albeit more for the unbeatable location than for the service. Reserve months in advance. The place feels like a private home, with simple bedrooms, a sitting room decorated with local handicrafts, and a shaded patio where home-cooked meals are served in summer. The downside is that, aside from the Alhambra itself, it's not near Granada's real life. It's a long hike or a taxi to the Albayzín, Sacromonte, and the Realejo. ✉ *Real de la Alhambra 53, Alhambra, 18009,* ☎ *958/227471,* 🖷 *958/227470. 13 rooms. Restaurant. MC, V. Closed Dec.–Feb.*

**$$–$$$** 🏨 **Casa del Aljarife.** This gem, hidden in one of the Albayzín's prettiest squares, is a carefully restored 17th-century house with lovely wooden floors, a flower-choked garden, and spectacular views over the Alhambra from some rooms. Galleries opening onto a typical Andalusian courtyard help create the feeling of a private home, and the owner-proprietors are gracious hosts with helpful suggestions about Granada. Park in nearby Parking San Agustin on the Gran Vía de Colón before entering the Albayzín on foot. The owners, by prior arrangement, will collect you in Plaza Nueva. ✉ *Placeta de la Cruz Verde 2, El Albayzín, 18010,* ☎ 🖷 *958/222425,* 🌐 *www.granadainfo. com/most. 3 rooms. Dining room. AE, DC, MC, V.*

**$$–$$$** 🏨 **Triunfo Granada.** This comfortable hotel is at the far end of the Gran Vía de Colón. The public rooms have gleaming marble floors, deep sofas, and copious paintings; guest rooms are traditional, with dark wood and pink or light-green curtains and bedspreads. The handsome Puerta Elvira Restaurant serves typical Andalusian dishes. ✉ *Plaza Triunfo 19, Centro, 18010,* ☎ *958/207444,* 🖷 *958/279017,* 🌐 *www.h-triunfo-granada.com. 37 rooms. Restaurant, cafeteria, meeting rooms, parking (fee). AE, DC, MC, V.*

**$$** 🏨 **Alixares.** Large and modern but not unattractive, the Alixares has a prime location between the Alhambra and the Generalife. The cream-color rooms are contemporary and functional; those on the fourth and fifth floors have the best views. The staff is friendly and professional. In summer, the rooftop barbecue is an added dining option. ✉ *Avda. Alixares del Generalife 27, Alhambra, 18009,* ☎ *958/225575,* 🖷

958/224102. *176 rooms. Restaurant, cafeteria, pool, meeting room. AE, DC, MC, V.*

**$$**  ⊞ **Reina Cristina.** Occupying the former Rosales residence, where the
★   poet García Lorca was arrested after taking refuge at the outset of the
Spanish Civil War, the Reina Cristina is near the lively Plaza de la
Trinidad. Plants trail from the windowsills of the reception area, a cov-
ered patio where a marble fountain splashes beneath a Moorish lamp.
A marble stairway leads to the bedrooms, which are simply but cheer-
fully furnished with red fabrics on a white background. The restaurant,
El Rincón de Lorca, is one of the best in Granada, serving classic local
dishes in a setting reminiscent of an elegant old home. ⊠ *Tablas 4, Cen-
tro, 18002,* ☎ *958/253211,* 𝖥𝖠𝖷 *958/255728,* 𝖶𝖤𝖡 *www.hotelreinacristina.
com. 43 rooms. Restaurant, cafeteria, bar, parking (fee), some pets al-
lowed. AE, DC, MC, V.*

**$-$$**  ⊞ **Macía Plaza.** The small reception area is dull, but it opens out onto
one of the liveliest squares in Granada, the Plaza Nueva, at the foot
of the Alhambra hill. Location comes at a price, though: the square
gets very noisy, especially on weekend evenings, which detracts from
the charm of the eight rooms with balconies overlooking the square
(sans double glazing). Interior rooms without the view are the quieter
option. All rooms are simply but comfortably furnished, with carpet-
ing and air-conditioning. ⊠ *Plaza Nueva, 4, El Albayzín, 18010,* ☎
*958/227536,* 𝖥𝖠𝖷 *958/227535,* 𝖶𝖤𝖡 *www.maciahoteles.com. 44 rooms.
Cable TV, meeting room. MC, V.*

**$**  ⊞ **Hotel Molinos.** Registered in the Guinness Book of Records as the
world's narrowest hotel—five meters (16.5 ft) wide at its narrowest
point and just 20 centimeters more at its widest—this slender stack of
rooms is nevertheless a well-designed and happy little spot. Rooms are
contemporary and simply but comfortably furnished with good air-conditioning. Conveniently located in the Realejo district just off Plaza del
Príncipe, this is good choice for both budget and comfort. ⊠ *Calle Molinos 12, Campo del Príncipe, 18009,* ☎ *958/227489,* 𝖥𝖠𝖷 *958/227367.
9 rooms. Cafeteria, parking (fee). AE, DC, MC, V.*

**$**  ⊞ **Suecia.** This flower-covered villa tucked into a quiet residential
alley near the Campo de Príncipe has the feel of a garden retreat ma-
rooned in the middle of downtown Granada. The atmosphere is friendly
and informal. Rooms vary in size, so you may want to look at several
if offered a choice. You'll be within walking distance from some of
Granada's most popular taverns in the Campo del Príncipe and the
Realejo. Safe (and free) parking in the street by the front gate is usually easy to find, and the perennial jasmine in the garden makes this
*huerta* (garden) a year-round floral display. ⊠ *Huerta de los Angeles
8 (off C. Molinos), Campo del Príncipe, 18009,* ☎ *958/225044,* ☎
𝖥𝖠𝖷 *958/227781. 12 rooms, 8 with bath. Dining room, free parking,
some pets allowed. MC, V.*

**$**  ⊞ **Verona.** This small hostal near the center of Granada is good bud-
get choice for dependable, adequate lodging in a modern building well
equipped with elevators, air-conditioning, televisions and the full range
of modern conveniences.⊠ *Recogidas 9, Centro, 18005,* ☎ *958/
255507,* ☎ 𝖥𝖠𝖷 *958/255507. 14 rooms. Meeting room, parking (fee).
MC, V.*

## Nightlife and the Arts

Get the latest on arts events, including diversions for young people, at
the **Area de Cultura** (City Department of Culture), in the Palacio de
los Condes de Gabia (⊠ Plaza de los Girones 1, Centro, ☎ 958/
247383, 𝖶𝖤𝖡 www.dipgra.es).

## Classical Music and Dance

The **Festival internacional de música y danza** (International Festival of Music and Dance, ☎ 958/221844, FAX 958/220691, WEB www.granadafestival.org), held annually from mid-June to early July, is Granada's star cultural event, featuring top ballet, flamenco, classical, and early music performers from around the world. Book far in advance for this exquisite combination of world-class music and dance held in Andalusia's most romantic architectural treasures, from the Alhambra's Patio de los Arrayanes to the Moorish palaces of the Albayzín. Tickets are available at the Corral del Carbón on Mariana Pineda, one block from Reyes Católicos, as well as by phone and on-line.

Granada's orchestra performs often in the **Centro Cultural Manuel de Falla** (⊠ Paseo de los Mártires, Alhambra, ☎ 958/222188). Contact the tourist office for information on the **November Jazz Festival.**

## Flamenco

Flamenco offerings in Granada range from the commercial *zambras* (song and dance) and *tablaos* (shows) of Sacromonte to the *peñas* (clubs) and cultural centers where, if you're lucky, you might stumble across a memorable performance when you least expect it.

For zambra performances by Gypsies in the Sacromonte caves, join a tour through a travel agent or your hotel. If you want to go to a Sacromonte flamenco show on your own, try **Cueva María la Canastera** (⊠ Camino del Sacromonte 86, Sacromonte, ☎ 958/121183), which also doubles as a Sacromonte flamenco museum, open weekdays 4:30–7:30, weekends noon–2:30. There's a flamenco show nightly at 10:15 in the **Sala Albaicin** (⊠ Mirador de San Cristóbal, El Albayzín, ☎ 958/804646). Flamenco is performed at 10 and 11 nightly in the **Cueva La Rocio** (⊠ Camino de Sacromonte 70, Sacromonte, ☎ 958/227129) for the reasonable €20, including bus and drink. **Cueva los Tarantos** (⊠ Camino del Sacromonte 9, Sacromonte, ☎ 958/224525) puts on regular zambra shows, bookable through hotels. Call ahead for performance times, and be prepared to part with lots of money. **Venta el Gallo** (⊠ Barranco de los Negros 5, Sacromonte, ☎ 958/220591) offers a dependably good nightly *zambra gitana* with dinner included at the legendary Casa Juanillo (overlooking the Alhambra) next door for €30, or with drink only for €20.

For more intimate and authentic amateur flamenco performances, try the **Peña de la Platería** (⊠ Plaza de Toqueros 7, El Albayzín, ☎ 958/210650). One of the oldest of Andalusia's flamenco peñas, this popular spot has free performances on Friday night. **La Chumbera** (⊠ Camino del Sacromonte, Sacromonte, ☎ 958/248140) is a cultural center dedicated to Gypsy studies that offers free flamenco performances on Saturday night.

## Theater

Plays are performed at the **Teatro Alhambra** (⊠ Molinos 56, El Realejo, ☎ 958/220447). The **International Theater Festival,** organized by Granada's ayuntamiento (⊠ Plaza del Cármen, Centro, ☎ 958/229344), fills 10 days each May. The main multipurpose auditorium complex is the **Palacio de Exposiciones y Congresos** (⊠ Paseo del Violón s/n, Ciudad Jardín, ☎ 958/246700).

## Nightlife

The *tapeo, copa,* music bar, disco, and after-hours scenes in Granada thrive thanks to the city's large student population (60,000 of the city's 250,000 inhabitants are 18- to 25-year-olds). Campo del Príncipe, a large plaza in the Realejo district surrounded by typical Andalusian taverns, is prime carousing country, and the streets around Plaza el Cármen (especially Escudo del Cármen and Navas) are known for lively tapeo and vino spots. Some of the trendiest bars in town are in converted houses in the Albayzín along the Paseo de los Tristes (next to the Darro River, between the Plaza Nueva and the Cuesta del Chapiz). In the upper Albayzín, Plaza Larga and Plaza de San Miguel Bajo are popular watering holes. In the modern part of town, on Pedro Antonio de Alarcón and Martinez de la Rosa, there are clubs and bars to investigate, and near the Glorieta de Arabial, the Taberna Taurina Laly draws bullfight aficionados into the wee small hours. Even farther out of the center is the cluster of terraces, discos, tapas emporiums, and restaurants wedged under the Granada bullring.

MUSIC BARS

**La Industrial Copera** (⊠ Crtra. de Armilla s/n, Armilla, ☎ 958/220134), on the outskirts of town, offers dance of every persuasion and the odd disc jockey on tour. **La Fontana** (⊠ Carrera del Darro 19, El Albayzín, ☎ 958/227759) is a lively forum to start the evening. **La Estrella** (⊠ Cuchilleros 6, El Albayzín, ☎ 958/225961), in Plaza Nueva, is always booming with students.

DISCOS

**Granada 10** (⊠ Carcel Baja 10, El Albayzín, ☎ 958/224001) is a former theater converted into a discotheque. **El Camborio** (⊠ Camino de-Sacromonte 47, Sacromonte, ☎ 958/221215) is the place to dance to the brink of oblivion and back. **Lla** (⊠ Santa Bárbara 3, Centro, ☎ 958/295763), near Plaza del Triunfo, is the place for rock.

# Outdoor Activities and Sports

## Baths

The **Hammam** (⊠ C/Santa Ana 16, El Albayzín, ☎ 958/229978), officially known as the Baños Arabes Al Andalus, is a fine, traditional Moorish bathhouse. You can also dine here at the tearoom or the restaurant that are part of the facility.

## Golf

Granada's 18-hole **Club de Golf de Granada** (⊠ Las Gabias, ☎ 958/584436) is 8 km (5 mi) south of the city center in Las Gabias, just off the N323 road to the coast at Motril. Greens fees are €36 on weekday mornings, dropping to €20 after 1:30. Weekend fees are €50, and tee times are hard to come by. While no Valderrama, this is nevertheless a better than average course.

## Swimming

Just outside Granada is **Aquaola** (⊠ Crta. Antigua de Sierra Nevada Km 4, ☎ 958/486189, WEB www.aquaola.com), a good water park with numerous attractions and facilities. It's open June 15 to September 15, and charges €9 for adults, €7 for children on weekdays, €10.50 and €8 on weekends.

# Shopping

Granada's handicrafts are very much a legacy of the Moors, whose aesthetic influence shows up in brass and copperware, ceramics, marquetry, and woven textiles. The main shopping streets, centering on the Puerta Real, are **Reyes Católicos, Zacatín, Ángel Ganivet,** and the **Gran Vía de Colón.** Most of the antiques stores are on **Cuesta de Elvira.**

**Cerámica Fabre**(⊠ Plaza Pescadería 2, Centro, ☎ 958/261558), near the cathedral, has a full range of the typical Granada ceramics, with their blue-and-green patterns on a white background and a symbol in the center representing a pomegranate, the emblem of the city. **Fajalauza**

(⊠ Fajalauza 2, Haza Grande, ☎ 958/200615) has been producing ceramics for 400 years; you'll find ovens on site as well as showrooms. For a good selection of wicker baskets and esparto mats and rugs, head for **Espartería San José** (⊠ Calle Jaudenes 22, ☎ 958/267415). For locally made guitars, go to **A Morales** (⊠ Cuesta de Gomerez 9, Centro, ☎ 958/221387), with other guitars at Nos. 26 and 29. **La Alacena de Andalucia** (⊠ San Jerónimo 3, Centro, ☎ 958/206890), near the cathedral, sells local gastronomic products, including wines, olive oil, vinegar, cheeses, and cookies. For fine air-cured hams from nearby Trevélez, sample slices at **Mantequería Castellano** (⊠ Almireceros 6, Centro, ☎ 958/224840). Spain's ubiquitous department store, with souvenir and gourmet sections, is **El Corte Inglés** (⊠ Carrera del Genil 20–22, San Matias, ☎ 958/217600). For books in English, visit **Librería Metro** (⊠ Gracia 31, Centro, ☎ 958/261565).

# SIDE TRIPS FROM GRANADA

Immediately around the city of Granada are several easy visits for travelers preferring to remain based in the capital while exploring the countryside and villages nearby. Farther afield are the main geographical regions within the province: El Poniente Granadino to the west, Sierra Nevada looming over Granada to the east, La Costa Tropical south on the Mediterranean, La Alpujarra mountains between Sierra Nevada and the coast, the flatlands of Guadix y Marquesado north of Sierra Nevada, and the high steppes and mountains of El Altiplano to the northeast.

## Santa Fe

**38** *8 km (5 mi) west of Granada, just south of N342.*

As much for the key historic events that have been played out here as for the well-preserved monumental *casco histórico* (historic urban center), Santa Fe is an important Granada landmark. Founded in winter 1491 as a campground for Ferdinand and Isabella's 150,000 troops as they prepared for the siege of Granada, Santa Fe was originally planned as a model fortified town, laid out in the shape of a cross with monumental entryways at the four extremities. The four arched entryways are the Puertas of Sevilla to the south, Loja to the west, Jaén to the north, and Granada to the east, each inscribed with Ferdinand and Isabella's initials and crowned with octagonal watch towers. At the center of the stronghold are the public buildings: La Casa Real (the Royal House), the parish house, the hospital, and *alhóndiga* (granary). The town has long since transcended its original boundaries, though the four gates remain, simultaneously visible from Plaza de España next to the neoclassical 18th-century Iglesia de la Encarnación at the center of the old town.

It was in Santa Fe, on November 25, 1491, that the Nasrid rulers of Iberia's last Moorish kingdom, Kings Abdallah and Boabdil, signed the treaty surrendering Granada to the Catholic Monarchs. It was also in Santa Fe, in April 1492, that Isabella and Columbus signed the agreements that financed his historic voyage, and thus the town has been called the Cradle of America.

## Fuentevaqueros

**39** *10 km (6 mi) northwest of Santa Fe.*

Federico García Lorca was born in this village on June 5, 1898, and lived here until the age of six. The **Casa Museo Federico García Lorca,** the poet's childhood home, opened as a museum in 1986, when Spain commemorated the 50th anniversary of Lorca's assassination and celebrated his reinstatement as a national figure after 40 years of nonrecognition during the Franco regime. The house has been restored with original furnishings, and the former granary, barn, and stables have been converted into exhibition spaces, with temporary art shows and a permanent display of photographs, clippings, and other memorabilia. A two-minute video shows the only existing footage of Lorca on film. ✉ *Poeta García Lorca 4,* ☎ *958/516453,* WEB *www.museogarcialorca. org.* ☞ *€2.* ☉ *July–Sept., Tues.–Sun. 10–1 and 6–8; Oct.–Mar., Tues.– Sun. 10–1 and 4–6; Apr.–June, Tues.–Sun. 10–1 and 5–7; mandatory guided tours hourly.*

The village of Valderrubio, not far from Fuentevaqueros, inspired much of García Lorca's early poetry, especially his *Romancero Gitano,* some of which was written in the house the poet's father bought here in 1907, now dubbed **Casa de Valderrubio.** One of García Lorca's best-loved plays, *La Casa de Bernarda Alba,* was modeled on the women he knew as a boy here. The García Lorca house in Valderrubio, having gradually recovered the furnishings lost when the family went into exile in 1936, offers a telling glimpse of the poet's family life between 1907 and 1909, and until 1925 as the family summer residence. ✉ *Valderrubio, Pinos Puente,* ☎ *958/454466,* ☞ *€2.* ☉ *By arrangement with Ayuntamiento, Pinos Puente.*

## Viznar

40  *9 km (5½ mi) northeast of Granada.*

If you're a García Lorca devotee, make the short trip to Viznar, heading northeast on N342 out of Granada, then turning left, then left again when you see signs for the town. The **Federico García Lorca Memorial Park,** 3 km (2 mi) from Viznar up a narrow winding road, marks the spot where Lorca was taken out and shot without trial by Nationalists at the beginning of the Spanish Civil War war in August 1936 and where he is probably buried. García Lorca, who is now universally venerated, was hated by Fascists for his active support of the Second Spanish Republic, his liberal ideas in general, and his homosexuality. A granite monolith and an olive tree mark the spot where the poet is thought to have fallen.

# EL PONIENTE GRANADINO

El Poniente (the west), where the sun *se pone* (sets), is Granada's borderland with Málaga, Córdoba, and Jaén. The castles at Loja, Moclin, Íllora, Zagra, and Montefrío bear witness to the final battles of this "last frontier" between Muslim and Christian Spain. From the trout streams of Riofrío and Cacín to the Arab baths at Alhama de Granada to the churches by Diego de Siloé and Ventura Rodríguez in Montefrío, El Poniente Granadino has a wide range of attractions.

## Loja

41  *55 km (34 mi) west of Granada, 40 km (25 mi) northeast of Málaga.*

Standing guard at the entrance to Granada's vega, halfway between Granada and Málaga on the A92, Loja is a traditional pit stop for travelers, who like to munch on the famous *roscos de Loja,* a hard, doughnut-shaped, sugar-coated pastry. The town's name comes from the "Lascivis" of Roman times, meaning "place of water and delight," and the town still has numerous fountains, including the 25-spout Fuente de los Veinticinco Caños.

Eight kilometers (five miles) west of Loja on A92 is the hamlet of **Riofrío,** next to a rushing trout stream. Trout and sturgeon raised at Riofrío's fish farm are enjoyed throughout Andalusia. Eight restaurants, all inexpensive, serve fresh trout in a variety of ways: *a la plancha* (grilled), *a la romana* (batter-fried), *a la navarra* (with ham), and *ahumado* (smoked).

### Dining and Lodging

$$$$ ★ ✕🏨 **La Bobadilla.** This luxurious complex 14 km (9 mi) west of Loja stands on its own 860-acre estate amid olive and holm-oak trees, a sumptuous island in the Andalusian hinterland. With white walls, tile roofs, patios, fountains, and an artificial lake, it resembles a Moorish village or a rambling Andalusian *cortijo* (ranch). The guest buildings surround a 16th-century-style chapel, whose 1,595-pipe organ is used for occasional concerts and weddings. Each room is individually designed and decorated and has its own terrace or garden. The elegant La Finca restaurant serves highly creative international cuisine, and a second restaurant, El Cortijo, has more down-to-earth regional fare. Prices are princely, but special deals are frequent, so it's worth inquiring. ✉ *Finca La Bobadilla (north of A92 between Salinas and Rute; exit north onto 334, toward Iznajar), 18300,* ☎ *958/321861,* FAX *958/321810,* WEB *www.la-bobadilla.com. 52 rooms, 9 suites. 2 restaurants, minibars, cable TV, 2 tennis courts, 2 pools (1 indoor), gym, hot tub, sauna, horseback riding, convention center; some pets allowed. AE, DC, MC, V.*

# SIERRA NEVADA

The Sierra Nevada is an easy and worthwhile excursion from Granada, as either a day trip or an overnight destination. The ski resort—with two stations, Pradollano and the higher Borreguiles—draws crowds from December to May, but the same slope is quiet in summer. In July and August you can drive right up to the summit of the Veleta on Europe's highest road. It's cold up here, so bring a warm jacket and scarf with your sunglasses, even if the weather in Granada is sizzling hot. The **Pico de Veleta,** Spain's third-highest mountain, stands at 11,125 ft, and the view from its summit across the Alpujarra range to the sea, at distant Motril, is stunning; on a very clear day you can even see the coast of North Africa. Away to your left, the mighty **Mulhacén,** the highest peak in mainland Spain, soars to 11,427 ft.

## Pradollano

42 *32 km (19 mi) southeast of Granada.*

Pradollano and the Sierra Nevada ski resort are virtually synonymous, with nearly all lodging, restaurant and after-ski resources found in this luxury hotel-filled Pradollano base camp. Everything from sports complexes with saunas and jacuzzis to skating rinks, classical music concerts and the Telecabina movie theater are available in this somewhat overdeveloped but still cozy Sierra Nevada clubhouse. The drive southeast from Granada to Pradollano along C420, by way of Cenes de la Vega, takes about 45 minutes. It's wise to carry snow chains even as late as April or May.

### Lodging

$$$$ 🏨 **El Lodge.** Built of Finnish wood—unusual for southern Spain, but perfectly appropriate in this alpine setting—this hotel has a warm and cozy, womblike quality. Rooms are not especially large, but ex-

tremely comfortable. Add to that a fantastic location next to the ski slopes, and a friendly, professional service, and you've got the best hotel in Granada's ski resort. ✉ *Calle Maribel 8, 18196,* ☎ *958/ 480600,* FAX *958/481314. 16 rooms, 4 suites. Restaurant, in-room safes, minibars, cable TV, gym, sauna, bar, meeting rooms. AE, MC, D. Closed May–Oct.*

### Skiing

**The Sierra Nevada** has one of Europe's best-equipped ski stations, having hosted the World Alpine Ski Championships in 1996. There are 21 lifts, 45 runs, and about 60 km (37 mi) of marked trails, not to mention a snowboarding circuit and two floodlit slopes for night skiing on weekends. A **children's ski school** and rental shop round out the facilities. Contact the **Sierra Nevada Information Center** (✉ Plaza de Andalucía 4, ☎ 958/249111, WEB www.sierranevadaski.com) for information; you can also call for **snow, weather, and road conditions** (☎ 958/249119).

# LA ALPUJARRA

South and east of Granada, the Alpujarra, on the southern slopes of the Sierra Nevada, is one of Andalusia's highest, most remote, and most picturesque areas. Here, whitewashed villages produce handsome crafts ranging from textiles to basketware to pottery and other goods. If you're driving, you'll find the road as far as Lanjarón and Orgiva smooth sailing; after that come steep, twisting mountain roads with few gas stations.

A few miles south of Granada on N323, the road reaches a spot known as the **Suspiro del Moro** (Moor's Sigh). Pause here a moment and look back at the city, just as Granada's departing "boy king," Boabdil, did 500 years ago. As he wept over the city he'd surrendered to the Catholic Monarchs, his scornful mother pronounced her now famous rebuke: "You weep like a boy for the city you could not defend as a man."

The Alpujarra region was originally populated by Moors fleeing the Christian reconquest (from Seville after its fall in 1248, then from Granada after 1492). It was also the last fiefdom of the unfortunate Boabdil, conceded to him by the Catholic Monarchs after he surrendered Granada. In 1568, rebellious Moors made their final stand against the Christian overlords, a revolt ruthlessly suppressed by Philip II and followed by the forced conversion of all Moors to Christianity and their resettlement farther inland and up Spain's eastern coast.

The villages of the Alpujarra were then repopulated with Christian soldiers from Galicia, who were granted land in return for their service against the Moors. To this day, the Galicians' descendants continue the Moorish custom of weaving rugs and blankets in the traditional Alpujarran colors of red, green, black, and white, and they sell their crafts in many of the villages. Houses here are squat and square; they spill down the southern slopes of the Sierra Nevada one on top of another, bearing a strong resemblance to the Berber homes in the Rif Mountains just across the Strait of Gibraltar in Morocco.

## Lanjarón

🔸 *51 km (30 mi) southeast of Granada.*

Marking the entrance to the Alpujarra, Lanjaró is a spa town famous for its mineral water, gathered from the melting snows of the Sierra Nevada and drunk throughout Spain. Lanjarón is also known for its wicker baskets and furniture. There are numerous hostals, but during the spa season (May–November) these cater mainly to people seeking cures for a variety of ailments, so the atmosphere can be less than festive.

# Orgiva

**44** *9 km (6 mi) east of Lanjarón.*

Orgiva, with a population of just under 5,000, is the largest village in the Alpujarra. It's known for its baroque church and Thursday farmers' market, and is a hub and jumping-off point for hiking, equestrian, and motor tours through the Alpujarra.

### Dining and Lodging

$–$$ ✕⊡ **Taray Alpujarra.** This friendly hotel on its own farm makes the perfect base for exploring the Alpujarra. The main hotel is a low, whitewashed building. A stone building was added in 1997, but the rooms with the best views (Nos. 1–15) are in the older wing. The sunny guest rooms are decorated with Alpujarran bedspreads and curtains; two have rooftop terraces. There's a pleasant common terrace, and most of the food served in the restaurant comes from the estate, including fresh trout and lamb. In season, you can pick your own raspberries for breakfast. ⊠ *Carretera Tablate–Albuñol, Km 18.5, 18400,* ☎ *958/784525,* FAX *958/784531. 28 rooms. Restaurant, pool. AE, DC, MC, V.*

# Capileira

**45** *80 km (48 mi) southeast of Granada, 16 km (10 mi) east of Orgiva.*

From Orgiva leave the C332, follow signs for Pampaneira and Capileira, and you'll find yourself in the Alpujarra Alta (High Alpujarra). Capileira, with a mere 576 inhabitants, is the main Alpujarran base camp for climbs to the peaks of Veleta and Mulhacén. The views down into the Barranco de Poqueira (Poqueira Gorge) below the village and up into the Sierra Nevada are equally astounding, and the Refugio de Poqueira, a six-to-eight-hour hike above Capileira, is the way station and staging point for the assault on Mulhacén's 11,427-ft summit.

Capileira's **Museo Alpujarreño,** has a colorful display of local crafts as well as an exhibit showing the similarity between the cubic, two-storied, flat-roofed, whitewashed houses and villages of the Alpujarra and those of North Africa. The looms in the workshops of nearby Pampaneira produce many of the characteristic bright textiles sold here. ⊠ *Mentidero s/n,* ☎ *958/763051.* ⊡ €1. ◷ *Tues.–Sun. 11:30–2.*

### Dining and Lodging

$ ✕⊡ **Mesón Poqueira.** This busy spot, part tavern, part art gallery, part inn and general store, is the nerve center of Capileira and the place to spend a night on the way onto or out of the sierra. Local cuisine based on partridge, trout, rabbit, wild boar, and other highland products is simply and well prepared here. ⊠ *Dr. Castilla 11, 18413,* ☎ FAX *958/763048. 13 apartments. Restaurant. MC, V.*

# Trevélez

**46** *17 km (10 mi) east of Capileira.*

Famous for its hams cured in the dry mountain air of the Sierra Nevada, Trevélez, perched at the tip of the road's sharpest incursion into the highlands, is the northernmost of the Alpujarran villages and, at an altitude of 4,843 ft, the highest village on the Iberian Peninsula. Trevélez has three levels, the Barrio Alto, Barrio Medio, and Barrio Bajo; the butchers are concentrated in the lowest section (Bajo). The higher levels are far more picturesque, with narrow cobblestone streets, whitewashed houses, and fewer shops. The valley is rich in trout streams and alpine scenery all within sight of North Africa.

### Dining and Lodging

$  ✕☷ **La Fragua.** Spotless rooms, some with balconies, fresh air by the lungful, and views over the rooftops of Trevélez are the rewards of this small, friendly hostelry in a typical village house behind the town hall. The restaurant, in a separate house up the street, serves regional dishes such as *arroz liberal* (hunter's rice), *lomo a los aromas de la sierra* (herb-scented pork loin), and *conejo al ajillo* (rabbit in garlic sauce). ✉ *San Antonio 4, Barrio Medio, 18417,* ☎ *958/858626,* ℻ *958/858614. 12 rooms. Restaurant. MC, V.*

## Bérchules

★ ㊸  27 km (16 mi) east of Trevélez.

This pretty, whitewashed town is one of the purest villages in the Alpujarras. Livestock clop through the streets before dawn, bringing milk down from the high pastures, and flocks of sheep ramble over the road crossing.

### Dining and Lodging

$  ✕☷ **Los Bérchules.** This is the most comfortable place in town, with a good restaurant ($$) and helpful owners Wendy Tamborero, a Briton, and her son Alejandro. Rooms are wood-trimmed, with colorful Alpujarran bedspreads and curtains, and there are views to the southeast over the slopes. ✉ *Crtra. de Bérchules 20, 18451 Bérchules,* ☎ *958/852530,* ℻ *958/769000. 13 rooms. Restaurant, bicycles, bar. AE, DC, MC, V.*

$  ☷ **La Posada.** A lovely little house in the upper part of Bérchules serves as a hikers' inn and way station with handsome twisted tree trunk beams (albeit whitewashed) and very friendly owners, Margarita Breimer and Miguel Ocaña. Meals are served for overnight guests only. ✉ *Plaza del Correo 3, 18451,* ☎ ℻ *958/852541. 4 rooms with shared bath. Restaurant. No credit cards.*

## Yegen

㊹  21 km (12 mi) east of Bérchules.

Yegen is a prototypical Alpujarran village with flat roofs, whitewashed walls, and geranium-covered windows overlooking the Sierra de Contraviesa to the south. The British Hispanist Gerald Brenan made Yegen famous when he moved here after the First World War. Author of, among other works, *The Spanish Labyrinth* (1943) and *South from Granada* (1957), Brenan lived in Yegen until his death in 1987. His house, below the road through the middle of town, bears the inscription honoring the writer who "universalized the name of Yegen and the customs and traditions of the Alpujarra."

### Dining and Lodging

$–$$  ✕☷ **El Rincón de Yegen.** This excellent table well merits planning a mealtime arrival around. The innovative interpretations of traditional Alpujarran and Andalusian culinary themes draw faithful diners from near and far. Rooms ($) are tastefully decorated in Alpujarran fabrics and wood-paneled. ✉ *Camino de las Eras, 18460,* ☎ ℻ *958/851270. 4 rooms, 3 apartments. Restaurant. AE, DC, MC, V.*

# LA COSTA TROPICAL

Granada's Costa Tropical has escaped the worst excesses of the property developers, and its tourist onslaught has been mild. A flourishing farming center thanks to the year-round mild climate, this area earns its keep not from tourism but from tropical fruit, including avocados, mangoes, papaws, and custard apples. Housing developments are generally inspired by Andalusian village architecture rather than concrete towers. You may find packed beaches and traffic-choked roads at the height of the season, but for most of the year the Costa Tropical is relatively free of tourists, if not devoid of foreign expatriates.

## Salobreña

**49** *74 km (44 mi) south of Granada.*

You can reach Salobreña either by descending through the mountains from Granada or by continuing west from Almería on the N340. A short detour to the left from the highway brings you to this unspoiled village of near-perpendicular streets and old white houses, slapped onto a steep hill beneath a Moorish fortress. It's a true Andalusian pueblo, well separated from the newer part of the village down on the beach, where you'll find most of the restaurants and bars.

## Almuñécar

**50** *85 km (51 mi) south of Granada.*

Almuñécar has been a fishing village since Phoenician times, 3,000 years ago, when it was called Sexi. Later, the Moors built a castle here to house the treasures of Granada's kings. Today Almuñécar is a small-time resort with a pebble beach, popular with Spanish and northern-European vacationers.

The road west from Motril passes through the former empire of the sugar barons who brought prosperity to the province in the 19th century. The cane fields are now giving way to litchis, limes, mangoes, papaws, and olives; avocado groves line your route as you descend into Almuñécar. There are actually two villages, separated by the dramatic rocky headland of Punta de la Mona. To the east is Almuñécar proper, and to the west is **La Herradura,** a quiet fishing community and a perfect place to relax. Between the two is the pretty Marina del Este yacht harbor, a popular diving center along with La Herradura.

With three millennia of history behind the town, practically any new building work results in the discovery of some new find. There is a Phoenician necropolis on the outskirts of the town, and a Roman fish-salting factory discovered by chance in the 1980s next to the town's El Majuelo park.

Crowning Almuñécar is the **Castillo de San Miguel.** A Roman fortress once stood here, later enlarged by the Moors, but the castle's current aspect owes more to additions during the 16th century. It suffered heavy bombardment during the Peninsular War at the beginning of the 19th century, and what was left became the village cemetery until the 1990s, when excavation and restoration began in earnest. You can wander around the ramparts and peer down into the dungeon (the skeleton at the bottom is a copy of human remains that were discovered on the spot). ⊠ ✉ €2 *(includes admission to archaeological museum).* ☉ *Tues.–Sat. 10:30–1:30 and 5–7:30; Sun. 10:30–1:30.*

A large vaulted stone cellar of Roman origin, the **Cueva de Siete Palacios** houses Almuñécar's archaeological museum, with a small but interesting collection of Phoenician, Roman, and Moorish items. It's below the Castillo de San Miguel. ⊠ ✉ €2 *(includes admission to castle).* ☉ *Tues.–Sat. 10:30–1:30 and 4–6:30; Sun. 10:30–1:30.*

### Dining and Lodging

$$$ ✕ **Jacqui-Cotobro.** This small establishment at the foot of the Punta de la Mona is one of southern Spain's most acclaimed French restaurants. The cozy dining room has bare brick walls and green wicker chairs; you can eat on a beachfront terrace in summer. The best bet for sampling the imaginative French-Andalusian cooking is to order the *menú de degustación,* with a selection of three courses plus dessert; it changes weekly but might include such dishes as breast of duck in sweet-and-sour sauce, followed by *hojaldre de langostinos con puerros* (shrimp pastry with leeks) and *suprema de rodaballo* (turbot). ⊠ *Edificio Río, Playa Cotobro,* ☎ *958/631802. MC, V. Closed Mon. Sept.–June.*

$$$ 🏨 **Los Fenicios.** The location near the beach in La Herradura is a highlight of this modern Andalusian-style hotel: you get views of the bay and the cliffs of Punta de Mona to the east and the rocky headland of Cerro Gordo to the west. A gleaming white entrance with an enormous Moroccan-style ceiling lamp sets the scene. Each room has a terrace and a small sitting area with wicker chairs; ask for a room with a sea view. There's a swimming pool on the roof. ⊠ *Paseo de Andrés Segovia, 18697 La Herradura,* ☎ *958/827900,* 𝔽𝔸𝕏 *958/827910,* 𝕎𝔼𝔹 *www. somelia.es. 42 rooms. Restaurant, cafeteria, pool, meeting room. AE, DC, MC, V.*

$$ 🏨 **Casablanca.** There's something quaintly old-fashioned about this family-run hotel with a neo-Moorish facade. The rooms come in all different sizes and shapes, with an eclectic selection of antique or just plain old furniture along with modern fittings. Rooms on the top two floors are newer, having been added in 2000. The hotel is next to the beach in the very center of town. Some rooms have balconies with sea views. ⊠ *Plaza San Cristóbal 4, 18690,* ☎ *958/635575,* 𝔽𝔸𝕏 *958/ 635589. 35 rooms. Restaurant, bar. AE, DC, MC, V.*

# GUADIX Y MARQUESADO

The region due north of Sierra Nevada known as Guadix y Marquesado is Granada's middle grounds, neither high sierra, nor fertile vega, nor arid steppe, nor lush tropical coast. Closer in character to, if anything, the parched plains of the Altiplano, this deeply ravined and eroded borderland is named for the onetime feudal holdings of the Marqués de Zenete and the Arabic word for "river of life" or "green river," *oadias,* which became Guadix in the early Spanish romance dialect.

## Guadix

🔟 *47 km (30 mi) east of Granada on A92.*

Guadix was an important mining town as far back as 2,000 years ago, and it has its fair share of monuments, including a cathedral (built between 1594 and 1706) and a 9th-century Moorish alcazaba. But Guadix and the neighboring village of **Purullena** are best known for their cave communities. Around 2,000 caves were carved out of the soft, sandstone mountains at various times, and most are still inhabited. Far from being troglodytic holes in the wall, they are well furnished and comfortable, with a pleasant year-round temperature; there's even a cave hotel. A number of private caves have signs welcoming visitors to inspect the premises; a tip is expected if you do. Purullena is also known for ceramics. Follow signs to the **Cueva Museo,** (⊠ Plaza de la Constitución s/n, ☎ 958/669300; 🎟 €1.50; ◷ Mon.–Sat. 10–2 and 5–7; Sun. 10–2) a small cave museum, in the heart of Guadix's cave district. Near the Guacix town center, the **Cueva la Alcazaba** (⊠ San Miguel s/n, ☎ 958/664767; 🎟 €2; ◷ Mon.–Sat. 10–12 and 5–7; Sun. 11–2) cave museum also houses a ceramics workshop.

### Dining and Lodging

$ ✕🏨 **Comercio.** This 1905 building in the center of Guadix holds the town's most charming establishment, an enchanting little family-run hotel. Rooms have thick bedspreads in rich red, marble floors, and modern bathrooms. The public areas include an art gallery, a concert room, and the best restaurant ($–$$) in Guadix, serving such local specialties as roast lamb with raisins and pine nuts. ⊠ *C. Mira de Amezcua 3, 18500,* ☎ *958/660500,* 🆑 *958/665072,* 🕸 *www.moebius.es/ hotelcomercio. 24 rooms. Restaurant. AE, DC, MC, V.*

$–$$ 🏨 **Cuevas Pedro Antonio de Alarcón.** There's not much of a view, but what do you expect from a cave? Located not in Guadix's main cave district but in a cave "suburb" outside town, this unique lodging consists of 19 adjoining caves. Each of the 20 suites (which sleep two to five) has a kitchenette, and the honeymoon cave has a whirlpool bath. The whitewashed walls are decorated with charming Granadino crafts, colorful rugs cover the clay-tile floors, and handwoven Alpujarran tapestries serve as doors between the rooms. The restaurant, also subterranean, serves regional dishes. ⊠ *Barriada San Torcuato, 18500,* ☎ *958/664980,* 🆑 *958/661221,* 🕸 *www.andalucia.com/cavehotel. 20 suites. Restaurant, some pets allowed. AE, MC, V.*

# EL ALTIPLANO

This northeastern corner of the Province of Granada is officially titled Baza, Huescar: El Altiplano. With the main towns of Bazar and Huescar, the archaeological site at Orce, and the Parque Natural de la Sierra de Castril, there are some attractions in this wild tundralike steppe, though, all things considered, it probably ranks last in Granada's hierarchy of destinations.

## Baza

**⑤²** *105 km (63 mi) northeast of Granada, 41 km (25 mi) northeast of Guadix on A92.*

Baza is known for its prehistoric archaeological treasures, notably the **Dama de Baza,** the sculpture of an Iberian goddess unearthed in 1971 and dating from between 500 and 400 BC, and the 1982 discovery (in Orce, 40 km northeast) of a fragment of a human skull thought by some to be one of the first humans to inhabit the European continent one and a half million years ago. The **Museo Arqueológico** (⊠ Plaza Mayor s/n, ☎ 958/703555), open weekdays 10–2 and 6–8, exhibits an interesting assortment of archaeological treasures. The **Museo Palenteológico de Orce** (⊠ Castillo de las Siete Torres s/n, ☎ 958/344380), open weekdays 11–2 and 6–8, shows finds from the historic dig that allegedly produced Europe's oldest human. Baza's **Colegiata de Santa María** is a Renaissance gem with a plateresque portal and an imposing 18th-century tower.

### Lodging

$ 🏨 **Anabel.** This simple spot may not merit a detour, but if you're interested in one of Granada's semisecret destinations (or the early September fiesta during which oil-anointed young men pursue an equally oily Guadix resident called "El Cascamorras" through the streets), it will do. Rooms are modest in size and taste but clean and comfortable. ⊠ *María de Luna 3, 18800,* ☎ 🆑 *958/860998. 18 rooms. Restaurant. AE, DC, MC, V.*

OFF THE
BEATEN PATH

**PARQUE NATURAL SIERRA DE CASTRIL –** At Granada's northeastern limit is a trout-fishing, hiking, and mountain retreat composed of 29,285 acres of reforested highlands with a dozen 6,500-ft peaks and the Río Castril running north–south for some 20 km (12 mi) through the heart of the park. El Cortijillo (⊠ Parque Natural Sierra de Castril, ☎ 958/344157) is a campground and inn some 15 km (9 mi) up the river from the town of Castril.

# GRANADA PROVINCE A TO Z

*To research prices, get advice from other travelers, and book travel arrangements, visit www.fodors.com.*

### AIR TRAVEL

Granada Airport is 18 km (11 mi) west of the city. Iberia, Spantax, and Air Europa all have daily flights to and from Madrid, Barcelona, Palma de Mallorca, and Melilla, and a summer-only service to Tenerife.

J. González buses leave from the Palacio de Congresos, stopping at Gran Vía across from the cathedral and at two stops along Av. de la Constitución (at Hotel Vincci and in Plaza de la Caleta). Bus schedules vary from day to day according to flights and leave 1¼ hours prior to scheduled takeoffs. Buses to the airport cost €3 and take about 45 minutes; to taxis cost €15 and reach the airport in 30 minutes.

➤ AIRPORT INFORMATION: **Granada Airport** (☎ 958/245200). **Iberia Líneas Aereas** (⊠ Plaza Isabel la Católica 2, ☎ 958/227592; 958/245238).

➤ TAXIS AND SHUTTLES: **Tele Radio Taxi** (☎ 958/280654). **ServiTaxis** (☎ 958/400199). **Radio Taxi Genil** (☎ 958/132323).

### BUS TRAVEL

If you're not driving, buses are the best method of transportation in this region. They run to most of the outlying towns and villages, and their connections between major cities are generally faster and more frequent than those of trains. If you're taking public transportation to the villages of the Alpujarras, check bus schedules and accommodations carefully with Granada's tourist office and the Alsina Gräells bus company before you set off.

Buses connect Granada with Madrid and all major cities throughout Andalusia. Buses run from Granada to Orgiva seven to nine times a day, from Granada to Capileira three times a day.

Granada's Estación de Autobuses (bus station) is on the highway to Jaén. The main company, Alsina Gräells, serves Madrid, Algeciras, Málaga, Córdoba, Seville, Jaén, Motril, and Almería. At 9 daily Autobús Sierra Nevada has a service to the Sierra Nevada ski slopes. For buses to the rest of Europe, including service to London leaving at 11:30 on Monday, Thursday, and Saturday, contact Eurolines.

➤ BUS INFORMATION: **Alsina Gräells** (☎ 958/185480). **Autobús Sierra Nevada** (☎ 958/465022). **Eurolines** (☎ 958/153198). **Granada Estación de Autobuses** (⊠ Ctra. de Jaén s/n, ☎ 958/185480).

### CAR RENTAL

Hertz, Avis, and Europcar have branches at Granada's airport.

➤ LOCAL AGENCIES: **Alquiauto** (⊠ Reyes Católicos 47 (Alhambra Viajes), Centro, Granada, ☎ 958/215467, WEB www.alquiauto.es). **Atesa** (⊠ Avda. de Andaluces, Centro, Granada, ☎ 958/288755; ⊠ Aeropuerto de Granada, ☎ 958/446290; ☎ national: 902/100101). **Autos Fortuna** (⊠ Infanta Beatriz 2, at Camino Ronda, Centro, Granada, ☎ 958/260254). **Autos Guldeva** (⊠ Pedro Antonio de Alarcón 18, Centro, Granada, ☎ 958/251435). **Avis** (⊠ Recogidas 31, Centro, Granada, ☎ 958/252358; ⊠ Aeropuerto de Granada, ☎ 958/446455). **Europ-**

car (⊠ Avda. del Sur 2, Centro, Granada, ☎ 958/295065; ⊠ Aeropuerto de Granada, ☎ 958/245275). **Hertz** (⊠ Avda. Fuente Nueva s/n [Hotel Granada Center], Centro, Granada, ☎ 958/204454; ⊠ Aeropuerto de Granada, ☎ 958/245277).

## CAR TRAVEL

Be prepared for parking problems. The layout of smaller towns dates from Moorish times, and is hardly suited to modern-day traffic. Often the best policy in major cities is to drive to the center of town and, if no legal street parking is evident, use an underground parking lot. In Granada, added to parking space scarcity is the ever-present threat of break-ins. Underground parking is all but required unless you are staying at the Parador, Casa Morisca, or the Suecia, which have easy parking at the door. In Granada, it's simpler to walk or take a taxi up to the Alhambra or into the Albayzín than to tackle the extremely complicated one-way system and narrow Moorish streets in a rental car.

The route from Granada to Jaén, Baeza, Úbeda, and Cazorla is one of Andalusia's least tourist-clogged, though you'll probably encounter the odd tour bus between Granada and Jaén. The roads are smooth, and driving through this region is one of the most pleasant ways to see the countryside. Driving through the Alpujarra is a challenge, the mountain roads tight and sinuous. Surfaces are, however, excellent, and as long as your objective is merely to stay on the road and enjoy the views, rather than making time, everything flows by nicely.

## EMERGENCIES

➤ CONTACTS: **Fire, Police, or Ambulance** (☎ 112). **Police** (☎ 092 or 091).

## MAIL AND SHIPPING

➤ POST OFFICE: **Granada** (⊠ Correos, Puerto Real 1, Centro, ☎ 958/224835).

## TOURS

In Granada, contact a multilingual guide through the Asociación Provincial de Guías. Horseback-riding tours—some with English guides—are offered in the villages of the Alpujarra and the Sierra Nevada and sometimes elsewhere. Contact tourist offices for information. A respected equestrian outfitter in the Alpujarra is Rutas a Caballo. Based at Capileira in the Alpujarra, Nevadensis offers guided tours of the region on foot, horseback, and mountain bike.

➤ FEES AND SCHEDULES: **Cabalgar Rutas Alternativas** (⊠ Bubión, ☎ 958/763135, FAX 958/763136). **Asociación Provincial de Guías** (⊠ Plaza Nueva 2, 2D, Centro, Granada, ☎ 958/229936, FAX 958/228685). **Nevadensis** (⊠ Plaza de la Libertad, Pampaneira, ☎ 958/763127, FAX 958/763301). **Rutas a Caballo** (⊠ Dallas Love, Bubión, ☎ 958/763038).

## TRAIN TRAVEL

The high-speed AVE (named for *Alta Velocidad,* high speed, and also for bird, *ave*) connects Madrid with Córdoba in less than two hours. Train service from Córdoba to Granada, however, is poor, and there is no service at all between Granada and Jaén.

➤ TRAIN INFORMATION: **RENFE** (⊠ Estación de Granada, Avda. de Andaluces s/n, Pajaritos, ☎ 958/271272; national line 902/240202, WEB www.renfe.es).

## TRAVEL AGENCIES

➤ CONTACTS: **Halcón Viajes** (⊠ Calle de las Recogidas 24, San Antón, Granada, ☎ 958/520707; national line 902/433000, WEB www.

halconviajes.com). **Viajes Ecuador (WagonsLits Cook)** (✉ Cuesta de Gomérez 1, Granada, ☎ 958/222058, WEB www.viajesecuador.com).

## VISITOR INFORMATION

If you plan to visit a number of the sites in Granada, you should purchase a Bono Turístico from a Granada tourist office, €18 if booked in advance and €20 if not, which gives entry to several of the main sites, including the Alhambra (but *not* an advance reservation through the BBVA), and also 10 rides on city buses. It is valid for a week.

➤ TOURIST INFORMATION: **Andalusian Regional Tourist Offices** (✉ Corral del Carbón, Mariana Pineda s/n, Centro, 18009 Granada, ☎ 958/221022 or 958/225990, FAX 958/223927; Generalife s/n, beside Alhambra ticket office, Granada, ☎ 958/229575, FAX 958/228201; WEB www.andalucia.org). **Granada Province Tourist Office** (✉ Plaza Mariana Pineda 10, 2Z, Centro, 18009, Granada, ☎ 958/026800, FAX 958/026803, WEB www.dipgra.es). **Granada Municipal Tourist Office** (✉ Avda. de Andalucia, between airport and city center on corner with Calle de Circunvalación, La Chana, 18014 Granada, ☎ 958/278398). **Information Kiosk** (✉ Plaza de Bib-Rambla, Centro, Granada).

**Alhama de Granada** (✉ Calle Vendederas s/n, ☎ 958/360686). **Almuñécar** (✉ Palacete de la Najarra, Av. de Europa s/n, ☎ 958/631125, WEB www.almunecar.info). **Baza** (✉ Casa de la Cultura, Arco de la Magalena s/n, ☎ 958/700691, WEB www.altipla.com). **Guadix** (✉ av. Mariana Pineda s/n, ☎ 958/662665, WEB www.guadixymarquesado.org). **Lanjarón** (✉ Avda. de la Alpujarra s/n, ☎ 958/770282). **Loja** (✉ Centro de Interpretación Histórica, Plaza de Arriba, ☎ 958/321520). **Montefrío** (✉ Plaza de España 1, ☎ 958/336004). **Motril** (✉ Casa de la Palma, Calle Marquesa de Esquilache s/n, ☎ 958/823591). **Riofrío** (✉ Calle Ribera de Riofrío s/n, ☎ 958/323177). **Salobreña** (✉ Plaza de Goya s/n, ☎ 958/610314). **Sierra Nevada** (✉ Plaza de Andalucía s/n, Monachil, ☎ 958/249119, WEB www.sierranevadaski.com). **Sierra de Castril (Parque Natural)** (✉ Centro de Visitantes, Crta. Castril–Pozo Alcón Km 0.2, Castril, ☎ 958/720059).

# 9 ALMERÍA PROVINCE

The easygoing city of Almería is the
gateway to the scenic coast of the Cabo
de Gata Nature Reserve and the arid but
dramatic landscape of its inland desert,
the setting for countless movies. Other
main attractions here are unspoiled pueblos,
fine handicrafts, and delicious seafood.

By Mark Little

Revised by
AnneLise
Sorensen

**F WHEN TRAVELING** through the landscape of Almería you have the feeling you've been here before, it could be you saw it in a movie. Film directors have used the dramatic backdrops of the Cabo de Gata coast and the desert of Tabernas to make hundreds of films: Peter O'Toole blew up trains here in *Lawrence of Arabia,* Harrison Ford and Sean Connery fought off the bad guys in *Indiana Jones and the Last Crusade,* and Clint Eastwood emptied his sharpshooter in *The Good, The Bad and the Ugly.*

Gazing on the vast, sun-bleached emptiness that covers much of the province, you might think nothing much ever happened here before the moviemakers moved in. You couldn't be more wrong. Prehistoric men dwelt here, leaving mysterious paintings on rock faces in its sierras. Later, the region gave rise to the first civilization in Iberia, at the ancient city of Los Millares. Later still Romans and Moors tapped Almería's vast mineral resources.

Today, the desert continues to yield up hitherto untapped riches. Modern farming methods have turned a good slice of the province into the market garden of Europe. Megawatts of sun power are harnessed at the continent's biggest solar power station, in the Almería desert. In Calar Alto, at one of the highest points in the province, consistently clear skies allow scientists to probe the farthest corners of space from the peninsula's most advanced astronomical observatory.

Almería keeps its treasures well hidden, its attractions appearing when you least expect them: a unique geological site here, an impossibly deserted, pristine beach there, and just when you need it, a white pueblo that seems the creation of a cubist painter.

## Pleasures and Pastimes

### Dining

Almería has its fair share of fine restaurants, but they face heavy competition from the countless tapas bars serving typically Andalusian snacks. Almería's tapas are outstanding both for their variety and their generous portions, and furthermore they are included in the price of your drink, a custom that sadly has disappeared in most other parts of Andalusia.

Almería's cuisine combines Andalusian specialties with the flavors of Murcia, its northern neighbor. Rice dishes, including paella, are well represented. Almería also shares with Murcia a passion for salt-dried fish, in particular tuna (*mojama*) and ling roe (*huevas de maruca*), traditional delicacies since Phoenician times.

Grilled or fried fish is the order of the day at numerous simple beach restaurants (*chiringuitos*) that line the Almería coast. The famous *gambas* (shrimp) from Garrucha are served plainly boiled or grilled, or incorporated into dishes such as *garbanzos marineros* (chickpeas with shrimp).

Renewed interest in regional cuisine has revived local specialties such as *gurullos* (a pasta roughly the size and shape of a large grain of rice), served in a stew with partridge or rabbit; *olla de trigo* (a stew incorporating whole, boiled grains of wheat) and *pelotas* (corn dumplings). The signature dish is *ajo colorao,* which incorporates skate, potatoes, tomatoes, and dried peppers seasoned with garlic and cumin. Almería's wealth of vegetables appears both raw in salads and in cooked dishes.

| CATEGORY | COST* |
| --- | --- |
| $$$$ | over €18 |
| $$$ | €13–€18 |
| $$ | €8–€13 |
| $ | under €8 |

*per person for a main course at dinner

## Lodging

Almería's largest concentration of hotels is on the southern coast, in the beach resorts of Aguadulce and Roquetas de Mar, mainly large establishments geared to the beach holiday market, comfortable enough but not what you would call an authentic Andalusian experience. Elsewhere in the province, scattered hotels range from dreary roadside inns and humble village pensiones to a handful of establishments of true character. Almería's only parador, in Mojácar, is a modern hotel with a good beachside location. A few miles north, in Vera, is Spain's first nudist hotel. Inland, in Laujar de Andarax, Almería's Villa Turística is the newest, and one of the best, in this regional network of country resorts.

| CATEGORY | COST |
| --- | --- |
| $$$$ | over €140 |
| $$$ | €100–€140 |
| $$ | €60–€100 |
| $ | under €60 |

*All prices are for a standard double room, excluding tax.

## Exploring Almería Province

Almería occupies the southeastern corner of the Iberian peninsula. The rain clouds that sweep in from the Atlantic to water western Andalusia rarely reach this far, and it shows. Much of the province is an awesomely barren landscape, eroded by the elements, scorched by 3,000 hours of sun a year.

Mountain ranges cross the province and plunge dramatically to the sea along the rugged coastline of the Cabo de Gata. The occasional torrential winter downpours run down the slopes of the sierras to shape wide *ramblas* (riverbeds), which are bone-dry most of the year but can become treacherously raging torrents in winter.

### Great Itineraries

#### IF YOU HAVE 3 DAYS

Spend your first morning exploring ⊡ **Almería** ①, then head north to view the desert of **Tabernas** ⑤, stopping along the way to see the archaeological site of **Los Millares** ②. Return to Almería in the evening for a round of tapas. On Day 2, head east for the **Cabo de Gata** ⑦, visiting San José and **Agua Amarga** ⑧ and perhaps enjoying a splash in the sea. Continue north to ⊡ **Mojácar** ⑨ and **Vera** ⑩. On the final day, head back to Almería along the inland highway, making short detours to see the caves of **Sorbas** ⑥ and visit the crafts town of **Villa de Níjar** ④.

#### IF YOU HAVE 5 DAYS

Devote a full day to exploring ⊡ **Almería** ①. The following day, see the archaeological site of **Los Millares** ② on your way to Laujar de Andarax in the ⊡ **Valle del Andarax** ③. On Day 3, backtrack to explore the desert of **Tabernas** ⑤ and, at its northern fringe, **Sorbas** ⑥ and its caves. Engage in some serious crafts shopping at **Villa de Níjar** ④ before heading to the ⊡ **Cabo de Gata** ⑦ for the night. Spend Day 4 following the coastline of the Cabo de Gata park as you head north to

## Almería Province

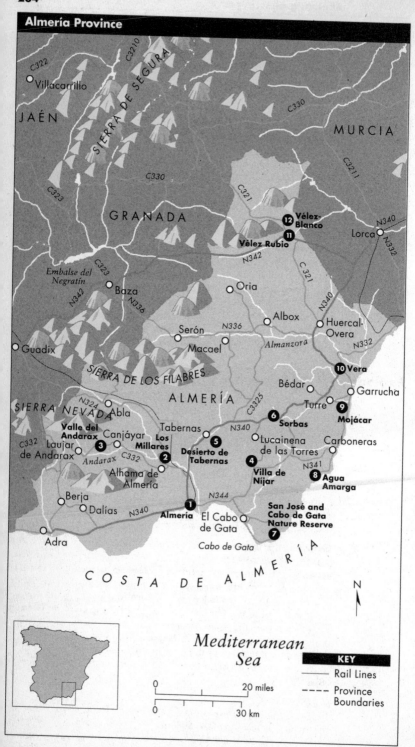

**Villacarrillo** C322

**JAÉN**

SIERRA DE SEGURA

C3210

C330

**MURCIA**

C323

C330

**GRANADA**

C321

C3211

N340

**Lorca** N332

C323

Embalse del Negratín

N342

N336

**Baza**

**Oria**

**Albox**

**Huercal-Overa**

C321

N340

N332

Almanzora

**Guadix**

SIERRA DE LOS FILABRES

**Serón**

N336

**Macael**

**⑩Vera**

**SIERRA NEVADA**

N324

**Abla**

**ALMERÍA**

**Bédar**

**Garrucha**

**Turre**

C3325

**⑥Sorbas**

**⑨Mojácar**

**Valle del Andarax**

**Canjáyar**

**Tabernas**

**Los Millares**

**⑤**

N340

**Lucainena de las Torres**

**Carboneras**

**Laujar de Andarax** C332

**③**

**②**

**Desierto de Tabernas**

Andarax C332

**Alhama de Almería**

**④**

**Villa de Níjar**

N341

**⑧Agua Amarga**

**Berja**

**Dalías**

N340

**①**

**Almería**

N344

**El Cabo de Gata**

**San José and Cabo de Gata Nature Reserve**

**⑦**

**Adra**

Cabo de Gata

**COSTA DE ALMERÍA**

N

Mediterranean Sea

**KEY**

Rail Lines

Province Boundaries

0 — 20 miles

0 — 30 km

☒ **Mojácar** ⑨ and **Vera** ⑩. From Vera, take the highway north toward Murcia, then head west on the A-92 highway as far as **Vélez-Rubio** ⑪ and ☒ **Vélez-Blanco** ⑫, to wander around the villages, see the prehistoric paintings in the Cueva de los Letreros, and explore the Sierra María–Los Vélez mountains.

## When to Tour

Almería can be enjoyed year-round. Although winter brings occasional heavy rains, wet weather is interspersed with long spells of sunshine. However, many hotels and restaurants along the coast close for winter. The sea is warm enough for swimming from May to October. You might prefer to avoid the holiday crowds of July and August.

# ALMERÍA AND ENVIRONS

Shelthered in its placid bay, the city of Almería was first settled by seafaring Phoenicians 3,000 years ago. The conquering Romans called it Portus Magnus (Port of Ports), whereas the Moors who arrived later gave it the more poetic name of Al-Maryat (Mirror of the Sea). At one time the capital of a great Moorish kingdom, Almería today is an easygoing provincial capital basking in the sunniest climate in Andalusia.

Just north of the capital, the otherworldly landscape of Tabernas, Europe's only desert, can mesmerize you with its stark beauty, just as it's done for the makers of countless Western movies. The mineral riches of the surrounding mountains gave rise to Iberia's first true civilization, whose capital can still be glimpsed in the 4,700-year-old ruins of Los Millares. The towns of Níjar and Sorbas maintain an ages-old tradition of pottery making and other crafts, and the western coast of Almería has tapped unexpected wealth from a parched land, thanks to modern farming techniques. In contrast to that inhospitable landscape, the mountain-fringed Andarax valley has a cool climate and gentle landscape, both conducive to making fine wines.

## Almería

❶ *166 km (103 mi) southeast of Granada, 183 km (114 mi) east of Málaga, 560 km (347 mi) southeast of Madrid.*

The very image of a small Mediterranean city, Almería has a modern, youthful feel to it, even though it has been inhabited since Phoenician times. The city has tree-lined boulevards and landscaped squares, and at its core are distinctly Moorish flat-roofed houses forming a maze of narrow, winding alleys.

Almería was Spain's major port in the days of the Moorish Córdoba caliphate, trading with Syria, Egypt, France, and Italy. After the caliphate disintegrated, the city became the capital of an independent Moorish kingdom encompassing Murcia and much of eastern Andalusia, and was a leading producer of silk. More recently, in the 19th and early 20th century, the port thrived on shipping iron ore mined from the neighboring mountains, but today, with mining activity at a standstill, the large harbor is eerily empty and underutilized.

Almería's sights can easily be explored on foot. A good place to start is **Nicolás Salmerón,** officially described as a "park" but actually a long, leafy boulevard that separates the old city from the port. Here you will find the regional tourist office, where you can pick up maps and brochures.

★ Dominating the city is Almería's main historical monument, the **Alcazaba,** which rises on a hill to the west of the city center. This Moorish castle is noteworthy both for its size and its admirable state of repair. The original castle, constructed in 955 at the height of the reign of the first caliph of Córdoba, Abd-al-Rahman III, was the largest fortress built by the Moors in Spain, originally covering 269,000 square ft.

Your climb from Nicolás Salmerón, up Calle de la Reina, to the entrance of the Alcazaba will be rewarded with splendid views of Almería and its bay. The castle consists of three successive enclosures: the second of them held the mosque, baths, and other public buildings, and the third and highest housed the palace, which was torn down after Almería's conquest by Queen Isabella and King Ferdinand's army to make way for improved fortifications and artillery emplacements to ward off attack from the sea. ⊠ *Calle Almanzor s/n,* ☎ *950/271617.* ⊡ *€1.50, free for EU citizens.* ☉ *Apr.–Sept., Tues.–Sun. 9–8:30; Oct.– Mar., Tues.–Sun. 9–6:30.*

The pleasant pedestrian Plaza de la Constitución, known commonly as the **Plaza Vieja** (old square), is on the way from the Alcazaba into town. On one side is the elegant 19th-century *ayuntamiento* (town hall). The monument in the center of the square honors those executed in 1824 for opposing the repressive regime of King Fernando VII.

Construction of Almería's **Catedral** (cathedral), two blocks south of Plaza Vieja, started in 1513 and dragged on for 2½ centuries, which explains the mixture of Gothic, Renaissance, and neoclassical styles. Its most striking feature is its fortresslike aspect, complete with buttressed towers. The building doubled as a castle in times when the threat of attack by Barbary pirates was ever-present. Inside, there's some interesting art (none of it marked with identifying labels), including the marble tomb of Diego Fernandez de Villalan, the 16th-century bishop and founder of the cathedral. The most pleasant part of the complex is the cloister, the last section to be built. Note the carved figure of the sun on the cathedral's eastern facade; it's known as the **Sol de Portocarrero** and is an emblem of the city. ⊠ *Plaza de la Catedral,* ☎ *609/ 575802.* ⊡ *€2.* ☉ *Weekdays 10–4:30, Sat. 10–1.*

The **Aljibes,** Moorish baths dating from the 11th century, have had their stonework and brick arches restored, and now the space is a venue for art exhibits and music concerts. You can get there from the cathedral by way of Calle Real, going through a district with many worthwhile tapas bars. The street turns into Calle de las Tiendas, and off it is where you'll find the baths. ⊠ *Calle Tenor Iribarne,* ☎ *950/273039.* ⊡ *Free.* ☉ *Tues.–Sat. 10:30–1:30.*

The **Paseo de Almería,** the city's main shopping thoroughfare, begins at the busy **Puerta de Purchena** square. At its bottom, it merges with the **Rambla de Belén,** once a dry riverbed, now covered to become a wide, modern boulevard graced with contemporary sculpture.

## Dining and Lodging

$$–$$$   ✕ **La Gruta.** The main draw of this restaurant is its distinctive location, in a series of four tunnels carved out of the cliff face 4 km (2 ½ mi) west of Almería on the old coast road to Aguadulce. It specializes in grilled and roast meat, including beef, wild boar, lamb, and kid, although a number of cod preparations and other fish dishes are available. ⊠ *Carretera Nacional 340, Km 436,* ☎ *950/239335. AE, DC, MC, V. No lunch. Closed Sun.*

$$   ✕ **Club de Mar.** The upstairs restaurant in Almería's yacht club has long been a mainstay of the local culinary scene. There are sweeping views of the harbor from the picture windows in the spacious dining area. In keeping with the setting, the menu concentrates on fish dishes such as *zarzuela de pescado y marisco* (seafood stew). Top off the meal with

the tangy *sorbete de limón* (lemon sorbet), the house dessert specialty. ✉ *Club de Mar, Playa de las Almadrabillas s/n,* ☎ *950/235048. AE, DC, MC, V.*

**$$** ✕ **Valentin.** This central spot serves fine regional specialties. *Cazuela de rape* (monkfish baked in a sauce of almonds and pine nuts) is a typical entrée. The decor is Andalusian: white walls, wood, and glass. Valentin is popular, so be on the early side (around 9) to get a table. ✉ *Tenor Iribarne 7,* ☎ *950/264475. AE, MC, V. Closed Mon.*

**$$** ✕ **Veracruz.** In El Zapillo, Almería's beach barrio, this popular, excellent seafood restaurant has its own tank for oysters, clams, prawns, and lobsters. Its specialty is *parillada de pescado,* a mixed grill of everything that swims in the Mediterranean. ✉ *Avda. Cabo de Gata 119,* ☎ *950/251220. AE, MC, V.*

**$** ✕ **Torreluz.** This bustling little eatery in the Torreluz III hotel is an excellent value. Famous among locals for its robust portions and brisk lunchtime service, the Torreluz serves a good cross-section of southeastern fare. Try the *pollo al ajillo con arroz* (garlic-sauteed chicken with rice) or the *zarzuela de marisco a la marinera* (mixed seafood in a zesty red marinade). ✉ *Plaza Flores 1,* ☎ *950/281425,* FAX *950/281428. AE, DC, MC, V.*

**$$–$$$** 🏨 **Gran Hotel Almería.** These rooms have brightly painted walls and chintz coverings to complement their fine views over Almería's harbor. The huge, marbled reception rooms evoke the hotel's golden age, when it hosted film directors there to make spaghetti Westerns. ✉ *Avda. Reina Regente 8, 04001,* ☎ *950/238011,* FAX *950/270691,* WEB *www. granhotelalmeria.com. 108 rooms. Restaurant, pool, bar, meeting rooms. AE, DC, MC, V.*

**$–$$** 🏨 **Torreluz III.** Good value is the overriding attraction of this comfortable
★ and stylish modern hotel. The rooms are slick and bright, with the kind of installations for which you'd expect to pay more. There are in fact two hotels, in two separate buildings on the same square, rated two and three stars and sharing the same reception. The cheaper two-star hotel is just as comfortable, but lacks some amenities such as minibars. Also worth trying is the inexpensive basement restaurant. A second restaurant across the square serves more expensive, creative Mediterranean fare. ✉ *Plaza Flores 1-3, 04001,* ☎ *950/234399,* FAX *950/ 281428,* WEB *www.torreluz.com. 94 rooms. 2 restaurants, cafeteria, bar, parking (fee). AE, DC, MC, V.*

**$** 🏨 **Hostal Sevilla.** If you want an inexpensive, comfortable place to stay, this is it. Located within the labyrinth of the old town, Hostal Sevilla gives healthy doses of Andalusian ambience, style, and charm. The whitewashed rooms vary—those on the street side have small terraces, whereas those on the quieter interior look over the courtyards and rooftops of the old town. All have ceramic-tile floors. ✉ *Granada 25, 04001,* ☎ *950/230009. 37 rooms. MC, V.*

### TAPAS BARS

Almería is one of the best places in Andalusia for sampling tapas. Many good spots are within easy walking distance of each other in the old town center. The price for a glass of wine or a beer with a tapa is €1.20–€1.50. An extra tapa costs around €0.90.

Located near the top of Calle Real and decorated with typical Andalusian tiles and old bottles, **Casa Puga** (✉ Calle Jovellanos 7, ☎ 950/231530; closed Sun.) claims to be the city's oldest bar, in business since 1870.
★ For variety, quality, and ambience, you can't beat **El Quinto Toro** (✉ Calle Juan Leal 6, ☎ 950/239135). Established by a retired bullfighter in 1952 and now run by his two sons, this small bar offers an unbelievable selection, serving more than 500 tapas on an average day.

**Bodega Las Botas** (✉ Calle Fructuoso Perez, 3, ☎ 950/262272; closed Mon.), named for the up-ended wine barrels that serve as tables and decorated with bullfighting memorabilia and hanging hams, is a good place to enjoy cured ham, sausage, or cheese. Nearby, **Bodeguilla Ramón** (✉ Calle Pedro Alonso Torres 4, ☎ 950/270126; closed Mon.) is one of Almería's most colorful, traditional taverns, serving *pulpitos* (small fried octopus), *caracoles* (snails), and other tidbits.

The **Baviera** (✉ Calle Tenor Iribarne, 10, ☎ 950/273008) specializes in fried fish, including *calamares* (squid), *salmonetitos* (baby red mullet) and *boquerones* (anchovies). The tiny **El Ajoli** (✉ Calle Padre Alfonso Torres 7, ☎ 950/251213) is one of the friendliest places in town, serving wine from the barrel and specializing in salted fish and a baked potato with sauce, which is a meal in itself.

## Los Millares

❷ *11 km (7 mi) north of Almería.*

The archaeological site of Los Millares is 2.3 km (1½ mi) from the village of Santa Fé de Mondújar. This collection of ruins scattered on a windswept hilltop was the birthplace of civilization in Spain, nearly 5,000 years ago.

In 1891 workers laying a railway line came across the remains of ancient stone walls. Hearing of the discovery, Luis Siret, a Belgian mining engineer working in the area, devoted the rest of his life to unraveling this hitherto unknown chapter of Spanish history. Large, dome-shaped tombs show that the community had an advanced society, and the existence of formidable defense walls indicate they had something to protect. A series of concentric fortifications shows that the settlement increased in size over the generations, eventually holding some 2,000 people. They were active in trade and were the first in Spain to master copper smelting. The town was inhabited from 2700 to 1800 BC, and came to dominate the entire region.

Go to the reception center at the edge of the site, where a guide will take you on a tour of the ruins. It is advisable to phone in advance. ✉ ☎ 608/957065. 🎟 *Free.* 🕒 *Tues.–Sat. 9:30–4.*

## Valle del Andarax

❸ *Laujar de Andarax: 45 km (28 mi) west of Los Millares; 48 km (30 mi) north of El Ejido.*

From Alhama de Almería, north of the city of Almería, the A-348 road runs parallel to the Andarax River. As you head into the mountains, the road becomes windier, the landscape greener, and the villages prettier.

**Laujar de Andarax** is the main town in the upper Valle del Andarax, which marks the eastern extreme of the Alpujarra region, and falls within the Sierra Nevada National Park. At 900 meters (2,950 ft) altitude, the air is cooler and fresher, the scenery more bucolic than in the desert regions below.

Laujar de Andarax has an impressive 18th-century **ayuntamiento** with three tiers of arches gracing its facade, and a Mudéjar-style church, **Iglesia de la Encarnacíon**, dating from the 17th century. A narrow lane leads from the village to **El Nacimiento,** the source of the Andarax River, a pleasant, leafy area with waterfalls and picnic facilities.

### Dining and Lodging

**$$**  ✕ 🏨 **Villa Turística de Laujar.** This pleasant country holiday complex,
★ 1 km (⅗ mi) from Laujar, is part of the regional network of Villas Turís-
ticas. Accommodations are in 31 semidetached units, sleeping two to
six, attractively arranged like a small self-contained village. In the
main building, cool blue-green furniture creates a relaxing ambience.
The restaurant, with views over the countryside, serves such regional
specialties as *cabrito ajillo alpujarreño* (kid fried with garlic) and
*salteado de conejo en salsa de almendras* (sauteed rabbit in almond
sauce). ✉ 04470, Laujar de Andarax, ☎ 950/513027, FAX 950/513554,
WEB *www.serinves.es/villalaujar. 31 units. Restaurant, kitchenettes, ten-
nis court, pool, bar, playground, meeting room, some pets allowed. AE,
MC, V.*

## Villa de Níjar

**4** *32 km (20 mi) northeast of Almería.*

Although it is the administrative capital of a large municipality en-
compassing most of the towns in the Cabo de Gata area, including San
José and Agua Amarga, Villa de Níjar strikes you as an unassuming
village, clustered around its 16th-century church, Nuestra Señora de
la Anunciacíon.

Níjar's main attraction is found on the Avenida Federico García Lorca,
the main street leading up to the village, with more than a dozen shops
selling the crafts for which the village is famous throughout Spain, in-
cluding ceramics, colorful *jarapas* (blankets made from scraps of fab-
ric), wicker baskets, and items fashioned from esparto grass. One
block south of the avenue is the Barrio Alfarero, where most of the
workshops are located. The typical glazed ceramics of Níjar are dec-
orated with blue, green, and yellow patterns, and are surprisingly light
and frustratingly fragile. Not many shops produce the authentic arti-
cle anymore; most sell sturdier, more modern ceramics.

### Shopping

The shops along Níjar's Avenida Federico García Lorca and the par-
allel Calle Real de la Eras (signposted *barrio alfarero,* or potters' quar-
ter) are the perfect place to load up on typical Almería crafts. The
**Francisco Góngora López** workshop (✉ Calle Real de Eras 66, ☎ 950/
360381), where you can watch the ceramacist at work, is one of the
few places that still make the delicate traditional ceramics of Níjar, using
a Moorish-style wood-fueled kiln. **Angeles López Cazorla** (✉ Avda. Fed-
erico García Lorca s/n, ☎ 950/360288) is one of the best sources of
jarapas, made at their own workshop.

## Desierto de Tabernas

**5** *25 km (15 mi) north of Almería.*

The Desierto de Tabernas north of Almería is billed as the only true
desert in Europe, receiving an average of 8 inches of rainfall a year.
The striking, almost lunar landscape of ramblas and parched hills
bears a similarity to the American desert—a fact not lost on film-
makers. More than 300 movies were made in the area between 1950
and 1990, most of them of the "spaghetti western" genre.

Several of the old film sets still stand, and two of them are open to the
public. **Mini Hollywood** is a Wild West theme park, complete with sa-
loon, sheriff's office, general store, bank robbery (site of regular staged
robberies), bars, restaurants, and two museums, one devoted to
Almería's filmmaking past, the other to old wagons and vintage cars.

Adjoining the Western town is a wildlife reserve, included in the admission, where you'll find lions, elephants, and other species. ⊠ *Ctra. N-340 Km 364,* ☎ *950/365236.* 🎟 *€16.* ☉ *Tues.–Sun. 10–7.*

At the turnoff to Guadix, the setting for Sergio Leone's iconoclastic epic *The Good, the Bad and the Ugly,* **Western Leone** is now a small, rough-and-tumble attraction that in the off-season is practically deserted. For €8 an hour (on top of the €6.50 admission), you can explore the desert on horseback and pretend you're a film extra. ⊠ *Carretera A-92 Km 378.9,* ☎ *950/165405.* 🎟 *€6.50.* ☉ *Daily 10–sundown.*

Just north of the town of Tabernas—a dusty place overlooked by a ruined castle—is an example of how Almería is deriving riches from its desert. The **Plataforma Solar,** Europe's largest experimental solar station, generates electricity by beaming reflected sunlight from hundreds of mirrors onto a collector at the top of a 260-ft tower. You can visit on weekdays by phoning ahead for an appointment; in the summer, you should phone at least a month in advance, because school groups usually fill the schedule to capacity. ⊠ *Carretera de Senes, Km 350,* ☎ *950/387900.* 🎟 *Free.* ☉ *By appointment.*

## Sorbas

**❻** *27 km (17 mi) east of Tabernas; 35 km (21 mi) north of Níjar.*

The village of Sorbas cuts a striking image with its houses dangling at the edge of a deep ravine carved by the Río Aguas. Rising over the typical whitewashed homes are 17th-century palaces that once belonged to the Duke of Valoig and the Duke of Alba, who spent the occasional summer here.

Sorbas, like the neighboring town of Níjar, is famous for its pottery, and signs point you to the **Barrio Alfarero** at the eastern edge of the village. At one time there were two dozen potteries in the village. Now there are only two left, one of which, Jaime Mañas, still uses a traditional Moorish wood-burning kiln.

★　The underground wonders of the **Cuevas de Sorbas** are the main draw of the town. Sorbas stands on one of Europe's richest deposits of gypsum, a sulphate used for plaster of paris, and these caves were formed millions of years ago when what was once an inland sea drained, leaving hundreds of cavities whose walls are covered with crystallized gypsum, glittering like diamonds. You can tour some of the caves.

The reception center is 1 km (⅗ mi) east of Sorbas. Tours run daily, every hour, but groups are limited, so it's a good idea to book ahead (one day's advance notice is usually sufficient). There are three different tours, of varying degrees of difficulty. The 1½-hour "basic" tour is negotiable by visitors who are reasonably fit, including children. The "combined" tour, which involves some climbing and crawling through crevices, is described as being suitable for "young people and agile adults," and the "technical" tour should be attempted only by those with some experience in climbing or caving. ⊠ *Paraje Barranco del Infierno,* ☎ *950/364704,* 🌐 *www.cuevasdesorbas.com.* 🎟 *Basic tour: €7.81.* ☉ *Mid-June–Sept., daily 10–8; Oct.–mid-June, daily 10–2 and 4–6.*

# EASTERN ALMERÍA

In other times the refuge of pirates, who lurked in coves hidden by volcanic headlands, the eastern shores of Almería constitute Andalusia's most dramatic coastline. The riches of its sea contrast with an unyielding, sunbaked hinterland where few crops can grow. Villages such as San José and Agua Amarga, in the Cabo de Gata Nature Reserve, originated as humble fishing hamlets in the 18th century. Now they are attracting increasing numbers of visitors who seek some of the most scenic, least crowded beaches in Andalusia.

North of the nature park, the hilltop village of Mojácar enchants travelers with its Moorish flavors, and the nearby coast of Vera has become the nudist capital of Spain.

## San José and Cabo de Gata Nature Reserve

★ ❼ *San José: 43 km (26 mi) east of Almería.*

The Cabo de Gata-Níjar Nature Reserve is a protected area taking in the eastern coast of Almería, a landscape formed eons ago by intense volcanic activity. Though from all appearances dry and barren, it is home to numerous wild plant species, some found nowhere else (not so the abundant agaves and prickly pear cactus, which were introduced from America).

Cabo (Cape) de Gata itself is a rocky headland on the southeastern tip of the province, 40 km (25 mi) east of Almería, marked by a lighthouse. Stretching north of here is a scenic coastline of cliffs, isolated coves, and fishing villages. Although more and more vacationers are discovering the area, outside July and August the region is relatively quiet.

The main town on the coast is San José, 12 km (7 mi) north of the cape. Once a tiny, remote hamlet, it has become a popular tourist destination, with half a dozen hotels and *hostales* in addition to vacation apartments and a campground, plus bars, boutiques, and an Internet café. It's a relaxed village perched over a bay, perfectly placed to take advantage of the all-but-deserted beaches nearby.

The visitor information center on Plaza Génova is a good place to pick up maps and information on the Cabo de Gata park. You can also sign up for four-wheel-drive tours of the area here. The village's small yacht harbor is a base for scuba-diving activities, and there are also boat trips along the coast available during summer (and by appointment the rest of the year).

For beach action, follow signs south to the **Playa Los Genoveses** and **Playa Monsul**; a dirt track (not navigable by car) follows the coast around the spectacular cape. There are more scenic beaches north of San José, in **Los Escullos** and **La Isleta**.

### Dining and Lodging

$$$ ✕🏨 **Cortijo El Sotillo.** Don't miss the opportunity to establish tempo-
★ rary headquarters in this newly restored 18th-century country estate at the very entrance of San José. Many guests visit El Sotillo to take advantage of its modern equestrian facilities and myriad riding trails that run through the Cabo de Gata Nature Reserve. The restaurant serves a varied menu of fine fish and meat dishes. Depending on the fresh catch of the day, fish dishes on offer may include *calamares* (squid) or *rod-aballo* (turbot); *cordero al horno* (oven-baked lamb) is a meat specialty. ⊠ *Entrada de San José 04118,* ☎ *950/611100,* ℻ *950/611105,* 🕸 *www.hotelsotillo.com. 17 rooms, 3 suites. Restaurant, tennis court, pool, billiards, archery, horseback riding, Ping-Pong. AE, MC, V.*

$$ 🏨 **Atalaya.** This modern midrange hotel has a bright, Mediterranean look, with a blue-and-white color scheme in its common areas and rooms. Some rooms face the street, but the best ones look onto an open patio at the back and have their own terraces. ⊠ *Calle Correos s/n, 04118*

*San José,* ☎ *950/380085,* FAX *950/380552,* WEB *www.atalayadelsur. com. 26 rooms. Some pets allowed. MC, V.*

### Outdoor Activities and Sports

The rocky headlands of the Cabo de Gata coast provide some of the best snorkeling and scuba-diving conditions in southern Spain. The **Centro de Buceo Alpha** scuba center (☎ 950/380321 or 608/057968) in the port in San José offers guided dives and equipment rental for licensed divers, and scuba-diving courses for the uninitiated.

## Agua Amarga

**❽** *22 km (14 mi) north of San José.*

Agua Amarga is perhaps the most pleasant village on the Cabo de Gata coast. Like other coastal hamlets, it started out in the 18th century as a tuna-fishing port. Today it attracts more visitors, but remains a fishing village at heart, less developed than San José. One of the coast's best beaches is just to the north: the dramatically named **Playa de los Muertos** (Beach of the Dead), a long stretch of fine sand bookended with volcanic outcrops.

### Dining and Lodging

**$$$** ✕ **La Chumbera.** This stylish restaurant in a villa off the coastal road
★ just north of Agua Amarga requires reservations, but phoning a day ahead or even on the same morning should secure you a table at one of the province's finest dining spots. The menu changes almost daily, but will always include a deliciously imaginative and eclectic selection, such as tunafish sashimi with sesame seed and ginger, breast of capon with foie gras and truffles, or sautéed loin of kangaroo with artichokes, tomatoes, and olives, impeccably served in an ambience of relaxed elegance. ✉ *Los Ventorrillos,* ☎ *950/168321. MC, V. Closed Mon.–Tues. Dinner only July–Aug.*

**$$$$** 🏨 **Mikasa.** Set in a resplendent modern villa of typical Almería design, this small and smart hotel has become a byword for tasteful decor and attention to detail. Each room is different, but they all share a distinctly design-conscious look. Some have terraces, some have king-size beds. In keeping with a "peace and silence" policy, cell phone use isn't allowed in public spaces, and the rooms don't have telephones, though you can use the reception phone. ✉ *Carretera de Carboneras s/n, 04149,* ☎ FAX *950/138073. 20 rooms. 2 pools, tennis, gym, hot tub, Turkish bath; no room phones. AE, MC, V. Closed Jan.–Mar.*

**$–$$** 🏨 **Hostal Family.** Two hundred yards from the beach, this small, intimate hostelry tucked down a quiet lane just south of Agua Amarga has simply furnished but pleasant lodgings. The five higher-priced rooms on the second floor are larger and have a view of the sea. The cheerfully decorated restaurant (no lunch weekdays) serves a small menu with a choice of dishes at a fixed price of €14. ✉ *Calle La Lomilla, 04149,* ☎ *950/138014,* FAX *950/138070. 9 rooms. Restaurant, pool, some pets allowed; no room phones. MC, V. Closed Nov.–mid-Dec.*

## Mojácar

**★ ❾** *32 km (20 mi) north of Agua Amarga; 93 km (58 mi) northeast of Almería.*

Perched on a hillside overlooking the sea, Mojácar is a cluster of whitewashed cubic houses attesting to the town's Moorish past. The North African aesthetic has been carefully preserved, although the only part left of the original town is the **Antigua Puerta de la Ciudad,** a whitewashed archway that was once the entrance to the village. The village's principal monument is the **Santa María** church, which, typical of this coast, doubled as a fortress, but the picturesque streets, alleys, and plazas are the true attraction of Mojácar.

Down on the coast 3 km (2 mi) from the village is the **Playa de Mojácar**, a beach lined with shops, restaurants, hotels, and nightspots. Less developed, more secluded beaches are to be found just south of here.

Life in the seaside town of **Garrucha**, 7 km (4 mi) north of Mojácar, centers on its busy fishing port. The restaurants lining the portside promenade serve some of the best seafood in eastern Andalusia, and the gambás from Garrucha are famous throughout the region.

## Dining and Lodging

**$$$$**  ✕ **Al Almejero.** At the most famous seafood place on the port of Garrucha, the informal dining room is always busy. Specialties include the gambas, *pargo a la sal* (sea bream baked in a crust of coarse salt) and *arroz caldoso* (a soupy version of paella). Service is brisk, bordering on brusque. ⊠ *Explanada del Puerto s/n, Garrucha,* ☎ *950/460405 or 950/132011. AE, MC, V.*

**$$–$$$**  ✕ **El Palacio de Mojácar.** Installed in an old white house with exposed beams and fireplace, this restaurant serves highly inventive cuisine, generally with an international twist. The friendly chef-owner doesn't produce a large menu, but whatever *is* on offer is consistently good. ⊠ *Plaza del Caño 1,* ☎ *950/472846. AE, MC, V. Closed Sun. (except in July–Sept.), and Nov. and Feb.*

**$$–$$$**  ✕ **Rincón del Puerto.** Here you'll find one of the most pleasant places to eat in the port of Garrucha. Although meat dishes are available, the specialty, naturally, is fresh seafood. Many fish dishes are sold by weight, so inquire about the price when ordering to avoid surprises. Two specialties have to be ordered in advance and serve two people: *caldereta de langosta* (lobster stew) and *arroz negro* ("black rice," a paellalike dish with squid ink). Both the interior dining room and the terrace have harbor views. ⊠ *Puerto Deportivo, Garrucha,* ☎ *950/ 133042. AE, MC, V.*

**$$**  ✕▥ **Mamabel's.** Isabel ("Mamabel") Aznar, the owner of this restaurant and small hotel at the edge of Mojácar, is something of a local institution. Specialties at the restaurant include a vegetable paella, fish in caper sauce, and *solomillo Mamabel* (fillet steak with wild mushrooms in a wine, garlic shoot, and raspberry sauce). The lodgings show a similar flair. Rooms vary in size and decor, but all have views, and some have terraces. Note that there's a long flight of stairs down to reach the place. ⊠ *Calle Embajadores 5, 04638,* ☎ FAX *950/472448,* WEB *www.mamabels.com. 8 rooms. Restaurant. MC, V.*

**$$$**  ▥ **Parador de Mojácar.** If you prefer to sleep by the sea rather than in the old town, this rambling, white modern parador is the best option in Mojácar. The public rooms are spacious and tasteful, with open fireplaces adding a rustic touch. Bedrooms are bright, with Castilian furniture. ⊠ *Carretera de Garrucha Carboneras, 04638 Playa de Mojácar,* ☎ *950/478250,* FAX *950/478183,* WEB *www.parador.es. 98 rooms. Restaurant, tennis court, pool, bar, meeting room. AE, DC, MC, V.*

**$–$$**  ▥ **El Puntazo.** For a beachfront location, this friendly family-run establishment is an excellent value. There are actually two hotels, separated by a garden: a more modern three-star and an older, simpler one-star that shares many of the services with its neighbor. ⊠ *Paseo del Mediterráneo 258, 04638 Playa de Mojácar,* ☎ *950/478265,* FAX *950/478285,* WEB *www.hotelelpuntazo.com. 3-star hotel 45 rooms, 1-star hotel 25 rooms. Restaurant, pool, bar, meeting room. MC, V.*

**$**  ▥ **Pensión El Torreón.** This tiny pensión above the old Moorish arch in Mojácar is a delight. The rooms are simple and tasteful, some furnished with antiques, but the real appeals are the wonderful atmosphere and friendly service. Breakfast on the terrace with views of the coast is a memorable experience. Note that there is one bathroom, shared by the five rooms; each room is equipped with a sink. ⊠ *Calle Jazmín 4–6, 04638 Mojácar,* ☎ *950/475259. 5 rooms without bath. Some pets allowed; no a/c, no room phones, no room TVs. No credit cards.*

### Outdoor Activities and Sports

#### GOLF

The 18-hole **Cortijo Grande** (⊠ Urbanizacióon Cortijo Grande, ☎ 950/479176), near Turre, wends its way among citrus groves. The **Marina Golf Mojácar** (⊠ Urbanización Marina de la Torre, Avda. del Mar s/n, Playa de Mojácar, ☎ 950/133235), opened in 2001, is on the coast, with some of its 18 holes overlooking the sea.

#### HORSEBACK RIDING

You can hire a horse or sign up for a horseback excursion at **Torre Cabrera** (⊠ Turre, ☎ 950/528807), a small country holiday complex next to a small lake near Turre, 4 km (2 ¼ mi) from Mojácar. The center also has tennis, rowing, and biking activities.

## Vera

❿ *20 km (12 mi) north of Mojácar; 90 km (41 mi) northeast of Almería.*

Vera's chief claim to fame is as the site of Spain's first nudist hotel, opened in the late 1980s on the coast 7 km (4 mi) from the inland village. Hiring local staff to work in the hotel was a major hurdle at first, but now Vera prides itself on its status as the nudist capital of Spain, and the hotel has since been joined by a spread of holiday apartment complexes for nudists, lining the **playa naturista** (nudist beach). Those who prefer to cover up when on the beach should follow the signs to the *playa textil,* south of the nudist area.

### Dining and Lodging

$$ ✕🏠 **Terraza Carmona.** The main reason many people visit the town
★ of Vera is to dine here, at what's widely considered the best restaurant in the province. Terraza Carmona was instrumental in reviving many classic Almerían dishes, including *ajo colorao* (a cumin-flavored paste made with fish, potatoes, and vegetables) and *gurullos con conejo* (pasta with rabbit). More conventional Spanish fare, including lots of fresh seafood, is also available. It's all served in a spacious dining room, the walls crammed with artifacts, photos, and culinary prizes. The adjoining hotel has comfortable if not luxurious rooms, dressed in floral fabrics and each with a small balcony. ⊠ *Calle Manuel Giménez ,1, 04620,* ☎ *950/390760,* FAX *950/391314,* WEB *www. terrazacarmona.com. 38 rooms. Restaurant, bar. AE, DC, MC, V. Restaurant closed Mon.*

$$$ 🏠 **Vera Playa Club.** Spain's first—and only—nudist hotel, on the beach, is popular with northern Europeans attracted by the informal, family atmosphere and the sunny climate. The only rules are that no clothing is allowed in the pool area, whereas dress is required after 8 PM and in the restaurant at all times. Otherwise, guests go as they please. The rooms are cool and comfortable, done in cheerful yellow tones, and have terraces, some looking onto the officially designated nudist beach, others with views of the garden and large swimming pool. ⊠ *Carretera Garrucha–Villaricos s/n, 04620,* ☎ *950/467475,* FAX *950/ 467476,* WEB *www.hotelesplaya.com. 281 rooms. Restaurant, snack bar, in-room safes, some kitchenettes, 2 pools (1 indoor), hot tub, bar, dance club, some pets allowed. AE, DC, MC, V.*

# NORTHERN ALMERÍA

The less explored northern half of Almería, ranging from the Sierra de Filabres down to the Almanzora valley (source of the finest marble in Spain) and beyond to the Sierra María mountains, also has its attractions. The standout among these is Vélez-Blanco, a dazzling white village overlooked by one of Andalusia's most impressive castles, and a base for viewing rare prehistoric rock paintings and for exploring the province's northernmost nature park.

## Vélez-Rubio

⓫ *127 km (79 mi) north of Vera.*

Vélez-Rubio is a pleasant town just off the main A-92 highway linking Granada to the eastern coast of Spain. Although a major center in Moorish times, most of it is of more recent vintage. Baroque is the predominant style in its monuments, foremost among which is the impressive 18th-century **Iglesia de la Encarnación**, the main church.

## Vélez-Blanco

★ ⓬ *136 km (85 mi) north of Vera.*

Vélez-Blanco, 9 km (5½ mi) north of Vélez-Rubio, is a picturesque maze of narrow streets, many with gushing fountains. Make your way to the **Almacén de Trigo** (⊠ Avda. Marqués de los Vélez s/n, ☎ 950/415354) a former wheat warehouse that is now headquarters for the local tourist office, where Friday through Sunday you can pick up information on the surrounding attractions.

Towering over Vélez-Blanco is the awe-inspiring profile of the **Castillo de los Fajardo.** Although a Moorish *alcazaba* originally stood here, most of the present Renaissance-style fortress was built between 1506 and 1515 by Pedro Fajardo, the first marquis of Vélez. Seeking to curb the power of the nobility, the Spanish crown had issued a decree forbidding the construction of new castles, but the wily marquis got around this by putting in a request to carry out some "minor repairs" on the old castle, and ended up with an inexpungible fortress. Inside, the once-lavish Renaissance inner courtyard is missing: it was ripped out and ended up in the Metropolitan Museum of New York in 1913. ⊠ *Just off Carretera 321,* ☎ *607/415055.* ☎ *€0.90.* ☉ *Mon.–Tues. and Thurs.–Fri. 11–1 and 4–8, weekends 11–8.*

The **Cueva de los Letreros** (Cave of Signs), 1 km (⅗ mi) south of Vélez-Blanco, is not in fact a cave, but a sheltered rock face that neolithic men adorned with mysterious symbols and figures some 6,000 years ago. To visit on the weekend, you need to contact the Almacén de Trigo information office (☎ 950/415354) to collect the key, leaving your passport as deposit. To visit on weekdays, pick up the key at the Vélez-Blanco ayuntamiento (⊠ Calle Corredera 38, ☎ 950/614800), open Monday to Friday from 8 to 3. The most famous neolithic figure was discovered in a rock shelter nearby: the **Indalo** shows a man with outstretched arms holding aloft an arch or a rainbow. ⊠ *Carretera 321, 1 km south of Vélez-Blanco,* ☎ *Free.* ☉ *Apr.–mid-June, Tues.–Fri. 10–2, Sat. 10–2 and 6–8, Sun. 10–2; mid-June–mid-Oct., Fri.–Sun. 10–2 and 6–8; mid-Oct.–Mar., Tues.–Fri. 10–2, Sat. 10–2 and 4–6, Sun. 10–2.*

Vélez-Blanco is the gateway to the **Sierra María-Los Vélez Nature Park.** This pine-covered mountain landscape is the only place in southern Spain where you can spot the rare red squirrel. Guided tours on foot or in four-wheel-drives can be arranged through the Almacén de Trigo information center (☎ 950/415354).

## Dining and Lodging

**$$–$$$**  ✕ **Mesón El Molino.** Cuisine from Castile—featuring grilled and oven-cooked meats and game—is the specialty at this rustic, down-home restaurant, with sturdy wooden tables, a fireplace, and—true to its name—a small *molino* (windmill) as part of the decor. Hearty dishes include *cochinillo* (oven-roasted suckling pig), grilled lamb, and *perdiz en escabeche* (marinated partridge). Fish specialties are *rodaballo a la plancha* (grilled turbot topped with a sauce of garlic and pine nuts) and grilled cod. ⊠ *Calle Curtidores s/n,,* ☎ *950/415070. AE, DC, MC, V. No dinner Thurs. (except in Aug.).*

**$$**  🏨 **Casa de los Arcos.** Splendidly located at the edge of a ravine in the heart of Vélez-Blanco, this friendly, informal hotel is installed in a restored 18th-century mansion, with good views of the castle. Rooms are simply furnished, with wrought-iron beds, but are spacious and pleasant, and some have small balconies. ⊠ *Calle San Francisco 2, 04830 Vélez-Blanco,* ☎ *950/614805,* ☒ *950/614947,* 🌐 *www.casadelosarcos. net. 14 rooms. No a/c. MC, V.*

# ALMERÍA PROVINCE A TO Z

To research prices, get advice from other travelers, and book travel arrangements, visit www.fodors.com.

### AIR TRAVEL

Almería's airport has direct scheduled links with Madrid, Barcelona, and Melilla (on the north African coast), served by Iberia and its regional affiliate, Binter. Those traveling from outside Spain have to take a connecting flight in Madrid or Barcelona.

➤ AIRLINES AND CONTACTS: **Iberia** (☎ 902/400500).

### AIRPORTS AND TRANSFERS

Almería Airport is 8 km (5 mi) east of Almería. There is a regular city bus line between the airport and Avenida Federico García Lorca in downtown Almería. The taxi fare is around €9.

➤ AIRPORT INFORMATION: **Almería Airport** (☎ 950/213700).

### BOAT AND FERRY TRAVEL

Almería's port has direct ferry links to Nador (Morocco) and the Spanish city of Melilla on the north African coast, in Morocco, run by the Ferrimaroc and Trasmediterránea companies. Ferrimaroc travels to Nador three times daily from late June to early September, and once daily during the rest of the year. Trasmediterránea sails to Melilla at 11 PM Monday–Saturday.

➤ BOAT AND FERRY INFORMATION: **Ferrimaroc** (☎ 950/274800). **Trasmediterránea** (☎ 902/454645).

### BUS TRAVEL

There are regular bus services between Almería and Málaga, Granada, Seville, and Córdoba, operated by the Alsina Graells Sur company. Within the province, if you don't have a car, the bus is the only means of public transport between most towns. Autocares Andreo runs services between Almería and many of the towns in the province, including Fondón, Mojácar, Ohanes, and Tabernas. Autocares Bernardo services destinations along the Cabo de Gata coast. All are based in Almería's Estación Intermodal.

➤ BUS INFORMATION: **Estación Intermodal** (bus and train station, ⊠ Plaza de la Estación, ☎ 950/262098). **Alsina Graells Sur** (☎ 950/

235168). **Autocares Andreo** (☎ 950/221784). **Autocares Bernardo** (☎ 950/264292).

## CAR RENTAL

A car is the best way to explore the province of Almería without having to depend on not-so-frequent buses. The major international car rental companies have offices in the Almería airport or the Estación Intermodal bus and train station.

➤ LOCAL AGENCIES: **Avis** (✉ Aeropuerto de Almería, ☎ 950/224126). **Almería Rent-a-Car** (✉ Avda. la Estación 20, ☎ 950/261533). **Europcar** (✉ Aeropuerto de Almería, ☎ 950/292934). **Hertz** (✉ Aeropuerto de Almería, ☎ 950/292500). **National Atesa** (✉ Estación Intermodal, ☎ 950/252275;✉ Aeropuerto de Almería, ☎ 950/293131).

## CAR TRAVEL

The main access to Almería from Madrid and northern Spain is via Jaén, Granada, and Guadix, or, from Barcelona and the eastern coast, the Autovía del Mediterraneo highway.

Almería is 560 km (347 mi) from Madrid; 809 km (502 mi) from Barcelona; 166 km (103 mi) southeast of Granada; and 183 km (114 mi) east of Málaga, along the N-340 coastal road.

The four-lane N-340 connects the coastal regions of Almería. Smaller roads are in generally good condition, but in mountainous regions can be winding and narrow, especially in the Cabo de Gata area. In these areas, there can be long distances between gas stations, so always fill up before you set out. There is often heavy truck traffic on main routes.

## EMERGENCIES

In case of an emergency, you will find local police helpful. Report the loss or theft of documents or other belongings immediately.

➤ CONTACTS: **Ambulance** (☎ 950/274440). **Fire Department** (☎ 080 and 950/62148). **Hospital Torrecárdenas** (✉ Almería, ☎ 950/212100). **Local Police** (☎ 092 and 950/621205). **Medical Emergencies** (☎ 061). **National Police** (☎ 091).

## TRAIN TRAVEL

Almería's combined train and bus terminal is the Estación Intermodal. There are train connections operated by RENFE between Almería and Granada, Madrid and Barcelona, although for travel between Andalusian destinations the bus is the better method.

➤ TRAIN INFORMATION: **Estación Intermodal** (✉ Plaza de la Estación, ☎ 950/262098).

➤ CONTACTS: **RENFE** (☎ 950/251135; general inquiries: ☎ 902/240202, WEB www.renfe.es).

## VISITOR INFORMATION

There are three tourist information offices in the city of Almería, run by the local, provincial, and regional governments.

➤ LOCAL TOURIST OFFICES: **Almería** (Regional tourist office: ✉ Parque Nicolás Salmerón s/n, ☎ 950/274355; Provincial tourist office: ✉ Plaza de Bendicho s/n, ☎ 950/621117; Municipal tourist office: ✉ Rambla Federico García Lorca, ☎ 950/280748). **Laujar de Andarax** (✉ Centro de Visitantes, Ctra. Laujar-Alcolea Km 1, ☎ 950/513548). **Mojácar** (✉ Plaza Nueva, ☎ 950/475162). **San José** (✉ Grupo J126, Plaza Génova s/n, ☎ 950/380199). **Sorbas** (✉ Calle Terraplén 9, ☎ 950/364476). **Vélez-Blanco** (✉ Centro de Visitantes, Almacén de Trigo. Calle Marqués de los Vélez s/n, ☎ 950/415354).

# 10 BACKGROUND AND ESSENTIALS

Portraits of Andalusia

Books and Movies

Chronology

Spanish Vocabulary

# FLAMENCO: THE MUSIC OF ANDALUSIA

Andalusia's flamenco is a musicologist's dream, a passionate mix of Arabic, African, Jewish, Hindu, and Spanish influences that became the musical signature of the Gypsies of southern Spain after their arrival from northwestern India in the 15th century. The derivation of the term *flamenco* is as uncertain as the origins of the music itself. In Spanish, *flamenco* means, literally, Flemish; one theory suggests that the histrionic carrying on of Charles V's courtiers, from Flanders, may have led to the use of the word to describe louche behavior in general. Another theory links flamenco with the bitter lament of the *felag mengu*, Arabic for "homeless peasant," after the 1492 expulsion decree left uprooted and fugitive Moriscos wandering throughout southern Spain.

The word *flamenco* was first used to describe music and dance in the mid-18th century. Gypsy artists were the rule, and their colorful lives made perfect subject matter. The Gypsies may not have created flamenco, but they have been its primary custodians and innovators. *Cante* (flamenco song), the original base from which dance and guitar later stemmed, has characteristics that are clearly eastern: repetition of the same note, as in ritual chant; variations around a pivotal note to stress a lyric; and sliding notes falling between the fixed points in western scales. Indeed, the unaccompanied *saeta* (a kind of cante, literally an arrow—a dart of emotion coming straight from the heart) has been likened to the call to prayer still heard from minarets around the Mediterranean.

*Cante jondo* (deep song), a fiery lamentation on pain and loss, is at flamenco's core. Within cante jondo, *soleares* (from *soledades*, loneliness) and *siguiriyas* (from *seguidillas*, folk songs) are the main song forms, the first addressing solitude and alienation and the second attacking the great existential problems of lost love and death. Each cante is performed to a different *compás* (rhythmic pattern), traditionally marked with *palmas* (hand clapping), which Andalusians learn from the cradle and can perform in astounding intricacy. *Taconeo* (heels), knuckles, and staffs are the other traditional com-

pás markers, with the guitar appearing only in the late 18th century. Spontaneous as flamenco is, there is nothing improvised about the compás. For example, a *buleria* is a song based on 12s—like blues. The emphasis may seem erratic, but it's mathematically consistent: one *two*, one two *three* four five six *seven eight* nine *ten,* one *two,* one two *three . . .*

Flamenco dance came about as an illustration of the emotions of the cante. Whereas ballet soars and seeks to elude gravity while liberating arm and leg gesture from the body, flamenco's fierce footwork struggles to connect with the earth while the limbs pull inward to the body.

Mid-19th-century *cafés cantantes* produced the *cuadro flamenco,* or performing troupe, the guitar becoming more important in marking both compás and harmonic progression. With a resurgence of the Spanish classical guitar in the 1870s, flamenco guitar gained stature, and today's virtuosos Paco de Lucía and Manolo Sanlúcar are stars in their own right. Once flamenco became show business, this art form's most extraordinary facet, *duende,* the "witch" or demon that transports the performer to a mystical level, became an endangered species.

Properly seeing and hearing flamenco today is not easy. Experts debate the pros and cons of pure flamenco, flamenco fusion, *zambras* (flamenco for tourists), and *juergas* (parties unleashed for the sheer joy of it). Estrella Morente is the female cante jondo hope of the moment, and if you hear her you will have heard the best in Spain. *Tablaos* (commercial flamenco venues) can be disappointing, though the artists are usually technically excellent. For authentic flamenco, find your way to a *peña,* a flamenco club in a semiprivate bar where, if you keep a low profile, you'll eventually find yourself in the midst of this raging, blueslike Andalusian musical culture, at its best bringing you face to face with the human mysteries of love and death and loss. It's a raw, exciting feeling that even *payos* (non-Gypsies) can sometimes understand.

—George Semler

# GRANADA'S MARTYR-POET

The execution in Granada of Spain's most famous poet, Federico García Lorca (1898–1936), was one of the most resounding tragedies of Spain's 1936–39 Civil War. His poetry and plays were, though addressing passionate and violent themes, so irrepressibly filled with life that the destruction of this vital spirit was a perfect metaphor for the premeditated murder of the Spanish Second Republic and its progressive and democratic ideals by the Spanish army, church, and oligarchy.

The military rebellion that overthrew the Republic didn't hesitate to get rid of García Lorca: his charm was such that, except in the most conservative circles, even his open homosexuality was regarded as endearing. As director of La Barraca, an itinerant theater troupe formed by the Cultural Ministry to bring classical theater to the working class, García Lorca was an inspirational voice on the progressive side of 1930s Spanish politics.

García Lorca's joyous, wide-ranging poetry and plays espoused the causes of the poor, the underprivileged, and the oppressed. His 1928 *Romancero Gitano* (Gypsy Ballads) made him the most popular poet of his generation at the age of 30. *Llanto por Ignacio Sanchez Mejías* (Lament for the Death of a Bullfighter), published in 1935, and *Poeta en Nueva York* (Poet in New York), published posthumously in 1940, were his later collections of poetry. His ability to synthesize tradition and invention, past and future, natural and human themes in language filled with music and color made his poetry at once popular and erudite. His plays, notably *Yerma, Doña Rosita la Soltera, La Casa de Bernarda Alba,* and *Bodas de Sangre* (Blood Wedding), written in the early '30s, all dramatize the plight of the weak, the outcast, and the disenfranchised: peasants, workers, women, and Gypsies.

García Lorca's fame grew along with the Republican cause. He, Salvador Dalí, and the actress Margarita Xirgu were all darlings of the Frente Popular, the most progressive elements in Spain, just as Spanish politics became increasingly polarized between 1934 and 1936. In Granada, the rightists won the elections, but the results were overturned in Las Cortes, Spain's

parliament, because of electoral abuses and fraud. In the new elections, the right lost, further infuriating local fascists. García Lorca, in an interview published in *El Sol* on June 10, 1936, five days short of his 38th birthday, was quoted as saying that "in Granada, Spain's worst bourgeoisie is agitating."

These bourgeois considered García Lorca *el maricón de la pajarita* (the little gay with the bow tie). His play *La Casa de Bernarda Alba* criticized landowners in his adopted village of Valderrubio. The circle began to close. After the assassination of Spanish senator Calvo Sotelo in the early morning of July 13, García Lorca, deeply worried, took the train to Granada, finding refuge with his family. On July 18, the military revolt finally took place. The local army captured Granada and began one of its worst purges, executing thousands of political opponents. García Lorca moved to the house of his friend, poet Luis Rosales, but the "worst bourgeoisie in Spain" easily discovered his hiding place. He was arrested and jailed, accused of supporting the Frente Popular, of friendship with the radical Fernando de los Ríos, and of homosexuality. General Queipo de Llano approved the execution with the enigmatically coded order, "*Dale café, mucho café*" (Give him coffee, lots of coffee).

During his last, long night in prison, García Lorca conversed freely with one of his jailers, who recalls the poet saying that he was not afraid so much of dying as of no longer being. "When you sleep, you are not; and to be, that is everything."

The poet was taken to a spot between the villages of Viznar and Alfacar, near Fuente Grande, or, in Arabic, Aynadamar (Fountain of Tears). There, along with a local schoolmaster and two anarchists, he was shot to death in the predawn hours of August 18, 1936.

Parque de Alfacar fills every August 18 for a piano, guitar, or cante jondo concert and a reading of the poet's verses. Federico García Lorca, more than a century after his birth, remains an important presence in Granada and beyond.

—George Semler

# IN PURSUIT OF THE PERFECT ANDALUSIAN TAPA

The tapa may be to cooking what poetry is to prose, and Andalusia—from Federico García Lorca to Rafael Alberti to cineast Luis Buñuel—is nothing if not poetic.

It is generally agreed in Spain that Andalusia is the birthplace of the *tapeo,* a nomadic wandering from bar to bar, tavern to tavern, *tasca* to *tasca,* in search of the perfect prawn or the freshest baby shrimp to go with a shot of wine, beer, or dry sherry. As the Iberian corner where the tapa has most evolved into a culinary art form, all of Andalusia is superlative, but the triangle with its apex in Seville and feet in Cádiz and Sanlúcar de Barrameda, surrounding Jerez de la Frontera and El Puerto de Santa María, is Andalusia's prime tapa grazing ground.

## Orgins

The origins and evolution of Spain's most emblematic and original contribution to world cuisine have been much debated. A piece of ham or cheese used to *tapar* (cover) a glass of wine to keep flies out and stagecoach drivers upright? A medical prescription for 13th-century Spanish King Alfonso X *El Sabio* (The Wise, or Learned) requiring sporadic minimeals with wine? A trick to *tapar* (contain) hunger? Cervantes called them *llamativos* (lures or attention getters) in his 1605 masterpiece *Don Quijote de la Mancha,* tidbits meant to provoke thirst and appetite. These explanations, neither discountable nor fully convincing, are regarded warily by Spanish historians and culinary cognoscenti.

Jaume Fàbrega, author of *La Cuina Mediterránea,* an 11-tome study of cooking around the Mediterranean, suggests more substantial reasons why Andalusia should have been the birthplace for this itinerant form of feasting. "Cádiz, and Andalusia in general," he wrote, "in close contact with eastern civilizations—Egyptians, Turks, Arabs—always showed a preference for small portions of a variety of appetizers, never favoring the tradition of the formal sit-down meal."

Moorish musician, poet, chef, and culinary sage Ziryab, who worked in the Caliphate of Cordoba during the 9th century, is credited with introducing into Europe the Arab practice of dining in various stages on different dishes: appetizers, a vegetable course, a meat course, and dessert. Even today, Moroccan and North African dining seems more a picnic than a feast, taking place on divans or couches loosely strewn around a jumble of dishes on a low table, which may in earlier days have been a carpet on the floor of a tent.

Fàbrega also cites Andalusia's traditional social structure, where class differences have historically been more pronounced than in the rest of Spain. "There was no prosperous peasant in Andalusia, as there was in northern Spain or in Europe. Many of these rural serfs, all but slaves, had no table to gather around nor great quantities of produce to put on it. Thus, they became accustomed to eating when and where they could. Gazpacho, for example, was a peasant invention, an example of poverty stimulating creativity in the kitchen, a way to make something delicious out of little or nothing.

"Tapas are a kind of fast food, really," Fàbrega concludes, "a way to eat and continue to work or party."

Andalusian Gypsy *juergas* (wild parties) endure for days; the juergistas dance, sing, have a *fino* (dry sherry from Jerez de la Frontera) or a Manzanilla, take a bite of something, and dance and sing some more. To adjourn for a real meal would completely break the rhythm of the party, as well as of the make-it-up-as-you-go-along nature of life in general as perceived by Andalusians. Tapas are largely a reflection of this non–western European view of life. Why become encumbered with a slumber-inducing, preplanned, prescheduled, sit-down event when you can allow the evening to develop along more natural and spontaneous lines?

The main difference between tapas in Andalusia and tapas in the Basque country or Madrid is that Andalusians frequently substitute the tapeo for dinner, whereas in most other parts of Spain tapas are considered mere preliminaries, *aperitivos* (literally, "openers") for the main event. Which are better—Basque, Madrid, or

Andalusian tapas? The question is never taken lightly, and the answer is usually prefaced with an allowance for personal taste. After all, Basque cuisine is perenially admired and respected as Spain's finest, and Madrid has been known for attracting all of the Iberian Peninsula's best produce and practices since it became the royal court in 1561.

"For me," explained Fermin Puig, culinary maestro of the Hotel Majestic's Drolma, one of Barcelona's premier gourmet restaurants, "Basque tapas, which are of course spectacular and exquisite, and perhaps decorate the top of the bar with greater color and variety, tend to be somewhat bulkier, heavier, more prone to creams, puddings, sauces, and pastes or combinations using these ingredients, whereas the Andalucían tapa is nearly always pure raw material, simply the freshest possible fish, crustacean or shellfish cooked quickly in very hot oil with plenty of salt and garlic."

Tapas are handled slightly (if not radically) differently all over Spain. Whereas in Barcelona they were nearly unheard of until the 1990s, in Madrid and points south you may be automatically served a tapa of the barman's choice on ordering a glass of wine or a *caña* (a glass of draft beer)—a piece of cheese, a few olives or anchovies, even a cup of *caldo* (hot broth), in winter. Tapas terminology covers a wide range of small-format cuisine. *Tentempies* are small hits of food designed to "keep you on your feet"; *pinchos* are morsels impaled on toothpicks; *banderillas* are the same thing but with colorful wrappings on the toothpicks that recall the barbed sticks or darts used in bullfighting. *Montaditos* are canapés, inventive combinations of anything from hake eggs to caviar, set up ("mounted") on toast or a slice of bread. A *ración* is a portion larger than a tapa, and a *cazuelita* is a small concoction served hot in an earthenware casserole. Restaurants all over Spain sometimes offer a selection of small dishes "*para picar*" (literally, to pick at) as a first course or appetizer. *Entretenimientos* are an assortment of small delicacies—nuts, cheeses, sausage—used as a starter. The postmodern gourmet *menu de degustación* is little more than a succession of heavy tapas.

## El Faro: Tapas Non Plus Ultra

Cádiz's seminal tapas emporium, El Faro, in the heart of the quarter of the old part of town known as la Viña, for the vineyards that once grew there, is the place to begin an exploration of Andalusian tapas. Don Gonzalo Córdoba is patriarch and *patrón* of what has become, along with his sons' restaurants Ventorillo "El Chato" in nearby San Fernando and El Faro de El Puerto in Puerto de Santa María, the area's most powerful culinary dynasty. He shows no hesitation in describing the tapeo as a growing phenomenon.

"You should have seen the bar at midday, entire families, kids and all. I think it's the variety and the movement that appeals, a sort of gastronomic promiscuity. The bay of Cádiz is so rich in marine life that produce seems to simply swarm out of the Atlantic. For over 3000 years of steady fishing, the abundance of fresh materials is extraordinary. My 17-year-old grandson brought me 25 kilos of squid yesterday, hunted underwater right around Cádiz."

The bar at El Faro is a tapa anthology, problematic only in that the place is hard to leave, although the itinerant quality of the tapeo depends so fundamentally on movement. A mirror placed over the fresh seafood displayed on a prow-shaped tray behind the counter gives a seductive view of the *chocos* (cuttlefish), *acedías* (small sole), *pijotas* (small hake), *gambas* (shrimp), *puntillitas* (tiny squid), and *cazon de conil* (miniature dogfish) that can be ordered by the single tapa, half ration, or ration. Further complicating any chance of departing from El Faro hungry are such fish opportunities as *dorada, besugo, lubina,* or *pargo,* and the *revueltos* (scrambled eggs) with *jabuguitos* (chunks of free-range Iberian pig) and potatoes, ham and mushrooms, salmon and shrimp, or *bacalao y patatas cerillas* (cod with shoestring potatoes). A hit of *jamón de pata negra,* Spain's very best acorn-fed "black hoof" ham, costs about €20 a plate (100 grams), but provides a perfect counterpoint for the seafood.

And to drink? Manzanilla, of course, the sherrylike fortified wine made from palomino grapes in nearby Sanlúcar de Barrameda, where the Manzanilla vineyards cover 500 hectares of the hillsides over the estuary of the river Guadalquivir as it joins the Atlantic. Manzanilla has a fresh salty-tangy maritime taste and is even said to combat hangover as a result of the vitamin B–rich yeast deposit under which it ferments. It's said to travel poorly and to be at its best in Sanlúcar (especially in the lower part of town), but according to the Barbadillo bodega oenologists, the export product simply needs to be more filtered and protected from the rigors of transport, whereas the local version is a less adulterated blend.

The bar at El Faro always has a bottle of Barbadillo Solear in a bucket of ice behind the counter, chilled to perfection, just short of frozen. Manzanilla, and its cousin fino, are compact and contemplative drinks that, perhaps partly as a result of the vitamin B, seem perfect for the long haul. Neither as filling as beer nor as complex as wine, Manzanilla is easy to sip slowly, and naturally accompanies the local seafood specialties.

A few steps down Calle San Félix into la Viña is another not-to-be-missed tavern, Casa Manteca, at the corner of Correlón de los Carros (No. 66), specializing in *chacina variada* (different cuts of Iberian ham), which they serve in the old style, on sheets of waxed paper over the rough wooden counter. Casa Manteca couldn't be more different than El Faro: rustic Andalusia, bullfighting and flamenco posters and photographs haphazardly stuck to the walls, a selection of tapas noteworthy mostly for its brevity, and yet a perfectly complementary tasca after El Faro's polish and plenty.

## Sanlúcar de Barrameda

Sanlúcar's Bajo de Guía beach (*bajo*— low—because it was once a marshy lowlands, and *guía*—guide—for La Virgen de Guía, patron saint of local fishermen) is an all but sacred spot in this part of the world: *una copa de Manzanilla y unos langostinos de Sanlúcar en la playa de Bajo de Guía* (a glass of Manzanilla and jumbo Sanlúcar shrimp on the Bajo de Guía beach) rank high among last mortal desires for Spain's true epicureans. Sanlúcar was the 1498 jumping-off point for Christopher Columbus's third voyage to the New World, as well as for Magellan's 1519 circumnavigation of the globe (which he did not survive, killed in the Philippines in April 1521, his voyage completed by Basque navigator Juan Sebastián Elkano).

The afternoon fish auction in the port just upriver from town is a chance to watch piles of fish, squid, shrimp, shellfish, and crustaceans of every shape and size separated and sold off to bidders from the area's many restaurants. The atmosphere crackles with excitement—the harvest is home and, for the excited bevy of young women, their seagoing *novios* (boyfriends) as well.

Downriver on the Bajo de Guía beach, restaurants start to open as the sun drops into the Atlantic. Burly ships glide down the estuary along with the fishing fleet headed back out for the night shift. Paco Hermoso, owner with his brother Fernando of Casa Bigote (so-named for their father's mustache), hands-down top spot on the Bajo de Guía waterfront, started out in the original wooden *chiringuitos* or shacklike restaurants that used to stand on stilts at the edge of the tide.

"Until 1967, the *lonja*, or fish auction, was held right here in the sand, and the restaurants stood right over the water and served fish as it came in from the sea. The August horse races came right down the beach, as they still do, and the restaurants served as grandstands."

Casa Bigote is now more than a tavern with superb tapas. The Hermoso brothers have moved into the building across the street and made it into a virtual museum of the history of Sanlúcar and the fishing industry. Paco seems to know every sea creature in this corner of the Atlantic, where it comes from, what kind of bottom it prospers in, what it feeds on, and how it tastes. As much as a chef, he seems a marine biologist, an aficionado of every aspect of fishing. It is said that when in bad weather there are as few as three fish brought in by the fleet, two of them will end up at Bigote's. Fires crackle in fireplaces at either end of the dining room as diners begin to fill the room, the walls thick with vintage photographs of early times on the Bajo de Guía.

Casa Bigote is the perfect spot for some exquisitely prepared chocos or a plate of pata negra ham after a sunset stroll on the beach. Paco's version of the origin of the tapa adds new insight on this popular topic: "In the old days there was extra fish around that had no market value, so taverns would give it away with drinks to help sell more wine, placing the fish on top of the wine glass on a little bit of waxed paper that *tapaba*, covered, the top of the glass."

Bajo de Guía ia an imperative Sanlúcar visit (along with the Fábrica de Hielo—Ice Factory—where the ice used for transporting fish was once made, now an excellent museum devoted to Spain's most important wildlife and habitat preserve in Doñana National Park just across the Guadalquivir). But the evening tapeo in Sanlúcar centers around Plaza del Cabildo and Casa Balbino, the true town forum and nerve center.

The plaza and the neighborhood around it rage until all hours on weekends, action centered around Casa Balbino, La Gitana next door, and, on the plaza's upper corner, the cozy and rustic Barbiana, boasting the world's best *papas aliñá* (Andalusian for *patatas aliñadas,* potatoes in olive oil, vinegar, onion, and parsley).

Casa Balbino is almost perfect tapeo habitat, with stand-up tables sprinkled around, tiny corners tucked here and there, plenty of bar space, outside tables on the plaza, blackboards with daily specials chalked in, and a big board at the end of the bar with well over 50 choices of tapas, montaditos, raciónes, revueltos, and tortillas, including *ortiguillas* (sea anemones), *tortilla de camarones* (crisped flour and egg and baby shrimp), *cazón en adobo* (fried dogfish), *pulpo aliñado* (squid pickled in onion and vinegar), *sangre encebollada* (black pudding with onions), *salmorejo* (a gazpacholike cold vegetable soup made with almonds), and *calamares* (fried cuttlefish).

La Gitana across the way, named for a Manzanilla bodega, serves an ample selection of tapas, although not of the same variety or caliber as those of Casa Balbino, and there are bars and restaurants worth checking out all around the square and down the neighboring streets of Tartaneros and Ramón y Cajal. The Barbiana is the only reasonable competition for Casa Balbino, for its papas aliñá and for rustic appeal of the place.

## El Puerto de Santa María

El Puerto de Santa María, just 23 km (15 mi) south of Sanlúcar, was home of Christopher Columbus and source for the name of one of his three ships. It's now known for its bullring, its 13th-century castle, its wineries, its *palacios* (elegant town houses), and, of course, for its tapas.

Romerijo—on the Ribera del Río (riverfront) promenade, nicknamed Ribera del Marisco (shellfish front)—is a sort of combination seafood supermarket and tavern, none too charming, but with an impressive display of some two dozen varieties of marine morsels to choose from. Crab, shrimp, prawns, sea snails, goosebarnacles, mussels . . . the list is long and colorful. You pick what looks appetizing and they cook it for you. Nautically decorated Casa Flores just down the street is a good spot for a hit of *jabugo,* cured Iberian ham from Romero Carvahal, the 5 J's on the label around the hock standing for the top quality, purely acorn-fed pata negra hams sold for some €400 a piece. These free-range pigs, one of the few mammals that develop fat deposits in muscle tissue, thus giving the meat its taste and lubricity, are also known to favor their left hind legs, which are therefore bigger, tastier, and more expensive.

El Puerto de Santa María's waterfront leads west past La Cañita at Calle Palacio 1, once the house of Christopher Columbus, now a promising tapas bar with outside stand-up tables, and into Plaza Alfonso X el Sabio to the Castillo de San Marcos and its crenellated battlements. One block in, Calle de la Misericordia leads back through a gauntlet of irresistible tapas bars and restaurants, including Bodega la Antigua at No. 12, Bar "Er Beti" at No. 7, and Mesón El Asador at No. 2; the latter serves hunks of beef cooked on small charcoal burners placed at each table. El Faro de El Puerto, Fernando Córdoba's contribution to the family empire, is excellent, though it will take you off the tapas track and back inland.

## Jerez de la Fontera

The *vaporcito* (little boat), once a steamboat, is one way back to Cádiz, but the next stop should be Bar Juanito in Jerez de la Frontera, a mere 12 km (8 mi) inland. Bar Juanito is yet another fabled tapas spot, maybe the most famous of all, with 100 selections of tapas and raciónes every day covering every conceivable combination from berza (a hearty stew with garbanzos, black sausage, chard, celery, sausage, pork, veal, and carrots) to *alcachofas en salsa* (artichokes in sauce), for which Juanito's son Faustino Rodriguez won a National Gastronomy Prize in 1995. Just off central Plaza Arenal in the tiny tunnel-like Calle Pescadería, Juanito has equally inviting tables outside in the passageway and inside on the patio. Meanwhile, next door, Las Almenas, with a bar carved into the 12th-century city walls, puts together a superb gazpacho. Though Bar Juanito has the tapas market in Jerez well cornered, La Parra Vieja, off the other side of Plaza Arenal, is also deservedly famous for meat cooked over coals as well as seafood.

## Cadíz

Back in Cádiz, a secret spot with a crypto-specialty can be found at Calle Sacramento (No. 16). "El Kuki," Juan Rodriguez, at Mesón La Cuesta will be happy to serve you his excellent *urta a la piedra* (sea bream with shrimp), a fish found only in and around the Straits of Gibraltar, known to live in stony habitat and feed exclusively on crustaceans. "El Kuki" adds most of the the urta's own diet of shrimp, crab, clams, and baby squid to green peppers, onion, tomato pulp, white wine, ground white pepper, and parsley, and the result is a superbly thick, dark stew.

Cádiz's tapas resources are vast: Grimaldi, near the Mercado Central, is the place to start, especially on flea market mornings around the west side of the market. Known for its fine produce fresh from the bustling cornucopia across the street, Grimaldi serves *pimientos de piquillo rellenos de gambas* (red piquillo peppers stuffed with shrimp), *tortillitas de camarones* (baby shrimp tortillas), *pulpo caletero a la gallega* (squid Galicia style), and *almejas finas al Grimaldi* (tiny clams Grimaldi), not to mention the nearly irresistible *tarta de queso con frambuesa* (cheesecake with raspberries).

North of the market is El Nuevo Almacen, at Calle Barrie 17, a delicatessen specializing in jabugo ham with a bar, tables, and a brilliant selection of more than 80 surprises ranging from *revuelto de ajetes jabugo* (scrambled eggs with young garlic and jabugo ham) to *morcón* (blood sausage) to *anchoas con bacalao y tomate* (anchovies with cod and tomato). From El Nuevo Almacen over to La Perola on Canovas del Castillo 13 there is barely time for a deep breath; moderation and pacing are key to achieving a tantric, pleasure-extending state of tapeo nirvana.

La Perola—perhaps Cádiz's best, most gourmet tapas sanctuary—is the creation of Francisco Leal, whose recipes combine traditional home cooking with modern and Moorish themes. Leal describes his *garbancitos con acelgas* (a stew of chard, garbanzos, garlic, cumin seed, sweet red peppers, fried tomato, and vinegar) as a *guiso mozarabe* (a recipe from the Mozarabs, Christians under Arab rule). The *tortilla de la Hermana Pascuala* (tortilla from Sister Pasquale), originated in a convent of barefoot nuns, is a power tortilla including ham (or chorizo or shrimp), parsley, bread, potato, and onion. *Tortilla de harina de trigo* (wheat flour tortilla), *pastela* (a sweet Moroccan filo pastry with chicken, pine nuts, almonds, and raisins), *pâté de cañaillas* (sea snail pâté), *albóndigas con roquefort* (meatballs with Roquefort cheese), and *pâté de rape y gamba* (shrimp and monkfish pâté) are just a few of the inventive minor wonders created at La Perola.

At the northwest corner of nearby Plaza de Mina is Calle Zorrilla, possibly the spot that best catches the spirit of the Sunday morning aperitivo. Here the sun comes in perfectly at midday and the street fills with the tapeo faithful and sidewalk vendors of *quisquilla* (baby shrimp), *cañaillas* (sea snails), *caracoles* (snails), and *mojama* (dried salt tuna). Surrounded by local bars, most notably El Cartucho, famed for its exclusively local dishes such as *berza y queso de payoyo* (chard stew and a local goat cheese), the top of this short alley leading out to the sea walls becomes an open-air street party. Clusters of Manzanilla tipplers hold their glasses delicately by the stems and crunch quisquilla fragrant with the salty sea smell of the nearly 360 degrees of Atlantic ocean surrounding Cádiz while discussing what they might eventually have for lunch, or the next and possibly definitive tapa fantasy around the corner.

In Andalusia, tapas, much more than fast food, are a way of life.

—George Semler

# BOOKS AND MOVIES

Washington Irving's 1832 *Tales of the Alhambra* is one of the earliest English-language accounts of Andalusia's romance and passion, and the first English guidebook on Spain, Richard Ford's 1845 *Handbook for Travellers in Spain,* is fascinating for the Spanish and Andalusian idiosyncrasies that have endured. George Borrow's *The Bible in Spain* is a profoundly wise and funny view of 19th-century Spain through the eyes by a Bible-peddling Briton.

Larry Collins and Dominique LaPierre's *Or I'll Dress You in Mourning* tells the rags-to-riches saga of one of Córdoba's most famous modern bullfighters, the 1960s "matador-yé-yé" Manuel Benítez El Cordobés.

Gerald Brenan portrays Andalusia before and during the Franco years in the *The Face of Spain, The Spanish Labyrinth,* and *South from Granada. Moorish Spain,* by Richard Fletcher, details the cultural and intellectual riches of the Islamic era. Titus Burckhardt's *Moorish Culture in Spain* is a study of Islamic art and architecture in Andalusia and beyond. *Farewell España,* by Howard Sachar, covers the Sephardim, the Spanish Jews who were forced to flee after the 1492 expulsion decree. Journalist John Hooper examines the post-Franco era in *The New Spaniards.*

Alastair Boyd's *The Sierras of the South* is a lively personal account of mid-20th-century life around Ronda and the Sierra de Grazalema. Nicholas Luard paints a careful picture of La Janda and upland Cádiz in his 1984 *Andalucía: A Portrait of Southern Spain. Inside Andalusia* by David Baird is a series of portraits of places and players.

For flora and fauna, look for *Birds of Iberia* by Clive Findlayson and David Tomlinson and *A Selection of Wildflowers of Southern Spain* by Betty Molesworth Allen. *Walking in Andalucía* by Guy Hunter-Watts shows the reader through 34 walks in six of Andalusia's nature parks. *Andalusian Landscapes* by Tim Gartside captures the full range of the Andalusian countryside in brilliant color photography. *Made in Andalucía* by Bob and Ruth Carrick is a guide to the arts and crafts of southern Spain. The greatest flamencologist, Spanish or foreign, is the American Don Pohren, whose books *Lives and Legends of Flamenco, Paco de Lucía and Family,* and *A Way of Life* explore the roots, romance, and musicology of Andalusia's most emblematic music.

Irish Hispanist Ian Gibson's *The Assassination of Federico García Lorca* meticulously reconstructs the poet's final moments and the dramatic Spanish, Granada, and personal history that led up to it. *Federico García Lorca: A Life* is Gibson's comprehensive biography of the poet. In *En Granada, Su Granada . . .* Gibson traces the poet's life and times in his native city.

The tragic bullfighting novel *Blood and Sand* by Vicente Blasco Ibáñez has three Hollywood adaptations: the first starring Rudolph Valentino, the second Tyrone Power, the third Sharon Stone. The last version shows quite a bit of Andalusia.

Cinema from Andalusia includes Carlos Saura's beautifully crafted classics consisting mostly of dance—*Carmen, Bodas de Sangre* (Blood Wedding), and *El Amor Brujo* (Love Bewitched). Saura's 1992 *Sevillanas* films 11 short performances by famous flamenco dancers, singers, and guitarists ranging in age from 8 to nearly 80. *Flamenco* (1995) is Saura's presentation of 13 flamenco rhythms performed for fellow artists, and for the camera.

Luis Buñuel's *Un Chien Andalou* (An Andalusian Dog) is still a hallmark of surrealism, and *Belle de Jour, Tristana,* and *That Obscure Object of Desire* contain haunting psychological studies. The last has lovely photography of Seville.

Though set in 1930s Galicia, José Luis Cuerda's gorgeous *Butterfly* (released in the United Kingdom as *The Butterfly's Tongue*) shows how the Spanish Civil War divided communities throughout Spain before the first shots were fired.

The darling of Spanish cinema is Pedro Almodóvar, whose *Women on the Verge of a Nervous Breakdown, Tie Me Up! Tie Me Down!, All About My Mother,* and *Talk to Her* were greeted enthusiastically on both sides of the Atlantic.

# ANDALUSIA AT A GLANCE

| | |
|---|---|
| **2,000,000 BC** | Hominid remains found in Orce, in Granada's Altiplano, accepted as earliest evidence of human presence in Europe. |
| **1,000,000–750,000 BC** | Stones carved by hominids found in Puerto de Santa María, Cádiz. |
| **50,000 BC** | Neanderthal man placed in Gibraltar. |
| **25,000–18,000 BC** | Paleolithic (Old Stone Age) settlement. Cave paintings by *homo sapiens* discovered. |
| **7,000 BC** | Arrival of Neolithic colonists from the north of Africa. Agriculture introduced on the Iberian Peninsula. |
| **4,000 BC** | Tombs found in the Cueva de los Murciélagos (Bat Cave) in Zuheros, Córdoba, with Neolithic remains, straw sandals, and religious offerings. |
| **ca. 2300 BC** | Copper Age culture. Stone megaliths built. Funeral dolmens found in Los Millares, Almería. |
| **ca. 1100 BC** | Earliest Phoenician colonies, including Cádiz, Villaricos, Almuñecar, and Málaga. Native peoples include Iberians in the south, Basques in Pyrenees, and Celts in the northwest. |
| **800–700 BC** | The golden age of Tartessus (Tharsis) in the estuary of the Guadalquivir River west of Seville. |
| **ca. 650 BC** | Greeks begin to colonize east coast at Empuries, in northern Catalonia, with colonists reaching as far south as the coasts of Andalusia. |
| **237 BC** | Carthaginians land in Spain, found Cartagena circa 225 BC. |
| **206 BC** | Romans expel Carthaginians from Spain and gradually conquer peninsula over next two centuries. Spain becomes one of Rome's most important colonies. The Roman city of Itálica is founded near Seville. |
| **200 BC** | Romans conquer the southern part of the Iberian Peninsula, reaching Cádiz. |
| **61 BC** | Julius Caesar named governor of Hispania Ulterior (Outer Spain), the western part of Rome's empire on the Iberian Peninsula. |
| **55 BC** | Seneca the Elder born in Córdoba. |
| **AD 55** | Seneca the Younger commits suicide on Nero's orders. |
| **74** | Roman citizenship extended to all Spaniards. |
| **380** | Christianity declared sole religion of Rome and her empire. |
| **409** | First Barbaric invasions. |
| **419** | Visigothic kingdom established in northern Spain, with capital at Toledo. |

## Moorish Spain

| | |
|---|---|
| **711–12** | Christian Visigothic kingdom destroyed by invading Muslims (Moors) from northern Africa. Moors create emirate, with capital at Córdoba. |
| **756** | Independent Moorish Emirate established by Damascus-born Ummayyad heir Abd al-Rahman I at Córdoba. |

**778** Charlemagne establishes Frankish rule north of Ebro.

**785** Córdoba's Mezquita begun.

**822–852** Reign of Abd al-Rahman II.

**912–61** Reign of Abd al-Rahman III: height of Moorish culture (though it flourishes throughout reconquest).

**961–976** Al Hakam II creates a major library in Madinat al-Zahra and enlarges the Mezquita.

**976–1002** Military strongman Al Mansur takes power.

**1010** Berber mercenaries sack and pillage Madinat al-Zahra.

**1012** The Moorish empire splinters into the Rule of the Taifas.

**1031** The Caliphate disappears.

## The Reconquest

**1085** Alfonso VI of Castile captures Toledo.

**1086** The Almoravid dynasty of Northern Africa invades Andalusia.

**1099** Death of Rodrigo Díaz de Vivar, known as El Cid, who served both Christian and Muslim kings; buried at Burgos Cathedral (completed 1126), first Gothic cathedral.

**1126** Birth of Averroës, Arabic thinker, in Córdoba.

**1135** Birth of Maimónides, Hebrew scholar, physician, and philosopher, in Córdoba.

**1137** Aragón unites with Catalonia through marriage.

**1147** The Almohads succeed the Almoravids as reigning dynasty in Andalusia.

**1175–1200** The Almohads reach the zenith of their power. Construction of La Giralda and La Torre de Oro.

**1209** Moors found first Spanish university, in Valencia.

**1212** Victory over the Almohads at Las Navas de Tolosa by united Christian armies: Moorish power crippled.

**1236–48** Valencia, Córdoba, and Seville fall to Christians.

**1270** End of main period of reconquest. Portugal, Aragón, and Castile emerge as major powers.

**1350–1369** Reign of Pedro I (the Cruel) de Castilla, who rebuilds Seville's Alcázar in Mudéjar, or neo-Moorish, style.

**1469** Isabella, princess of Castile, marries Ferdinand, heir to the throne of Aragón.

**1478** Spanish Inquisition established.

**1479–1504** Isabella and Ferdinand rule jointly.

**1492** Granada, the last Moorish outpost, falls. Christopher Columbus, under the sponsorship of Isabella, "discovers" America, setting off a wave of Spanish exploration. Ferdinand and Isabella, also known as the Catholic Monarchs, expel Jews and Muslims from Spain.

**1494** Treaty of Tordesillas: Portugal and Spain divide the known world between them.

**1499** Publication of *La Celestina*, by Fernando de Rojas, considered most important literary precursor to *Don Quixote*, which would not appear until 1605.

**1502** Rebellion of Los Moriscos, Moors who had been permitted to remain in Andalusia after 1492, in the Alpujarra mountains of Granada.

**1516** Death of Ferdinand. His grandson and heir, Emperor Charles I (Charles V of the Holy Roman Empire), inaugurates the Habsburg dynasty and Spain's golden age.

## The Habsburg Dynasty

**1519** Charles I of Spain is elected Holy Roman Emperor as Charles V. From his father, Philip of Habsburg, he inherits Austria, the Spanish Netherlands, Burgundy, and nearly continuous war with France. Hernán Cortés conquers the Aztec Empire in Mexico.

**1519-22** First circumnavigation of the world by Ferdinand Magellan's ships completed by Basque navigator Juan Sebastián Elkano.

**ca. 1520-1700** Golden age. Funded by its empire, Spain's culture flourishes. Artists include El Greco (1541-1614), Velázquez (1599-1660), and Murillo (1617-82). In literature, the poet Quevedo (1580-1645), dramatists Lope de Vega (1562-1635) and Calderón (1600-81), and novelist Miguel de Cervantes (1547-1616) are known throughout Europe. Counter-Reformation Catholicism takes its lead from St. Ignatius of Loyola (1491-1556), founder of the Jesuit order (1540), and the mystic St. Teresa of Ávila (1515-82).

**1531** Pizarro conquers the Inca empire in Peru.

**1554** Charles's heir, Philip, marries Queen Mary of England ("Bloody Mary").

**1556** Charles abdicates in favor of his son, Philip II, who inherits Spain, Sicily, and the Netherlands. Holy Roman Empire goes to Charles's brother Ferdinand. Philip II leads cause of Counter-Reformation against Protestant states in Europe.

**1561** Capital established at Madrid.

**1571** Spanish fleet stops westward advance of Ottoman Empire in naval battle of Lepanto—afterward regarded as the high-water mark of the Spanish Empire.

**1588** Philip attacks Protestant England with *"Invencible"* Spanish Armada, which is destroyed in the English Channel.

**1598** Death of Philip II.

**1599** Velazquez is born in Seville.

**1605** Publication of first part of Miguel de Cervantes's masterpiece, *Don Quijote de la Mancha*, generally considered the first modern (psychological) novel.

**1609** Under Philip III, Moriscos (converted Muslims) expelled and independence of Netherlands recognized.

**1617** Murillo born in Seville.

**1618** Beginning of Thirty Years' War. Originally a religious dispute, it became a dynastic struggle between Habsburgs and Bourbons.

**1621-65** Reign of Philip IV. Count-Duke Olivares reforms regime on absolutist model of France.

**1630** Madrid becomes Europe's largest city. Zurbarán moves to Seville.

**1640–59** Revolt in Catalonia; republic declared for a time.

**1648** End of Thirty Years' War; Spanish Netherlands declared independent.

**1659** Treaty of the Pyrenees ends war with France and Spanish ascendancy in Europe.

**1680** The Guadalquivir River silts in and becomes marshland. Shipping commerce switches to Cádiz, while Seville declines.

**1665–1700** Reign of Charles II, last of the Spanish Habsburgs, who dies without heir.

## The Bourbon Dynasty

**1701–14** War of the Spanish Succession: claimants to the throne are Louis XIV of France, Leopold I of Bavaria, and Philip of Anjou. Treaty of Utrecht, 1713, recognizes Philip as Philip V, first Bourbon king. Barcelona and Catalonia fall after a yearlong siege to a combined Castilian and French army under the command of Philip V. By Treaty of Rastatt, 1714, Spain loses Flanders, Luxembourg, and Italy to Austrian Habsburgs.

**1756–63** Seven Years' War: Spain and France versus Great Britain. 1756: Spain regains Minorca, lost to Great Britain in 1709. 1762: In Treaty of Paris, Spain cedes Minorca and Florida to Great Britain and receives Louisiana from France in return.

**1771** La Real Fábrica de Tabacos, where 3,000 *cigarreras* (female cigar-makers who made most of Europe's cigars) were inspiration for Mérimée's and Bizet's *Carmen,* closes in Seville.

**1779–1783** Siege of Gibraltar.

**1805** Battle of Trafalgar.

## Napoléonic Intrusion

**1808** King Charles IV abdicates in favor of Joseph Bonaparte, Napoléon's brother. Napoléon takes Madrid in December.

## The Peninsular War

**1809–14** Reconquest of Spain by British under Wellington.

## Restoration of the Bourbons

**1812** Spain's Liberal Constitution approved in Cádiz.

**1814** Bourbons restored under Ferdinand VII, son of Charles IV. Like other restored monarchs of the era, he is a reactionary and crushes all liberal movements.

**1833** Ferdinand deprives brother Don Carlos of succession in favor of his infant daughter, Isabella; her mother, María Cristina, becomes regent.

**1834–39** First Carlist War: Don Carlos contests the crown and begins an era of upheaval.

**1840** Coup d'état: Gen. Baldomero Espartero becomes dictator, exiles María Cristina, and ushers in a series of weak and unpopular regimes.

**1843** Espartero ousted; Isabella II restored to throne.

**1846–1849** Second Carlist War.

## Period of Troubles

**1868** Revolution, supported by liberals, topples Isabella II but ushers in the Period of Troubles: attempts to establish a republic and find an alternate monarch fail.

**1873** First Spanish Republic declared; three-year Third Carlist War begins.

## Restoration of the Bourbons

**1874** Alfonso XII, son of Isabella, brought to throne.

**1876** Composer Manuel de Falla born in Cádiz.

**1881** Pablo Picasso born in Málaga.

**1892** Peasant revolt, inspired by anarchist doctrine (to be repeated in 1903).

**1893** Guitarist Andrés Segovia born in Jaén.

**1895** Revolution in Cuba, one of Spain's few remaining colonies. Spain moves to suppress it.

**1898** Spanish-American War: United States annexes Spanish colonies of Puerto Rico and the Philippines. Cuba is declared independent as U. S. protectorate.

**1902–31** Reign of Alfonso XIII. Increasing instability and unrest.

**1914** Spain declares neutrality in World War I.

**1923** Coup d'état of Gen. Manuel Primo de Rivera, who models his government on Italian Fascism.

## Republic, Civil War, and Fascism

**1930–31** Primo de Rivera is ousted. Republic is declared, and Alfonso XIII is deposed. Liberals attempt to redistribute land and diminish the power of the Church.

**1936–39** Spanish Civil War: electoral victory of Popular Front (a coalition of the left) precipitates rightist military insurrection against the Republic, led by Gen. Francisco Franco. Europe declares neutrality, but Germany and Italy aid Franco, and the USSR and volunteer brigades aid (to a lesser extent) the Republic. More than 600,000 die, including the poet Federico García Lorca. Franco is victorious and rules Spain for the next 36 years.

**1939** Fascist Spain declares neutrality in World War II.

**1940** Franco denies Hitler permission to attack Gibraltar from Spanish soil.

**1945** Spain is denied membership in the United Nations (but is admitted in 1950).

**1953** NATO bases are established in Spain in return for economic and military aid.

**1962** Mass tourism development begins on the Costa del Sol.

**1969** Franco names Prince Juan Carlos de Borbón, heir to the vacant throne, his successor. Spain closes border with Gibraltar.

**1973** Franco's prime minister, Carrero Blanco, is assassinated by Basque separatists.

## Restoration of the Bourbons

**1975** Franco dies and is succeeded by Juan Carlos, grandson of Alfonso XIII.

**1977** First democratic elections in 40 years are won by Center Democratic Union.

**1978** New constitution restores civil liberties and freedom of the press.

**1981** Attempted coup by Col. Antonio Tejero.

**1982** Spain becomes a full member of NATO. Socialists win landslide victory in general election.

**1985** Frontier with Gibraltar reopened.

**1986** Spain enters European Union. Socialists win for a second time.

**1989** Camilo José Cela awarded Nobel Prize for Literature. Socialists lose majority but continue in office.

**1992** The Universal Exposition held in Seville; Olympic Games held in Barcelona.

**1993** Socialists win last victory in general election.

**1995** Elena de Borbón, eldest daughter of King Juan Carlos I, marries Don Jaime de Marichalar in the Seville cathedral.

**1996** Popular Party, Spain's conservative party, wins general election, ending 14 years of Socialist rule. World downhill skiing championships held in Granada's Sierra Nevada.

**1999** Popular Party reelected with a clear majority, curtailing the power of the Catalonian nationalist party.

**2000** Juan Carlos celebrates 25 years as Spain's king.

**2002** Granada's Alhambra Palace ranked as Spain's most visited monument.

# SPANISH VOCABULARY

| English | Spanish | Pronunciation |
|---|---|---|

## Basics

| English | Spanish | Pronunciation |
|---|---|---|
| Yes/no | Sí/no | see/no |
| Please | Por favor | pohr fah-**vohr** |
| May I? | ¿Me permite? | meh pehr-**mee**-teh |
| Thank you (very much) | (Muchas) gracias | (**moo**-chas) **grah**-see-as |
| You're welcome | De nada | deh **nah**-dah |
| Excuse me | Con permiso/perdón | con pehr-**mee**-so/ pehr-**dohn** |
| Pardon me/ what did you say? | ¿Perdón?/Mande? | pehr-**dohn**/mahn- deh |
| Could you tell me . . . ? | ¿Podría decirme . . . ? | po-**dree**-ah deh-**seer**-meh |
| I'm sorry | Lo siento | lo see-**en**-to |
| Good morning! | ¡Buenos días! | **bway**-nohs **dee**-ahs |
| Good afternoon! | ¡Buenas tardes! | **bway**-nahs **tar**-dess |
| Good evening! | ¡Buenas noches! | **bway**-nahs **no**-chess |
| Goodbye! | ¡Adiós!/ ¡Hasta luego! | ah-dee-**ohss**/ **ah**-stah-**lwe**-go |
| Mr./Mrs. | Señor/Señora | sen-**yor**/sen-**yohr**-ah |
| Miss | Señorita | sen-yo-**ree**-tah |
| Pleased to meet you | Mucho gusto | **moo**-cho **goose**-to |
| How are you? | ¿Cómo está usted? | **ko**-mo es-**tah** oo-**sted** |
| Very well, thank you. | Muy bien, gracias. | **moo**-ee bee-**en**, **grah**-see-as |
| And you? | ¿Y usted? | ee oos-**ted** |
| Hello (on the phone) | Diga | **dee**-gah |

## Numbers

| | | |
|---|---|---|
| 1 | un, uno | oon, **oo**-no |
| 2 | dos | dohs |
| 3 | tres | tress |
| 4 | cuatro | **kwah**-tro |
| 5 | cinco | **sink**-oh |
| 6 | seis | saice |
| 7 | siete | see-**et**-eh |
| 8 | ocho | **o**-cho |
| 9 | nueve | new-**eh**-veh |
| 10 | diez | dee-**es** |
| 11 | once | **ohn**-seh |
| 12 | doce | **doh**-seh |
| 13 | trece | **treh**-seh |
| 14 | catorce | ka-**tohr**-seh |
| 15 | quince | **keen**-seh |
| 16 | dieciséis | dee-**es**-ee-**saice** |

| | | |
|---|---|---|
| 17 | diecisiete | dee-**es**-ee-see-**et**-eh |
| 18 | dieciocho | dee-**es**-ee-**o**-cho |
| 19 | diecinueve | dee-**es**-ee-new-**ev**-eh |
| 20 | veinte | **vain**-teh |
| 21 | veinte y uno/ veintiuno | **vain**-te-oo-noh |
| 30 | treinta | **train**-tah |
| 32 | treinta y dos | train-tay-**dohs** |
| 40 | cuarenta | kwah-**ren**-tah |
| 50 | cincuenta | seen-**kwen**-tah |
| 60 | sesenta | sess-**en**-tah |
| 70 | setenta | set-**en**-tah |
| 80 | ochenta | oh-**chen**-tah |
| 90 | noventa | no-**ven**-tah |
| 100 | cien | see-**en** |
| 200 | doscientos | doh-see-**en**-tohss |
| 500 | quinientos | keen-**yen**-tohss |
| 1,000 | mil | meel |
| 2,000 | dos mil | dohs meel |

## Days of the Week

| | | |
|---|---|---|
| Sunday | domingo | doh-**meen**-goh |
| Monday | lunes | **loo**-ness |
| Tuesday | martes | **mahr**-tess |
| Wednesday | miércoles | me-**air**-koh-less |
| Thursday | jueves | hoo-**ev**-ess |
| Friday | viernes | vee-**air**-ness |
| Saturday | sábado | **sah**-bah-doh |

## Useful Phrases

| | | |
|---|---|---|
| Do you speak English? | ¿Habla usted inglés? | **ah**-blah oos-**ted** in-**glehs** |
| I don't speak Spanish | No hablo español | no **ah**-bloh es-pahn-**yol** |
| I don't understand (you) | No entiendo | no en-tee-**en**-doh |
| I understand (you) | Entiendo | en-tee-**en**-doh |
| I don't know | No sé | no seh |
| I am American/ British | Soy americano (americana)/ inglés(a) | soy ah-meh-ree-**kah**-no (ah-meh-ree-**kah**-nah)/in-**glehs**(ah) |
| My name is . . . | Me llamo . . . | meh **yah**-moh |
| Yes, please/ No, thank you | Sí, por favor/ No, gracias | **see** pohr fah-**vor**/ no **grah**-see-ahs |
| Yesterday/today/ tomorrow | Ayer/hoy/mañana | ah-**yehr**/oy/mahn-**yah**-nah |
| This morning/ afternoon | Esta mañana/tarde | **es**-tah mahn-**yah**-nah/**tar**-deh |
| Tonight | Esta noche | **es**-tah **no**-cheh |
| This/Next week | Esta semana/ la semana que entra | **es**-tah seh-**mah**-nah/lah seh-**mah**-nah keh **en**-trah |
| This/Next month | Este mes/el próximo mes | **es**-teh mehs/el **prok**-see-moh mehs |

| How? | ¿Cómo? | **koh**-mo |
| When? | ¿Cuándo? | **kwahn**-doh |
| What? | ¿Qué? | keh |
| What is this? | ¿Qué es esto? | keh es **es**-toh |
| Why? | ¿Por qué? | por **keh** |
| Who? | ¿Quién? | kee-**yen** |
| Where is . . . ? | ¿Dónde está . . . ? | **dohn**-deh es-**tah** |
| the train station? | la estación del tren? | la es-tah-see-**on** del **train** |
| the subway station? | la estación del metro? | la es-ta-see-**on** del **meh**-tro |
| the bus stop? | la parada del autobus? | la pah-**rah**-dah del oh-toh-**boos** |
| the bank? | el banco? | el **bahn**-koh |
| the hotel? | el hotel? | el oh-**tel** |
| the post office? | la oficina de correos? | la oh-fee-**see**-nah deh-koh-**reh**-os |
| the museum? | el museo? | el moo-**seh**-oh |
| the hospital? | el hospital? | el ohss-pee-**tal** |
| the bathroom? | el baño? | el **bahn**-yoh |
| Here/there | Aquí/allá | ah-**key**/ah-**yah** |
| Open/closed | Abierto/cerrado | ah-bee-**er**-toh/ser-**ah**-doh |
| Left/right | Izquierda/derecha | iss-key-**er**-dah/dare-**eh**-chah |
| Straight ahead | Todo recto | **toh**-doh-**rec**-toh |
| Is it near/far? | ¿Está cerca/lejos? | es-**tah** sehr-kah/**leh**-hoss |
| I'd like . . . | Quisiera . . . | kee-see-**ehr**-ah |
| a room | una habitación | **oo**-nah ah-bee-tah-see-**on** |
| the key | la llave | lah **yah**-veh |
| a newspaper | un periódico | oon pehr-ee-**oh**-dee-koh |
| a stamp | un sello | **say**-oh |
| How much is this? | ¿Cuánto cuesta? | **kwahn**-toh **kwes**-tah |
| A little/a lot | Un poquito/mucho | oon poh-**kee**-toh/**moo**-choh |
| More/less | Más/menos | mahss/**men**-ohss |
| I am ill | Estoy enfermo(a) | es-**toy** en-**fehr**-moh(mah) |
| Please call a doctor | Por favor llame un medico | pohr fah-**vor** ya-meh oon **med**-ee-koh |
| Help! | ¡Ayuda! | ah-**yoo**-dah |

## On the Road

| Avenue | Avenida | ah-ven-**ee**-dah |
| Broad, tree-lined boulevard | Paseo | pah-**seh**-oh |
| Highway | Carretera | car-reh-**ter**-ah |
| Port; mountain pass | Puerto | poo-**ehr**-toh |

| Street | Calle | **cah**-yeh |
| Waterfront promenade | Paseo marítimo | pah-**seh**-oh mahr-**ee**-tee-moh |

## In Town

| Cathedral | Catedral | cah-teh-**dral** |
| Church | Iglesia | **tem**-plo/ee-**glehs**-see-ah |
| City hall, town hall | Ayuntamiento | ah-yoon-tah-me-**yen**-toh |
| Door, gate | Puerta | poo-**ehr**-tah |
| Main square | Plaza Mayor | plah-thah mah-**yohr** |
| Market | Mercado | mer-**kah**-doh |
| Neighborhood | Barrio | **bahr**-ree-o |
| Tavern, rustic restaurant | Mesón | meh-**sohn** |
| Traffic circle, roundabout | Glorieta | glor-ee-**eh**-tah |
| Wine cellar, wine bar, wine shop | Bodega | boh-**deh**-gah |

## Dining Out

| A bottle of . . . | Una bottella de . . . | **oo**-nah bo-**teh**-yah deh |
| A glass of . . . | Un vaso de . . . | oon **vah**-so deh |
| Bill/check | La cuenta | lah **kwen**-tah |
| Breakfast | El desayuno | el deh-sah-**yoon**-oh |
| Dinner | La cena | lah **seh**-nah |
| Menu of the day | Menú del día | meh-**noo** del **dee**-ah |
| Fork | El tenedor | ehl ten-eh-**dor** |
| Is the tip included? | ¿Está incluida la propina? | es-**tah** in-cloo-**ee**-dah lah pro-**pee**-nah |
| Knife | El cuchillo | el koo-**chee**-yo |
| Large portion of tapas | Ración | rah-see-**ohn** |
| Lunch | La comida | lah koh-**mee**-dah |
| Menu | La carta, el menú | lah **cart**-ah, el meh-**noo** |
| Napkin | La servilleta | lah sehr-vee-**yet**-ah |
| Please give me . . . | Por favor déme . . . | pohr fah-**vor** **deh**-meh |
| Spoon | Una cuchara | **oo**-nah koo-**chah**-rah |

# INDEX